PEACEBUILDING

Published in association with the Field Diplomacy Initiative

Field Diplomacy Initiative (FDI) is an independent, pluralistic organization that highlights the role of field diplomacy in sustainable peacebuilding. It considers participatory action research as a tool for peacebuilding and believes that more effective cooperation between researchers and practitioners can raise the "peacebuilding learning curve" considerably.

FDI is developing and generating case study–based training material and concepts and tools for conducting conflict-impact assessments; monitoring democratic transitions, negotiation, and mediation; and developing sustainable peace processes.

Luc Reychler, Chairman
Patrick Dupont, coordinator of the *Peacebuilding: A Field Guide* project

PEACEBUILDING

A FIELD GUIDE

edited by
Luc Reychler and Thania Paffenholz

LYNNE
RIENNER
PUBLISHERS

BOULDER
LONDON

Published in the United States of America in 2001 by
Lynne Rienner Publishers, Inc.
1800 30th Street, Boulder, Colorado 80301
www.rienner.com

and in the United Kingdom by
Lynne Rienner Publishers, Inc.
3 Henrietta Street, Covent Garden, London WC2E 8LU

Library of Congress Cataloging-in-Publication Data
Peacebuilding : a field guide / edited by Luc Reychler and Thania Paffenholz.
　　　p.　cm.
Includes bibliographical references and index.
ISBN 978-1-55587-912-9 (hc. : alk. paper)
ISBN 978-1-55587-937-2 (pbk. : alk. paper)
　　1. Conflict management.　2. Peace.　I. Reychler, Luc.　II. Paffenholz, Thania.
HM1126.P43　2000
303.6'9—dc21
　　　　　　　　　　　　　　　　　　　　　　　　　　　　　00-031092

British Cataloguing in Publication Data
A Cataloguing in Publication record for this book
is available from the British Library.

Printed and bound in the United States of America

　　　The paper used in this publication meets the requirements
∞　　of the American National Standard for Permanence of
　　　Paper for Printed Library Materials Z39.48-1992.

10　9　8　7

Foreword

Elise Boulding

I congratulate the authors of this handbook. They are helping to address a serious gap in peace research. Peace scholars have given a great deal of attention to the causes of war, the conditions of peace, the analysis of conflict processes, and even to the role of nongovernmental organizations (NGOs) and civil society in working for disarmament. However, they have given very little attention to the work of practitioners in the field and to the growing reality of Track 2 diplomacy in conflict situations. This lack of connection between research and practice has left practitioners on their own, learning as they go, and in fact doing an impressive job of learning by doing. Given the exploding demand for competent field-workers in a great variety of conflict situations, it is definitely time to bring together the wisdom and skill that has accumulated in recent decades, and make it available for future practitioners and policymakers. Equally important, peace-movement NGOs need to have this knowledge if their own peacebuilding work is to continue to contribute effectively to the development of alternatives to war.

The coverage of this handbook is impressive and many outstanding professionals and NGO field-workers active in current peacebuilding, working in hotspots around the world, have contributed articles. Because peacebuilding is a broad concept that includes monitoring, humanitarian aid, and development, as well as actual conflict resolution and conflict transformation, the conceptual analysis of the subject by the editors is a very important prelude to the fine section on the actual training of peacebuilders.

The section on fieldwork brings together a distinguished group of pioneers in many types of on-the-ground peacebuilding, making it clear to readers that there are many different strategies, tools, and roles available to field-workers. The need for outside peace-workers to respect and be willing to listen to and learn from local groups, relating to them when possible as partners, comes out over and over again. No peacebuilding can be effective if it is not based on the best insights and resources of local communities in conflict situations. Seeking out the local peacemakers—faith groups and women's groups, teachers, health and human services professionals, and local elders—is a must. Field-workers who do not do this will not only be ineffective, but they may actually do harm. The fact that peacebuilding NGOs must learn to collaborate in the field rather than compete for resources is clearly spelled out. Not only must NGOs cooperate with each other, they must learn to work with the military and with government officials. There are excellent essays on the many field problems in dealing with civil-military authorities.

Processes of healing from past traumas and developing images of a better future that can empower action in the present are critical to peacebuilding, as are processes of dealing with victimizers and efforts for restorative justice. These difficult subjects are covered by authors with an outstanding record of having dealt with them in the field. So are the issues of personal survival of field-workers.

Given that NGO peacebuilding fieldwork on the scale that we currently find in the modern world is a new phenomenon, there is a great deal of social learning going on that needs to be documented and shared, not only within the NGO peacebuilding community but also with governments and the UN. Lessons learned must be passed on! This book is a very important contribution to that process.

Foreword

Cyril Ramaphosa

In an African continent in which both civil wars and multinational conflicts stretch from southern Sudan to Angola's southern borders, the publication of this book is helpful and timely. Great-power diplomacy can sometimes bring protagonists to the negotiating table, and statesmen can craft the compromises that bring into effect cease-fires, accords, settlements, and constitutions. To turn such agreements into sustainable peace, however, requires a much wider range and distribution of skills.

In South Africa we learned to negotiate our way to peace step by step, first in the arena of industrial relations, later in the broader context of localized communal conflict, and finally around the process of making a constitution. In each of these undertakings we absorbed lessons through a process of trial and error. One key consideration in the relative success of our experience of peacemaking was that the key decisions were made by local actors, not international agencies: we decided between ourselves about the terms and principles around which negotiations should be conducted. But this could only happen because most of the adversaries in our conflict even before the formal process of peacemaking began had accepted that the process would have to be as inclusive as possible and that it must involve compromises.

This book draws on the lessons of a decade of peacemaking and conflict management in some of the most troubled regions of the world. There are no simple formulas or prescriptions offered in its pages. Readers who engage with its contents will acquire a deeper understanding of the complexities and the challenges that confront agencies and individuals who seek to bring about political and social reconciliation, while at the same time addressing the issues that underlie profound and protracted conflict. Sustainable peace cannot be reconciled with the perpetuation of social injustice. Justice, though, will not achieve reconciliation if it merely secures revenge.

Peacebuilding is a process of learning, which should never conclude. Keeping the peace requires us to maintain our commitment to expanding the frontiers of such knowledge. I welcome the publication of this book as an important contribution to such an undertaking.

Preface

Luc Reychler and Thania Paffenholz

Two-thirds of the countries in the world today suffer tension and latent violent conflict. In 200 flashpoints, people are killing one another. These human-made disasters cause massive destruction, they are extremely expensive, and they pose a serious threat to global stability. The international community is increasingly becoming aware that it can no longer afford such conflicts and that there are, moreover, limits to just how much violence can be tolerated. Consequently, governmental and nongovernmental organizations have been paying more attention to the prevention and management of violent conflicts. But however well-intended these peacebuilding efforts, they are not always wholly effective. Indeed, in some instances, they may even be counterproductive. Often the outcome is a mere pile of peacebuilding stones rather than a sustainable peace.

We genuinely believe that any action in or around existing or potential conflict areas has an influence on war and peace. Building sustainable peace is not just a matter of direct intervention through mediation. It also requires indirect intervention through development and relief aid, media coverage, or any other activity relating to existing or potential violent conflicts. *Peacebuilding: A Field Guide* therefore aims at making the reader aware of the bigger picture involved in the building of sustainable peace, while also providing some real guidelines on how to maximize all contributions to peacebuilding.

The basic messages of the book are simple: (1) more attention should be paid to the invaluable contribution to peacebuilding made by people working in the field; (2) there is a need for a better peacebuilding architecture; (3) sustainable development cannot succeed without sustainable peacebuilding; (4) more adequate preparation of field-workers could significantly increase the chances of successful peacebuilding; and (5) the learning curve could be shortened if debriefings of people who have acquired peacebuilding experience would be taken more seriously. Intended mainly for current and prospective field-workers as well as those working at the headquarters of organizations involved in peacebuilding, it reflects the expertise of more than fifty people with practical experience in different areas of peacebuilding.

The book is divided into four parts. Part 1, "Preparing for the Field," introduces concepts and tools for sustainable peacebuilding. Part 2, "Working in the Field," focuses on seven specific peacebuilding activities. Part 3, "Surviving in the Field," addresses the problems that field-workers are confronted with on an almost daily basis. And the Conclusion provides an overview of the essential lessons learned from the wisdom that the authors have generously shared with us.

All the articles are of a how-to nature, providing the reader with practical guidelines. We invite our readers to share with us their own experiences, suggestions, and comments via e-mail: fdi@ngonet.be.

There are many to whom we owe a great amount of gratitude and without whom this project could never have come to fruition. Many people have offered encouragement along the way. A special thanks goes to Reginald Moreels, a mind without boundaries, who inspired the writing of this book, and to the Belgian Department of International Cooperation for its financial support of the project.

We thank the numerous authors—scholars and practitioners—who shared their experiences. Our gratitude goes also to the Field Diplomacy Initiative staff: to Patrick Dupont for coordinating the project, to Jo Govaerts for her careful cooperation and translations, and to Joyce Wayua Munyao for her service as a dedicated intern. We would also like to mention our families, who have been extremely patient and supportive during the editing of the book.

PART I

Preparing for the Field

CHAPTER 1

From Conflict to Sustainable Peacebuilding: Concepts and Analytical Tools

■ 1.1

Conceptual Framework

Luc Reychler

HOW TO PREVENT VIOLENT CONFLICT

Conflict Is a Driving Force in Human History

Conflict has led to destruction, but it is also a strong motivating force for peacebuilding. In the first half of the twentieth century, Europe was one of the most violent places in the world; in the Guinness book of violence, it scored all the records. It caused two world wars, set up totalitarian regimes, built concentration camps, and had civil wars. In the second half of the twentieth century, a European community was created. It became one of the most free, secure, and well-off places on the globe.

Conflicts signal problems that need to be taken care of. If serious conflicts are not resolved effectively, they can become destructive and cause a great deal of suffering. Today one can visit nearly 200 places in the world where people kill people. A great number of seemingly peaceful countries suffer from serious tensions and latent conflict.

Violence Is Costly

The high costs of violence have led to an increase in the efforts to prevent conflicts from crossing the threshold of violence. This is called *proactive violence prevention.* This is more cost-effective than *reactive violence prevention.* The aim of reactive conflict prevention is to prevent a further escalation of the conflict by controlling the intensity of the violence, by reducing the duration of the conflict, and by containing or preventing geographic spillover. Also in the postconflict phase, violence-prevention efforts could be needed to avert a new flaring up of the conflict.

When a conflict crosses the threshold of violence, the costs and the difficulty of managing them increase significantly. Violence becomes the cause of more violence. A comprehensive analysis of the costs of the violence gives an idea of reconstruction and peacebuilding efforts that will have to be made when the violence ends. Not only are there human and economic costs but also social, political, ecological, cultural, psychological, and spiritual destruction (see Exhibit 1.1-1).

Exhibit 1.1-1   Costs of Violent Conflicts

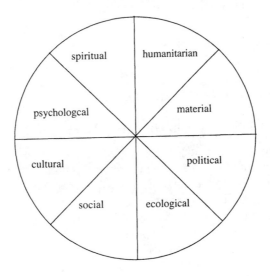

What Is Violence?

To understand violence prevention, it is essential to analyze the violence that exists and the instruments for committing violence. The term *violence* refers to a situation in which the quantitative and qualitative life expectancy of individuals or communities is intentionally reduced. Indicators of this are the average life expectancy of the members of a group, infant mortality, daily calorie intake, access to schooling, and so on.

There are different ways to hurt people. The most visible is armed violence. Armed violence is intended to deter, coerce, wound, and even kill people. Psychological violence aims at the minds and hearts and tries to incapacitate the sentimental power of people. Psychological violence is often intended to produce mental suffering or spread fear and hate. Structural violence differs from the two preceding types in that it is an indirect type of violence. Here, violence is built into the social structure and is less visible than physical or psychological violence. The previous apartheid regime in South Africa or the remaining caste system in India are textbook examples. A fourth instrument, cultural violence, refers to those aspects of the culture that legitimize the abuse of the instruments of violence cited above. Violence is approved of in the name of revolution, in the name of religious fanaticism, and in the name of political ideologies, such as nationalism and communism (see Exhibit 1.1-2).

To achieve sustainable peace, we must first study how and to what extent each of the four types of violence is used. Peace requires more than the absence of armed violence. In fact, the absence of armed violence may mask all sorts of frustrations and even a potential for armed violence. An analysis limited to the study of armed violence can lead to surprises.

Exhibit 1.1-2   Four Instruments for Committing Violence

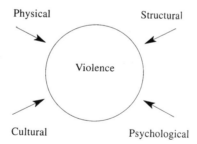

DIAGNOSIS OF A CONFLICT

By *conflict* we mean the pursuit of incompatible goals by different groups. For a diagnosis of a conflict, one can make use of the 4 + 1 model. This model indicates four necessary preconditions for a violent conflict: (1) interdependent parties, (2) who experience the interdependence as negative, (3) who have the opportunity to use armed violence, and (4) who consider the use of violence as the most cost-effective policy option. Once a conflict becomes violent, violence begets violence.

Actors

The first thing one needs to identify are the parties involved and their constituents: the owners and the stakeholders. This is not always an easy task. There are internal and external parties. Among the internal parties, one can distinguish the internal core parties who are directly involved in the conflict, the internal concerned individuals and groups who wish to play a role in facilitating conflict resolution, and the internal uninvolved. Among the external parties, one can single out the external involved parties, the external concerned parties who wish to and can play an active role in resolving the conflict, and the external uninvolved.

Interests and Issues

After identifying the parties, we need to learn what issues or interests are at stake for the parties. Competing interests are at the center of any conflict, yet there can also be common interests. Conflicts of interests can be expressed in different ways. For example, they can be presented as scarce goods (territory, power, resources); a definition of various situations, means, ends, values, and collective identity; or even as irrational issues.

For the sake of problem solving, it is useful to distinguish the terms *problem, interpretation, interest, position,* and *issue.* The problem is the immediate source of the conflict (barking dog); the interpretation explains the other party's behavior (my neighbor is unfriendly, inconsiderate); the position refers to demands, threats, fixed solutions, proposals, or points of view (buy a muzzle); the interest refers to why is *x* a problem (I am not sleeping well); and the issue is the topic the parties need to discuss and decide (how to control the barking at night).[1]

Opportunity Structure

What does the opportunity structure look like for the parties involved in the conflict? Here we examine the power relations between the parties and the objective conditions in the conflict environment that enhance or inhibit the use of violence. The political, strategic, legal, economic, geographic, and cultural environment in which the conflict is embedded can raise or decrease the chances of war and peace. The chances of violence are higher in a nondemocratic versus a democratic environment. In a security community, conflicts tend to be handled constructively. In a crisis climate, good decisionmaking becomes more difficult.

Strategic Thinking

How do the actors define the present situation and how do they see the future? How do they assess different ways and means for handling the conflict? What do they consider as their best alternatives to a negotiated agreement (leave the situation as it is, refer to higher authority, or use power)? What are possible solutions for the parties in question? Solutions can be defined as actions that will resolve a given piece of the problem or the whole problem.

Most of the analysts differentiate five major styles (and variants) of handling conflicts.[2] They can be distinguished in terms of *assertiveness,* defined as behaviors to satisfy one's own concerns, and *cooperativeness,* defined as behaviors intended to satisfy the other party's concerns. The *forcing/competing style* is high on assertiveness and low on cooperativeness: the party places great emphasis on his or her concerns and ignores those of the other. The basic desire is to defeat the other. The *accommodating style* is unassertive and cooperative: the party gives in to the other at the costs of his or her concerns. This orientation has also been called appeasement or smoothing. An *avoiding style* is unassertive and uncooperative: the party simply withdraws and refuses to deal with the conflict. This style has also been called flight. A *compromising style* is intermediate in both assertiveness and cooperativeness: both parties give up some and split the difference. It has been referred to as sharing or horse trading. A *collaborating style* is high on both assertiveness and cooperation: the party works to attain a solution that will meet the needs of the parties involved. This style has been called the problem-solving or the integrative style.

All the styles are considered useful under different circumstances. The selection depends on the answer given to five questions: How important are the issues for the party? How important are the issues to the other party? How important is maintaining a positive relationship? How much time pressure is there? To what extent does one party trust the other?[3]

Conflict Dynamics

Finally the outcome of a conflict is determined by the dynamics of the interaction between the parties. Some conflicts transform constructively; others end up in a violent confrontation. Some are transformed in a mutually satisfactory way (win-win); others end up frustrating one or all parties involved (win-lose, lose-lose). One should not only make a static conflict analysis but also a diagnosis of the conflict's dynamics. Once a conflict has acquired a certain dynamic (for example, escalatory, de-escalatory, violent, or peaceful), the dynamic tends to feed on itself and become prolonged.[4] Escalation tends to further escalation, and war is the cause of further war. Peacebuilders ought to monitor indicators of positive or negative developments.[5] Changes in each of the 4 + 1 variables can be classified as forces for or against a constructive transformation of the conflict (see Exhibit 1.1-3). The length of the arrow could depict the strength of these forces. The longer it is, the greater the influence it exerts.

Exhibit 1.1-3   Forces Influencing Escalation and De-escalation

Forces For	Actors	Forces Against
Hawks/generals take over	→ ←	Dove/diplomat leaders
Spoilers	→ ←	Local peace capacity increases
Polarization of political spectrum/alliances formed	→ ←	Third parties are mediating

Forces For	Issues	Forces Against
Number of issues grow	→ ←	Limited issues
Parties expand their demands	→ ←	Concrete specific demands
Growing dissatisfaction with interdependence	→ ←	Growing satisfaction with interdependence

Forces For	Opportunity structure	Forces Against
Communications channels interrupted/selective information	→ ←	Communications channels open/ effective arms control
	←	Democratic embedment of conflict
Arms expenditures increase	→	
	←	Balance of power
Embedment of conflict in undemocratic environment	→	
Imbalance of power	→	

Forces For	Strategic thinking	Forces Against
Zero-sum perceptions	→ ←	Win-win perceptions
Negative stereotyping "enemy perceptions distortions"	→ ←	Deconstruction of stereotypes
	←	Tactics: persuasion, problem solving, integrative
Tactics: threats, violence, exclusive	→	
	←	Goals: doing well
Goals: hurting the other, winning	→	
	←	War weariness increases/ perception of stalemate
Violence is perceived as most cost-effective option	→	
	←	No fear of losing face
Fear of losing face	→	

Forces For	Process	Forces Against
Confrontations become destructive	→ ←	Relations positive/ neutral
	←	Cease fire
Violence escalates	→	

CONFLICT IMPACT ASSESSMENT

What Is Conflict Impact Assessment All About?

The aims of a conflict impact assessment system (CIAS)[6] are (1) to assess in time the positive and/or negative impact of different kinds of intervention (or the lack thereof) on the dynamics of the conflict; (2) to contribute to the development of a more coherent conflict prevention and peacebuilding policy; (3) to serve as a sensitizing tool for policyshapers and policymakers, helping them to identify weaknesses in their approach (such as blind spots, incoherence, bad timing, and inadequate priority setting); and (4) to further the economy of development and peacebuilding efforts. CIAS is about reminding people involved in matters of development and conflict prevention.

Concerns and Critics

Despite the self-evident usefulness of a CIAS, one still senses resistance and reservations with respect to the development and the implementation of such a tool. Some of the reticence is caused by the preference of governmental and nongovernmental organizations for leaving popular and appealing terms such as *peace* and *conflict prevention* undefined. Other reservations are based on the conviction that conflict dynamics are much too complex to be tracked by a CIAS. Still others fear that an adequate assessment will be a time-consuming exercise and/or inhibit flexibility. There is also the apprehension by some, stated less explicitly, that a CIAS would expose the limited or negative impact of one's policies on the peace process and thereby reduce the chances for funding. All these comments suggest that the road to the development and implementation of an assessment system will not be a smooth one. Anyway, the overall aim of CIAS is to sensitize the decisionmakers and opinion leaders about the complexity of peacemaking, peacebuilding, and peacekeeping and to help them formulate or design a more coherent, efficient, and effective peace policy.

Levels of Assessment

Conflict assessment could be done at three levels. At the policy level, one studies the overall impact of the different peacebuilding efforts on the realization of a sustainable peace in a country or region. At the sector level, one looks at the impact of different peacebuilding efforts on one of the sectors of a sustainable peace in a country or region. At the project level, one focuses on the impact of a particular project on the realization of a sustainable peace. In the following section, some guidelines are suggested for performing a conflict impact analysis at the policy and project levels.

Conflict impact assessment at the overall policy level. A conflict impact assessment system at the policy level uses six criteria to evaluate policies with respect to their peacebuilding potential. Ideally, a good policy should have the following:

- A clear and compelling definition of the peace one wants to achieve and a valid conceptual framework indicating the conditions enhancing or inhibiting the realization of the aim.
- A comprehensive assessment of the needs or of the presence or absence of the above-mentioned conditions in the conflict region.
- A coherent action plan.

- An effective implementation of the action plan.
- Recognition and inclusion of the owners and stakeholders in the conflict-transformation process.
- An awareness and dismantling of the sentimental walls inhibiting the satisfaction of all of the above.[7]

Conflict impact assessment at the project level. Step 1: How and to what extent does the project contribute to the goals of the peace and development policy and satisfy the needs? An answer to this question necessitates an adequate conflict analysis of the country and region where the project will be implemented, a clear idea of the peace one intends to realize, and a comprehensive needs analysis.

Step 2: What is the impact of the conflict on the project? In this phase of the CIAS at the project level, the attention is focused on the concrete environment in which the project will be implemented. Here we are looking at a series of variables in the situation, which could negatively and/or positively influence the implementation of the project.

Step 3: What is the impact of the project on the conflict dynamics? In this phase of the conflict impact analysis, we research how and to what extent the intervention reinforces or weakens the preconditions of sustainable peace (consultation and negotiation system, political and economic structures, security and moral-political climate); the effectiveness of targeting the people; and the coherence and the synergetic quality of the project.

Step 4: Generating alternative options and decisionmaking. In this phase, a decision is made with respect to the project proposal. The project can be approved and given a green light, amended, and linked to supporting other measures, postponed, turned down, or stopped. Efforts are also made to redesign the project to prevent or reduce the negative impact of projects and to raise the "peace added value" of the interventions. Development workers could become field diplomats. They could help to set up an adequate early warning system, sensitize the donors for the benefits of conflict prevention, and help people to build a durable peace. They could, using Mary Anderson's terms, support existing capacities for peace and promote incipient ones. Projects can be redesigned to convey the message that cooperation is mutually benefiting; and they can bring people together to discuss the problems and reduce misunderstandings; they can help to create a safe space where people can air and resolve their problems; they can help to build peace-enhancing political and economic structures; they can help to heal the past and raise confidence and hope in the future. For generating alternative options and redesigning projects, active listening and creativity are essential.

For Whom Is the CIAS Intended?

Ideally, all peacebuilders in conflict-prone regions should use the CIAS. Donors might use it to guide project selection, funding decisions, and monitoring; operational organizations could use it to design projects and guide implementation; and the recipient communities in conflict-prone areas could make use of CIAS to assess the utility and relevance of outside-sponsored development projects.

Who Should Do CIAS?

Taking into account the sensitivity and complexity of CIAS, the assessment should be performed by a limited team, consisting of people with adequate conflict expertise and knowledge of the project and of the country and region where the project will be implemented. An adequate analysis should also make use of the input of the recipient parties, the stakeholders (who will have to live with the consequences and/or whose interests are at stake), and other donors who operate in the area.

When and Where Should CIAS at the Project Level Be Applied?

Undertaking a CIAS should not be determined by the types of project but by the nature of the environment in which the intervention is planned. CIAS should be considered in environments characterized by incipient, latent, and manifest violence. CIAS should be performed in the preconflict, conflict, and postconflict phase.

Where Does CIAS Fit in the Project Process?

Conflict impact assessment should be done in all phases of the project cycle. CIAS should be done before the project is implemented, during its implementation in the field, when the project has ended, and even much later (ten to twenty years) for monitoring long-term effects. In the pre-project phase CIAS allows us to decide to go in or not in the conflict-prone region. It helps us also to redesign project proposals with a minimum of negative side effects and a maximum of peace added value. The aim of CIAS in the implementation phase is to monitor progress and identify and resolve unexpected problems more effectively. Equally important is CIAS after the project has finished. The purpose is to learn from the experience and to use the lessons to design better projects.

Methods?

An effective CIAS makes use of several sources and methods: existing country studies, active listening, informal in-depth interviews and discussions, questionnaires, and problem-solving workshops. To assess the impact of the project in the implementation phase, one can invite the project leader and other coordinators to keep a diary.

SUSTAINABLE PEACEBUILDING

Transforming Conflicts

The overall aim of peacebuilding is to transform conflicts constructively and to create a sustainable peace environment. Transforming a conflict goes beyond problem solving or managing a conflict.[8] It addresses all the major components of the conflict: fixing the problems, which threatened the core interests of the parties; changing the strategic thinking; and changing the opportunity structure and the ways of interacting. Through peacebuilding, the conflict is not merely resolved—the whole situation shifts. It tries to make the world safe for conflicts. The term *peacebuilding* refers to all the efforts required on the way to the creation of a sustainable peace zone: imagining a peaceful future, conducting an overall needs assessment, developing a coherent peace plan, and designing an effective implementation of the plan. A useful overview of peacebuilding tools is presented in Michael Lund's contribution.

Sustainable Peace

The term *sustainable peace* refers to a situation characterized by the absence of physical violence[9]; the elimination of unacceptable political, economic, and cultural forms of discrimination; a high level of internal and external legitimacy or support; self-sustainability[10]; and a propensity to enhance the constructive transformation of conflicts.

Preconditions for a Sustainable Peace

The essential requirements for the creation of a sustainable peace can be clustered in four groups.

Effective communication, consultation, and negotiation at different levels. The first precondition for establishing a sustainable peace is the presence of an effective communication, consultation, and negotiation system at different levels and between the major stakeholders. Effective negotiations can be distinguished from less effective negotiations by looking at the process, outcome, and implementation[11]: there is no destruction or wasting of time and means; the relations between the parties do not deteriorate and improve; the outcome is perceived mutually satisfactorily, and—with the exception of initial external support—the agreement is self-sustaining.

Peace-enhancing structures.   Essential for the establishment of a sustainable peace is the establishment of series of peace-enhancing structures.[12] The first is of a political nature: it is the establishment of a consolidated democracy. Such a democracy consists of ten building blocks and internal and external support systems. The second structure necessary for the establishment of a sustainable peace is an effective, legitimate, and restorative justice system. The creation of a restorative justice system has been strongly promoted by Howard Zehr.[13] The third structure that needs to be built is a social, free market system. The chances of establishing a sustainable peace are greater in a social, free market system than in a centralized or pure free market economic environment. Of great importance are the privatization process and the creation of a vibrant economic society. The fourth structure that needs attention is the education, information, and communication system. Here we look at the degree of schooling, the level of discrimination, the relevance of the subjects and the attitudes held, the control of the media, the professional level of the journalist, the extent to which the media play a positive role in the transformation of the conflicts, and the control of destructive rumors. Finally, structures are needed to cope with refugee problems in a satisfactory way.

An integrative moral-political climate.   The term *integrative moral-political climate* refers to a political-psychological environment characterized by a "we-ness" feeling or the existence of multiple loyalties, expectations of mutual benefits as a consequence of cooperation, reconciliation of the past and the future, a dismantling of sentimental walls, a reconciliation of the values that will guide the future, and a commitment to cooperate. An integrative moral-political climate enables a community to solve its problems constructively.

Is there hope for a better future? Does one expect mutual benefits as a consequence of cooperation? What hope-raising measures have been taken?

How strong is the nationalism? Is the political commitment inclusive or exclusive? Is there a we-ness feeling? Is the political engagement of the people characterized by multiple loyalties? How strong is and how far does the we-ness feeling reach? How much social capital is available? The term *social capital* refers to a culture of trust and cooperation that makes collective action possible and effective. As Robert Putnam says, it is the ability of a community, to develop the "I" into the "we." A political culture with a fund of social capital enables a community to build political institutions with a real capacity to solve collective problems. Where social capital is scarce, even an elected government will be viewed as a threat to individual interests.[14]

How much progress has been made with respect to the healing of past wounds and reconciliation? Is the reconciliation process oriented toward the future, here and now, and/or the past?

Which sentimental walls obstruct the way to a sustainable peace? Victims with despair, pluralistic ignorance, and political inefficacy? Offenders with historical falsification, stereotyping, dehumanization, distrust, indifference, wrong assessment of the consequences of decisions (optimism/pessimism), preference falsification and pluralistic ignorance, obstacles of a religious nature? Third parties with neutralism/passivity/non-intervention, cultural arrogance, a moral-legal approach, a wait until the conflict is ripe? Analysts with a one-dimensional approach who use invalid theories, the influence of "scientific" doctrines/myths/taboos, an elitist analysis, a wrong assessment of future developments?

How compatible are the values of the parties? What are the basic values (peace, economic welfare, democracy, justice, truth, forgiveness, and dignity) that will guide the future of the community when reconciled?

Objective and subjective security. Here we look at the ingredients necessary for enhancing real and perceived security. Both could be enhanced by several measures, such as cease-fires, arms control and disarmament, confidence- and security-building measures, the creation of regional security arrangements, and the like.

Very important in the creation of a sustainable peace environment are efforts to also create these conditions at the regional level. Internal and external peace is indivisible. One of the secrets of the European Union is that a great deal of its political, economic, and security problems are managed at a multilateral level. Another secret is the role played by a new type of leadership. The creation of a sustainable peace environment requires a new type of internal leader, such as Jean Monet, George Marshall, or Nelson Mandela. These leaders are able to project a clear and compelling image of the future and the ways and means to get there. Equally important are courageous followers standing up to and for the leaders. Irresponsible followership remains an obstacle to a successful transformation of conflicts. Evil is stoked and fanned by followers who abandon their empathy with the suffering of others, either through fear or through seduction by a leader. Ira Chaleff suggests four principles on the basis of which a courageous follower operates within the group and a fifth dimension outside the group: the courage to assume responsibility, the courage to serve, the courage to challenge, the courage to participate in transformation, and the courage to leave.[15]

NOTES

1. J. Beer and E. Stief, *The Mediators Handbook* (Gabriola Island, Canada: New Society Publishers, 1997).

2. J. Folger, et al., *Working Through Conflict*, 3d ed. (New York: Longman, 1997).

3. Folger, *Working Through Conflict,* 199–203.

4. This phenomenon could be called conflict inertia. Without external intervention some conflicts seem to stay on the same track.

5. Mark Anstey, *Practical Peace Making: A Mediators Handbook* (Cape Town: Juta and Co., 1993).

6. Luc Reychler, "Conflict Impact Assessment," paper presented at the IPRA conference, 1996, Durban, South Africa.

7. To analyze and transform conflicts, more attention needs to be paid to political-psychological variables. More efforts in particular should be undertaken to identify and dismantle sentimental walls. The term *sentimental wall* refers to concepts, theories, dogmas, attitudes, habits, emotions, and inclinations that inhibit democratic transition and constructive transformation of conflicts. The existence of sentimental walls increases the chances of misperceiving the situation, misevaluating the interests at stake, lowering the motivation to act on the opportunity to do something about it, and developing the necessary skills and know-how. From the words *sentiment* and *mental,* "sentimental" makes people aware of the emotional roots of many cognitions and attitudes. Making people aware of the existence of sentimental walls and efforts to dismantle them can provoke lots of resistance. Anyway, conflict prevention requires not only learning but also a lot of unlearning.

8. The term *conflict management* refers to efforts to limit, mitigate, and contain a particular conflict. Conflict resolution goes further and implies that the root causes of a conflict are addressed and resolved.

9. This could also be positively defined as a situation characterized by objective and subjective security (people are and feel secure).

10. Although external support may be necessary in a particular phase of the peacebuilding process, in the end people should be able to support it themselves.

11. See Luc Reychler, *Democratic Peacebuilding: The Devil Is in the Transition* (Leuven: Leuven University Press, 1999).

12. For a more elaborate description of the peace-enhancing structures, including a series of checklists, see Reychler, *Democratic Peacebuilding,* 12.

13. Howard Zehr, *Changing Lenses* (Waterloo, Ont.: Herald Press, 1990).

14. R. Putnam, *Making Democracy Work: Civic Traditions in Modern Italy* (Princeton, N.J.: Princeton University Press, 1993).

15. Ira Chaleff, *The Courageous Follower: Standing Up to and For Our Leaders* (San Francisco: Berrett-Koehler Publishers, 1995).

A Toolbox for Responding to Conflicts and Building Peace

Michael Lund

Responding to violent conflicts requires two steps: knowing what tools are effective in which circumstances; and devising and implementing multi-tooled, place-specific strategies to move a country toward a durable peace (tool profiles).

Conflicts can have multiple causes. They can be at various stages of escalation or de-escalation. Interventions can be undertaken at any point in the peace-conflict-peace continuum and can be performed by third parties. We are most familiar with interventions that third parties take at the height of violent conflicts such as shuttle diplomacy, peacekeeping, or, in times of full-blown war, direct military intervention. Yet efforts to intervene in conflicts can be and are taken by any party at all stages of the conflict—previolent, violent, or postviolent. Successful intervention depends on whether actions are appropriate to the conflict's sources and stages.

TOOLS FOR PEACEBUILDING

Policy tools are methods to prevent or mitigate a conflict and to build peace. Policy tools can comprise several projects, procedures, programs, policies, or mechanisms. Each tool operates on a conflict's sources and manifestations by manipulating different kinds of influence—"carrots" or "sticks." Tools can be implemented through different organizational channels: some are sponsored by actors outside a region in conflict, some by national governments, and some locally. Tools vary in the aspects of conflicts they address and in their effectiveness and efficiency in achieving results.

Policy Tools and Functional Areas

Tools directed at the same causes of conflict can be operated through different *functional areas* such as official diplomacy or military measures, to name two examples. Exhibit 1.2-1 organizes ninety policy tools by major functional categories.

Exhibit 1.2-1   Tools for Peacebuilding

Official Diplomacy

Mediation
Negotiation
Conciliation
Good offices
Informal consultations
Peace conferences

Unilateral goodwill
   gestures
Conflict prevention or
   management centers
Special envoys
Diplomatic sanctions
International appeal/
   condemnation

Crisis and war diplomacy
Coercive diplomacy
Diplomatic recognition
Withdrawal of recognition
Certification/decertification
Hot lines

Nonofficial Conflict Management Methods

Mediation
Support to indigenous dispute
   resolution and legal
   institutions
Conflict resolution or
   prevention centers
Peace commissions

Civilian peace monitors
Visits by eminent
   organizations,
   individuals/ "embarrassing
   witnesses"
"Friends" groups
Nonviolent campaigns

Nonofficial facilitation/
   problem-solving workshops
Cultural exchanges
Civilian fact-finding missions
Humanitarian diplomacy

Military Measures

Preventive peacekeeping
   forces
Restructuring/integration of
   military forces
Professionalization/reform of
   armed forces
Demobilization and
   reintegration of armed
   forces
Military aid
Military-to-military programs

Alternative defense strategies
Confidence-building and
   security measures
Nonaggression agreements
Collective security or
   cooperation arrangements
Deterrence
Demilitarized zones

Arms embargoes or blockades
Threat or projection of force
Disarmament
Arms control agreements
Arms proliferation control
Crisis management procedures
Limited military intervention
Peace enforcement

Economic and Social Measures

Development assistance
Economic reforms
Economic and resource
   cooperation
Intercommunal trade

Joint projects
Private economic investment
Health assistance
Agricultural programs
Aid conditionality

Economic sanctions
Humanitarian assistance
Repatriation or resettlement of
   refugees and displaced
   people

Political Development and Governance Measures

Political party building
Political institution building
Election reform, support, and
   monitoring
National conferences

Civic society development
Training of public officials
Human rights promotion,
   monitoring, and
   institution building
Power-sharing arrangements

Decentralization of power
Trusteeship
Protectorates
Constitutional commissions and
   reform

Judicial and Legal Measures

Commissions of inquiry, war
   crimes tribunals
Judicial/legal reforms

Constitutional commissions
Police reform
Arbitration

Adjudication
Support to indigenous legal
   institutions

(continues)

Exhibit 1.2-1 (continued)

Communications and Education Measures

Peace radio, TV	Promote alternative	Peace education
Media professionalization	information and	Exchange visits
Journalist training	communication sources	Training in conflict
International broadcasts	Civic education	management, resolution,
	Formal education projects	and prevention

Tools for Peacebuilding According to Principal Sources of Conflict Addressed

Some policy tools aim directly at immediate triggers of conflicts such as an ethnic group leader's hostile rhetoric. Others target potential sources of conflict, for instance, antipoverty programs intending to rectify disparities in resource distribution and living standards. Exhibit 1.2-2 classifies policy tools for peacebuilding in terms of whether they chiefly address systemic or structural conditions such as material resource deficiencies and conditions; proximate or enabling factors such as institutions and processes, perceptions and attitudes, the means of coercion and force, and substantive issues in dispute; and immediate causes such as actions or behavior.

Exhibit 1.2-2   Tools for Peacebuilding by Principal Source of Conflict Addressed

Tools Addressing Systemic (Structural) Causes

Main aim and target: To increase the aggregate, conserve and/or redistribute natural, economic, and human resources—land, water, food, infrastructure, technical skills—to improve material conditions.

- General or targeted development assistance
- Economic reforms, including social safety nets
- Economic integration/cooperation
- Intercommunal trade
- Private economic investment in conflict-prone areas
- Humanitarian aid

- Human resource development programs such as job training
- Public/private health assistance such as sanitation facilities
- Agricultural productivity promotion programs
- Resource management/cooperation

Tools Addressing Proximate (Enabling) Causes

Main aim and target: To create or strengthen general political, social, and economic institutions, rules, procedures and other decision processes through which societies define their public problem agenda, set goals, form policies, allocate authority, implement public decisions, and settle grievances.

- Constitutional commissions/reforms
- Judicial/legal reforms
- Support to local indigenous dispute resolution and legal institutions

- Political institution building
- Training public officials
- Civic society development
- Conflict-prevention centers

(continues)

Exhibit 1.2-2 (continued)

Tools Addressing Proximate (Enabling) Causes (continued)

- Human rights promotions, institution building, and monitoring
- Election reform, monitoring, and support
- National conferences

- Power-sharing arrangements
- Decentralization of power

Tools Addressing Proximate (Enabling) Causes

Main aim and target: To reduce and put prior restraints on specific means of armed force or coercion that could be used to carry out violent conflicts.

- Coercive diplomacy/economic and diplomatic sanctions
- Human rights monitoring
- International condemnation
- Police reform
- Restructuring/integration of military forces
- Demobilization/reintegration/reduction of military forces
- Military professionalization/reform
- Nonaggression agreements
- Security agreements
- Demilitarized/peace/nuclear-free zones

- Trusteeships
- Protectorates
- Arms embargoes
- Surgical power projection/threat of force
- Disarmament
- Arms control agreements
- Arms proliferation controls
- Military aid
- Alternative defense strategies
- Preventive peacekeeping forces
- Targeted deterrence policies
- Permanent war crimes tribunals

Tools Addressing Immediate (Triggering) Causes

Main aim and target: To regulate parties' manifested conflict behavior directly—actions, speech, and interactions.

- Special envoys
- Mediation
- Negotiation
- Arbitration
- Conciliation
- Good offices
- Adjudication
- Civilian fact-finding missions
- Conditionality
- Humanitarian diplomacy
- Sanctions
- Arms blockades
- International moral appeals/condemnation
- Informal consultations
- Support to indigenous conflict management/resolution mechanisms

- Crisis management procedures
- Peacekeeping forces
- Conflict management and resolution training
- Peace commissions/committees
- Peace conferences
- Reciprocated goodwill gestures
- Nonofficial facilitation/problem-solving workshops
- Peace monitors
- Internationally sponsored peace consultations
- Conflict resolution/prevention centers
- Visits by eminent organizations/individuals/ "embarrassing witnesses"
- Threat or use of force
- Limited military intervention

TOOL PROFILES

Any peacebuilding tool offers strengths and weaknesses; successful application depends on the conflict context and associated conditions. Effective peacebuilding requires choosing tools carefully, that is, with care; this choice in turn must rest on a thorough understanding on how each tool operates. To assist practitioners in considering a tool's applicability to the particular situations they encounter and in implementing chosen tools, tool profiles are organized according to a consistent set of elements.

- A description of the tool—objectives, expected outcome or impact, and relationship to conflict prevention or mitigation.
- A discussion of the tool's implementation—organizers, participants, activities, cost considerations, other resource considerations, set-up time, and time frames to see results.
- A summary of the conflict context in which the tool should be applied—stage and type of conflict, cause of conflict the tool addresses, and prerequisites for the tool's effective implementation.
- In-depth illustrations of past practice in using the tool.
- An evaluation of the tool's effect on conflict or peace—strengths, weaknesses, and lessons learned.
- A list of references and resources.

NOTE

This text is an adapted version of "Part III: A Toolbox to Respond to Conflicts and Build Peace," in Creative Associates International, Inc., *Preventing and Mitigating Violent Conflicts: A Revised Guide for Practitioners*, 25 April 1997, 3.1–3.9.

CHAPTER 2

Selecting People

■ 2.1

Motivation and Qualifications

Katarina Kruhonja, interviewed by Margareta Ingelstam

Katarina Kruhonja, Ph.D., heads the project Building a Democratic Society Based on a Culture of Nonviolence—Postwar Peacebuilding in Eastern Croatia, run by the Osijek Center for Peace, Nonviolence, and Human Rights. She is former president of the center. In the project, twenty-four people—Croats, Serbs, Bosnians, and internationals—will have been actively involved for two years (1999–2000) in five peace teams in the rural areas of eastern Croatia.

In an interview with Margareta Ingelstam (MI), program secretary of the Swedish Council of Churches, Katarina Kruhonja (KK) gives her views on what values, motivation, skills, and qualifications to look for when selecting people for work in conflict and crisis areas. This interview is inspired by key elements of the peace project Katarina is directing: active listening, needs assessment, dialogue, negotiation, mediation, active nonviolence, human rights monitoring and education, psychosocial support, women and youth empowerment, and income-generating activities.

MI: You have a very varied experience of both peacebuilding and of work in violent situations?
KK: Yes, we started as a small group of people during the war, who felt the need to explore possible ways out of the culture of war and violence and to contribute to a culture of peace and nonviolence. This was in 1991. Now we have some experience with working in conflict areas. For instance, we have learned what it means to have "external" people come and assist you. In a way, you can say that we are trying to assist the people in the rural areas of eastern Croatia in the same way as people from other countries have assisted us.

MI: So what have you learned?
KK: It is very important to have a *vision*. According to us, when you want to work toward a new society, your work should build on and be motivated and inspired by people's own experiences, people's existing problems and needs, people's knowledge of alternatives and will to create a society according to their dreams. If you make this vision very clear and understandable for everybody and if you keep it alive, it is a powerful driving force in your work. Then you need to formulate the mission and find and select the people who are committed to the vision.

MI: Ideally, how do you see a recruitment procedure?
KK: It is crucial to spend enough time and energy on the *recruitment process*. First, a *comprehensive application form* should be provided so that the candidates can write about themselves, their commitment, motivation, experience, education and training, values, attitudes, skills, and qualities.

The recruitment procedure should include feedback from the *reference persons*, *individual interviews* with a larger group of applicants, and a *recruitment seminar*. Such a seminar should include exercises, role-playing and discussions, unveiling the various personal qualities.

In the case of the project that I am currently directing, the final recruitment decision was ideally made after the ten-week *preparatory course* by the people in charge of the project on the one hand and by the applicants themselves on the other.

MI: As part of the selection process, you mentioned "commitment" and "motivation" first. What kind of motivation are you not interested in when dealing with applicants?
KK: There are people who are trying to run away from their own past. Maybe they are hoping that while "working for peace" they will be "healed." Maybe they are looking for acceptance that they do not find in their own group. Or maybe they seek some self-fulfillment by exposing themselves to danger; maybe they would like to become heroes. These people may be one by one valuable persons with real needs and problems, but I am not sure whether they apply with the right motivation. In the end, the peacebuilding activities might experience major difficulties.

There are also unemployed people who say they would do any job and people who apply, not so much for the actual job but to improve their curriculum vitae.

MI: What kind of commitment and motivation are you looking for?
KK: I am aware that professional experience is often very important. And yet I believe that commitment comes first. Commitment includes motivation—they go together. The Croatian word for commitment is *posvecen*, the

root of which is "saint," *svet,* and it means "a person who is ready to give," "a person who takes from himself to give to somebody else." For me, commitment implies readiness to share your time, energy, and material resources for an idea, a cause connected to people, the community, the society. To me, commitment is always linked to people, to people who are suffering, and to social change. It is often the motivation which determines the success or failure of an action.

Commitment is an inclusive word: it implies a work for somebody with somebody. Therefore, I hesitate using concepts like "field diplomacy," not because I have a prejudice against diplomacy. But I prefer using "service"—service for development and peace. The task of our peace teams is to assist people in exploring their basic needs, to enhance communication and cooperation between different ethnic and religious groups, and to encourage people to create the social change they seek.

MI: Are there some basic values and attitudes that should be expected from all peace workers?
KK: Yes, I believe in an absolute commitment to truth and a striving toward openness and transparency in work. We expect a commitment to nonviolent social change and participatory democracy. This includes a respect for every human being—making no discrimination on grounds of gender, religion, race, ethnic background, nationality, and trusting every person as part of the solution.

MI: The word commitment *makes me think about written commitments that people have made. In the civil rights movement, people who were willing to participate in actions of civil disobedience were asked to sign a vow, which included promises to practice active nonviolence, to give money to the struggle, to pray for the struggle daily, to practice "a soldier's discipline."*
KK: A commitment is a promise that I make to myself, consistent with the vision and mission and for the benefit of the community I want to work with and for. This leads to a special behavior. I believe that the behavior of people, which has been growing from within without strict rules from the outside, will make a significant difference in all our work for social change.

MI: What do you mean by saying that the behavior must be consistent with the vision and mission?
KK: If you are working as a rescue team in a crisis area where people are cold and hungry, you do not dress in expensive clothes and eat expensive food. If you are involved in mediation and reconciliation processes, you also need to work on the conflicts within your own organization. Sometimes it is good to have some rules of behavior—but they should be developed in relation to the people with whom you work, taking into

account the situation, the culture, the experience of people—namely, traumatic war experiences.

MI: In the early 1990s when you and your colleagues were within the war zone, you started to look for solidarity from the outside!
KK: Yes, people came to us, people who did not come with ready-made solutions but who were able to explore our needs and to listen carefully. They used the right questions, which made us trust our own knowledge, our experience, our analysis, and inspired us to find our own possible solutions to the problems.

A question like "How can I help?" which sounds right can be very wrong. Because people inside a crisis do not know how somebody coming from the outside can help. Most people who have come to us have been very much aware of the danger of pushing us in the role of victims. Instead, they have met every one of us with respect—men, women, youth, and children.

MI: This kind of attitude implies quite a lot of maturity. What is that?
KK: Maturity has much to do with emotions. A person can be very good at intellectual analysis, but if she is immature, a conflict area is not the right place. A person is mature when she has a certain amount of self-awareness; when she has respect for or confidence in herself; when she knows how to make decisions herself, not needing to fall back on authorities; when she is taking on responsibilities in a group, keeping in mind the needs of others; when she is not imprisoned by her own perceptions and behavior—but able to be open and flexible and to adjust to situations which are different from her own; when she is aware of the way human perceptions are distorted by anger, fear, hate, and other strong emotions roused in conflict; and when she is able to deal with these emotions—both with herself and with others. Maturity also involves good communication skills, above all an ability to listen with empathy to others.

MI: All these capabilities are also prerequisites for conflict transformation skills.
KK: Of course, working in a conflict area demands these kinds of skills and many others, such as facilitating and organizational skills. I am reluctant to emphasize the demand for special skills at the expense of personal characteristics and values, as reflected in presence and action. What is expected of peace workers is a sincere commitment to nonviolence, a power used to heal, to liberate, and to empower. As a philosophy or principled stance toward life, nonviolence expresses a conviction that truth and love are powerful social forces and are meant to ground all our interactions with other members of the human community and with earth itself.

To change a violent society in a nonviolent way implies working systematically to change the very assumptions and perceptions of the people involved, and creating opportunities for new ways of living and acting.

MI: I know you believe in building and nursing the personal relationships in your peace work.
KK: Many people who have been working with us keep in touch. It is essential to keep this human contact. It prevents us from feeling hurt, from thinking that the warmth and trust we felt was not real, from losing faith in humanity.

That is why I think it is very important that people who come from other parts of the world to work with us should really look for and find at least one person whom they can rely on in a personal way and with whom they can build a mutually enriching relationship. If this occurs, these people will commit themselves much easier for a long time, exploring new ways of cooperation. In a way, long-term commitment is like adopting a child. The child brings "her world" with her into the new family—the child changes the whole life of the family—that family's life will never be the same. There are people in the safer parts of the world, daring to get involved in such a joint long-term adventure, taking the risk of personal revolution. This gives me hope.

MI: Somewhat paradoxically, we are told that people who come from safer parts of the world to work in conflict areas should be impartial. Is that what you think, too?
KK: No, I do not think so. To be impartial means not to take sides for anybody, to keep a certain distance to be able to be more objective. I believe in *compassion* and *inclusion*. This means: I am close to you, I feel with you, but I do not exclude others because of that. We are all part of one another. Such an attitude is not less but more effective in order to better understand the situation.

MI: Could you highlight some other attitudes or skills that are important in peace and development work?
KK: Reflecting on what I have said before, one of the most important skills is the belief that you yourself and the people you work with are able to change. Having had this experience oneself, and having acquired this basic belief, adds a lot of value to work in difficult situations.

Adam Curle, a mentor and friend of our Peace Center and an experienced mediator, told us once how he prepared for a dangerous meeting with a very cruel mass murderer. He spent many hours preparing himself to be able to see that person as a human being worthy of compassion and to be able to trust that person's eventual agreement with negotiation and peaceful conflict transformation.

We have learned that our perception of human nature—especially our own—is of overarching importance. It is indeed an absurd illusion to think that we can work for peace (which means to be actively involved with people who are behaving in an unpeaceful way) or to think that we can help people change their lives for the better if we are inwardly turbulent and ill at ease.

We have also learned that it is possible to go from insecurity to confidence, from feelings of worthlessness to feelings of dignity, from mistrust to trust, from guilt to forgiveness, from hate to reconciliation, from fear to love. During the last decades we have witnessed these changes and we know now that they do not need to take a lifetime. It is possible to intensify such changes.

MI: Another issue is, how do you relate to the need of a certain amount of security in a risk zone?
KK: The context and the situation can vary a lot from mission to mission—compared, for instance, to medical assistance in a crisis area or a training session in more stable circumstances. The organization in charge has to provide information about the risk level and foreseeable developments. The organization should at all times contribute to minimizing risks by not selecting people who have the wrong motivations. When an applicant has received all relevant information and is accepted for a project, it is up to her to make the final very personal decision.

A person can be very well prepared. On the basis of written and oral information provided, she can quite rationally analyze and calculate risks. Still, when she decides to enter a conflict area, she has to accept and be prepared for potential and unexpected security risks. When I stayed in a shelter during the bombing of Osijek, I prepared myself day by day, internalizing the conviction that whatever happened to me, there was no such situation in which I could not rely on a greater power than myself, which I call God. In similar dangerous situations, this insight was a source of hope and courage.

MI: You have mentioned values, attitudes, and personal characteristics that you desire for people working in conflict areas. Most persons do not have all these gifts.
KK: Some people have some gifts, possess some skills, have some capabilities. When people work in teams and are committed, they complement and influence each other in a synergetic way. This complementarity is heavily taken into consideration when constituting our peace teams.

MI: Before I met you I had read an article about the Peace Center, which had just started. You were asked what you saw as the most important part of its work. You answered, "Education, education, and education." How do you look at education today?

KK: Education, training, and empowerment, including psychosocial development, are the key elements of our work. Education is crucial for the peace teams; it offers a continuous process of learning and empowerment for all people involved.

To be empowered, we believe, is to recognize one's power to take charge of one's own life. For this, a person needs to learn about specific situations and to develop specific personal and interpersonal skills. She needs to acquire self-confidence and, above all, sufficient self-awareness to understand what has been done and what she can do and be in order to escape from the oppression trap. We have noticed that people whom we consider empowered perceive much better their own and other people's difficulties and possibilities.

REFERENCES

Center for Peace, Nonviolence, and Human Rights. (1997, 1998). *Annual Reports.* Osijek, Croatia.

Curle, Adam. (1995). *Another Way. Positive Response to Contemporary Violence.* Oxford: Jon Carpenter.

Jegen, Mary Evelyn. (1966). *Sign of Hope: The Center for Peace, Nonviolence, and Human Rights.* Uppsala: Life and Peace Institute.

"Working to Establish Civil Society: The Center for Peace, Nonviolence, and Human Rights in Osijek, Croatia." (1999). In *People Building Peace: Thirty-five Inspiring Stories from Around the World.* A publication of the European Center for Conflict Prevention in cooperation with the International Fellowship of Reconciliation and the Coexistence Initiative of the State of the World Forum, 186–191.

Who Should Go Where? Examples from Peace Brigades International

Luis Enrique Eguren

Mario Calixto was president of the Human Rights Committee of Sabana de Torres, a small town in central Colombia. He was under heavy threat from the local paramilitary forces due to his open denouncement of the acts committed by these groups.

On the night of December 23, 1997, two armed men came to Mr. Calixto's house, intimidated and threatened him, and demanded that he go with them. (Such methods are widely used in Colombia to kill human rights activists.) However, the gunmen did not achieve their goal; two international observers from Peace Brigades International (PBI) were in Mr. Calixto's house at the time. They had been staying with him for several weeks. The PBI officials intervened and asked the gunmen to leave, which they did.

After this incident, Mr. Calixto had to move with his family to another part of the country, but grateful for his life, he was even more willing than ever to continue his fight against human rights violations in Colombia. This was of course good news, particularly in a country where dozens of human rights activists are murdered every year.

This incident was merely the tip of the iceberg of the twenty-two international PBI observers' work in the midst of the protracted armed conflict in Colombia. It is certainly a good example of the evident conflict between presence (strategy) and reaction (perception). The PBI observers' presence—the only foreigners in a small town who are in contact with other nongovernmental organizations (NGOs), civilian authorities, and security forces—conflicted with the reaction of the armed men who became dissuaded from acting in the presence of the two foreigners. This interaction between strategy and perception is one of the essences of PBI's peacebuilding work.

PBI's peacebuilding paths go beyond uncharted territories. Therefore, we as PBI activists have to carefully question ourselves in order to follow a sensible direction; and we also have to learn directly from our own experiences in the process. As third party intervenors, we more specifically have to ask ourselves the following questions: How do we select a conflict?

When do we engage someone in a potentially violent environment? How do we select people?

Some answers are given below, based on our PBI experience as an NGO providing international observers in internal armed conflicts for the past sixteen years in Guatemala, El Salvador, Sri Lanka, Haiti, Colombia, and elsewhere. PBI observers have played an important role in protecting human rights defenders, trade union and NGO activists, and activists in organizations of displaced people, refugees, and others. PBI observers contribute to violence control, peacekeeping, and interpositioning. They have also played a part in low-level mediation, Track 2 diplomacy, observation, monitoring and verification, and training and in the dissemination of useful information.

HOW TO SELECT A CONFLICT

When selecting a conflict, we first need to thoroughly analyze the situation and the perceptions. Only then will we be able to come up with an appropriate action plan. We also need to bear in mind that every third-party action program will have an impact that needs to be assessed very carefully. Although this statement may seem obvious, it is striking to see how often we find examples of a lack of impact analysis. As a basic requirement, we should carefully study the potential consequences of our work and avoid harming or aggravating the conflict dynamics.

Conflict Mapping

The first set of questions focuses on the context in which we have to operate:

- Is there any trustworthy information and material available for conflict analysis? What is the ideological context of the conflict?
- Who are the main actors in the conflict? What are their main interests and strategies?
- Which groups are affected by the conflict? Are they at all organized and, if so, how? What are their interests, strategies, differences, perceptions, and levels of cooperation?

Third-Party Intervention

The second set of questions addresses the existing niches for third-party intervention:

• Do the parties involved in the conflict accept the intervention? Did any of the affected actors ask for such an intervention? Unarmed international third-party intervention—be it through NGOs, intergovernmental organizations (IGOs), or governmental organizations—requires at least a certain degree of consent by the parties involved in the conflict, especially the armed ones. The consent can be explicit (formal permissions and visas issued by a government) or implicit. The degree of consent will be high if an armed actor expects benefits from the external presence, or low if he expects political costs due to such a presence. If the armed actor is not keen on external presence, his consent will be determined by the political costs of expelling the intervenors. The balance between the political costs of expelling the intervenors and letting the latter do their work will define the intervenors' freedom of action.

• What are the expectations, objectives, biases, and stereotypes of the affected groups about peacebuilding intervention?

• What are the expectations, biases, and stereotypes of the antagonists (especially the armed parties) concerning peacebuilding intervention?

• Mapping of potential counterparts and others: Do all peacebuilding actors work in the conflict setting? This mapping is important for two reasons. First and conceptually, civil society should not be considered or approached only as the "recipient" of external peacebuilding initiatives or as the "victim" of a conflict but as the major actor in any peace process. The ultimate responsibility for resolving a conflict lies within the local society. Second and strategically, the presence of active local peacebuilding initiatives is a key factor for the success of any third-party intervention.

• Who are the other (potential) allies? Which other third parties or international entities are working in the area or are following up on the situation? What are their interests, experiences, strategies, and results?

Organizational Aspects

The third set of questions refers to the characteristics and organizational aspects of the third-party intervenors:

- What are the expectations, objectives, and biases of the organizations involved and of the prospective workers/volunteers in light of the conflict, the actors, and the affected groups?
- What are the prerequisite characteristics for personnel, such as linguistic abilities and physical demands?
- Can the organizations find, train, coordinate, and support enough qualified personnel to meet the demands in the short and the long run?

SECURITY RISKS AND SENDING PEOPLE INTO THE FIELD

It is quite impossible to find a perfect balance between involvement and security in fieldwork. It may be relatively easy to exclude obvious risks, but this is only one part of the solution. Most of the decisions have to be taken in a "gray area," where the dividing lines are blurred by the complexities of the conflict environment, the impossibility of knowing and analyzing all relevant information, and the changing and unpredictable nature of the decisionmaking processes of key actors such as the armed forces. Decisions are affected by subjective elements (personal perceptions, biases, or prejudices) and by poor communication, bureaucratic inertia, and internal power struggles.

Protocol of Operations

Everyday operations require a lot of decisionmaking, mainly about tactics to be used as part of a general strategy. Those strategies should be linked to so-called protocols of operations that are to be the main source of security and stability. A protocol of operations is, for example, the set of questions and prevailing factors we have to consider when receiving a request for a peacebuilding mission in a region we are less familiar with. Or, for example, the set of elements we evaluate before starting a fact-finding mission in a remote area—namely, defining a route; informing the security forces, the government, or the embassies about the peacebuilding intervention; ensuring effective systems of communication; and establishing an alternative emergency plan.

Such protocols should include effective feedback systems to enable the rethinking of a strategy as the scenario might change. And risk indicators for measuring, detecting, and avoiding insecure aspects in the fieldwork might need to be refocused.

Protocols of operations are also of use to the central office, which may be lacking accurate information because, for instance, it is too far removed from the conflict setting. In any case and as a general rule, if there is no agreement between the field team and the central office on how to proceed, conservative decisions should prevail. Either one of the parties may be wrong, but the consequences may be a lot worse if a proactive role is assumed.

How to Determine When to
Visit a Conflict-Struck Region

It is important to first determine whether the local armed forces are in any way affected by external presence. Are they sensitive to international pressure and to the presence of third-party intervenors such as human rights observers? If the armed forces' interests are not likely to be affected by international pressure, the international presence will not make a difference and could possibly even prompt an attack by the former, who are keen on keeping "their" territory free of "strangers."

The armed forces' perception of international presence must be re-evaluated in a rapidly changing political context. This implies that when a military actor feels seriously threatened, his actions toward the international presence may worsen without him evaluating the political costs. This may be the case, for example, during an exacerbation of an armed conflict. Similarly, an armed actor may act against a disturbing international presence if he perceives an "opportunity" for reducing the costs of his actions. This happens, for instance, if the third-party intervenor is accused of an illegal action or if there is a vacuum of power and consequently no one has to assume the political costs of an attack.

Communication with State and Nonstate Actors

External peacebuilders should maintain constant communication lines with government officials, security forces, religious institutions, and NGOs present in the field. Communication is a key factor in ensuring that all actors fully understand the role of the peacebuilders and in correcting possible misperceptions.

The Dissemination of Human Rights Information

What is the security risk for third-party intervenors of transmitting information on human rights or humanitarian law violations? How may this risk compromise peace intervenors' fieldwork in the long run? Which criteria can be used to assess the associated risks?

On the one hand, human rights protection in any conflict situation is a major prerequisite for building a sustainable peace. On the other hand, if third-party intervenors disseminate firsthand information on human rights violations, the response of the transgressors (the security forces, the government, or the armed actors) may seriously compromise their own and other peacebuilders' presence in the field. To develop a proper strategy to ensure human rights protection while maintaining presence in the field, careful analysis is of paramount importance.

In order to do effective human rights promotion work, information transmission is not sufficient. Other suitable means that have proven effective, if properly coordinated, include:

- Lobbying and holding periodic meetings with civil and military authorities, carefully posing to them the main concerns regarding the protection of the affected population and the safety of the humanitarian workers.

- Facilitating the work of human rights activists and organizations—both local and international—which may include the investigation and denouncement of human rights violations.
- Distributing already published information on the main aspects of the rights of the affected population(s).

Taking these activities into account, third-party intervenors should communicate, network, and coordinate their work with local and international NGOs and IGOs, embassies, and other groups.

A general criterion for assessing the security risk of human rights protection and promotion work is to avoid public denouncements of human rights violations, provided that these human rights violations do not directly affect the local population or the peacebuilders. Avoid as much as possible to be the first source or the only source of denouncement of a human rights violation.

HOW TO SELECT FIELD-WORKERS

Specific personal qualifications and qualities are required of prospective field personnel.

> We cannot guarantee that our presence will prevent acts of violence, rather we hope it will lower the probability of such acts. . . . Do not think, as many do, that you are safe because you are an international. . . . Your ability to respond to a violent or tense situation could well depend on how honestly you have accepted the danger and prepared yourself. [From a letter sent by PBI to its prospective volunteers for the Guatemala team.]

A basic requirement for an external peacebuilder is to be able to cope with a violent situation and with the risk of getting hurt. We already pointed out that there must be an organizational and strategic approach to general and specific security risks; however, the "human factor" lies beyond such an approach. It is of utmost importance that a peacebuilder be able to recognize and accept potential risks and be flexible enough to adapt. This requires a certain degree of personal maturity and a lot of common sense. Furthermore, a peacebuilder should have strong analytical and interpersonal communication skills in order to share and contrast his/her perceptions and analyses with others and be able to cope with the stress or fears that arise from living in a violent conflict setting.

Motivation and commitment are key elements for preparing oneself to take up personal security risks. Experience shows, moreover, that personal commitment is of vital importance and cannot be replaced by any other element. In terms of organizational origins, the "ideal" peacebuilder should be a professional worker as well as a grassroots activist.

"Do not join to do someone a favor." This is another one of PBI's recommendations to prospective volunteers. It may sound harsh, but the feelings of paternalism or guilt that may motivate some volunteers hinder effective peacebuilding work. Prospective peacebuilders should be able to find a balance between total personal commitment (which may lead to a lack of overall perspective and objective judgment) and disinterest or apathy (which will prevent him or her from having the necessary flexibility required for peacebuilding work).

NOTE

I would like to thank Teresa Panepinto, who reviewed the first English-language draft of this article.

SUGGESTED READING

Mahony, Liam, and Luis Enrique Eguren. (1997). *Unarmed Bodyguards: International Accompaniment for the Protection of Human Rights.* West Hartford, Conn.: Kumarian Press.

CHAPTER 3

Training People

■ 3.1

Training Peacebuilders and Peacekeepers

Arno Truger

THE NEED FOR A SOUND
PREPARATION OF CIVILIAN PERSONNEL

The increasing number of intrastate conflicts with various societal roots and conflicting parties makes them very difficult to understand and handle. It has become obvious that a sole reliance on the traditional resources associated with diplomatic or military strategies is not adequate. There is a lack of appropriate concepts, structures, methods, and instruments including a prepared manpower. There is a need, therefore, for a comprehensive peacebuilding approach, including humanitarian aid and the development of cooperation and conflict transformation (to transform conflicts to a less violent stage). Peacebuilding needs to be coordinated on an international level; related to the needs of the population in the conflict area; compatible with civil society and other actors in the field; nonviolent and distinct from enforcement actions; flexible and practical; and capable of counteracting violent escalations at an early point. To meet these goals, the following peacebuilding activities are needed:

- Mediation and confidence building among the conflict parties.
- Humanitarian assistance (including food aid, water, sanitation, and health care).
- Reintegration (including disarming and demobilization of former combatants and the assistance to displaced persons, refugees, minorities, and vulnerable groups).
- Rehabilitation and reconstruction.
- Stabilization of economic structures (including the establishment of economic links).

- Monitoring and improving the human rights situation and the empowerment for political participation (including election monitoring and assistance).
- Interim administration for short-term stability improvement.
- Information and the establishment of educational structures and programs designed to eliminate prejudices and enemy images.
- Campaigns informing and educating people about the peacebuilding activities at hand.

These tasks have to be fulfilled by international and local mission staffs in a conflict environment that is shaped by stark prejudices and enemy images, proneness to violence, inadequate health care and supply systems, refugee problems, and a lack of a sufficient infrastructure. The severe mission conditions challenge the personal as much as the social abilities of the peacebuilders, who perform far away from their "normal life" with family and friends. They have to cooperate closely with colleagues from all over the world with a different cultural background and problem approaches, and with the population on-site.

Therefore, skills related to managing complex situations within pluralistic cultures and deeply divided societies are needed in addition to task-specific knowledge. A "normal" professional background is not sufficient. The multidimensional and multilevel characteristics of conflicts, applicable conflict transformation strategies and practices, and the professional and personal challenges that peacebuilders will face, require non-mission-specific knowledge and a multitude of skills for all mission personnel. These go far beyond traditional diplomatic and professional skills used in democracies. Hence, regardless of which mission civilian personnel will be seconded to, all civilians who are willing to serve and who are fulfilling certain requirements should receive basic preparation. However, what is offered at the moment for civilian personnel are pre-mission briefings, but no real preparation. At best civilians are introduced to their mission tasks through short-term courses. There is a lack of comprehensive training programs that fit the needs of field operations. Furthermore, the institutions that are involved in recruiting people for field missions should enhance their cooperation with the aim of constituting a pool of adequately trained, qualified, and skilled civilian experts to be sent to specific missions on short notice.

STAGES OF PREDEPARTURE
TRAINING OF CIVILIAN PERSONNEL

In order to meet the requirements and objectives mentioned in the previous article, preparation should include three stages: general preparation, task-specific preparation, and mission-specific preparation. In addition, predeparture training will also rely on the results of postmission debriefings and ongoing scientific review.

General Preparation

General preparation aims at the creation of a pool of trained personnel familiar with a fundamental knowledge of field operations and the respective personal roles—irrespective of the specific mission and the professional mission assignments they might get involved in. This includes the development of skills usable under extreme conditions and applicable to a wide array of conflict situations. In terms of general preparation, the two-week foundation course of the International Civilian Peacekeeping and Peacebuilding Training Program (IPT) of the Peace Center in Burg Schlaining, Austria, can serve as a model. The IPT foundation course explores the following elements:

- Introduction: introduction to the program and the participants; communication, intercultural, and cross-cultural understanding; the nature and task of peacebuilding.
- Strategies of various actors in international conflict transformation: the role of governmental and intergovernmental organizations in civilian peacekeeping and peacebuilding; and the role of nongovernmental organizations (NGOs) in peacebuilding.
- Human rights protection: history and concept of human rights, promotion, fact-finding, and monitoring.
- Project planning and project management: identifying needs, planning and setting up a project.
- Workshop on conflict transformation: nature and task of conflict; various forms of third-party intervention; conflict partnership facilitation.
- Case studies on particular conflicts: analysis of the conflict situation and of the activities and strategies of UN and Organization for Security and Cooperation in Europe missions with a focus on the importance of cooperation between various intergovernmental, governmental, and nongovernmental actors involved in the respective areas.
- Excursion to the Austrian Military Academy: cooperation with the military, security issues, and mine awareness.
- Communication and cooperation with the civilian police: role of the civilian police and practical exercises (e.g., radio communication, four-wheel car driving).
- Evaluation of the course.

Task-Specific Preparation

Regardless of which mission civilian personnel will be seconded to, all experts who are willing to fulfill a certain task in field missions should receive task-specific preparation. IPT offers two-week task-specific training courses as listed below. Those specialization courses are offered in an alternate sequence. The participation in a foundation course is a precondition for the participation in a specialization course.

- Election observation and assistance: concepts and practice of democracy, elections and election observation in various societies.
- Empowerment for political participation: democratic institution building, relationship between state and civic initiatives, promotion of personal political engagement.
- Human rights protection and promotion: definition and concept of human rights, international human rights procedures, cultural differences, fact-finding, promotion, monitoring, and technical assistance.
- Humanitarian assistance: dilemmas, approaches, methods, instruments, and political implications for delivering emergency help—food aid, water, sanitation, and health care.
- Information dissemination: acquisition and distribution of information in crisis regions, communication among the actors in the field, dealing with political instrumentalization of media.
- Postconflict reconstruction: concepts and practice of sustainable reconstruction—repatriation, rehabilitation, dealing with trauma and shock, rebuilding civil society.
- Third-party intervention: mediation, facilitation, negotiation, arbitration.

Mission-Specific Preparation

To perform successfully during their assignment, peacebuilders need to adapt as much as possible to the specific conditions in the mission area and to link their activities to the prevailing conflict situation and the actors involved. Therefore, thorough knowledge of the roots of a conflict and of the societal background and context of a specific mission is of the utmost importance to peacebuilders. Such knowledge constitutes the peacebuilders' working basis and can be of important use during their conflict de-escalation efforts. Especially in multidisciplinary peacekeeping operations (PKOs), peacebuilders face the problem of increasingly complicated mandates and organizational structures. In addition, the problem of communication among the different actors of multifunctional missions and related activities increases.

The specific conditions that peacebuilders will encounter and the specific roles and tasks of the organizations they will be seconded to require a familiarization with the following details prior to deployment:

- Mission-specific objectives (mandate), strategies, structures, logistics, and instruments.
- The specific political, legal, social, cultural, and economic conditions relative to implementation and realization.
- Logistics: procedures for security assessment, regulations required to follow the rational for the mandate, resource management, reporting.
- Medical conditions in mission areas.
- Basic language skills.

The development and organization of mission-specific courses are the responsibility of the organization responsible for the field operation. However, this organization could be supported by external training institutions, especially with regard to information on the specific political, legal, social, cultural, and economic conditions in a mission area.

However, details on certain mission-specific tasks, and the conditions under which they will be implemented, have to be learned "on the job." Such a training will merely have the character of supervision, of established regular contacts among the organization's experts and of visiting the peacebuilders and talking about their needs.

Postmission Debriefing and Ongoing Scientific Review

All preparation stages mentioned above should include elements of postmission debriefings and of scientific review and evaluation. The aim of the latter is to provide continuous feedback and to continuously update applicable and relevant field knowledge that can be of use during the different training programs.

The lessons learned by organizations and field experts during past missions should be made available to relevant institutions and individuals so that the organization that was in charge of a specific mission before and that will be responsible for another field operation in the future can integrate these lessons learned in its future activities and thus perform better; that training institutions can optimize their training programs; and that the peacebuilders who come back from the field can better understand and learn from their own and from others' experience.

A training institution should also conduct a lessons-learned exercise to strengthen the link between the reality in the field and the contents of its programs. That is why every IPT program is subject to a verbal and a written evaluation by the participants. Furthermore, to assess the field relevance and usefulness of the IPT courses, all former participants are encouraged to report on their missions. On the basis of past reports, a need for training in handling practical problems was assessed. Negotiation and personal communication skills were also regarded as crucial. Training before deployment, during a mission, and after finishing a particular assignment (debriefing) were all considered important.

TRAINEES' PROFILE

Applicants for training programs should possess certain characteristics that match the characteristics required for field staff. The aim should be a large number of trained people recruited for field missions after the training. That is why sufficient care, time, and energy should be spent on selecting course participants. Acceptance to a specific course could be subject to the following conditions:

- Personal characteristics: prepared to work in conditions of physical and psychological hardship; able to engage in intensive teamwork and intercultural communication; record of motivation and commitment; prepared to be at disposal on short notice.
- Professional qualifications.
- Technical skills (e.g., driving license).
- Language: good knowledge of English and possibly other languages.
- Previous mission experience in conflict areas would be an additional advantage.

Evaluation instruments can be the review and screening of application forms including application essays, questionnaires, letters of reference, health certificates, and interviews.

Considering the wide range of activities to be trained for and the multicultural and multiorganizational setting of a mission, mission-preparation courses should reflect diversity. IPT's experience underlines the advantage of course participants with a heterogeneous background in terms of country of origin, profession, institution, and experience.

The success of a training course can be measured by the degree of international recruitment. It is of significant advantage to recruit participants with different cultural backgrounds, including individuals from conflict areas. Such diversity helps participants learn about approaches that are not culturally single-minded, and it fosters an awareness of multicultural settings commonly found in protracted conflicts.

The IPT programs gain from the participation of a wide range of professionals, such as administrators, logistic experts, health personnel, educators, engineers, development workers, and economists. For instance, the involvement of a few soldiers or police officers in its courses has contributed to a better understanding and cooperation in the field. However, large-scale and more intensive joint training programs for civilians and military and police personnel are considered useful only for these high-level administrative and management tasks where civilian, military, and police staff need to cooperate intensively.

IPT courses include participants from both governmental organizations and NGOs. IPT especially considers applicants who show a strong record of field experience in developing countries and/or conflict areas (development organizations, religious organizations, human rights groups, etc.). This enhances cooperation between different organizations in the field.

METHODOLOGICAL AND ORGANIZATIONAL ASPECTS OF TRAINING

Methodology

The personal and professional characteristics mentioned above reflect the importance of so-called contact skills, namely, skills that are practiced in direct interaction with people. That is why preparatory training needs to be based on a highly interactive methodology. The information should be provided as a mix of lectures, working groups, exercises, and readings and should enhance interaction, reflection, and integration.

Basic written information about organizations and organizational structures relevant to field operations should be made available to the participants in advance to help the latter prepare for the lectures. Lectures should primarily use the case study approach and focus on recent field missions. In addition, working groups give participants the opportunity to consolidate topics dealt with in the lectures. Workshops will enhance communication skills and intercultural understanding and encourage the participants to learn how to deal with their own role within a team and vis-à-vis conflicting parties. Participants can practice conflict analysis and resolution skills and gain experimental knowledge of different conflict management concepts by analyzing conflict escalation and de-escalation cases and by participating in focused interactive exercises (simulations, role-playing, etc.).

This methodology requires resource persons to be more than academic experts in peacebuilding. The IPT experience proves that they should, in addition, have strong practical field experience and, of course, have excellent pedagogical skills.

Duration of Training

The longer a preparatory training lasts, the broader and more detailed will be its scope. Long training will, however, have a negative effect on the number of applicants that are qualified for training programs According to IPT's experience, a high-quality preparatory program should involve at least five weeks of training: two weeks of general introductory training, two weeks of task-specific training, and one week of mission-specific briefing. To maximize the peacebuilders' performance from the outset, mission-specific training should take place shortly before the mission begins. Assuming the trainees will already have had basic training, mission-specific preparation prior to deployment does not need to be an extended process.

RECRUITMENT FOR FIELD OPERATIONS

For a recruitment that fits the needs of field operations in assigning the right people to the appropriate jobs, comprehensive criteria are needed based on the mission-, mandate-, and personnel-specific requirements for field operations; these requirements run parallel to the ones for successful training programs. In addition, a coordinating mechanism would be advantageous to ensure that the different field-operational institutions recruit along the same high-standard lines.

In order to achieve this, there should be common agreement on a number of basic recruitment criteria, such as job description of every major peacebuilding task; description of general skills and knowledge required for field operations; description of special skills and knowledge needed for every major peacebuilding task; and specific requirements such as language skills and previous experience, including hardship experience and age. Further, rules on setting up expert rosters and agreement on a number of guidelines related to recruitment procedures and the assessment of applicants' qualifications will eventually enhance the quality of field missions.

Finally, the more that administrative and financial support including job security can be provided to people qualifying for field operations, the higher the chances that the most suitable persons will participate in these missions. Because civilian personnel unlike military personnel normally have to take leave from their regular job and have to arrange deployment individually in order to participate in field missions, specific government support can be useful. Legal and financial steps could be taken by governmental and other organizations, such as the European Union, to provide job security, medical coverage, and logistical and travel support.

Training Humanitarian Aid Workers

Jo Wouters

As an international organization, the Red Cross works with expatriate staff. The Red Cross/Red Crescent Movement is composed of the International Committee of the Red Cross (ICRC) and the International Federation of Red Cross and Red Crescent Societies (Federation) and more than 170 National Societies. The ICRC is mainly involved in conflict areas, whereas the Federation deals with natural disasters, refugee issues, and development work in times of peace. For their field activities, both the Federation and the ICRC rely on the National Societies to provide them with experienced expatriate staff. The need for predeparture training is obvious: it adds to the efficiency, effectiveness, and competency of the staff.

For more than fifteen years, Belgian Red Cross–Flanders has played an active role in providing personnel for different tasks within the Red Cross movement. These people are called "delegates." In terms of training, a basic training is set up by the respective National Societies, while an advanced training is organized at the international level.

SELECTION PROCEDURES

Each year, several hundred people apply for working with the Red Cross by sending in their curricula vitae. Subsequently, candidates are screened on a number of general requirements, such as a minimum age of twenty-five and a maximum age of fifty-five; relevant formal education/training; a minimum of three years' work experience; and the ability to communicate (work) well in English and/or French.

The Red Cross is continuously searching for colleagues who have a sincere desire to help people in need. Candidates who pass the first screening are invited for an interview, where a closer look is taken at their motivation, language skills, professional qualifications and experience, international field experience, computer literacy, availability, and technical core competencies. A potential delegate should also be in good physical and mental shape and have a sense of adventure.

Still, a candidate who meets these requirements does not automatically make a good candidate. All staff dealing with recruitment are familiar with applicants motivated mainly by unemployment, boredom, or problems at home. These are the worst motivations for successful future delegates. A Red Cross delegate does not join a delegation to do his or her specialist job during "working hours" only; above all, a delegate must be adaptable and flexible, appreciate and respect other cultures, communicate well, and be a team worker.

BASIC TRAINING COURSE

A Basic Training Course (BTC) is organized each year by National Societies involved in the recruitment and training of delegates for assignments with the International Red Cross/Red Crescent Movement. The BTC is a standard training course, with a substantive input from resource persons from the organizing National Society, the Federation, and the ICRC. These resource persons spend an entire week with the participants. They are usually desk officers with extensive field experience, who have also followed a special "training the trainers" workshop.

For the past ten years, systematic reading material has been developed for the course. The idea of writing a course manual consisting of a number of modules arose in the early 1990s. Previous courses and the general experience of National Societies showed that there was a need and a demand for a standard approach. The purpose of this manual is to outline the standard approach for BTCs and provide the necessary support to organize and conduct such courses. It is meant to offer a framework that is flexible enough so that each National Society can adapt it to its own particular situation. It is essentially a practical and "living" tool, offering a collection of ideas, guidelines, and materials for preparing and conducting Basic Training Courses. The manual includes:

- An introduction to the standard BTC approach.
- An introduction to the different modules.
- A checklist for organizers and resource persons.
- Training tips for the resource persons and for each module: guidelines for organizers and resource persons defining the objective, key learning points, other specific advice and reference material; a set of overheads with notes for resource persons on how to present basic concepts; a set of exercises, case studies, games, and sketches, each accompanied by instruction notes for the resource persons on how to conduct the exercises; and a set of handouts to be distributed to the participants.

Likewise, Belgian Red Cross–Flanders organizes a one-week Basic Training Course every year. Out of all the people interviewed since the last course, about twenty to twenty-five candidates are selected for a new course. They are informed about their selection two to three months in advance. Selection is also determined by the need for specific profiles in upcoming missions.

Aim and Objectives of a BTC

The overall aim of a BTC is not so much to teach the participants specific technical skills but to prepare them for fulfilling their role as Red Cross/Red Crescent (RC/RC) delegates in the field. That is why the main focus of a BTC is an introduction to the RC/RC framework; the relief and development context in which the delegate will work; and the profile and identity of an RC/RC delegate.

The key objectives of the course are to increase participants' understanding of and commitment to RC/RC structure and principles; to discuss issues, problems, and challenges participants may meet in situations of conflict, disasters, and development; to provide participants with knowledge and practical tips to help them work effectively in a delegation; to help develop participants' skills in relation to relief and development issues and dilemmas; and to provide participants and the National Society with the opportunity to reassess their suitability to work as RC/RC delegates.

The course lasts five to six days and is residential in order to enhance team building.

Methodology

Extensive use is made of personal experiences, case studies, group work and discussions, short presentations, and videos. The course is designed to involve participants as much as possible, with particular emphasis on their role within a team. The whole course is focused on specific situations in which delegates may find themselves—concepts and theory are used when considered useful to increase understanding. In general, a BTC is designed according to the following principles:

- Specific situation: wherever possible, the topic should be initiated with a specific case in which future delegates may find themselves. These situations can be presented in the form of case studies, personal experiences, or a video.
- Problems and dilemmas: the above cases are used to illustrate the typical problems, challenges, frustrations, issues, and dilemmas that a delegate may face.
- Solutions: the participants should be encouraged to find solutions to specific problems, assisted by the resource persons present.
- Conceptual framework: resource persons can present the theory

provided that it is limited in time, applied to particular cases, and
meant to raise awareness.

A typical BTC organized by the Belgian Red Cross–Flanders last year is
shown in Exhibit 3.2-1.

Exhibit 3.2-1   Basic Training Course

	Day 1	Day 2	Day 3
Morning		Module 2—RC/RC framework: history and origin of the movement; principles; international structure; rules of international humanitarian law	Continuation of Module 3
Afternoon		Continuation of Module 2 Module 3—conflict situations: role and activities of the ICRC in preconflict situations and international and noninternational armed conflicts	Module 4—disaster situations: types of disasters and effects; initial assessment; concept of vulnerability: the most vulnerable
Evening	Arrival of participants Module 1—opening of the course: welcome, aims, objectives, and practical arrangements	Stress management	Exchange of experiences

	Day 4	Day 5	Day 6
Morning	Continuation of Module 4— rules and principles of RC/RC relief assistance; role of the International Federation of Red Cross and Red Crescent Societies	Module 6—working in a delegation: purpose and organization of delegations, security, safety, stress management, and support; teamwork and life in a delegation Module 7—working relationships in the field: relations within the RC/ RC movement	Module 8—development: development within the RC/RC context; dimensions of development (human/institutional); rules and principles of RC/RC development assistance
Afternoon	Module 5—cultural awareness: cultural sensitivity, culture shock, and cultural pressure points; skills for cultural assimilation	Continuation of Module 7—relations with other NGOs and UN agencies and with the media Camp management	Continuation of Module 8 Module 9—practical information: recruitment procedures; briefings; regulations and employment conditions; health and personal arrangements
Evening	Free	Role plays	Social evening

As teamwork will be of major importance when involved in the field, this issue is stressed during the training course. Role-plays and group work are focused on checking the participants' ability to function as part of a team. Next, the specific mandate and tasks of the Red Cross delegates are defined during the course, as is the relationship of the delegates with the National Societies in the field. Finally, intercultural games are played to raise cultural awareness.

At the end of the course, the participants are individually evaluated by the resource persons. Their suitability for the different positions in the field and for particular kinds of operations as well as their weaker and stronger points are discussed. Although the course does not aim to be a selection instrument as such, occasionally participants will be excluded after the course from further employment possibilities within the organization.

EMPLOYMENT FOR MISSIONS AND FURTHER PREMISSION TRAINING

National Societies that regularly put delegates at the disposal of the other components of the movement regularly receive lists of open positions in the field from both the Federation and the ICRC. They may propose suitable candidates after carefully checking the candidate's qualifications for a particular job description (currently there are about sixty standard job descriptions) and, of course, after having discussed the job description and circumstances with the respective candidate.

In Geneva, where both the Federation and the ICRC have their headquarters, the final choice is made as to which candidate gets the particular job. This decision is made by their human resource officers, in coordination with the respective technical departments and desk officers.

Delegates can be employed in operations for various positions:

- Coordinating positions: head of delegation or head of subdelegation, relief coordinator, medical coordinator, or logistics coordinator.
- Supervisory or executive positions: relief administrators, finance-administrative delegates, telecommunication specialists, surgeons, anaesthetists, nurses, dissemination officers (delegates who are responsible for the dissemination of the principles and international humanitarian law), and information officers.
- Advisory positions: development delegates and disaster preparedness delegates who assist other National Societies with carrying out disaster preparedness activities and development programs and with setting up local Red Cross societies.

Belgian Red Cross–Flanders gives candidates who have been accepted by one of the Geneva institutions a contract of limited duration (mostly ranging from six months to one year). Besides, Belgian Red Cross–Flanders also takes care of their visa application, transport tickets, and insurance. After their first briefing at Brussels headquarters, the delegates leave for Geneva, where another extensive briefing is given before moving to the field. In case they leave for the Federation, so-called first-timers, that is, people who leave for the field for the first time, have to follow an induction course in Geneva, which lasts one week.

This training was introduced in 1998 with the aim of introducing new delegates to the Federation culture, mandate, policies, rules, and procedures as contained in the *Handbook of Delegates;* of developing a sense of group identity and giving new delegates an opportunity to familiarize themselves with the secretariat of the Federation and meet senior managers of the organization; and of reinforcing information introduced at the BTC.

Finally, in case they leave for the ICRC for a mission of more than six months, delegates follow a three-week integration course in Geneva to become familiar with the complete range of activities performed by the ICRC.

SPECIFIC TRAINING FOR THE FIELD

Training beyond the basic level (beyond the BTC) was started only after BTCs were common in all sending National Societies (1993). This training can be either position oriented (health, finance, information, etc.) or context specific (security, training of trainers, etc.). Furthermore, at the management level, specific training sessions can be organized. The common goal of such second-level training is to allow the delegates to improve their professional performance in the field.

The broad objectives of this second-level training are to strengthen the delegates' feeling of a professional and social context within the RC/RC movement, giving them a sense of identity and belonging; to update delegates on the most recent developments in policies and procedures within the movement in general and developments specifically related to their field; and to train delegates in specific fields in which there seem to be general problems for the group in question.

Some of the second-level training courses take place in Geneva; other sessions are organized at regional field headquarters. In recent years there has also been a tendency to outsource a number of these training activities to interested National Societies because of managerial, logistical, and financial constraints.

CONCLUSION

The Red Cross/Red Crescent Movement puts a lot of emphasis on training—not only to inform potential staff members and to train (future) delegates, but also to optimize performance and flexibility and to adapt to rapidly changing situations. As for the future, on-the-job training will increase in importance, mostly on a decentralized scale with regional delegations in charge. Finally, to prepare the Red Cross delegates even better for the new challenges that will be coming up in the near future, a lessons-learned approach will need to be intensified—taking into account and integrating into training programs and policies past experiences and participants' course and field evaluations. After all, human resources are the main capital of an organization.

CHAPTER 4

Creating Awareness

■ 4.1

Preparing for a Multicultural Environment

Angelika Spelten

MANAGEMENT OF COMMUNICATION
BEHAVIOR BY MEANS OF LEARNED MODELS

Verbal and nonverbal communication are the core forms of behavior that we use to establish a connection with our social environment and come to terms with the world around us. We want to be able to make contact, to comprehend the interactions in our surroundings, and thus be able to react to them in a way that makes us understood. In order to do this, we must be capable of learning the rules, patterns, and models that our fellow human beings use to regulate their world and make it comprehensible; we must be able to ascribe a specific meaning to events; and we must be able to connect the events to one another.

Without our being aware of it, many areas of our everyday life are normed: they are oriented to codes of behavior and *sociocultural models* that we have learned. In the family, in the community, in our profession, but also in special spheres such as the church or mosque, people adapt their behavior to particular rules and come to have similar expectations of others in their social environment. If we are able to meet these expectations to a certain extent, the result is a consensus that makes community life predictable and imparts a sense of security within social relationships.

Thus, we learn the codes of behavior that enable us to determine what the father expects from his eldest son in a given situation, what the neighbors expect from someone who has just moved in, or what the religious community expects from its members. We learn to adjust to these rules and to adopt them as our own. Such sociocultural models consequently influence not only our perceptions and the manner in which we assimilate information but also the way we act.

We generally know not only whether we should pay a gratuity to the authorities to speed our business along but also how such a gesture should be made so as not to give offense. Or, again, knowing that the police in a particular area want to avoid any charge of antifeminist or gender-insensitive behavior, we can drive on with less delay when the police pull us over by drawing the officers' attention to the pregnant passenger in the back seat.

Communication Patterns Are Linked to Cultural Identity

Such examples also reveal that the roots of sociocultural models are to be found in historical and cultural values, material circumstances, experiences, and traditions. They are, therefore, dependent upon the cultural communities in which people grow up and become socialized. The members of a cultural community have common models and patterns of behavior; however, each person keeps an individual note through minor variations. Large cultural communities may give rise to subgroups and subcultures. Every sports club, business, organization, or circle of friends has elements of a specific code of behavior that sets it apart from both the society at large and from other subgroups and strengthens the internal bonds among the members through a sort of corporate identity. The increasing cultural differentiation within a society through political and economic pluralism, greater division of labor, increased internal mobility, or international interchange all multiply the range of subcultures.

Subcultures are refinements of a larger overall culture and are possible and distinct only in contrast to it: the larger cultural common ground remains even in the face of partial negation. When members of different subcultures meet, each may experience the behavior of the other as strange or alienating, yet as a rule the common frame of reference and superordinate overall culture help make understanding possible without any great difficulty. The dynamics of action and reaction remain relatively calculable for all involved.

THE CHALLENGE OF INTERCULTURAL UNDERSTANDING

It is a different matter altogether when the members of entirely different cultures encounter one another. In such cases, the usual models for structuring and interpreting information or for selecting patterns of behavior no longer correspond to the reactions and codes of behavior of the other person or persons. And the less the behavioral patterns within the two cultures correspond, the more difficult it becomes to adjust one's own behavior to the other's expectations and to interpret and evaluate the other's behavior. Let us clarify this principle with the following example: Can you ever satisfy the police?

A student from an African country governed by a military regime spends several years in western Europe. The police frequently stop him to check his papers. Because of the negative experiences he has had in his own country, he is always somewhat nervous and takes particular care not to make a bad impression on the officers or to provoke them in any way. He seeks to achieve this by being appropriately respectful and maintaining his composure. Specifically, he strictly avoids looking the policemen in the eyes and is careful to respond to their questions quietly, briefly, and simply. This behavior is appropriate to the patterns in his cultural community, where it is considered disrespectful to establish eye contact with a more highly ranking person or to say any more than is strictly necessary. But despite his efforts and the fact that his papers are in order, the student feels that he is being summoned to the police station for further review of his status more than is usual or necessary. He often spends hours there.

From the point of view of the officers, the student is making an entirely different impression than he intends. When someone fails to maintain eye contact, responds to questions hesitantly, quietly, or in monosyllables, this indicates, in terms of the social signals and behavioral patterns familiar to the police, uncertainty and lack of sincerity and leads to the suspicion that something is being concealed. That such persons are submitted to more detailed questioning is no longer so surprising when interpreted in this light.

In this instance, both the student and the police are applying without modification the interpretative and behavioral models customary in their own cultural spheres to another cultural sphere. The anticipated correct response from the other person(s) is not forthcoming, however, for the two respective models display interpretation patterns that are to some extent contradictory. Mutual understanding and behavior appropriate to the situation can only succeed in intercultural situations when existing interpretation and behavioral models have been expanded by elements from the foreign culture, thus leading to the creation of context-related variations of interpretative models. Discriminatory behavior or behavior hostile to foreigners can be characterized by a basic disposition to judge every deviation from familiar or local reaction patterns as deficient or as intentional provocation. What is lacking is the capability or readiness through reflection on one's own cultural precepts to recognize foreign behavior as an equally legitimate and valid alternative for social order and communication behavior.

THE CULTURAL ROOTS OF ONE'S OWN BEHAVIOR

Intercultural training programs aim to inject greater flexibility and breadth into current sociocultural behavioral models. A starting point for this is the study of one's own behavioral patterns and the norms and values they are based upon. Hence, in theory every communication situation can be broken down into four steps: perception, interpretation, evaluation, and reaction. The decisionmaking process in the situation described above—from the moment when the policeman asked for the student's identification papers to the decision to take him along to the station—follows this pattern.

Perception

In the first step, perception, certain bits of information were selected from the available mass as being relevant in terms of the specific background of culture and life experience. Within the perception category, three levels may be distinguished. The content of the policeman's questions and the student's answers are on a *factual level,* namely address, date of birth, and so on. The nature of the interaction—that the policeman considers himself authorized to ask questions while the student only answers without looking at him directly—defines a certain relationship between the two persons (*relationship level*). And, finally, the context is an important aspect of perception. If the police control point is on the periphery of a political demonstration and involves checking a number of people with all sorts of backgrounds, the student would surely have been less nervous than if he had been driving somewhere alone late at night (*context level*).

Interpretation and Evaluation

In the second step, interpretation, the signals entering from the three perception levels are classified, with the aid of the models, into the learned significance categories; causality is established; and the whole series is reshaped into new statements. The policeman in the example above links his two perceptions together—"avoids eye contact" and "gives hesitant answers"—and classifies both in the category of "bad conscience and uncertainty." Together with the interpretations of the two other perception areas (the factual level and the context level), this information is evaluated rationally and emotionally in the third step, with a negative result in our example, "suspicious: should be checked further."

Reaction

This is the point of orientation for the policeman's reaction and for his decision to take the student along to the police station. In reality, the series of events that make up such a reaction take place very quickly and often sub-consciously, and the individual steps may overlap in the process. We frequently make a judgment, such as "this person appears suspicious to me," without knowing ourselves what kind of behavior on the part of the other person gives us this impression. Thus, on the one hand, sociocultural models guide our behavior in situations to which we must react, and, on the other hand, they constitute the basis for our own behavior in situations in which we want to evoke certain reactions from others. Our student used this perspective in planning his own behavior. He wanted to prompt the police officers to react by taking a brief look at his papers and then letting him go his way and turning to someone else. He thought he would be able to achieve this outcome through respectful behavior—that is, on the relationship level. He did not consider it relevant that the data he gave concerning his person—on the factual level—were insufficient. And to influence the (in his mind) important relationship level positively, he sent certain signals (avoidance of eye contact and very limited speech), which he assumed the police officers would interpret the same way he did. This, however, did not turn out to be the case.

The pivotal challenge of intercultural communication lies, first, in being able to recognize the basic rules and evaluation patterns that determine the communication behavior of other people and, second, in being sufficiently flexible to adjust one's own behavior to them.

ORIENTATIONAL AIDS FOR PREPARING FOR ASSIGNMENTS IN INTERCULTURAL CONTEXTS

The best preparation for an assignment in a country located within a different cultural sphere is several weeks of intercultural training with instructors from the region concerned. However, even without a specific training program, it is possible to adapt oneself to the new social environment and to the appropriate communication behavior. To be considered in this process are general models for communication behavior and models related to specific tasks. In both cases, the extent to which—in particularly relevant models—one's own norms diverge from those of the host country should be reviewed and the limitations in terms of mutual understanding and joint action identified. Because it is perfectly possible that people may view certain communication rules in a foreign job location as a restriction of their own rights, the individuals involved should also consider which behavioral modifications they are willing to accept.

A comparison of a few fundamental differences between communication models in different cultural spheres should result in increased awareness of the range of variation among meaning and interpretation models. In the process, however, the description of cultural standards can serve as an orientational aid only to the decoding of real-life models.

General Models for Communication Behavior

The function of communication.   Generally speaking, in every cultural sphere there are various speech communication situations that serve distinct objectives, as in the difference between a declaration of love and a professional meeting. In addition, within each culture there are also basic attitudes or tendencies that distinguish the rules that apply to different cultural spheres. An important characteristic in this regard is the function given to verbal communication.

In the United States and western Europe, for example, the interest in an exchange of information is primary. The speakers tend to focus their attention on the factual level and are more aware of their own signals on this level than they are of the information they are conveying on the relationship or context levels. In extreme cases, the conveying of facts can take on such significance that sacrifices on the relationship level may be accepted in the process (IFIM 1991, 3).

In an African or Asian environment, contrariwise, the relationship level tends to be more important to persons talking together than is the exchange of factual information. The content of conversation is chosen on the basis of whether the dialogue partners will be positively affected and whether a good relationship will result. Factual information or topics that might displease the other person are often softened somewhat and thus altered, or they are not brought up in the first place. When people focus particularly on the relationship level in conversation, the mode of communication, which person introduces the topics, the observation of courtesy, and the division of the amount of speech among the participants all constitute important information in themselves. When partners in communication enter a discussion with widely divergent expectations about the course it should take and its results (exchange of information versus creation of good feelings), misunderstandings and misinterpretations are unavoidable.

These problems in mutual understanding can possibly be reduced when both dialogue partners are prepared for a different mode of exchange. It is helpful before entering such a conversation situation first to examine one's own patterns of behavior. What communication function does one usually emphasize? What significance is ascribed to a particular context and/or the environment in which the dialogue takes place? When these questions have been answered, one can give some thought as to how the same questions would be answered by people from a different cultural sphere and which variations in one's own speech behavior are possible in response to other expectations and codes of behavior.

It is particularly important to be familiar with the forms of courtesy. How does one express respect, gratitude, the decline of an offer, or criticism? Are there set verbal formulae such as dialogue rituals for greeting other persons or taking one's leave?

Self-portrayal. Closely related to the function that we ascribe to communication situations generally is our own role-playing. We would like to make ourselves acceptable or interesting to the persons with whom we speak and to communicate to them an image of ourselves, our wishes, and our role. We can only succeed in doing so, however, if we communicate to them both verbally and nonverbally the kind of information that they, too, perceive as personal qualifiers—characteristics that rate us appropriately. A comparison between recommended behavior for interviews in Germany and in East Africa shows that here, too, fundamental differences may exist.

The code of behavior in East Africa would generally be based on the assumption that employment depends on how applicants would fit into the company's social structure, whether they can employ their technical capabilities in such a way that the work atmosphere is positively influenced, how loyal they would be to the company leadership, and whether they will be accepted by their fellow workers. Applicants that can present themselves as being loyal, reliable, modestly adaptive, and reticent tend to have the best chances. Applicants can make a better impression on their potential boss with information about their background and previous professional connections than with details about their qualifications in their field or the challenges they hope to confront in their new job. Applicants who adopt a reticent, modest, and rather passive mode of behavior during the interview will be more likely to leave a positive impression than those who appear dynamic and talkative.

The recommended mode of behavior for a similar situation at a German firm is based on the assumption that an applicant with the best qualifications, personal commitment, and a reasonable amount of self-confidence is likely to have the best chances for employment. In this context, a person who appears performance- and success-oriented, innovative, dynamic, and even critical will be more likely to get a hearing and a positive response. The interviewer expects detailed information about the applicant's professional qualifications and his successes to date, and indications of what he or she expects from the new position. Information about the applicant's background and current family situation are usually of secondary significance. For the applicant, it is therefore advantageous to participate in actively steering the interview, to be sure and ask questions, and not to appear overly deferential and certainly not obsequious.

In regard to working relationships in an intercultural context, it can be helpful to orient one's own communication behavior to how one's function or position is perceived within the social environment and to existing expectations in terms of roles and behavior. The qualities that lend a person authority can be very diverse. In some social environments, the only persons who are accepted as authority figures are those who have good contacts to traditional dignitaries and otherwise maintain a certain aloofness. In other cultural spheres, being able to hold one's drink and cultivate social contacts may be indispensable attributes. Knowing how to gain others' confidence also facilitates cooperation, as does familiarity with the rules for passing on information.

Behavioral Models Relating to Special Tasks

In ordinary daily life, verbal communication is significant for the interaction of both individuals and groups, but it can be a matter of survival for those working in politically tense situations or where there is potential for violence. In preventive peace efforts, in mediation methods, or in conducting negotiations, verbal adroitness assumes a particularly high value. Even when the processes and procedures have been adapted to the relevant cultural context, there is no assurance that all participants will be speaking the same language. M. Abu-Nimer points out that some mediation and facilitation techniques derived from the European-American context can encounter resistance in, for example, rounds of talks in an Arab setting. He numbers among these the usual language rule of using "I messages," of imparting feelings, too, in formulating the various points, and applying the rules of reflective listening. These standards were rejected by Arab workshop participants as too individualistic, self-centered, and formalistic (Abu-Nimer 1998, 109).

The basic attitude toward conflicts in general and the acceptance of third parties also varies within the cultural context and can be a key influence on the success or failure of peacebuilding activities. Hence, certain basic Western assumptions about conflict resolution directly conflict with the points of view held in, for example, the Arab cultural sphere (Abu-Nimer 1996, 29ff).

Western Assumptions:

Conflict is positive and normal and can bring growth and spur creativity.

Conflict needs to be dealt with in a planned and structured manner.

Addressing the individual's interests, position, needs, and desires is pivotal to conflict resolution.

Arab Assumptions:

Conflict is negative and dangerous: it brings destruction and disorder.

Conflict should be avoided.

Conflict resolution processes are based on group identities and social patterns such as the family

	or clan; these need to be safeguarded and not called into question by the process itself.
Successes in the conflict resolution process should be sealed with a written agreement.	Commitments and agreements are sealed by the establishment or renewal of social or cultural values.

Mediation attempts that ignore the differences and/or characteristics unique to each respective cultural sphere have but little hope of success.

In the context of peacebuilding activities, staff members are often confronted with critical situations in which their communication behavior can influence other persons' tendencies toward violence. For example, reports about unanticipated shifts during negotiations or events at military checkpoints or hostage crises have shown that the parties' readiness for dialogue or violence can be influenced by the communication behavior of the interlocutor. Although the outcome of such critical situations depends upon a number of factors, for those in the victim's position, often communication remains the last chance for action to avert violent escalation. Nonviolent resistance methods and know-how of intercultural communication and mediation can help to make more conscious use of this extra latitude. To prepare for potentially dangerous situations, it appears advisable to gather specifically relevant information and to practice modes of behavior appropriate to the situation.

Try to answer the following questions in order to raise your own awareness of possible difficulties ahead:

1. How should I behave when confronted with members of the military, rebel movements, or an angry mob? In the particular region you are working in at a particular point in time, is it helpful to point out to members of the military, rebels, or an angry population that one belongs to an international aid organization? Would it be more advisable not to refer to the organization but to stress that one is acquainted with the military/rebel movement, already has established contact with several high-ranking persons (name-dropping), and that as yet neither side has got in the other's way?

2. How much do you know about current political constellations, political figures, and their relations to one another? Are there major political decisions at hand that might threaten you? Are there set bases for the actions of certain groups to which one can confidently refer as a (more or less) shared value or objective? Are there verbal expressions that one should avoid, if possible?

3. How can one reduce tensions and uncertainty? Will the person who

appears with rather authoritarian rules and makes procedural proposals be listened to? Can this behavior contribute to a de-escalation, or would a more humorous playing down of tensions and potential dangers tend to be more appropriate in damping hysteria and further escalation? Will women have a chance to be heard, or is it advisable to always send teams of mixed gender and to leave the communication in certain situations to the men?

Behavioral communication models have a pivotal influence on interaction in conflict situations. Intercultural training is, therefore, a necessary element of preparation for peacebuilding in the field. Nevertheless, it should be noted that culture-related codes of behavior undergo a constant process of change and that the strictness with which they must be applied can also vary. Consequently, they present an aid to orientation only and not a set formula of any kind.

REFERENCES AND SUGGESTED READING

Abu-Nimer, M. (1996). "Conflict Resolution in an Islamic Context." *Peace and Change* 21, no. 1 (January): 22–44.

———. (1998). "Conflict Resolution Training in the Middle East: Lessons to Be Learned." *International Negotiation* 3: 99–116.

Augsburger, D. W. (1992). *Conflict Mediation Across Cultures, Pathways and Patterns.* Louisville, Ky.: John Knox Press.

Bennett, M. J. (1993). "Towards Ethnorelativism: A Development Model of Intercultural Sensitivity." In R. Michael Paige, *Education for the Intercultural Experience.* Yarmouth, Me.: Intercultural Press, 21–69.

Bittner, A., and B. Reisch. (1990). "Kulturstandards, Ein Orientierungssystem für das Leben und Arbeiten im Ausland." Working paper, Institute for Intercultural Management, Königswinter, Germany.

Flechsig, K.-H. (1998). "Kulturelle Schemata und interkulturelles Lernen." Working paper no. 3, Institute for Intercultural Didactics, Göttingen University.

Hofstede, G. (1991). *Cultures and Organizations: Software of the Mind. Intercultural Cooperation and Its Importance for Survival.* London: McGraw Hill.

IFIM (Institut für Interkulturelles Management). (1991). *KS-10.* Germany: IFIM.

Kiel, E. (1997). "Die Entwicklung interkultureller Kommunikationskompetenz aus der Sicht der Interkulturellen Didaktik." Working paper no. 2, Institute for Intercultural Didactics, Göttingen University.

Landis, D., and R. S. Bhagat, eds. (1996). *Handbook of Intercultural Training, Issues in Theory and Design.* London: Sage.

Skabelund, G. P., S. M. Sims, and P. Brown, eds. (1992). *Culturegram '92.* Provo: David M. Kennedy Center for International Studies, Brigham Young University.

Thomas, A., S. Kammhuber, and G. Layes. (1997). *Interkulturelle Kompetenz—Ein*

Handbuch für internationale Einsätze der Bundeswehr, München. Munich: Verlag für Wehrwissenschaften.

INSTITUTIONS/UNIVERSITIES/ORGANIZATIONS

Institut für Interkulturelles Management (IFIM), Im Mühlenbruch 1, 53639 Königswinter, Germany. This institute operates within the private sector and offers materials on cultural and communication standards for different countries and regions, as well as training seminars mainly held in German, with some in English as well. URL: http://www.ifim.de.

International Academy for Intercultural Research. The aim of the academy is to provide a forum where senior intercultural researchers, academics, and trainers can exchange ideas, theories, research, and successful training approaches. In this way the academy fosters high-level research and scholarship on intercultural issues. All disciplines are welcome in the academy. URL: http://www.interculturalacademy.org.

John Brown University, Department of Intercultural Studies. The department offers courses designed to cultivate an awareness of the cultural, political, economic, linguistic, and spiritual diversity of our interdependent world and prepare Christian leaders to live and serve effectively in an intercultural community. URL: http://www.jbu.edu/sbs/ics/.

University of Hawaii at Manoa, Department of Communication. The department faculty educates its students in the social communication sciences. It focuses not only on interpersonal and intercultural communication but also on management, international communication, and telecommunication. It also provides a comprehensive list of intercultural communication-related Web sites. URL: http://www2.soc.hawaii.edu/css/com.html.

Institute for Intercultural Didactics at Göttingen University. The institute focuses on didactical methods for teaching people from different cultural backgrounds. URL: http://www.gwdg.de/~kflechs/iikdarbeitsgebiete.htm.

■ 4.2

Mainstreaming a Gender Perspective

Beth Woroniuk

This article is designed to provide guidance to organizations working in the field of conflict management (which includes prevention, containment, resolution, reconciliation, and reconstruction). It is an attempt to draw operational lessons from our increasing understanding of the interrelationship of gender-equality issues, conflict, and peacebuilding. Based on a review of reports and published sources, it sets out questions to be asked and issues to explore. The Canadian International Development Agency (CIDA) framework itself will evolve. It assumes that participatory approaches are more effective than top-down initiatives and that both women and men must be involved in building peace and gender equality.

BACKGROUND

Gender Equality and Mainstreaming

Gender equality has been adopted as a vital goal for development cooperation agencies and their programs, with mainstreaming used more and more as a strategy to support that goal.

> Gender refers to the socially constructed roles and responsibilities of women and men. [It] . . . includes the expectations held about the characteristics, aptitudes and likely behaviours of both women and men (femininity and masculinity). These roles and expectations are learned, changeable over time, and variable within and between cultures.[1]

Gender equality requires equal enjoyment by women and men of socially valued goods, opportunities, resources, and rewards. Gender equality does not mean that men and women become the same but that their opportunities and life chances are equal. The emphasis on gender equality and women's empowerment does not presume a particular model of gender equality for all societies and cultures; rather, it reflects a concern that women and men have equal opportunities to make choices about what gender equality means and work in partnership to achieve it.

Because of current disparities, equal treatment of women and men is insufficient as a strategy for gender equality. Achieving gender equality will require changes in institutional practices and social relations through which disparities are reinforced and sustained. It also requires a strong voice for women in shaping their societies.

Mainstreaming is a strategy to support the goal of gender equality. It has two general dimensions: (1) the integration of gender-equality concerns into the analyses and formulation of all policies, programs, and projects; and (2) initiatives to enable women as well as men to formulate and express their views and participate in decisionmaking across all development issues.[2]

The Emergence of a New Form of Peacebuilding

This framework is grounded in a broad definition of peacebuilding:

> Peacebuilding refers to those initiatives which foster and support sustainable structures and processes which strengthen the prospects for peaceful coexistence and decrease the likelihood of the outbreak, reoccurrence or continuation of violent conflict. This process typically contains both immediate and longer term objectives. . . . Peacebuilding is a two-fold process requiring both the deconstruction of the structures of violence and the construction of the structures of peace.[3]

Why Look at Gender Equality Issues in Peacebuilding Initiatives?

It is important to ensure that gender-equality issues are taken into consideration in peacebuilding initiatives for several reasons. First, gender is a relevant dimension in peacebuilding. Conflict is a gendered activity. There is a strong gender division of labor; women and men have differential access to resources (including power and decisionmaking) during conflicts; and men and women experience conflict differently. This was recognized by the international community and highlighted in the final document of the Fourth World Conference on Women (Beijing, 1995), the Platform for Action (PFA): "While entire communities suffer the consequences of armed conflict and terrorism, women and girls are particularly affected because of their status in society as well as their sex" (para 135).

Second, women (as well as men) have a fundamental stake in building peaceful communities. Their contributions to peacebuilding should be encouraged and supported; given women's economic and political marginalization, they are not always well placed to play an effective role.

Third, gender perspective should be part of peacebuilding initiatives. The PFA states: "In addressing armed or other conflicts, an active and visible policy of mainstreaming a gender perspective into all policies and programmes should be promoted so that before decisions are taken, an analysis is made of the effects on women and men, respectively" (para 141).

Last, peace is a prerequisite to achieve the goal of gender equality and women's empowerment, and some would argue that gender equality is necessary for true peace (broadly defined).

Gender Issues in Conflict Situations

All conflict/peacebuilding situations are different, hence there is always a need to analyze each case individually. Factors such as gender, religion, age, class, nationality, ethnicity, race, and sexual orientation will come together in different ways. Exhibit 4.2-1 provides some examples of ways that gender differences and inequalities may be relevant in conflict situations.

WHAT TO DO?

What are the implications of our increasing understanding of both the gender dimensions of conflict and peacebuilding and the role of development assistance in facilitating peacebuilding processes? There are two fundamental dimensions. First, all initiatives should:

- Incorporate a gender analysis into the assessment of the situation.
- Ensure that gender-equality considerations are present at the level of results (in other words, gender-equality issues should not be restricted to one component of a project; rather, they should be part of and influence the primary direction of the initiative).
- Increase women's participation in conflict resolution at decision-making levels.
- Promote women as actors and protagonists (rather than as a "vulnerable group").
- Provide, where feasible, sex-disaggregated data (of participants, beneficiaries, etc.).

Second, there is also a need for specific initiatives to strengthen women's capacity to participate in peacebuilding initiatives in a meaningful fashion, to improve the capacity of organizations to deal with gender differences and inequalities, and to reduce gender inequalities. This could involve initiatives and/or components that directly target women (including skills training and improving the capacity of women's organizations) and/or men (such as sensitization and analyses of links between notions of masculinity and violence).

Exhibit 4.2-1   Elements of Conflict Situations and Possible Gender Dimensions

Elements of Conflict Situations	Possible Gender Dimensions

During Preconflict Situations

Increased mobilization of soldiers.	Increased commercial sex trade (including child prostitution) around military bases and army camps.
Nationalist propaganda used to increase support for military action.	Gender stereotypes and specific definitions of masculinity and femininity are often promoted. There may be increased pressure on men to "defend the nation."
Mobilization of pro-peace activists and organizations.	Women have been active in peace movements—both generally and in women-specific organizations. Women have often drawn moral authority from their role as mothers. It has also been possible for women to protest from their position as mothers when other forms of protest have not been permitted by authorities.
Increasing human rights violations.	Women's rights are not always recognized as human rights. Gender-based violence may increase.

During Conflict Situations

Psychological trauma, physical violence, casualties, and death.	Men tend to be the primary soldiers/combatants. Yet in various conflicts, women have made up significant numbers of combatants. Women and girls are often victims of sexual violence (including rape, sexual mutilation, sexual humiliation, forced prostitution, and forced pregnancy) during times of armed conflict.
Social networks disrupted and destroyed—changes in family structures and composition.	Gender relations can be subject to stress and change. The traditional division of labor within a family may be under pressure. Survival strategies often necessitate changes in the gender division of labor. Women may become responsible for an increased number of dependents.
Mobilization of people for conflict. Everyday life and work disrupted.	The gender division of labor in workplaces can change. With men's mobilization for combat, women have often taken over traditionally male occupations and responsibilities. Women have challenged traditional gender stereotypes and roles by becoming combatants and taking on other nontraditional roles.
Material shortages (shortages of food, health care, water, fuel, etc.).	Women's role as provider of the everyday needs of the family may mean increased stress and work as basic goods are more difficult to locate. Girls may also face an increased workload. Noncombatant men may also experience stress related to their domestic gender roles if they are expected, but unable, to provide for their families.
Creation of refugees and displaced people.	People's ability to respond to an emergency situation is influenced by whether they are male or female. Women and men refugees (as well as boys and girls) often have different needs and priorities.
Dialogue and peace negotiations.	Women are often excluded from the formal discussions given their lack of participation and access in preconflict decisionmaking organizations and institutions.

(continues)

Exhibit 4.2-1 (continued)

Elements of Conflict Situations	Possible Gender Dimensions
During Reconstruction and Rehabilitation	
Political negotiations and planning to implement peace accords.	Men's and women's participation in these processes tends to vary, with women often playing only minor roles in formal negotiations or policymaking.
Media used to communicate messages (peace accords, etc.).	Women's unequal access to media may mean that their interests, needs, and perspectives are not represented and discussed.
Use of outside investigators, peacekeepers, etc.	Officials are not generally trained in gender-equality issues (women's rights as human rights, how to recognize and deal with gender-specific violence). Women and girls have been harassed and sexually assaulted by peacekeepers.
Holding of elections.	Women face specific obstacles in voting, in standing for elections, and in having gender-equality issues discussed as election issues.
International investments in employment creation, health care, etc.	Reconstruction programs may not recognize or give priority to supporting women's and girls' health needs, domestic responsibilities, or needs for skills training and credit.
Demobilization of combatants.	Combatants often assumed to be all male. If priority is granted to young men, women do not benefit from land allocations, credit schemes, etc.
Measures to increase the capacity of and confidence in civil society.	Women's participation in community organizations and nongovernmental organizations is generally uneven. These organizations often lack the capacity and interest in granting priority to equality issues.

Gender Analysis in Peacebuilding Initiatives

In recent years, significant work has been done in developing gender frameworks and analytical tools. Exhibit 4.2-2 distills some of this thinking into questions to be asked in peacebuilding initiatives. To be most effective, the questions should not be asked in a mechanistic manner. They are meant to spark discussion and action on how best to incorporate a gender-equality perspective and improve peacebuilding initiatives.

Entry Points

In attempting to link gender-equality objectives to general peacebuilding objectives, there are numerous possible entry points. Exhibit 4.2-3 offers an initial list that builds on the potential peace and conflict impact assessment areas.

Exhibit 4.2-2   Gender Analysis in Peacebuilding Initiatives

Key Questions to Ask	Why Ask This Question?
How and why is gender equality relevant to the proposed results/impacts of the project?	All too often gender-equality issues are considered as a subset or a marginal issue. Experience has shown that it is important to bring equality issues into the main proposed results for an initiative. In many programs, attention has focused on increasing women's participation in project activities rather than considering the overall impact on gender inequalities.
Has there been an analysis of how women can contribute to peace in this situation and how the peacebuilding initiative can contribute to gender equality?	Consistent with the move toward mainstreaming strategies, gender-equality issues should be brought into the core of the initiative. For example, an economic reconstruction program should look at how women participate in the overall program, not merely set aside a marginal amount of money for "women's projects."
Has contact been made with local/regional peace organizations, especially those involving women?	It is important to build on local initiatives and draw on relevant expertise.
Is there a clear understanding of people's differential conflict experiences both between women and men and among different groups of women?	Research has clearly demonstrated that women and men experience conflict differently. (Exhibit 4.2-1 outlines numerous gender-equality issues.) Gender imbalances in access to power are reflected in numerous ways. It is important that these differences be recognized in the general analysis and design of interventions.
Does the analysis include a consideration of the gender division of labor, differential access and control of resources, and include domestic work in the calculations of work?	Despite the recognition of the importance of gender analysis, it is rarely done as part of the project preparation. Yet this type of analysis should be seen as routine and part of the crucial information necessary to understand a specific situation.
Have women participated in a meaningful fashion in the design of the project? Have the project holders/partners established a "channel of access" to women and demonstrated a capacity to involve women?	Participatory methodologies will not automatically ensure that women's voices are heard or that their perspectives are represented in project design. It is important to understand the obstacles women face when participating in programs or political processes and work to minimize these obstacles.
Are women viewed as actors and protagonists rather than as victims?	Development cooperation organizations have often focused on women as victims rather than on strengthening their capacity to survive, act, articulate alternative visions, and rebuild.

Exhibit 4.2-3   Entry Points to Support Gender Equality in Peacebuilding

Institutional Capacity to Manage/Resolve Conflict and Build Peace

Support for women's role in peacebuilding: What is the role of women both in mixed organizations and women's organizations in peacebuilding initiatives—both formally and informally? (Even when women have been excluded from the formal discussions, they have often played an important role through civil society institutions in trying to hold governments accountable for their commitments.) Are women involved in early warning systems? Do women, as well as men, receive training in mediation, facilitation, and alternative dispute resolution? Is there an analysis of the barriers that women face when attempting to participate in peacebuilding initiatives? Is there a role for women-specific activities?

Institutional capacity to work with a gender-equality perspective: Do local and international organizations have the capacity to recognize and work with gender-equality issues? For example, do investigators of war crimes take full consideration of gender-based violence, and do witness protection programs consider the safety of witnesses testifying in cases relating to gender-based violence? Do organizations working with refugees have the capacity to implement the United Nations High Commissioner for Refugees (UNHCR) guidelines on refugee women? Do Canadian organizations providing support and assistance have the capacity to work with gender issues?

Human Security

Individual security: Are the basic physical security needs of women and girls being met? Is there a recognition that women and girls face specific dangers primarily related to their sex? Is there a consideration of women's sense and definition of security? (Specific issues for attention include violence against women and girl refugees, prostitution, gender-based violence, rape, etc.) In addressing basic human needs and survival strategies, is there consideration of needs of both women and men (based on their health needs and domestic roles and responsibilities)?

Public and state security: Do public security forces receive adequate training on women's rights and violence against women? Do women have equal access to employment in public security forces? Do they have equal access to membership in civilian review boards? Do oversight institutions (ombudsmen, complaints boards, etc.) have the mandate and authority to investigate violations of women's rights related to the conflict?

Political Structures and Processes

Women's involvement: Will the project support women's participation and decisionmaking within political structures, organizations, and other institutions? Will nongovernmental organizations gain insight into how better to represent their female members? Will women's organizations gain new skills and capacity in articulating policy alternatives, holding governments accountable, and being advocates for change?

Human rights: Do all human rights initiatives recognize and support women's rights as human rights?

Legal framework: Special support can be directed to ensuring that the legal system complies with international norms and conventions on women's legal and human rights (including the Convention on the Elimination of All Forms of Discrimination Against Women [CEDAW] and the Beijing Platform for Action).

Women within state structures: Will women have equal access to state employment and advancement at all levels?

Economic Structures and Processes

Economic reconstruction: Do reconstruction programs allow for equitable participation by women? Are these programs designed so that women can take advantage of new resources and/or opportunities? Will women's productive roles be supported by these programs?

(continues)

Exhibit 4.2-3 (continued)

Social Reconstruction and Empowerment

Support the gains women might have made: In some conflict situations, women might have moved into nontraditional occupations or made other gains. Development assistance can play a role in helping ensure that there is no movement back. Support can be provided to women's organizations, and efforts can be made to grant legitimacy to these new roles.

Women's empowerment: Is there support for women's empowerment generally (as defined by international conventions including CEDAW and the Beijing Platform for Action)? Do projects anticipate and attempt to minimize backlash?

Anticipated Results

Anticipated results should be developed in close cooperation with the people involved in a specific initiative. They will also depend on the situation, the institutions involved, and the scope of the project.

Ideally, a gender-equality perspective should be part of the primary anticipated results of an initiative. For example, if a project aims to help restore the political, legal, security, and civil structures necessary for the establishment of peace,[4] gender-equality dimensions must include:

1. Enhancement of human security: the initiative distinguishes between the security of women and men (as well as boys and girls) and ensures that everyone's security is enhanced.
2. Increased capacity of local leadership to assume responsibility for peace: local leadership includes both women and men; local leadership has the capacity to recognize the needs and potential participation of both women and men.
3. Empowerment of civil society: women are active participants in civil society organizations; organizations represent both their female and male members; vibrant women's organizations and other equality-seeking organizations are active in setting policy agendas.
4. Increased trust in, reliance on, and functioning capacity of political and legal systems: legal systems are based on and promote women's rights; both women and men have trust in the political and legal systems; there is increased participation of women in the political system.
5. Demilitarization of society and conversion of war economies: both women and men benefit from economic promotion initiatives; demilitarization is ensured at all levels (including the household). A similar analysis could be carried out for other primary expected results.

Indicators

In general, sex-disaggregated indicators can offer some of the differential impacts of initiatives on women and men. For example, asking how many peace negotiators were women, or the voting rates of women and men, or the male/female ratio of a group of displaced people can offer insights into gender differences and the varying impact of a project on women and men. Indicators of more equal gender relations and women's increased role in setting a peacebuilding agenda are more difficult to frame. In part, they will be situation specific, as they will relate to what each project is intending to achieve. However potential indicators could be based on:

- Increased participation of women in peacebuilding.
- Respect for women's human rights; institutions able to deal with women's complaints relating to human rights abuses.
- Ratification and implementation of international agreements on women's rights and empowerment.
- Improved infant and maternal mortality figures.
- Number of women standing for election and the number elected.
- Percentage of new businesses started by women.

A third set of indicators offers guidance on whether attention has been given to gender-equality considerations in specific projects: (1) expected results should include a gender-equality dimension; (2) resources must be provided to ensure that the gender-equality dimension is delivered during the implementation phase; and (3) the implementing organizations must have a demonstrated capacity to work with equality issues.

NOTES

This article was written by the author for the Canadian International Development Agency's (CIDA's) Peacebuilding Unit (Multilateral Programs Branch) and CIDA's Gender Equality Unit (Policy Branch), April 1999. Comments and feedback are welcome. Please contact: peacebuilding@acdi-cida.gc.ca. It is reprinted here, with minor changes, with kind permission from the author and CIDA.

1. From CIDA's *Policy on Gender Equality,* 1998.

2. Gender equality and mainstreaming definitions are from *DAC Guidelines for Gender Equality and Women's Empowerment in Development Cooperation,* 1998.

3. Kenneth Bush, "A Measure of Peace: Peace and Conflict Assessment (PCA) of Development Projects in Conflict Zones," working paper no. 1, the Peacebuilding and Reconstruction Program Initiative and Evaluation Unit, IDRC, Ottawa, 1998.

4. These sample results are taken from Anne-Marie Laprise, *Programming for Results in Peacebuilding: Challenges and Opportunities in Setting Performance*

Indicators. Prepared for the Strategic Planning Division of the Policy Branch, CIDA, 1998.

REFERENCES AND SUGGESTED READING

Background Documents

BRIDGE. (1996). *Gender, Emergencies and Humanitarian Assistance.* Commissioned by WID desk, European Commission, Directorate General for Development.

————. (1996). *Gender, Conflict and Development.* Vol. 1: *Overview.* Vol. 2: *Case Studies.* Report nos. 34 and 35. Prepared for the Netherlands' Special Program on WID, Ministry of Foreign Affairs.

Canadian Peacebuilding Coordinating Committee. (1998). *Gender and Peacebuilding: A Discussion Paper.* See http://www.cpcc.ottawa.on.ca/cgend-e/htm.

Date-Bah, E. (1996). *Sustainable Peace After War: Arguing the Need for Major Integration of Gender Perspectives in Post-Conflict Programming.* Action Program on Skills and Entrepreneurship Training for Countries Emerging from Armed Conflict, International Labour Organization.

Grenier, S. (1997). *Bibliography on the Rights of Women in Situations of Conflict.* Montreal: International Center for Human Rights and Democratic Development. See http://www.ichrdd.ca/publicationsE/biblioWomen.html.

Manning, K., and B. Arneil. (1997). *Engendering Peacebuilding.* See http://www.dfait-maeci.c.ca/virtual/foreignpolicy/english/gender.htm.

Nordstrom, C. (1997). *Girls and War Zones: Troubling Questions.* Uppsala: Life and Peace Institute.

Sorensen, B. (1998). *Women and Post-Conflict Reconstruction: Issues and Sources.* The War-Torn Societies Project. Occasional paper no. 3. UNRISD, Geneva.

SIDA. (1997). *Overview: Gender Equality and Emergency Assistance/Conflict Resolution.* Stockholm.

UNESCO. (1997). *Expert Group Meeting on Male Roles and Masculinities in the Perspective of a Culture of Peace.* 24–28 September, Oslo. See http://www.unesco.org/cpp/uk/projects/oslotoc.htm.

Women's Rights Unit, United Nations Division for the Advancement of Women. (1998). "Sexual Violence and Armed Conflict: United Nations Response." *Women 2000* (April). New York. See http://www.un.org/womenwatch/daw/public/cover.htm.

International Agreements and Guidelines

Beijing Platform for Action. Critical Area of Concern: Women and Armed Conflict. Strategic objectives:

- E.1: Increase the participation of women in conflict resolution at decision-making levels and protect women living in situations of armed and other conflicts or under foreign occupation.
- E.4: Promote women's contribution to fostering a culture of peace.

- E.5: Provide protection, assistance, and training to refugee women, other displaced women in need of international protection, and internally displaced women.

Full text available at http://www.un.org/womenwatch/daw/beijing/platform/armed.htm.

The Vienna Declaration and Program of Action (1993). Article 38: "Violations of the human rights of women in situations of armed conflict are violations of the fundamental principles of international human rights and humanitarian law." For complete text, see http://www.unhchr.ch/html/menu5/d/vienna.htm.

Declaration on the Protection of Women and Children in Emergency and Armed Conflict (1974). Available at: http://www.unhchr.ch/html/menu3/b/24.htm.
UNHCR. (1991). *Guidelines on the Protection of Refugee Women*. Geneva.
UNHCR. (1995). *Sexual Violence Against Refugees: Guidelines on Prevention and Response*. Geneva.

PART 2

Working in the Field

CHAPTER 5

Selecting Approaches to Mediation

■ 5.1

Western Approaches to Negotiation and Mediation: An Overview

Thania Paffenholz

Mediation as an instrument of peaceful conflict resolution in Western societies has existed since early history. But it was not until the twentieth century that mediation was institutionalized in international law as a means of peaceful resolution of interstate conflict. Although the debate on mediation became concentrated on states and diplomacy in the late 1970s, different mediation approaches, more social psychology oriented, entered the debate on mediating wars. The actors were now civil society representatives.

As a result of this historical development, Western approaches to mediation make a distinction between actors on the state level (governments and international or regional organizations) and actors on the civil society level (international or local nongovernmental organizations [NGOs], research institutes, churches, or individuals). Whereas states as mediators (called Track 1) use only one approach to mediation, civil society mediators (called Track 2) use a variety of approaches.

This distinction between the two levels of actors has been in place for a long time, yet modern Western approaches to mediation have tried to bring the two levels together: these complementary approaches argue that, in reality, both levels, Tracks 1 and 2, are needed for successful conflict resolution. Lately, a new type of approach has been developed, leading to a process-oriented understanding of mediation and peacebuilding. The development of Western approaches to mediation can be illustrated in Exhibit 5.1-1:

Exhibit 5.1-1   The Development of Western Approaches to Mediation

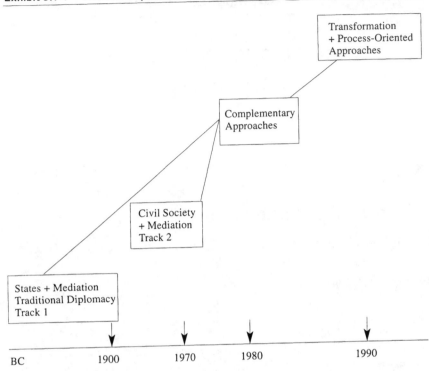

DIFFERENT TYPES OF MEDIATION

Mediation by states is practiced in the form of official or quiet diplomacy. The usual types of mediation are good offices, facilitation, consultation, negotiation, and *mediation*.[1] The mediators are diplomats.

Good Offices are low-intervention mediation efforts. Facilitation occurs prior or parallel to the negotiations, when facilitators try to bring conflicting parties together; facilitators talk to the parties separately, often through shuttle diplomacy. Within consultations, mediators acts like advisers to the conflicting parties. Negotiation is a type of mediation, when a third party is involved and both sides are present. A negotiator tries to bring the different views of the conflicting parties together and helps them to formulate an agreement. *Mediation,* mainly on the level of states, is more interfering than other types of mediation, because mediators give their own opinions of the process and usually try to develop their own plan for resolving a conflict.

TRACK I, STATES AND MEDIATION: TRADITIONAL DIPLOMACY

How States Mediate: The Outcome-Oriented Approach

States mediate with the so-called outcome-oriented approach. The aim of this approach is to identify the representative leaders of the conflicting parties and to bring them together to negotiate or mediate a cease-fire and a peace accord.

The outcome-oriented approach has been the focus of various criticisms: John Paul Lederach highlights that states tend to concentrate solely on the top leadership of the conflicting parties in the negotiations.[2] Norbert Ropers claims that states as mediators in internal wars are not neutral because they have the priority to favor outcomes within a state perspective.[3] Mark Hoffman and many others think that the outcome-oriented approach overlooks deep causes of conflicts. According to him, this approach cannot guarantee long-term stability.[4] Although those critiques are valid, this approach remains a major instrument in ending a large number of wars.

Power Mediation: A Special Form of the Outcome-Oriented Approach

Power *mediation* has all the criteria of the outcome-oriented approach plus the explicit possibility of use of power, including force. States that are able to bring resources (financial "carrots" or military "sticks") into the negotiations can practice this approach. One of the most important key concepts related to this approach is the concept of ripeness.[5] A conflict is ripe for resolution when a hurting stalemate is reached. Two types of stalemate can be distinguished: a plateau and a precipice. A plateau starts when one party cannot reach its aims anymore. The plateau is reached when all parties involved experience the same. A precipice starts when a conflict situation changes suddenly. This could, for example, be the death of a leader of one of the conflicting parties or a natural disaster such as a drought.

What can mediators in such a situation do? They should try to make the stalemate more salient for the parties. In a lot of cases there is already a stalemate present, but the conflicting parties do not realize it. Consequently, the mediators can try to convince the conflicting parties that it is more profitable to negotiate for peace than to continue with war (win-win outcome). Mediators can also make use of sticks and carrots to underline these efforts. Sticks can be any sort of military or financial threat. Carrots are usually linked to financial promises and commitments for reconstruction.

A good example of power mediation is the U.S.-generated peace treaty for Bosnia in the summer of 1995 when the United States linked financial support to reconstruct war-torn Bosnia to a peace agreement by the warring parties. The United States announced it would bomb Bosnian Serb artillery in case no agreement was reached. Another example is the mediation in Haiti, when former U.S. president Jimmy Carter mediated an agreement while U.S. troops were ready to intervene.

TRACK 2: CIVIL SOCIETY AND MEDIATION

Nonofficial mediation is practiced by many different types of actors, from academics to international or local NGOs and nonorganized individuals. All of these actors do not represent a government or an international organization.[6]

On the Track 2 level, there are many more approaches to mediation than on the Track 1 level. Yet the aim of both tracks is to work on the deeper causes of conflicts in order to develop long-term solutions. The third parties here are nondirective and try to empower the conflicting parties to find their own solutions. The approaches are long-term and relationship-oriented because they aim at rebuilding destroyed relationships between the conflicting parties.

One of the most popular approaches is the problem-solving workshop (PS workshop).[7] The aim of these workshops is to improve the relationship between the conflicting parties and to get at the root causes of conflicts. In spite of the diversity of different workshops, the core ideas are always the same. Usually representatives of the conflicting parties are invited who have access to the top leadership. The selection of the participants is tremendously important.

The approach concentrates also on the needs of the parties. To do this, John Burton developed a human needs theory.[8] The premise is that, in violent conflicts, fundamental human needs, like security, identity, or participation, are not satisfied. With the help of a needs assessment, efforts can be made to identify the unfulfilled needs of the conflicting parties and bring them into an agreement.

Mediators are usually a team of academic professionals with conflict-resolution expertise or regional or technical expertise. To be successful, it is important to conduct a series of PS workshops with the same target groups and mediators.

States are often critical of these approaches. They consider these approaches too long-term in their orientation to be able to stop wars.[9] Another criticism is that improving communication and building relationships between conflicting parties do not necessarily result in agreements to end wars.[10]

COMPLEMENTARY APPROACHES: BRINGING TRACK I AND TRACK 2 TOGETHER

The aim of complementary approaches is to integrate the Track 1 and Track 2 approaches. The premise of these approaches is that both of them can make important contributions to mediation and peacebuilding. It is necessary to identify the appropriate actor and approach at a certain time in the conflict. At different phases of escalation in conflicts and wars, complementary approaches try to identify the most efficient mediators at a given time.

On the basis of Friedrich Glasl's conflict intervention model,[11] Ronald Fisher and Loraleigh Keashly developed a contingency model for third-party intervention in armed conflicts.[12] The aim of this model is "to intervene with the appropriate third party method at the appropriate time."[13] According to Fisher and Keashly, mediation is not a question of the right approach but of finding the right time to intervene. They believe that the right time for relationship-oriented approaches is during the prenegotiation phase. When the conflict escalates further, more power mediation should be used. After a peace accord has been reached, it is time to build peace by using relationship-oriented approaches again. To make conflict intervention more effective, Fisher and Keashly suggest coordination among the various mediators involved. Critics of this approach say that in the practice of mediation, different types of interventions can take place at the same time.[14]

Jacob Bercovitch and Jeffrey Rubin developed an approach similar to the contingency approach. They merely changed the perspective from approaches to actors.[15] According to them, it is not important which mediators are the most effective but who is more effective at different stages of the conflict. The results are similar to those of Fisher and Keashly: the more the conflict escalates, the more powerful the third party should be. The problem with this approach, however, is that the issue of coordination is not looked into.

TRANSFORMATION-ORIENTED APPROACHES

The basis of transformation-oriented approaches is a different understanding of peacebuilding and mediation. The aim is neither short-term ending of wars nor long-term resolution of conflicts. The task is to transform violent conflicts into peaceful conflicts. These approaches do recognize the existence of unresolvable conflicts. Therefore, they suggest replacing the term *conflict resolution* with the term *conflict transformation*.[16]

John Paul Lederach developed the most comprehensive transformation-oriented approach. His peacebuilding approach divides the society in the conflict country into three levels, which could be approached with different mediation and peacebuilding strategies.[17] The top leadership level could be accessed by mediation on the level of states (Track 1) and the outcome-oriented approach. The middle-range leadership level could be approached with problem solving workshops, peace commissioners, or "partial insiders." Those partial insiders are prominent individuals from inside the society of the conflict country. A prominent partial insider, for example, is the South African bishop, Desmond Tutu. The third level, the grassroots level, represents the majority of the population and can be approached by a wide range of mediation measures.[18]

The aim of Lederach's peacebuilding approach is to identify representative individuals or groups on the middle-range level and empower them by means of mediation and other peacebuilding measures. Another aim is to build a long-term infrastructure for peacebuilding through supporting the available mediation and reconciliation potential of the society. To maximize the peacebuilding potential, third-party intervention should concentrate on support and coordination. Developing sensitivity for the culture of the conflict country is a necessary requirement as well as a long-term time frame for enhancing an elucidative type of conflict transformation.

CONCLUSION

This overview of Western approaches to mediation demonstrates that all the different approaches can potentially contribute to peacebuilding. However, it is necessary for all the actors to be aware of the options and potentials of the various approaches. The practice of mediation has shown that it can take place at any time and should not wait until a conflict is ripe for resolution, because ripe moments cannot be used or become missed opportunities when there is no process already in place.

NOTES

1. Mediation is used as a general term throughout this article. When it appears in italics, it refers to a special form of mediation used within mediation (as explained further in the text).
2. See John Paul Lederach's article in this book.
3. Norbert Ropers, "Die friedliche Bearbeitung ethno-politischer Konflikte. Eine Herausforderung für die Staaten- und die Gesellschaftswelt," in Norbert Ropers and Tobias Debiel, eds., *Friedliche Konfliktbearbeitung in der Staaten- und Gesellschaftswelt* (Bonn, 1995), 214.
4. Mark Hoffman, "Konfliktlösung durch gesellschaftliche Akteure. Möglichkeiten und Grenzen von Problemlösungs-Workshops," in Ropers and

Tobias, *Friedliche Konfliktbearbeitung in der Staaten- und Gesellschaftswelt*, 284–303.

5. William, I. Zartman, *Ripe for Resolution, Conflict and Intervention in Africa* (New York: Oxford University Press, 1985), 267ff.; Dean G. Pruit and Jeffrey Rubin, *Social Conflict: Escalation, Stalemate and Settlement* (New York: Random House, 1986); Jeffrey Rubin, "The Timing of Ripeness and the Ripeness of Timing," in Louis Kriesberg and J. Thorsen, *Timing the De-escalation of International Conflict* (New York, 1993), 239ff.

6. Sidney Bailey, "Non-official Mediation in Disputes: Reflections on Quaker Experience," *International Affairs* 61, no. 2 (1985): 205; and Stephen John Stedman in Roy Licklider, *How Civil War Ends* (New York, 1995).

7. See the article by Herbert Kelman in this book.

8. On the basis of Paul Sites's need research.

9. Jacob Bercovitch, *Social Conflicts and Third Parties: Strategies of Conflict Resolution* (Boulder, Colo.: Westview Press, 1984), 116.

10. Ibid.

11. Friedrich Glasl, *Konfliktmanagement* (Bern/Stuttgart, 1990).

12. Ronald Fisher and Loraleigh Keashly, "The Potential Complementarity of Mediation and Consultation with a Contingency Model of Third-Party Intervention," *Journal of Peace Research* 28, no. 1 (1991): 29–42.

13. Ibid., p. 36.

14. David Bloomfield, "Towards Complementarity in Conflict Management: Resolution and Settlement in Northern Ireland, *Journal of Peace Research* 32, no. 2 (1995): 151–164.

15. Jacob Bercovitch and Jeffrey Rubin, *Mediation in International Relations: Multiple Approaches to Conflict Management* (Bassingstoke, UK: MacMillan, 1992): 64–96.

16. See Kumar Rupesinghe, *Conflict Transformation* (New York: St. Martin's, 1995).

17. See his article in this book.

18. See John Paul Lederach, Chapter 6.1.

Multitrack Efforts in Burundi

Jan Van Eck

A PERSONAL CASE STUDY IN
TRACK 2 FACILITATION: BURUNDI, 1995–1999

I developed an interest in the protracted Burundian conflict during a week-long visit to this small land-locked country in June 1995, when I was still a member of Parliament for the African National Congress (ANC) in the South African Parliament. Consequently, I decided to return to learn more about the origin of the conflict. One visit led to another, and in early 1996 I retired from Parliament to be able to commit myself virtually full-time to Burundi.

I Arrived with No Formalized Role Specified

From the outset I made it clear that I was there to listen and learn how Burundians saw the nature of the conflict, its origins, and how it developed. And because theirs was basically a conflict driven by the different political elites, I focused on the senior political role-players within all the conflicting parties. Also, I made it clear that, in spite of their interest in the South African transition and my role in that transition, and some of the similarities between my country and theirs, that I was not there to "sell" the South African model to them—although I stated that there were indeed lessons to be learned from the process (rather than the end product) that we followed during our transition.

Having decided not to play the role of human rights activist—which was my role in South Africa—but rather contribute to conflict resolution, I adopted the approach that I was not there to decide who was "right" or "wrong," "good" or "bad" (both sides have after all committed terrible wrongs); that I did not represent the interests of my own government or any other government or organization; and that the two nongovernmental organizations (NGOs) who supported my "project," the Center for Conflict Resolution (Cape Town) and the Washington-based Search for Common Ground, had given me the right to operate without being dictated to.

With regard to any future role I might be able to play, I adopted the principle that if the Burundian parties found my involvement of use to them and if they felt comfortable with my presence, the kind of role I would play would sooner or later become clear or—preferably—be identified by the Burundians themselves. This lack of an up-front role, considered strange by many international actors, proved to be a tremendous advantage.

Being Trusted by the Burundians Was Critical

Without the necessary trust, I would obviously not have been able to play any constructive role. In view of their experience of so many foreigners who, after a mere two or three days in their country, turned into instant experts on their country, Burundians had and still have a healthy suspicion of foreigners who seemingly come "to help."

My low-key approach of "no formal role" and "merely listening and learning" helped to allay people's fears; the fact that I was a white South African *and* an ANC member of Parliament convinced both the minority and the majority that I understood the minority's fears and the majority's aspirations. This provided me with an invaluable and truly unique entry point.

Engaging in In-Depth, Ongoing Analysis in an Attempt to Understand

Although it is easy to be informed about the numerous daily manifestations of the conflict (the visible symptoms), it takes a tremendous amount of time and energy to really understand, not only the hundreds of historical events such as uprisings, massacres, revenge massacres, and coups, but the state of mind—even the collective state of mind—that these events have created on different sides of the political divide.

And because I was able and willing to use my intensive program of one-on-one discussions with a multitude of Burundians to go into great depths about Burundian recent history and events in neighboring countries that played a major role in shaping the state of mind of Burundians, I believe I was able to understand that no solution would be durable unless the fears, especially the hidden, unspoken fears, were addressed. In brief, unless people were empowered to undergo a mind-shift away from these paralyzing fears, there would be no solution.

The more than twelve months' long initial period of intensive analysis helped me understand that Burundians were unwilling to move forward due to two main reasons: (1) the virtual complete breakdown in trust between the opposing political/ethnic forces caused by the numerous acts of horrendous violence, broken promises, and bad faith; and the virtual complete loss in negotiations as a viable way of reaching durable solutions, due to the complete and disastrous failures of previous attempts, such as the democratization process of 1991–1993, and the Convention of Government of 1994.

It was this understanding that enabled me to realize that there would be no progress toward a peaceful, negotiated solution unless a minimum degree of trust was first restored, and the failures of the democratization and negotiation processes were seen not as a reflection of negotiations and democratization but rather of the inappropriate and overhasty processes that Burundians followed at that time. Therefore, when confronted with their concerns, I could respond with confidence by suggesting that the negotiations process should at least be considered again—but on condition that it be done properly and that a minimum of trust be restored. In other words, make sure you do it properly this time, regardless of how much the external players may again be trying to push you into hasty agreements.

Promoting Dialogue Among the Key Role-Players

The fundamental premise was that, although accepted facilitators could assist Burundians in discussing and debating the issues, the Burundians would ultimately have to work through these issues themselves and reach their own conclusions. All one could do was to facilitate these discussions and debates and make useful suggestions when appropriate. In the end, the Burundians would have to be empowered to reach well-thought-through decisions themselves in order for them to own the decisions and the process that would automatically emanate from this.

Although the Burundians had not invented the concept of dehumanizing one another, they had definitely perfected it to a fine art. The language in 1994–1995 and 1996 was pure demonization, with both sides labeling the other as being either putschists or *génocidaires*. When people have demonized and dehumanized one another to such an extent, it is obviously completely unrealistic to expect them to want to negotiate in good faith—and even if they negotiate an agreement, they will obviously expect the other to renege on it sooner rather than later.

When I introduced the principle of negotiations into the debates in 1996, the response was so hostile that I invented what I called "TDN," which stood for "talks/dialogue/negotiations," and asked them to choose the word they preferred. Virtually everyone chose the seemingly soft option: talks. As the dialogue and debate continued mainly in private, in numerous small group discussions at my house and elsewhere, after some significant public seminars in early 1997, and as trust building and rehumanizing started taking place, I saw a small but significant shift among the power elite away from talks to dialogue and eventually to "we will *try* negotiations again" (the emphasis on "try").

Once Burundians Adopted These Concepts, the Process Became Theirs

It was indeed an incredible experience to see how the Burundian parties, once they had overcome their initial misgivings and had developed a belief that it was possible to rebuild some trust and negotiate a truly durable agreement, made this process theirs.

Internally, the key role-players on both sides of the divide created an interim grand coalition government, called the Internal Partnership, between the government of President Pierre Buyoya (who came to power during a bloodless coup in July 1996) and the majority party, Frodebu, which lost its power in the very same coup. The objective was not to legitimate minority/illegitimate rule but to ensure that those with power and those who lost power would cooperate to take Burundi back to a representative/democratic government. Most important of this Internal Partnership was that the internal opposing political/ethnic groupings were proving that building minimum trust with former "enemies"—and now opponents—and cooperating as partners toward the creation of a new Burundi was possible. This created the belief among the minority that talks and even negotiations with the exiled leaders might soon become possible.

Because of this launch of the Internal Partnership, the government decided to return to the external Arusha-based multiparty negotiations for Burundi under the mediation chairmanship of former Tanzanian president Julius "Mwalimu" Nyerere. Both internal and external peace processes are continuing today. And although Burundians have in the period of two years moved light-years ahead, much more needs to be done to continue building the still very fragile trust that has been built and strengthening the resolve to try again to negotiate in good faith.

Tensions with Track 1 Role-Players

Within the Burundian context my "organic" approach to peacemaking frequently created tension between myself and Track 1 role-players. The main reasons were that the latter had a preprepared "solution" to the Burundian conflict; they knew who the guilty parties were, and they were in a hurry to have the parties sign an agreement regardless of whether there was minimum trust, a genuine desire to negotiate, or whether such an agreement would be durable. When I warned in a press interview at the end of July 1997 that the government delegation might withdraw from the negotiations because the mediation initiative was fatally flawed (especially due to the perceived bias of the mediation), those international role-players who were critical of my action were more concerned about me criticizing and alienating the mediator than taking steps to do something about the flaws in the mediation process—something they all agreed on, but only in private. Coincidentally, the government delegation actually pulled out from Arusha a few days after my warning was published.

My problem was that I was far better informed about the real dynamics on the ground and therefore about what was possible and what was not. Although we were able to manage most of these tensions, some tensions remained. As someone who is committed to play a true Track 2 facilitator role, and who is therefore primarily interested in the ability of the "patient" (Burundi) to recover (at his/her own speed), I am inclined to be less tolerant about the foreign doctors (regional and international Track 1 players) who may (knowingly or unknowingly) be administering the wrong medicine.

TRACKS I AND 2: INCOMPATIBLE OR COMPLEMENTARY?

It needs to be accepted at the outset that there will be tension between actors from Track 1 and Track 2 intervening in the same conflict. The only question that needs to be answered is whether this tension can be managed in such a way that both can play a constructive and therefore complementary role in helping the conflicting parties to reach a truly durable agreement.

It also needs to be stated that Track 1 intervenors normally try to bring an immediate end to the kind of open, violent, and unacceptable conflict that guarantees prime-time coverage on CNN, and do not have the time/mandate to try and end it in a way that will establish a durable peace. Track 2 facilitators, by their very nature, see violent conflict as a mere symptom of deeper problems and, when they intervene, try to address those fundamental, underlying causes of the violence. But because this approach requires more time, their efforts are normally ignored.

A Durable Peace Process Takes as Much Time as It Needs

Because Track 1 diplomats operate at the behest of governments and other international and/or regional powers, they are generally interested in the quickest possible end to hostilities. For example, in the case of small, "marginal" countries, they are in a hurry to get a "quick fix" solution, as when the crisis in the Democratic Republic of Congo erupted in August 1998 and very few international players retained the same intensity of interest or involvement in the small neighboring country of Burundi.

Track 1 intervenors also have a substantive amount of clout and power, which they frequently use or sometimes misuse to force conflicting parties to agree to ending hostilities or signing agreements, regardless of whether they are truly ready to do so. Track 2 facilitators approach peacemaking/building much like a courtship between a man and a woman who think they might want to get married—eventually. The hard facts are: it is normally a long process during which the two individuals try and see if they are compatible and have the same vision of a common future. To summarize: it takes as long as it takes, and if one or the other breaks trust or behaves in an inappropriate way, the "yes" word will never be uttered. Making peace is a similar process; it takes as long as it needs. Peacemaking is a process, not an event.

With regard to their clout and power, Track 2 intervenors obviously do not have much or any. Contrary to popular wisdom, this can be an advantage—as was stated by the Rome-based San Egidio Community when it mediated successfully in the Mozambique conflict. The lack of clout results in Track 2 facilitators more readily being able to assess the real feelings of the key actors instead of the sanitized diplomatic version frequently given to Track 1 intervenors by the conflicting parties. Due to this lack of power, they are also more able to *persuade* the parties instead of *bullying* them into agreements.

Conflict Analysis Is Essential in Deciding Which Interventions Are Appropriate

While Track 2 facilitators have the ability (luxury?) to conduct an intensive and ongoing conflict analysis, very few, if any, Track 1 intervenors have the time to do this; consequently, they have to automatically rely on either their government's representatives in the specific country or on analysts far removed from the terrain. This frequently results in a faulty or incomplete analysis of the nature of the conflict on behalf of some Track 1 intervenors or—even worse—an inability to agree on the nature of the conflict and what appropriate measures could be taken. While Track 2 intervenors can readily admit their analysis and prescription as faulty, Track 1 intervenors, with the honor of governments at stake, do not have this freedom to back-track without losing face.

Taking Sides Nullifies Attempts to Mediate a Peaceful Resolution

While Track 2 facilitators are also tempted to take sides in conflicts, very few Track 1 intervenors even try or have the freedom to adopt a nonpartisan role in intranational conflicts. For example, in the Horn of Africa, both Uganda and Eritrea are disqualified from mediating in the conflict in Sudan (as part of the regional peace initiative led by the Intergovernmental Authority on Development), due to their open and active support for the Sudanese rebel movement, the Sudan People's Liberation Army, in its attempt to overthrow the Sudanese government.

The United States, due to its virulent anti-Castro, -Gaddafi, -Hussein, and -Milosevic position, is automatically disqualified from playing the role of peace facilitator in the mentioned presidents' countries. Some European countries are handicapped in the same way. It needs to be stressed that the obsession with the removal of one leader and the belief that his removal will end the country's problems is also not found in any conflict resolution material.

In the ongoing crisis in the Democratic Republic of Congo, the military intervention of at least six countries does not even pretend to be an attempt to help the Congolese people solve the internal political, economic, and social problems but is merely motivated by their own perceived national interests.

The ease with which Western countries resort to the use of force to "solve" a conflict, as in Iraq or Kosovo, is setting an extremely dangerous example. As an African who is deeply concerned about the nearly entrenched culture of using force to come to and stay in power, namely in the countries of the Great Lakes region, it is indeed deeply disturbing that Western nations, instead of promoting dialogue, negotiations, and compromise, are actively reinforcing the fallacious argument that conflicts can be resolved by the use of force.

In such cases where Track 1's coercive diplomacy completely takes over, Track 2 facilitators have difficulty not only in effectively playing their own role but in playing any role at all. In such situations there is, after all, no plan for trying to reach an acceptable durable peace. All that is left seems to be: "Sign the agreement (however unacceptable) or we bomb you." This is a trend that should concern all who are interested in resolving conflicts in a durable way, for it will completely sideline those who are trying to practice sustainable conflict resolution principles.

Conflicting Parties Must Agree on a Solution

Peace can only be made in the final analysis by the parties in conflict (something that is readily accepted by most Track 2 facilitators) and not primarily or even exclusively through coercion, threats, force, or bullying (strategies frequently too readily adopted by some Track 1 intervenors). The roles played by the Economic Community of West African States Monitoring Group in the West African countries of Liberia and especially Sierra Leone are examples of how the use of force has merely aggravated existing conflicts.

The final and only really relevant test of a peace agreement is whether, once the foreign intervenors have left, the parties will still be willing to continue implementing the signed agreement. If not, then the whole exercise has been useless.

There are numerous examples in conflict resolution literature that demonstrate that imposed agreements not only fail, but worse, once they fail countries frequently descend into deeper chaos and anarchy, which makes the prospects for any future peaceful resolution even more difficult. In the case of Rwanda, the Arusha peace negotiations were virtually immediately followed by the 1994 Rwandan genocide.

CONCLUSION

I have tried to highlight some of the conflict resolution principles that need to be upheld if we truly want to assist countries in conflict to find durable solutions to their problems. I have also touched on the way in which Track

1 intervenors and Track 2 facilitators respond to these principles. It should be clear that if we want Track 1 and Track 2 intervenors to play separate but complementary roles in conflict resolution in the same country (a goal worth striving for), then much work needs to be done to reach some agreement on:

- What the fundamental principles of conflict resolution are.
- Whether peacemaking is an event or a process.
- Whether being partisan helps to resolve or aggravate a conflict.
- Whether in-depth analysis is essential to decide on an intervention strategy.
- Whether peacemaking belongs to the parties or external actors.

Although Track 2 initiatives are frequently also far from perfect (especially when Track 2 intervenors try and behave like Track 1 intervenors, suffer from delusions of grandeur, or are more interested in empire building or winning peace prices), in most cases they try hard to apply the fundamental principles of conflict resolution. But once Track 1 intervenors adopt a hardline attitude toward one party in conflict, conflicting parties are inclined to dig in their heels, resulting in the role of Track 2 facilitators being actively undermined.

A suggested solution for further discussion is the creation of a framework that provides for key, experienced Track 2 facilitators who have no link to any governmental or other international organizational structures to be given the task of drafting an appropriate conflict intervention process for the specific country in conflict. If the process that leads to the drafting of such a process is done properly, then this would provide Track 1 intervenors with the basic framework within which they can apply their strengths (even force where needed) to assist the conflicting parties in finding a durable, negotiated, compromise settlement.

By an appropriate conflict intervention process, I mean a process that will be multifaceted, that is, if there is a need for a military component in the peacemaking process, then this should be preceded by the implementation of or at the very least an agreement on a political peacemaking process. Military intervention can only play a constructive role if it is a subcomponent of a broader political/diplomatic peacemaking process. Above all, such a process has to be agreed upon by all the national political actors involved in the conflict with agreed-upon foreign actors playing a supportive role only, meaning the warring parties must feel that they own the process.

Other principles that are essential for a successful mediation process include:

- The acceptability to all parties of the mediator.
- The venue.
- The agenda.
- Absolute nonpartisanship of the mediation process—both with regard to the reality and the perception of the parties.
- The inclusion of *all* relevant parties who have the ability to make or break an agreement.
- Allowing conflicting parties to reach an agreement that they believe in, instead of imposing a solution from the outside.
- Continuous monitoring whether the delegations involved in the negotiation process actually still have a mandate from their constituents.
- Actively monitoring the interests that neighboring and other foreign powers and multinational companies have in the conflict and the kind of solution they are openly or quietly working toward.

Because the duration of most peacemaking processes is difficult to predict and is generally longer than shorter, the agreed-upon process should be flexible enough to survive major obstacles, deadlocks, and a major upsurge in violence.

NOTE

The original version of this text was presented by the author at a code of conduct conference organized by the European Center for Conflict Prevention, Life and Peace Institute, Berghof Center, International Alert, Soesterberg, Netherlands, 25–27 April 1999.

Field Diplomacy Initiatives in Cameroon and Burundi

Luc Reychler

BACKGROUND

The term *field diplomacy* refers not to something new but pays attention to the grossly underestimated and valuable work done by many people in the field. The initiative to promote field diplomacy was triggered by several factors.[1]

First, there was the observation that most official and Track 2 diplomats were predominantly operating from abroad. R. Moreels, past president of Doctors Without Borders, in Belgium, coined the term. While working as a surgeon in conflict zones, he was struck by the fact that official and Track 2 diplomats were not in the field, where peace services were urgently needed. The conviction grew that there was a serious gap in the peacebuilding process, that there was a deep-felt need for field diplomacy.

People need to be empowered to get rid of the conflict entrepreneurs and to strengthen the local peace potential. At the middle and the local levels, peacebuilding efforts need to be facilitated and supported. Field diplomacy is not an alternative to traditional and Track 2 diplomacy but is complementary. The successful transformation of the conflicts in, for example, Northern Ireland and South Africa is the result of different forms of diplomacy.

Second, there was the perception that the peace efforts of people in the field, some of them known but most unknown, have long been overlooked. The conviction grew that these efforts needed to be highlighted, upgraded, and supported. The main rationale of using the term *field diplomacy* was to draw attention to the valuable but grossly underestimated work done by local people in conflict areas.

Third, there was the growing awareness that external intervention (development, humanitarian aid, election monitoring, mediation, etc.) had a significant impact on the conflict dynamics and that some well-intentioned interventions were causing harm. It became clear that soon there would be a strong demand for the development of a more effective conflict impact assessment system (CIAS) and the design of effective ways and means to reduce the negative impact of the external interventions and to raise their peace-added value.

A fourth factor was the observation that all the peacebuilding efforts were not adding up to sustainable peace. In many conflicts, one sees huge piles of peacebuilding stones but not the expected peacebuilding. Peacebuilding requires a clear and compelling vision of the peace one wants to create, a comprehensive assessment of what is needed to realize this peace, a coherent plan, and an effective implementation of the plan. Some people in the field are not aware that they play a role in the peace process. Others feel lost; they don't know how and to what extent their activities contribute to the peacebuilding process. This affects their motivation negatively and reduces effective peacebuilding.

Field diplomacy focuses on local peacebuilding capacity as well as external peacebuilding efforts. The latter include not only the so-called peace services but also the efforts of the people engaged in other fieldwork (humanitarian, development, political, military, etc.).

FIELD DIPLOMACY INITIATIVE

Field Diplomacy Initiative (FDI) considers fieldwork as essential for peacebuilding, the creation of a sustainable peace as its goal, and the involvement of people in the peace process as very important. It strives toward a more cost-effective peace policy and a greater accountability of the policymakers. It questions the fragmented piecemeal approaches and pleads for the development of more integrative and coherent peace architecture. To implement these goals, several things are required.

A Credible Presence in the Field

Field diplomacy requires a credible presence in the field. One has to be in the conflict zone to get a better insight into the dynamics of the conflict and to facilitate the transformation of the conflict more effectively. The building of trust or of a network of people who can be relied on is essential to prevent a destructive transformation of a conflict. Building trust takes a great deal of time and effort. When a conflict erupts, it can be too late.

Commitment to Sustainable Peacebuilding

Field diplomacy implies a serious commitment to a constructive transformation of a conflict. One cannot adopt a conflict for a week or a month; it is a long-term commitment and likely a difficult journey. The efforts need to be credible. It can be stressful and risky. An appropriate motivation and adequate backup is necessary to enhance the effectiveness of fieldwork. The overall aim of peacebuilding is to construct a sustainable peace environment. Such an environment is characterized by the absence of armed violence; the absence of structural, psychological, and cultural discrimination; the possibility of conflicts to transform constructively; and internal and external legitimacy. A sustainable peace environment requires an effective system of communication, consultation, and negotiation; peace-enhancing structures; an integrative moral-political climate; and objective and subjective security.

Engagement of the People in the Peace Process

A third characteristic of field diplomacy is the engagement of the people in the peace process. A sustainable peace is a legitimate peace that relies on the support of the people. It is the result of an elicitive, not a prescriptive, process. Not only the highest but also the middle and grassroots levels of the conflicting groups need to be involved.

Pursuit of More Cost-Effective Peacebuilding

A fourth characteristic of field diplomacy is the pursuit of a more cost-effective peacebuilding policy. Peacebuilding could become more cost-effective through (1) a more systematic and proactive use of a CIAS; (2) the development of a more comprehensive cost and benefit accounting system; and (3) efforts to make decisionmakers accountable for the their handling of conflicts. It is difficult to understand the conflict dynamic if one does not have an idea of the cost-and-benefit calculations of the stakeholders in the conflict.

A comprehensive analysis of costs distinguishes humanitarian, economic, political, social-psychological, environmental, cultural, and spiritual costs. Not only the costs but also the benefits need to be assessed. Conflicts last as long as powerful actors, the so-called spoilers or conflict entrepreneurs, expect to profit from them. The chances of creating a more effective conflict prevention regime could be significantly raised if the conflicting parties could be convinced that a proactive prevention of violence is not only more cost-effective than reactive violence but mutually benefiting as well.

Development of an Integrative and Coherent Peace Architecture

The last characteristic of the peace thinking of field diplomats is related to the architecture of peacebuilding. Today's conflict prevention is low on clarity, integration, coherence, and coordination. Most violence prevention or peacebuilding efforts are compilations of unidimensional measures. Peacebuilding requires peace architecture: a clear and compelling vision of the peace one wants to create; a comprehensive assessment of what is needed to realize this peace; a coherent plan; and an effective implementation of the plan. This is not a plea for a master plan controlled by a peace authority but for a more comprehensive and creative approach in which the different components are validated and integrated into a more effective peacebuilding process. The improvement of coherence relates to:

- The domains in which peacebuilding efforts are undertaken (diplomatic, political, economic, legal, psychological, military, humanitarian).

- The timing and time perspectives involved.
- The higher and deeper layers of the conflict.
- The system levels that need to be involved (local, middle, national, regional, international).

Field diplomats perceive peacebuilding from a wide time perspective: forward and backward. A sustainable peace requires a reconciliation of the past, present, and future. Historical wounds that are left unhealed tend to mortgage future cooperation. A joint expectation of future benefits resulting from cooperation helps not only living with the past but also the creation of a sustainable peace. The development of a new conflict culture, in which competing values—such as peace, truth, mercy, welfare, and justice—are reconciled, is crucial, too.

Attention needs also be paid to deeper layers of the conflict. When we consider the underlying layer of motives, apprehensions, and often ideology, we enter the realm of chaotic emotional unreason. War engenders a mental environment of desperation in which fear, resentment, jealousy, and rage predominate.[2] Consequently, building peace requires not only attention to the hardware of conflict (the political-diplomatic, military, legal, economic, and ecological) but also to the softer and less visible layers of the deep conflict. Signing a peace agreement does not guarantee a sustainable peace. An approval at the psychological and emotional levels helps. Peace must feel good.

Also significant is the spiritual layer. Here, peacebuilding means transforming despair into hope, hate into love, nihilism into meaningfulness, condemnation into forgiveness, and alienation into belonging and understanding.

Finally there is the problem of the levels, internal and international, on which peacebuilding efforts are undertaken. Field diplomats recognize the complex interdependence between seemingly different conflicts. The artificial legal distinction between internal and international conflicts and the propensity to conceptually isolate or quarantine closely interwoven conflicts is seen as problematic. Despite the strong empirical correlation between the internal and international-regional democratic transition, the North prefers to promote the former and avoid the latter. Most of the conflicts in the developing countries cannot be reduced to pure internal conflicts. They are influenced by decisions made at both the regional and the global level. The establishment of a sustainable peace in, for example, the Great Lakes area requires not only peacebuilding efforts within the area but also at the subregional, African, European, and global levels.

ACTIVITIES OF FDI

The activities of FDI relate to setting up an accessible documentation and information center, training of people working in conflict areas, facilitation of the working of local peacebuilding nongovernmental organizations (NGOs), applied research, evaluation and capacity building, conflict impact assessment, and networking. In 1997 and 1998 several trainings were organized to prepare human rights and election monitors for working in conflict zones.

FDI also tries to raise funds for projects of local NGOs. It organized with International IDEA on March 24, 1999, in the Belgian Senate a conference, "Electoral Observation and Assistance: Instruments to Consolidate Democracy?" The purpose was to draw lessons and to highlight the best practices. From June 10 to 17, 1999, it invited electoral administrators of five Southern African countries to observe and comment on the electoral process in Belgium. In 1998 and 1999, several briefing and debriefing sessions were organized for election monitors. It also tried to adopt two conflicts in Cameroon and Burundi.

Monitoring Democratic Peacebuilding in Cameroon

In 1997, two members of FDI, Huib Huyse and myself, were invited by Norbert Kenne to help facilitate a workshop on conflict transformation in Cameroon. The ecumenical organization Service Humanus, assembled in Bamenda, from June 29 to July 6, 1997, thirty opinion leaders. The theme of the workshop was religion and sociopolitical mediation. There were six Catholics, five Protestants, four Muslims, three members of political parties, two of the administration, three of the civil society, and seven resource persons, including Hizkias Assefa. The main concerns of the participants were to find out how and to what extent religious organizations could enhance the democratic transition of their country and how to make Cameroon a democratic, secure, and affluent country.

Our contribution consisted of presenting a conceptual framework for analyzing conflicts and conflict transformation, assessing the needs for building a sustainable peace, and making a diagnosis of democracy and of the factors inhibiting and/or enhancing the democratic transition. To analyze the level of democracy, the participants used the democratic building block matrix. The most dynamic and fruitful part of the workshop started when the participants met in small groups and reflected on their own country: on the status of democracy in Cameroon, on the obstacles on the way to a consolidated democracy, and on the role religious actors could play to enhance the democratic peacebuilding process. The participants were satisfied. The workshop became a think tank that made a thorough analysis of the democratic peacebuilding process in Cameroon, and concrete action plans were generated for promoting a more democratic and affluent country.

Conflict Impact Assessment of Burundi

In 1998–1999 FDI, in cooperation with the University of Leuven, did a conflict impact study of Burundi. The team consisted of Tatien Musabyimana, Stefaan Calmeyn, and myself. The aim was to find out how to stop this protracted conflict and how to create a sustainable peace. We engaged more than fifty people who were well acquainted with the situation in Burundi (thirty-four Burundians and eighteen external experts). Using questionnaires and in-depth interviews, we were able to make a comprehensive need analysis, assess the impact of external interventions, and generate concrete suggestions for establishing a sustainable peace. The suggestions related to what we consider the four pillars of a sustainable peace: (1) effective communication, consultation, and negotiation systems; (2) peace-enhancing structures, political and economic; (3) an integrative moral political climate; and (4) security.

When the preliminary report was ready, it was sent to the participants for evaluation and feedback. In addition, the Burundians were invited to a one-day-long round table at the University of Leuven to discuss the CIAS methodology and the content of the report.[3] The participants concluded that the analysis was not biased and that it provided a comprehensive and systematic overview of what needed to be done to create a sustainable peace. The group also suggested to meet more frequently to generate concrete proposals for solving specific issues related to, for example, the problem of power sharing, dealing with the past and impunity, the creation of the economic society, and regional integration. The results of this project will be published as a book titled *Burundi: Le défi de la paix.*

Besides learning how to conduct an impact assessment, we were surprised by the will and the capacity of the diaspora to contribute to the peacebuilding process. The diaspora should not be neglected and could be more constructively engaged, for example, as a diaspora think tank.

NOTES

1. In 1993 Reginald Moreels made a plea for field diplomacy. The first field diplomacy initiative, named "International Dialogue," started in 1995 with the support of Médicins Sans Frontiers in Belgium.

2. Adam Curle, *Tools for Transformation: A Personal Study* (Stroud, UK: Hawthorne Press, 1990).

3. Twenty-five diaspora Burundians living in different parts of Belgium representing the political spectrum participated.

Interactive Problem Solving in the Middle East

Herbert C. Kelman

For more than twenty-five years, my colleagues and I have been developing and applying an unofficial, academically based, third-party approach to the analysis and resolution of international and ethnic conflicts, which I have come to call *interactive problem solving*. The approach is derived from the seminal work of John Burton.[1] It is anchored in social-psychological principles and follows a scholar/practitioner model. Our practice is informed by theoretical analyses and empirical studies of international conflict, social influence, and group interaction. The experience gained in practice, in turn, contributes to theory building and to the evaluation and refinement of our intervention model. The work thus represents an integration and continuing interaction between practice, research, and theory building.

The fullest—in a sense, the paradigmatic—application of the approach is represented by *problem-solving workshops*, which bring together politically influential members of conflicting parties in a private, confidential setting for direct, noncommittal communication. Workshops are designed to enable the parties to explore each other's perspective and, through a joint process of creative problem solving, to generate new ideas for mutually satisfactory solutions to their conflict. The ultimate goal is to transfer the insights and ideas gained from these interactions into the political debate and decisionmaking processes in the two communities.[2]

Problem-solving workshops are not negotiating sessions, and they are not intended to simulate and certainly not to substitute for official negotiations. Their unofficial, nonbinding character clearly distinguishes them from formal negotiations, which can only be carried out by officials authorized to conclude binding agreements. At the same time, such workshops and similar mechanisms for interactive problem solving are closely linked to negotiations and play an important complementary role at all stages of the negotiation process: in the prenegotiation phase, they can help create a political atmosphere conducive to movement to the table; in the active negotiation phase, they can help in overcoming obstacles to productive negotiations and in framing issues that are not yet on the table; in the post-negotiation phase, they can contribute to implementation of the negotiated agreement and to long-term peacebuilding. It is precisely the nonbinding character of workshops that is the source of their unique contribution to the larger negotiation process: they provide an opportunity for sharing perspectives, exploring options, and joint thinking that is not readily available at the official negotiating table.[3]

SOCIAL-PSYCHOLOGICAL ASSUMPTIONS

The practice of interactive problem solving is informed by a set of assumptions about the nature of international or intercommunal conflict and conflict resolution, derived from a social-psychological analysis. These assumptions enter into the formulation of the structure, the process, and the content of problem-solving workshops. Five general assumptions are central to our approach.

1. Although war and peace—and international relations as a whole—are societal and intersocietal processes, which cannot be reduced to the level of individual behavior, *there are many aspects of international conflict and conflict resolution for which the individual represents the most appropriate unit of analysis.* Most important, the satisfaction of the needs of both parties—the needs of human individuals as articulated through their core identity groups—is the ultimate criterion for a mutually satisfactory resolution of their conflict.[4] Unfulfilled needs, especially for identity and security, and existential fears typically drive the conflict and create barriers to its resolution. By pushing behind the parties' incompatible positions and exploring the identity and security concerns that underlie them, it often becomes possible to develop mutually satisfactory solutions, for conflicts about identity, security, and other psychological needs are not inherently zero-sum.

Both in our theoretical work and in our practice, we need to determine the relevant points of entry for psychological analysis—those points in the theoretical model or in the diplomatic process at which the cognitions, emotions, and intentions of individuals and the interactions between individuals can play a direct role in determining outcomes. Thus, we can identify certain processes central to conflict resolution—such as empathy, insight, creative problem solving, and learning—that of necessity take place at the level of individuals and interaction between individuals. Problem-solving workshops provide a setting in which these processes can occur. Changes at the level of individuals—in the form of new insights and ideas—resulting from the microprocess of the workshop can then be fed back into the political debate and the decisionmaking in the two communities, thus becoming vehicles for change at the macrolevel.

2. *International conflict must be viewed as not merely an intergovernmental or interstate phenomenon but also as an intersocietal phenomenon.* Insofar as the conflict is between two societies, it becomes important to examine what happens within each society. In particular, this view alerts us to the role of internal divisions within each society in international conflicts—namely, the crucial relationship between *intragroup* and *intergroup* conflict. Internal divisions place serious constraints on decisionmakers in the pursuit of peaceful solutions, yet they also provide opportunities and levers for change. They challenge the monolithic image of the enemy that parties in conflict tend to hold and enable them to deal with each other in a more differentiated way. Conflict-resolution efforts that are sensitive to the role of intra- and intersocietal processes require analysis of the dynamics of public opinion on both sides and of the requirements for consensus building within and coalition forming across the conflicting societies.[5]

An important implication of the intersocietal view of conflict is that negotiations and third-party efforts should ideally be directed not merely to a settlement of the conflict in the form of a brokered political agreement but to its resolution. Conflict resolution in this deeper and more lasting sense implies arrangements and accommodations that emerge out of the interaction between representatives of the parties themselves, that address the basic needs of both parties, and to which the parties are committed. Only this kind of solution is capable of transforming the relationship between societies locked into a protracted conflict that engages their collective identities and existential concerns.

The conception of international conflict as an intersocietal phenomenon also suggests a broader view of diplomacy as a complex mix of official and unofficial processes. The peaceful termination or management of conflict requires binding agreements that can only be achieved at the official level. Unofficial, noncommittal interactions, however, can play a constructive complementary role by exploring ways of overcoming obstacles to conflict resolution and helping to create a political environment conducive to negotiations and other diplomatic initiatives.[6]

3. *Conflict is an interactive process with an escalatory, self-perpetuating dynamic.* The needs and fears of parties involved in an intense conflict relationship impose perceptual and cognitive constraints on their processing of new information.[7] A major effect of these constraints is that the parties systematically underestimate the occurrence and possibility of change and therefore avoid negotiations, even in the face of changing interests that would make negotiations desirable for both. Images of the enemy are particularly resistant to disconfirming information. The combination of demonic enemy images and virtuous self-images on both sides leads to the

formation of mirror images, which contribute to the escalatory dynamic of conflict interaction and to resistance to change in a conflict relationship.[8] Moreover, interaction between conflicting parties is governed by a set of "conflict norms" that encourage each party to adopt a militant, uncompromising, threatening posture, which reinforces the enemy's hostile image and creates self-fulfilling prophecies. The conflict dynamics tend to entrench the parties in their own perspectives on history and justice; dehumanization of the enemy makes it even more difficult to acknowledge and access the perspective of the other.

Conflict-resolution efforts require promotion of a different kind of interaction, capable of reversing the escalatory and self-perpetuating dynamics of conflict through sharing of perspectives, differentiation of the enemy image, and insight into the processes that contribute to escalation. At the microlevel—in problem-solving workshops or similar fora—such interaction can contribute to the development of a de-escalatory language, of ideas for mutually reassuring gestures and actions, of commitment to reciprocity, and of proposals for win-win solutions. At the macrolevel, such products can translate into a new discourse among conflicting parties, characterized by a shift in emphasis from power politics to mutual responsiveness, reciprocity in process and solutions, and invitation to a new relationship.

4. *Conflict resolution requires a wider range of influence processes than those typically employed in international conflict relationships.* It is necessary to move beyond influence strategies based on threats and to expand and refine strategies based on promises and positive incentives. Conflict resolution efforts, by searching for solutions that satisfy the needs of both parties, create opportunities for mutual influence by way of responsiveness to each other's needs. They can demonstrate the possibility of influencing the other through one's own actions. A key element in this process is mutual reassurance. In existential conflicts, in particular, parties can encourage each other to negotiate seriously by reducing both sides' fears—not just, as more traditional strategic analysts often suggest, by increasing their pain. At the macrolevel, this broader conception of influence processes calls for a shift in emphasis from deterrence and compellence to mutual reassurance. The use of influence processes based on responsiveness to the other's needs and fears and the search for ways of benefiting the other can do more than affect specific behaviors of the other. It can contribute to a creative redefinition of the conflict, to joint discovery of win-win solutions, and to transformation of the relationship between the parties.[9]

5. This expanded conception of influence processes in a conflict relationship is based on the further assumption that *international conflict is a dynamic phenomenon, marked by the occurrence and possibility of change.*

Conflict resolution efforts are geared, therefore, to discovering possibilities for change, identifying conditions for change, and overcoming resistances to change. Such an approach favors an attitude of strategic optimism—not because of an unrealistic denial of malignant trends but as a part of a deliberate strategy to promote change by actively searching for and accentuating whatever realistic possibilities for peaceful resolution of the conflict might be on the horizon.[10]

PROBLEM-SOLVING WORKSHOPS

The assumptions that I have just summarized are reflected in the composition, the ground rules, and the procedures of problem-solving workshops.[11] Problem-solving workshops are intensive meetings between politically involved and, often, politically influential but unofficial representatives of conflicting parties, drawn from the mainstream of their respective communities. Thus, in our Israeli-Palestinian work, participants have included parliamentarians, leading figures in political parties or movements, former military officers or government officials, journalists or editors specializing in the Middle East, and academic scholars who are major analysts of the conflict for their societies and some of whom have served in advisory, official, or diplomatic positions.

The number of participants has varied; our workshops generally include three to six members of each party, as well as a third party of two to eight members. The third party consists of a panel of social scientists knowledgeable about international conflict, group process, and the Middle East region. The third party's skills and knowledge in these areas and its academic status serve as the basis of its credibility. The credibility as well as the effectiveness of the third party are also enhanced by ethnic balance on the panel. In the past few years, for example, I have worked closely with Nadim Rouhana, whose Palestinian-Arab background provides a helpful balance to my own Jewish background. The third party in our model does not offer solutions but enacts a strictly facilitative role.

Recruitment of participants is one of the most important tasks of the third party. The effectiveness of our recruitment process depends on intimate familiarity with the two communities and their political elites, on the establishment of links to various networks within these communities, and on the maintenance of both parties' trust in our evenhandedness, integrity, and knowledge of the region. Depending on the occasion and the political level of the participants, we may discuss our plans for a workshop with relevant elements of the political leadership on both sides in order to keep them informed, gain their support, and solicit their advice on participants and agenda. Recruitment, however, is generally done on an individual basis, and participants are invited to come as individuals rather than as formal representatives. An essential part of the recruitment process is a personal discussion with each participant about the purposes, procedures, and ground rules of the workshop before obtaining his or her final commitment to the enterprise.

A typical workshop consists of a preworkshop session of four to five hours for each of the parties and joint meetings for two and a half days. The workshops take place in an academic setting. Most of our workshops have been carried out under the auspices of the Harvard Center for International Affairs. The university has the advantage of providing an unofficial, nonbinding context, with its own set of norms, to support a type of interaction that departs from the norms that generally govern interactions between conflicting parties.

The discussions are completely private and confidential. There is no audience, no publicity, and no record, and one of the central ground rules specifies that statements made in the course of a workshop cannot be cited with attribution outside of the workshop setting. These and other features of the workshop are designed to enable and encourage workshop participants to engage in a type of communication that is usually not available to parties involved in an intense conflict relationship. The third party creates an atmosphere, establishes norms, and makes occasional interventions, all conducive to free and open discussion, in which the parties address each other rather than third parties or their own constituencies, and in which they listen to each other to understand their differing perspectives. They are encouraged to deal with the conflict analytically rather than polemically— to explore the ways in which their interaction helps to exacerbate and perpetuate the conflict, rather than to assign blame to the other side while justifying their own. This analytic discussion helps the parties penetrate each other's perspective and understand each other's concerns, needs, fears, priorities, and constraints.

Once both sets of concerns are on the table and have been understood and acknowledged, the parties are encouraged to engage in a process of joint problem solving. They are asked to work together in developing new ideas for resolving the conflict in ways that would satisfy the fundamental needs and allay the existential fears of both parties. They are then asked to explore the political and psychological constraints that stand in the way of such integrative, win-win solutions and that, in fact, have prevented the parties from moving to (or staying at) the negotiating table, or from negotiating productively. Next, they are asked to engage in another process of joint problem solving, designed to generate ideas for "getting from here to there." A central feature of this process is the identification of steps of mutual reassurance—in the form of acknowledgments, symbolic gestures, or confidence-building measures—that would help reduce the parties' fears of entering into negotiations whose outcome is uncertain and risky. Problem-solving workshops also contribute to mutual reassurance by helping the parties develop a nonthreatening, de-escalatory language and a shared vision of a desirable future.

Workshops have a dual purpose. First, they are designed to produce changes in the workshop participants themselves, in the form of more differentiated images of the enemy, greater insight into the dynamics of the conflict, and new ideas for resolving the conflict and for overcoming the barriers to a negotiated solution.[12] These changes at the level of individual participants are not ends in themselves but vehicles for promoting change at the policy level. Thus, a second purpose of workshops is to maximize the likelihood that the new insights, ideas, and proposals developed in the course of the workshop are fed back into the political debate and the decisionmaking process within each community.

One of the central tasks of the third party is to structure the workshop in such a way that new insights and ideas are likely to be generated *and* to be transferred effectively to the policy process. The composition of the workshop is crucial in this context: great care must be taken to select participants who, on the one hand, have the interest and capacity to engage in the kind of learning process that workshops provide and, on the other hand, have the positions and credibility within their own communities that enable them to influence the thinking of political leaders, political constituencies, or the general public.

A basic assumption of interactive problem solving is that solutions emerging out of the interaction between the conflicting parties are most likely to be responsive to their needs and to engender their commitment. However, the facilitative role of the third party is essential—at least at certain stages in the conflict—to making that interaction possible and fruitful. The third party provides the context in which representatives of parties engaged in an intense conflict are able to come together. It selects, briefs, and convenes the participants. It serves as a repository of trust for both parties, enabling them to proceed with the assurance that their confidentiality will be respected and their interests protected even though—by definition—they cannot trust each other. It establishes and enforces the norms and ground rules that facilitate analytic discussion and a problem-solving orientation. It proposes a broad agenda that encourages the parties to move from exploration of each other's concerns and constraints to the generation of ideas for win-win solutions and for implementing such solutions.

Furthermore, though the third party tries to stay in the background as much as possible once it has set the stage, it is prepared to intervene in order to help keep the discussion moving in a productive, constructive direction. Thus, if the discussion goes too far afield, becomes repetitive, or systematically avoids the issues, the third party—usually with the help of some of the participants—will try to bring it back to the broad agenda. At times, we also make substantive interventions in the form of suggestions for potentially useful conceptual handles or observations about the content and process of the interaction. Content observations are designed to summarize, interpret, integrate, clarify, or sharpen what is being said in the group. Process observations, which suggest how interactions between the parties "here and now" may reflect the dynamics of the conflict between their communities, are among the unique features of problem-solving workshops. They generally focus on incidents in which one party's words or actions clearly have a strong emotional impact on the other, leading to expressions of anger and dismay, relief and reassurance, understanding and acceptance, or reciprocation. The third party can use such incidents, which are part of the participants' shared immediate experience, as a springboard for exploring some of the issues and concerns that define the conflict between their societies. Through such exploration, each side can gain some insight into the preoccupations of the other and the way these are affected by its own actions. Process observations must be introduced sparingly and make special demands on the third party's skill and sense of timing. It is particularly important that such interventions be pitched at the intergroup, rather than the interpersonal, level. Analysis of "here and now" interactions is not concerned with the personal characteristics of the participants or with their personal relations to each other but only with what these interactions can tell us about the relationship between their national groups.

The nonbinding character of workshops makes it possible for new understandings and ideas to emerge out of the interaction between the parties. Although workshops are clearly separate from negotiations, they *are* intended to contribute to the negotiation process. The nature of their potential contribution depends on the status of the negotiations—on whether, for example, the parties are engaged in a prenegotiation phase, in early negotiations, in advanced negotiations, or in an implementation phase. Whatever phase the negotiations are in, however, maximizing the political impact is a central consideration in defining the purpose of a particular workshop, shaping its agenda, steering the discussion, and selecting the workshop participants.

Most of our work on the Israeli-Palestinian conflict—that is, all of our workshops before the fall of 1991—took place during the prenegotiation phase. The primary function of this work was to help create a political environment conducive to negotiations. Participants in the workshops that we have conducted over the years, as well as many analysts of the Arab-Israeli conflict, seem to agree that our program has indeed contributed, in a small but significant way, to paving the way to the negotiating table. Workshops have enabled the parties to penetrate each other's perspective and thus gain insight into the other's concerns, priorities, and constraints. They have con-

tributed to a more differentiated image of the other side, to a greater awareness of changes that have been taking place, to the discovery of potential
negotiating partners, and thus to the sense that there is someone to talk to
on the other side and something to talk about.

More concretely, workshops have contributed to the development of
cadres of individuals with experience in productive communication with
the other side and the conviction that such communication can be fruitful.
Representatives in the various Israeli-Palestinian negotiating sessions that
have been conducted since the fall of 1991 have included a considerable
number of individuals who took part in our workshops and other Israeli-
Palestinian unofficial meetings over the years. In particular, many members
of a continuing workshop (to be described further on), which met periodi-
cally between 1990 and 1993, have been actively involved in the official
peace process as negotiators or advisers.[13] "Alumni" of our workshops
have served in the Israeli cabinet, Knesset, and foreign ministry, and in
leading positions in various official Palestinian agencies.

Workshops have also contributed to creating a political environment
conducive to negotiations through the development of a de-escalatory language, based on sensitivity to words that frighten or humiliate and words
that reassure the other party. Anecdotal evidence for this effect is provided
by the changes in the tone of the political discourse among Palestinians and
Israelis in recent years. Moreover, workshops have helped in the identification of mutually reassuring actions and symbolic gestures, often in the form
of acknowledgments of the other's humanity, national identity, ties to the
land, history of victimization, sense of injustice, genuine fears, and conciliatory moves. The workshops have contributed to the development of
shared visions of a desirable future, which help reduce the parties' fears of
negotiations as a step into an unknown, dangerous realm. They have generated ideas about the shape of a solution to the conflict that meets the basic
needs of both parties, as well as ideas about a framework and set of principles for getting negotiations started. Perhaps the greatest value of these
workshops was that, for the short run, they helped to keep alive a sense of
possibility, a belief that a negotiated solution remained within the parties'
reach; for the long run, they helped to begin the process of transforming the
relationship between former enemies.

CONTRIBUTIONS OF UNOFFICIAL EFFORTS
TO THE ISRAELI-PALESTINIAN PEACE PROCESS

The Israeli-Palestinian agreement of September 1993 represents a fundamental breakthrough in the longstanding Arab-Israeli conflict. The crucial
element of this breakthrough is the mutual recognition between Israel and

the Palestine Liberation Organization (PLO), expressed in the exchange of letters between the late prime minister Yitzhak Rabin and chairman Yasir Arafat and in the opening of formal negotiations between the two sides. Israel's recognition of the PLO constituted acceptance of Palestinian nationhood and signaled—to Palestinians, Israelis, and the rest of the world—that the most likely eventual outcome of the negotiations, after a peaceful transition period, will be a Palestinian state. PLO recognition of Israel constituted a formal acknowledgment of the legitimacy of the state of Israel within its pre-1967 borders and opened the door to the recognition of Israel by the Arab states and acceptance of its rightful place in the region.

The significance of this act of mutual recognition becomes apparent in the light of the history of the Israeli-Palestinian conflict, which was marked by mutual denial of the other's nationhood and systematic efforts by each side to delegitimize the other. The conflict had been perceived by the two parties as a zero-sum conflict over national identity and national existence, in that each saw acknowledgment of the other's national rights and even the other's existence as a nation to be antagonistic to its own national rights and existence.[14] The September 1993 agreement thus represented a conceptual breakthrough. To be sure, the process that it set into motion is not irreversible; any political process is potentially subject to change. But the fact that what has been unthinkable for the entire history of this conflict has now not only been thought but spoken and acted upon at the highest level of each community and in the international arena has created a new historical reality that cannot be completely undone. Moreover, the political costs of reversing the process that has been set into motion with the peace agreement would be extremely high for the leaderships on both sides. There is no doubt that Rabin and Arafat (though apparently not Benjamin Netanyahu) made a strategic decision to bring an end to the conflict through a historic compromise and that each staked his political future and his standing in history on the achievement of this goal. In doing so, they responded to a widespread—though far from unanimous—sense within each community that continuation of the conflict does not serve its fundamental needs and long-term interests.

Our workshops and related activities over the past two decades made a modest but not insignificant contribution to this breakthrough in the Israeli-Palestinian conflict.[15] They did so through the development of cadres prepared to carry out productive negotiations; the sharing of information and the formulation of new ideas that provided important substantive inputs into the negotiations; and the fostering of a political atmosphere that made the parties open to a new relationship. The continuing workshop of 1990–1993 greatly enhanced these contributions and strengthened the political relevance of our work, both because it represented a sustained effort of joint Israeli-Palestinian exploration of key issues and because of the high level of the participants in terms of their political influence and their intellectual power.

With the onset of the negotiations, we found ourselves at an important new turning point. Unofficial communication, far from being irrelevant under the new circumstances, became a potentially important vehicle for helping to create the momentum that was still lacking in the negotiation process and to develop ideas to sustain the process and improve its outcome. The participants in the continuing workshop, given their role in the negotiations and their increasing political influence in their respective communities, were particularly well situated to make such contributions.

Despite the historic breakthrough of September 1993, there is a continuing need for the potential contributions of unofficial diplomacy. The Israeli-Palestinian negotiations are by no means complete, and enormous obstacles have yet to be overcome. Implementation of the interim agreement and conclusion of a final agreement will inevitably be a long and arduous process. The difficulties are exacerbated by sharp divisions within each society. Ideological opponents of the peace process who want to hold out for sole possession of the entire land, although they represent only a minority on each side, are strengthened by the existential fears and profound distrust of the other side that pervade both communities. Under these circumstances, the peace process is particularly threatened by acts of violence, which heighten the public's sense of vulnerability and its dread that the leadership has embarked on an uncertain and dangerous course. For Palestinians, such acts of violence reinforce the feeling that the peace process is not producing the hoped-for changes in their daily existence; for Israelis they help to erode the belief that the process can succeed in transforming the status quo into a state of peaceful coexistence. Delays and difficulties in negotiating details of an agreement and in implementing it are inevitable in a conflict with such a long history of bitterness and distrust.

Therefore, a great deal of effort and skill are still required—at the levels of diplomacy, political decisionmaking, and public education—if the major breakthrough of September 1993 is to fulfill itself through implementation of a viable interim agreement, passage of a peaceful transition period, conclusion of a mutually satisfactory final agreement, and establishment of a new relationship between the two nations. A successful transaction of these tasks calls for a systematic process of mutual reassurance responsive to both sides' existential fears and creative reframing of the final-status issues so that they become amenable to negotiation. Unofficial efforts, such as those that my colleagues and I are engaged in, can make useful contributions at this stage, particularly by (1) facilitating a joint Israeli-Palestinian forum for addressing the obstacles and constraints that impede implementation of the interim agreement and negotiation of the final agreement; (2) developing principles and options for resolving the difficult political issues left to the negotiations over the final agreement; and (3) exploring the requirements for building a new relationship between the two communities.

In conclusion, let me return to my conceptual analysis to summarize the two ways in which interactive problem solving can potentially make such contributions to peacemaking in the Middle East and elsewhere. First, it provides a microprocess that can generate new insights into the conflict and new ideas for advancing negotiation and for shaping mutually satisfactory solutions; it can also infuse these insights and ideas into the political debate and the decisionmaking processes in the two communities. The special value of these ideas is that they emerge from a process of interactive problem solving—of joint thinking—by politically influential, mainstream members of the parties themselves.

Second, interactive problem solving contributes to the development of new approaches to conceptualizing and conducting the macroprocess of conflict resolution and international relations in general. The central features to this reconceptualization are (1) a view of conflict resolution as an attempt to change the relationship between the conflicting parties, which, in turn, implies the principle of reciprocity in the process and product of conflict resolution; (2) a new kind of political discourse in international relations—one that involves a shift in emphasis from power politics to joint problem solving; and (3) a new view of the influence processes employed in international relations—one that involves a shift in emphasis from deterrence and compellence to mutual reassurance.

NOTES

The original version of this article appeared as Herbert C. Kelman, "Interactive Problem Solving: An Approach to Conflict Resolution and Its Application in the Middle East," *PS: Political Science and Politics* 31 (June 1998): 190–198. It has been reprinted here with minor adaptations with kind permission of the American Political Science Association.

    1. See Burton 1969, 1979, 1984; and Kelman 1972.

    2. For a fuller description of problem-solving workshops, see Kelman 1979, 1986, 1992a, 1996b, 1997a; Kelman and Cohen 1986; and Rouhana and Kelman 1994. For a review of other work within this general framework, see Fisher 1989, 1997.

    3. Kelman 1996a.

    4. Burton 1990; and Kelman 1990.

    5. Kelman 1993.

    6. Saunders 1988.

7. Kelman 1997b.
8. Bronfenbrenner 1961; and White 1965.
9. Kelman 1997b.
10. Kelman 1978, 1979.
11. Kelman 1979, 1986, 1992a.
12. Kelman 1979, 1986, 1992a.
13. Rouhana and Kelman 1994.
14. Kelman 1992b.
15. Kelman, 1995.

REFERENCES

Bronfenbrenner, Urie. (1961). "The Mirror Image in Soviet-American Relations: A Social Psychologist's Report." *Journal of Social Issues* 17, no. 3: 45–56.

Burton, John W. (1969). *Conflict and Communication: The Use of Controlled Communication in International Relations.* London: Macmillan.

———. (1979). *Deviance, Terrorism and War: The Process of Solving Unsolved Social and Political Problems.* New York: St. Martin's Press.

———. (1984). *Global Conflict: The Domestic Sources of International Crisis.* Brighton, Sussex: Wheatsheaf.

———, ed. (1990). *Conflict: Human Needs Theory.* New York: St. Martin's Press.

Cohen, Stephen P., et al. (1977). "Evolving Intergroup Techniques for Conflict Resolution: An Israeli-Palestinian Pilot Workshop." *Journal of Social Issues* 33, no. 1: 165–189.

Fisher, Ronald J. (1989). "Prenegotiation Problem-Solving Discussions: Enhancing the Potential for Successful Negotiations." In Janice Gross Stein, ed., *Getting to the Table: The Processes of International Prenegotiation.* Baltimore: Johns Hopkins University Press.

———. (1997). *Interactive Conflict Resolution.* Syracuse: Syracuse University Press.

Kelman, Herbert C. (1972). "The Problem-Solving Workshop in Conflict Resolution." In Richard L. Merritt, ed., *Communication in International Politics.* Urbana: University of Illinois Press.

———. (1978). "Israelis and Palestinians: Psychological Prerequisites for Mutual Acceptance." *International Security* 3, no. 1: 162–186.

———. (1979). "An Interactional Approach to Conflict Resolution and Its Application to Israeli-Palestinian Relations." *International Interactions* 6, no. 2: 99–122.

———. (1986). "Interactive Problem Solving: A Social-Psychological Approach to Conflict Resolution." In William Klassen, ed., *Dialogue Toward Interfaith Understanding.* Jerusalem: Ecumenical Institute for Theological Research.

———. (1987). "The Political Psychology of the Israeli-Palestinian Conflict: How Can We Overcome the Barriers to a Negotiated Solution?" *Political Psychology* 8, no. 3: 347–363.

———. (1990). "Applying a Human Needs Perspective to the Practice of Conflict Resolution." In John W. Burton, ed., *Conflict: Human Needs Theory.* New York: St. Martin's Press.

———. (1992a). "Informal Mediation by the Scholar/Practitioner." In Jacob Bercovitch and Jeffrey Z. Rubin, eds., *Mediation in International Relations:*

Multiple Approaches to Conflict Management. New York: St. Martin's Press.

———. (1992b). "Acknowledging the Other's Nationhood: How to Create a Momentum for the Israeli-Palestinian Negotiations." *Journal of Palestine Studies* 22, no. 1: 18–38.

———. (1993). "Coalitions Across Conflict Lines: The Interplay of Conflicts Within and Between the Israeli and Palestinian Communities." In Stephen Worchel and Jeffrey A. Simpson, eds., *Conflict Between People and Groups.* Chicago: Nelson-Hall.

———. (1995). "Contributions of an Unofficial Conflict Resolution Effort to the Israeli-Palestinian Breakthrough." *Negotiation Journal* 11: 19–27.

———. (1996a). "Negotiation as Interactive Problem Solving." *International Negotiation: A Journal of Theory and Practice* 1, no. 1: 99–123.

———. (1996b). "The Interactive Problem Solving Approach." In Chester A. Crocker and Fen Osler Hampson, eds., with Pamela Aall, *Managing Global Chaos.* Washington, D.C.: U.S. Institute of Peace.

———. (1997a). "Group Processes in the Resolution of International Conflicts: Experiences from the Israeli-Palestinian Case." *American Psychologist* 52: 212–220.

———. (1997b). "Social-Psychological Dimensions of International Conflict." In I. William Zartman and J. Lewis Rasmussen, eds., *Peacemaking in International Conflict: Methods and Techniques.* Washington, D.C.: U.S. Institute of Peace.

Kelman, Herbert, C., and Stephen P. Cohen. (1986). "Resolution of International Conflict: An Interactional Approach." In Stephen Worchel and William G. Austin, eds., *Psychology of Intergroup Relations.* 2d ed. Chicago: Nelson-Hall.

Rouhana, Nadim N., and Herbert C. Kelman. (1994). "Promoting Joint Thinking in International Conflicts: An Israeli-Palestinian Continuing Workshop." *Journal of Social Issues* 50, no. 1: 157–178.

Saunders, Harold H. (1988). "The Arab-Israeli Conflict in a Global Perspective." In John D. Steinbruner, ed., *Restructuring American Foreign Policy.* Washington, D.C.: Brookings Institution.

White, Ralph K. (1965). "Images in the Context of International Conflict: Soviet Perceptions of the U.S. and the U.S.S.R." In Herbert C. Kelman, ed., *International Behavior: A Social-Psychological Analysis.* New York: Holt, Rinehart and Winston.

First- and Second-Track Diplomacy in Northern Ireland

Mari Fitzduff

The population of Northern Ireland is roughly 1.5 million, about one-fifth that of London. Given its size, it is hard to believe how dialogue and mediation between conflicting parties and groups can be so difficult. But because of the divided nature of the society where Catholics/Nationalists and Protestants/Unionists usually live, learn, pray, and socialize separately, open and honest dialogue between either individuals or communities from differing political and cultural backgrounds is rare. Even where sectarian divisions are not total, and work or sometimes social contexts permit mixing (more often in the more middle-class mixed urban areas or those few villages and towns that remain shared), individuals have developed very effective ways of not relating to each other. For example, by the age of eleven, children have begun to be competent in the clues that will enable them to know which "side'" they are talking to, and they will temper their communications accordingly.[1] It has been frequently noted that there is almost a schizoid character to relationships in Northern Ireland.[2] So, while there is often a collective and public level of both verbal and sometimes physical expressions of sectarian hostility, at a private level, relationships are usually characterized by politeness and silence about contentious issues.[3]

It is even more difficult for those who are politicians, paramilitaries, or parties associated with paramilitaries to involve themselves in personal dialogue with each other, as they are very closely watched by their communities. Political dialogue between politicians usually happens only at a public level, and it is usually addressed to one's own constituency, who, many politicians fear, are watching, listening, and waiting lest their politicians betray their beliefs.

Added to the above is the difficulty that circumstances will often dictate to whom one is "permitted" by one's constituencies to talk, and the decades in Northern Ireland have shown a consistent pattern of such refusals. Unionists have at times refused to talk to all other non-Unionist parties and the British government; the Social and Democratic Labor Party (SDLP) has refused to talk formally with others in the assembly (1982–1986); and churches, government ministers and others have usually refused to talk to Sinn Fein for most of the conflict.[4] Fashions for such permissions changed in the light of paramilitary atrocities, or political developments. Also, because Northern Ireland is such a small place, it can almost be guaranteed that such talking cannot be done with any degree of privacy. Individuals or groups wishing to cross sectarian boundaries often receive threats from members of their own community if they decide to talk with their enemies. In addition, the media are often watching for such moves, and their scrutiny can often be very destructive to the development of dialogue.[5]

It can therefore be seen why dialogue and mediation of either a formal (Track 1) or more informal (Track 2) nature is so difficult. On the one hand, Track 1 initiatives, that is, the formal efforts of governments and political parties to achieve a solution by negotiation, have been limited by the huge ignorance and distrust between the representatives of the political parties. The very public and formal nature of many such processes was to prove cumbersome in developing an inclusive dialogue process. In addition, the problematic nature of including paramilitaries or political parties perceived to be aligned with paramilitaries at the negotiating table has severely hampered and delayed progress toward a solution in Northern Ireland. On the other hand, Track 2 initiatives, though more capable of flexibility and privacy in a way that is impossible for Track 1 initiatives, have often suffered from lack of resources and the necessary authority to translate successful informal initiatives into agreed and formalized agreements. Yet the interplay between the two has been vital for the eventual success of the peace process.

FIRST TRACK INITIATIVES

In general, first-track initiatives were conducted between governments and political parties. Until 1985, the British government was the main player in Track 1 initiatives and resisted any externalization of the conflict. However, the Anglo-Irish agreement of 1985 eventually acknowledged the interest and positive role of the government of the Republic of Ireland in seeking a solution to the conflict. And in the mid-1990s, the British government also began to realize the usefulness of using the goodwill of the United States in finding a solution. Both liaisons were to prove extremely productive, as formal and informal representatives from the Irish and U.S. governments were able to widen and deepen the necessary dialogues between political parties, and subsequently, between governments, politicians, paramilitaries, and communities. In addition, the eventual, often painfully slow development of creative political solutions to issues of constitutional and identity conflicts was extremely important to achieving an agreement. Equally necessary was the development by government of what were often very complex and tortuous dialogue processes for involving paramilitaries in political negotiation without compromising democracy.[6]

First Efforts, 1972–1982

Until 1994, formal talks were conducted only with constitutional parties, those who eschewed violence in the pursuit of their political aims.[7] In 1972, the British government dismissed the Unionist government, which had had regional control in Northern Ireland since 1921, because of its unwillingness to address issues of inequality and the counterproductive nature of its security response to the demands of the civil rights movement. In 1974 the government tried to reintroduce devolved government to the region, but such government failed following a general strike organized by Loyalist paramilitaries, which led to the return of direct rule by the British government.[8]

As violence in the region subsequently rose, efforts at settling the conflict were mainly focused on security approaches to deal with the daily dosage of bombings, shootings, and the consequent destruction of life and property. Although some efforts were made in 1972 to engage with the Irish Republican Army (IRA) through secret negotiations, these were unsuccessful, as no common ground could be agreed between the British government representatives and the IRA.[9] And, although in 1982 the British government announced it was going to set up a new assembly for dialogue between the constitutional parties, this suggestion was rejected by the SDLP on the basis that power sharing within it was not mandatory, and it excluded an Irish governmental dimension to the solution.

British-Irish Cooperation, 1995

As the conflict continued into its second decade, the British government, which had formerly resisted any involvement of the Irish government in seeking a solution to the conflict (believing it would impinge on its sovereign status), eventually realized that there might be some merit in a cooperative approach, as both parts of the island were suffering from the ongoing violence. So in 1985 the Anglo-Irish Treaty was signed by the two governments. This recognized that any change in the status of Northern Ireland could only come about with the consent of the majority of people in Northern Ireland, and it established an intergovernmental conference where both governments could discuss matters of policy affecting Northern Ireland.

The agreement was rejected by the Unionists, who saw it as diluting the union with Britain, and by Sinn Fein, who saw it as confirming partition. Despite such opposition, the agreement has, in fact, functioned as a very useful vehicle through which concerted efforts and assorted disagreements were dealt with by both governments. Such cooperation was to be of considerable significance in the years that followed.

In 1989 a particularly energetic and committed secretary of state, Peter Brooke, began another series of meetings with all the political parties, except for Sinn Fein, which was still excluded because of its refusal to condemn the use of violence.[10] During these talks, it was agreed that there should be three strands to any eventual solution: the internal structures for Northern Ireland, the all-Ireland context, and the British-Irish relationship.

Ultimately, however, the differences between the parties on the formation of new political structures proved too difficult to surmount, and these talks ended without any agreed political framework in 1992.

Including the Paramilitaries, 1988–1998

One of the major difficulties in the talks was that they excluded Sinn Fein, whose leaders were believed to be spokespersons for the IRA. In 1988, the SDLP and Sinn Fein held a series of meetings to see if they could resolve their differences, particularly over Sinn Fein's support for the use of violence. Following the breakdown of the interparty talks in 1992, John Hume, leader of the SDLP, and Gerry Adams, the leader of Sinn Fein, restarted their talks in March 1993 to see if they could achieve a breakthrough in the stalemate that saw violence continue.

It had been obvious for some time that there were those within Sinn Fein who no longer believed that a military offensive on their part would necessarily achieve a British withdrawal, and a few of their leaders had begun to explore the option of a much more widely based Nationalist front in order to progress their aim of a united Ireland. Sinn Fein began to change the nature of its demands by softening its statements on the need for a stated time frame for such British withdrawal, recognizing the need for Unionists to consent to a united Ireland, and asking the British government to be persuaders to that consent. Despite significant hostility from most Unionists and some Nationalists, Hume continued his dialogue with Adams for most of 1993, and they eventually agreed upon a series of principles that they hoped would make it possible for Sinn Fein/IRA to end the violence with some sense of political success.

Meanwhile, other dialogue processes that were directed at Sinn Fein were gathering momentum. Particularly useful were the dialogue opportunities opened up by West Belfast priests and Sinn Fein, which helped to open communication between Sinn Fein and the Dublin government. And toward the end of 1993, it was revealed that the British government, through some intermediaries, had been having talks with Sinn Fein in secret. These talks had focused on how Sinn Fein could be included in political discussions once they had renounced violence.

In the end, most of the principles agreed upon by Hume and Adams were incorporated into the Downing Street Declaration issued by both governments in December 1993. The declaration once again reiterated the commitment of the British government to maintaining the union until the greater number of the people in Northern Ireland decided otherwise. This decision could be ratified by referenda both north and south of the border, thus allowing for the "self-determination by the people of the Island of Ireland" that Sinn Fein had said was necessary if the violence of the IRA was to cease. It also provided for North-South cooperation on a variety of issues, and, once again, it provided for a devolved government in Northern Ireland.

Cease-Fire and Subsequent Talks, 1994–1998

In August 1994, the IRA declared a cease-fire, followed six weeks later by a cease-fire commitment by the Loyalist paramilitaries. This paved the way for further political progress. In February 1995 the British and Irish governments produced a document that outlined the British government's perspective on a possible framework for an internal power-sharing government in Northern Ireland, a political agreement between the two governments, and cooperation on an island-wide basis.

The proposals, and in particular those concerned with North-South cooperation, were greeted with anger by many Unionists, who felt they represented another step on what many of them saw as the road to a united Ireland. But paramilitaries on both sides reiterated their commitment to maintaining the cease-fires and committed themselves to pursue political progress through democratic means. The continued involvement of the Loyalist paramilitaries in the process had been considerably assisted by the efforts of a Dublin trade unionist who had, during the mid-1990s, opened up channels of communication between the Dublin government and Loyalists.

In early 1995, talks began between the civil servants of the British government and Sinn Fein and with parties representing the Loyalist paramilitaries, which explored some possibilities for involving them in political dialogue with other political parties as well as reassurances from them about their commitment to decommissioning arms. In May 1995, the government entered into ministerial dialogue with Sinn Fein, which also committed itself to discussing arms decommissioning.

Given such agreements, talks involving parties representing paramilitaries now became possible. Elections were held to select representatives for the all-party talks due to start in June 1996. Although Sinn Fein secured 15.5 percent of the vote, they were initially excluded because the IRA cease-fire broke down when the IRA, angered by the delays in political progress, bombed in the heart of London in January 1996. But after the Labor Party was returned to power in an election in May 1997, contact with the British government was renewed again. The IRA declared a new cease-fire in July 1997, and Sinn Fein finally entered the multiparty talks in September 1997.

After an intensive eight months of talking, the parties finally agreed to the Belfast Agreement on April 10, 1998. This agreement provides for the future shared governance of Northern Ireland, with various bodies to address issues of rights and equality; a variety of cross-border bodies to ensure that the Republic of Ireland and Northern Ireland work together on issues of mutual concern; and an East-West body to address issues of collective concern to the islands of Britain and Ireland. Six weeks later, more than 71 percent of the population of Northern Ireland voted yes to the agreement, and a timetable was set in place for setting up the political arrangements agreed, as well as bodies to deal with contentious issues such as policing and decommissioning.

TRACK 2 INITIATIVES

Many of the above initiatives were achieved through the efforts of governments, politicians, and civil servants, assisted in some cases by members of civic society. But, in addition, there were a variety of second-track mediation initiatives that significantly assisted first-track processes. Many of these concentrated on trying to develop fruitful contact between the politicians, between the paramilitaries and governments, and between politicians and civic society.

The Role of Community Mediators

Throughout the conflict, there have been many hundreds of initiatives aimed at achieving contact or shuttle diplomacy between the participants to the conflict.[11] Indigenous mediators undertook most of these initiatives, although there were some very useful interventions by people from outside of Northern Ireland and particularly by some who came from a Quaker or Mennonite tradition. Such mediators tried to provide safe and unthreatening opportunities for politicians to look at issues of mutual concern such as social issues, or the economy, or conflicts elsewhere. Such processes were designed to increase the trust that could develop between them, without necessarily burdening them by initiating direct mediation, as direct mediation on political possibilities was often deemed by politicians to be more appropriately the concern of Track 1 initiatives.

In addition, there were also thousands of people involved in community initiatives aimed at achieving dialogue between communities, and in the early 1990s, these numbers increased significantly.[12] Training for such dialogue was developed by many organizations, and hundreds of local workshops took place that brought together people from all sections of the community to look at a variety of issues, including political options, for their future together.[13] Many other initiatives that aimed to stimulate dialogue through drama, music, and art also proliferated.[14] It is notable that the years preceding the agreement were marked by a large increase in cross-community attendance at the funerals of victims of political and sectarian assassinations, and huge public demonstrations organized by trade unionists and others against continuing violence. Such initiatives contributed significantly to the development of a context that made it possible to achieve the readiness in the community on the part of both paramilitaries and politicians for a political agreement.

Academics

Although many within the academic community stayed aloof from the conflict, there were a few who were committed to very constructive dialogue processes. One such initiative was undertaken by academics who were located at the University of Ulster, and which facilitated a collective look between the parties at the development of a Northern Ireland Center in Brussels in the early 1990s.[15] Because the parties were able to focus on common issues of concern, the center was successfully established under the auspices of both the political parties and the business community and enabled some levels of knowledge and trust to be developed between them.

During the 1990s, academics and others were also very useful in organizing workshops for politicians to meet in places like the United States or South Africa to address issues of conflict resolution. These conferences often provided opportunities for relationships to form between the politicians, which were difficult to form at home in Northern Ireland given the restricted nature of society and the watchful eyes of the media.

Initiative 92—Community Consultation

In 1992 a major program, called Initiative 92, asked local communities and other interested bodies and individuals to express their views about ways forward for the future for Northern Ireland on a political, economic, and social level. Although condemned by most politicians (who initially saw it as irrelevant or threatening), the initiative was a significant success in achieving its objective of stimulating discussion. It received over 500 submissions from people and groups in Northern Ireland, many of which had been developed on a cross-community basis, and it held public workshops at which various contributors were given an opportunity to expand on their ideas. The submissions were eventually contained in a huge ideas book for Northern Ireland called the Opsahl Report.[16] Many of these ideas were to prove fruitful in eventually generating the agreement.

The Role of the Churches

Although the churches themselves had in the main contributed little to dialogue processes, there were some exceptions.[17] In addition to the work by some members of the Catholic clergy in opening up and developing dialogue with Sinn Fein in order to end violence, confidential workshops were held over a period of several years in the mid-1990s between Sinn Fein and members of the Protestant/Unionist clergy. Although there was significant hostility to such dialogue by many within the Unionist community when they were eventually disclosed, the workshops provided a useful context within which Sinn Fein could address the reality of the perceptions and fears of the Unionist community and take them into account in developing their strategies.

Business Community

A late but effective newcomer to the peace process was the business community. In the mid-1990s, leaders in the business community began to cooperate with each other and with the trade unions to see if a more strategic approach could be implemented that would put pressure on both Republican and Loyalist paramilitaries to end their campaign of violence. They also publicly encouraged all parties to get involved in political negotiations. Groups such as the Chamber of Commerce, the Confederation of British Industry, the Institute of Directors, and the trade unions involved themselves in dialogue with Sinn Fein and the Loyalist parties, often on issues of the economy. Their influence was very helpful, particularly as it also put pressure on the political parties to enter into serious dialogue.

The United States

During the 1990s, many people from the United States were also of assistance in developing dialogue processes—initially with Sinn Fein but subsequently also with the Loyalist parties. Although for the first few decades of the conflict, the United States had primarily appeared to be sympathetic to the politics of the Nationalist community in Northern Ireland, during the 1990s, many from the United States began to develop an inclusive process of political dialogue that could end the violence. Various members of Congress and business leaders brought pressure to bear upon Sinn Fein to end the violence, enter into dialogue, and engage with the Unionist community. Such dialogue efforts were significantly assisted by the efforts of President Bill Clinton and Senator George Mitchell. Mitchell became chairman of the multiparty talks that were eventually successful in reaching an inclusive agreement between the parties.

CONCLUSION

Without doubt, the major difficulty in Northern Ireland has been achieving sufficient dialogue between politicians and communities to engender enough understanding and trust to find solutions to issues of equality and political choices. Both sides felt threatened by each other, and fears turned into anger, exclusion, recrimination, and the murder of more than 3,500 people. Starting and continuing the debates about the development of a shared and pluralist society has been extraordinarily difficult.

Although Track 1 efforts are and should be preeminent, the experience of Northern Ireland has been that such initiatives would never have succeeded without the plethora of Track 2 initiatives, which developed the context for more formalized initiatives. It was Track 2 initiatives that broke the logjam of nondialogue between governments and paramilitaries. It was also the creativity and courage of many informal actors such as academics and business and community people who developed contexts in which politicians could meet each other away from the destructive glare of the political spotlight. And it was the enormous number of dialogue efforts by hundreds of community groups that enabled many of the politicians to engage in dialogue in the knowledge that such dialogue would not be political suicide.

Relationships between the two tracks have not always been easy. Frustration with the lack of political leadership has been an abiding complaint of many involved in Track 2 work. Many politicians have complained about the lack of appreciation for how difficult their task has been. Both sides have often been reluctant to acknowledge the contribution that each has made to the development of the peace process, and such tensions continue. Since the agreement, many within civic society who feel that they have contributed an 'enormous amount to the development of the peace have felt excluded from the considerations of the newly elected assembly. Although the agreement provided for a civic forum, where community, business, trade union, and church groups will have a chance to contribute to the assembly, the newly elected politicians have, with few exceptions, been noticeably cool about its development.[18] Politicians are now anxious to prove that they can deliver on the implementation of the agreement and are keen to exercise their newly elected power.

Such tensions are understandable and need to be recognized, understood, and anticipated by those involved in the processes. But without the courage and commitment of the many thousands of people involved in Track 2 initiatives, the reality is that the Belfast Agreement would never have been reached. Given the tensions that have continued between the political parties since the agreement was signed, it is equally unlikely that the agreement can be sustained without a continuing commitment by politicians, civic leaders, and others to the continuance of both Track 1 and Track 2 initiatives in the difficult years ahead. Conflicts do not end—they merely change. In the new order of Northern Ireland, although the bombs and the bullets are falling increasingly silent, the need for dialogue at all levels will continue to be a priority, and will need all the complementary approaches that can be brought to bear on the continuing divisions in society if peace in the years ahead is to be secured.

NOTES

1. Cairns 1994.
2. Harris 1972; and Murphy 1978.
3. "Whatever you say, say nothing" is a line from Northern Ireland poet Seamus Heaney that is usually used to exemplify the silence between people in Northern Ireland.
4. The SDLP is a constitutional, nationalist, party committed to achieving a United Ireland by solely democratic means. Sinn Fein is a political party believed to be closely allied with the Irish Republican Army.
5. Kelly 1998.
6. For an interesting account of the frustratingly slow processes of the 1996–1998 talks, see *Making Peace* by the chairman, Senator George Mitchell (1999).
7. It must be noted that even so-called constitutional parties often accused each other of inciting violence or colluding with those who used violence.
8. *Loyalists* is the term usually used to denote Unionists who are prepared to countenance political violence.
9. For an account of these efforts, see Bardon 1992, 694–695.
10. The secretary of state is the major representative of the British government in Northern Ireland.
11. Shuttle diplomacy is where a mediator tries to increase understanding of differing perspectives through sequential conversations with the participants, rather than through contact between them.
12. Fitzduff 1996.
13. Such work included contact work, rumor clarification, institutional antisectarian work, rights work, church dialogue work, work on issues of identity, and political discussion work.
14. Community Relations Council reports, 1990–1998.
15. This center deals with all European Community issues of concern to Northern Ireland.
16. Pollack 1993.
17. Morrow 1994.
18. The civic forum was the idea of the Northern Ireland Women's Coalition, a party set up in 1996, and dedicated to cross-community dialogue between the political parties. They have two elected members in the assembly.

REFERENCES

Arthur, Paul. (1992). "Multiparty Mediation: Northern Ireland as a Case Study." In Hampson FO Crocker and P. Aail, eds., *Herding Cats: The Management of Complex. Mediation*. Washington, D.C.: United States Institute of Peace.

Bardon, Jonathon. (1992). *A History of Ulster.* Belfast: Blackstaff Press.

Cairns, Ed. (1994). *Caught in the Crossfire: Children in the Northern Ireland Conflict*. Belfast: Appletree Press.

Community Relations Council. (1990–1998). *Annual Reports.* Belfast, Northern Ireland: Community Relations Council.

Fitzduff, Mari. (1996). *Beyond Violence: Conflict Resolution Processes in Northern Ireland.* Tokyo: United Nations University Press.

Harris, Rosemary. (1972). *Prejudice and Tolerance in Ulster.* Manchester: Manchester University Press.

Kelly, Grainne. (1998). *The Art of Mediation.* Ulster: INCORE, University of Ulster.

Mitchell, George. (1999). *Making Peace.* Portsmouth, N.H.: Heinemann Press.

Morrow, Duncan. (1994). *The Churches and Inter-Community Relationships.* Ulster: Center for the Study of Conflict, University of Ulster.

Murphy, D. (1978). *A Place Apart.* Dublin: John Murray.

Pollak, Andy. (1993). *A Citizens Inquiry. The Opsahl Report.* Dublin: Lilliput Press.

▓ Thirteen Characteristics of Successful Mediation in Mozambique

Thania Paffenholz

This article presents thirteen factors of successful mediation by different internal and external actors that led to the ending of the war in Mozambique. The lessons drawn from these factors can be of interest to people involved in actual mediation processes because they give many ideas to overcome breakdowns in different phases of mediation. Before presenting the success factors, the text gives a brief overview of the war and the peace process.

THE WAR AND ITS CAUSES

In October 1992 a peace accord ended thirty years of war in Mozambique. The war started as an anticolonial fight in 1964 with the communist Frelimo (Frente de Libertaçao de Moçambique) being the only liberation movement. Since winning the liberation struggle and gaining independence in 1975, Frelimo has been running the government.

However, the war continued as Renamo (Resistençia National Moçambicana) was fighting against Frelimo soon after independence. Renamo was made up of smaller groups that had split off from Frelimo. It remains unclear whether the Rhodesian Intelligence Service under Ian

Smith founded or supported Renamo in order to control Rhodesian opposition groups inside Mozambique and to destabilize the new state.[1]

After the independence of Rhodesia (Zimbabwe) in 1980, Renamo received support from South Africa. As a consequence, the war escalated. Mozambique's government responded by a massive strengthening of its army.[2] During the following years, until the peace accord in 1992, Renamo controlled large areas of the country.

Three main causes of the war can be identified. The first cause was apartheid. The aim of the apartheid states, Rhodesia and South Africa, was to maintain their economic and military power in the region. South Africa saw the newly independent states of Angola and Mozambique as potential threats. Destabilizing these countries was therefore the aim of South African foreign security policy, the so-called Total National Strategy. The support for Renamo must be seen within this context.[3] The second cause of the war was related to the domestic and social policy of Frelimo. The Marxist/communist-inspired policy led to an overcentralization of the state and minimized the power of the local administration. The Frelimo party and the capital Maputo, located in the south, dominated the whole country. Equally questionable was the reform of the agricultural system. Many people were forced to move into collective villages and to abolish traditional forms of agriculture. Finally there was the antireligious policy of Frelimo.[4]

THE PEACE PROCESS: MANY ACTORS CONTRIBUTED TO SUCCESSFUL MEDIATION

The Preparation Phase

The peace process started at the end of the 1970s with the involvement of the Mozambican churches.[5] The Catholic Church of Mozambique started a campaign for peace with pastoral letters, public meetings, and talks with the government. The Mozambique Council of Churches, the umbrella organization of the Protestant churches in Mozambique, started its support for peace with the establishment of the Commission for Peace and Reconciliation in 1984. In comparison to the Catholic peace initiative, the Protestant one remained more informal, and it also involved secret talks with the government.

At the beginning of the peace process, the churches supported peace separately. Their activities were not coordinated. However, from 1988 on they started a common initiative to involve Renamo in the peace process. This was not an easy task, because Renamo was hidden somewhere in the bush and any contact was forbidden by the government. At this stage the Kenyan government functioned as a focal point for contacts with Renamo. It provided Good Offices and helped the church delegations establish contacts and offered passports and accommodations for the Renamo delegations. The first talks with Renamo began in 1988.

The Facilitation Phase

In 1989, the churches met with Renamo representatives several times in Nairobi. Consequently, the churches were asked by Mozambique's president, Joaquim Chissano, to become formal facilitators. Then in August 1989, President Chissano nominated Zimbabwe's president, Robert Gabriel Mugabe, and Kenya's president, Daniel arap Moi, as facilitators. But the talks ended unsuccessfully because Frelimo refused to hold direct talks with Renamo. As a result, the churches and the Italian and U.S. governments made various attempts to convince Frelimo to negotiate directly with Renamo. From mid-1990 the Italian Catholic lay organization San Egidio became involved, too. They provided facilitation and Good Offices. San Egidio had previous experience and had already mediated in a conflict between Frelimo and the Catholic Church at the beginning of the 1980s.

The Negotiation Phase

In March 1990, President Chissano agreed—after a visit to the United States—to hold direct talks with Renamo. From July 1990 until October 1992, Frelimo and Renamo held direct negotiations in Rome. The Italian government, San Egidio, and the Catholic Church of Mozambique acted as mediators. The negotiations took place in the community of San Egidio.

The Parallel Facilitation Phase in Rome

The success of this negotiation process was not only the result of these negotiation sessions but also by other efforts: whenever the negotiations stopped or were delayed, the U.S. government, the Italian government, the Mozambique Council of Churches, and later the Portuguese government initiated efforts to facilitate a renewal of the negotiations. They supported the mediators and the delegations of the warring parties in Rome, and they influenced the leaders of both sides.

The U.S. government had appointed the first secretary of the U.S. embassy to the Vatican as a contact person for the Mozambique negotiations in Rome. During the negotiations, he became a focal point for the delegations and the external mediators and facilitators. Furthermore, other representatives of the State Department contacted the presidents of the warring parties in the region and provided expertise on mediation to the mediators in Rome and to the delegations of the warring parties.

San Egidio requested that the Italian government support the negotiations logistically. Italy in turn provided one of the mediators, was part of the external actions around the negotiations in Rome, and cooperated close-ly with the United States. The Portuguese government came into the negoti-ations at a later stage and had a minor role by mainly providing technical advice for military questions concerning the cease-fire.

The Parallel Facilitation Phase in the Region

The government of Malawi was providing Good Offices for the secret meetings in the region. At a later stage in the process, Malawi became the focal point for meetings with Renamo. Several times the mediators and facilitators met with Renamo's president, Alfonso Dhlakama, in Malawi.

The German Friedrich Ebert Foundation made a successful contribu-tion by funding and initiating a study on the possible future role of the UN in Mozambique. Soon after the study was presented at a workshop in July 1992, the Mozambique government asked the UN to join the negotiations. Before that time, the UN was not involved in the process at all.

Good Offices and facilitation were also offered by individuals such as Andre Thomashausen, Renamo consultant, and the president of the British-Zimbabwean multinational Lonrho, Tiny Rowland. When Renamo was not allowed to enter Maputo, Thomashausen became an envoy, carrying mes-sages between Renamo and the government. Rowland provided air trans-port for the Renamo delegations to different facilitation meetings and had a certain influence on Dhlakama.

The Postagreement Phase—Mediation Continued

In October 1992 the peace talks resulted in a peace accord. However, medi-ation efforts continued to cope with difficulties in implementing the accord. The postwar phase was characterized by a lack of confidence between the conflicting parties, the difficult transformation of Renamo into a political party, the slow demobilization process, and many problems concerning the preparation for the elections. After the peace accord, the UN became the leading actor for the implementation of the peace accord with the United Nations Operation in Mozambique mission. UN envoy Aldo Ajello mediat-ed in a lot of detailed conflicts, and UN Secretary-General Boutros Boutros-Ghali intervened personally at a certain critical stage. The former mediators also continued to mediate when it was necessary.

CONCLUSION

From the first church initiatives in the late 1970s to the peace treaty, more then ten years were needed to come to an agreement. During the whole period the process was in danger of breaking down because at different stages the warring parties expected to be able to win the conflict by military means. Even after the peace treaty, this propensity did not disappear.[6]

A series of factors prevented the breakdown of the peace process:

1. Many mediators were involved. Fourteen different actors, eight states and six nongovernmental organizations (NGOs), were involved in the mediation process at the same time or at different times in the process. This gave the warring parties a choice.

2. The dynamics of the process played an important role. Due to the number of actors and mediation initiatives, the process could be kept going because a dynamic was created that made it increasingly difficult for the conflicting parties to abandon dialogue.

3. The existence of parallel mediation networks enhanced communication. Before, after, and parallel to the Rome negotiations, there had been two other networks. One was the facilitation, which took place to bring the parties to or back to the negotiation table. The other was the parallel consultancy, providing technical support and advice for the delegations in Rome and the presidents of the warring parties. This was mainly done by the U.S. and Italian governments.

4. The central role of internal actors was vital. One major reason for the success of Mozambique's mediation process was the involvement of the Mozambican churches as internal actors (partial insiders). They were the only mediators involved in every stage of the process, and they are still continuing this task.

5. The involvement of external actors was needed, too. Despite the importance of internal actors, the involvement of external mediators was relevant. They supported the internal actors by providing advice to both the warring parties and the mediators, and they also facilitated the ongoing involvement.

6. Ripeness was useful but not sufficient. There had been many moments in Mozambique's mediation process when the warring parties were open to negotiations and facilitations, when the conflict was ripe for resolution.[7] This always happened when a change in the external situation influenced the military balance of power. But the simple existence of ripe moments was not enough. When ripe moments occurred, progress within the mediation process was only possible because complex mediation networks already existed.

7. The process was enhanced by the establishment of humanitarian corridors. The Red Cross introduced the idea of these war-free corridors into the negotiations for humanitarian reasons. Because war-free corridors were not directly a peace issue, the warring parties agreed to their establishment. This quickened the peace process, because after having agreed on

a partial cease-fire, the expectations grew that the conflicting parties were ready to agree on a general cease-fire.

8. The efficiency of the process depended on the entrance way. States as mediators were more successful when they had been invited by both sides. On the contrary, NGOs and internal actors could mediate successfully even without invitation.

9. The existence of a relationship between the mediators and the warring parties before the beginning of the process was relevant. It was not relevant for a mediator to have a relationship with both parties, yet a relationship to at least one party was needed. Only the U.S. government and the UN needed no previous relationship at all.

10. No mediation could exist without the individual interests of the mediators. All involved mediators had their own interests in the mediation. In contrary to many assumptions, neutrality was not a precondition for mediation in the case of Mozambique. Individual interest was relevant; otherwise there was not enough motivation to continue the mediation.

11. Coordination speeded up the process. Coordination between the mediators contributed to success. The most effective coordination existed in the U.S.-Italian focal point for the negotiations in Rome. Information sharing was at some moments the basis for coordination.

12. Postagreement mediation was essential. Without the establishment of a flexible mediation network for the implementation and monitoring of the peace accord, the chances would have been high for a collapse of the process.

Peacebuilding is a long-term process. The disappearance of the external causes of conflict after the end of the East-West conflict changed the regional situation positively. However, several internal causes, such as the overcentralization of the state and the power dominance of one party, remain to be resolved. Since the elections, which were won by Frelimo, the situation continues to be problematic; the opposition is still not included in the government and frequently not even in the political process. This mitigates the success of the mediation process and shows clearly that peacebuilding is a longer process than just the mediation phase.

NOTES

1. See Alex Vinces, *Renamo: Terrorism in Mozambique* (London, 1991), p. 11.
2. See Africa Watch, *War, Famine and the Reform Process in Mozambique* (London, 1992), 65.
3. See Joseph Hanlon, *Beggar Your Neighbours: Apartheid Power in Southern Africa* (Bloomington: Indiana University Press, 1986).

4. Gucorgui Derluguian, "Social Decomposition and Armed Violence in Postcolonial Mozambique," *Review* 8, no. 4 (1990): 439.

5. For the role of the churches, see Sabine Derluguian and Thania Paffenholz, "Kirchen können in Kriegen vermitteln," *Der überblick* 3 (1994): 116–119; and Alex Vinces and Ken Wilson, "Churches and the Peace Process in Mozambique" (paper presented at the conference "The Christian Churches and Africa's Democratization," University of Leeds, 20–23 September 1993).

6. For more detailed conclusions, see Thania Paffenholz, *Konflikttransformation durch Vermittlung* (Mainz, Germany: Matthias-Grünewald-Verlag, 1998).

7. For the concept of ripeness, see the article by Thania Paffenholz, "Western Approaches to Negotiation and Mediation: An Overview," in this book.

Traditional Approaches to Negotiation and Mediation: Examples from Africa

▓ Burundi, Rwanda, and Congo

Filip Reyntjens and Stef Vandeginste

Reconciliation is a process that ideally involves not only political and military players at the macrolevel but society as a whole. It may be assumed that all societies develop their own ways of dealing with internal conflicts at the microlevel, such as interpersonal conflicts or conflicts between families, clans, neighborhoods, or other groups. These society-rooted conflict resolution mechanisms, which supposedly enjoy an important degree of popular support, may sometimes also turn out to be an instrument or source of inspiration for macrolevel conflict settlement. However, the cases of Rwanda and Burundi, which we will examine below, illustrate the limits of traditional conflict resolution and reconciliation mechanisms. Their improper use, very often combined with a top-down, public sector intervention in and modification of their structure, composition, functions, and operation modalities, may not only render them inadequate for their "new" purpose but also deprive them of their popular support and credibility (two key aspects of their traditional reconciliatory role). Both traditional mechanisms will be compared to a more "modern," nevertheless community-based, negotiation and reconciliation mechanism in a discussion of the role of civil society in the 1993 crisis in the northern Kivu province in eastern Congo (former Zaire).

RWANDA: *GACACA* AND ITS USE FOR GENOCIDE PROSECUTION

Description

Defining *gacaca* is difficult. As a society-rooted phenomenon, it is more appropriate to describe than to define. Its setting strongly depends on the community in which it operates. A *gacaca* is not a permanent judicial or administrative institution; rather it is a meeting that is convened whenever the need arises and in which members of one family, or of different families, or all inhabitants of one hill participate. There are generally no applicable rules or criteria to determine the number of participants in the discussions. However, traditionally, unless women are party to the conflict to be solved, only male adults take part in the proceedings. These proceedings are chaired by family elders, supposedly wise old men, who will seek to restore social order by leading the group discussions that, in the end, should result in an arrangement that is acceptable to all participants in the *gacaca*.

The "modern" distinction between judges, parties, witnesses, and audience is hardly applicable: given the disruption of social order, all members of society are affected and, as a consequence, parties to the conflict. The objective is, therefore, neither to determine guilt nor to apply legal regulations in a coherent and consistent manner (as one expects from state courts) but to restore harmony and social order in a given society. The outcome of the *gacaca* thus may not be at all in accordance with the state laws of the country concerned.

Generally, the types of conflict dealt with by the *gacaca* are related to land use, land rights, cattle, marriage, inheritance rights, loans, and damage to properties caused by one of the parties or animals. Most conflicts would thus be considered to be of a civil nature when brought before a court of law. However, conflicts amounting to criminal offenses—generally of a minor kind, such as theft, but sometimes even murder—may also be settled, though they will not result in a typically criminal sanction (imprisonment) but in some sort of civil settlement, for instance, an amount of compensation, possibly exceeding the damage incurred by one of the parties.

Despite the *gacaca*'s traditional roots, it gradually evolved to an institution that, though not formally recognized in Rwandan legislation, has found a modus vivendi in its relation with state structures. The *tribunal de canton* (or cantonal tribunal, situated at the bottom of the hierarchy of judicial institutions) is considered the appropriate forum to deal with conflicts that are not solved by the *gacaca* or to file appeals against *gacaca* decisions. Also, *gacaca* meetings were gradually held at more regular intervals, and decisions were registered in writing.

Postgenocide *Gacaca*

Following the war (which started in October 1990) and the genocide (April–June 1994) that devastated the country, there were—and still are—a large number of legal and other conflicts to be settled. Yet the capacity of the national justice system was extremely limited, even more than was already the case before 1990. In its action plan on justice, the new

Rwandan government—which took over in July 1994 and was largely dominated by the Rwandan Patriotic Front (RPF), the predominantly Tutsi, former armed rebellion—hoped for a revalorization of the *gacaca* to promote a peaceful settlement of disputes and to reduce the number of cases submitted to the formal judicial structures.

However, for the *gacaca* to be operational, some preconditions must be fulfilled. As a traditional, community-based conflict resolution mechanism, it is based on certain common values and norms of reciprocity. It has been rightly argued that the genocide and other crimes against humanity have not only caused an exceptionally high number of deaths, refugee movements, and internal displacements, destroying existing communities, but that these events have also destroyed the fundamental value structures that formed the basis of the *gacaca*. This illustrates how a conflict can substantively alter or even reduce the availability of existing traditional reconciliation mechanisms.

An evaluation study of postgenocide *gacaca* has shown that, in many villages, the *gacaca* has been reactivitated; this is due in part to the lack of functioning state courts, but its nature has also been fundamentally altered because of new circumstances, such as those related to the new composition of the local population after the genocide. Also, the *gacaca* has been modernized through the introduction of formal procedural modalities and the behavior of "arbitrators," as if they were civil servants.

It can be concluded, on the one hand, that traditional conflict resolution schemes were a useful instrument to make up for the lack of a formal judicial structure to deal with "ordinary" conflicts that did not relate to the genocide. On the other hand, the traditional mechanism has severely suffered from the crisis, which may seriously undermine its credibility and its popular acceptance for the resolution of the types of conflict it was traditionally dealing with.

The Use of *Gacaca* for Genocide Prosecution Purposes

The Rwandan government currently proposes the use of so-called popular *gacaca* arbitration tribunals to reduce the bottleneck of cases to be heard by the formal judicial structures and to include a component of reconciliation in the enormous postgenocide justice challenge. In fact, as of April 1999, an estimated 125,000 persons had been held in illegal detention, awaiting trial for their alleged involvement in the 1994 genocide. Two years after the start of the trials, in December 1996, approximately 1,200 genocide suspects, that is, less than 1 percent of all detainees, had been convicted or acquitted on the basis of national genocide legislation. This legislation categorizes suspected perpetrators under four different categories, ranging from genocide leaders and planners (Category 1 suspects) to "small fish" who committed offenses against properties only (Category 4 suspects).

A draft amendment to the law now proposes to establish popular *gacaca* tribunals to judge persons suspected of committing homicide (Category 2 suspects), other serious assaults against persons (Category 3 suspects), and Category 4 suspects. These popular tribunals will be established in a pyramidal structure at various levels corresponding to existing administrative units (*cellule*, sector, commune, prefecture). At the lowest level, *cellule*, 100 members elected among the local population will participate in the hearings; the *gacaca* tribunals at higher echelons will be composed of delegates elected at the lower echelons. Presidents will be elected. Secretaries, rapporteurs, and members of a coordinating committee will be appointed and receive payments. The *gacaca* tribunals will be formally vested with the combined powers of the prosecutors and judges. Limited appeal procedures are included in the draft law. Criminal sentences, up to life imprisonment, but also community works or other reparation measures can be imposed.

The establishment of this so-called participatory justice mechanism, modeled after the traditional *gacaca,* is intended to speed up the judicial process, to add to the people's perception that justice is done, and to include an element of reconciliation (i.e., public hearings and collective healing-oriented confrontations of relevant parties) and an element of reparation (i.e., alternative sentencing and community work) at the local community level. The potential risks of such an operation are manifold:

• As illustrated above, the nature of the *gacaca* is subject to radical changes in the proposed legal regulation. This may cause serious harm to the traditional *gacaca* in its role as a conflict resolution scheme for other, namely, nongenocidal, types of conflict. For instance, the genocide *gacaca* tribunal will be expected to apply state law; the traditional *gacaca*, however, does not seek to operate in accordance with state law.

• The use of popular mechanisms to impose reconciliation by decree and through what amounts to a top-down approach is no guarantee of its success.

• The use of the *gacaca* for the prosecution of genocide or other wide-scale crimes of a political nature was never envisaged under the traditional mechanism and may result in, or be perceived as, an organized popular revenge.

• The establishment of *gacaca* tribunals may hide one important side objective of the government. Given the increased donor fatigue to fund a judicial operation that, at the current rate, can take more than 200 years, the government seeks to raise funds (the estimated budget of the whole *gacaca* tribunals operation roughly amounts to U.S.$36.3 million) through a mechanism that it rightly considers to be attractive among donors: the use of a society-rooted, tradition-inspired, and widely accepted reconciliation mechanism.

- The usual due process of law or fair trial guarantees that are embodied in international human rights instruments ratified by Rwanda may be circumvented by this type of popular justice mechanism in which the role of state institutions is seemingly minimal. It is, for instance, as yet unclear which role, if any, a defense lawyer may play under this new type of *gacaca* proceeding. One could argue that *gacaca* never used to involve attorneys. Yet *gacaca* never resulted in the sort of criminal sanctions currently envisaged either.
- Elections will be held to compose the coordinating committees. It is as yet undecided how these elections will be conducted. If the voting procedure is secret, votes may well be cast along ethnic lines (the Hutu demographic majority outweighing the Tutsi minority, except for the urban centers) as has been the case in previous elections in Rwanda and Burundi. If people have to line up behind their preferred candidate, with the military openly supervising the operation, people may be under pressure to select certain (Tutsi) candidates.

In conclusion, it seems clear that the proposed mechanism is far from traditional and, though nominally referring to the *gacaca*, has very little to do with it.

BURUNDI: THE INSTITUTION OF THE *BUSHINGANTAHE* AND ITS EROSION

Traditional Concept of *Bushingantahe*

In the traditional Burundese society, the *bushingantahe*, of which the origins go back to a premonarchical era, played a critical role in promoting social integration. The Council of Notables was composed of representatives of the most powerful lineages on a hill and included both Hutu and Tutsi. Although all evidence indicates that it was encouraged by the Tutsi monarchy, it was a major constitutive element of civil society and a counterbalance for the power of the central state. According to some observers, the "notables" constituted the democratic core of traditional Burundese society. As a natural leader, a *mushingantahe* (plural *bashingantahe*) played an important role in adjudicating local disputes, reconciling individual persons or families, representing the local population at higher level, and "officializing" all sorts of contracts, such as marriages, gifts, and inheritance.

Further on, we will indicate how the *bushingantahe* institution has gradually been eroded through its increased institutional role in relation to national judicial and political party structures, and how, as a consequence, its current potential for conflict resolution is limited.

The *Bushingantahe* Vis-à-Vis the Formal Judicial Structures

In 1943, the *bushingantahe* were integrated by the colonial power as assessors of the *tribunaux de chefferie* (chief's tribunals), which somewhat reduced their long-standing independence vis-à-vis the local chiefs. In the postcolonial era, it was not until the adoption of the new code on judicial organization and jurisdiction in 1987 that the Council of Notables was officially re-established as an auxiliary judicial institution. This development is strongly linked to its political treatment, which we will describe below.

At the level of each *colline de recensement* (census hill), a council was established. In a civil action, any claimant has to submit his or her case to the council prior to introducing it before the *tribunal de résidence* (the court situated at the bottom of the hierarchy of judicial institutions). The council makes an attempt to reconcile the parties involved and proposes a solution to the dispute. In case the parties do not agree with the proposed solution, the claimant can submit the case before the tribunal, which will then adjudicate independently but with due attention to the council's recommendations. The composition and the procedure before the council are not determined by law but are done in accordance with local tradition. The idea behind the 1987 legislation was that local notables are much more familiar with the local context and are, as a consequence, more likely to adjudicate in a judicious manner.

The *Bushingantahe* Vis-à-Vis the Political Party Structures

Prior to the formal reintroduction of the *bushingantahe* as an auxiliary judicial institution in 1987, Unité et Progrès National (UPRONA), the single political party of Tutsi presidents Michel Micombero, Jean-Baptiste Bagaza, and Pierre Buyoya, during its political congress of 1979, had recommended that the judicial responsibilities of the *bushingantahe* be given to those notables who were associated with the local structures of UPRONA. This recommendation was not implemented, and under the second republic of President Bagaza, efforts were made to eliminate the *bushingantahe*, partly because of their mixed ethnic composition and their close connection with the Catholic Church.

The third republic of President Buyoya (who took power in 1987), however, attempted to transfer the legitimacy of the *bushingantahe* to local party organizations The above-mentioned *colline de recensement* level, which was used to reintroduce the traditional *bushingantahe*, corresponded in fact to a lower level within the UPRONA. Beginning in 1988, UPRONA cells were formally invested with the functions normally performed by the Council of Notables. Members of the cell committees were called *bashingantahe*, and their cooptation by local party members was the occasion for a ceremony similar to the traditional *bashingantahe* investiture. According to most observers, the use of tradition to strengthen local party organizations was not successful and eroded the traditional conflict resolution potential and popular credibility of the *bashingantahe*.

> Rather than speak of the reorganisation of the bashingantahe, it would be more accurate to speak of their annihilation and demolition: all that is left is their outer shell. . . .The new bashingantahe, mandated and legitimized from above, are regimented by the party and no longer accountable to the local communities.[1]

Current Conflict Resolution Potential

The *bashingantahe* continue to enjoy a great deal of credibility among the population. However, the traditional institution has severely suffered from the two above-mentioned types of intervention: under the second republic, it was nearly uprooted, and under the third, it was politically dominated. The *bashingantahe* can obviously be perceived as an institution embodying pluralism, tolerance, and moral authority in Burundese society if they are seen to represent a political party. This is all the more true in a multiparty system that, in Burundi, was introduced in 1992. More fundamentally, a *mushingantahe* is much more a way of life than a political mandate. This makes it extremely hard to determine its use by law or by political party decision. Its adaptation to a more modern, sometimes more anonymous social context will be a natural process, or will not be at all.

The current political negotiation process taking place in Arusha (Tanzania) is nearly exclusively at the macropolitical and urban level. The role of the *bashingantahe* might possibly be to "translate" the achievements and the advantages and disadvantages of the compromise to the society at large and to highlight the importance of traditional values (the common good) in the postconflict society. This role strongly depends on what is left of the traditional credibility and moral authority of the *bashingantahe* among the population. Steering and transforming it, for instance, in the framework of the ongoing Arusha peace talks, may only do more harm to what is left of it.

Some initiatives are currently taking place to study the current position and role of the *bushingantahe* in certain regions. Simultaneously, field research efforts are intended to raise awareness among the population on the traditional concept, the current role, the denaturation and distortion, and the possible revalorization of the *bushingantahe*. Reference can be made to a program conducted by the Centre de Recherches pour l'Inculturation et le Développement (CRID) in Bujumbura.

KIVU: CIVIL SOCIETY AS A MODERN COMMUNITY-BASED RECONCILIATION MECHANISM

The violence in Rwanda and in Burundi can certainly not be considered as a consequence of failed states. On the contrary, it has been amply demonstrated how a strong public administration in Rwanda has been very effective but, unfortunately, used for the wrong purposes. Rwanda and Burundi strongly differ from Zaire, which is an example of a failed or collapsed state. In this particular context, it is interesting to note how, from the early 1980s onward, the east Zairean Kivu region has seen the emergence of a civil society, mainly built around nongovernmental organizations (NGOs) that have taken over some typical state functions (including conflict management and resolution) before being overwhelmed by the influence of an external element, namely the massive influx of Rwandan refugees in 1994 and the ensuing regionalization of the Rwandan armed conflict.

Their initial initiatives were centered around activities to improve the living conditions of the populations through the promotion of agricultural and other economic development. The success of their activities and the absence of the central state at the local level turned them into the privileged partners of multilateral and bilateral development cooperation agencies. In the context of the national conference, the NGOs also prevented local politicians from imposing their straw men as representatives of the local civil society. The NGOs became increasingly visible and important in local conflict mediation, also because land rights and use of land are among the most conflicting elements in both the northern and southern Kivu region. With the support of foreign donors, a number of civil society components increasingly engaged in popular human rights education, grassroots training on democracy, and good governance–related issues.

In early 1993, the northern Kivu province was the scene of a violent conflict structured along ethnic lines. It opposed so-called autochthonous Hunde, Nyanga, and Nande ethnic groups and the Banyarwanda (people of Rwandese origin, both Hutu and Tutsi). The reasons for the conflict were mainly related to land rights and land tenure relations, as well as to the exclusion of Banyarwanda from the political democratization process. This exclusion was closely linked to a nationality question and the enjoyment of other political rights by the Banyarwanda. Partly due to inflammatory speeches by the provincial authorities, the violence reportedly caused at least 14,000 deaths and tens of thousands of internally displaced persons. The ethnic violence ceased when President Mobutu Sese Seko sent in 500 troops of his elite force in May and June 1993. This military intervention obviously did not address the root causes of the conflict.

From September 1993 onward, initiatives were taken by representatives of the Catholic Church and NGO leaders to launch a negotiation process between the conflicting groups. Interestingly, these conflict mediation efforts did not bring together just politicians but also representatives of local groupings, teachers, NGO people, priests, traditional chiefs, and local administrators. In addition, the initiative did not limit itself to well-intended but impractical seminars on democracy, peace, and other values of a general nature. Through the technique of objective-oriented intervention planning, the design of problem trees and solution trees commonly used in development project identification and formulation, the interests, fears, and needs of the various ethnic groups and actors involved were identified. Through this innovative approach, issues such as nationality, land rights, and power positions were analyzed from the different perspectives; recommendations, including administrative reforms, legal amendments, and judicial action, were put forward. On certain critical issues, including nationality legislation and the legitimacy of autochthonous customary chiefs, opinions differed, and implementation of recommendations turned out to be highly problematic. But in general, the civil society initiative, through its society-born and innovative bottom-up approach, resulted in an overall positive outcome: acute tension and conflict-prone behavior of relevant actors were strongly reduced, and dialogue replaced confrontation as a strategy. The initiative set the example for various other meetings of representatives of civil society to deal with acute or potential conflict matters in 1993 and early 1994.

Unfortunately, the massive influx of Rwandese refugees in eastern Zaire in July 1994 set in motion a series of cross-border military confrontations that, as of early 1999, had resulted in "conflict management" by foreign armed forces (Uganda and Rwanda) and armed rebel groups (Rassemblement Congolais pour la Democratie, Maï Maï, etc.) rather than by civil society.

CONCLUSION

From the case studies, a number of general conclusions can be drawn. First, traditional reconciliation mechanisms can definitely play a useful role in fostering a spirit of tolerance, pluralism, and cooperation at the community level and in restoring the social tissue in a postconflict society. Second, there is, however, a vulnerable form of social capital that can easily be destroyed by the negative impact of political and armed conflict. Finally, attempts in Rwanda and Burundi to steer, reform, and control them indicate how minimally effective these traditional mechanisms for other than their own "natural" purposes may be, and how, at the same time, these attempts may erode their value for their traditional purposes.

Politically inspired ethnic or other armed conflicts require a political solution. Traditional, society-based mechanisms, insofar as they survived these conflicts and have adjusted themselves to the postconflict situation, can no doubt play a healing role at their appropriate level, but outsiders' expectations or interventions (through excessive funding, streamlining, modernizing, etc.) risk to suffocate and deprive them of their natural value and credibility more than anything else.

The Kivu case study has shown the potential use of modern society-based mechanisms. It is important to note that this experiment took place in the context of a failed or collapsed state and that something similar may be less likely in states with a strong central control. The absence of the state, which created room for this innovative approach, constituted at the same time one of its main weaknesses when consolidation of its achievements and implementation was needed.

In the current context of a regional military conflict with multiple players and easily shifting alliances, the potential leverage of the remaining (traditional and modern) society-based conflict resolution mechanisms seems, unfortunately, quite limited.

NOTE

1. T. Laely, cited in Lemarchand 1996, 168.

REFERENCES

Jyoni Wa Karega, J., et al. (1996). *Gacaca. Le droit coutumier au Rwanda*, Rapport pour le Haut Commissariat des Droits de l'Homme des Nations Unies. Vols. 1 and 2. Kigali.

Lemarchand, R. (1996). *Burundi. Ethnic Conflict and Genocide.* New York: Cambridge University Press.

Manirakiza, Z., O. Nkurunziza, and A. Ntabona. (1999). *Les Bashingantahe dans la région traditionnelle du Buyogoma.* CRID, Bujumbura, Burundi.

Marysse, S., and F. Reyntjens, eds. (1996). *Conflits au Kivu: Antécédents et Enjeux.* Centre d'étude de la région des grands lacs d'Afrique. Anvers.

Ntabona, A. (n.d.). *Institution des Bashingantahe à l'heure du pluralisme politique africain.* Bujumbura, Burundi.

Ntampaka, C. (1995). "Le retour à la tradition dans le règlement des différends: Le gacaca du Rwanda." *Dialogue* (October–November): 95–104.

Reyntjens, F. (1990). "Le *gacaca* ou la justice du gazon au Rwanda." *Politique Africaine* (December): 31–41.

Willame, J. C. (1997). *Banyarwanda et Banyamulenge: Violences ethniques et gestion de l'identitaire au Kivu.* Brussels and Paris: Institut Africain, L'Harmattan.

Roots of Reconciliation in Somaliland

Ahmed Yusuf Farah

The experience with traditional peacebuilding in Somaliland illustrates the importance of local peacemaking initiatives. While most of Somalia was in a state of war, traditional reconciliation mechanisms in the northern part of the country, in Somaliland, led to the successful re-establishment of peace and security in the region.

Important elements in the peace process have been the peace agreements and the roles of the traditional elders, *akils;* the councils of elders, *guurti;* and paramount heads and religious leaders. Of special interest are also the adjustments to the penalty code, which enable control to be regained; the role of women in peacemaking; and the influence of traditional poetry as a powerful medium for encouraging peacemaking.

These types of peacemaking initiatives should be encouraged, and external assistance should be handled carefully to preserve the self-help effort of local initiatives. Although it is obvious that local peace processes are not likely to be a panacea, the establishment of modern political structures must take into account the moral authority of the elders and the progress achieved so far in establishing local level peace agreements.

THE SOMALI CONTEXT

The former head of state, Mohammad Siad Barre, fled the city of Mogadishu in January 1991, leaving the capital and much of Somalia in the hands of competing armed militias who rapidly established clan fiefdoms in areas dominated by their social groups. Strife and fragmentation have continued ever since. The dismemberment of Somalia has been most pronounced in Mogadishu itself, where hostile warlords have divided the city in two. There have been, and continue to be, serious efforts by Somalis to bring about reconciliation in Mogadishu and other parts of the country. Peacemaking initiatives in the north, however, in the self-proclaimed "Republic of Somaliland" have been relatively successful compared with the rest of Somalia.

The severity of the government assault on this area before Barre's departure, and the disruptive legacy of the 1977–1978 war with Ethiopia, have thrown the clans of Somaliland back on their own cultural and institutional resources in order to tackle the disorder that prevailed after January 1991. A key to the visible progress in the north has been the spontaneous adoption by the general public of a bottom-up approach to the restoration of peace and stability, involving representative authorities and institutions at all levels of society in Somaliland.

THE ROLE OF TRADITIONAL LEADERS UNDER SIAD BARRE

Under Major General Mohammad Siad Barre, a system of divide and rule, formulated and implemented by the centralized state, undermined the ability of traditional leaders in Somalia to settle local disputes and keep the peace.

Through a system of incentives, Barre drew many such leaders into the regime, just as colonialism had wooed them in the past. However, their association with the regime diminished their standing among their own communities. The Barre government, meanwhile, sought to impose a homogeneous modernity on the culture of clan and lineage. References to one's clan or common ancestors were strenuously discouraged. The regime officially outlawed one of the key traditional judicial instruments in Somalia: the collective compensation, known as *dia*, by lineage groups in case of misconduct by their members. By the mid-1970s the regime claimed that it had abolished the clan system throughout Somalia.

EVOLUTION OF CLAN STRUCTURES DURING THE WAR

During the civil war, the authority of clan elders was actually strengthened in the north. The guerrillas who fought Barre's despotic regime were drawn from northern subclans and clan militias within the Somali National Movement. This returned traditional figures to prominence. In a period of turmoil and uncertainty, and in the absence of legitimate state institutions, clans and subclans have had recourse to their own traditional structures. Particular emphasis has been given to the appointment of sultans—a secular political office, sanctioned by religion. There are now more than twice the number of sultans in Somaliland than at independence in 1960. It has also been noticed that the lineage elders, who led smaller units within the clan, are alive and well despite a period of eclipse under the Barre regime. The return to tried and tested systems of governance has enabled Somalis in the north to break the momentum of war and opportunistic plunder. The mediating authority of *akils*, or heads of *dia*-paying lineage groups—an office abolished in the early 1970s—is now firmly re-established, and its functions have expanded into the vacuum left by the collapse of the Barre administration.

All clans in Somaliland and some of the larger subclans now have their own supreme council of elders, known as *guurti*. These fulfill a dual role as legislature and executive, with responsibility for everyday questions arising within the clan and also for arbitration between different clans.

HOW THE PEACE CONFERENCES HAVE WORKED

In November 1992, some 400 delegates representing the Eastern Habar Yonis and the Warsangeli met at Jiideli. By the end of the conference they had agreed that each clan would be responsible for maintaining law and order in its own territory. A joint local committee of thirty members would be responsible for settling conflicts according to the terms laid down at the conference (see Exhibit 5.2-1). If more rain fell in the land of one clan, the guest community attracted by the pasture would be responsible for the protection of the lives and livestock of the host community.

Elders had also decreed that responsibility for paying damages for the actions of armed groups should be directly shouldered by the families of persistent offenders, rather than, as normally, extend to the whole *dia*-paying group. If an armed robber is unable to pay compensation, the burden falls upon his father and brothers. There are many instances of crimes committed by younger men being dealt with by clan elders. In some cases offenders have been executed by their own kin.

The various interclan peace conferences in the north of Somalia culminated in the Boroma national conference at which a national (Somaliland) peace charter was agreed and basic provisions for law and order were formulated. Following the collapse of the regime, a new government was appointed by the elders. This was politically the most telling achievement to date of northern local-level clan democracy.

The Boroma conference received international support, but all of the other successful clan conferences in the north have been financed by the communities. This happened in striking contrast to the high-profile UN forums in the south of the country and abroad, all of which have failed to produce a plausible settlement. Perhaps this accounts for the caution

Exhibit 5.2-1   Regulations Agreed to at a Special Conference Between the Warsangeli and Eastern Habar Yonis at Shimbirale, 8–18 November 1992

With effect from 18 August 1992 any property stolen or looted should be returned immediately.

Anybody who suffers injury cannot take revenge on the tribe of the criminal but will seek payment from the individual responsible or from his immediate subclan.

Those who suffer casualties should take no retributive measures themselves but inform the standing committee on peace. If they take steps by way of revenge, they will be treated as bandits.

The standing committee on peace will use the services of the peace forces when needed.

Anyone killed or injured while involved in acts of banditry will be treated as a dead donkey and should be denied any rights.

Any subclan engaging in acts of banditry that cause death or material loss should pay for whatever damages they have caused. In addition, they will pay a bond of 100 female camels. This bond will be made over to the joint administration of the two sides, for common use.

expressed by the Eastern Alliance Elders in Garadag in 1992 against a unilateral UN military intervention in the north "without the consent of the leaders of local clans."

SUCCESS FACTORS OF TRADITIONAL PEACEBUILDING IN SOMALILAND

Local Initiatives

The mechanisms for establishing peace depend on joint community committees formed at the local level, empowered to implement agreements reached by the councils of elders. Another local authority know as "the committee that uproots unwanted weeds from the field" is responsible for dealing with banditry and minor disturbances. This localized approach to peacekeeping began with a series of interclan reconciliation conferences in 1991 and gradually advanced to district, regional, and "national" levels. The authorization of agreements at peace conferences is given by clan elders, but other traditional leaders—politicians, military officers, and particularly religious men and poets—have also played a crucial role in the peace process. Religious figures, such as *sheikhs* and *wadaads*, or Islamic scholars, take their duties as peacemakers seriously. Their authority is based on the esteem in which they are held as spiritual leaders, as distinct from *akils* and sultans, whose status is more secular. Spiritual leaders are seen as ideal and neutral arbiters with allegiance to universal Islamic values that transcend clan loyalties. They do not settle disputes themselves or sit in judgment. This is the work of elders in council. Instead, their task is to encourage rivals to make peace. To this end, independent delegations of renowned holy men have taken part in all the major peace initiatives between previously hostile clans in Somaliland.

The Power of Poetry

Poetry, which is the most celebrated and respected art form in Somalia, has also been marshaled to the cause of peacemaking. Through metaphor and allusion, oral poetry can tap the richest reserves of Somali discourse; it is widely understood and enjoyed and, like the mass media in the West, it has the power to influence opinion. It has been noticed that in major clan reconciliations, distinguished national poets recited poems advocating peace at the inaugural and closing ceremonies.

The Importance of Women

Women have also played a significant part in peacemaking. After marriage, a woman retains her kinship ties with her father's group and—even though they are often denied—the property rights that these entail. The dual kinship role conferred by marriage has often existed across two neighboring but warring clans, with the result that women have suffered unduly in Somalia's upheaval. It has also meant that women have taken on a new and active function as ambassadors between rival groups—the group that they married into and the group they were born into. This is a function of their traditional role in systems of exchange.

Often, at the height of the civil war, women provided the only means of communication between rival clans, as their status allowed them to cross clan boundaries. Twenty-four days after the Dhulbahante council of elders failed to appear at the agreed site for the first peace forum, the Habar Yonis, with whom they were supposed to meet, sent a delegation of kinsmen born of Dhulbahante women, who persuaded suspicious maternal relatives among the Habar Yonis to attend.

Traditionally, women were exchanged to seal a peace treaty between two parties. A daughter was offered as a sign of trust and honor to mark the pact between giver and receiver. Likewise, when blood has been shed, Somalis regard the gift of a marriageable partner as material and symbolic compensation for the loss of life. Such traditions have persisted in Somaliland and have strengthened some of the major peace agreements, including that of the Habar Yonis and the Isa Musa, each clan providing fifty eligible women for the other.

Tradition and the Help of Modern Technology

Modern technology has also been instrumental in the relative stability of Somaliland. In the past, radio communication was the monopoly of the government and international organizations. Recently, however, the elders of several bitterly embattled clans in Somaliland have remained in constant radio contact during periods of tension, and radio links have provided vital channels for negotiation.

CONCLUSION

Incorporation of Traditional Structures into Modern Statebuilding

The efforts of clan leaders in northern Somalia over the years to bring about peace have raised popular hopes for positive change. The moral status and customary skills of the elders are a vital component in tackling the many problems that prevail in Somaliland. The participation of lineage leaders enables the representation of local groups in the administration to be balanced, ensures the equitable distribution of political and economic resources, and allows for a more effective demobilization of armed groups. This participation must not be allowed to be marginalized as a modern state and professional infrastructure develops. The task of reconstructing basic services should start at the district level rather than from the top downward. This approach is attuned to the decentralized system of governance, which is enshrined in the interim national charter for Somaliland formulated by the elders at the Boroma conference.

Sensible External Support Needed

The traditional structures on their own are not a complete panacea for the problems that are faced. Traditional peacemaking is sturdy, but it is also slow and cumbersome and will always benefit from logistical assistance. The initiatives in the north need to be supported. Such external support, however, needs to recognize the sensitivity of the recovery process. Although much has been achieved in terms of restraining freelance banditry and interclan strife, the security situation remains delicate, which in turn suggests pitfalls for any hasty attempt at a program of comprehensive reconstruction. For the time being, external assistance must supplement rather than overwhelm the kinds of local grassroots initiatives that already exist. To do so it will have to be timely and discerning, and acknowledge the progress that an alliance of popular will and traditional leadership has already achieved in northern Somalia.

BIBLIOGRAPHY

Farah, A. Y. (1994). *The Milk of the Boswellia Forests: Frankincense Production Among the Pastoral Somali.* Uppsala: EPOS.

Farah, A. Y., with I. M. Lewis. (1993). *Somalia: The Roots of Reconciliation. Peacemaking Endeavours of Contemporary Lineage Leaders: A Survey of Grassroots Peace Conferences in Somaliland.* Original research commissioned by ACTIONAID, London.

————. (1997). "Making Peace in Somaliland." This paper is a shortened version of *Somalia: The Roots of Reconciliation,* ACTIONAID, London, 1993, published in *Cahiers d'Etudes Africaines* 37, no. 2: 349–377.

Lewis, I. M. (1961). (1982). *A Pastoral Democracy.* London: Oxford University Press.

————. (1994). *Blood and Bone: The Call of Kinship in Somali Society.* Lawrencivlle, N.J.: Red Sea Press.

CHAPTER 6

Identifying Key Actors in Conflict Situations

■ 6.1

Levels of Leadership

John Paul Lederach

THREE LEVELS OF LEADERSHIP

I find it helpful to think of leadership in a population affected by a conflict in terms of a pyramid (see Exhibit 6.1-1). An analytical perspective such as the one suggested here will always rely to some degree on broad generalizations that provide a set of lenses for focusing in on a particular concern, or for considering and relating a set of concepts. In this instance, we are using lenses to capture the overview of how an entire affected population in a setting of internal armed conflict is represented by leaders and other actors, as well as the roles they play in dealing with the situation. The pyramid permits us to lay out that leadership base in three major categories: top level, middle range, and the grassroots.

We can use the pyramid as a way of describing the numbers within a population in simplified terms. The pinnacle, or top-level leadership, represents the fewest people, in some cases perhaps only a handful of key actors. The grassroots base of the pyramid encompasses the largest number of people, those who represent the population at large. On the left-hand side of the pyramid are the types of leaders and the sectors from which they come at each level. On the right-hand side are the conflict-transformation activities that the leaders at each level may undertake. Each of these levels deserves further discussion before we look at the broader implications of the pyramidal model for our conceptual framework.

Exhibit 6.1-1   Actors and Approaches to Peacebuilding

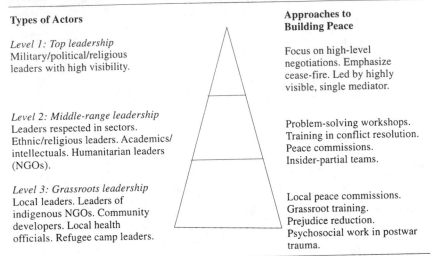

Types of Actors	Approaches to Building Peace
Level 1: Top leadership Military/political/religious leaders with high visibility.	Focus on high-level negotiations. Emphasize cease-fire. Led by highly visible, single mediator.
Level 2: Middle-range leadership Leaders respected in sectors. Ethnic/religious leaders. Academics/intellectuals. Humanitarian leaders (NGOs).	Problem-solving workshops. Training in conflict resolution. Peace commissions. Insider-partial teams.
Level 3: Grassroots leadership Local leaders. Leaders of indigenous NGOs. Community developers. Local health officials. Refugee camp leaders.	Local peace commissions. Grassroot training. Prejudice reduction. Psychosocial work in postwar trauma.

Level 1: Top-Level Leadership

Level 1 comprises the key political and military leaders in the conflict. In an intrastate struggle, these people are the highest representative leaders of the government and opposition movements, or present themselves as such. They are at the apex of the pyramid, the spokespersons of their constituencies and for the concerns that, they argue, generate and will resolve the conflict. It is crucial to recognize that in most instances, they represent a few key actors within the broader setting. Certain features are common to this level of leadership.

First, these leaders are highly visible. A great deal of attention is paid to their movements, statements, and positions. They receive a lot of press coverage and air time. In this era of CNN worldwide news, these leaders sometimes find themselves elevated from virtual obscurity to international prominence and even celebrity status. One could argue that this media dynamic possesses a symbiotic and dialectic nature that is related to the legitimacy and pursuit of top-level leaders' personal and political ambitions.[1] A legitimate base of representation for a constituency or a set of concerns establishes a leader as such. Publicity and profile are essential for establishing the concerns of that constituency, yet the focus of the publicity is on the leader. Such publicity and profile further consolidate and maintain a leader's base of legitimacy. Visibility and profile thus become essential components descriptive of this level, and they are actively sought by this level, both to represent the concerns of a leader's constituency and to secure his or her own position of influence.

Second, by virtue of their high public profile, these leaders are generally locked into positions taken with regard to the perspectives and issues in conflict. They are under tremendous pressure to maintain a position of strength vis-à-vis their adversaries and their own constituencies. (By "position" I am referring to the almost static viewpoints about solutions that are demanded by each side in order to resolve the conflict.)[2] This, coupled with a high degree of publicity, often constrains the freedom of leaders operating at this level to maneuver. Acceptance of anything less than their publicly stated goals or demands is seen as weakness or loss of face. For the leaders, this means that every move represents a high-stakes decision for both their careers and the stated goals of their government or movement.

Finally, these leaders are perceived and characterized as having significant, if not exclusive, power and influence. Certainly, top leaders and individuals do tend to have more influence and power than other individuals. Equally, however, the picture is more complex than initially meets the eye. On the one hand, top leaders benefit from visibility and publicity, and their statements do carry enormous weight, both in the framing of issues and processes and in decisionmaking. On the other hand, in international affairs in general and in protracted settings of conflict in particular, power is primarily perceived in the form of a hierarchy in which top leaders are in a position to make decisions for, and to deliver the support of, their respective constituencies. I say "perceived" because the international community most often seeks out and relates to hierarchical leaders on all sides of an internal conflict as if they had exclusive power, even when, as is often the case, power may be far more diffuse and fractionated. In situations such as Bosnia, Somalia, and Liberia, the degree to which hierarchical power is operational is decidedly unclear. There are many leaders at different levels of the pyramid who may not fall in line behind the more visible leaders. In these situations, action is often pursued and taken in far more diffuse ways within the society, even though peace accords that may be negotiated assume hierarchical representation and implementation.

Level 2: Middle-Range Leadership

In the middle range are persons who function in leadership positions within a setting of protracted conflict but whose position is defined in ways not necessarily connected to or controlled by the authority or the structure of the formal government or major opposition movements.

Middle-range leadership can be delineated along several different lines. One approach is to focus on persons who are highly respected as individuals and/or occupy positions of leadership in sectors such as education, business, agriculture, or health. A second approach is to consider the primary networks of groups and institutions that may exist within a setting, such as those linking (formally or otherwise) religious groups, academic institutions, or humanitarian organizations. These networks contain individuals who lead or are prominent within a particular institution—such as the head of an important indigenous nongovernmental organization, the former dean of a national university, or a well-known priest in a given region— who may be well recognized and respected within that network or geographic region. A third approach is to concentrate on the identity groups in conflict and to locate middle-range leaders among people who are well-known as belonging to a minority ethnic group, or who are from a particular geographic region within the conflict and enjoy the respect of the people of that region but are also known outside the region. Yet another approach is to focus on people from within the conflict setting but whose prestige extends much further—for example, a well-known poet or Nobel laureate.

Important features of this level characterize the key actors within it. First, middle-level leaders are positioned so that they are likely to know and be known by top-level leadership, yet they have significant connections to the broader context and the constituency that the top leaders claim to represent. In other words, they are connected to both the top and grassroots levels. They have contact with top-level leaders but are not bound by political calculations that govern every move and decision made at that level. Similarly, they vicariously know the context and experience of people living at the grassroots level, yet they are not encumbered by the survival demands facing many at this level.

Second, the position of middle-range leaders is not based on political or military power, nor are such leaders necessarily seeking to capture power of that sort. Their status and influence in the setting derives from ongoing relationships—some professional, some institutional, some formal, and others regarding friends and acquaintances. Consequently, middle-range leaders are rarely in the national or international limelight, and their positions and work do not depend on visibility and publicity. By virtue of this, they tend to have greater flexibility of movement and action; certainly, they can travel with an inconspicuousness denied to top-level leaders.

Third, middle-range actors tend to have pre-existing relationships with counterparts that cut across the lines of conflict within the setting. They may for example, belong to a professional association or have built a network of relationships that cut across the identity divisions within the society.

In sum, middle-range actors are far more numerous than are top-level leaders and are connected through networks to many influential people across the human and physical geography of the conflict.

Level 3: Grassroots Leadership

The grassroots represent the masses, the base of the society. Life at this level is characterized, particularly in settings of protracted conflict and war, by a survival mentality. In worst-case scenarios, the population at this level is involved in a day-to-day effort to find food, water, shelter, and safety.

The leadership at the grassroots level also operates on a day-to-day basis. Leaders here include people who are involved in local communities, members of nongovernmental organizations (NGOs) carrying out relief projects for local populations, health officials, and refugee camp leaders. These people understand intimately the fear and suffering with which much of the population must live; they also have an expert knowledge of local politics and know on a face-to-face basis the local leaders of the government and its adversaries.

In many instances, the local level is a microcosm of the bigger picture. The lines of identity in the conflict often are drawn right through local communities, splitting them into hostile groups. Unlike many actors at the higher levels of the pyramid, however, grassroots leaders witness firsthand the deep-rooted hatred and animosity on a daily basis.

Before turning our attention to the peacebuilding approaches associated with each level, two broad observations should be made about the pyramid population. First, while many of the fundamental conditions that generate conflict are experienced at the grassroots level—for example, social and economic insecurity, political and cultural discrimination, and human rights violations—the lines of group identity in contemporary conflict are more often drawn vertically than horizontally within the pyramid. In most armed conflicts today, identity forms around ethnicity, religion, or regional geography rather than class, creating group divisions that cut down through the pyramid rather than pitting one level against another. Correspondingly, leaders within each level have connections to their "own people" up and down the pyramid and, at the same time, have counterparts within their own level who are perceived as enemies.

Second, there are two important inverse relationships in the conflict setting. On the one hand, a higher position in the pyramid confers on an individual greater access to information about the bigger picture and greater capacity to make decisions that affect the entire population. It also means, however, that the individual is less affected by the day-to-day consequences of those decisions. On the other hand, a lower position increases the likelihood that an individual will directly experience the consequences of decisionmaking but reduces the ability to see the broader picture and limits access to decisionmaking and power. These two inverse relationships pose key dilemmas in the design and implementation of peace processes, to which we now turn our attention.

APPROACHES TO PEACEBUILDING

Level 1: Top-Level Approaches

On the right-hand side of the pyramid are various features of, and approaches to, peacebuilding. At the top level we find what we might call the "top-bottom" approach to peacebuilding. This approach has the following characteristics.

First, the people who emerge as peacebuilders, often seen as intermediaries or mediators, are eminent figures who themselves possess a public profile. They are often backed by a supporting government or international organization such as the UN, which lies outside the relationships embroiled in the internal conflict. More often than not, actors at this level operate as single personalities.

Second, the goal is to achieve a negotiated settlement between the principal high-level leaders in the conflict. These peacemakers tend to operate as third parties who shuttle between the protagonists. What transpires is a process of high-level negotiations in which top-level leaders are identified and brought to the bargaining table. Getting to the table and setting the agenda for negotiations become guiding metaphors of the peacemaker's work.[3]

Level 2: Middle-Range Approaches

The middle range offers what might be called a "middle-out" approach to peacebuilding. It is based on the idea that the middle range contains a set of leaders with a determinant *location* in the conflict who, if integrated properly, might provide the key to creating an *infrastructure* for achieving and sustaining peace. To my knowledge, a theory of literature of middle-range peacebuilding as such has not yet been developed. We do, however, have a number of parallel examples to draw on of middle-range approaches to peace. These fit into three categories: problem-solving workshops, conflict resolution training, and the development of peace commissions.[4]

Some illustrations of practical applications will highlight the role middle-range training has played in peace strategies. In the South African context, for example, the Center for Conflict Resolution (formerly Center for Intergroup Studies) has undertaken an extensive training program directed at providing a conceptual framework and skills for dealing with conflict in the postapartheid "New South Africa." In some cases, the organization has trained leaders of political movements such as the African National Congress; in others, it has targeted sectoral actors such as religious and civic leaders; and in a third approach, it has provided training that has brought together former antagonists, such as liberation movement leaders and policemen.[5]

Paula Gutlove and other members of the Harvard-based Balkan Peace Project undertook a program of training middle-level leaders across former Yugoslavia.[6] Here the threefold goal was to create for participants an opportunity to reflect on the experience of the conflict; to deal with psychological dimensions inherent in their experience of the conflict; and to develop skills for dealing with conflict in alternative ways.

A third example is the vast array of training approaches and events that have emerged in Northern Ireland.[7] Here, the training has not only provided skills but also endeavored to identify Irish approaches and experiences for dealing innovatively with the sharp sectarian divisions.

Another example is the efforts by the All Africa Conference of Churches, principally in collaboration with the Nairobi Peace Initiative, to combine the roles of convener and trainer.[8] Middle-range leaders from church communities who found themselves on different sides of the conflict in countries such as Mozambique and Angola were brought together to share their perceptions and experiences of the conflict, analyze their own role in it, and develop approaches for encouraging and supporting reconciliation in their context.[9]

What these approaches suggest is that although training is generally thought of as the dissemination of knowledge and imparting skills, it becomes a strategic tool as it promotes the development of peacebuilding capacities within the middle-range leadership. This potential is further enhanced when training, serving a convening function, brings together people from the same level of society but on different sides of the conflict.

The third category of middle-range peacebuilding involves the formation of peace commissions within conflict settings. These commissions have been as varied in form and application as their settings. Two situations will illustrate the point: Nicaragua in the late 1980s and South Africa in the early 1990s.

Throughout the 1980s, multiple internal wars raged in Central America. In an innovative approach that built upon the efforts of the earlier Contadora peace process, the Central American peace accord, which was signed in Esquipulas, Guatemala, by the five countries in the region, provided mechanisms that dealt with the internal situations of each country but did so simultaneously, through a coordinated plan.[10] Among the provisions of the plan was a process whereby each country would establish a national peace commission made up of four prominent individuals representing different sides of the conflict. The Nicaraguan government moved quickly, not only to set up its national commission but also to devise a more extensive internal structure that included region-specific commissions and an extensive network of local commissions.[11]

The most extensive of the regional efforts within the country was the establishment of a conciliation commission to deal with the East Coast of

Nicaragua. The commission was established to prepare and then facilitate the negotiation and conciliation efforts between Yatama (the umbrella organization of the East Coast indigenous resistance) and the Sandinista government. The conciliation commission was composed of the top leadership of two Nicaraguan religious networks: the Moravian Church, which had its roots in the East Coast; and the Evangelical Committee for Aid and Development (CEPAD), an ecumenical arm of the Protestant churches that was based in Managua.[12]

The model for this conciliation effort was that of an insider-partial mediation effort.[13] (An insider-partial approach involves intermediaries from within the conflict setting who as individuals enjoy the trust and confidence of one side in the conflict but who as a team provide balance and equity in their mediating work.) As a member of the conciliation team, I experienced how "partiality" is not always a detriment to intermediary work and can in fact be a significant resource. The insider-partial approach we saw in operation in the Sandinista-Yatama conflict involved "insider" intermediaries such as Andy Shogreen, who was from a Creole-Miskito family, had been superintendent of the Moravian Church during the war in the 1980s, and was a close childhood friend of Brooklyn Rivera, the Miskito leader of Yatama. Guastavo Parajon, by contrast, was from Managua and had been appointed by President Daniel Ortega as the "notable citizen" on the national conciliation commission. The middle-range religious leaders on whom the conciliation commission drew were able to use their personal and institutional networks within the context to create a successful response to the conciliation needs of the regional aspects of the overall national conflict.

A parallel example can be drawn from the national peace accord structure that emerged in postapartheid South Africa. In this instance, the rubric of formal negotiations between top-level leaders set in motion a process of transition and sociopolitical transformation that specifically contemplated numerous levels of activity across society. The accord created at least seven major levels of activity, ranging from a national peace committee to regional and local committees.[14] It contemplated, for example, jointly operated communication centers to monitor and, where possible, preempt community violence that was threatening to undermine the peace process.[15] Such an effort was a move toward identifying key people in critical locations who, working through a network, would begin to build an infrastructure capable of sustaining the general progression toward peace. Central to the overall functioning of the peace process was the development of institutional capacities through the training of a broad array of individuals to respond to the volatile period of transition.

What the above approaches suggest is that the middle range holds the potential for helping to establish a relationship- and skill-based infrastructure for sustaining the peacebuilding process. A middle-out approach builds on the idea that middle-range leaders (who are often the heads of, or closely connected to, extensive networks that cut across the lines of conflict) can be cultivated to play an instrumental role in working through the conflicts. Middle-range peacebuilding activities come in varied forms—from efforts directed at changing perceptions and floating new ideas among actors proximate to the policymaking process to training in conflict resolution skills and to the establishment of teams, networks, and institutions that can play an active conciliation role within the setting.

Level 3: Grassroots Approaches

Grassroots approaches face different challenges from those confronting the top- and middle-range levels. First, at this level are massive numbers of people. At best, strategies can be implemented to touch the leadership working at local and community levels, but more often than not, these strategies represent points of contact with the masses rather than a comprehensive program for reaching them. Second, many of the people at this level are in a survival mode in which meeting the basic human needs of food, shelter, and safety are a daily struggle. Although unresolved human conflict is a central cause of their suffering, efforts directed at peace and conflict resolution can easily be seen as an unaffordable luxury. Nonetheless, important ideas and practical efforts do emerge at this level. We will consider here an outline of a bottom-up approach to peacebuilding and several concrete examples of programs targeted at the grassroots-level population.

A concrete case of a bottom-up approach has been clearly delineated in the Somali context. First articulated by the Somali members of the Ergada—a forum of Somali intellectuals for peace created in 1990—the bottom-up perspective was later rearticulated more by international and Somali resource groups convened by the Life and Peace Institute of Uppsala, Sweden,[16] to advise the UN in its reconciliation work in Somalia between 1991 and 1993.[17]

The approach was rooted in an assessment of three important features of the situation in Somalia. First, since the fall of President Mohammad Siad Barre in 1991, the formal, political infrastructure of the country had for all practical purposes disintegrated. Second, in the post-Barre years, Somalis had come to rely directly on clan and subclan structures for security and subsistence. Third, Somalis have a rich history of traditional mechanisms for dealing with interclan disputes.

Given this background, efforts to identify national leaders or convene peace conferences relying on common diplomatic devices, such as bringing together key militia leaders, would create a superficial structure unable to sustain itself. Instead, the most promising approach would be to develop a process that would build on the traditions of the Somali people.[18]

In brief, the bottom-up approach involved a process of first achieving discussions and agreements to end the fighting at local peace conferences by bringing together contiguous and interdependent subclans, guided by the elders of each subclan. These conferences not only dealt with issues of immediate concern at local levels but also served to place responsibility for interclan fighting on the shoulders of local leaders and helped to identify the persons considered to be rightful representatives of those clans' concerns. Having achieved this initial agreement, it was then possible to repeat the same process at a higher level with a broader set of clans. Characteristics of these processes were the reliance on elders, lengthy oral deliberations (often lasting months), the creation of a forum or assembly of elders (known in some parts of the region as the *guurti*), and careful negotiation over access to resources and payments for deaths that would re-establish a balance among the clans.

A number of other important efforts aimed at promoting peacebuilding at the grassroots level suggest a broader scope of possibilities. These efforts can be divided chronologically according to whether they were launched before or after a formal peace structure had been achieved in a conflict situation.

Two examples of peacebuilding efforts targeted at the grassroots level *before* formal peace and electoral structures were established took place in Mozambique, where initiatives emerged from both the Christian Council of Mozambique (CCM) and the United Nations Children's Fund (UNICEF). The CCM-initiated program Preparing People for Peace was conceived as a way to open and deal with conflict issues in Mozambique's setting, with a specific focus on the provincial and district levels.[19]

The CCM program began with a national seminar in summer 1991 that brought together representatives from all the provinces; these representatives were then given the responsibility for implementing seminars at local levels. An integrated approach was taken regarding the content of the seminar discussions, which ranged from religious perspectives on war and peace to family and church involvement in conflict and resolution to issues of youth, displaced persons and their return, land reform, public health, human rights, and the impact of violence and war on children. On average, each seminar involved thirty to fifty participants, both pastors and laypersons, and lasted for two weeks. Over the course of sixteen months (toward the end of which the national peace accord was signed), more than 700 people participated in the seminars, several of which were held in refugee camps in neighboring Zimbabwe.

The second example from Mozambique was the UNICEF project

Circus of Peace.[20] The aim in this case was to deal innovatively with the conflict, violence, and militarization facing the local communities, especially their youth. Like a circus, the project was organized as a traveling show that wove drama and the arts into its explorations of nature and the challenges of war and conflict and the possibilities of reconciliation, including the skills of resolving conflict. The show not only captivated audiences but also served as a way to publicly grieve over the losses the country had suffered, to address the concerns of the people, and to set the stage for changes and movement toward peace.

NOTES

This is a redrafted version of chapter 4, "Structure: Lenses for the Big Picture," by John Paul Lederach, in *Building Peace: Sustainable Reconciliation in Divided Societies* (Washington, D.C.: U.S. Institute of Peace Press, 1997). It is redrafted and reprinted with kind permission from the U.S. Institute of Peace.

1. Michael Parenti, *Inventing Reality: The Politics of the Mass Media* (New York: St. Martin's, 1990).

2. Roger Fisher and William Ury, *Getting to Yes* (Boston: Houghton Mifflin, 1981), 3.

3. See Thania Paffenholz, "Thirteen Characteristics of Successful Mediation in Mozambique," in this book.

4. On problem-solving workshops, see Herbert Kelman, "Interactive Problem Solving in the Middle East," in this book.

5. Ron Kraybill, interview by author, June 1994.

6. Paula Gutlove and Joe Montville, "Toward Sustainable Peace in the Balkans," Balkans Peace Project, Cambridge, Mass., 1992.

7. Mare Fitzduff, *Beyond Violence: Conflict Resolution Process in Northern Ireland* (Tokyo: United Nations University, 1996).

8. Hizkias Assefa, *Peace and Reconciliation as a Paradigm* (Nairobi: Nairobi Peace Initiative, 1993); Harold Miller, *Peace and Reconciliation in Africa* (occasional paper no. 19, Mennonite Central Committee, Acro., Pa., July 1993).

9. "Peace and Reconciliation in Angola and Mozambique" (communiqué from participants in Lusophone Consultation, Limuru, Kenya, 20–27 September 1990).

10. Jack Child, *The Central American Peace Process, 1983–1991* (Boulder, Colo.: Lynne Rienner, 1992).

11. Paul Wehr and John Paul Lederach, "Mediating Conflict in Central America," *Journal of Peace Research* 28, no. 1 (February 1991): 85–98.

12. Bruce Nichols, "Religious Conciliation Between the Sandinistas and the East Coast Indians of Nicaragua," in *Religion: The Missing Dimension in Statecraft* (Oxford: Oxford University Press, 1994).

13. Wehr and Lederach, "Mediating Conflict," 97.

14. Lauri Nathan, "An Imperfect Bridge: Crossing to Democracy on the Peace Accord," *Track Two* 2 (May 1993).

15. Proshaw Camay, "The JOCC Solution," *Track Two* 2, no. 4 (November 1993): 16–17.

16. See Johan Svensson, "Designing Training Programs: The Life and Peace Institute Approach in Somalia," in this book.

17. John Paul Lederach, "Tapping the Tradition: Cultural Elements of the Peace Process in Somalia" (paper presented at the National Conference of Peacemaking and Conflict Resolution, Portland, Ore., May 1993), 8.

18. See Ahmed Yusuf Farah, "Roots of Reconciliation in Somaliland," in this book

19. Alta Brubaker, "Preparing People for Peace" (report no. 4 of the Program of Work by the Peace and Reconciliation Committee of the Christian Council of Mozambique, Nampula, Mozambique, 1993), 4.

20. Barbara Kolucki, *Circo da Pa* (New York: UNICEF, 1993).

■ 6.2

Stakeholders and Owners

Ahmedou Ould Abdallah

The consequences of a country's historical past—borders separating ethnic/religious groups, poverty, overpopulation, and ancient or present foreign meddling—are common throughout the world. The borders between Finland and Sweden, France and Spain, Hungary and Romania, and Bulgaria and Turkey that divide ethnic groups are among the many good illustrations of this. However, with the exception of the Balkans, these countries have not necessarily experienced all-out devastating civil wars as seen in Africa. Hence, Africa and Africans cannot keep blaming others for their present wars.

OWNERSHIP OF CIVIL CONFLICT

In reality, most civil conflicts are the result of incompetent political leadership. By leadership, I mean in particular the leaders of the majority, but also to a certain extent the leaders of the opposition and of civil society organizations. Incompetent leadership—greedy, nepotistic, myopic—is the main reason behind civil wars. Therefore, from its early stages, an internal conflict is fully "owned" by the country, or at least by its national leaders. In the face of these conflicts, the ultimate objective is to ensure that a solution be "owned" by the population and by a new and more accountable leadership. Having said this, it should also be stated that each conflict is specific and should be addressed against its own background and within its own context. Generalization with regard to approaches and solutions in this domain could have devastating consequences.

The causes of conflict are rooted in bad policies of governments and political parties. Political, economic, and social exclusion, lack of tolerance and dialogue, and impunity from justice all are determined and carried out by successive leadership. The desire to share both political power and economic resources forces those who feel unfairly excluded to seek a better bargaining position. Government inflexibility in response to these aspirations makes confrontation unavoidable in the long run. In addition, respect for human rights and promotion of democracy in Africa were not a priority in the agenda of Cold War actors. As a consequence, this international indifference facilitated the ascendancy of despots in many countries. Violence and oppression often went unchecked throughout the continent, followed by civil wars with the opening up of the political systems in the 1990s.

USE OF LOCAL WISE PERSONS

When I arrived in Burundi in November 1993, the president had been assassinated one month earlier, and many Burundese, 50,000 to 100,000, had been killed in the subsequent interethnic violence. At the same time, 850,000 nationals were refugees in Rwanda, Tanzania, and Zaire and nearly 500,000 were internally displaced in camps within Burundi. The civil war was temporarily on hold while protagonists prepared themselves for the next round of violence.

To address the political vacuum and constitutional chaos, proposals were made to hold new elections to replace the assassinated president elected only four months earlier. I rejected the idea as costly, unproductive, and essentially conducive to exacerbating further the already tense and violent situation. A fresh presidential campaign would have sparked renewed killings. Yet I did support a national mediation undertaken by a group of prominent Burundese from the church and the business communities. I worked closely with them to devise an approach based on an amendment of the constitution that would allow parliament to elect a new president instead of having a direct popular vote. As the main external mediator, I had to convince national players through discussions with the leadership of each party, though not by limiting myself to confidential dialogue with only its chairman and secretary-general.

Ownership, therefore, means involving a significant group of leaders from each party so as to reach out to as many of its members as possible. This approach has major advantages; by bringing into the negotiations a larger number of party members, it helps democratize these members, or at least opens them up to further dialogue within their own ranks and with others. In addition, it comforts the moderates in each party by demonstrating the need to reach out to all national players. Finally, it increases the magnitude of political transparency within the society.

Because a civil conflict is in a way essentially a family feud, with all its intricate schemes, paranoia, and mutual accusations of betrayal, a lasting solution can come only from within. It is therefore imperative that an external player understands the deep causes of the conflict at hand. To this end, he could rely on a dedicated and widely accepted group of local personalities, wise and capable, for bringing together the leaders of the various factions. The group understanding of the background of the conflict is equal or better compared to that of the protagonists and greater than that of any newcomer. It can help put pressure on the belligerents, whom they know well enough to understand which kind of pressure to exert. Moreover, the wise persons can also appeal to the patriotism of the faction leaders.

Despite its important role, there is, however, a limit to national mediation. First, there is always suspicion—justified or not—that a member of this group of wise persons is acting in his or her own interest, seeking pre-eminence or political position. Second, as they necessarily belong to one clan or another, individuals in a group are naturally subject to accusations of bias. Finally, fear of reprisal from their own clan could lead to silencing the group. In view of these intricacies, the selection of the wise persons should be made in consultation with members of their own communities but without making them their delegates. Acceptable to their own group of origin, the wise persons are not rejected by the other side. In addition, they have the capacity to propose compromises. Therefore, once serious contacts have been re-established between faction leaders, the role of an external mediator becomes essential. Having no vested interest to defend and no reason to promote beyond that of peace, this external mediator should move toward a negotiated settlement, taking his or her role very seriously and being neutral in both approach and action. Avoiding a quick fix, the mediator should be able to devise a peace process that will bring both an end to the conflict and lay the ground for a lasting peace on a credible political arrangement.[1]

INVOLVEMENT OF EXTREMISTS

Dealing with extremists is not an easy task. They represent political sensitivities that are difficult to ignore because they run through the veins of a society and through each ethnic group. Furthermore, there is no doubt that a strong and credible settlement calls for the inclusion of all parties with a stake in the conflict, including the most vocal ones and even those with a background of gross human rights and humanitarian violations. At the same time, these extremist parties enlist ruthless individuals who use fear and murder as a vehicle to further their political ambitions. Consequently, I have strong objections to incorporating extremists into a serious peace process. By extremists I am referring to those political leaders with no patience for dialogue, negotiations, or compromise. They have only one single item on their agenda: the exclusion of the other.

Bringing in real hard-liners can only worsen an already shaky political environment because their participation at official negotiations is tantamount to a recognition of their "right" to blackmail, kill, and abuse the rights of others. In this context, it should be noted that extremists start by exerting violence not against their adversaries but within their own community. To impose themselves as leaders, they first terrorize their neighbors whom they know best. Once their reputation as ruthless is confirmed, they move in on other groups. Thus, their exclusion seems to be the right decision. The price of their participation in a negotiation is too high and a painful one to ask moderate and neutral leaders to digest. Indeed, an atmosphere of fear and terror in a negotiation room stifles frank and conciliatory dialogue. Moreover, by raising the stakes higher and higher, the tactics of extremist groups usually consist of frightening their adversaries into submission or forcing them into a refugee situation. Their presence at a peace process can only lead to more violence and hatred. Moreover, parties being threatened and blackmailed by extremists will themselves generate extremist factions within their ranks. This contagious effect will poison the peace process.[2] Finally, even if extremist leaders were co-opted into the negotiation, this would be met by the formation of splinter groups breaking away from the main extremist body. This endless speculative outbidding would reduce the peace process to an exercise manipulated by hard-liners.

For all these reasons, my policy during my tenure in Burundi was not to incorporate declared extremists into the peace process. I was, however, always prepared to meet with them, and I have done so on a bilateral basis. I would then explain to them why they were not acceptable and never would be unless they changed their way of addressing national issues. I also never hesitated to warn them that they would be on the short list of unwanted persons in democratic countries and, moreover, so would members of their families. Threatening with denying entry visas into democratic countries was a strong deterrent. Finally, to prevent them from exploiting to their advantage the discussion with me, I always ensured that the government and other parties be immediately and completely briefed.

Extremists may evolve in view of difficulties encountered and of the global context. Once they accept that violence is not the only means to achieve political success, and once they look for common grounds for cohabitation, former extremists could have their seat around the negotiating table. Of course, there is always the risk that their acceptance is only a tactic to get honorability before taking up their arms again. I think that as long as declared extremists renounce resorting to violence, they should be invited in. If they renege on their position, they discredit themselves and lose credibility.

After I left Burundi in October 1995, extremists were included, maybe without conditionality, in the peace process. Not only did violence increase, but political parties began to disintegrate into more extremist groupings: each one out for its own political gain. In the end, a military coup took place in July 1996. It seems to me that, had the extremists been excluded, President Pierre Buyoya would not have seized power. Furthermore, once the coup was consummated, Buyoya and his colleagues from parliament would have achieved their successful internal partnership at an earlier stage and on a more solid foundation. The partnership was signed only in June 1998, two years after the coup.

Finally, to strengthen the role of the main mediator and weaken the hold of extremists, there is a need to work closely with all representatives of the international community present in the country, including non-governmental organizations (NGOs). Cooperation and information sharing among members of the international community help send a nonambiguous message to all the belligerents. It also prevents them from using one organization against another. A code of conduct for all foreign actors should ensure that they do not play their own game for the benefit of their organization and against the peace process.

LESSONS TO BE LEARNED: GUIDELINES FOR EXTERNAL ACTORS

There are many lessons to be learned from a country afflicted by a deeply rooted civil conflict. Below are a few:

Modesty and Humility

None is more important than the lesson of modesty and humility. After seeing death and despair, families divided and traumatized, the plight of refugees and displaced persons, the destruction of habitat and infrastructure, and the irrational behavior even within educated elites, one can only be humble and caring. This humility encourages giving priority to essentials: life and property, stability, and lasting peace over political partnership and etiquette considerations. One practical lesson is that external actors and their closest associates should always have a decent and sober manner during their stay in the afflicted country. In the face of the trauma and suffering endured by the local populations, a show of concern and respect by external actors would be most productive.

Open-Mindedness

A serious effort should be undertaken to help understand the country concerned and the background of the crisis. History, geography, culture, and the deep causes of the crisis should be given enough space and time. Even if books and reports on the country have been read, external actors should come to the country with an open mind. They should not arrive with preconceived or stereotyped ideas on what groups or policies are right or wrong. They should be prepared to listen to the main groups and build their own ideas and approaches. Finally, external actors should not forget that despite similarities, each crisis is specific and should be addressed against its own background. Caution and personal judgment are most important.

Conflict Prevention

Another critical lesson to be learned is that, in a politically fragile country, it is essential not to minimize the negative impact of any political claim or of any land or tribal dispute. In other words, prevention is the key, regardless of the difficulty in achieving it effectively.[3] Obviously, this does not mean that we should let extremists hold a country ransom to the threat of civil war. It is wise, nevertheless, not to underestimate how quickly people can turn against one another and how quickly neighbors can turn guns against neighbors, often for trivial motives. In a fragile country, we should promote dialogue and ongoing contact between different groups of people.

Democratic Transition

An additional lesson to be learned is that, at a political level, a wise reading of the constitution is advisable. Hence, at the political level, it is essential to recognize the need for a period of democratic transition. During that transition, solutions to crucial issues such as political tolerance, including freedom and responsibility of the press, funding of political campaigns, and alternating the power, should be devised. Power sharing, alternating the power, and participatory democracy are ingredients against violence. Women and youth associations deserve special attention, for their role in war and peace is important and, so too, is that of the press.

Intensive Communication

It is also important that efforts be made by external players to establish and maintain good lines of communication between political, business, church, and civil society leaders. As the main ingredients for conflicts are rumors, fear, and stereotypes—all fueling hatred and mistrust—communication is a good instrument for preventive action. Two approaches should be undertaken simultaneously. In the long term, education and training on tolerance should start at school and in the workplace. In the much-needed short and medium terms, external actors in full cooperation between themselves and local actors should make use of all opportunities to bring together leaders and members of different groups and communities. All events—such as visits of high-level dignitaries, commemorations, birthdays, and weddings—are reasons for inviting them and making them meet and talk to each other on casual and serious issues as well. The ultimate objective of these gatherings is to win over fear, suspicion, and rumors. Many times a week, people from various backgrounds should be able to leave their ethnic and political ghettos and see other men and women and listen to different opinions.

Code of Conduct for Foreign Actors

Finally, because of prevailing mistrust between communities, the effective presence and action of an external mediator should always aim at preventing conflict from erupting. His or her personal behavior in public as well as in private is a matter very closely watched by local populations in times of troubles. In the context of civil conflict, every foreign actor from a government, an intergovernmental organization, or an NGO is perceived as a mediator. As a consequence, there is an absolute need for those in the field to adhere fully to a code of conduct. During the past few years, a number of organizations have approved and signed codes of conduct formalizing rules and regulations for their activities in the field. All external actors, even those not belonging to signatories, should abide by the rules of the code of conduct. In reality, beyond these codes of conduct there is the moral obligation for a strict respect of ethical behavior. This ethical behavior helps the credibility and also the physical security of the foreign actors. Therefore, exchange of information between partners is most advisable. Moreover, a legitimate search for a higher profile should not push external actors to secretly support one group against the others or to undertake negotiations parallel to that of the main negotiator.[4]

NOTES

1. One major first step in a peace process is to avoid a political vacuum. Therefore, by helping put in place a government, the mediator sends to the population and the faction leaders a strong signal of normality. A message that power is not anymore for grabs should end the infighting of the leadership that destroyed countries like Somalia and Afghanistan. The new government and other parties should then discuss a lasting and credible settlement. In September 1994, I helped the Burundese have a government (convention of government) that in its Article 52 calls for the initiation of real negotiations for a durable settlement (the national debate).

2. The experience of negotiations with declared extremists in Bosnia (Radovan Karadzic and General Ratko Mladic) has shown the danger and futility of such an exercise. By the end of the Dayton negotiations, both men were on the list of most-wanted criminals.

3. For conflict prevention, refer to the important distinction made by Professor Luc Reychler between proactive prevention (before a conflict) and reactive prevention (once the conflict has erupted) in "Field Diplomacy: A New Conflict Prevention Paradigm?" (paper presented at the conference of the International Peace Research Association, Brisbane, Australia, 1996).

4. For too long, Burundese and Rwandese have been presented solely as belonging to particular communities, almost species, with specific behavioral patterns. This approach, which may have academic merit, has monopolized the debate on the Great Lakes region, occulting a political approach conducive to a peaceful settlement. Time has certainly come to try to understand and assess this unfortunate region in the same way as other human societies. Its political leadership (majority, opposition, civil society) should be evaluated in relation to other leaderships in Africa with their strengths and weaknesses instead of being seen only as Hutu and Tutsi. The fundamental problems (political power, resource redistribution, development issues) faced by these countries should be analyzed and addressed under a human perspective (namely, incompetence, greed, nepotism, and the like) and not only under the specific angle of ethnic characteristics. To me, there are no genetic or "programmed" behaviors in Burundi and Rwanda except those demonstrated around the world by incompetent leaders.

SUGGESTED READING

Ould Abdallah, Ahmedou. (1996). *La diplomatie pyromane: Burundi, Rwanda, Somalie, Bosnie . . . , Entrietiens avec Stephen Smith.* Paris: Calmann-Lévy.

The Role of the Business Community in Northern Ireland

Ray Mullan

The "Troubles" in Northern Ireland have left more than 3,000 people dead since 1969 and countless thousands injured and maimed. Although paramilitary cease-fires are currently in place, and local politicians are close to establishing a form of partnership government, the depth of the sectarian divisions between Northern Ireland's Protestant/Unionist and Catholic/ Nationalist communities remains as a problem to be addressed if peace is to firmly established.

The Northern Ireland Community Relations Council (CRC), a non-governmental organization formed in 1990, has sought to play a leading role in addressing communal divisions in Northern Ireland by empowering local people and organizations to deal with difference in positive ways. The CRC was created after a report (by H. Frazer and M. Fitzduff in 1986) from the Northern Ireland Standing Advisory Commission on Human Rights. The report recommended that a new agency should be established to support and encourage the efforts of all those individuals and groups concerned to improve communication, understanding, and tolerance between communities in Northern Ireland and to initiate new work in this area.

The CRC receives financial support from the British government and the European Union but was created as an independent organization. Its board of directors (approximately twenty members) consists of individuals from all sections and sectors of the community, including peace groups, churches, trade unions, community groups, academia, business, and public bodies. The CRC employs twenty professional and administrative staff.

Much of the CRC's work has focused on supporting community relations projects initiated by voluntary and community groups, including local peace and reconciliation organizations. More than 4,000 projects have been supported since 1990, approximately 500 per annum. Since 1996 these have included projects funded by the European Union's Special Support Program for Peace and Reconciliation for which the CRC is an intermediary funding body. But increasingly the CRC has also sought to "mainstream" community relations work by persuading major institutions in the public sector and in the business community to put community relations on their agenda.

The CRC has no statutory authority and thus no power of compulsion. Rather its approach has been to engage major institutions and agencies by demonstrating that the divided and segregated nature of Northern Ireland society poses particular problems for all those working and operating there. Those problems require the development of proactive strategies, policies, and practices based on antisectarianism. The CRC has offered to work in partnership with organizations in producing these.

One example of this approach has been the Doing Business in a Divided Society initiative developed by the CRC in partnership with nine major business institutions. Opportunities for inward investment and tourism have been missed in the past as a result of the image of violent conflict and political instability, although the recent paramilitary cease-fires and the interparty agreement on Good Friday 1998 have created a new business optimism. Sectarian intimidation within the workplace and communal tension related to disputes over parades have also affected many local businesses and have produced public statements of condemnation from business leaders.

In 1997 the CRC met with a number of business organizations with the intention of developing a collective initiative from the business community that would help address the issue of sectarian division. The initiative took as its premise the notion that handling division positively was good management practice.

The organizations involved in the project included the Institute of Directors, the Northern Ireland Chamber of Commerce and Industry, the Institute of Management, the Institute of Personnel and Development, the Chief Executives Forum, the Federation of Small Businesses, the Northern Ireland Quality Center, the Confederation of British Industry, and Business in the Community. In meetings in 1997 and 1998, various committees met to agree to a set of guidelines of good practice for managers and employers in dealing with the sectarian divisions as they affected business life. These included guidelines for relations within the workplace, with customers, with suppliers, and with the community. The CRC participated in the work of the committees but was careful to allow the suggested guidelines to come from business people themselves. The various drafts were fully tested in pilot exercises before being prepared for publication. One of the four sets of guidelines was Good Practice in Managing the Workplace. It contained the following checklist:

- Has your business considered how sectarianism in the workplace could affect performance?
- Does your business have knowledge of the extent to which sectarianism is having an impact within your workplace, for example on

morale, motivation, team performance, absenteeism, and labor turnover?

- Has your business made an unequivocal commitment to being anti-sectarian?
- Does your business engage in discussions with staff, employee representatives, and on-site contractors about the need for antisectarian policies and practices?
- Does your business clearly communicate its antisectarian policy to all people in the workplace, including full-time staff, seasonal staff, visitors, customers, suppliers, and contractors?
- Does your business have a thorough understanding of fair employment legislation, and is this translated into proper practices for recruitment, training, and promotion?
- Does your business have senior staff who are seen consistently to practice antisectarianism within the workplace?
- Has your business developed ways by which managers and staff learn to work within an antisectarian environment?

The Doing Business in a Divided Society guidelines for managers and employers were published in a public launch in April 1998, only ten days after the Good Friday Agreement among the politicians at Stormont. The publication was cosponsored by the two main morning newspapers in Northern Ireland, the *Newsletter* (Unionist), and the *Irish News* (Nationalist), to give it added cross-community appeal and local publicity. Furthermore, copies of the guidelines were posted through the membership lists of each of the partner organizations involved in the project with cover letters from that organization. In this way 10,000 copies of the guidelines were sent to local businesses and agencies by nine leading business institutions and promoted as a good business practice. This was likely to be much more effective than a mail shot by the CRC of a publication drawn up by the CRC alone.

The guidelines are the start of a process rather than the end of one. Follow-up work now needs to be done in terms of developing appropriate training and resources for business management, but interest has been created that hopefully the CRC can build upon.

The mainstreaming model of identifying a common interest with other sectors and working with partners to adapt community relations concerns and interests to priorities within that sector is being applied by the CRC to a variety of areas in addition to business. These include sport, institutes of further and higher education, health and social service agencies, housing, job training agencies, regional planning, local government, churches, and museums.

Focused community relations projects organized by voluntary and community groups will continue to be necessary in building up the cross-community contacts, opportunities, and skills at a community level. But if community relations values of respect for differences, acknowledgment of interdependence, and regard for principles of equity are to be fully accepted as part of a new culture of tolerance in Northern Ireland, then public bodies and the major institutions of civil society need to mainstream this work in their policies and practices.

With the possibility of a locally elected government executive based on cross-community partnership, the CRC's hope is that mainstreaming community relations within all aspects of government activity will become the pattern for the future. The CRC's role will be to help them in that process.

■ 6.4

A Role for Religious Communities

Rienzie Perera

In this article, my intention is to share some lessons learned during my years working for peace and justice in Sri Lanka.

The island of Sri Lanka has a population of 17 million people. Because of Sri Lanka's religious and ethnic diversity, one can say that it is a multireligious, -ethnic, and -cultural country. Sri Lankan diversity is its richness. Yet because of political manipulations of religion and ethnicity, this diversity has become a major source of conflict. With the escalation of the conflict and the continuation of war, suspicions and divisions have become visible, and the disintegration of society is rapidly taking place. It is within this context one has to work for peace and justice in Sri Lanka.

INVOLVE THE CONGREGATION

In 1988, I was posted to the south of Sri Lanka to serve one of the oldest Christian communities in a village called Baddegama. I served this church until 1992 and then was invited by the National Christian Council of Sri Lanka to serve as its general secretary from 1992 to 1998. The situation in the country during these ten years challenged me to realize that my ministry was to the whole community and that I should not confine my work only to Christians. I had to explain this to the members of my church and win their support to devote my time to the community as a whole. This was not an easy task, but I managed to both win the support of the majority and get them involved in justice and peace work.

The lesson I learned was the necessity to get one's own religious community involved in the work one does and to rely on their solidarity. At the same time, one also has to realize that it will be almost impossible to get the unanimous support of any religious community to be involved in peacebuilding and physically join the work one does for the victims of violence.

BUILD BRIDGES OF SOLIDARITY

During these years in the south, we experienced the pain of people, especially those who have lived in the east of Sri Lanka for generations but had to abandon their homes and return to the south for security reasons. Although they were originally from the south of Sri Lanka, they had no roots there because they belonged to the second or third generation of persons who had migrated from the south to the east of Sri Lanka. Over these years a number of interethnic marriages had taken place, and it was therefore a well-integrated community. This integration enabled them to transcend ethnic and religious barriers.

The Tamil militants wanted them to leave that part of the country where they had lived for generations and return to the south. They were driven away from that region because they belonged to the dominant ethnic group, the Singhalese, whom the Tamil militants look upon as the oppressors. Through fear they left everything and came to the south for refuge and in search of their roots. Their desperate situation demanded an immediate response.

I invited the leaders of these families—women and men, young and old—to the church hall to discuss their plight and plan a program of relief and rehabilitation. The program planned by the Christians was called into question by some of the leading Buddhist monks and Buddhist lay leaders. The argument of the monks was that I, a Christian priest, was trying to convert these Buddhist refugees by offering them relief. Their accusation was based on the premise that the missionaries during the colonial era used similar methods to convert people. I was convinced that my intentions were not to convert but to help these uprooted people. I had no intention to exploit the vulnerability of these victims of violence for conversion. The Buddhists were not convinced, however.

This encounter made me realize that, although love and compassion are at the heart of the majority of religions, there are deep-seated suspicions and hatred that divide and keep us apart. Very often our own religious histories are against us. Therefore, it is important to avoid past mistakes of our forefathers and mothers and create new history. I learned from experience that if our true intention is to serve the victims in a broken society and, especially, if the victims are from different faith communities, then we need to win the confidence and the support of religious leaders of all faiths in a given situation.

In any inter-religious context one needs to build bonds of solidarity among the religious communities to serve the people better. In many inter-religious contexts the arrogance and the bigotry of religious leaders contribute to the perpetuation of suffering. In my context, I realized that the only way to win the confidence and support of religious leaders, whether Buddhists, Christians, Muslims, or Hindus, was to make friends with them and involve them at the initial stage of discussions and planning.

If we can consciously plan and implement our work of peacebuilding with this inter-religious mentality, then many possibilities will open up and inter-religious solidarity will pave the way for justice and peace to blossom in our societies. However, a joint venture will serve the people better. The humility of the founders of our religions should enlighten our minds and inspire the work we do for the innocent victims of conflict. The lesson I learned was that, in an inter-religious context, if one's work on relief and rehabilitation were to reach its target groups, one has to work in partnership with people of all faiths and no faiths. If such partnerships are built at the grassroots level, the resources of each religious community could be shared to alleviate the suffering of people.

UTILIZE DIFFERENCES

On another occasion the National Christian Council had arranged to transport dry rations to the Tamil refugees who were living in camps in Vavuniya, in the northwestern province. A few days before we were to transport the dry rations, the Tamil militants attacked a Sri Lankan Army camp, and few hundred soldiers were killed. As the bodies of the soldiers—the majority of them Singhalese—were brought to the south, the feelings of the majority community against the Tamils were running high, and the country was tense with racial hatred. A mischief maker made use of the opportunity and informed the police that certain banned items were being loaded onto a lorry by Christians for transport to the north, where they would be handed over to Tamil militants. Based on this information the police raided the church premises where the dry rations were being loaded and took into custody the two lorries with the dry rations along with the drivers and the laborers.

The church tried to explain the facts but in vain. Then we requested that some of the friendly and enlightened Buddhist monks intervene on behalf of the National Christian Council, and they obliged. The result was that the lorries along with the dry rations were released. We also appealed to the monks to assist us in transporting the goods to Tamil refugees. The monks accepted our offer.

The result of this episode was that the dry rations were taken to the northwestern refugee camps—about 200 kilometers from the capital—by the monks, without being stopped at any of the security checkpoints for inspection. This was possible simply because the transportation was done by Buddhist monks who form the dominant religious group in Sri Lanka. Yet it was the first time in the history of Sri Lanka, as far as I am aware, where Buddhist monks had transported dry rations to Tamil refugees. It was a mission of compassion and mercy. A lesson learned from these experiences was the importance of inter-religious cooperation to overcome barriers especially when the victims whom you want to serve happen to be people of diverse religious beliefs.

POOL INTER-RELIGIOUS RESOURCES

All of these experiences made some of us who are in the forefront of peace-building realize that we need to transcend our religious differences and forge bonds of solidarity and pool our spiritual and material resources if we are to serve the people who have become victims in our war-torn societies. Having this ideal in mind, we formed an organization and named it the Inter-religious Peace Foundation. The thrust and vision of the organization was built on our experience of inter-religious cooperation and solidarity. As an organization, decisionmaking power is shared by all religious communities, and the chairpersonship is also jointly shared by a Christian/Muslim, Buddhist/Hindu, Christian/Buddhist, and Hindu/Muslim on a rotating basis.

Some of the main aims of the organization are (1) peacebuilding through inter-religious and ethnic cooperation, (2) intervention in conflicts on an inter-religious and ethnic basis, (3) formation of inter-religious and ethnic clusters at the district level for peace building, (4) using spiritual resources in each religion for peace and community building, and (5) sharing the material resources of each religious community to assist victims of violence and the poor.

At the beginning it was difficult for us to discuss and plan together, travel together, and intervene in conflicts together. Over the years, however, we have learned from one another, and an inter-religious culture of peace, harmony, and partnership has been built. This bond has enabled us to break diverse forms of barriers and taboos and becomes a way of life and a source of spiritual strength to walk the rough path of peacemaking and peacebuilding. I believe, that, in a world where religions have been at the center of conflicts, they can also become a source for healing of nations, mending of communities, and transformation of conflicts. This process can take place if the devotees of these religions are immersed and nurtured in the liberating spiritualities of their respective religions. This has become the foundation to build a culture of peace in Sri Lanka.

SUGGESTED READING

Hurley, Michael, ed. (1993). *Reconciliation in Religion and Society.* Belfast: Queen's University.
Jeffrey, Paul. (1998). *Recovering Memory, Guatemalan Churches and the Challenge of Peacemaking.* Uppsala: Life and Peace Institute.

CHAPTER 7

Designing the Mediation Process

■ 7.1

Principles of Good Process Design

Ron Kraybill

People and organizations are usually more sensitive about *how* a decision is reached than *what* the decision itself is.

Consider the following situation. It is tea time at a meeting of professional colleagues. The chair suggests a thirty-minute break, calls out the names of three women, and asks them to go and prepare the tea. These women are all from the same racial group, a minority in the community and the professional group. At tea time, others from this minority gather in a corner and angrily discuss the problem of racism. After the tea break, they confront the chair and the entire group.

In another organization, it is also tea time. Here, too, the leader announces the names of three minority women chosen to serve tea. But here the women laugh good-naturedly as they rise to undertake their duties. Why? Their names were chosen randomly by pulling straws. The *outcome* was the same in both groups—individuals were chosen to serve tea against their preferences. But in one, the outcome was accepted because the *process* was fair.

Democracy is built on the latter principle. In every democratic election there is a group of people whose candidate lost. For the loser and his or her supporters, an outcome has been reached that they had actively opposed. Nevertheless, in a democracy losers rarely stage a rebellion, even where the stakes are vast. "Losers" can almost always be counted upon to step aside and allow the "winners" to move ahead, if the process of the elections has been agreed upon in advance by all the key parties and the ground rules have been observed.

But the converse holds as well. People will reject almost any outcome—even a wise and fair one—that they feel is the result of a bad process. "It's not that we oppose the idea of further development in our community," complained a leader in a community dispute. "What we resent is the high-handed way the planners go about ramming this proposal down our throats. This is our community and we want to be a part of decisions affecting us." A great deal of group conflict is simply the consequence of bad process, for key parties will reject even the best of ideas and proposals if they are created in processes they find objectionable. Thus, peacebuilders need a strong capacity to assist groups to interact on principles of good process.

1. *Good process requires careful thought, consultation, and planning.* Haste is a major enemy of good process.

2. *Good process asks, "Who should be involved?" not "What are we going to do?"* Here are some questions to guide planning about whom to involve in the discussion process:

- Who will view themselves as deeply affected by this negotiation, project, or decision? (Almost always this group should be at the heart of the decisionmaking process.)
- Who is in a position to block implementation if they are unhappy with decisions? (They should always at least be consulted, and often they need to be an active part of the decision process.)
- Whose advice or assistance will be valuable? (Consultation is called for.)
- Whose approval will be required to enable this project to proceed? (Inform and consult.)
- What are the interests or motivations of each of the above groups?

3. *Good process calls for joint information gathering, joint education, and joint problem definition.* The purpose of joint information gathering and/or joint education is to engage in a process of information gathering, thus laying the groundwork for problem solving later. It is preferably done jointly with all the parties working together in hearing each other and gathering data. Alternatively, it is done by an impartial third party. Typical general activities:

- "Story-telling"—taking turns sharing perspectives and listening.
- Field trips.
- Interviews of key parties conducted by the facilitator in the presence of other parties (or separately, if the tension is high

and facilitators feel unsure of their skills to facilitate joint meetings; in this case, some effective way must be found to report key issues to the parties).

- Gathering data and issuing reports by joint study groups.
- Authorizing studies by outsiders; interviewing experts.

Helpful leadership or facilitator activities:

- Make sure everyone understands the purpose of this stage: to get educated about the issues and needs *as perceived* by key parties. It is not to argue about "what's *really* going on," not to debate solutions.
- Establish ground rules such as there will be no interruptions until a speaker is finished; responses to presentations will be limited to clarifying questions.
- Involve parties in deciding how they would like to go about educating each other about their issues and needs.
- Provide strong and clear facilitation to prevent slipping into bargaining or attacking.

Joint problem definition is to agree on what problems need to be resolved before beginning serious discussions of solutions. Typical general activities:

- List problems, issues, or needs on paper.
- Create one list of problems that is specific and that incorporates the concerns of all key parties.
- Assign joint working groups for each problem area and ask each group to return with a list of key problems needing to be addressed.
- List possible problems, then come back and mark with a C those that are *causes* and an S those that are *symptoms*. Causes usually deserve the most attention as problems; symptoms usually fade if causes are addressed.
- Alternative approach: plan backward. Parties are asked to define "the ideal relationship" or their dream for their community or government in ten (or two, five, whatever) years. If there is agreement on the desired *end,* parties can then plan backward from there to the present. "What needs to happen in five years to reach the goal set for ten years?" "What must happen in two years?" and so on.

Helpful leadership or facilitator activities:

- Provide clear facilitation.
- Use newsprint or a blackboard.

- Educate parties about the difference between a *problem state-ment* and a *solution,* and keep focused at this stage on the for-mer.

4. *Good process is conducted under auspices acceptable to all.* If a community is complaining about police brutality, a program for dialogue between police and community is unlikely to earn community trust if it is sponsored solely by the police. Good process design would call for such a program to be sponsored by an independent organization or jointly by the police and a trusted community organization.

5. *Good process involves key parties (or their representatives) not only in the process of negotiation and decisionmaking but in the design of the process itself.* Suppose you were leader of a key faction involved in a community dispute over what to do with the vacant lot next door. One Saturday you receive a polite invitation announcing that your chief oppo-nent would be convening a meeting at his house next Wednesday to "bring together responsible citizens in order to make decisions critical to the future of our community." Would you go?

You are likely to be less than thrilled about the invitation, given the lack of consultation with you. Typically key parties are skeptical of any proposed discussion in which they have not had a role in sorting out such issues as where, when, involving whom, and under the auspices of whom. Then, too, you are likely to sense that if the meeting succeeds in bringing together key people from the community and enabling a good discussion, your opponent is likely to gain considerable stature as a consequence.

Suppose your opponent takes a different approach and announces plans to convene a commission to discuss the problem. He invites suggestions on the commission. How do you respond now? Well, it's better than it used to be—at least he seems open to suggestions. But even so, you are not likely to be pleased. Your archrival is still in the role of making the final decision about how the talks will be arranged, plus he gets the credit if anything suc-cessfully results.

Key parties are more likely to trust facilitators and participate in talks if they have been consulted extensively and feel that they have helped design the negotiation forum. It is often wise to give them a fundamental role at every level of process design. Go to them and say, "We are wonder-ing about building a forum in which all of us can talk. Would you be inter-ested? What should it look like? Who should be there? When and where should we meet? Who should convene it? Should it be on the record or off the record?" Don't build and then try to "sell" a process to the parties.

Whether the conflict is in a religious congregation or a political ward, if the parties indicate an openness to talk, one of the most effective ways to ensure that it is designed and conducted in ways to foster cooperation is to create a process committee. Made up of thoughtful representatives of all key parties, this group has the task of planning, announcing, and coordinating the process.

Design and build consensus around the process so that it is understood and supported by all key parties. Typical general activities:

- Identify the parties, including anyone capable of blocking an agreement.
- Conduct one-on-one interviews with key leaders regarding what kind of process would be acceptable.
- Provide good information about the process to those participating or affected. Devise and circulate a proposal regarding the process that covers the purpose of the process, what will happen when (a timeline is useful here), participants (who, how, and how many), ground rules, and who facilitates.
- Avoid announcing a process and then "selling" it to key actors. Rather, involve key actors in informal decisions to design the process, then ask for formal commitment to it. *Create* the process *jointly*.
- Key parties must agree on the "decision rule": who will make the final decision and what kind of decision rule applies (51 percent majority, 67 percent majority, consensus, modified consensus, unanimity, etc.). Consider when to decide this. All of these things usually cannot be decided at the beginning of the process, but they should be clarified as early as possible.

Helpful leadership or facilitator activities:

- Educate parties about the importance of good process.
- Insist on consultation with all key parties before process is announced.
- Urge that the process be designed and accepted by key parties before the next stages begin.
- Ask repeatedly of all parties: "Can you support this process? Can you help us improve it?"
- Insist on clarity about goals or purposes of the process.
- Provide ideas/stories from parallel experiences.
- Make sure there is adequate provision in the timeline for consultation between negotiators and their constituencies.
- Initiate the process by one-on-one interviews.
- Write the process proposal.

6. *Good process offers more than one kind of forum for those people affected to express and evaluate problem-solving options.* In institutional settings, use large group discussion, small group discussion, polls or ques-

tionnaires, study circles, and personal interviews. In community or political settings, in addition to the above, use conferences, community forums, publications, and study materials. These forums should allow for the generation and evaluation of problem-solving options.

Generate problem-solving options to generate a comprehensive list of options available for resolution. Typical general activities:

- Brainstorm.
- Individuals list ideas on paper, and then all are posted on a board (Delphi technique).
- Go around the room and everyone adds an idea to the list.
- Consult experts and the experience of others.
- Appoint a task force for each of several problem areas.

Helpful leadership or facilitator activities:

- Stress that the goal is to get a range of options listed, not to agree on any one option.
- Be firm about holding a debate on the options until the next stage (evaluation). The whole value of separating the task of generating options from evaluating them is lost if the facilitator is not firm on this.
- Use newsprint or a board for lists.
- Know how to facilitate brainstorming. It is especially important to emphasize that no criticisms of ideas are wanted at this stage.
- Persist in getting beyond the same old "pet" solutions. The more options created, the greater the chances of finding an acceptable resolution to problems.

Evaluate problem-solving options to examine thoughtfully the strengths and limits of each option. Typical general activities:

- Review lists of options and reduce to a "short list."
- Do a "pluses/minuses" or "benefits/costs" list for each option.
- Do an "anticipated impact" list for each option.
- Parties "rank order" the options from most to least acceptable.
- Parties state what criteria they are using in deciding whether a solution is acceptable.
- Parties jointly create a list of objective criteria that any solution chosen must fill.
- Seek out the experience of others as a basis for evaluating options.
- Ask an expert.

Helpful leadership or facilitator activities:

- Stress that the goal is not yet to agree on any option but to assess each option.
- Use newsprint or a board.
- Facilitate evaluation discussion; propose tools to do so like those above.

7. *Process maintains trust through careful reporting back to the people affected.* Use open discussions, surveys, nonbinding votes, questionnaires, and interim reports during the negotiation or discussion process to keep people informed about the trend of the discussion before the decision is final. If people are shocked at the outcome of a decisionmaking process, it is usually a sign that designers of that process have failed to build adequate report-back mechanisms into the process. Disappointment is inevitable in decisionmaking. Being shocked is not, and it almost always brings charges of unfair process.

Give frequent opportunities for people to comment about how they feel about the process, whether it is fair, and whether they understand the next steps.

Never conduct a formal query process (e.g., questionnaires, interviews, or meetings designed to find out what people want) without reporting back to those queried about what information or preferences the query process revealed.

Follow-up at the end: report to people about the outcome/decision finally reached, solicit evaluation of the process used, and report what monitoring or implementing process will be used.

The purpose of follow-up is to ensure that things agreed to in a negotiation forum are supported by the constituencies represented there and to keep agreements on track. Typical general activities:

- Look for ways of consulting with constituencies on key issues throughout the process. The more consultation there has been, the more likely are the constituencies to support decisions they are not thrilled with.
- It is important to plan from the beginning for ways of reporting to constituencies both during and at the end of the process.
- Agree jointly on mechanisms to monitor agreements or to renegotiate elements that prove unworkable.
- Agree on the means to evaluate the outcome of the negotiations and/or the process used to reach decisions.

Helpful leadership or facilitator activities:

- Impress on the parties how important it is not to relax too early. Many good agreements fall through because the negotiators assume that the problem is resolved. Now is when the real work begins: implementing an agreement in a fragile atmosphere.
- Stress the importance of negotiators consulting with and reporting to constituencies.
- Stress the importance of agreeing on monitoring mechanisms.

APPENDIX: PEACEBUILDING PROCESS—PHASES IN PEACEBUILDING

Phase of Conflict	Adversarial Struggle	Acceptance of Interdependency	Dialogue	Talks About Talks	Negotiation	Developing Broad Support for Peace Settlements	Implementation, Reconstruction
Characteristics of Phase	• low awareness of interdependency • win/lose struggle • goal: to defeat or destroy the opponent	• growing numbers of people on both sides becoming aware that they cannot defeat the enemy	• focus is on developing relationships and understanding the other side • usually informal and private; key leadership keep a safe distance (but are interested in hearing outcomes) • solutions may be discussed but only informally • no mandate to negotiate	• discussion begins about the possibility of talks; the focus is on technicalities: when, where, with whom, regarding what, etc.	• negotiation takes place by people with a mandate to speak on behalf of leaders and/or constituencies • public appearances of polarization often increase as each side seeks to win the battle for public opinion	• leadership consults with their supporters • ideally consultation has been taking place throughout the negotiation process rather than only at the end (unfortunately the latter is often the case) • ideally leaders work carefully to establish bilateral committees and opportunities for contact at grassroots and middle levels of constituencies	• the major pieces of the agreement are implemented • a secondary round of negotiations begins about the details of the agreements • institutions and processes for implementation are jointly created and managed by formal antagonists • broad relationship building between formerly divided groups takes place • ongoing mechanisms or procedures for dealing with "normal" conflicts are created

(continues)

Phase of Conflict	Adversarial Struggle	Acceptance of Interdependency	Dialogue	Talks About Talks	Negotiation	Developing Broad Support for Peace Settlements	Implementation. Reconstruction
Dynamics That Help to Move to the Next Phase	• if powers become balanced, it assists in moving toward the next phase • growing awareness of costs of struggle • fatigue • outside pressure • voices of morality	• a few courageous, realistic people begin to see the need for developing relationships with the other side, and they begin to seek forums for dialogue	• awareness develops that there are sensible, responsible human beings on the other side • word of useful encounters in informal dialogue strengthens, moderates, and increases pressure on leadership to begin formal talks	• success in working out the technicalities of talks increases the willingness of key leaders to enter formal talks	• if negotiation leads toward settlement, the need not to appear to be a "sellout" drives leaders to build public support for a settlement	• if leaders are effective in interpreting and winning support for the agreement, constituents are informed about the settlement and are ready and able to support it in the implementation phase	
Possible Peacebuilder Activities	• help weaker side find advocates • assist weaker side think through strategy • assist in coalition building within the weaker side • work with media to reduce inflammatory or biased news coverage • provide nonviolence training • mobilize voices of morality • conciliation	• support analysis and documentation of the costs of violence • have a good understanding of the ways the groups are interdependent; communicate this broadly • pay attention to the victims of violence; know their realities; be effective in making others aware of them;	• arrange relationship-building encounters, joint trips, joint workshops (usually not with official leaders) • conduct problem-solving workshops • arrange constructive media reporting of some dialogue events; this broadens the impact and may bring contacts	• look for timely moments to expand dialogue to analysis of when and how talks could begin • convey ideas for how talks could be held back and forth between key leaders • advocate principles of good process design • think about ways to bring a respected outsider	• sometimes facilitate talks • provide training in negotiation skills • there are many instances of peacebuilders spending informal time with one or both sides, analyzing the situation, thinking through constructive strategy, helping understand the other side's concerns, etc.	• be aware that it is often at this phase that many peace processes fail • advocate peacebuilding strategies that work at top, middle, and grassroots levels throughout the negotiation process, so there is a framework for bringing constituencies on-board with major agreements when	• be aware that the hardest work often begins after the "big" settlement; encourage others to be aware of this as well • encourage a proactive stance, i.e., anticipate problems that might arise and put response structures in place to deal with them • mobilize many sectors to assist (business, religious, educational, etc.); to the extent that these

(continues)

Phase of Conflict	Adversarial Struggle	Acceptance of Interdependency	Dialogue	Talks About Talks	Negotiation	Developing Broad Support for Peace Settlements	Implementation, Reconstruction
Possible Peacebuilder Activities (con't)	(separate meetings with each side to hear their fears and concerns and encourage awareness of the same in the other side)	assist in organizing humanitarian aid • develop relationships with and support "natural peacemakers" • conduct conflict-analysis-and-resolution workshops separately with each side (assuming that people are not yet ready for joint workshops)	from key people looking for assistance in meeting their counterparts • train facilitators of dialogue events	into the picture who might be able to secure an agreement on the technicalities of when and how to begin talks • explore the possibility of pulling together a group of respected people representing all key factions (or at least acceptable to all key factions) who could as a group advocate talks, conduct "talks about talks," and perhaps facilitate the talks • conduct negotiation skills–training workshops	• help provide needed information to the parties about the conflict • encourage parties to consult extensively with their grassroots throughout the negotiation process to reduce the dangers of "top-down" settlements being rejected later • in general, seek to mobilize peacebuilding strategies at top, middle, and grassroots levels, and encourage coordination among the levels • encourage negotiators to take a long-term perspective on their task and not assume that a political settlement will be reached swiftly	they are achieved • be a resource to leadership to plan and conduct consultation processes • assist in educating the public about talks • draw the media into this task • seek ways to draw in many sectors, not just rely on the political or military groupings of the leadership	groups have been taken seriously in the earlier negotiations process, it is easier to involve them in long-term reconstruction

Undue Pressure: International Mediation in African Civil Wars

Laurie Nathan

In the past decade there have been numerous attempts to resolve intrastate conflict in Africa through mediation. Most of these efforts have failed, with one or more of the parties spurning negotiations, being unwilling or unable to reach a settlement in the course of mediation, or subsequently violating agreements that had been concluded. The factors that might account for the lack of success in each case include the history, nature, and causes of the conflict; the goals and conduct of the disputant parties; the role of neighboring states and foreign powers; and the style and methods of the mediator.

This article focuses on the mediator's strategy and tactics as variables that enhance or diminish the prospect of success. I argue that state and intergovernmental mediators frequently deviate from the logic of mediation and resort instead to power-based diplomacy. They are insensitive to the psychological dynamics of conflict and appear to be unfamiliar with mediation techniques for managing and transforming those dynamics. As a result, the mediators' endeavors heighten the suspicion, fear, and anger of beleaguered disputants and are consequently ineffectual or counterproductive.

The critique is organized around seven strategic principles of mediation: (1) mediators must not be partisan; (2) the parties must consent to mediation and the appointment of the mediator; (3) conflict cannot be resolved quickly and easily; (4) the parties must own the settlement; (5) mediators must be flexible; (6) mediators must not apply punitive measures; (7) and mediation is a specialist activity. These principles are explored with reference to mediation initiatives in African civil wars and the experience of community mediation conducted by the Center for Conflict Resolution (CCR) in Cape Town.

By "mediation" I mean a process of dialogue and negotiation in which a third party helps disputants, with their consent, to manage or resolve their conflict. In the context of civil war, the process is deemed successful when it leads to the advent of democratic and inclusive governance. "Confidence-building mediation" indicates a style of mediation oriented toward raising the parties' confidence in each other, in negotiations, and in the mediator.

MEDIATORS MUST NOT BE PARTISAN

Individuals and groups locked in conflict tend to regard each other with intense suspicion and animosity. They are reluctant to engage in dialogue even when they are contemplating ways of resolving the conflict. Alternatively, they might enter into talks but be unable to move beyond mutual recriminations. The utility of mediation lies in creating a comparatively calm and safe space to address their concerns with the support of a trusted intermediary. Mediation can be viewed as a confidence-building exercise, with the mediator acting as a bridge between the parties. Their trust in the mediator rests on the assumption that he/she will treat them fairly. This is a critical consideration especially for weaker parties that fear being outmaneuvered in the course of negotiations. If mediators are biased against one of the parties, they break that bond of trust and jeopardize the success of the process.

This emphasis on impartiality reflects an ideal that is not fully attainable. CCR mediators naturally have personal, cultural, and professional values; they are always concerned about the equity of agreements reached; and they invariably acquire positive or negative opinions of the antagonists in a specific dispute. Yet one of their professional values, declared expressly to the parties, is a commitment to facilitate the process in a nonpartisan manner. If they are unable to honor that commitment in a given conflict, they will refrain from playing a mediating role.

Some scholars claim that the principle of impartiality does not apply to international mediation. W. Smith presents the following version of the argument. Whereas the impartiality of mediators in domestic settings stems from the fact that they have no extended relationship with the parties and no interest in the dispute beyond its peaceful resolution, states have little motivation to mediate in international conflicts other than because they have a relationship with the adversaries and an interest in the details of a settlement.[1] International mediators are thus probably always biased to some degree. The bias may enhance the acceptability and effectiveness of the mediating state because its interest in its relationship with both of the disputants gives each of them a measure of leverage over it and vice versa. The less-favored party cooperates in the hope that the mediating state will extract concessions from the party with which it enjoys closer ties.

This argument is analytically and empirically incomplete. First, it does not distinguish between a partial mediator who is imposed on the parties and one whom they accept without duress; there can be no objection if they agree to use a mediator who is affiliated to one of them, and in this regard no distinction need be drawn between international and domestic mediation. Second, it considers the problem of bias primarily in terms of the mediator's interest in the dispute and prior relationship with the parties when the problem relates more to the mediator's conduct during the peace-making process. Third, it disregards the fact that a mediator may succeed precisely because of a lack of bias, as in the case of the Community of Sant' Egidio in Mozambique in 1990–1992. According to Father A. Romano, "Our strength was exactly not having to defend any vested interest in the country but the one of a solid peace."[2] Fourth, it ignores the evidence, illustrated below, of a mediator's acceptability and effectiveness being diminished greatly by their partisanship.

In 1989 Liberia was plunged into civil war when rebels led by Charles Taylor sought to oust Samuel Doe who had seized power in a coup ten years earlier. The Economic Community of West African States (ECO-WAS) formed a standing mediation committee to resolve the conflict. When its initial peacemaking bid failed, the committee established a military force known as the ECOWAS Monitoring Group (ECOMOG). Over the next six years ECOMOG became embroiled in the fighting, prolonging the war and contributing to wider regional instability. Dominated by Nigeria, which had backed the despotic Doe, it destroyed its claim to neutrality by targeting Taylor and arming rival factions.[3] According to A. Nyakyi, former UN special representative to Liberia, the enmity between Taylor and Nigeria was the main impediment to securing a lasting peace agreement.[4]

When the elected Hutu government in Burundi collapsed in 1996, Major Pierre Buyoya and the predominantly Tutsi army staged a coup. Neighboring states imposed sanctions on the country with the endorsement of former president Julius Kambarage Nyerere of Tanzania, the official mediator for Burundi. While the Buyoya regime pursued negotiations and forged agreements with its internal opponents, it resisted the external peace process led by Nyerere. It called repeatedly for his resignation as the mediator on the grounds of bias. Prior to the suspension of sanctions in 1999 as a result of pressure from the United Nations Security Council, the tension between Buyoya and Nyerere, and the controversy around the embargo, threatened to overshadow the conflict in Burundi itself.[5]

In 1993 the second United Nations Operation in Somalia (UNOSOM II) was launched with objectives that included peacebuilding and the promotion of reconciliation. After Pakistani peacekeepers were killed in an attack, the UN embarked on a campaign to capture General Mohammad Farrah Aidid, the faction leader deemed responsible. In their bid to hunt him down, UN forces bombed a house and killed more than fifty clan members. K. Menkhaus asserts that "efforts to arrest or marginalize warlords failed to account for the deep-rooted notion of collective responsibility in Somali political culture. . . . Actions taken against a clan's militia leader were seen by Somalis not as justice done to an errant individual, but as a hostile action against the entire clan."[6] Having compromised its impartiality, the UN became too discredited to pursue its mandate and departed Somalia in ignominy.

In the situations described above, the mediator's bias may well have been justified. Nevertheless, a mediating body that undertakes punitive action will be mistrusted by the targeted party as surely as a soccer team mistrusts a jaundiced referee. It sacrifices its status as an "honest broker" and becomes a party to the conflict. Smith acknowledges that a biased domestic mediator will be viewed with suspicion and hostility by the disfavored disputant and may make the conflict more intractable.[7] This logic applies equally to international mediators. As argued further below, enforcement and mediation functions should be performed by different actors.

THE PARTIES MUST CONSENT TO MEDIATION AND THE APPOINTMENT OF THE MEDIATOR

Paradoxically, mediation is most threatening to disputant parties when it is most required. Where a conflict escalates to the point that its negative consequences are manifestly serious, independent observers might regard mediation and negotiations as obvious means of overcoming the impasse. At this stage, however, the adversaries are likely to view the conflict in zero-sum terms. From their perspective, mediation entails talking to "the enemy" and the prospect of compromising fundamental principles in order to reach a settlement. The parties fear losing face, being outmaneuvered by their opponent's negotiating tactics, and being pressured by the mediator to abandon their goals.

Given these dynamics, the CCR undertakes mediation only with the consent of the disputants. It may be called in the first instance by one of the parties or by some authority with an interest in ending the conflict, but its staff will then meet with all the parties to ascertain their willingness to engage in mediation under the CCR's auspices. This approach raises the disputants' confidence by giving them a strong measure of control over the process: they can select a mediator whom they trust, and any one of them can dismiss the mediator at any stage. There is the further advantage of setting an early precedent of decisionmaking by consensus because the protagonists have to agree on the potential benefit of dialogue and on the appointment of the mediator.

Although the voluntary and consensual nature of mediation is widely endorsed as a matter of principle, it is often ignored in practice. When a conflict within or between states reaches a certain level of intensity, third-party countries and multinational bodies tend to assume the role of mediator and appoint envoys to that end without consulting the protagonists. The parties may not be receptive to mediation or they may be ready for talks but lack confidence in the host agency or its envoy. In either event they are likely to regard the endeavor as a form of interference and thereby feel threatened. More striking still is the refusal of mediators to step down when a disputant objects to their presence on the grounds of bias. The mediator's persistence in these circumstances can become a significant secondary source of conflict and an obstacle to resolving the primary conflict.

Peacemakers naturally play uninvited roles where a party refuses to enter into talks, seeking to persuade it otherwise or acting as an interlocutor. Where all the disputants are willing to engage in negotiations, in contrast, enabling them to select the mediator is clearly preferable to imposing one on them. An intermediary could invite each protagonist to nominate a number of third parties to serve in that capacity, the matter being settled quickly if there are any common nominations. If this is not the case, further iterations would be required. Through a process of elimination, the disputants might settle either for a balanced team of mediators or for a single mediator who is not completely unacceptable to any of them.

The approach advocated here may be difficult to implement, but it is no more difficult than any other aspect of mediation and it is not without precedent. When San Egidio convened the first meeting of the Mozambican peace talks in 1990, Renamo insisted that its patron, Kenya, be appointed as the mediator. Frelimo would accept Kenya only if its own ally, Zimbabwe, were a co-mediator. Renamo rejected such involvement by Zimbabwe, a combatant in the war. Renamo also dismissed Frelimo's proposal that they proceed without a mediator. Following shuttle diplomacy by members of the San Egidio team, the parties agreed at the third round of talks to upgrade San Egidio's status from "observer" to "mediator."[8]

CONFLICT CANNOT BE RESOLVED QUICKLY AND EASILY

The CCR mediators are seldom able to resolve community conflicts swiftly. Apparently irreconcilable interests and values, exacerbated by intense mistrust, defy simple solutions. The degree of complexity rises considerably where the conflict has a national character, the adversaries believe that their survival is at stake, large-scale violence has occurred, and the principal causes of the conflict are structural.

Without discounting the UN's mistakes in Somalia, Menkhaus insists that certain of the organization's goals and strategies were inherently incompatible and bound to generate conflict because of objective circumstances; peacemakers were confronted by "unique political dilemmas and thus a menu of very unpalatable options, all of which posed a high probability of failure. There were, in short, no easy and obvious reconciliation strategies."9 This argument has broad applicability to civil wars. For example, mediation and reconciliation efforts may entail courting groups responsible for atrocities and affording them formal recognition; this may alienate sectors of society and be perceived as rewarding violence. However, excluding the groups is likely to ensure their resistance to both the peace process and its outcome.

The complexity of intrastate conflict and peacemaking poses two main challenges to international mediators. First, they should acquire a thorough understanding of local history, politics, cultures, and personalities before assuming a substantive role. Second, they should refrain from rushing the process and making precipitate interventions. However critical of the situation, they should not attempt to thrust solutions on the parties or pressure them into signing an accord prematurely.

Mediators deployed by states and international bodies consistently ignore these challenges and pursue quick-fix solutions. Their confidence that they can quickly bring the parties to their senses through a combination of reason and leverage is naive and arrogant. Underestimating the passion of the belligerents and the intricacies of the conflict, such mediators are more likely to muddy the waters than make a positive impact. Conclusions of this kind have been drawn in respect of international mediation in the Sudanese civil war in the 1990s, the ECOWAS intervention in Liberia, UNOSOM II in Somalia, and Henry Kissinger's attempt to broker a settlement in former Rhodesia.10

In summary, a failure to appreciate the complexity of conflict leads inevitably to a flawed analysis and misguided strategy. The argument presented here relates largely to the structural dimensions of civil wars and the inescapable dilemmas of peacemaking. The following section considers the problem from the perspective of the parties. Mediators who seek quick-fix solutions display a lack of respect for the disputants and will consequently fail to win their respect and cooperation. Because denying citizens the opportunity to be fully involved in political decisionmaking is a primary cause of civil wars, it makes little sense to reproduce the problem in efforts to resolve such conflicts.

THE PARTIES MUST OWN THE SETTLEMENT

In many conflict situations, independent observers might view the stance of one or more of the parties as unreasonable and the solution to the underlying problems as fairly obvious. If the parties shared these views, there would be no need for mediation. Adversaries are typically motivated by an acute sense of injustice, by real or imagined threats to their security, or by other unmet needs that they regard as fundamental. Moreover, basic human needs are not limited to material imperatives like food and shelter. Individuals and groups crave respect, affirmation, and acknowledgment. They want to be involved in decisions that affect their lives and resent being treated as the object of some other body's plans.

A mediating body will alienate the parties if it fails to take seriously the importance they attach both to their positions and to the process of resolving the conflict. Mediators should therefore refrain from prescribing solutions. Their job is not so much to solve problems as to facilitate problem solving by the disputants. Agreements that are not shaped and embraced by the parties have little chance of enduring. Romano recalls that Sant' Egidio resisted pressure to end the Mozambican talks quickly because the "pathology of memory could not easily be cancelled" and because "there is no use in forcing people to agree on anything. The only way the process could have been successful and the reason that made it successful was that all the actors involved gained ownership [of] the process."[11]

State and multinational mediators, in contrast, tend to be more concerned with securing a settlement than with the process by which this is done. They regard their function as persuasion rather than facilitation and rely on the authority and muscle of the body that appointed them to press for rapid results. This invariably gives rise to perceptions of partisanship and coercion. The use or threat of sanctions or military force might compel the parties to reach a settlement, but it will be short-lived if they are not genuinely committed to it.

Less extreme versions of a peremptory approach can also have unhappy consequences, as illustrated by Kissinger's bid to broker peace in former Rhodesia. According to S. Stedman, Kissinger arrived in South Africa in April 1976 confident that his diplomatic skills and the strength of the United States would lead to success where others had failed.[12] Insisting publicly that he was merely an interlocutor and would not be prescriptive, he had in fact devised a formula for majority rule. His objective, he later revealed, was to co-opt the program of "moderate evolutionary reform" and isolate the "ideological radicals." The immediate goal was to obtain Ian Smith's approval of the plan, through various threats and promises, before the U.S. presidential election in November. The initiative was counterproductive. Kissinger's proposals emboldened the minority regime, were rejected by the liberation movements, and culminated in what his British counterparts described as a "mess."[13]

A related problem arises when international actors seek to forge a settlement among political elites without fully engaging local communities. B. Kiplagat notes the absence of public participation in the failed Ugandan peace talks of 1985 and its presence in successful peacemaking at grassroots levels in Sudan and Kenya. He describes a traditional approach to mediation through public gatherings that constitute a "community in discussion." Leaders and affected communities participate equally in the process; there is an emphasis on healing relationships rather than on bargaining; and a spiritual dimension is introduced to promote reconciliation. Community involvement puts pressure on leaders to make peace and abide by peace agreements.[14]

MEDIATORS MUST BE FLEXIBLE

Whatever the validity of general propositions on conflict, the actual dynamics of conflict differ markedly from case to case as a result of historical developments and diverse personalities, social relations, cultural perspectives, and material conditions. Because these factors are not immutable, and because conflict is an open system, its thrust and contours change over time. Mediators must therefore be sufficiently flexible to adapt their style and methods to the circumstances, the protagonists, and the evolution of the conflict. The need for flexibility is reinforced by the view that mediators should facilitate problem solving by the parties rather than craft and sell solutions to them.

The UN and regional bodies like the Organization of African Unity (OAU) lack the requisite flexibility when their mediation efforts are subject to decisionmaking by member states. S. Touval observes that intergovernmental organizations tend to adopt only those measures on which consensus is possible; that such consensus is often ambiguous, reflecting compromises based on the lowest common denominator; that decisions cannot be modified easily in response to new developments; and that the compromises and discord weaken the coherence and credibility of a mediation exercise.[15] In some instances the organization is rendered impotent by divisions within its ranks or by the formal or informal veto of a powerful state. In other cases disparate state interests within the mediating body are exploited by the disputants and have the effect of exacerbating the conflict.

The inflexibility of a multinational body can also stem from its principles. For example, a 1964 resolution of the OAU Assembly of Heads of State and Government forbids secession and irredentism, proclaiming the inviolability of African borders imposed by the colonial powers. This position derives partly from the justified concern that legitimizing the redrawing of boundaries would provoke intra- and interstate violence. Nevertheless, it offers little scope for easing the ongoing tensions induced by incongruous borders. It ignores the possibility that ethnic groups might agree to partition a state; it has precluded OAU mediation in civil wars; and it has led to the anomalous situation of OAU envoys trying to resolve a secessionist struggle while opposing the main demand of one of the protagonists, as occurred in the Comoros in 1998.[16] Arguing that the problems outlined above are inherent limitations of intergovernmental bodies, Touval concludes that the UN should refrain from mediating in complex international disputes and rather sponsor "unilateral mediation by great powers or other states who have a vested interest in conflicts within their sphere of influence."[17] This is a strange conclusion as Touval acknowledges that third-party countries may be unwilling to play that role, that disputants may be wary of such meddling, and that they sometimes choose a multilateral mediating body precisely to avoid a state mediator attempting to force on them an undesired settlement.

In many situations the better structural solution would lie in the UN Secretary-General undertaking mediation independently of the institution's deliberative organs, an option supported by Boutros Boutros-Ghali.[18] This approach would meet the dual imperatives of legitimacy and flexibility. C. R. Vance and D. R. Hamburg propose strengthening the Secretary-General's authority and capacity to utilize personal envoys, without being undermined by second-guessing from the Security Council, as a low-cost and low-risk means of averting and ending crises.[19] They note that resistance from the United States and other governments to such proposals has more to do with the politics of the Security Council than with the prevention and resolution of deadly conflict.

MEDIATORS MUST NOT APPLY PUNITIVE MEASURES

The question of punitive action requires further comment because one or more of the parties to a civil war is typically resistant to mediation and engages in conduct deemed unacceptable by the international community. In these circumstances, external actors might apply enforcement measures against the offending party. As in the case of apartheid South Africa, sanctions can help to weaken an authoritarian regime to the point that it becomes receptive to negotiating a democratic settlement. In other cases the aim might be to impel a belligerent, such as Unita, to adhere to the terms of a peace agreement it has signed.

Further comment is required also because many diplomats and scholars believe that effective international mediation depends on the political power and leverage of the mediator. Smith, citing only one successful case in support of this view, concludes that "it's therefore logical to expect that great power mediation will be generally more successful than small power mediation."[20] J. Bercovitch draws the same conclusion while making contradictory assertions about the utility of "carrots and sticks" and the noncoercive nature of mediation.[21] Touval maintains that the UN's lack of political leverage contributes to its ineffectiveness as a mediator, its threats of punishment, and promises of assistance having little credibility because it has no readily accessible military or economic resources.[22] According to Vance and Hamburg, representatives of the UN Secretary-General should be familiar with "techniques to pressure parties to negotiate (e.g., sanctions or threats of force)."[23]

This position is flawed in several respects. First, mediators can achieve a great deal where they have no formal political power and their credibility emanates instead from moral stature. Examples here include the accomplishments of the World Council of Churches and the All African Council of Churches in Sudan in 1971–1972, of San Egidio in Mozambique, and of representatives of the UN Secretary-General in a variety of conflicts.[24] Romano attributes San Egidio's achievement to the "weakness" of nongovernmental mediating bodies that lack the capacity to threaten the disputants.[25]

Second, sanctions and the threat or use of force do not easily deter groups that believe they are fighting for their survival. Punitive action may even be counterproductive. The experience of ECOMOG in Liberia illustrates how peace enforcement operations can broaden, deepen, and prolong hostilities.[26] In the case of Burundi, sanctions have undermined Tutsi confidence in reconciliation, strengthened extremist positions within the army and the minority community, and exacerbated poverty and inequality of wealth, which are counted among the root causes of the conflict.[27]

Third, general claims about the utility of leverage ignore a range of distinctions with respect to the nature, timing, and purpose of external intervention. Consider, for example, a powerful state terminating military aid to a belligerent, offering it financial inducements to abandon hostilities, attempting to bully it into peace talks through sanctions, providing resources to facilitate negotiations, and acting as a guarantor in respect of agreements reached. These interventions, all covered by the term *leverage*, have such different strategic and psychological import that it is misleading to regard them as examples of a single category. The problem is especially evident in the notion of carrots and sticks as a synonym for leverage. The idiom implies that rewards and punishment are similar or complementary strategies when it would seem to be a trite observation that people react to coercion and encouragement in manifestly dissimilar ways.

Fourth, and most important, a mediating body will almost certainly be mistrusted by a disputant against whom it threatens or applies sanctions or military force. As argued earlier in respect of Somalia, Liberia, and Burundi, it loses credibility as a peace broker and becomes a party to the conflict. This is not to say that punitive action is intrinsically invalid. Rather, the point is that where it is deemed necessary, it should be undertaken by an agency other than the mediator. G. Picco thus proposes that the UN's management of force should not lie with the Secretary-General but be subcontracted to a military alliance, as occurred in the Gulf War. This would allow the Secretary-General to play the "good cop" negotiator, with the Security Council playing "bad cop" if negotiations fail.[28]

Some division of labor is inevitable in complex intrastate conflicts because the activities associated with peacemaking are too many and too varied to be conducted by the same agency.[29] In the case of Mozambique, partisan states put pressure on their allies to engage in talks (Zimbabwe in respect of Frelimo, and Kenya in respect of Renamo); a nonpartisan religious body facilitated the talks (the Community of Sant' Egidio); powerful states provided resources and played the role of guarantor in respect of agreements reached (Italy, Portugal, the United States, and the UK); and the UN oversaw the implementation of the peace plan.

MEDIATION IS A SPECIALIST ACTIVITY

In the CCR's experience, effective mediators have a particular combination of personal traits. A high level of empathy and sensitivity is required to maintain the trust of the disputants and discern the concerns that underlie their formal demands. Mediators must also have sufficient confidence to maintain control of meetings when tempers flare and to avoid being bullied by powerful parties. At the same time, they must be able to keep their egos in check and refrain from becoming too assertive or too anxious to achieve a settlement. Flexibility and creativity are prized because conflict is dynamic and no two cases are identical. These attributes contribute to the art of mediation.

Domestic mediation can also be regarded as a professional discipline in the sense that it encompasses a body of theory, comparative research, case studies, and tested techniques. If the principles outlined above reflect the strategic dimensions of mediation, then the techniques are the tactical elements that constitute the essence of the profession. They relate to diagnosing the causes of the conflict; engaging in shuttle diplomacy where adversaries refuse to talk directly to each other; designing and convening the mediation process; setting agendas and conducting meetings; identifying common ground between the parties; and generating options for resolving deadlocks. Many of the techniques are intended to overcome the psychological barriers to effective communication and cooperative problem solving.

States and multinational bodies do not view mediation as a specialized activity, however. Major policy statements on peace and conflict by UN Secretaries-General invariably present a perspective on early warning, military deployment, and other topics but say little about mediation.[30] Whereas discussion around humanitarian aid, sanctions, and peace operations occurs within and between academic, political, and activist circles, debates on mediation are confined mainly to scholars and professional mediators; one of the debates concerns the question of professionalizing domestic mediation, but the question is not posed in respect of international mediation. In practice, the principal methods of international mediation are persuasion, bargaining, and the exercise of leverage. No clean distinction is drawn between mediation and enforcement, with the result that mediation is reduced to power-based diplomacy. It follows that international mediators are appointed on the basis of their political stature rather than their experience and competence as mediators.

It is not intended here to rarify mediation or fetishize professions. The aim is rather to highlight the emphasis that professions place on specialists' qualifications and training. Mediation of intrastate conflicts is usually undertaken in situations of imminent or actual violence where the stakes and risks are high. It seems absurd that states and intergovernmental bodies that would not deploy untrained soldiers, police, or doctors in these situations, or in any other circumstances for that matter, are willing to utilize untrained peace brokers.

Because the stature of a mediator is important in the context of intrastate crises, it is understandable that heads of state and senior diplomats are entrusted with this task. In some instances they may be effective because of their interpersonal skills and the ripeness of the conflict for resolution. Yet the success rate might be higher if the mediators were proficient in mediation techniques. African diplomats have acknowledged their lack of expertise and confidence when engaged in complex mediation, and a number of foreign affairs officials have raised the need for comprehensive training in mediation and related skills.

A structural solution to this problem might lie in establishing expert mediation units within the offices of the UN and OAU secretaries-general. As standing entities they would provide greater depth and continuity than ad hoc missions. A host of additional benefits might accrue if they operated independently of the plenary organs of the UN and the OAU: they could engage in low-profile mediation long before a conflict reaches crisis proportions and attracts the attention of the Security Council; their flexibility would not be constrained by the interests of member states; they could more easily make contact with disputants that had acquired pariah status; and their impartiality and lack of coercive power might make their efforts less threatening to the parties. The units' staff could also serve as technical advisers to the secretaries-general and to heads of state and senior diplomats engaged in high-profile mediation.

CONCLUSION

The experience of peacemaking in African civil wars suggests that international mediators are ineffective, if not counterproductive, when they deviate from the logic of mediation and apply undue pressure on the parties. Individuals and groups tend to resist coercion under most circumstances. This is especially the case where they are in conflict over issues related to freedom, justice, security, and survival. While external pressure may be unavoidable because of a disputant's intransigence or aggression, a mediator who threatens a party will lose that party's trust and inhibit the resolution of the conflict.

This is not to say that the mediators were primarily responsible for the lack of success in the cases cited above. Establishing the reasons for failure in each case would entail a more thorough investigation than has been presented in this article. In any event, even the most accomplished mediator can do little if one of the parties has no inclination to reach a settlement. Nevertheless, the more modest point is that an inexperienced mediator can blow opportunities for progress and exacerbate the conflict.

The thrust of this article is that mediators diminish the prospect of ending conflict when they deviate from the principles of mediation and are unfamiliar with its techniques. Mediation is a specialized activity that is not a mystical affair, reducible to common sense or synonymous with power-based diplomacy. Assuming good faith on the part of the mediator, strategic and tactical errors are not inevitable. The stronger conclusion, then, is that international actors should acquire greater proficiency in the art and science of mediation. This could be achieved at little expense through comprehensive training, by deploying qualified mediators alongside prominent personalities involved in peacemaking, and by establishing expert mediation units within the UN and the OAU.

NOTES

This is an abridged and revised version of a paper presented at the African Mediation Seminar, Independent Mediation Service of South Africa and Center for Conflict Resolution, Johannesburg, 3–5 November 1998.

1. Smith 1985.
2. Romano 1998, 7.
3. Howe 1996/1997; Ofuatey-Kodjoe 1994; and Nyakyi 1998.
4. Nyakyi 1998.
5. Van Eck 1997; International Crisis Group 1998; Evans 1997; and Mthembu-Salter 1998.
6. Menkhaus 1996, 59.
7. Smith 1985.

8. Hume 1994, 32–43.
9. Menkhaus 1996, 43.
10. Deng 1997; Howe 1996/1997; Ofuatey-Kodjoe 1994; Menkhaus 1996; and Stedman 1991.
11. Romano 1998, 5–7.
12. Stedman 1991.
13. Stedman 1991, 105–106.
14. Kiplagat 1988.
15. Touval 1994.
16. Organization of African Unity 1998, 11.
17. Touval 1994, 45–46.
18. Boutros-Ghali 1992.
19. Vance and Hamburg 1997.
20. Smith 1985, 367.
21. Bercovitch 1996.
22. Touval 1994.
23. Vance and Hamburg 1997, 14.
24. Assefa 1987; Romano 1998; and Rivlin and Gordenker 1993.
25. Romano 1998.
26. Nyakyi 1998; and Howe 1996/1997.
27. International Crisis Group 1998.
28. Picco 1994.
29. Mitchell 1993.
30. Boutros-Ghali 1992; and Annan 1998.

REFERENCES

Annan, K. (1998). "The Causes of Conflict and the Promotion of Durable Peace and Sustainable Development in Africa." Report of the United Nations Secretary-General to the Security Council, 16 April. New York: United Nations.

Assefa, H. (1987). *Mediation of Civil Wars: Approaches and Strategies—The Sudan Conflict*. Boulder, Colo.: Westview Press.

Bercovitch, J. (1996). "Understanding Mediation's Role in Preventive Diplomacy." *Negotiation Journal* 12, no. 3: 241–258.

Boutros-Ghali, B. (1992). *An Agenda for Peace*. New York: United Nations.

Deng, F. (1997). "Preventive Diplomacy: The Case of Sudan." *Preventive Diplomacy Series* 1. Durban: ACCORD.

Evans, G. (1997). "Responding to Crises in the African Great Lakes." *Adelphi Paper* 311. International Institute for Strategic Studies. London: Oxford University Press.

Howe, H. (1996/1997). "Lessons of Liberia: ECOMOG and Regional Peacekeeping." *International Security* 21, no. 3: 145–176.

Hume, C. (1994). *Ending Mozambique's War*. Washington. D.C.: U.S. Institute for Peace.

International Crisis Group. (1998). "Burundi Under Siege: Lift the Sanctions: Relaunch the Peace Process." *Burundi Report* 1, 28 April.

Kiplagat, B. (1988). "Is Mediation Alien to Africa?" *Track Two* 7, no. 1: 4–7. Center for Conflict Resolution, Cape Town.

Menkhaus, K. (1996). "International Peacebuilding and the Dynamics of Local and

National Reconciliation in Somalia." *International Peacekeeping* 3, no. 1: 42–67.

Mitchell, C. (1993). "The Process and Stages of Mediation: Two Sudanese Cases." In D. R. Smock, ed., *Making War and Waging Peace: Foreign Intervention in Africa*. Washington, D.C.: U.S. Institute for Peace, 139–159.

Mthembu-Salter, G. (1998). "A Policy Passed Its 'Sell-By' Date: An Assessment of Sanctions Against Burundi." Report prepared for ActionAid, December.

Nyakyi, A. (1998). Untitled paper presented at Learning from Conflict Resolution in Africa, Workshop on the Experience of Individual and Institutional Mediators, Mwalimu Nyerere Foundation and the Tanzanian Ministry of Foreign Affairs and International Cooperation, Arusha, 21–23 January.

Ofuatey-Kodjoe, W. (1994). "Regional Organisations and the Resolution of Internal Conflict: The ECOWAS Intervention in Liberia." *International Peacekeeping* 1, no. 3: 261–302.

Organization of African Unity. (1998). *Resolving Conflicts* 2, no. 4 (March–April). OAU Political Department, Addis Ababa.

Picco, G. (1994). "The UN and the Use of Force: Leave the Secretary-General Out of It." *Foreign Affairs* 73, no. 5: 14–18.

Rivlin, B., and L. Gordenker, eds. (1993). *The Challenging Role of the UN Secretary-General: Making "The Most Impossible Job in the World" Possible*. Westport, Conn.: Praeger.

Romano, A. (1998). "Peace Is Possible: Lessons from the Mozambique Peace Process." Paper presented at Learning from Conflict Resolution in Africa, Workshop on the Experience of Individual and Institutional Mediators, Mwalimu Nyerere Foundation and the Tanzanian Ministry of Foreign Affairs and International Cooperation, Arusha, 21–23 January.

Smith, W. (1985). "Effectiveness of the Biased Mediator." *Negotiation Journal* 1, no. 4: 363–371.

Stedman, S. (1991). *Peacemaking in Civil War: International Mediation in Zimbabwe, 1974–1980*. Boulder, Colo.: Lynne Rienner.

Touval, S. (1994). "Why the UN Fails." *Foreign Affairs* 73, no. 5: 44–57.

Van Eck, J. (1997). "Brokers in Burundi: Broadening the Nyerere Mediation Initiative." *Track Two* 6, no. 5: 17. Center for Conflict Resolution, Cape Town.

Vance, C. R., and D. A. Hamburg. (1997). "Pathfinders for Peace: A Report to the UN Secretary-General on the Role of Special Representatives and Personal Envoys." A report of the Carnegie Commission on Preventing Deadly Conflict, Washington, D.C.

CHAPTER 8

Monitoring

■ 8.1

Human Rights Monitoring: How to Do It and Lessons Learned

Karen Kenny

This article will focus on three issues: how to do diagnostic human rights monitoring; what lessons can be learned from human rights monitoring; and how to improve human rights monitoring in the field.

DIAGNOSTIC MONITORING

This section will focus on diagnostic monitoring, which accurately identifies what the human rights situation is and the root causes of that situation at various levels, with a view to prescribing appropriate action. We will highlight some of the professional techniques and sensitive issues that arise in carrying out effective monitoring of this kind, such as recording, cross-checking, reporting, and following-up information regarding possible violations or attempts to improve observance of human rights. The benefits of drawing on the complementary skills of field human rights partners are emphasized.

Four key principles are involved in diagnostic human rights monitoring: (1) *detail and precision* in the information collected, cross-checked, and reported; (2) *confidentiality* of information and sources (actual and perceived); (3) *objectivity and impartiality* in all aspects of field human rights work; and (4) *sensitivity to the physical and psychosocial security* of the victim-witnesses and other sources.

In general, diagnostic monitoring is carried out by establishing and maintaining contact with reliable sources of information and with alleged victims. This is followed by the corroboration and analysis of information received, which is then transmitted for reports. This process may involve several different information-gathering techniques and different types of analysis, all of which come together to present an overall picture. One reason for this variety is the range of human rights violations that exist: economic and social as well as civil and political. Also, we are usually asked to monitor the human rights situation—identifying not only violations but also attempts to improve the situation made in good faith by the host authorities.

On the basis of comprehensive, reliable information, we can identify weak links in the chain of responsibility for human rights protection and make recommendations for how to improve the situation. This analysis should form the basis of action by host authorities, civil society, international field partners, donors, and international political decisionmakers to carry out the range of activities that contribute to human rights development.

Accuracy is vital in diagnostic monitoring. The basic facts of the case/situation must be clear so that the information can be useful to you, your superiors, and especially to the host authorities in seeking corrective action. Fundamentally, accuracy is essential to ensure that recommendations and follow-up action are well targeted.

Finally, a golden rule of diagnostic monitoring is to be prompt, thorough, and impartial while protecting sources of information.

Fact-Finding: A Cornerstone of Diagnosis

The basis of all activities should be well-informed analysis. Thus, the cornerstone of human rights fieldwork is an ongoing diagnosis of where the weaknesses and strengths lie in the human rights situation, namely the human rights needs of the host society.

It is important to clarify that fact-finding is not a police investigation. Contrast what happens in the movies when detectives carry out a murder investigation with what is the normal situation facing human rights factfinders in the field. On TV there are usually many elements of information available as leads: the murder scene; the corpse; forensic evidence such as fingerprints and hair samples; powers of search and seizure; and a network of police informers.

For human rights fact-finders these types of information are not generally available. Very often we do not have speedy access to the scene of the alleged human rights violation—if at all. For example, a mass grave may remain indefinitely under the control of the alleged perpetrator (such as de facto authorities, during combat, or in a prison), where access may be refused or delayed; or the body of the alleged deceased victim has not been found and generally you have no power to compel the production of evidence, witnesses, or documents. Of course we cannot force witnesses to cooperate. We do not have a system of subpoenas at our disposal, a witness protection program offering "deals" to accomplices or informers, or the possibility of arresting suspects.

Another key difference is that, unlike the happy situation of investigations conducted by national police, we almost never have the opportunity to interview suspects. Our key interviews are with other sources of information.

These differences exist because as human rights fact-finders our function is not the same as the national police. Unlike on the national level, our witnesses may not know who we are or understand our role (we are not wearing a familiar police uniform), and often we do not have language or cultural patterns in common. Therefore, we must take care to explain a great deal more to witnesses. The reliability of an allegation may have to be assessed in the first instance on the basis of the statement of a single witness. This is why the interview with that witness may be all important. Conducting such interviews requires in-depth consideration.

Mandate

No matter what our precise function is, whether we are a UN civilian police officer, Civil Affairs representative, human rights officer, soldier, or humanitarian field officer, we are likely to undertake the following:

- Use our presence as influence, even unconsciously.
- Record information collected (see Recording, p. 205).
- Communicate the information (see Reporting and Communicating, p. 207) to our superiors and/or some of the human rights field partners.

As precise mandates will vary, we speak here in terms of generic principles. In every case, these principles will need to be adapted to the local realities and priorities determined by the types of violations of the most urgent nature.

For international organizations, a host state agreement for the mission will usually contain provisions of particular importance for the ways in which we can carry out diagnostic monitoring. Frequently it will contain guarantees of free access to any person, place, or material relating to a reported human rights violation. There may be guarantees of access for spontaneous visits to prisons, agreed terms such as access to speak to prisoners in privacy, and freedom of movement throughout the whole territory. Other terms guaranteeing a form of diplomatic immunity for human rights field officers—especially limiting the power of the host government to search or seize mission documents, offices, or residences—are also typical. When the agreement is being drafted, particular attention should be paid to terms such as these, which are necessary for the operation to effectively fulfill its human rights functions.

Identify Priorities

Traditionally, human rights fact-finders give priority to civil and political rights, such as freedom from torture or freedom of association. Some mandates, like that for the international mission in Haiti, give express priority to certain named human rights, such as freedom of expression and the right to life. Important choices may have to be made to prioritize resources. This is because, almost by definition, human rights operations take place in states with very widespread, usually systematic violations. You must identify priorities from your mandate according to the most urgent reality on the ground. Preserving life and preventing torture may be more immediate than, say, freedom of expression or freedom of assembly. Problems arise where the priorities of a human rights operation are not necessarily the same as those of the host society, which may regard other rights (food/shelter) as more urgent.

Dialogue with Host Society

The priorities should vary over time, as the priority needs of the host society vary as the situation evolves. This was a particularly cogent criticism of the UN's human rights operation in Rwanda, which had no mechanism for meaningful input from the host society on the question of what the mission's human rights priorities were to be. It thus appeared distant from some urgent human rights issues facing the population, such as the discrimination in obstacles to women's ownership of land in a country where 80 percent of the survivors of the genocide were women and dependent children who needed access to the land for survival.

Without a dialogue with the host society in whose name human rights operations are deployed, there is no guarantee that the work will evolve as needed, that it will be relevant, or that it will have a sustainable impact. The lack of methodology developed internationally and applied in fieldwork to effectively deal with economic, social, and cultural rights through techniques such as diagnostic monitoring has also been a handicap for ensuring that relevant priorities are set.

With limited resources and usually faced with daunting human rights problems, we should not spread ourselves too thin by trying to cover the entire range of human rights. We should stimulate and facilitate the local expectations, processes, and institutions that will ensure human rights improvements after we are gone. We need to prepare for that day from the outset. Hard choices will have to be made to identify priority substantive rights; once made, these should be monitored thoroughly and actively.

Draw on the Skills of Other Human Rights Partners

In this section, we are not discussing the role of human rights specialists but rather those who are specialized in other areas who have their own contribution to make as human rights actors. For instance, we may come across an incident directly or receive information regarding an alleged incident, and we will gather as much detail with as much accuracy as possible and then pass it to a specialist who knows what the legal elements of the internationally accepted definitions are. If we are not human rights specialists, legal analysis may be needed. This is where human rights field partners come in, and this is one of the reasons why it is in our interests to ensure that there is a specialist human rights monitoring component to our work— or working alongside us—whether before, during, or after hot conflict.

Thus, knowing our mandate means not only knowing the list of human rights by name (life, torture, expression, shelter, food, association, etc.) but also understanding that these are legal terms whose parameters are defined by international human rights law. For example, what does the right to a fair trial really mean, and when can the term *torture* be used? Torture applies to acute suffering (mental or physical) that is intentionally inflicted by a public official or other person acting in an official capacity (or on their instigation or with their consent or acquiescence), and which is not incidental to lawful sanctions. The legal prohibition of torture applies under any circumstances—there is never a legal justification for inflicting torture (see Article 1, Convention Against Torture and Other Cruel, Inhuman or Degrading Treatment or Punishment).

Who can commit a human rights violation? We draw on the skills of our human rights partners who know that a range of actors may be involved in violence in a host state. In the classical situation, there are armed agents of the state using violent, unilateral repression against the civilian population. However, the situations that we face may be "complex emergencies" characterized by mutually violent confrontations between the army/police and "civilians" who are, in fact, armed opposition groups or secessionist rebels. There may be violence between different sectors of the population, without any obvious involvement of the apparatus of the state, such as the police. Or, there may be violence between some or all of such groups and armed criminal gangs/private armies such as narco-traffickers. Each of these situations raises complex legal questions. Thus, the key to advancing matters beyond basic fact-finding is to draw on the complementary skills of human rights legal specialists to add to our own. Often, our role may be to act as pathfinder, to alert others to a situation or an incident, so that they can follow-up our leads. It is therefore important to be familiar with how fact-finders work.

What Is a Source of Information?

Any person with direct or indirect knowledge relevant to a specific allegation or a structural defect in human rights protection may be a source: victims-survivors, witnesses, relatives, or perpetrators. Yet it also could be a newspaper article, a radio broadcast, a nongovernmental organization (NGO), a community leader, the staff of international organizations, or sometimes officials of a local authority.

In some cases of torture, there may only be two direct witnesses: victim and perpetrator. However, even those persons who have only indirect knowledge can be very valuable sources by providing background information or leads to other sources. The general rule may seem self-evident: identify what the best possible sources are. From an initial report or rumor, try to identify eyewitnesses (from thirdhand to secondhand to firsthand— one source leading to another). Beware of simply accumulating sources at the same level because they may all be getting their information from the same source or even from each other.

The Need to Actively Seek Information

We can passively receive information by observing what happens before our eyes and also by having others approach us with information. Such passivity is inadequate to get a comprehensive picture of the human rights situation needed for a reliable diagnosis. The active approach requires the participation of human rights partners, with a special emphasis on local participation.

Even if there is a very well-developed and well-resourced network of civil society (NGOs, church groups, women's groups, lawyers, youth organizations) gathering information and providing it to you, such a network of contacts will have had to be actively established and nurtured; passivity will not create trust. Such a network is adequate only if you are sure it geographically covers the whole country, together with completely systematic coverage of all human rights substantive issues, so that priorities can be amended as the situation evolves. In addition, you must ensure that every piece of information that the network gives you has been thoroughly checked and impartially gathered in all circumstances. Thus, we need to be very active if we are to ensure that the information we work with is full, factually accurate, and politically unbiased.

Networks and credibility.   One of the keys to diagnostic monitoring is networks combined with credibility. This is because the amount and quality of information received depends a great deal on the networks of local organizations with whom we build relations of trust. Good relations must be established—especially with any local human rights, political, economic, religious, and church organizations, and cooperatives, trades unions, and hospitals—working in the area. This means actively contacting them, arranging regular meetings, and creating an active network where information and advice flow in all directions as much as possible.

Individual complaints, systematic visits, and interviews.   One method of fact-finding is to actively seek, gather, record, and analyze information on individual cases. These cases are important in and of themselves but more important for distinguishing any general patterns of human rights violations that may exist. This involves gathering statements and individual complaints.

Certain types of human rights require other fact-finding techniques such as a program of systematic visits to places where human rights violations frequently take place (or where indicators of such violations may be found) rather than merely gathering individual allegations. For example, a program of routine though preferably irregular visits may be established to monitor courts, trials, prisons, police lock-ups, hospitals, morgues, or political meetings, assemblies, and demonstrations. These visits are an important part of systematic monitoring, helping to reduce the element of chance in the information received. They may also help deter violations, although this should never be assumed.

Each type of systematic visit has its own sensitivities, and guidance through training and standard operating procedures will be necessary from management to minimize the risk of exacerbating tensions or increasing the risk of reprisals against victims, as well as using common methodology to ensure that accurate and cross-comparable information is gathered.

A key building block in any human rights monitoring is the interview. This is the method that underlies the gathering of information through individual cases; it is also often a part of systematic visits and is frequently used in cross-checking information. Here, "interviews" means any kind of oral exchange with another person, whether formal or informal. These will vary a great deal according to the kind of information to be sought, the persons to be interviewed, and the aim of the interview. The interview is central to fact-finding.

Recording.   What information is to be noted and recorded when carrying out fact-finding? Above, we illustrated what the elements of the absolutely prohibited act of torture are. Those elements tell us the kind of information that is required to allow analysts to determine what the situation is regarding torture. There are as yet no standard formats in universal use, whether for noting details of individual cases or for noting relevant information from systematic visits. The language used in recording information is important; we must always be careful to think of an alleged violation, the alleged victim, and the alleged perpetrator. This is part of the discipline of being impartial, and it also emphasizes the necessity of cross-checking all the information. Nothing should be taken at face value.

Generally speaking, records in individual cases should, as far as possible, include:

- The alleged victim's name, age, and place of residence (preferably using a case code with a separate master list of names).
- The alleged incident.
- The motivation for the alleged violation, such as being targeted because of gender, race, or political opinion.
- The context and circumstances of the alleged violation.
- The alleged perpetrators.
- The alleged action (or lack of action) by responsible authorities (police, prosecutor, tribunal).
- The sources of information and any other leads for follow-up.

Never act without cross-checking.   Take nothing on its appearance. There is one exception: act when life is at risk and when experience and common sense tell you that the allegation, such as a disappearance, may be true, but always remembering the four key principles mentioned earlier.

In seeking to check an allegation, we are seeking to corroborate (confirm) or refute (deny, rule out) the information received. In many cases we will not be able to do so, yet we will still record the allegation and factor it into our records in case information arises later that casts new light on the matter. What is sufficient or enough information in any case depends on what the aim of gathering it is. Is it for reporting? Is it to present to authorities? Is it for prosecution?

If inquiries show that there was no human rights violation, a case file may be closed. This does not mean that inquiries were fruitless. It may be that the report that was followed up was typical of the rumor in circulation. Are these deliberate attempts to create a climate of insecurity among the population? Are the rumors in fact deliberately organized to incite hatred of one group against another? Do they indicate rising tension or fear in a locality that could lead to actual rights violations unless active measures are taken to defuse the fear or tension? Throughout inquiries, improvements in respect for human rights should be verified, noted, and assessed over time.

Cross-checking the source itself.   When seeking to cross-check, three main types of information arise: witness statements; documents (death certificate, medical records, driving license, prison register); and physical material (spent bullets, gravesite, weapon, vehicle).

We need to assess the reliability of sources. Are they each related to each other, that is, are they members of the same family or political group? Do they have some kind of vested interest in the outcome of the complaint? What motivates the source to come to you? All information received, especially if provided by political parties and other groups that might attempt to use the operation as an instrument for their own ends, should be evaluated with caution. However, the mere fact that it suits a source to have you agree with the lead they give, does not mean that the information is automatically untrue. Impressions of a source's comportment must be used with caution, especially if the source is the alleged victim. Cultural differences and the effects of trauma can mislead an interviewer into thinking that the interviewee is exaggerating or is not really believable, as they do not show signs of being "upset." Detailed training should be sought on the sensitivities of interviewing.

Sometimes we will receive several secondhand allegations relating to the same apparent event. It sometimes happens that all these accounts are based on the same original (unreliable) source. Be careful to avoid seeing corroboration where there is, in fact, no independence among sources. Precautions: before contacting a possible source, consider how best to do so—whether to contact directly or indirectly.

After allegations have been followed-up.   If public officials or institutions have tried to block, hinder, or delay an inquiry, or they directly prevent cross-checking of sources, it may be reasonable for inferences regarding state involvement in, or tolerance of, violations to be drawn from that circumstance. Such inferences may be drawn to avoid a situation where authorities can avoid responsibility by simply blocking human rights inquiries. We recall here the voluntary nature of the undertakings that the host state has given in inviting/allowing the operation onto its territory— and in (probably) providing the necessary guarantees (of free movement, etc.) in the host state agreement.

Reporting and Communicating

Communication of information depends on the nature of the case and the objectives to be achieved. The information may concern serious and urgent cases, individual cases, or the general human rights situation. The nature and frequency of internal reports to the operation's headquarters or public reporting will depend on the organizational charts of management within which you work, as well as the reporting instructions contained in your mandate. Broadly, three types of reporting arise. These written communications help avoid a lack of precision or misunderstandings:

- Communicating information on serious and urgent cases for immediate action. If you are not within a specialist human rights operation, it may mean urgently communicating with field partners who are.
- Reporting on individual cases.
- A periodic report (e.g., weekly) evaluating the general human rights situation in the region/geographic area within which you work with a representative sampling of cases to illustrate trends or deep-rooted problems.

The most important reason for ensuring precision and detail is that we collect information for diagnosis and action, and the efficacy of that action depends on the quality of information. The more detailed the information, the easier will be the task of making appropriate recommendations with target dates for compliance and follow-up. For example, if the patterns of human rights violations suggest bad faith by the authorities, or they suggest lack of resources to improve the situation, different recommendations will be required.

LESSONS LEARNED FROM HUMAN RIGHTS MONITORING

A lesson is only learned once it has been effectively acted upon. Generally, internal opposition to learning processes per se is common because learning involves change. This opposition may stem from a manager's fear of being undermined, fear of failure, and so forth. There will be some inertia to be avoided and minimized. *Very few organizations reward inquiry. When was the last time anyone was promoted for asking tough questions that challenged established policies and practices?*

Debriefing of Staff Within Field Organizations

Those who have either been involved in fieldwork relating to human rights or who have spent time listening to those who have will be struck by the fact that they have learned a great deal from working in challenging environments. However, while they as individuals have learned, it is frequently the case that their organization has not. The absence of channels for feedback from staff is widely credited as a factor in staff frustration and burnout. This omission is especially serious when combined with a lack of systematic support to address cumulative and post-traumatic stress from working in dangerous or crisis environments.

Such ongoing feedback (debriefing) of field personnel is an essential step to expand the base of valid information on which decisionmaking is founded in the Office of the High Commissioner for Human Rights (OHCHR) and by others involved in fielding such operations. Instead, currently field methods evolve day by day on the ground, adjusting to the environment based on an individual staff member's capacities. Without systematic feedback from staff, each individual remains a closed learning cycle, and others outside that cycle are not benefiting from that learning. Internal feedback is not systematically gathered and woven into the evolution of doctrine and training cycles of that organization. Thus, there is an inadequate link between actual experience in the field and the content of training carried out for others, or for the organization's own staff. As such, field methods and doctrine are not continuously evolving, as new, varying, and fast-moving situations require.

The range of ways to ensure ongoing feedback from staff should be explored by field operators and tested in practice. These include addressing (1) issues of principle (such as independent debriefers); (2) procedures to ensure that representative information is received and to encourage full and frank feedback; and (3) substantive areas to cover, such as recruitment, training, administration, logistics, speed of deployment, and tasks assigned.

Debriefing Is Not Enough

Even if it were in place, systematic feedback or debriefing does not ensure learning. This becomes clear after examining the ways in which many UN agencies and other field operators manage their efforts at learning from field experience, such as UNICEF, the High Commissioner for Refugees (UNHCR), the Department of Peacekeeping Operations, the volunteer program, as well as the Organization for Security and Cooperation in Europe (OSCE) and a cross-section of NGOs.

First, broader inputs are needed. A range of sources of information must be sought out and developed, beyond the routine feedback from all staff, at headquarters and in the field. These include:

- Host society input of priorities, views, suggestions, proposals, and evaluations regarding the field operation's work. The voice of the rights-holders in whose name field operations act should be actively sought regarding ways in which the relevance, impact, and effectiveness of operations can be improved.
- Partner UN and other international agencies, such as the OSCE and the European Union (EU).

- NGOs.
- Academic research networks. Indeed, in the absence of internal channels nurturing feedback from the experience of staff, several former human rights officers have written in the academic literature, yet through this channel there still is no focal point responsible for considering the practical application of their recommendations.

Thus, debriefing will change nothing where there is no clear responsibility for ensuring learning. Although internal reviews or evaluations are now more common, alone these are not adequate. They usually lack a follow-up mechanism and independence or distance from the work being evaluated; they are not linked to individual or organizational accountability for performance; and they do not have a responsible proponent to ensure implementation of needed changes in a defined time period.

Beyond clear responsibility for learning, the proactive creation of a learning, questioning culture is needed within each organization. The effectiveness of field operations is not merely limited by financial constraints. Such limits also flow from what has been called a culture of impunity, a tendency toward defensiveness in response to criticism, an atmosphere that does not encourage creativity, initiative, or an effective auditing of the implementation of improvements.

The Need for the OHCHR to Provide Leadership in Learning

The learning units mentioned have developed in isolation from each other, and there is no cross-fertilization among them. Inputs from various human rights field presences need to be pooled. At present, this is not the case, even among operations fielded by the same organization, which results in a lack of harmonized policies, methodology, procedures, doctrines, and principles among them. Each time, the wheel is reinvented and often disimproved in the process.

Thus, beyond the individual learning needs of field operators, in the system as a whole, there is no effective guidance or leadership in the development of policies, doctrines, and field methods. For example, such pre-mission training as there is remains ad hoc, with a range of unconnected initiatives in different countries. The subjective experience of an individual trainer does not create coherent teams when these various trainees are put together to work, frequently in a crisis. Most attention is going to this most expensive and least effective type of training: that which is generic predeployment training, not mission and task specific. The fact that so many courses are now being run on a generic level gives the impression of much activity regarding training for field human rights work. More attention and more rigor is needed from funders, trainers, and the organizations intended as end-users of the trainees in evaluating the operational relevance effectiveness and impact of such training. To address this requires leadership in the system.

The human rights actor with the mandate to provide leadership as a focal point for all UN human rights activities is the OHCHR in Geneva. The High Commissioner intends to ensure leadership on the integration of human rights across the UN system, fully in keeping with the mandate she received from the General Assembly and the Vienna Declaration and Program of Action in 1993. In addition, the UN Secretary-General is committed in his Program for Reform to the integration of human rights in all UN activities. The UN's human rights work takes many forms and is spread through many agencies.

The High Commissioner has stated that:

> While I realis[e] that not all UN agencies and programmes [speak] the technical language of human rights, they all [do] work on human rights ... the United Nations, in many ways and under many names, is undertaking the difficult work to strengthen human rights and reach people in practical ways daily so as to better own their own lives.[1]

The full implications of the Secretary-General's Program for Reform have yet to be worked out in terms of what it should, or will, mean for the Office of the High Commissioner.

Establishment of a Learning Resource Center

Each field human rights actor, whether an NGO or intergovernmental organization (IGO), should consider adapting the proposals below for their work in their own organization. The approach is particularly necessary for the Office of the High Commissioner if it is to give the leadership and support required for integrating human rights in the humanitarian assistance, development, and peacekeeping work of the UN.

There is a need for a permanent, continuous learning cycle, located and managed within the OHCHR. This cycle would involve analyzing a broad range of inputs (missing "voices" such as those described above) to identify trends indicating new issues to be addressed and issues for improvement; proposing concrete solutions; pilot testing their application; following through in support of implementation; and evaluating the outcome.

The complete process should be coordinated by a single authoritative unit within the Office thereby ensuring that information is centralized; that no trends are missed; and that there is clear responsibility to ensure that the outputs are appropriately acted upon. It is proposed that a Learning Resource Center be established in the Office to carry out those tasks. The Learning Resource Center would benefit not only the Office's human rights methodology but also the clarity of its mandate, the division of labor within the Office and with other partners, as well as its administration and support and policymaking. Benefits that would assist all field actors include:

- Facilitating operational issues, including the development of standard operational procedures and ongoing testing of training content.
- Developing transparency regarding impact, benchmarks to measure success, and a focus on effectiveness rather than activity.
- Facilitating informed policymaking throughout the UN system, including, for example, the integration of human rights impact assessments into all lessons-learning practices.

The function of the Learning Resource Center should be clear: its success would be measured in increased effectiveness of the OHCHR in fulfilling its mandates and contributing to the sustainable improvement of human rights through all aspects of the Office's work. It will not produce reports or recommendations or run training workshops as ends in themselves. It would be expected to achieve change as well as developing the mechanisms to measure it.

To ensure that the output of the learning process is actually effective in achieving those improvements, the Learning Resource Center will need to have a number of features:

Credibility, authority, independence: The quality of the impact of the Learning Resource Center is a function of its credibility. This includes reporting directly to the High Commissioner, clearly working with her authority, and providing input directly into policy discussion. Here, states have an important role in contributing to the Learning Resource Center's authority. Several learning units have emphasized that they did not wish for more resources but rather wished that responsible member states, including donors, would discuss the application of their recommendations when meeting senior management responsible for implementation, and ask, "What has been done about this?"

Five steps: The learning process has five essential steps: information (voices), analysis, output, validation, and evaluation. The process of learning would be daily, continuous, and the concern of all staff. Routine information flows from staff are emphasized, as well as the need to be proactive in building relationships with external sources such as NGOs and academic networks specializing in the areas of human rights work. The adaptation of effective participation methods from the field of development is needed to ensure meaningful host society input at all stages.

Pool learning with others systemwide: An effective learning cycle is not only essential for the OHCHR's own credibility. As yet, where several units are examining learning from the same country situation or the same issue, they do not pool experience or lessons to be learned. Nor is the human rights framework of UN work typically understood in the lessons-learning processes concerning, for example, military peacekeeping, as illustrated by the 1998 review by the United Nations Department of Peacekeeping Operations Lessons Learning Unit of the United Nations Transitional Authority in Eastern Slavonia. In the case of humanitarian aid, even where a crisis is quite clearly a human rights crisis, evaluations are frequently approached without that framework. The Learning Resource Center would, as its name implies, be a resource for learning units systemwide, from the United Nations Development Programme to the Department of Peacekeeping Operations, providing both the stimulus and the resources such as a mobile team of facilitators to encourage the process. The Learning Resource Center would be the central location for these other units to address in order to pool human rights experience for the benefit of that Office, and the UN generally.

The potential inherent in the UN Secretary-General's commitment to integrate human rights throughout the activities of the UN is such that it should *transform* the way all UN agencies and bodies work—whether relief aid, development, police, military, or human rights specialists. In addition, it should greatly enhance the coherence of these actors working together. Supporting the integration of human rights across the UN system should be a core function of the OHCHR.

Beyond the UN system, other obvious potential beneficiaries of the work of the Learning Resource Center are regional IGOs fielding peace support operations, including the Organization of American States, the EU, the OSCE, and the Organization of African Unity; as well as field NGOs. There is a general need to develop a stronger human rights framework for such work, and it is increasingly understood that common challenges are being faced by the several organizations involved in mandating, fielding, or funding human rights operations. There is a need to pool common experience and contribute to better practices in areas such as training, coordination from the field to headquarters levels, and in national administrations. Such regional bodies should be encouraged to be actively involved by providing inputs and validating outputs of the Learning Resource Center. In turn, the Learning Resource Center should facilitate common mutual training to help rationalize scarce resources and maximize coherent actions once in the field.

CONCLUSION

Often the urgency and scale of human rights problems in the field seem daunting. It has been suggested that the OHCHR is like a forester, so overwhelmed by the number of trees he feels he has to cut down that he does not take time to stop and sharpen his axe, nor to reflect on whether he really should be cutting that tree or indeed whether he is working in the right forest. It is not easy to learn in such circumstances, yet one thing is clear: learning is not merely an option, but an imperative. There is real enthusiasm for the direction of these proposals and clear commitment to give the needed political and financial support to the High Commissioner in implementing them.

NOTES

The author gives permission to reproduce this article, provided that the source is fully acknowledged.

1. For the OHCHR, see http://www.unhchr.ch/html. The quote from the HCHR is from the statement by Mary Robinson, UN High Commissioner for Human Rights, to the Third Committee of the General Assembly, New York, 14 November 1997. On the Program for Reform, see UN Doc. A/RES/52/12, 12 November 1997; and UN Doc. A/52/L.72/Rev.1, 19 December 1997.

REFERENCES

The concepts expressed in this article are discussed in more detail in the following publications of the International Human Rights Trust (IHRT), which may be contacted at kkenny@compuserve.com: "Learning to Integrate Human Rights," a report of IHRT, 1999; and Karen Kenny, "Towards a Human Rights Partnership for Effective Field Work," a policy discussion paper, 1998; for background and a bibliography, see Karen Kenny, *Towards Effective Training for Field Human Rights Tasks: Recommending an Ongoing International Process to Codify Best Field Practice*, Nottingham, England: International Human Rights Trust, 1996.

Texts of international human rights treaties and other relevant links can be found at www.un.org.

Samples of Guidance Developed by a Broad Range of Actors

International Commission of Jurists. (n.d.). "A Note on the Right to a Fair Trial." Trial observation sheet, Geneva.

"Principles on the Effective Prevention and Investigation of Extralegal, Arbitrary, and Summary Executions." (1989). *UN New York* (24 May).

"Methods of Work of the Working Group on Involuntary Disappearances." (1995). United Nations Center for Human Rights, now the Office of the High Commissioner for Human Rights, UN, 1211 Geneva 10, Switzerland. Fax: 41 22 9170123 (1993).

"Cooperation Between Non-government Organizations and the International Criminal Tribunal for the Former Yugoslavia." *ICTY.* Office of the Prosecutor, The Hague, 25 September.

Books

Blewitt, Graham T. (1996). "The Relationship Between NGOs and the International Criminal Tribunals." In Médecins Sans Frontières, *Conference on Co-operation Between Humanitarian Organisations and Human Rights Organisations*. Final report of the conference held in Amsterdam, the Netherlands, 9 February; plenary discussion; minutes of Working Groups 1, 2, and 3, "Collecting, Sharing, and Passing Information on Violations of Human Rights Law and Humanitarian Law: How Could the System Work?"

Evidence and Casework Skills, Inns of Court School of Law (The Council of Legal Education). (1993–1994). England: Blackstone Press.

Guidelines for the Conduct of UN Inquiries into Allegations of Massacres. (1995). Sales no. E.DPI/1710 (includes the "Minnesota protocol"). New York: UN Office of Legal Affairs.

Methods of Work of the Special Rapporteur on Torture. (1994). Geneva: UN. E/CN.4/1994/31.

Methods of Work of the Special Rapporteur on Summary, Arbitrary or Extra-judicial Executions. (1990). Human rights fact sheet no. 11. Geneva: UN Center for Human Rights.

Methods of Work of the Working Group on Arbitrary Detention as of December 1993. (1994). Geneva: UN. E/CN.4/1994/27.

Thoolen, Hans, and Bert Verstappen. (1986). *Human Rights Missions: A Study of the Fact-Finding Practice of Non-Governmental Organisations*. Dordrecht: Martinus Nijhoff Publishers/Netherlands Institute of Human Rights.

Articles

Franck, Thomas M., and H. Scott Fairley. (1980). "Procedural Due Process in Human Rights Fact-Finding by International Agencies." *American Journal of International Law* (April): 308–345.

Kenny, Karen E. (1995). "Formal and Informal Innovations in the United Nations Protection of Human Rights: The Special Rapporteur on the Former Yugoslavia." *Austrian Journal of Public and International Law* 48: 19–77.

Monitoring Democratic Transitions

Luc Reychler

The power of a state is invaluable when contained democratically. If not, it always carries the risk of catastrophe. Democracy is a prime peacebuilder and an effective confidence-building measure. A study of 233 internal conflicts in the world found that democracies had a far better record for handling internal conflicts peacefully than alternative systems. The fact that democracies are far less likely to go to war with each other lends support to the relationship between democracy and violent conflict. Authoritarian or totalitarian regimes tend to try to deal with conflicts by ignoring or denying them, by suppressing or attempting to eliminate them. Authoritarian systems can present the illusion of short-term stability, but they are unlikely to be sustainable over the long term.[1]

The transition, however, from a nondemocratic to a consolidated democratic environment is not without difficulties. There are successes but also a considerable number of failures. The international community has taken this message seriously, and much effort is being put into supporting the transition to democracy in nondemocratic countries.

The suffering that people can experience during the transition period can be so negative that they wish it never happened. The growing awareness that democratization tends to be not a smooth ride but a rough journey has led researchers and practitioners to look for ways to increase the chances of a successful transition process.

CONTENDING DEFINITIONS OF DEMOCRACY

A systematic monitoring of democratic transition requires consensus about what democracy is all about and a good set of monitoring instruments. *Democracy* remains a contested term. The dispute over the operational definition influences the transformation process to a large extent. The differences in the discourse about democracy can be depicted along four dimensions: broad, multidimensional, continuum, and international.

In contrast to the *broad* definition of democracy, the *narrow* definition lacks depth and breadth and tends to focus on the formal building stones of democracy while paying less attention to the substantive democracy.[2] It also has a tendency to reduce democracy to a limited number of building blocks that make up a genuine democracy.

The second dimension of the discourse on democracy relates to the *uni-* or *multidimensional* nature. In multidimensional discourse, one does also not accept the separation of the political system from the social order or the functional autonomy of the political, social, and economic spheres. In the absence of progressive social reform, the term *democracy* is considered devoid of content.

The third dimension in the democratic discourse concerns the treatment of democracy as *dichotomous* or as something that could vary on a *continuum.* It may be convenient to divide the world into democracies and nondemocracies or, as during the Cold War, into communist, authoritarian, and democratic states. But from an analytical point of view, these simple classifications should be rejected because they hide the real shades of difference and the mixed systems that share features of both.

The last dimension, *internal,* on which differences in the democratic discourse can be depicted, relates to the system level at which the democracy building is aimed. Most of the attention and investments in democracy building (with the exception of the European Union) are focused on the national and subnational levels. The discourse about the democratization of the *international* system remains a taboo and nonstarter in international discourse.

ASSESSING DEMOCRATIC PROGRESS

How can one assess the impact of the democratization efforts on the democratic transition process and on the establishment of a stable/sustainable democracy? A democracy audit could focus on the outcome and/or the process.

Outcome

Overall outcome: from undemocratic to consolidated democracy. Democratization efforts can end up with nondemocratic or pseudo-democratic regimes; they can be halted in the course of the development and get into an impasse; they can involve considerable violence and a deterioration of the economic security of the people. Responding to this, researchers have been trying to map transition dynamics to get a better insight into them. Three phases are being distinguished:

- *Liberalization:* the authoritarian elite relaxes its grip, allowing the opposition to organize.

- *Transition:* the old regime is dismantled, a new system of government is agreed upon, and founding elections are held.
- *Consolidation:* all actors become used to the new democracy and accept it as the only game in town. The degree of consolidation can be assessed by looking at three types of indicators. Behaviorally, a democracy is consolidated when no significant national, social, economic, political, or institutional actors spend resources attempting to achieve their objectives by creating a nondemocratic regime or by seceding from the state. Attitudinally, a democratic regime is consolidated when a strong majority of public opinion, even in the midst of major economic problems and deep dissatisfaction with incumbents, holds the belief that democratic procedures and institutions are the most appropriate way to govern collective life and when support for the antisystem alternatives is quite small or is more or less isolated from pro-democratic forces. Constitutionally, a democratic regime is consolidated when governmental and nongovernmental forces alike become subject to, as well as accustomed to, the resolution of conflict within the bounds of specific laws, procedures, and institutions that are sanctioned by the new democratic process.[3]

The successful installation of the building blocks. A review of the literature concerning the main building blocks of democracy indicates that there is no consensus but a considerable convergence of opinion. A preliminary synthesis of the major building blocks of democracy can be found in the following list for depicting the democracy profile of a country or region.

1. Free and fair elections.
2. Separation of powers.
3. Open and accountable government.
4. Decentralization.
5. Appropriate power-sharing arrangement.
6. Human rights.
7. Civil society.
8. Rule of law.
9. Good governance.
10. Inclusive citizenship and participation.

Transition Process

Despite the fact that democratization has become a credo in diplomatic discourse, transition efforts have not always led to the installation of democratic regimes. The devil is in the transition. The democratic transition can be mapped by looking at different transition roads and factors influencing the transition process and outcome.

Different transition roads. Democratization is not an either-or, unilinear, and inevitable progression toward a Western-style democracy but a continuum of regimes situated between authoritarianism and democracy, with multiple starting points, multiple routes to get there, and a variety of democratic endpoints. Serious efforts are needed to develop more sophisticated analytical frameworks and policies to deal with these complexities. The various roads to democracy can be described as follows: (1) the transition can be violent or peaceful; (2) it can take a very long or a relatively short time; (3) the interaction between the incumbent group and the opposition can be conflictual or characterized by cooperation (compromise or intense negotiations); (4) the transition can be gradual or abrupt; (5) it can be progressive or characterized by impasses, ruptures, ups and downs, or by a one-way regression; (6) it can be accompanied by a successful or not so successful economic transition and development; and (7) the transition can be predominantly influenced by internal or external factors.

The factors influencing the transition process and the outcome. Several factors influence the process and the outcome of the democratization efforts. Some of the most important internal political variables are the preceding regime; the elite base; the actors who start and control the process; the missing players; the civil-military relations; responsiveness to the mass public; the leadership of the principal actors; and the role of spoilers and supporters.

The democratic transition is also significantly influenced by four democratic support systems: the resolution of ethnic conflict, the socioeconomic environment, the political-cultural context, and the objective and subjective security. The most important external factors include international security, the moral-political climate, foreign intervention, and the role of transnational civil society.

CONCLUSION

If recent developments are any guide, the period of quick and easy gains for democracy is over. We seem to have entered a long period of considerable regime instability. The new democracies are now facing the more difficult challenge of building solid democratic institutions and developing a democratic culture. Most countries will probably make incremental progress toward consolidation, others will continue to regress or perform very poorly, and some will break down. Although it is good to provide further international assistance to foster and consolidate democracy, it should be clear that the installation of an internal democracy does not necessarily guarantee a high-quality society.[4] More and other efforts at different levels are needed. No democracy can assure successful entrepreneurs, skillful bankers, creative scientists, good physicians, fine artists, honest judges, or a free and fair international trading system or a secure international environment. Despite the limits of democratization, consolidating the third wave democracies remains one of the major challenges for building a stable and secure international environment. The greatest challenge of the twenty-first century will be to integrate whole regions democratically and to initiate the democratic transition of the world order.

NOTES

Excerpted from Luc Reychler, *Democratic Peacebuilding: The Devil Is in the Transition* (Leuven, Belgium: Leuven University Press, 1999).

1. P. Harris and B. Reilly, eds., *Democracy and Deep-Rooted Conflict: Options for Negotiators* (Stockholm: International Institute for Democracy and Electoral Assistance, 1998).

2. For a distinction between formal and substantive components of democracy, see Mary Kaldor and Ivan Vejvoda, *Democratization in Central and Eastern European Countries* (Sussex: European Institute, September 1996).

3. J. Linz and A. Stepan, "Toward Consolidated Democracies." In Larry Diamond et al., eds., *Consolidating the Third Wave Democracies: Themes and Perspectives* (Baltimore: John Hopkins University Press, 1997), 16.

4. Ibid., 30–31.

SUGGESTED READING

Beetham, David , ed. (1994). *Defining and Measuring Democracy.* London: Sage.

Beetham, David, and Keven Boyle. (1995). *Introducing Democracy: Eighty Questions and Answers.* Cambridge: Polity Press/UNESCO.

Dahl, Robert A. (1998). *On Democracy.* New Haven, Conn.: Yale University Press.

Diamond, Larry, and Marc F. Plattner. (1999). *Democratization in Africa.* Baltimore: Johns Hopkins University Press.

Diamond, Larry, et al., eds. (1997). *Consolidating the Third Wave Democracies.* Vol. 1, *Themes and Perspectives.* Vol. 2, *Regional Challenges.* Baltimore: Johns Hopkins University Press.

Di Palma, Guiseppe. (1990). *To Craft Democracies: An Essay on Democratic Transitions.* Berkeley: University of California Press.

LeDuc, Lawrence, Richard G. Niemi, and Pippa Norris, eds. (1996). *Comparing Democracies: Elections and Voting in Global Perspective.* London: Sage.

O'Donnell, G., and P. Schmitter. (1995). "Transitions from Authoritarian Rule: Tentative Conclusions About Uncertain Democracies." In Neil J. Kritz, ed., *Transitional Justice: How Emerging Democracies Reckon with Former Regimes.* Washington, D.C.: United States Institute of Peace.

Norris, Pippa, ed. (1999). *Critical Citizens: Global Support for Democratic Governance*. London: Oxford University Press.

Reynold, Andrew, and Ben Reilly, eds. (1997). *The International IDEA Handbook of Electoral Systems Design*. Stockholm: International IDEA.

Sisk, Timothy D. (1996). *Power Sharing and International Mediation in Ethnic Conflicts*. Washington, D.C.: USIP.

Sisk, Timothy D., and Andrew Reynolds, eds. (1998). *Elections and Conflict Management in Africa*. Washington, D.C.: USIP.

Election Monitoring

Patrick Vander Weyden

International election monitoring takes place when noncompetitive political systems (after a period of dictatorship or civil war) convert into competitive political systems. The international community, in particular the European Union (EU), the United Nations (UN), and the Organization for Security and Cooperation in Europe (OSCE), is often invited to observe the first democratic election process. The aim of an election-monitoring mission is to judge the "free and fair" character of an election process.

According to most current typologies, two types of election monitoring can be identified: short-term and long-term observation. Short-term observation usually refers to the observation activities on election day and a part of the counting process. Long-term observation implies an involvement of several months by the observers who are to monitor the entire election process[1]: registration of voters and political parties/candidates, the campaigning period, the voting and counting process, and the installation of the elected bodies.

There is a general consensus that long-term observation is preferable to short-term observation. Indeed, the potency of manipulation and fraud is even more plausible in the phases before election day than on election day itself. However, international public opinion leaders are often only interested in the latter. Nevertheless, the registration of voters and political parties and the campaigning period are crucial steps for free and fair elections. But the counting process, immediately after election day, is very important, too, and often offers opportunities to manipulate the election results. Still, the international community opts for a combination of a limited number of long-term observers and a greater number of short-term observers because of financial and logistical reasons. The basic requirements for effective monitoring are:

- Excellent knowledge of the electoral law of the guest country. The electoral law(s) should be the basic document for the evaluation of the election process.
- Act according to the code of conduct and carry out tasks, respecting the instructions of the international organization in charge of the observation mission.

- Language skills and knowledge of the observation mission, common sense, empathy, and self-control.[2]

This article can be of use for people involved in setting up observation missions. The underlying idea is that the observers' professionalism will arise from the professionalization of the management of monitoring missions.

Election monitoring can be improved if more attention is paid to evaluation of the electoral law and the support for the election process; knowledge of the electoral regulations; the problem of reporting; the deployment (within the country) of the observers and the observation period; the monitoring problem of the counting process; and postelection monitoring.

EVALUATION OF THE ELECTORAL LAW AND THE SUPPORT FOR AN ELECTION PROCESS

Electoral law usually includes the rules with regard to the different phases of the election cycles: appointment of electoral commissioners, registration of voters and candidates, campaigning, the electoral system, polling stations, the counting process, and so forth. Electoral regulations can be taken up in a range of sources—constitutional law, electoral law(s), and rules and regulations of the national election commissions. It is preferable that these regulations are included as much as possible in the constitutional or electoral law(s), and that administrative bodies, such as election commissions, only deal with administrative procedures.

When fundamental rules are not included in the electoral law, this can cause serious problems. We can illustrate this with an example from the last general elections in Cambodia in 1998. It was stated in the electoral law that the electoral formula (which translates votes into seats) must be a formula of proportional representation. However, the particular kind of formula was not specified in the electoral law and was consequently subject to the national election commission's interpretation. One month before the elections, the commission decided to opt for the D'Hondt method of division.[3] However, the commission did not proceed very carefully and did not produce a full example of a D'Hondt divisor method. The result was that after the elections, the parties from the opposition and the leading government party were using different formulas. This led to a chaotic postelection period, as most parties did not want to accept the results of the elections.

Before the international community decides on participating in an election-monitoring mission, it should carefully evaluate the electoral laws in order to judge the probability of a free and fair election process. At this stage, specialists in electoral laws must be involved. On the basis of their analysis of the strong and weak points in the electoral legislation, the international community should be able to decide whether to participate. Their report should be public so that improvements and amendments can be suggested and integrated.[4]

Finally, a needs assessment must be organized before making a decision on participation in a mission. This study should show the extent of support for the elections and the electoral law by a given country's population and leaders of political parties and civil society.

Such studies must be conducted professionally and independently—and preferably not by private consultants who may have financial interests in the organization of an election observation mission.

KNOWLEDGE OF THE ELECTORAL REGULATIONS

Once the international community decides to observe the electoral process, long-term observers are sent out. Their most important task is to judge the process in the context of the electoral law. That is why they need to have an excellent knowledge of the regulations at hand.

Each mission should start with an extensive briefing on the electoral law.[5] We regret that, too often, too little attention is paid to the transfer of this specific kind of knowledge to the observers.[6] This briefing should be taken care of by a team of specialists. The aim of the briefing is to familiarize the observers with the electoral law of the guest country so that they consider the latter, and no longer their home country's electoral law, as a norm.

THE PROBLEM OF REPORTING

A lot of mistakes are made during reporting. In general, the reporting techniques differ for the voting and counting process (done by short-term observers) on the one hand and for the other steps in the electoral process (done by long-term observers) on the other hand. The long-term observers' reports are very often open reports (with open questions)—without clear instructions on how to make an analysis of the situation. The short-term observers' reports are mostly based on questionnaires (yes/no questions, scaling methods).

In general, too little attention is given to the formulation of the questionnaires and to the way the observers should handle these. This is profoundly regretted. There is a close link between the reporting methods used by the observers in the field and the validity of the analysis of the questionnaires by the statisticians at headquarters. As far as I know, up to today, in none of the missions were observers intensively and explicitly trained in filling out the questionnaires. Consequently it should be no surprise that the observers, who come from a variety of countries, interpret the questions in the questionnaires in a variety of ways and that observers' influence/interpretation can appear in the statistical analyses. This cannot be our intention. If the international community wants to come to a valid conclusion on the basis of the observers' reports, all observers must observe univocally.

Some would argue that looking at the election process from different angles leads to statistically valid observation results, but I do not agree. It is useless to observe ten polling stations from an Indian point of view and another ten polling stations from a Belgian point of view. The questionnaires should be made in such a way that Belgian, Indian, British, German, Swedish, American, and other observers interpret and fill out the questionnaires in the same way. This is only possible with closed questionnaires (yes/no questions, scaling methods), with some room for personal comments and interpretations (open questions).

Of course, the observers must be briefed on how to interpret and fill in the questionnaires. At headquarters, more attention must be paid to the way in which the questionnaires are drawn up. Still too often questionnaires are drafted only a few days before the observers' arrival in the host country. Moreover, questionnaires must be tested. This can be done by organizing simulated voting and counting processes.

The same logic applies to the reporting by the long-term observers. Coordinators and analysts from headquarters must train the long-term observers on reporting techniques and on the main reporting elements. Reporting is the observers' main task. That is why headquarters should get more involved than it is today. Qualitative reporting includes the following criteria:

- Clear and tested questionnaires.
- Extensive training on interpreting and filling out the questionnaires.
- All observers must interpret and fill out the questionnaires in the same way.
- The reports of long-term observers must be standardized, too. A separate section for personal interpretations and comments can be attached.
- The analytical unit within the mission should be responsible for the development of the questionnaires in cooperation with the electoral specialists and the head of mission.

PROBLEM OF DEPLOYMENT

Deployment entails the spread of observers throughout the country and the selection of polling and counting stations. In most missions, security reasons are the main criterion for deciding the appointment of observer teams to polling stations. In dangerous areas, relatively few observers are appointed.

The ideal situation is, of course, one observer in one polling or counting station. For financial and logistical motives, though, this cannot be realized. In Russia, for instance, there are more than 10,000 polling stations. But in the 1997 and 1998 elections in Bosnia-Herzegovina, the OSCE did, however, appoint one supervisor to one polling station with a mandate to control the entire voting and counting process from the opening of the polling station until the completion of the counting forms.[7]

In most missions a selection of polling station must be made, preferably in a statistically relevant manner. To do this and to determine how long one observer must be present in a polling station, there should be a close cooperation between analysts/statisticians on the one hand and other personnel (logisticians, security staff) on the other. Obviously, the better the deployment of the observers, the more representative will be their observation reports.

OBSERVATION OF THE COUNTING PROCESS

The counting process is one of the most crucial steps in the election process. Because of media pressure, international organizations are compelled to issue a statement immediately after the closing of the polling stations. Often, the observation reports on counting are neglected. The counting procedure is considered to be of minor importance, because counting is often a long and boring process that can last until late in the morning of the next day. In 1996, during the Palestinian elections, some of the short-term observers, who were operating under the umbrella of the EU, had to take their plane back to Europe in the early morning of the day after the election. Some of them were more worried about packing their luggage than observing the counting process.

It is essential that observers monitor a counting station from the first voter until the conclusion of the counting process. The elections in Bosnia-Herzegovina were a positive example, with the supervisors present during the entire voting and counting process in one and the same polling and counting station. Of course, the role of "standard" observers is different—but at least, in order to monitor possible fraud, they should receive a copy of the official results of the counting station they observed.

POSTELECTION MONITORING

After votes are counted and translated into individual parliamentary seats, parliamentary work starts. If one party receives a majority of the seats, a government can easily be installed. When two or more parties are necessary to form a government, coalition talks will follow the election process. The aftermath of the election process can vary from an easy and smooth event to a complex yet crucial process. Because elections may result in losers and winners, the first step is that political parties accept the results and do not use other than peaceful political means to support or oppose the government.

A smaller group of highly qualified observers should be responsible for observing the postelection process, which mainly implies (1) the observation of the inauguration of parliament, (2) the formation of a government, and in the long run, (3) the functioning of parliament and government. In most missions, headquarters observes the first two steps. Parliamentary and governmental work during the first legislature does not get sufficient attention—despite the fact that the political dynamics after a first competitive election have a major impact on the democratic successfulness of a later competitive election. For that reason, a very small team of observers should remain in the country until the second election. Their main tasks should consist of observing the relations between parliament and government and the competitive relations between political parties. The denser their network in state organizations and civil society, the more successful they will be in their activities.

NOTES

1. The entire election process comprises different steps, beginning with the proclamation of the elections, the creation of the election law, and the appointment of a national (and/or regional and/or local) electoral commission.

2. Such skills seem obvious. However, reality is that some observers have participated in a mission without, for instance, understanding the mission language. Fortunately, we can now take that up in their training. In addition to that, although to a lesser extent, the selection of international observers has been improved and professionalized in the past couple of years.

3. According to the D'Hondt system, "seats are awarded sequentially to parties having the highest 'average' numbers of votes per seat until all seats are allocated. Each time a party receives a seat, its 'average' goes down. These 'averages' are not the averages as they are normally defined but depend on the given set of divisors that a particular divisor system describes. The D'Hondt formula uses the whole numbers 1, 2, 3, 4 and so on" (Lijphart 1994, 153).

4. For a detailed checklist of electoral legislation, we refer to the excellent ACE (Administration and Cost of Elections) project produced by the International Institute for Democracy and Electoral Assistance (IDEA), the International Foundation for Election Systems, and the United Nations.

5. Short-term observers need to be briefed, especially on the voting and counting procedures.

6. Especially those long-term-observers, who have extensive Third World experience but who are not always acquainted with electoral processes, should be briefed intensively.

7. In this article, we only described the tasks of observers and not of supervisors. The main difference between the two is that observers may only observe the electoral process whereas supervisors are allowed to intervene in that process.

REFERENCES

Carothers, Thomas. (1997). "The Rise of Election Monitoring: The Observers Observed." *Journal of Democracy* 8, no. 3: 17–31.

European Union Observation Unit in Cambodia. (1998). *Observer Manual.*

Hendrick, Diane Theresa. (1997). *Report on the Training Programme for Election Observation Action Managers.* Stadtschlaining: Austrian Study Center for Peace and Conflict Resolution.

Lijphart, Arend. (1994). *Electoral Systems and Party Systems: A Study of Twenty-Seven Democracies 1945–1990.* Oxford: Oxford University Press.

OSCE/ODIHR. (1997). *Election Observation Handbook.* Warsaw: OSCE.

Smeets, Hans, and Janet Exel. (1997). *The 1996 Bosnia-Herzegovina Elections: An Analysis of the Observations.* Dordrecht: Kluwer Academic Publishers.

SUGGESTED READING

Baxter, Joe. (1994). "Techniques to Effective Election Management." Paper presented at the African election administration colloquium, Victoria Falls, Zimbabwe, 15–18 November.

Dupont, Patrick. (1998). *Policy of Donor Countries Regarding International Electoral Administration.* Antwerp: Center for Development Studies.

Elklit, Jorgen, ed. (1997). *Electoral Systems for Emerging Democracies: Experiences and Suggestions.* Copenhagen: Ministry of Foreign Affairs.

Elklit, Jorgen, and Palle Svensson. (1997). "What Makes Elections Free and Fair." *Journal of Democracy* 8, no. 3: 32–46.

Electoral Monitoring and Electoral Systems: A Brief Guide. (1994). Brussels: Friedrich Naumann Stiftung.

Gould, Ron. (1994). *Reference Guide for Election Observers.* Ottawa: Commonwealth Parliamentary Association.

Hanf, Theodor, et al. (1995). *Observing Democratic Elections: A European Approach.* Freiburg: Arnold Bergstraesser Institut.

International IDEA. (1998). *Guidelines for Determining Involvement in International Electoral Observation.*

———. (1999). *The Future of Elections Observation: Lessons Learned and Recommendations.* Future of Elections Observation conference, Copenhagen, 26–27 October 1998.

Nevitte, Neil, and Santiago A. Canton. (1997). "The Role of Domestic Observers." *Journal of Democracy* 8, no. 3: 47–61.

OSCE Office for Democratic Institutions and Human Rights. (1998). *The OSCE/ODIHR Election Observation Handbook.*

United Nations Center for Human Rights. (1994). *Human Rights and Elections; A Handbook on the Legal, Technical and Human Rights Aspects of Elections.* Professional training series no. 2.

Monitoring Minority Conflicts: The Role of the OSCE High Commissioner on National Minorities

H. Gajus Scheltema

THE ESTABLISHMENT OF THE INSTITUTE

The rapid change that the Organization for Security and Cooperation in Europe (OSCE) went through in the early 1990s after the collapse of the Berlin Wall and the subsequent revolutions on the European continent resulted in a thorough reappraisal of this forum at the Helsinki meeting of 1992. What had until then been largely a process of negotiating between two blocs, a reflection of the status quo during the Cold War, was increasingly resembling an organization aimed at conflict prevention in the broadest sense of the word.

The radical turnovers in that period posed two challenges for the OSCE. On the one hand, the iron division of the continent had disappeared, creating previously unheard of possibilities for cooperation. On the other hand, the traditional balance of power had made way for new dangers: small-scale conflicts caused by emerging nationalist tendencies, regional old sores that had lain hidden for decades under communism (including those relating to national minorities), and new demarcation lines that emerged as genuine borders through the disintegration of a number of states (the Soviet Union, Czechoslovakia, Yugoslavia).

The response formulated by the member states of the OSCE at the Helsinki meeting was threefold. First, existing forums and institutions were strengthened and new ones created, with the purpose of developing an adequate consultative and decisionmaking structure for addressing the new challenges. Second, a separate chapter of the final act was devoted to early warning, conflict prevention, and crisis management (including peacekeeping) in which new decisionmaking mechanisms were developed. By means of the aforementioned concepts, different phases of the crisis spectrum were distinguished, including the smoldering initial phase, which was referred to as "early warning." Finally, the meeting decided to appoint a High Commissioner on National Minorities (HCNM).

Developments in the previous years had shown that ethnic conflicts often lay at the heart of the tensions that had manifested in Europe after 1989. As early as June 1990, at the OSCE conference in Copenhagen, it was recognized and even emphasized that, with regard to the human dimension, minority issues were of immediate relevance to international peace and security. Nevertheless, it took a while before this recognition was translated into an institutional response. This response was finally formulated by the then Dutch minister of foreign affairs, Hans van den Broek, at Helsinki.

Although the idea of charging an international figure with minority issues was not new, it was first presented in detail during the follow-up meeting in Helsinki (March–July 1992). The experiences of a disintegrating Yugoslavia and ensuing tensions in the region, combined with fears that such ethnically based tensions might also emerge elsewhere in Europe, provided ample rationale for the proposal and contributed to its eventual adoption. This experience reconfirmed yet again that if the international community wished to play an effective role in controlling interethnic tensions, an instrument needed to be developed that would allow one to gain greater insight into and understanding of the complex reality of contemporary Europe. Such an instrument would have to negotiate independently, impartially, and authoritatively between the parties involved in a smoldering conflict and try to defuse potentially dangerous situations before tensions ran too high.

Although the above needs were generally recognized, not all countries agreed with the Dutch proposal for a mandate. Some pointed at problems relating to definitions, others denied that there were ethnic minorities on their territory, and others argued about the notions of collective versus individual minority rights. A number of nations (Hungary, Albania, Russia) had special historical links with minorities in neighboring states (so-called kin states), while others feared that the establishment of a special institution would draw more attention to the issue than was desirable, which would only aggravate the situation. In addition, there was the question of the use of violence (terrorism).

These and other objections resulted in a text that inevitably resembled a compromise, although the original proposal as a whole did remain intact. Consequently, the mandate could be defined in the decisionmaking documents of the aforementioned Helsinki meeting of July 10, 1992; at the end of that same year, the former Dutch minister of foreign affairs, Max van der Stoel, was appointed as the first High Commissioner.

THE MANDATE

The mandate of the HCNM added a previously unknown dimension to the right to intervene in the domestic affairs of participating states. Save for a few exceptions, the mandate entitled international institutions to visit a country uninvited by the nation concerned or the OSCE in order to check the conditions of a minority or minorities living there. The HCNM may decide independently whether to get involved in a minority issue. As such, he is able to intervene early on, in a discreet and constructive fashion, when a minority issue has given rise to tension and is threatening to escalate to a full-blown conflict. Besides unearthing the roots of these tensions, the HCNM may also play an active role by promoting dialogue, trust, and cooperation between all parties involved. However, if a situation were to deteriorate despite these efforts, he would have to inform the OSCE (the former warning function in the formal sense, to be distinguished from the aforementioned early warning as a phase in a conflict).

Despite the significant degree of autonomy, the mandate also determines the limits of intervention. First and foremost, the HCNM should only get involved in minority issues if these carry in them a risk of escalation. This has meant in practice that, though not a fixed rule, most minority issues in Western Europe have not led to intervention. However, the HCNM must not get involved in interethnic conflicts marked by violence. The so-called terrorism clause was adopted mainly at Turkey's request, but it also applies to conflicts in the Basque provinces, Nagorno Karabakh, and Chechnya. The underlying principle for this was, of course, that the HCNM would be most effective in situations where one could mediate in the earliest stage of the conflict through silent diplomacy, persuasion, and international authority. Hence, the requirement that a High Commissioner must be an individual with international authority who is prepared to operate discreetly.

The independent position of the HCNM, which has until today been unique within the OSCE, does not affect his accountability. The chapter of the mandate that deals with this matter mentions frequent consultations with the OSCE chairman in office through confidential reports. In addition, there is a customary bimonthly report to the Permanent Council in Vienna, while it has also become customary for the HCNM to inform the Permanent Council of any recommendation made and the subsequent response from the government in question.

The requirement of confidentiality, which has contributed significantly to the success of the HCNM, is not absolute in other senses either. Besides the aforementioned reporting to the chairman in office and the Permanent Council, the HCNM may also opt to make certain recommendations public; in recent times, it has become customary for these recommendations to be published at the HCNM Web site (part of the OSCE Web site) in due course. To an extent, his oral reports to the Permanent Council are an exception, as is the possibility provided for in the mandate to deliver a formal "early warning" to the Permanent Council. Recently, the HCNM made use of the latter instrument in relation to the situation in the former Yugoslavian Republic of Macedonia (FYROM), the first time he has done so in the six and a half years that he has been in office. However, such a public action is rare, as he generally shuns the media—certainly if it concerns minority issues in specific countries. After all, experience has shown that opposing parties tend to come together more easily if the matter of dispute has not been publicized and hence they have not been forced to take a public stance.

The limited perceptibility of the activities of the HCNM, however intentionally chosen as a tool for preventative diplomacy, can sometimes mean that he receives little recognition for results achieved. The fact that the public at large is unfamiliar with his activities may result in politicians, to whom public opinion is a measure of success, feeling insufficiently compelled to act on the recommendations of the HCNM. In order to reduce this risk, one sometimes strives toward cooperation with other organizations, while the aforementioned accountability to the Permanent Council also results in explicit declarations of support from third parties.

The HCNM receives information about relevant minority issues from various sources. The rather extensive description of these sources in the mandate has in practice added little to what he would have to do anyway to obtain this information. The determination of possible partners, the traveling conditions for the HCNM, and the involvement of experts in his activities, too, have developed naturally in the course of his activities. Although in retrospect the mandate is rather needlessly explicit on these areas, one could say that the actuality of the mandate as such has remained unchanged.

DEVELOPMENTS SINCE 1993

Initially almost a one-man operation, the HCNM has seen his staff grow due to increasing activities. At present, the institute of the HCNM, which is based in The Hague, employs a staff of fifteen, including seven advisers, four of whom deal with specific regions. In addition, the HCNM has two legal advisers and one personal adviser at his disposal. The HCNM has, in the past, also called on the services of external experts on specific cases. Nevertheless, the office of the HCNM can hardly be compared to other OSCE institutions, if only because the HCNM marks such a personal stamp on activities because of his own political accountability.

As might have been expected, the activities of the HCNM have increased over the years and changed somewhat in nature. While the emphasis in the early period was still partly on the acquisition of knowledge and fact-finding, the aspect of direct mediation between opposing parties soon came to the fore. This requires a strong personal involvement and therefore more traveling. The latter element in particular is not quite as outspokenly present anywhere else within the OSCE, with the possible exception of the chairman in office. Moreover, there has also been a development toward an increasing number of separate travels by the HCNM's advisers, for example, to discuss draft legislation with the parties concerned.

Besides its internal administration, the HCNM also has a foundation at his disposal, namely the Foundation for Interethnic Relations. The original purpose of this foundation, which was to be incorporated into the office of the HCNM in 1999, was mainly to conduct research into more fundamental minority issues.

Especially in recent years, the foundation has, at the HCNM's request, implemented a number of projects in countries such as Croatia, the FYROM, Romania, Kazakhstan, and Kirghizia. The goal of all of these projects is to offer support at the local level to minority policies, for example, in the field of education, and by monitoring possible interethnic tension.

PRACTICE

Without going into specific minority issues with which the HCNM has been or still is involved, the scope of the organization's activities can only be illustrated with real examples.

The HCNM has always been involved in the Baltic region, in particular Estonia and Latvia, because of the sizable Russian-speaking minority that lives there. His interventions encompass a great many aspects of the difficult integration process of that minority, but focus predominantly on legislation. Crucially important in this respect was the amendment of the citizenship act, with the purpose of allowing a more rapid naturalization of the minority, namely, children born within this minority group after the declaration of independence on the part of the Baltic republics.

In Central Europe, the Hungarian-speaking minority living outside the borders of Hungary, more specifically in Romania and Slovakia, plays an important role. The HCNM has been involved in these two countries, both in a general political and directional sense and in the field of education. The latter was also the subject of recommendations by the HCNM in FYROM. The interethnic opposition between Macedonians and Albanians, which was clearly visible due to a lack of integration of the two populations, was naturally put to a further test by developments in neighboring Kosovo. On May 12, 1999, the HCNM issued a formal warning to the OSCE Permanent Council in Vienna that the influx of refugees from Kosovo might well destabilize the situation in FYROM, unless the international community was willing to contribute significantly to the reception of refugees elsewhere and continue to offer support to the United Nations High Commissioner for Refugees (UNHCR) and to FYROM directly.

In Croatia, the involvement of the HCNM has focused on, among other things, the return of displaced Serbs and their representation at the local level through the United Council of Municipalities. Another example of his activities in this region was the setting up of a project regarding legal aid to the Serbian minority in Knin, a project that was implemented by the previously mentioned Foundation for Interethnic Relations. Other activities of the HCNM concerned the position of the Crimean Tartars in Ukraine; the plight of the so-called Meskhetian Turks, who were driven from Georgia under Stalin's reign; and interethnic relations in Kazakhstan and Kirghizia. In the latter two countries, the Foundation for Interethnic Relations has set up monitoring projects so that the governments involved as well as the HCNM would receive a prior warning in case of negative developments.

A somewhat different problem is that of the Roma and Sinti, who live in many European countries in poor or even atrocious circumstances. After a first report in 1993, at the end of 1999 the HCNM decided to return to this issue, which resulted in a report that contained concrete recommendations to the OSCE in March 2000.

The above and other activities relating to specific minority issues—in which the HCNM often cooperated closely with other relevant international organizations such as the European Commission and the Council of Europe—are aimed primarily at improving the dialogue between government and the minorities in question by promoting specific existing or new structures to this end. A substantial and constructive dialogue between both parties and the actual participation of the minorities in public life are absolute conditions for successful conflict prevention. Besides encouraging such a dialogue, the HCNM has in many cases formulated advice during drafting of new legislation. The criterion that is applied in such cases is whether the legislation in question is in accordance with international norms and standards. Finally, an area that is crucial to the identity of minorities, and in which the HCNM has therefore repeatedly formulated specific recommendations, is education.

In the course of his activities, the HCNM discovered that it would be useful to issue a series of general (not country-specific) recommendations with regard to different aspects of policy on minorities. To this end, he invited a group of renowned experts, who formulated recommendations regarding education in 1996 (The Hague recommendations), regarding language issues in 1998 (the Oslo recommendations), and regarding general policy issues and participation of minority groups in public life in 1999 (the so-called Lund recommendations).

Also, in the period 1997–1999, the HCNM commissioned an extensive study of regulations concerning minority-language legislation in all OSCE nations by means of a questionnaire that was sent to all governments concerned. The ensuing report was published in March 1999.

CONCLUSION

The great expectations that were created in Europe after 1989 soon gave way to the realization that the following period would be marked by more rather than less conflicts, mostly of an interethnic nature. Nationalism, characterized by feelings of ethnic superiority and a refusal to respect the fundamental rights of other population groups, came in place of the earlier ideologies. In extreme cases, this has led to the horror of ethnic cleansing. The international community responded by, among other things, appointing a High Commissioner on National Minorities, an independent and impartial political figure who could mediate between opposing sides through silent diplomacy.

Mostly avoiding the publicity associated with such flashpoints as Bosnia, Kosovo, and Nagorno Karabakh, he has succeeded in making opposing parties in many a European country realize that it is in their mutual interest not to allow a conflict to escalate. In some cases, this required considerable powers of persuasion, sometimes in cooperation with other relevant organizations, such as the European Commission, which may contribute to finding solutions by applying their own arguments and tools.

History will tell whether the HCNM has succeeded in fulfilling his mandate. The hotbeds of modern Europe sometimes make one forget that, luckily, smoldering conflicts elsewhere in the world have been resolved before they could escalate. It is certainly the case that the HCNM is regarded as one of the most successful instruments within the OSCE, as is apparent from the significant support that he has received time and again from various OSCE presidencies, through the Permanent Council in Vienna and elsewhere. Insofar as the HCNM has succeeded in preventing tension from escalating to an open conflict, in bringing opposing parties to the negotiating table, and in putting forward solutions—sometimes even dealing with the root of a conflict—one can safely say that the HCNM is already a success. The High Commissioner has not yet made himself superfluous, but over the past seven years, much has been achieved—in part thanks to him—in reducing tensions between ethnic groups in Europe.

APPENDIX: THE HCNM IN SLOVAKIA

One of the issues in the Slovakian context with which the HCNM has dealt extensively is the Law on the State Language, which was adopted by parliament in 1995 under Vladimir Meciar's government. This law, which replaced a more liberal version, was a "compensation demand" of the nationalists within the government, after they had reluctantly approved a bilateral treaty of friendship with neighboring Hungary as part of the so-called Stability Pact of March 20, 1995. According to the coalition partner Slovak National Party, Meciar had made too many concessions to Hungary; a "strong" Law on the State Language was the price that had to be paid in return for their vote to ratify the treaty.

Although the Meciar government also restricted the rights of the Hungarian minority (10 percent of the population) in other ways, the state language law was a thorn in the side of Western Europe. Not only the HCNM protested against it, but the European Union (EU), too, regarded it as one of the most important reasons for rejecting Slovakia from the first group of entrants into the Union.

It was not until after the parliamentary elections of 1998, which led to the fall of Meciar, that matters began to change. Even before the Dzurinda government was in place, the HCNM organized a secret meeting with the principal future coalition parties (including Mikulas Dzurinda and the future president Rudolf Shuster) in Hainburg, Austria. At this meeting, a number of wishes of the HCNM were discussed, and it was agreed that the maligned state language law would be complemented with new legislation on the use of minority languages.

Despite the good intentions of the new Slovakian coalition government (in which the Hungarian population group was also represented), it took longer than anticipated before this new legislation was in place. Although the other coalition partners initially wanted to restrict the use of minority languages to official channels, namely, public institutions (as a result of which the state language law was incompatible with the constitution), the Hungarians strove toward an all-embracing law that also provided for the use of Hungarian in education and culture.

The HCNM and his advisers discussed the draft legislation with the various parties concerned between December 1998 and May 1999, not only in Bratislava but also by fax; representatives of the European Commission and the Council of Europe were also involved, because of their own perspective on the issue and to add weight to the international point of view. After the Hungarian side had already presented various elaborate drafts, the other coalition partners finally produced a text of their own by May (which was not to the liking of the Hungarians). The latter text was discussed in mid-June in The Hague by representatives of the Slovakian government, the HCNM, and the above-mentioned European institutions, and it was adapted in the sense that a number of Hungarian demands were incorporated.

During an emotional and tumultuous parliamentary debate, the opposition accused the government of selling out the Slovakian cause. Under pressure from the opposition, certain amendments were accepted that weakened the text somewhat. It was characteristic of the psychological atmosphere that none of the Hungarian amendments made it. Nevertheless, after a legal interpretation on the part of the Slovakian side, the HCNM considered the law to be a step in the right direction, and stated so publicly. An important stumbling block for further decisionmaking by the EU in Helsinki in late 1999 on accession talks with Slovakia was thus removed.

However, as far the Hungarians were concerned, the law did not go far enough. Not only in Slovakia but also in Budapest were protests lodged against the law, which was regarded as altogether insufficient. But while some reservations seemed well founded, there also appeared to be an element of tactics involved: pressure on interethnic relations is, after all, easily translated into pressure on the government in question to make further concessions.

CHAPTER 9

Relief Aid and Development Cooperation

■ 9.1

The Challenge of Linking Aid and Peacebuilding

Manuela Leonhardt

DEVELOPMENT AND CONFLICT

Most violent conflicts nowadays are taking place in developing countries. The costs of these wars are immense and can throw back a country's development efforts by years or even decades. Among them are human costs, peacekeeping and humanitarian costs, commercial and reconstruction costs, and political costs. As far as numbers can express human suffering, we may recall that during the Rwandan genocide of 1994, an estimated 800,000 persons were killed and more than 2 million were forced to flee their homes. Between 1990 and 1995, Rwandan exports dropped by 60 percent due to internal instability.[1] During the conflict in Bosnia-Herzegovina, 145,000 were killed, 174,000 injured, and 2.5 million people made refugees. The Bosnian gross domestic product plunged from an estimated $10 billion to $2 billion between 1990 and 1996, while the costs of reconstructing Bosnia have been estimated at several billion dollars.[2]

The rising number of conflict-related humanitarian emergencies also diverts scarce resources from long-term development to humanitarian assistance. While in the 1980s emergency relief accounted for only 3 percent of the total development cooperation budget of the Organization for Economic Cooperation and Development (OECD) countries, this proportion rose to 10 percent in the 1990s. At the same time, the total amount of international assistance fell sharply.

These trends prompted an intensive discussion within the development community on the relationship between aid and security. Highlighted in this debate was the need for socially sustainable development; the negative effects of aid; and a study of the reactive approach to conflict.

Socially Sustainable Development

Cases such as Rwanda, where well-established development structures were not able to prevent genocide, raise fundamental questions about the type of development being supported. There is an increasing consensus that development aid should foster not only economically but also socially sustainable structures. The prevention of violent conflict, therefore, should become an objective of long-term development strategies that include economic, social, political, and environmentally sound development.

Negative Effects of Aid

Aid frequently sustains a form of development that supports the elites and is dominated by them. Thus, it furthers structural instability. In situations of conflict, aid projects often inadvertently contribute to conflict while trying to achieve their internal objectives (see Mary B. Anderson in this volume). This was the case in Somalia, where emergency aid for the victims of drought and war actually subsidized the warring factions. Even ordinary development projects can increase tensions. They may exacerbate existing rivalries by, for example, ignoring established patterns of land use or injecting resources into one impoverished region while neglecting another. Methods are required to monitor and redress these potentially negative effects of development cooperation.

Reactive Approach to Conflict

In the context of shrinking budgets, aid agencies have been called to revise their largely reactive approach to complex emergencies. Given the huge costs of war, aid can be an extremely cost-effective way of conflict prevention. For this, development and humanitarian agencies need to identify and support opportunities for peace from an early stage. This corresponds to the general shift in development thinking toward "enabling environments," which emphasizes good governance, rights-based development, and a strong civil society.

This new proactive approach toward humanitarian aid, development, and violent conflict poses new challenges to aid agencies, for which they require additional instruments and tools. These include conflict analysis,

Exhibit 9.1-1   Risks and Opportunities of Development Aid in Conflict-Affected Regions

Thematic Area	Risks	Opportunities
Governance	Aid reinforces illegitimate political structures. Aid weakens local government by creating unsustainable parallel structures. Aid replicates authoritarian structures. Aid undermines local capacities and creates dependency.	Aid strengthens local formal and informal structures. Aid encourages participation and local ownership. Aid recognizes local ownership of the peace process. Aid agencies assume engaged but neutral position in conflict.
Economics	Aid distorts local economies. Aid cements existing socioeconomic divisions. Aid encourages unsustainable use of natural resources. Aid supports contentious claims to natural resources.	Aid strengthens local economy. Aid promotes more equal opportunities. Aid delivery encourages collaboration and cohesion. Aid encourages sustainable resource management. Aid strengthens equal access to resources.
Sociocultural Factors	Aid agencies duplicate and reinforce war images. Aid grafts Western conflict-resolution methods on local peace processes.	Aid agencies support trust building and reconciliation. Aid empowers people to resolve violent conflict in their own ways.
Arms and War Economy	Aid subsidizes the war economy.	Aid avoids instrumentalization by warlords. Aid develops alternative livelihoods to violence.

socially sustainable planning, identifying peace constituencies, and monitoring the conflict impact of aid activities.

THE ROLE OF AID IN PEACEBUILDING

How can development and humanitarian assistance help prevent violent conflict and build sustainable peace? It is important to recognize that aid cannot promote peace on its own but should be part of a package of foreign policy measures toward a conflict-affected country or subregion. Other relevant instruments include policy dialogue; preventive diplomacy; cultural, trade, and investment policies; and military cooperation. To be effective, policy coherence between these instruments is required, which means that they all should be applied with peace as the ultimate objective in mind.

There are three main areas, in which relief, rehabilitation, and development aid can play a positive role in promoting peace: long-term conflict prevention, supporting peace processes, and addressing localized violence.

Long-Term Conflict Prevention

Aid has the potential to address the structural conditions (or root causes) that produce violent conflict, such as social exclusion, lack of political participation, unaccountable public institutions, and lack of personal security. It can also support people in creating institutions for the peaceful resolution of social conflict and empower them to become involved in conflict prevention initiatives. Such fundamental social transformations can only be achieved in a long-term perspective. Despite ever-shortening funding cycles, aid does have the capacity to offer such long-term commitment and support to countries at risk of violent conflict.

Supporting Peace Processes

During war-peace transitions and in postconflict situations, aid can help prepare the ground for sustainable peace. Experience has shown that political negotiations (Track 1) are unlikely to lead to a lasting peace agreement if they are not supported by a peace process that goes down to the grassroots. The social groundwork for peace is based on the triangle of participation, material benefit, and security. In the early stages of the peace process, aid can support citizens in creating social spaces for dialogue, generating public pressure for peace, and formulating a people-focused peace agenda. During peace negotiations, their role as facilitators, mediators, and witnesses can be strengthened, while later their participation in the process of reconciliation and building structures to sustain peace is essential. Aid for postconflict rehabilitation and reconstruction can help build trust in the peace process by offering real material improvements to people (such as new business or employment opportunities) and making sure that the "peace dividend" is distributed equally among the population. The transformation from a culture of violence to a culture of peace requires that people can trust in their personal security and the institutions of justice. Prudent support for a reform of the security services can assist in bringing about this change.

Addressing Localized Violence

Development aid can support communities in dealing with localized forms of violence and conflict. Such violence can range from cattle rustling in rural Kenya to gang violence in the urban center of Latin America. These conflicts are often associated with a high number of unemployed (male) youth, the ready availability of small arms, and a deep disregard for the value of the individual life. In this context, aid can assist people to develop community-based security systems; it can address the material preconditions of violence and support local mediation efforts. Traditional ways of conflict resolution can be very effective in these situations and should be explored and strengthened.

Exhibit 9.1-2 provides an overview of the ways in which development aid can address the root causes of conflict and promote peace in pre- and post-conflict situations.

What does it mean to integrate a peacebuilding perspective into development and humanitarian assistance? There are two main operational challenges to aid agencies:

Linking peace and development initiatives: Until recently, development and peacebuilding were regarded as different types of activities. Development was mainly about economic development, although governance and social issues have increasingly been included. Peacebuilding, on the other hand, was mainly approached as an intangible process of building relationships and trust through intensive face-to-face interaction. Typical peacebuilding activities were peacebuilding training and conflict-resolution workshops. Grassroots peace workers have seen, however, that the poor simply cannot afford to participate in time-consuming conflict-resolution exercises without any immediate material benefits accruing from them. Therefore, it is important to link development and peace initiatives with each other so that they simultaneously address the material conditions of violence (lack of opportunities) and empower people to resolve their conflicts peacefully.

Sustaining peace processes: The conditions of peace work are very different from those of traditional development assistance. Peace processes take a long time, advance very slowly, and are full of setbacks. As far as peacebuilding is about changing perceptions and building relationships, few tangible results can be presented. As far as it is about justice, economic opportunities, and political participation, peacebuilding ventures into highly politicized fields and risks to become involved in local power politics. Usual project-type approaches with their short time frames and rigid performance requirements are inadequate in these conditions. Therefore, agencies need to develop more flexible and long-term frameworks to sustain peace processes.

TOOLS AND INSTRUMENTS
FOR LINKING AID AND PEACEBUILDING

In order to play a more proactive role in preventing violent conflict, aid agencies should review and strengthen their capacities for peacebuilding.

Exhibit 9.1-2   Peacebuilding Approaches in Pre- and Postconflict Situations

	Situation of Submerged or Rising Tensions	Postconflict Transition
Governance		
Legitimate government and good governance	Support democratic processes. Strengthen efficiency and accountability of public institutions. Promote political reform and stability in a balanced way.	Assist establishment of a legitimate and participative political system.
Pluralism and participation	Promote popular participation in the political process. Encourage protection of minority groups. Protect freedom of information. Empower civil society.	Strengthen civil control of the political process. Build civil society capacity for conflict resolution and reconciliation.
Channels for conflict management	Encourage an impartial and accessible justice system. Strengthen the rule of law and respect for human rights.	Support judicial and legal reform. Promote justice for victims of war and violence.
Positive and negative international engagement	Reduce external support for conflict. Prevent conflict spilling over into neighboring countries.	Strengthen regional security initiatives.
Economics		
Problems in managing transition and rapid change	Support economic stability and economic reform in a balanced manner. Assist integration of migrants and resettlers.	Strengthen social cohesion through economic and political participation. Aid reintegration of refugees and displaced persons.
Widening socioeconomic disparities	Promote equitable economic development. Meet basic human needs. Reduce social exclusion.	Ensure equal participation in "peace dividend." Assist conversion of war economy.
Competition over natural resources	Enhance environmental security. Help create sustainable-resource management systems.	Promote agreement on sustainable-resource management systems as a central part of the peace process. Support environmental rehabilitation.
Sociocultural factors		
Political exploitation of cultural and other differences	Support constructive social dialogue and cooperation.	Promote a culture of peace and reconciliation.
Security		
Legacy of violence	Promote individual and collective security. Transform the culture of violence.	Help heal the wounds of war.
Arms proliferation and irregular fighters	Control small arms proliferation. Monitor private and opposition armed formations.	Support land mines clearing. Assist disarmament, demobilization, and reintegration of former combatants.
Uncontrolled state armed forces	Promote security sector reform.	Help define a new role for the military in a democratic postwar society.

Clear Peacebuilding Objectives

Any form of external intervention in a conflict-affected area does have an impact on the dynamics of peace and conflict. Without a clear peace orientation, however, many development projects have failed to make full use of their potential for peacebuilding. Therefore, peacebuilding objectives should be integrated into any development initiative in a conflict-affected area.

Strategic Use of Old and New Instruments

To make a substantial contribution to peace, development programs need to be implemented in a strategic and coherent way. On the macrolevel, *strategic conflict analysis* or conflict appraisals should inform the preparation of the country assistance programs. On the microlevel, *conflict impact assessments* can help projects avoid and mitigate adverse effects on the conflict and make full use of opportunities for peace. Many traditional forms of development assistance can make important contributions to peacebuilding, if they are used in strategic ways. These include education and professional training, income generation for disadvantaged groups, community-based resource management systems, and community development. Each measure should be reviewed as to how far it can alleviate inequality, promote cooperation, and establish channels for resolving conflict issues. Newer areas of assistance such as human rights, democracy, security sector reform, and local capacity building can play a central role in creating enabling environments for peace.

Participation

Just and sustainable peace can only be achieved with the consent and participation of those most affected by conflict. Therefore, peacebuilding work should be seen as a way of empowering people to create the conditions for peace. This implies a participative approach to development work, which takes people's voices seriously and supports local initiative. Participatory methods and approaches such as community mobilization (see Vivien Erasmus in this volume), which have been developed within traditional development work, should be reviewed and adapted for use in conflict situations.

Values and Ethical Guidelines

Peace work can at times pose moral dilemmas. In these situations, clear statements of an organization's ethical orientation and central values can assist in making tough decisions. Codes of conduct and ethical guidelines have been developed both by individual organizations, such as the International Alert Code of Conduct for Conflict Transformation Work, and by the development and humanitarian community (e.g., SPHERE project). In situations of violent conflict, such values may sometimes be required to take "honorable risks," as the consequences of inaction may even be more devastating.

Good Practice and Learning

Peacebuilding is first of all a learning process. Short project cycles and high turnover rates among field staff, however, seriously restrict the capacity of development agencies to reflect on past experience. Agencies need to make a conscious effort to retain precious local knowledge and build an institutional memory of lessons learned from the past. More incentives for field staff and conflict-oriented monitoring and evaluation systems can play an important role in this regard. Compilations of good practice are another valuable way of drawing on past experience. The Development Assistance Committee has produced the most comprehensive of these guides to date on conflict, peace, and development cooperation.[3]

NOTES

1. Killick and Higdom 1998.
2. Ibid.
3. OECD/DAC 1998.

REFERENCES AND SUGGESTED READING

Anderson, Mary B. (1999). *Do No Harm: How Aid Can Support Peace—or War.* Boulder, Colo.: Lynne Rienner.
International Alert. (1998). *Code of Conduct for Conflict Transformation Work.* London.
Killick, Nick, and Simon Higdom. (1998). *The Cost of Conflict.* London: International Alert/Saferworld.
Leonhardt, Manuela. (1999). *Conflict Impact Assessment of EU Development Co-operation with ACP Countries: A Review of Policy, Literature, and Practice.* London: International Alert/Saferworld.
OECD/DAC. (1998). *Conflict, Peace, and Development Cooperation on the Threshold of the 21st Century.* Paris: OECD.

Community Mobilization
as a Tool for Peacebuilding

Vivien Erasmus

WHY COMMUNITY MOBILIZATION?

A noticeable fact, fundamental to many humanitarian crises seen today, is their underlying political nature. These crises are usually not short-lived. In many cases they have persisted for more than a decade: Sudan, Somalia, and Mozambique are classical examples. Sadly, for communities trapped in these intractable situations, the abnormal has become the norm. Individuals will be born and live out their lives during the course of the disaster.

Donor organizations, implementing agencies, and the general public have become increasingly concerned with the growing need to support the many humanitarian crises flaring worldwide. In the face of decreasing resources, securing adequate funds to cope with these emergency situations has become a serious problem for both donors and implementing agencies. The unending need for large amounts of humanitarian funds creates "donor fatigue." Therefore, the question that arises is whether resources currently deployed are used in the most cost-effective manner possible. Intertwined with this question is the complex issue of whether emergency interventions exacerbate conflict or promote peace.

The classical emergency approach of doing things for people (providing food, water, and shelter, and immunizing vulnerables) is valid in the early stages. It is, however, essential to move rapidly to enabling the community to return to a more normal and productive way of life. Not to do this creates dependency on external assistance and marginalizes traditional leadership and systems: the dreaded but all too common dependency syndromes.

Although initially humanitarian crises can be characterized as acute emergencies requiring urgent life-saving interventions, their long-term nature and fundamental attributes are those of a long-term or chronic disaster requiring a combination of relief, rehabilitation, and developmental interventions. (The term *complex emergency,* introduced in the UN in 1989 to describe these disasters, is, in my opinion, misleading and inappropriate: no emergency or disaster can be characterized as simple.)

Short-term emergency funds and emergency-oriented nongovernmental organizations (NGOs) often perpetuate the situation by the very nature of their humanitarian responses, usually at high cost to the international community. The deployment of these funds and the time-bound activities of these agencies frequently result in the dependency syndrome. Worse still, as Mary B. Anderson has so vividly documented in this volume, such interventions frequently intensify conflict and thus the emergency situation itself. Community mobilization is a means of tapping into the knowledge and resources of the local community and fostering a spirit of community ownership. It is a key strategy in re-empowering the community to make vital decisions by themselves, and to promote, support, and nurture a capacity within the community to once again care for their own vulnerables: doing things with people.

Failures in Community Mobilization: Somalia

Somalia is an example of how a disaster can be aggravated and to some degree perpetuated by classical short-term emergency approaches that lead to marginalization of the community. The government system operating in Somalia prior to its collapse resulted in two significant consequences to the community: (1) the development of a socio-politico-economic elite largely based in Mogadishu; and (2) the marginalization of the traditional community and its leadership.

This urban elite, largely based in Mogadishu, developed a disrespect and disregard for traditional Somali society. They were preoccupied with drawing on the benefits of international aid (often dictated by the Cold War) and supporting a government system that was the basis of their employment, business, and career development. The civil war forced the elite to flee Mogadishu and other towns in search of security to the very hinterland they had earlier deserted. Agencies, meanwhile, began to have more contact with the rural area, previously not so accessible. The urban elite was a godsend to the agencies: they spoke the foreigners' language and were familiar with the aid business and its methodology. They realized that jobs—and other benefits—were once again to be had.

To perpetuate their control of this windfall, these educated urbanized groups created a "wall" around the humanitarian agencies and, to a large extent, monopolized them. They became the main interlocutors between the community and the agencies, with resources flowing in directions controlled by and serving chiefly the elite. The traditional community could only look on in anger and frustration. The agencies thus found themselves trapped in a cycle of conflict and animosity. The urban elite had successfully hijacked international humanitarian programs.

The consequence was growing tension between the traditional community and the humanitarian agencies. Resources were often channeled to areas and groups with family or clan ties to Somali employees, causing grievances that could not be adequately resolved. Tensions between local factions and groups were thus inflamed, and humanitarian assistance was repeatedly misappropriated or wrongly deployed. Agencies, seen as necessary evils by many local persons, soon became victims of a society that frequently settles disputes, if all else fails, violently.

The response of the agencies to this difficult situation has been one of mistrust and isolation from the community, which simply exacerbates the situation. The end result is top-down programs, only partly relevant, and a widespread fear and condemnation of Somali society. By allying themselves to particular families or subclans, or attempting to exercise an almost paranoid control over resources, agencies promoted a perception that the programs being supported belonged to the agency. Community participation and ownership became largely impossible. Communities identified projects as foreign property that they were free to exploit as best they could. Sustainability and local contribution had little chance of success.

Community mobilization, and the building of local structures and their capacity and capability, though generally accepted as desirable, cannot be adequately initiated within this prevailing environment. The "real" community and its decisionmakers have been marginalized, and the atmosphere of mutual contempt and fear puts to rest any hope of a partnership between the communities and their external benefactors. The main beneficiary of the aid programs frequently turns out to be a privileged group of Somali service providers and their relatives.

Failures in Community Mobilization: South Sudan

The Sudan People's Liberation Movement/Army (SPLM/A) initiated the civil war in Sudan in 1983. Led by a group of ex-government army officers, the initial philosophy of the SPLM/A was that a military solution was possible. The military tendency thus enjoyed all control resulting in disempowerment of the community and its traditional system of self-governance: the liberators became the tyrants. It was only in 1993 that this approach was questioned, leading to a realization that the separation of the civil from the military, the promotion of democracy, and the establishment of governance were critical to conflict resolution at an internal level.

Meanwhile in 1988, James Grant, then executive director of UNICEF, promoted the establishment of Operation Lifeline Sudan (OLS). OLS was based on the premise that humanitarian assistance must be provided to all affected civilians, irrespective of who exercised factual control over the area they lived in, and that humanitarian assistance could promote peace. However, the structure was flawed in many ways: important aspects in hindsight are that OLS gave inordinate control to the regime in Khartoum and limited itself to an emergency agenda.

The OLS agenda once again resulted in the arrival of emergency donor funds and emergency humanitarian agencies in large numbers, with consequences similar to those described for Somalia. Their short-term emergency agenda dominated humanitarian assistance, with emphasis on the delivery of survival services and with little consideration for the community's intrinsic capacity to help itself. Combined with the military solution agenda of the SPLM, the humanitarian assistance program resulted in almost total marginalization of the community.

However, some agencies operating in South Sudan began, around 1991, to question the wisdom of tackling what was classically a chronic disaster situation with usual emergency approaches. Several interesting and successful projects have grown out of this questioning. They have, particularly in the agriculture and health sectors in western Equatoria, demonstrated that focusing on community-based approaches in environments where governance and administration are absent or at best ineffectual can have dramatic results on improving the quality of life of communities trapped in these conflict situations.

COMMUNITY MOBILIZATION

As defined earlier, community mobilization is a means of tapping into the knowledge and resources of the local community and fostering a spirit of community ownership. This is one of the most effective means of minimizing dependency and reducing conflict at the grassroots level.

Community mobilization is commenced as early as possible and is sustained throughout the intervention or program. It should continue as a standard principle and procedure even after the assistance program is withdrawn. The essence of community mobilization is dialogue between various stakeholders. Dialogue is achieved either formally or informally. The main output is a community that is a full member of the planning, implementation, and evaluation team that designs and implements a program for the benefit of the community. The purpose of community mobilization is:

- To create a dialogue between the community, donors, and service providers.
- To promote structures and systems for involvement of the community in planning, management, implementation, supervision, monitoring, and evaluation.
- To optimize utilization of existing community resources—technical, information/knowledge, management, human, material, and financial.

- To ensure full cooperation and collaboration between all stakeholders.
- To advance community empowerment and ownership.
- To resolve conflicts and grievances.

Prerequisites for Community Mobilization

Some important prerequisites for achieving good community mobilization are:

- An agency philosophy in which local authorities and communities are viewed as equal partners deserving of respect and transparency; a commitment to a significant time scale of involvement; a commitment to the concept of community ownership.
- Agency staff that has a long-term commitment to the project and shares the agency vision stated above.
- Donors who are sympathetic to the approach of community participation and ownership and are willing to provide adequate flexibility for a responsive project.

COMMUNITY MOBILIZATION IN PRACTICE

Consultation with Resource Persons

Before embarking on community mobilization, it is essential to be familiar with basic information about the community: stakeholder analysis. Identifying individuals who can explain the dynamics of the situation can be very difficult. Once such persons have been identified and are willing to be interlocutors as well, their help is invaluable. Initial information about the relevant history of the community; its important governance structures; various interest groups and stakeholders; and problems and issues can be collected and understood. At the same time information about the project/program objectives, strategies, resources available, and time frame can be shared. Feedback can also be obtained. This is often helpful in planning the next steps.

Needless to say, the value of resource persons depends largely upon who they are. Care must be exercised in deciding who is reliable and will not bias the project image in the mind of the community. It is useful to make as wide a contact as possible and to ensure that there is a clear understanding of the activities to follow. Emphasis on a broad-based process involving all interest groups must be made clear right from the beginning.

Meetings with Special Groups

Once the basic facts have been understood, dialogue must be widened to involve other groups. Local authorities should be adequately informed. Discussions with as many community leaders (elders, heads of local groups or organization religious leaders, relevant professionals) should be carried out, where possible, in groups. This will ensure transparency and clarity while minimizing rumors. A clear explanation of the project/program objectives, strategies, and management structure should be presented. Feedback on the opinions of these leaders is vital. The idea of the Community Leaders' Workshop should also be introduced along with suggestions for the agenda and participation.

Community Leaders' Workshop

This is a very important forum. If effectively managed, it can be the main mechanism for making important decisions about the project/program objectives, strategies, and management structures. Accountability and transparency are promoted, and grievances heard and dealt with. It is therefore necessary to hold it on a regular basis.

All program stakeholders constitute the Community Leaders' Workshop: local authorities; representatives of traditional community structures and community-based institutions; women; and religious leaders, relevant professionals, and humanitarian agencies. Even though large numbers may be a problem, the advantage of a broad-based representation far outweighs the disadvantages. An appropriate local person or authority best chairs the workshop, though an external facilitator may be desirable.

Some important issues that may be discussed at the workshop are listed below. It must be emphasized, however, that nothing of relevance or importance should be excluded.

Roles and responsibilities. One important source of conflict is an inadequate or incorrect understanding of roles and responsibilities of the three important stakeholders: the *community,* the *donor,* and the *service providers.* It is important to point out that the primary interest of the donors is to assist a community in need. The community assesses its needs and the essential resources it lacks as well as those available. This information needs to be communicated to the donors. Because the community may not have the capacity to formulate its needs in a form acceptable to the donors, service providers assist them.

Service providers are internal (local NGOs, government departments, etc.) or external (international agencies or foreign governments). External service providers usually have better contacts with external donors whereas the internal service providers have better relationships with the community. Together they form a "counterpart structure." The community, with the assistance of service providers, formulates the project proposal (participatory planning) and forwards it to the donor. If the donor is agreeable, it provides external resources as a project (a limited set of objectives, limited in time and resources) in support of the local program (a locally owned set of objectives and strategies, usually unlimited in time). It is vital that the community understands the difference between a donor project and the local program and the relative implications and ownership of each. This distinction is very helpful in avoiding conflict and promoting cooperation between stakeholders.

Sometimes the donor may also request the service providers to provide technical assistance to the community to ensure that the resources provided are adequately used, capacity is created, and management is sound. Service providers may also assist the community to formulate reports required by the donor from the community. If the reports are satisfactory, the cycle may be repeated and the project extended or renewed.

It is important also to emphasize that service providers are a necessary evil. Though their services may be essential to the success of the project, they are not usually the focus of donor assistance. If left unchecked, they will often represent or serve mainly their own interests. The community must monitor them carefully to avoid hijacking of the project.

It is encouraging how responsive the community is to this explanation of relationships. It is the first step in community empowerment. Once these issues are clear, the Community Leaders' Workshop is able to proceed to setting up an appropriate management structure through an agreement or set of agreements, which define how the project and program will work together.

Needs analysis.   The workshop is a good place to initiate needs assessment and involves the community in participatory planning. Various participatory rural appraisal (PRA) tools can be used to facilitate this process, such as focus group discussions and ranking. Differences between priorities of different social, ethnic, gender, or economic groups should be highlighted. It is essential during needs assessment to emphasize the limitations of the donor(s) and their sectoral or financial constraints, as well as their expectations for community contributions.

Program and project management structures.   A system for management of the project and program should be agreed and understood by all stakeholders. Responsibilities and authority should be clarified. Once a clear understanding exists and is documented, conflicts between the various stakeholders can be avoided or resolved.

Information sharing. The workshop is an excellent forum for broad-based information sharing. Since participation is broad, information can be clearly communicated and clarifications provided to avoid rumors and misunderstandings.

Conflict and grievance resolution. Some types of conflicts and grievances can be resolved at the workshop through discussion of project/program resource allocations or management systems. Accountability and transparency can be promoted, and cooperation and intersectoral collaboration built.

Participatory Planning

Participatory planning effectively promotes community mobilization. A major limitation is that involvement cannot be as broad as at the Community Leaders' Workshop. However, without participatory planning, community ownership with active participation and contribution is impossible. There are many ways of conducting participatory planning, ranging from community action plans drawn up through PRA methods to more sophisticated techniques for developing more complex plans at a district, regional, or even national level.

During participatory planning, community leaders representing various interests as well as technical/professional persons must be involved. Good facilitation is important to ensure that a wide participation among the participants is engendered. Technical information should be provided in a simple and clear manner to avoid intimidating participants.

It should be made clear that plans developed are the property of the local community and the embodiment of the locally owned program. External projects will accordingly support the local program depending on resources available and donor/agency mandates. Based on such plans, the community and its authorities can seek assistance from donors, coordinate agency projects to prevent duplication, and monitor progress. If plans are drawn up well and are broadly understood, a strong sense of ownership and commitment will be created among the participants. This sense of ownership contributes effectively to reduction of conflict and improved cooperation among stakeholders during its implementation.

Community Mobilization in South Sudan

Aktion Afrika Hilfe (AAH) is a German NGO with projects in South Sudan, Somalia, and northern Uganda.[1] Based on the principles and tools described above, AAH has attempted to use community mobilization as the key strategy to build community-based projects in primary health care (PHC), primary education, food security, and relief.

In South Sudan, under the OLS umbrella, international NGOs have focused primarily on providing emergency assistance. This high-cost approach involves large numbers of expatriate staff and little involvement of local counterparts. The AAH project in South Sudan, covering three districts in the Equatoria region, set out to extensively involve local communities and local counterparts trapped within a civil war to promote a capacity for self-help.

Initial contacts. The project in South Sudan commenced at a time when the SPLM/A was highly militaristic and centralized. Initial activities dealt with meeting emergency needs in an area that had received little or no assistance for years. The SPLA was extremely suspicious of expatriates, and contact with local communities was closely monitored. The project team succeeded in making contacts with key individuals in the SPLM/A, explaining the project strategy and approach. An SPLA physician became interested in the project and soon served as a key interlocutor, allaying suspicions and explaining the project to the local authorities. His interventions opened doors to other consequential officials. Suspicions about the motives underlying community mobilization were dealt with and an initial Community Leaders' Workshop was agreed. This process took approximately six months.

Community Leaders' Workshop. More than 100 participants representing chiefs and subchiefs, SPLA officers, religious leaders, cooperatives, women's groups, professionals, and administrators attended the first Community Leaders' Workshop. Lasting two days, the workshop agreed on a community-based PHC system, where the grassroots health facilities were owned and managed by the village community. Village-level health workers for these facilities were to be selected, employed, and supervised by the village. A written agreement (contract) was finalized and later signed by each village prior to the establishment of services. The system has persisted and spread to more than 200 PHC facilities in the region supported by at least four international NGOs. *Despite the war and an economy reduced to subsistence and barter trade, the community contribution to the PHC program between 1991 and 1996 averaged 15 percent of the total cost of the program.*

Participatory planning. Following the Community Leaders' Workshop, a participatory planning session was conducted to develop a medium-term strategic plan (master plan) for PHC services for the three districts. Again, broad participation was organized. The plan focuses on rehabilitation of PHC structures, human resources, and services. It is reviewed annually to confirm its relevance, and modifications are made if necessary. Each plan period is five years, with an annual operational plan being prepared after review of the master plan. In 1992, three other districts also requested to participate even though they were not within the AAH project area. It has since been the basis of PHC services in the region.

Village-level mobilization. Enlightenment and training of Village Health Committees (VHCs) in order to create motivation and capacity was the next important activity. This is an ongoing process, and much remains to be achieved. To support the VHCs, a cadre called the Community Support Officer (CSO) was developed, recruited, trained, and deployed. CSOs and PHC staff focus on resolving community problems and monitoring elections and meetings.

Formulation of health policy. In 1997, the New Sudan Relief and Rehabilitation Association (NSRRA, the humanitarian arm of the SPLM), based on the developments in PHC in the region, requested that AAH support them in developing a health policy. They wished to base this policy on the positive experiences of community mobilization, capacity building, and service provision seen in the project area. AAH together with the African Medical and Research Foundation (AMREF) through a participatory process involving Sudanese political and community leaders, health workers, women leaders, as well as external resource persons, formulated a draft policy. This policy, emphasizing community-based approaches and decentralized health services, has now been formally adopted by the SPLM as the health policy of the New Sudan.

Food security and relief. A similar experience was made in the agriculture and relief sectors between 1991 and 1996. The project area received more than 15,000 metric tons of food aid in 1991. With the distribution of seed and tools through reactivated farmers and women's groups, the area became a surplus producer within one year. The project purchased 75 metric tons of surplus in 1992. The arrival of displaced persons increased surplus procurement to 3,000 t in 1993 and 1994 for redistribution to them.

These displaced persons came from Bahr-el-Gazal. Pastoralist by tradition, they had lost virtually all their cattle. The few they possessed could not survive in the area due to disease. It is noteworthy that many considered this group to be incapable of cultivation and resistant to self-help. The resettlement area was remote and accessible only by air or by mud roads in appalling condition. With extremely limited resources and virtually impossible logistical conditions, the strategy of mobilizing community resources became key. Having been provided with seed and tools, a food ration and some nonfood relief items, the displaced were able, within a year, to accept a food ration reduction of 50 percent; malnutrition was reduced from more than 30 percent to less than 5 percent and health indicators were satisfactory. Other similar camps in Sudan, with similar groups, developed high levels of dependency, with the consequent social and psychological ill effects. Today most of the displaced have returned home or are still in the camp as self-settled persons requiring no special inputs.

Experience in Somalia

AAH experience in Somalia, though limited to slightly more than a year, has followed that of Sudan. AAH was requested, in 1995, to consider a project in three districts of Bari region, northeast Somalia. Several NGOs had been operating in the area but withdrew since relationships with the community had deteriorated to a point where kidnappings and looting had occurred. The departing NGOs left behind a considerable number of assets, and the elders of the local community had secured these. These were offered for use in any NGO project. Unfortunately there was an expectation amongst the laid-off staff that they must benefit from any new project. The combination of problems made NGOs reluctant to operate in the area.

The AAH analysis recognized that the community must be re-empowered so that the conflict between the elite and traditional groups could be avoided. Several key interlocutors were identified and provided very useful advice. AAH staff commenced a dialogue with community elders emphasizing that AAH was there to support them and their local programs. The resources available were made transparent. The intention to work as partners was stressed. The need to establish a clear "counterpart" and "management" structure was agreed. This process took three months.

Once the project approach had been clarified, a three-day Community Leaders' Workshop involving 180 community representatives, administrators, professionals, and women was held. This covered the principles of community participation, roles, and responsibilities of various stakeholders and a detailed examination of the structure for cooperation and management of the program. Considerable time was spent on separating the external donor-funded project and the local programs for health and primary education. A six-page agreement between the NGO and the local community was drafted and agreed. One significant achievement was that all local staff would be employees of the community and not the NGO. The approach and content of the workshop was appreciated by the community as this was the first time they had been involved in a frank and detailed discussion on these issues.

A participatory planning workshop followed at which five-year master plans for PHC and primary education were elaborated. These were probably the first such community-based documents developed in Somalia in the recent past. At the end of this process, spanning nine months, the districts are now generally seen as good partners for project implementation, and the process as a model to be followed in other parts of the region.

CONCLUSION

The AAH experience illustrates the point that failures in community mobilization, participation, and ownership are one root cause of conflict between NGOs and the community. Prolonged top-down emergency interventions lead to marginalization of community leadership and the dependency syndrome. Inadequate or inappropriate community participation also exacerbates conflict within the community itself. Appropriate community mobilization is therefore a key strategy in managing conflict and postconflict disaster situations and promoting peace.

NOTE

1. AAH was registered in Munich in 1996. Between 1991 and 1996, the projects were implemented by Aktion Afrika in Not (AAIN). AAIN was dissolved in 1996 and all projects handed over to AAH. The program vision, implementation structures, staff, and strategies remained the same.

■ 9.3

Enhancing Local Capacity for Peace: Do No Harm

Mary B. Anderson

Conflicts, especially those that occur within countries, are characterized both by intergroup divisions and by connections between the warring groups. In spite of their best efforts to maintain nonpartisanship in relation to the warring sides, international aid agencies inevitably affect these intergroup dividers and connectors. On one hand, they can exacerbate, reinforce, or prolong conflict by feeding into and worsening intergroup dividers or by ignoring and undermining intergroup connectors. On the other hand, their assistance can also help reduce intergroup dividers and/or build on and strengthen the connectors between people on different sides of a conflict. When provided with attention to the context of a conflict, humanitarian and development aid can do the good they are meant to do—alleviating human suffering and promoting sustainable enterprises—and, at the same time, encourage and enhance people's capacities to disengage from conflict and find nonwar options for solving problems.

These claims are neither theoretical nor speculative. They are based on the broad experience of many aid agencies providing assistance in many conflict areas in recent years and collected by the Local Capacities for Peace Project. Working collaboratively, a number of aid agencies joined together with support from several donor governments to understand how aid and conflict interact. In place after place, in spite of the differences that exist among cultures, types of wars, and aid agencies and projects, aid's effects on conflict followed similar and predictable patterns. In the few pages that follow, the patterns by which aid affects conflict—either negatively (reinforcing and prolonging it) or positively (supporting connectors)—are described and illustrated. Ways that aid agencies can avoid negative impacts and promote positive ones are also described.

HOW AID AFFECTS CONFLICT

Experience shows that aid affects conflict through two mechanisms: *resource transfers* and *implicit ethical messages.*

258

RESOURCE TRANSFERS

Aid resources represent economic wealth and political power. Thus, people at war always try to control them as a part of their effort to claim victory. The economic and political resources represented by aid affect conflict—negatively and positively—in five ways:

1. Aid resources can be stolen by warriors to support armies and buy weapons.
2. Aid affects markets, either reinforcing the war economy or reinforcing the peace economy.
3. The distributional impacts of aid affect intergroup relationships, worsening tensions or reinforcing connectors.
4. Aid can substitute for local resources that would have been required to meet civilian needs, and thus free them up for conflict.
5. Aid can legitimize people and their actions/agendas, either supporting the pursuit of war or the pursuit of peace.

Theft

Theft is the most widely recognized process by which aid feeds into conflict, though not necessarily the most important in terms of impact.

Aid workers have been extremely inventive in developing strategies to avoid theft of aid goods. Some deliver goods unannounced, according to no fixed schedule and never to the same location twice so thieves cannot know when or where to steal. Some lower the resale value of the aid goods (without damaging their usefulness), thus undermining the incentive to steal. Others make theft inconvenient so the effort is not worth the return. Some broadly advertise their planned aid deliveries, so that communities for whom the aid is intended can hold thieves accountable. This last strategy, relying on communities to thwart theft, not only reduces the resources available for conflict, it also reinforces the connectedness of civilian communities and, thus, strengthens them.

Aid Affects Markets

Wars reshape production, employment, trade, and service delivery from peacetime to war-related activities. Some people are enriched by war while many are impoverished. Some trade linkages are supported while others are disrupted.

Because of the wealth that aid represents and the systems it relies on, profits can be made by local people who are in a position to control the assets that aid needs. War disrupts distribution systems and routes, and aid agencies need these to reach at-risk populations. Individuals and groups who control delivery and access can gain both financially and politically. Whenever local individuals or groups gain economically from the presence of aid, whether it is because they gain employment or because they assist aid needs, the influx of massive aid can reinforce their interest in the perpetuation of the war economy. In addition, when aid agencies import goods that can be produced locally and distribute them for free, this can undermine peacetime economic incentives and reduce both opportunities and incentives for the return to peace.

To avoid reinforcing a war economy and undermining a peace economy, aid agencies should assess both the local capacity for supplying the goods they need and the impact of their purchases on war profiteering. To avoid undermining peacetime activities, they can buy aid goods locally rather than importing them. When such purchases support normal, peacetime economic activities (such as agriculture) rather than special, war-related enterprises (such as guard services), they can help maintain peacetime economic systems. When such purchases rely on or promote intergroup cooperation, it strengthens connectors. Agencies sometimes peg prices for local goods and services at peacetime rates in order to ensure the ease of transition back to peacetime by preserving indigenous productive capacity.

Some NGOs include training for local staff in professions that can become peacetime employment. Some reinforce such training by providing small-scale loans to help their local staff set up new enterprises during the transition from war to peace.

The ability of individuals to make unwarranted profits because of war conditions often involves an element of secrecy and threat. When aid agencies locate decisions about payments in a broad community base, this can limit people's incentives and opportunities to make unreasonable incomes from war. War profiteering may be best controlled by community accountability, which, again, can be used to reinforce intergroup connectors.

Distributional Impacts

Aid agencies usually target subgroups. With limited resources, they focus where need is greatest. However, experience shows that, when targeting criteria exactly match the subgroup divisions of the war, targeting aid can reinforce and worsen intergroup dividers.

The price and wage effects of aid discussed above can also reinforce intergroup tensions when ownership of the assets that aid needs is differentially distributed among local groups. For example, when aid agencies hire local people who can speak the foreign language of the agency, these benefits are often biased because foreign language ability is related to educational access that is, in turn, correlated to patterns of privilege and discrimination that underlies intergroup dividers.

To avoid exacerbating tensions this way, aid workers can organize aid delivery so that, for anyone to gain, everyone must gain. They can develop committees or rely on existing leadership structures where responsibility for making distributional decisions is broadly discussed and decided. When people are involved in making decisions about how to distribute aid, they often accept a system that favors the neediest even though they are of another group. Aid's resources can be directed toward linking people's interests and enlarging and reinforcing their economic interdependence. They can provide incentives for people to work together on nonwar activities and issues.

Substitution Effects of Aid

External aid can fill so great a proportion of civilian needs for food, shelter, safety, and health services that significant local resources are freed up for the pursuit of war. This economic substitution effect of aid has a further political impact. Experience shows that when external aid agencies assume responsibility for civilian survival, there is a tendency for warlords to define their responsibility only in terms of military control. Even if they began their struggle with a commitment to peacetime political leadership, as the international aid community takes over the job of feeding and providing health services and shelter for civilians, they increasingly relinquish responsibility for civilian welfare, focus on military ends, and over time define their roles solely in terms of physical control and violent attainment and maintenance of it.

To avoid the economic substitution effects, some aid agencies limit inputs to minimal levels. Rather than supplying resources from the outside, they focus support on local efforts to meet local needs.

The political substitution effect poses another challenge. In the next section, after we discuss how aid legitimizes people and actions, we describe how some aid staff have tried to encourage warriors to assume responsibility for civilian survival.

Aid Legitimizes People and Actions

When they control a given geographical area, commanders expect aid agencies to comply with the rules and restrictions they impose in that area. They may tax aid goods, impose duties, establish currency exchange rates, and restrict delivery sites and schedules. They often use the income to finance war; they use aid delivery sites to control where people live (or do not live) and to control people's loyalties. Further, when aid agencies depend on the permission of armed factions to gain access to people with whom they need to work, this reinforces factional power and legitimacy.

Aid agencies find it impossible to avoid dealing with the warriors who control areas where they work. The issue, thus, is *how* to interact with them. To understand how aid workers can avoid reinforcing the illegitimate power of warriors, it is important to understand *what* is illegitimate about their power.

As aid agencies, we do not want to support oppression inflicted through violence and threat. We do not want to legitimate self-serving power and greed. We do want to support the ability of communities to hold their leaders accountable for civilian welfare. And we do want to support people's nonwar activities and attitudes. It is not the responsibility of international aid agencies to govern, nor to presume that they know the appropriate systems of governance for the people with whom they work. This is the job of local people, not outsiders. All international assistance should be designed to leave behind a society strengthened by its interactions with aid rather than weakened by them.

From this perspective, the question is not how to avoid warlords but how to encourage (push?) them to assume responsibility for civilian welfare and reduce their thuglike behavior. There are no efforts to affect such changes that have produced immediate or total transformations. However, some aid workers have found that they can help lower the levels of threat and coercion that characterize situations of conflict by setting a "tone" in their interactions that emphasizes and demonstrates tolerance, respect, trust, and commitment to human welfare. To co-opt commanders into assuming responsibility for civilian welfare, they have set up systems and routines to involve warriors in bettering people's lives. For example, they meet regularly with commanders or their representatives to discuss their aid to civilians; they take "authorities" to visit project sites so that they interact with people there face to face; and they expose commanders to the real impacts of their policies on people's lives.

To do this without naiveté is tricky. In the following section, we discuss how aid's implicit messages offer possibilities for providing aid in war zones with an alternative tone.

IMPLICIT ETHICAL MESSAGES

Seven implicit ethical messages have been identified as exacerbating aid's negative impacts on conflict.

1. When aid agencies hire armed guards to protect their resources or their staff, the implicit message received by people in the conflict area is

that it is legitimate for arms to determine who has access to food, health services, and the other goods that aid agencies provide.

2. When aid agencies refuse to cooperate with each other in the field and when, worse, they actually compete for beneficiaries by differentiating their work as "good" and other agencies' work as "bad," the implicit message conveyed to people in the conflict zone is that one does not have to work with, or respect, people with whom one does not agree.

3. When aid workers use the resources at their disposal for their own welfare or entertainment (as when they use the agency vehicle for a much-needed weekend outing to the mountains), the message conveyed is that one can use whatever resources one controls for one's own benefit without accountability to anyone else, even those whose needs are greater. Such a message of impunity mirrors the impunity exercised by warriors.

4. When aid agencies produce emergency plans that call for evacuation of expatriate staff but leave local staff behind in time of danger, the message conveyed is that some lives are of greater value than others.

5. When aid workers disclaim responsibility for the impacts of their aid programs, saying "It's not my fault; my headquarters (or my donor) makes me do it this way," they reinforce the attitude of many participants in war who also claim not to be responsible for what they do because "others" make them do it.

6. When aid workers approach each checkpoint or interaction with warriors with hostility, suspicion, and belligerence, they reinforce the modes and moods of warfare whereby everyone assumes that no one can be trusted and that "those people" only understand power.

7. When aid agencies depict the horrors of war in terms that cite atrocities against innocent victims, they very often reinforce the sense that all wrong is done by one group while others are only "victims." This demarcation is seldom, if ever, accurate and the messages thereby further the tendencies of warfare whereby some demonize others for their own purposes.

Aid workers who recognize that the methods they employ to deliver aid convey such implicit ethical messages to the people they serve have found numerous small ways to avoid them. They have adopted behaviors that reinforce, instead, a mood of security, appreciation, respect for life, accountability, trust, and sympathy—in short, of connectedness—that allows others also to remember and sometimes act on these values.

CONCLUSION

The implications of these lessons about the impact of aid through resource transfers and through implicit ethical messages are clear. It is neither inevitable nor excusable that aid should worsen conflict. Aid agency staff have ample knowledge based on past field experience of how aid affects conflict. They can predict, and thus prevent, the repeated patterns by which aid worsens intergroup tensions. They can identify existing connectors among groups and design their programs in ways that build on and support these. Using the lessons they and their colleagues have learned, aid workers can, and should, hold themselves accountable not only for the intended consequences of their work but also for its side effects on the conflicts where they work.

As to the need for institutional change within aid agencies, the answer is nuanced. Many of these programmatic adjustments can be made by field staff in their daily operational work. However, for field staff to act on these guidelines, they must be encouraged to learn about them, try new approaches, and reflect with colleagues on these side effects of their aid work. Ultimately, they must be held accountable by their headquarters and by their donors not only for the lives that they save but also for the ways in which their life-saving activities affect the conflicts that prompted them. And, if field staff are to be expected to assume these new roles, then aid agency headquarters and aid donors will also have to be cognizant of how aid affects conflict, and they will have to adopt new policies and procedures that support and reinforce the best practices of field workers that incorporate and integrate the lessons about how aid and conflict interact, always seeking to reduce (rather than feed) intergroup divisions and to support (rather than undermine) intergroup connectedness.

NOTE

This article is based on and partially extracted from Mary B. Anderson, *Do No Harm: How Aid Can Support Peace—or War,* Lynne Rienner Publishers, Boulder, Colo., 1999.

Participatory Action Research as a Tool for Peacebuilding: The WSP Experience

Matthias Stiefel

The reflections that follow arose out of the four-year, global field experience of the War-Torn Societies Project (WSP).[1] They first examine the main challenges faced by societies in the rebuilding process, then the key elements of a postwar development approach, and finally the potential for participatory-action research as a tool for rebuilding.

UNDERSTANDING THE CHALLENGES OF REBUILDING WAR-TORN SOCIETIES

The challenge of rebuilding war-torn societies is infinitely more difficult and complex than is generally recognized. It exceeds by far the challenges of "normal" development processes that, in countries emerging from war, are amplified by the legacy of the conflict (physical destruction, lack of resources and manpower, institutional fragility, political volatility, social trauma), by the urgency of the problems, and by the simultaneous challenges of humanitarian relief and military security. It is this complexity that multiplies the number of actors and agendas present in any postconflict country and introduces logics and practices of assistance and intervention that often run counter to basic principles of development assistance.

Mending Relations and Restoring Dignity, Trust, and Faith

Societies emerging from war face a range of problems, all connected and urgent. But one overshadows and affects all the others: the destruction of relationships and the loss of trust, confidence, dignity, and faith. More than the physical, institutional, or systemic destruction that war brings, it is this invisible legacy, grounded in individual and collective trauma, that is most potent and destructive. It has the potential to undermine the solutions to all the other problems, be they economic, technical, institutional, political, humanitarian, or security related.

If people do not trust each other and lack trust and confidence in government and in the rebuilding process in general, then the best rebuilding strategies are likely to fail. Demobilizing and disarming combatants is likely to remain a sham if protagonists do not feel secure and have no trust in the political arrangements put in place. And the promotion of economic efficiency helps little if the confidence of investors and consumers in the stability of the system is not restored.

A case in point is Somalia, where mistrust among the Somali people for government institutions has been one of the major obstacles to the restoration of administration at any level. People are simply too afraid that real authority bestowed upon any power structure may be abused or used against them. Similarly, Guatemala is an example of a society emerging from decades of civil war where destruction is much less physical than psychological, social, and political. Rebuilding requires above all restoring confidence and trust in the legitimacy of public institutions.

Problems of relationships between people and institutions are compounded by the lack of neutral spaces in which they can meet and talk. The politicized context leaves few neutral or impartial spaces for dialogue, and postwar political systems rarely provide institutionalized mechanisms for dialogue and communication. Also, the authoritarian tendencies of many postwar governments are not conducive to constructive communication and genuine open dialogue. Often governments simply do not see the need to bring civil society in its widest sense into the policy debate and work on the basis that the urgency of the rebuilding task diminishes the need to take time for dialogue, and that civil society accepts this.

Problems of relationships between people are compounded by the difficulties of reconciliation. Painful and divisive memories of the conflict are difficult to set aside and are often exacerbated by inappropriate policies that are insensitive to the impact they may have on relationships and thus on the promotion of peace or of conflict. This is particularly apparent and serious in cases like Rwanda or the former Yugoslavia, where the scale of horrors perpetrated during the war left deep and seemingly indelible scars in the collective memory of people. But it is just as relevant and potentially destructive for the rebuilding process in most other societies emerging from war. Reconciliation, the healing of bitter memories, the mending of relations, and the restoration of trust is an infinitely complex and delicate exercise and may take a generation or more. The fact that people are ready to work together in rebuilding programs and projects does not necessarily mean that they no longer harbor resentments or that they feel reconciled with former adversaries. It often just shows that people are surprisingly pragmatic and ready to work with former enemies in the elementary pursuit of livelihood and security. Even the restoration of justice by itself does not heal relations, though it is likely to contribute to healing by attributing responsibility and punishing perpetrators of violence.

Rebuilding Is a Development Challenge in a War-Torn Society

Problems faced by different societies emerging from war are surprisingly similar: they are basically development challenges—related to growth, stability, and sustainability—amplified and compounded by the multiple impacts and legacies of the war and by the simultaneous presence of humanitarian and security issues: military presence, displacement, people seeking refuge, family breakdowns, increased health and sanitation problems, and the like. Challenges of political development linked to the mending, building, and clarifying of relationships among people and between people and institutions are at the heart of the rebuilding challenge. This is common to all postwar societies, though the political configuration of actors, and thus the range of possible solutions, varies considerably depending on the type of war and the type of peace. An unfinished civil war on which a cease-fire has been imposed from the outside, as in Bosnia or to some extent Mozambique, obviously produces a very different set of political actors and dynamics than a successful liberation war, such as in Eritrea, where a successful liberation movement acquires state power invested with the legitimacy and credibility of victory. A "failed state" like Somalia presents yet a different type, and so does Guatemala.

Observations of postwar development policies.   Because humanitarian and military security challenges are added to the developmental challenges, most postconflict problems involve multiple policy approaches and multiple actors at different levels, from the local to the international. Efforts are sometimes made to adopt integrated approaches to assistance, but they are always complex and potentially conflictual because they imply being able to accommodate vastly different agendas and logics of action. It is because actors are aware of this, and because so many different actors are involved, that sometimes nothing gets done, and sometimes all the problems are tackled at once.

As for humanitarian and security challenges, they are present and real, but usually they are temporary and do not alter the fundamentally developmental nature of the rebuilding challenge. Humanitarian needs often increase at the end of a war, mostly because of large-scale movements of people, and humanitarian relief aid responds to this, alleviating suffering and providing basic livelihood support. It helps people get through the most difficult phases after the war, but is probably not crucial in terms of the longer-term rebuilding process. As for military security challenges, they are largely a reflection of the challenge of political developments, and this itself reflects the primary need to mend relations and restore trust. They cannot be tackled by military means alone but require that the root causes

of distrust and insecurity—between communities and neighboring countries—be resolved.

POSTWAR DEVELOPMENT APPROACH

There are no blueprints for rebuilding societies after war. Although the
objective, technical challenges and problems faced by societies after war
are surprisingly similar in most postwar situations, the political context and
configuration of actors, and the quality and nature of relations between
actors and institutions, are unique to each case. Because it is precisely these
qualitative and invisible legacies of war that determine the extent to which
technical solutions can be applied to specific problems, it is not possible to
draw up a blueprint for tackling the many challenges facing a society after
war. At best, general guidelines about priorities and methods of approach
can be formulated. Nor is it possible to simply replicate policies that
proved successful in one case in a new situation, although it is obviously
possible to learn from past successes and failures. Concrete policy responses to specific rebuilding challenges must consequently be defined anew in
each case and in accordance with given political realities.

Developing an Approach Tailored
to the Requirements of Postwar Rebuilding

Such an approach must be based on a holistic and in-depth understanding
of the problems and the ways they relate to each other, of available
resources, and of actors and their respective agendas. It must also consider
the larger geographical influences and implications of problems and of possible policy responses. It must give particular consideration to political
development, which is as important as and crucial to social and economic
development.

Given the nature of the challenges, political development is particularly important but is often not given sufficient attention in rebuilding strategies. In the case of Somalia, the UN has recognized that the central problem of this country today is one of governance. Without some kind of
formula for the restoration of public administration, it will be impossible to
find ways to provide social services, regulate economic activity, protect the
environment, and promote reconciliation.

A new development approach will have to take into account and target
the root causes of war, as well as the tensions or problems that may emerge
and grow as an unintended result of the rebuilding process itself and that
may then become sources of conflict. It must also be based on a long-term
perspective and strategy, for rebuilding a war-torn society can take a gener-

ation or more. At the same time, it must be able to accommodate both the need for urgent action in response to urgent problems, and the need for patience and the ability to wait for solutions to mature. Both may be equally difficult and are not common in traditional development approaches. The ability to respond urgently, through emergency development responses, requires flexibility, room for pragmatic ad hoc solutions and decisionmaking, possibly downward transfer of authority, and special budgetary reserves. The ability to wait presumes exceptional sensitivity on the part of decisionmakers to the evolving political and societal dynamics and much flexibility in timetables and rebuilding plans. All this has major repercussions on structures and processes at headquarters level.

Building Relationships and Restoring Dignity and Trust Must Become Explicit, Overriding Policy Objectives

Mending relations and restoring trust have been identified as the primary challenge of postwar societies. Relations must also be mended between the present, the past, and the future to prevent bitter memories of the past from poisoning visions of the future. This does not mean restoring the past. It means defining new roles and sound relations between people, ethnic or religious groups, and between people and authorities. It means working out a new, common order of values. It means inventing a new and different future. The challenge of rebuilding, if approached as a common task, can heal relations and restore dignity, trust, and faith in the future as people learn to cope with the past together and regain control over the present and the future.

Relations can often be mended through the appropriate design of rebuilding strategies that pay proper attention to the political and relational context in which they are applied. Development or humanitarian rebuilding strategies should be designed and applied in such a way that they not only address their primary objective but at the same time improve relations and build trust. If they are poorly designed, they can fuel tensions and lead to new conflict.

Mending relations requires that ambiguous or unjust relations be clarified or rectified. This is one reason why it is so important to work out power-sharing arrangements between parties to a conflict. Third parties, often external actors, may need to play a mediating role. Power-sharing arrangements must be both realistic (reflecting the actual configuration of forces) and be perceived as equitable if they are to be sustainable and contribute to the consolidation of peace. Mending relations also requires that relations of trust be restored between the people and government and institutions. Setting up inclusive systems of governance and promoting consensual and participatory decisionmaking processes greatly contributes to this, as does establishing transparent and regular communication and neutral spaces for dialogue. Authoritarian systems and practices of governance are likely to exacerbate old tensions and fuel distrust and conflict. However, more than working together in common rebuilding schemes, it is necessary that bitter memories of the past linked to the horrors of war are healed. Justice alone cannot do this, but memories can stop hurting if there is reconciliation and the capacity to forgive. Reconciliation requires exposing, admitting the truth about atrocities of the past. This is why bodies such as the Truth and Reconciliation Commission in South Africa, the Comisión pare el Esclarecimiento Histórico in Guatemala, or similar bodies or mechanisms that publicly expose the truth about what happened are so important.

Postwar Development, External Assistance, and Peacebuilding

The quality of external assistance to war-torn societies can and must be dramatically improved if it is to contribute effectively to rebuilding. This requires major reform and explicit political commitment. Both the approach and the operational practice of aid need to change, although operational practice of reform is probably more important and more urgent.

It is the operational practice of external assistance at the field level that ultimately determines how effective it will be. Operating in unstable, volatile, risky, and politicized postwar situations is not easy, and it is not surprising that it is at the level of implementation of new policy approaches to postwar situations that international assistance most frequently fails. There is an urgent need for operational reform; not so much *what* is done but *how* it is done. There must be more listening and.discussion and less imposition, more facilitation and empowerment and less control, more sensitivity to intangible processes and less emphasis on output and measurable results. There needs to be more quality and possibly less quantity.

To help in the rebuilding of war-torn societies, external actors require in-depth, intimate knowledge and understanding of local and national actors, forces, and dynamics. Defining an assistance policy and implementing it starts with a clear analysis based on a holistic understanding of the postwar situation and the specific country context, the legacies of the war, the root causes of conflict, the different actors involved, and more generally the dynamics of peace and war. This is particularly important given the essentially political nature of rebuilding, which can turn the most trivial administrative task into a political act. The effectiveness of international assistance depends on the ability to understand the political context and to fit constructively into it. What is needed is more than technical knowledge but a deep understanding of postwar rebuilding, of the subtleties of inter-group relations, of issues of power sharing and of reconciliation. It requires extensive preparatory work before intervening and, ideally, a long-term or continuous presence in the country. At the field level, external actors must build informal networks of relations and trust. These can provide not only important insights into local realities but also open up informal and flexible lines of communication that are a vital prerequisite to operational success. It also implies better and more effective sharing of information and knowledge.

Work in postwar societies demands a great degree of flexibility and the capacity to adapt pragmatically to a volatile and rapidly changing context. This implies far-reaching changes in the way assistance programs are formulated, funded, and implemented. Therefore, it is necessary to define special and simplified administrative rules and regulations and accounting and financial procedures for work that gives more flexibility and allows for quick action in crisis and conflict countries. Changing needs and realities must be taken into account in the periodic adjustment of programs and delivery. This may imply rolling work plans and timetables that are regularly revised. Also, special budgetary reserves have to be created to allow operating budgets to be flexible so that they can be adapted at short notice in line with changing needs.

In joint or coordinated assistance operations, coordination forums and mechanisms such as strategic frameworks must include provisions for the flexible reallocation of funds between sectors and actors. Moreover, it implies delegation of authority from headquarters and capitals to field offices to allow operational decisions to be taken as near to the field as possible. Such delegation of authority must be accompanied by improved and more regular reporting and communication to ensure accountability.

Work in societies emerging from war requires specially trained and exceptionally qualified field staff to cope and succeed in such difficult and unstable contexts. Qualities required are the ability to take and manage risk, the analytical capacity to understand complex situations in a holistic way, political acumen and maturity, pragmatism and creativity in dealing with multiple actors in rapidly evolving situations, and exceptional commitment. Such work also requires intercultural, team-building, and communication skills. All this is more important than academic, technical, or administrative qualifications or indeed experience. A special system of rewards and sanctions for staff performance in crisis and postconflict countries must be elaborated that recognizes the special and difficult context of the work, rewards the taking and management of risk, and sanctions incompetence or dishonesty. Field staff in postwar situations require special headquarters support that can only be given if desk officers and managers at headquarters are themselves specially chosen and trained. They should be familiar with the specific country contexts their work relates to and with the special demands these contexts impose.

To be effective, external assistance must be carefully timed to local dynamics. The failure of external assistance projects is often due to wrong timing. It has to be noticed that there are important differences between the anthropological/political time in which reality in the field evolves and the chronological/bureaucratic time that governs international assistance agencies. Aware of these differences, it is important to adapt external assistance to local political timing. This may require activities to be accelerated or slowed down. It may also imply that external actors simply need to wait and do nothing until a situation has matured and the timing is right. Generally speaking, external assistance agencies must accept that rebuilding war-torn societies is a long-term process that evolves in often unpredictable and apparently irrational ways and that cannot therefore be easily planned. They must move away from a preoccupation with urgent action and quick fixes and define their role in a medium- to long-term perspective.

The promotion of local and national ownership of external assistance projects can, at times, become an objective in itself because it contributes in important ways to building local capacities and to restoring confidence and dignity. Promoting local or national ownership goes beyond participation. It implies transferring control from donors to recipients and accepting the implications this may have in terms of redefining objectives and priorities and nationalization of the project. It also implies a common learning process during which local and national actors gradually acquire the ability and confidence to direct, while the role of external assistance is reduced to back-up support, facilitating, providing advice, and, at times, mediating between local or national actors. As a result of this, administrative donor control is replaced by collective social control and responsibility on the part of the recipients.

PARTICIPATORY ACTION RESEARCH AS A REBUILDING TOOL

The basic principle of Participatory Action Research (PAR) is that researchers and social actors join forces in collective research and analysis. The social actors contribute their knowledge of the issues at stake and the researchers help to systematize this knowledge, carrying out targeted investigations to complete it, and leading the collective analysis exercise. Social actors, who traditionally are the objects of research, become at the same time the active subjects of the research. The potential importance and value of PAR as a research methodology is contained in the main assumptions on which it is based. It presumes, for example, that if researchers and social actors work together as a team in a collective effort of research and analysis, the results obtained are better and reflect reality more effectively, because the participants bring to the research exclusive knowledge and understanding that would not otherwise be available. This raises delicate questions of objectivity, but it is assumed that this bias can be addressed and excessive politicization of the research avoided. It also presumes that the research results and findings are more usable because the involvement of policymakers and other participants encourages them to apply the results and translate them into concrete policy and action.

PAR also presupposes that the very exercise of engaging social actors in such processes leads to political action, which is generated by and unfolds in the very process of research. It presumes to provide an answer to the problem of transferring ownership of the research results and processes to those ultimately intended to benefit from them, and that the value of this by far exceeds possible limitations on scientific rigor.

PAR can contribute to rebuilding not only in the traditional sense of generating insights and better understanding of complex problems—this any research is supposed to achieve. It also greatly increases the applicability and relevance of the research results and, beyond that, facilitates and leads to the integration of research findings into the policymaking process. Moreover, taking the form of inclusive policy debate and processes at national and local levels and involving a wide range of local and possibly external actors, it can contribute to promoting a better and more comprehensive understanding of complex postconflict situations. Such processes represent an invaluable source of information and tools for analysis. They can help in setting priorities and defining the responsibilities of internal and external actors and improve understanding between them. They can also provide a reality check for assistance actors and can help to limit and manage risk. Apart from their inherent merits, such processes can play a critical role in transforming relations and building trust among different actors by providing neutral spaces for communication and dialogue. They consequently also contribute to building a democratic culture and society.

PAR Can Promote Better Understanding of the Holistic Nature of Postconflict Problems

Intellectual and analytical clarity is particularly important for policymakers in postwar societies given the complexity and urgency of the challenges that they face. The active involvement in the research process of internal and external actors, representing different agendas, objectives, and mandates, facilitates the understanding of the holistic and interrelated nature of the problems faced in postwar societies. The participation of policymakers in participatory research processes may create problems of objectivity, but it provides access to information and increases the relevance and likely impact of the research. If the participatory research processes are led and animated by impartial researchers, then these cannot only counterbalance the subjectivity of participants but can contribute, or call on, specialized technical expertise if necessary.

PAR Can Facilitate the Search for More Integrated Policy Responses

Helping participants in a collective research process to see problems from the various actors' perspectives leads not only to a more holistic understanding but also quite naturally to more integrated policy responses. The fact that the actors are directly involved in the process and participate in the definition of policies greatly increases the chances that they will actually be applied. This is particularly the case if the PAR exercise can provide a neutral space that allows participants to depoliticize issues by examining them from a more objective technical and scientific perspective. The credibility of such a space is closely linked to the academic quality and the seriousness of the research that underpins the collective assessment exercise. It also depends on the perceived neutrality and impartiality of the researchers who provide the substantive support and impartially facilitate the process. Researchers must play multiple roles in such research processes: they must carry out preparatory research to provide substantive support for the discussions, animate the meetings, and mediate among antagonistic agendas. The real value and usefulness of such an exercise is linked to and increases with the informal, almost private character of the setting and the nonbinding nature of the agreements. However, it is important that such consultations remain complementary to formal processes of representation and decisionmaking and are not perceived by government as challenging these.

PAR Can Contribute to Consensus Building and to Promoting a Democratic Political Culture

The neutrality of the researchers and the research process is crucial. It must remain independent from any of the actors and institutions, including the government, and must be able to resist attempts by some actors to monopolize it, control it, and use it to further their own agenda. The research process must be inclusive, open to all the main actors, and must maintain a balanced representation. This can be difficult if, in the postwar period, the society develops rapidly and becomes more differentiated and complex with the emergence of new social and political forces. It is the inclusive nature of the process that provides it with the necessary political legitimacy. Also, the research process must continue over some time, at least a year or more, for the actors to get used to it, to dispel initial suspicion, and for participants to get to know each other. If such participatory research processes are well established and have gained respectability and legitimacy, they may also be able to play a role in preventing conflict. They can indeed provide an informal yet legitimate space—rare in postwar environments—where actors can discuss issues on which there is disagreement even if talks and negotiations are deadlocked on the formal political level. PAR collective research can neutralize politically divisive issues and allow protagonists to discuss them without losing face.

Bearing in mind the complexity of the development challenge and peacebuilding process, it is clear that PAR methods have an important contribution to make in loosening up the knot of problems faced by war-torn societies. However, it is only a tool, and its effectiveness depends very much on the people who are using it and their ability to adapt to the complexity of a postwar situation.

NOTES

These insights were initially put forth in "Rebuilding After War: A Summary Report of the War-Torn Societies Project," a WSP report written by Matthias Stiefel. This report was produced in late 1998 as part of the project's drawing of lessons exercise.

1. In 1994, WSP was established as a joint initiative of the United Nations Research Institute for Social Development and the Program in Strategic and International Security Studies of the Geneva Graduate Institute of International Studies. The objective of this pilot project has been to assist the international community and local authorities to improve their response to complex postconflict challenges by carrying out Participatory Action Research exercises in selected countries emerging from war. Between 1995 and 1998, country projects were carried out in Eritrea, Guatemala, Mozambique, and Somalia, with work in the latter continuing. The project served both to gain a better understanding of complex challenges, and to create experimental spaces for interaction between the different actors concerned with rebuilding.

During WSP's concluding year, in 1998, project activities were assessed and lessons were drawn from the WSP experience in the four countries and at the global level. Project results were then disseminated to audiences around the world through a series of workshops, conferences, and briefing sessions. It was agreed that WSP activities had been useful for the local, national, and international actors who had participated in the project and that WSP-type activities should be continued. In January 1999, WSP thus initiated a transition program to define the mandate and institutional structure and identity of a successor body. This new institution began work in January 2000.

REFERENCES

Kane, June. (1999). *The First Four Years (Eritrea, Guatemala, Mozambique, Somalia)*. WSP, Geneva, June.

Stiefel, Matthias. (1998). *Rebuilding After War: A Summary Report of the War-Torn Societies Project*. WSP, Geneva, October.

————. (1999). *Rebuilding After War: Lessons from WSP*. WSP, Geneva, October.

War-Torn Societies Project. (1994). *The Challenge of Rebuilding War-Torn Societies: Report on the Working Seminar at Cartigny, Geneva, 29 November to 1 December 1994*. WSP, Geneva, December. Photocopy.

————. (1998). *Improving External Assistance to War-Torn Societies: A Statement*. WSP, Geneva, July. Photocopy.

————. (1998). *Improving External Assistance to War-Torn Societies: Practical Recommendations for Managers of Multilateral and Bilateral Agencies*. WSP, Geneva, July. Photocopy.

————. (1999). *WSP in Practice*. WSP, Geneva, October.

CHAPTER 10

Training Local Peacebuilders

■ 10.1

The Challenge of Building Training Capacity: The Center for Conflict Resolution Approach in Burundi

Kent Arnold

In recent years, there has been an increasing emphasis on the "training of trainers" to build capacity for peacebuilding efforts. While the building of training capacity is a worthwhile endeavor, it raises a number of considerations for field diplomats who provide this type of training service. Anecdotal evidence suggests that training of trainers programs can have an important impact on the peacebuilding environment; still, there is much to be learned from the experiences of both providers and recipients of training of trainers initiatives.

This section will examine the training of trainers issues from two perspectives. It will deal with the challenges confronting *external trainers* (trainers who come from outside the conflict environment) in designing and implementing these programs. It will also address the needs of *local participants* (peacebuilders from within the system of conflict) in developing their training ability. The purpose of this section is to identify the particular challenges to building training capacity; program strategies that address some of these challenges; and guiding principles that can help trainers, especially those from outside the conflict environment, create a strong foundation for training of trainer programs.

The section is oriented toward field diplomats who are developing training of trainer programs in a foreign country. It is this type of initiative that often poses the most difficult challenges to trainers. A case study of a training of trainers program in Burundi will be used to illustrate various training issues. It was conducted by a South African nongovernmental organization (NGO) in partnership with two NGOs from Burundi whose staff were the recipients of the training. Their joint design and implementation of this program provides interesting insights into the process of building training capacity.

BUILDING TRAINING CAPACITY

The practice of peacebuilding is informed by many years of experience and research. People involved in various aspects of peacebuilding come to learn the body of knowledge and skills through a number of methods. Whether these techniques are learned through direct experience, observing others in action, or through a formal training or educational program, the process of learning is an ongoing endeavor. A training of trainers workshop is merely one of a number of possible steps for building training capacity. It is important for this type of approach to be supplemented with other activities. Even for very experienced peacebuilding trainers, keeping abreast of the debates in the field, studying new developments in peacebuilding, engaging in self-reflection, debriefing events with others, and soliciting feedback from participants and observers form a strong foundation for continued development as a peacebuilder.

The increasing emphasis on training trainers in peacekeeping, peace-making, and peacebuilding techniques arose, in part, due to the high demand for these techniques in conflict systems combined with the, too frequently, insufficient number of trainers and practitioners to meet the demand. As a result, the building of training capacity was given a higher priority. This approach assumed that there would be a training multiplier effect, that is, a greater number of trainers would more quickly meet the demand for peacebuilding knowledge and skills.

Although it seems obvious that increasing the number of peacebuilding trainers will have a positive impact on the conflict system, the building of this capacity is not so straightforward. Approaches to training trainers that underestimate the complexity of peacebuilding work or the process of becoming a trainer can lead to insufficient preparation and nurturing of the program's participants. For trainers who lack the necessary field experience, knowledge of the conflict context, and course content or institutional support to organize training events, there is an increased risk of conducting courses that negatively impact on the target audience. For external trainers, this risk is more acute. Initiatives designed by external trainers who are not sufficiently aware of the norms and ethics that should inform training efforts in a specific country, and the expectations and needs of local participants, can compromise the integrity of their mission.

Operating in systems that have or are experiencing destructive conflicts makes the trainer's work considerably more complicated. Communities in these environments usually have significant needs for reconciliation, reconstruction, and development, which are often exacerbated by mistrust, anger, fear, and despair. In communities with insufficient capacity to manage these competing concerns, human and material resources become thinly stretched. Trainers may find that they are overwhelmed by the demand for their services. The resulting tension between meeting the objectives of a specific training program and meeting the needs of the target audience can contribute to a number of problems, including (1) loss of strategic direction for training programs, which can lead to ad hoc training efforts that increase the number of people trained at the expense of depth of training; (2) trainer burnout due to a lack of time to properly organize, present, evaluate, and debrief training activities, which is often combined with a sense of frustration in not being able to meet all training requests; and (3) insufficient ongoing support of trainers and training participants, which can expose them to risks without opportunities for consulting, problem solving, and debriefing with experienced trainers or practitioners.

These concerns suggest that there are two critical dimensions to the design and implementation of training of trainer programs. The first dimension deals with the preparation, conduct, and approaches of external trainers. The second dimension deals with local participants, and it relates to how one approaches the challenge of building indigenous peacebuilding training capacity. Proper planning, program management, and local ownership can mitigate many of the typical problems. The following case study illustrates these issues in more detail.

CASE STUDY: TRAINING OF TRAINERS IN BURUNDI

In 1998, the Center for Conflict Resolution (CCR), a Cape Town–based training NGO, was invited to develop a training of trainers program for the staff of two NGOs based in Burundi. Burundi posed a number of special challenges for the CCR. First, there was a need to provide training in French. Second, it was a country still experiencing a significant amount of conflict. The related degree of suspicion between various parties to the conflict impacted considerably on the design and implementation of the program. Third, Burundi was a relatively new training environment for the CCR trainers. There was much that the trainers needed to know about the conflict and the needs of the training participants before they could properly design and develop this program.

The CCR had some experience with working in Burundi. One of its senior consultants had spent considerable time working at the government level on a Track 2 effort to facilitate dialogue. He was able to brief the trainers on the conflict and what it was like working and living in Burundi. The training staff were also given the opportunity to travel to Burundi a few times before designing the training of trainers program. Prior to discussions about this initiative, the CCR's trainers were invited to present a conflict resolution workshop to members of the Burundi parliament. Spending time in the country listening to Burundians talk about their conflict and having the opportunity to present a training workshop provided a strong foundation for developing this initiative.

In June 1998, the CCR's trainers met with the directors of their Burundi-partner NGOs, Search for Common Ground and Ligue Iteka. The discussion covered the needs of the participants, methodological approaches to training trainers, training content, funding, and logistical considerations for implementing the program. Although this meeting did not create consensus on all program objectives and strategies, it did identify sufficient common ground to get started. Over the next two months, the three organizations worked together to develop a three-phase training program and identify participants.

Because the CCR's experience in training trainers suggested that a smaller number of carefully qualified participants was better than a large number, it was decided that just seven people would be trained. These people were selected because they met the following criteria:

- They displayed an aptitude for peacemaking and a desire to do this kind of work.
- They had some experience in managing conflict situations in their professional lives.
- They had the self-confidence to work in front of groups.
- They were available and willing to conduct training courses both during and after the completion of the training program.

The conflict in Burundi has strong identity group characteristics; therefore, it was important to pay attention to this matter when selecting the team. The Burundi NGOs ensured that the team's diversity would meet the expectations of their potential training audiences.

Training Phase One: Basic Conflict Resolution and Training Methods

The first phase consisted of a nine-day training workshop that took place in August. The first week was spent training the trainers in basic conflict resolution theory and practice and training methods (see "Agenda for the Initial

Burundi Training of Trainers Workshop" at the end of this article). It also included team-building activities and the creation of a statement of commitment to the program by each of the participants. Training exercises were designed to prepare the participants for a briefing that they would conduct during the second week. Prior to the start of the training workshop, the participants were asked to set up a half-day meeting with a small group of people with whom they were familiar. The Burundian trainers worked with the CCR's trainers to design, develop, and present this briefing during the second week. These briefings were presented on consecutive days. Afterward, the CCR's French-speaking trainer used a videotape of the presentations to extensively review and debrief the sessions.

Prior to the first workshop, the CCR's trainers felt it would be important to include a local trainer with significant conflict resolution experience in the program. There were two reasons for this. First, it was felt that this person could provide local insight into the particular challenges to training Burundians in conflict resolution techniques. Second, especially when starting the process of development as a trainer, it is important to have close contact with experienced trainers to help discuss issues, debrief events, and problem solve challenges that arise. Because CCR trainers would not be generally available, it was necessary to find someone in Burundi who could play the support roles that the local participants would require.

The selected trainer was a person who the CCR had experience working with; however, their Burundi partners were not convinced that this person was an acceptable choice. For the first workshop, the partner NGOs agreed to allow this person to play the role of training observer. As trust was built and participants came to understand the value of having a senior trainer to assist them when CCR trainers were unavailable, he become more involved. In future training sessions, he presented simulations of traditional approaches to conflict, and he added valuable insights into the Burundian context.

Training Phase Two: Addressing More Advanced Topics

There was a three-month break between the first and second sessions. During this time, the Burundian trainers were asked to conduct another round of briefings and create conflict simulations that could be used for future training workshops. Both NGO teams started meeting together to provide support to one another. The participants from Search for Common Ground also had the opportunity to travel outside the country to attend conferences on conflict resolution. Their experiences formed the foundation for the second workshop. In November, the participants met with the CCR trainers again. The objectives for this workshop were to discuss the participants' experiences with briefing people about conflict resolution, address advanced conflict resolution and training topics, and prepare the trainers to present a half-day training workshop.

The November workshop focused more on the specific context in which the Burundi trainers were operating. It was designed to use their experiences of working with particular audiences to examine conflict resolution and training processes. The Burundian trainers facilitated many of the workshop sessions. The workshop was designed to allow time for debriefing their role as facilitator and allowing the team to offer coaching tips. Over the final two days, the Burundian trainers worked with their CCR counterparts to design and develop their own training material. Both NGO teams were given the opportunity to present a portion of their training workshop and have this session thoroughly debriefed.

On Monday and Tuesday of the following week, each team presented their workshop with the assistance of the CCR's trainers. These sessions were videotaped and debriefed over the following two days. The final day was set aside to discuss the needs of the participants, how they would continue their development as trainers, and what would be included in the final training session. The participants were encouraged to continue meeting with one another and continue conducting workshops. They were also asked to attempt to resolve a dispute in either their personal or professional lives.

Training Phase Three: Self-reflection, Problem Solving, and Future Considerations

The third training session was conducted in March 1999. This workshop focused on self-reflection. The trainers were given an opportunity to discuss personal issues as well as their training and intervention efforts. There was also time given to simulations, training preparation, and discussing traditional conflict-resolution practices. During the second week, the trainers worked together to conduct a two-day workshop. This was followed by a debriefing session and a discussion of the future needs of the training team. While this marked the completion of the three-phase program, there is a need for ongoing support as the trainers continue their process of development.

DEVELOPMENT OF THE BURUNDI TRAINING OF TRAINERS PROGRAM

The design and implementation of this training of trainers program in Burundi was informed by a number of principles that guide the CCR's training efforts. These principles have been derived from years of experience as both recipient and provider of training of trainer programs. They include principles related to the preparation of external trainers, their conduct, and the design of the training program. These principles can help external trainers address some of the particular challenges involved in building training capacity and reduce the risk of developing inappropriate training programs. While these principles are oriented toward the external trainer operating in a foreign environment, many of the principles have general applicability to the training of trainer programs.

Principles Related to Preparing Training Courses

Gain an understanding of the context in which the training will take place. Skills training is tightly bound to the environment within which the participants operate. To provide the most useful course, the trainer needs to understand this environment. It is important for the training program to address the typical issues that confront participants, build on indigenous methods for managing these issues, and help participants analyze how the environment impacts on their work. One of the more important aspects of an external trainer's preparation is spending time getting to know the training environment. For the Burundi program, CCR trainers read articles about the conflict in Burundi, visited the country, and discussed issues with people working in Burundi.

Build partnerships with credible, local organizations. Partnerships with credible, local organizations can provide critical support for a training initiative. In addition to helping external trainers understand the conflict context and the needs and expectations of participants, local partners lend their credibility to the training program. In conflict systems where there is a high degree of mistrust, *who* conducts the training is as important as *what* is being trained. Finding credible, local partners helps external trainers create an effective program and ensure that it is seen to be legitimate.

Develop the training program with local partners. Local ownership is, in part, fostered by including partners in the design, development, and implementation of the program. In the Burundi case study, local partners created a strong foundation for the program. They helped design it, determined who would participate, organized training workshops, and provided financial support. Without their involvement, the CCR would not have attempted to run this program. Fostering local ownership of training programs also helps ensure that there is a future purpose for the training. Partners are usually in a good position to provide institutional support, which sustains peacebuilding efforts long after the external trainer leaves the environment.

Principles Guiding the Conduct of External Trainers

Be respectful. External trainers are often viewed as experts in their field. How they manage this perception impacts considerably on the training program. In too many cases, the African experience as a recipient of training is one where ideas or methods are imported from other countries without due consideration of their appropriateness or the value of local methods. This can make participants suspicious of the purpose of the training or its usefulness. Local participants bring a considerable amount of knowledge and experience to the training setting. In addition, they are the experts of their context. Trainers who incorporate this local wisdom and skill create a richer, more effective training and show that they value the work of participants.

Be sensitive to social, political, and cultural issues. While understanding the training context is part of proper preparation, it is also important to incorporate this knowledge into the training program. In the Burundi case study, the partnering organizations were sensitive to matters such as the selection of participants, avoiding social taboos or inappropriate course topics and simulations, and what training methods were used. Even the location of the training venue was an important consideration. Social, political, and cultural factors often have a significant impact on the development of the program. Careful attention to these matters can reduce suspicion for participants and prevent disruption of training workshops.

Spend time in the training environment. Operating in a familiar environment increases a trainer's confidence and effectiveness. It also shows participants that the trainer has a strong interest in their unique circumstances. It takes time to get to know the people and the challenges they face, and it takes time to support them in their work. External trainers who spend a week or two presenting training programs in an unfamiliar country typically do not have enough time to become well acquainted with the training environment. Presenting concepts and skills that are not sufficiently grounded in the participants' experiences may be inappropriate in some cases; however, in destructive conflict systems, it can place participants in dangerous situations. Committing time and resources to acquiring a deep understanding of the training environment positively impacts on the effectiveness of training and, in turn, the trainer's reputation.

Work to build a local network. In addition to developing partnerships for training initiatives, it is useful to build a local network of people who can provide guidance, feedback, and support. As certain challenges emerge, this network can assist the trainer in problem solving and generating new ideas.

Members of the network may provide direct assistance in training workshops, or they may provide wise counsel or emotional support. Throughout the training of trainers program in Burundi, CCR trainers relied heavily on their internal network to test assumptions, evaluate training ideas, and debrief difficult events. They used an experienced Burundian trainer from their network to support participants during and between workshop sessions. Tapping into local resources enriches the program for both trainers and participants.

Trainers should be experienced practitioners as well as trainers. Training in new environments, and especially in places that have or are experiencing violent conflict, requires confidence, flexibility, and skill. Experienced trainers are best prepared to manage this type of training setting. Training organizations should take care not to send inexperienced trainers into international settings without an experienced trainer to assist them. There are two primary reasons for this: (1) experienced, confident trainers are usually better suited to manage misunderstandings or disputes that may arise over course objectives and strategies; and (2) they usually have the background necessary to determine what concepts and skills are applicable to certain types of situations and inappropriate for others.

Experienced trainers, especially those who are also practitioners, often pick up on nuances raised by participants that may be unnoticed or disregarded by less experienced trainers. During the training of trainers course in Burundi, for example, a simulation raised important questions about how parties in Burundi confront one another about conflict issues. A trainer's past experience in peacebuilding is a valuable asset in helping participants frame their questions and guide this type of problem-solving situation.

Principles Guiding the Design of Training of Trainer Programs

Adapt training materials, content, and methods. A significant aspect of developing any training program is identifying the target audience. After this is done, their training needs can be assessed. The assessment is then used to build a framework for training workshops. These steps are especially important for external trainers working in a new environment because the training needs and expectations can vary considerably. For example, the CCR's preparation for training in Burundi included translating their training materials into French, adding new topics on communication and traditional methods of conflict resolution, constructing simulations based on the experiences of the participants, and providing a more detailed explanation of their training methods. Each of these adaptations was made through consultation with local partners and training participants.

Select participants carefully.   Especially when developing training of trainer programs, the selection of participants is critical. It is important for candidates to be committed to the goals of the program, have time to participate, and have the skills and qualities needed to perform the work. Only seven participants were selected for the Burundi training of trainers. The primary reason for choosing a small number was that building training capacity is a resource-intensive effort. It requires close supervision, opportunities for practice, detailed debriefing and feedback sessions, and opportunities to conduct workshops with experienced trainers. Providing intensive support for selected trainers gives them the encouragement and direction needed to grow more confident. Without it, their development can become stunted through uncertainty, frustration, and failure. Careful consideration of selection criteria helps ensure that the training has maximum impact on participants both during and after the program.

Meet the participants' immediate and long-term needs.   Most training programs are designed to meet the immediate needs of participants. It is important for training of trainer programs, however, to place an emphasis on the long-term needs of the participants. Becoming an experienced trainer takes considerable time. The processes of acquiring knowledge and skills, understanding the debates in their field of expertise, learning new concepts, and gaining practical experience will continue throughout their development as trainers. Although much can be gained from a single workshop, this is only one step in the much larger process of building training capacity. When designing training of trainer programs, it is important to incorporate other developmental aspects as well.

Provide time for practice and debriefing.   Skills-based training is a cyclical process of practice, feedback, reflection, and learning. Training of trainers' programs need to provide participants with opportunities to serve in the trainer role and debrief these events. There is no shortcut to becoming a good trainer, and there is a danger in trying to develop trainers too quickly, both to themselves and the people they train. The Burundi training program was designed in three phases to provide a good start for the participants. During each of the phases, there was a well-defined limit to the theory and techniques that would be covered. All three phases included an opportunity for each participant to present a section of a training session. The phases were also spread over eight months to provide time for the participants to gain practical experience between workshops.

The program was designed to ensure that these experiences were debriefed with experienced trainers and the course participants. These debriefing sessions were a central aspect of the course design. The purpose of these sessions was to allow each of the participants to relate what they experienced during the preparation and presentation of their team's briefing; to provide participants a time of reflection and constructive feedback from team members and observers; and to identify future topics for the training of trainers program.

Providing time for debriefing is an important component in any activity that produces significant degrees of excitement and anxiety. When training trainers, it is crucial because debriefing sessions often provide participants with insights or lessons that cannot be replicated through other methods. This program incorporated considerable time for participants to reflect on and learn from their experiences in order to help them consolidate what they learned from a specific activity and to establish a pattern of debriefing as an important aspect of their development as trainers.

Provide opportunities for training and practice. A trainer's ability and confidence tends to grow through experience as both trainer and practitioner in their field of interest. A well-designed training of trainers program will provide or encourage participants to find opportunities to gain this experience. Training of trainer participants usually become very motivated to offer their skills. Typically, however, they need some institutional support to help them get started. Designing this support into the program helps them take advantage of their eagerness to use their training skills and gain experience while the training is fresh in their minds.

CONCLUSION

The Burundi training of trainers case study illustrates a number of approaches to building training capacity. The objective of that program was to provide a strong start for the participants in their development as conflict-resolution trainers. During this three-phase program, it was clear that the trainers made considerable progress and built up a great deal of confidence in their ability as both conflict-resolution trainer and practitioner. Still, there is a need to continue ongoing support of these trainers. This is now being considered. The CCR conducts training workshops in Burundi with some frequency. It is hoped that future CCR training sessions will be assisted by this team of trainers and that time will be allocated to debriefing their ongoing activities.

Although it is important for all training programs to meet the needs and expectations of the participants, with training of trainer initiatives, it is critical. These programs produce a ripple effect on the environment. If the program is poorly conceived or implemented, trainees and future participants of their training sessions may be negatively affected. If the program is well designed and supported, these ripples can create currents that constructively guide efforts at reconciliation, reconstruction, and development.

APPENDIX: AGENDA FOR THE INITIAL BURUNDI TRAINING OF TRAINERS WORKSHOP

Each training of trainers course is unique. There is no set agenda for a conflict-resolution training of trainers program that will suffice for all or even most audiences. A well-designed training of trainers course will ensure that the needs of the participants are identified, clear objectives are determined, and appropriate strategies to attain the objectives are implemented. This section provides an overview of the agenda for the first workshop of the Burundi training of trainers program. It is very important to note, however, that this workshop was tailored to meet the specific needs of this target audience.

For this program, most of the participants had experience as either school teachers or facilitators of community workshops. Much of their work was conducted at the grassroots level with either youth or women's organizations. Prior to the training of trainers program, participants were frequently called upon to facilitate workshops and run activities geared toward reconciliation between members of different identity groups. This program was designed to help prepare them for two additional roles: training others in conflict-resolution techniques and intervening in conflict situations.

The first workshop introduced participants to basic topics in conflict resolution and training. The following list provides a general overview of the activities and content covered during this workshop. Each day of the workshop started with a time for participants to raise ideas and concerns. Each day ended with a review of the day and a time for reflection and feedback.

Day One

- Welcome and introduction to project: objectives for the workshop; objectives for the project; and group contract.
- Understanding conflict: nature, causes, and functions.
- Approaches to resolving conflict.
- Communication: Forms of communication; techniques for intervenors identifying positions and interests; and experiential exercises.

Day Two

- Components of conflict resolution: conflict analysis; process design; identifying and clarifying issues; and problem solving (purpose and options).
- Simulations and exercises used throughout the day.

Day Three

- Different types of decisionmaking processes.
- Constructing agreements: purpose and key elements.
- Principles of conflict resolution to guide the participants' work.

Day Four

- Background on the training of trainers program.
- Participants' role as change agents.
- Training methods: participants' experiences as trainers and facilitators; overview of training methods; and advantages and disadvantages of various training methods.
- Components of workshop session design: purpose, objectives, audience, content, and method.
- Exercise: design of a one-half-day briefing session on conflict resolution.

Day Five

- Presentation of briefing session design.
- Continued preparation of briefing session: allocation of session slots; development of content and materials; and presentation practice, reflection, and feedback.

Day Six

- Continued preparation of briefing session.

Day Seven

- Briefing presentation by Ligue Iteka (videotaped).
- Debriefing session with review of video.

Day Eight

- Briefing presentation by Search for Common Ground (videotaped).
- Debriefing session with review of video.

Day Nine

- Facilitated discussion dealing with issues and concerns emerging from the presentations.
- Discussion regarding topics for the next training workshop.
- Evaluation of the workshop.
- Vision and commitments for the project.

The presentations, debriefing sessions, and group discussions over the final three days were used to determine priorities for the second workshop. The participants expressed an interest in focusing on communication and problem-solving techniques at this workshop. The CCR trainers asked the participants to develop conflict-resolution scenarios for this workshop that were based on their experiences. The continued emphasis was on ensuring that the training program was addressing the specific needs of the participants and that the content was relevant to their context.

Designing Training Programs: The Life and Peace Institute Approach in Somalia

Johan Svensson

BACKGROUND

The Life and Peace Institute (LPI) was founded in 1985 as a peace research institute. Due to its close relationship with the Church of Sweden and other agencies that had a major commitment to the Horn of Africa region, a research project focusing on the Horn of Africa was initiated in 1987. This initial project has developed into a full-fledged program where research is one important component in an action-oriented conflict-transformation program. The largest component of the program is capacity building for local peacebuilding through training, which is the focus of this article. The program experience from the Horn of Africa has brought a new dimension to the LPI as a whole, which now regards itself as the International Peace Institute for Research and Action.

The Guiding Philosophy of the LPI/Horn of Africa Program

The Horn of Africa Program (HAP) experience is not based solely on a theoretical framework made from an overseas office. Rather, it is based on a guided process where research and the input of people from conflict areas have converged. Furthermore, it is built on the vast experience from the region of the former program director, the Reverend Sture Normark, and our strong conviction of local people's potential capacity to build peace.

The underlying philosophy assumes that peace is a process that must involve the entire society toward transforming attitudes of members of the conflicting parties and society toward each other. It is not a condition that can be achieved by signing agreements between conflicting parties at conference tables.

The HAP's peacebuilding concept is based on the conviction that sustainable peace can only be built from within, by the people themselves, drawing upon their own resources, within the context of their own culture and tradition. The concept further underlines that this is a long-term process that can only be made sustainable by the people themselves. The

LPI/HAP's role is to act as a facilitator to strengthen and empower locally initiated efforts and actors for peace and participatory democracy.

The philosophy is furthermore built on the findings and recommendations of two expert consultations on Somalia, involving both external scholars and intellectuals from the region and the experience of John Paul Lederach, Ph.D., professor in sociology and conflict studies at the Eastern Mennonite University (see "Levels of Leadership" by John Paul Lederach in this book).

The implementation of this concept should enable local people's capacity to make use of their indigenous knowledge, cultural and social resources, and traditional structures in conflict transformation and peacebuilding. The HAP refers to a community-based building of peace and democracy.

The Example of Somalia

The initial LPI/HAP involvement in Somalia did not start as a training program for peacebuilders. It started as a learning process, and it continues as a learning process. Initially, two expert consultations were organized in 1992 to provide a deeper understanding on how to approach the Somali conflict: one consultation with international scholars on Somalia, one with Somali intellectuals. These expert consultations advised us on the importance of strengthening various groups in the civil society in order to enhance their role in the reconciliation and peacebuilding process in Somalia. They further stressed the importance of the involvement of traditional leaders and women and the particular role they could contribute toward peacebuilding; they also emphasized the need to involve other groups in the so-called civil society as actors in the peace process.

According to how we understand the nature of conflict in Somalia—and this is true for most of today's internal conflicts—it is not possible to await the settlement of disputes and conflicts before you engage yourself in peacebuilding activities. Instead, it is necessary, while the conflict is ongoing, to equip the people themselves with skills, tools, and the capacity to work as peace agents in order to solve their own conflict. It is also important to empower groups in the civil society to challenge and marginalize leaders of the worrying factions.

The learning process has continued with the planning and implementation of specific programs aimed at strengthening and empowering the various groups of the civil society in their work toward peace and reconciliation. The program now involves:

- Capacity building for local administrations.
- A women's program.
- A reconciliation program.

- Civic education.
- Advocacy.
- Evaluation, research, and documentation.

TRAINING ACTIVITIES

Selection of Trainers

When starting the work, there was no local institution or organization in Somalia that we could see as our counterpart. Hence, we chose to employ our own trainers. Because it is essential to know and understand the local, social, and cultural context of the society that we aim to address with our peacebuilding training program, we chose to work exclusively with local trainers. Thus, the trainers became our first target group.

The trainer is a key person, and it is essential that he or she understands the message and content of the training modules in order to adequately convey and sometimes be able to model the message in the training context. To be able to "listen in" to what the participants are contributing, and to know how they themselves are practicing what is taught is important and may be an easier task if the trainer comes from the community he or she is training.

When recruiting trainers for the HAP, the following criteria have been considered:

- They are respected in the community.
- They do not have ties to any faction and are not active in any political group.
- They have completed higher education.
- They believe in the HAP approach.
- The team of trainers should as fairly as possible represent the various communities in the area where they are working. This is more important when the training takes place in an area of conflict between different communities.

Training of Trainers

The capital you have in a training program is, of course, human resources. Therefore, much effort has to be put into the development of the trainers and other staff, especially if you have a long-term commitment to the area you are working in. Most of our trainers have a university degree, but few had any previous theoretical knowledge about conflict or peacebuilding. As a result, we are trying to emphasize ongoing training and upgrading of our trainers' knowledge.

The first training of trainers course lasted three weeks. Thereafter, a two-week course has been given each year for two years, focusing on the subject content for the training program. This year the two-week course will focus more on research methodology, evaluation, and documentation, as well as participatory training methodologies. The trainers have identified relevant topics during review and planning meetings.

Organizational Setup

The aim from the initial involvement in Somalia has been to work in the entire country with the training program. To be able to run such a program, we set up teams of trainers working out of zone offices. Each team covers a certain geographical area and the team arranges seminars and training workshops in various locations over the zone. The training teams receive support from the regional office in Nairobi.

The training venues are evenly distributed all over Somalia. We have seen that a training workshop can have an impact, not only on the participants, but it also can contribute to a positive change in the community where the training takes place. Bringing participants together from various communities may also contribute toward confidence building between the host community and the participants from other areas.

Identification of Target Groups

In the capacity-building program for district councils, the participants were already selected as local councilors by the traditional elders representing the various communities. The reason for choosing this target group developed as a result of a major attempt to build peace through the restoration of local institutions for governance in a "failed state."

In the civic education project, different Somali society groups have been identified as key groups on the basis of their capacity to become agents of peace. The target groups in the civic education training program involve teachers, media personnel, artists, women office workers, elders, business people, law enforcement personnel, and others. This identification of groups has been done with our field-based staff and upon recommendations and advice from people from various Somali communities. The relevance for each target group differs from area to area. In the program review, the target groups have been evaluated and sometimes changed in favor of other groups.

Selection of Participants

Some basic criteria have been established for the selection of participants. The individuals are chosen from the various local, ethnic, and religious groups of Somalia. This process is often done through community representatives such as elders, local councils, or respected women leaders. It is important to ensure that no individual groups are left out, something which could endanger the continued support from communities toward the peacebuilding program. For the selection of participants for the women's program, we rely on peace volunteers. They have previously gone through a two- to three-week training course.

Content and Methodology of Training

The LPI/HAP training program aims at empowering the local people, transforming their attitudes, and strengthening their efforts in peacebuilding. These may be some of the objectives valid for all different training sessions, whether it is for district councilors or for other groups of the civil society. The content of the training for district councilors involves also technical subjects such as public administration, planning, and budgeting and finance, but the basis for the peacebuilding training is civic education. Under this heading we have two subject clusters: participatory democracy and peacebuilding. The participatory democracy module contains subjects such as gender in development, human rights, and leadership. The peacebuilding module contains the topics of conflict transformation, environment, resource conflicts, and small arms awareness.

We aim at using a participatory methodology and are trying to build on the participants' realities in utilizing their vast experiences. We may use such tools as role-plays, case studies, poems and songs, and different forms of group work in order to achieve this. It is easy to fall into relying on a standard lecture format; therefore, we are attempting to strengthen the trainers' knowledge in participatory training methods. Because we give the same kind of topics to a wide range of people, we have to adopt the topics to suit each group separately. For example, in the elders' training, the trainers act more as facilitators than trainers when it comes to conflict transformation and reconciliation. Here, the participants have a vast knowledge of the traditional methods of reconciliation, from which the LPI trainers can build the session around. The topic of human rights also allows the possibility of tying the modern concept to traditional ways of respecting the rights of others.

Material Development

The curriculum has been developed as a joint exercise of the trainers, the field training coordinators, the women coordinators, the national officers, and the regional program officers. The same curriculum is used by the teams all over the country. The individual zone team is then modifying the material according to the target groups they aim at addressing.

Moreover, the trainers are developing handouts according to the local context.

Program Review and Planning

To incorporate feedback from the field into program development, quarterly coordination meetings and yearly planning meetings take place. Furthermore, every three years program review and planning meetings also involving relevant program staff from headquarters are held. We have now just concluded the second program review and planning meeting. The results of these meetings influence and determine how, and if, the program will continue and develop.

REFLECTIONS AND LESSONS LEARNED

Reflections

When the Somalia training program started, we did not have any local counterpart but had to recruit our own team of trainers. This may have been essential, and without doing so there had perhaps been no training in peacebuilding at all. However, we now ask ourselves how the ownership of an eventual continued program can be transferred to the Somalis themselves. In a similar civic education program for southern Sudan, we are collaborating with the churches and other organizations already working on the ground. Here, we have seen our role more as facilitators and supporters of others to enable them to organize their own training of peacebuilders.

Initially, we could not foresee that what started as a training program for district councilors should develop into a major training program in peacebuilding for various Somali civil groups and last for several years. A training program normally has a certain life span. When the trainees have acquired the aimed skill and knowledge, the program may close down. When it comes to training of peacebuilders, we are aiming toward the transfer of skills, but also, and perhaps more important, the change of attitudes not only among the trainees but also in the society at large. We have realized that peacebuilding takes time, and hence there is a need to plan from the beginning on the necessity to commit time and resources. It is also important to see the training program as one component in a more holistic way of approaching community-based peacebuilding. Other components and interventions are definitely needed and in some locations may provide the only option for community-based peacebuilding.

What is the impact of this kind of capacity-building program? We have yet not undertaken any external impact study, even if there has been an evaluation of the training program for district councilors. We see and believe that we have got good practical evidence suggesting that there is a change in attitudes among participants in the training sessions, and also some visible changes in the society at large in some instances. However, there is a need to develop clear impact indicators already in the beginning of the training program. Now, we are planning the impact study for our Somali program toward the end of the year.

Main Lessons Learned from the HAP Experience

Training in peacebuilding is possible during ongoing conflict. The Somalia experience has taught us that it is possible to conduct a major training program in peacebuilding in conflict areas during an ongoing conflict, although, often, the diplomatic skills of our field staff have been put to the test when representatives of the worrying factions wanted to stop the training. In some instances we have seen how the training session itself has constituted a forum for reconciliation and confidence building between participants from different conflicting constituents. And in some instances the seminar itself has directly contributed to the resolution of the conflict. For example, in a seminar for elders, the facilitating role of the LPI/HAP training team has led to a significant breakthrough in a potentially very dangerous local conflict.

More focus on follow-up. There is a need to select fewer groups to train, and to follow up and support these groups in their various peace activities. After conducting numerous training sessions for different social groups, we have realized that we may have neglected to follow up and support them in their continued activities. Therefore, we will devote more time on follow-up and conduct less new training sessions.

As a tool for follow-up we are now introducing an activity plan for all participants toward the end of the training workshop. The activity plan challenges the participants to think through and plan on how they will use the new knowledge in their daily life for the coming year. It also provides us with a tool for follow-up and impact assessment. This may also contribute toward strengthening local groups for peace work.

Need to strengthen the research component. A training program is always a learning exercise in two ways, both for the target group as well as for the organizers. We have seen that not enough efforts and resources were put into research and documentation of the entire exercise. We are therefore putting emphasis on these two subjects in this year's training of trainers.

Linking peacebuilding with relief and rehabilitation aid. In conflict areas, where emergency relief and rehabilitation aid is present, numerous international and local agencies are working. We have learned that in these situations, there is often a need to link peacebuilding with their activities. It is not only a concept of "do no harm." The idea is more about adding a component to the relief program in order to utilize the intervention also in peacebuilding exercises. Further studies in this area are essential.

HOW TO DO PEACEBUILDING TRAINING PROGRAMS

Ownership and Sustainability

Ensure the ownership and sustainability of a training program for peacebuilding. From the beginning, there is a need to assess if there is a credible local organization having a fair representation in the area of intervention. Or there may be a need to link up with several organizations that already have the knowledge and the experience from the area.

Time Commitment

Ensure that you have the time and resources not only to start a training program but also to be able to give continued support over a substantial period of time.

Work with Local Trainers

To train at the community level requires a deep insight and knowledge about the area you train in. It is very difficult for an external trainer to acquire all this knowledge about the local environment, culture, and social organization. Hence, the recommendation is to equip local trainers with the skills to do the training at this level.

Ensure a representation of different communities living in the area of intervention when selecting the persons who will be the trainers. An excellent training content may be rejected due to lack of trust and confidence if the trainers are seen as being exclusively from the other side.

The capital in a training program is human resources. Encourage and invest in the trainers by providing upgrading courses. This will also enhance and further develop the program.

Build on Indigenous Knowledge and Resources

Encourage the trainers to build on local good practices. All communities are likely to have some good indigenous practices when it comes to relations with others, in traditional reconciliation, and settlement of disputes. Be prepared to adapt the training material or handouts after local conditions.

Count on the participants' own resources. This ensures the feeling of true participation and ownership of the process. This may be applicable both in respect to material resources in arranging the seminar and in human resources during the training session.

Importance of Venue

Select training venue with a purpose. Sometimes the ongoing training program may have an impact on the present situation in the area. Do not shy away from the difficult spots, but count on the contribution that the occasion of training may have for the community as such.

Work in the Local Language

Utilize training materials or handouts in the local language. Remember that the material will most likely be read by many more than the one person who had the opportunity to attend the training.

Gender Balance

Make sure that there is a fair gender balance in the team of trainers as well as in the selection of participants. Remember that at least half of the adult population are women.

Incorporate Feedback Mechanisms

Make sure that there is some built-in mechanism in the program that allows for feedback from the participants. This is both to ensure the best possible training but also to create a sense of ownership, and not only a sense, rather a real possibility to influence and change in the ongoing program based on the experience and knowledge gained during the sessions by the trainers themselves.

Impact Study

Try to set up indicators on how to measure the impact of your training program when initially putting together the program document.

Research and Documentation

Learn from the process and be ready to share your experience with others. It may be good to incorporate a research and documentation component from the beginning of the program process. The trainers and program staff are likely to learn as much from the participants as they do during the training sessions.

CONCLUSION

It is important to realize that the training program is only one part of a more holistic way of working for community-based peacebuilding. Other activities of importance for a community-based peacebuilding program are advocacy in support of the activities on the ground and for the people of the area. Another intervention may be to support various indigenous groups (i.e., traditional leaders, women's groups, youth) in their activities for peace. Then, as we have mentioned, a training program in peacebuilding is a learning process in two ways. We must not forget that what is learned in one conflict area may provide suggestions for solutions in another. Hence, the research and documentation component is essential to maximize the benefit of the intervention.

CHAPTER 11

Media

■ 11.1

The Role of Media in Conflicts

Ellen Gardner

Though the media's conflict-resolution potential is largely underutilized, it has in many instances played an important role in conflict resolution or in helping to rebuild a society after the conflict has passed. Recognizing the potential power of the media, many international organizations and media groups are now advancing new ideas on the media's role in conflict prevention and resolution and ways in which the media might contribute toward developing an effective system of nonviolent problem solving or positive media participation.

The job of reporting on any conflict can influence the situation in many ways. Media coverage can strongly influence how the parties, both inside and outside, relate to a conflict and the "players" within it by the choice of stories that are covered or omitted, the sources used, and the stand that is taken toward ethical reporting. The complexities of war and the advent of new mass media technology have further complicated the role of the media, with economics likely to predominate.

MEDIA ECONOMICS AND COMPETITION

Mass media—leading to incredible competition in and between the media—and the economic constraints that many newspapers and radio and television stations are experiencing place huge demands on the media in general, particularly in conflict or war reporting. Cutting costs means that there is a reduction in the number of journalists sent abroad, especially to far-flung places. With these financial constraints, the media often do not become involved until a crisis is happening, is already out of control, or at high points of public interest.

Often, by the time the media are dispatched to a conflict area, it is too late for any kind of prevention simply by media coverage, as stated by Lindsey Hilsum after reporting from the unfolding conflict in Rwanda in April 1994: "I couldn't stop the smallest part of it. I am only slowly beginning to understand it. At the time I could only watch and survive."[1]

Good news is no news, but conflict sells. The battle for ratings and advertising revenue has led to competition not only between newspapers and stations but also between journalists. Conflict reporting, especially with the mass popularity of television, has given birth to the "star" reporter, with many reporters concentrating more on maintaining an image than on reporting. With commercial pressures and stretching of budgets dominating much of the media, if the conflict is at a low point in public interest or in a distant country, the agency may take only a passing interest.

The necessity to cover a conflict or to be seen as covering a conflict has led some organizations to use agency material, like Reuters, the Associated Press, and Worldwide Television News. These agencies provide the words and pictures for a pre-fixed price, and are usually assembled at base in a TV edit room, thus ensuring rapid coverage of a story, albeit, secondhand, well before a correspondent and crew can be assembled and sent to the conflict area.

The ability to analyze a conflict is a basic requirement of good professional journalism, but often reporters are sent to conflict areas at a moment's notice with no knowledge of the underlying histories or causes of the conflict in a particular region. Showing the public horrific and dramatic images of the atrocities of war but with no explanation or understanding of the histories or complexities of the conflict, therefore giving a one-sided or distorted view, journalists and the public risk becoming party to the propaganda of the warring sides.

The pressure of deadline journalism, or of being the first to get the "big" story before the competition, can lead to a deficiency in covering or checking sources, as well as options and resolutions, and can tend to make some journalists concentrate on conflict behavior rather than conflict resolution. Given these factors, journalists, both local and international, are facing more demands and complexities in reporting from within the conflict areas.

AUTHENTICATING INFORMATION

One of the basic rules in journalism is to authenticate and question any information that is unclear or dubious; however, with instant reporting this often precludes verification. Many reporters do go to great lengths to authenticate information in order to report objectively, but there are numerous incidences where the military, governments, and civilian entities have been grossly disillusioned and angered by the media's attitude toward ethical reporting in conflict situations.

Journalists have also been disillusioned by information given them by what they considered to be "informed officials." Many reporters in the conflict in the former Yugoslavia have stated that they were at times astonished by claims and information given them by United Nations Protective Force and that upon further "digging," they proved that the information was incorrect.

Though information may not be given with the intent to mislead, the military, politicians, warring factions, and the media have different agendas, and different interpretations of the same event can result. Even some top UN officers proved unreliable because they were not well informed about the conflict in which they found themselves and had neither the time, resources nor the responsibility to investigate the war's political or historical background and were unprepared to challenge explanations they heard in daily conversations. Political leaders and warring factions are well aware of the power of the media to further their political agendas.

MEDIA FREEDOM ISSUES

In many countries, governments continue to dominate the media from which most people get their news and information, and freedom of the press does not fully exist, even where the media establishments are so-called privately owned. Various methods are used to silence or control the media.

The international and national media often have to undergo extreme pressure and danger in order to report professionally. In some countries, media personnel are fearful for their lives and livelihood and are continuously harassed and threatened. Stations have been closed down; government people have been installed in high positions; licenses have been denied or revoked; visas have been denied or revoked; material has been denied or destroyed; and pressures have been placed on journalists to "toe the government line," with threats of detention, litigation, or loss of employment for outspoken journalists. Such actions serve to remind journalists that they are being closely watched.

FREEDOM OF SPEECH

"One conception of democracy has it that a democratic society is one in which the public has the means to participate in some meaningful way in the management of their own affairs and the means of information are open and free."[2] The most fundamental responsibility of the media is to enable the public to participate in democratic life by providing information.

Most people would agree that freedom of speech is a fundamental right, but freedom of speech must bear a responsibility, and in the hands of the unethical, it is a dangerous weapon. If democracy is to grant freedom of speech, at what price should freedom of speech be allowed if it infringes on an individual's right to operate freely and without fear in society?

HATE MEDIA

Hate media can be defined as encouraging violent activities, tension, or hatred between races, ethnic or social groups, or countries for political goals and/or to foster conflict by offering a one-sided or biased view or opinion, and/or resorting to deception. Hate media is a good example of how freedom of speech is abused to deliberately worsen existing tensions between and within countries by whipping up nationalistic feelings and/or ethnic hatred. The use of hate speeches and their role in helping start many conflicts and savage massacres have been well documented.

Hate speeches are not new; hate speeches via radio were used in Nazi Germany to whip up racial hated and prepare the ground for the Holocaust. More recent obvious examples of this are the prominent roles played by the local media in justifying, supporting, and sustaining the wars, genocides, and ethnic cleansing in Rwanda and the former Yugoslavia.

Radio is still one of the most powerful mediums in countries where much of the population is illiterate or televisions are rare, and it is the key means to reach the public with news and information that can influence people, positively or negatively. It can be transmitted to local audiences or across national boundaries and behind enemy lines. Because radio can reach large and varied targeted audiences quickly, it is useful for many types of operations. Radio broadcasts can be quickly prepared, which is important when attempting to capitalize on targets of opportunity. Illiteracy does not prevent the listener from receiving the messages and forming their own individual images and ideas, and a skilled radio announcer can exert tremendous influence on the listener simply by how the message is transmitted.

The power of radio, in particular hate radio, figured prominently and played a key role in starting the genocide in Rwanda. The owners and managers of Radio-Television Libre de Mille Collines (RTLM) used the power of the radio to further their political agenda by broadcasting political propaganda and hate speeches that were well planned before the genocide started. Privately owned but government controlled, RTLM was created in mid-1993, and its shareholders had strong ties to the ruling regime and its security forces.

From July to October 1993, RTLM broadcasts were reported to have consisted mostly of popular music with little news or commentary and were designed along the lines of Western-style radio shows; they were frequently listened to by a large section of Kigali's population. After the October 21 assassination of Melchior Ndadaye, the first democratically elected and first Hutu president of Burundi, RTLM programs quickly became inflammatory and began to incite ethnic hatred that did not go unnoticed. RTLM received several formal warnings about breaches of law and contract. In addition, members of the international diplomatic community informally expressed concern about RTLM. Jamming the radio station was discussed but not seriously considered. Nothing was done, and the radio station went on to transmit its messages of hate, reportedly for up to twenty-four hours a day during the first several weeks of the genocide.

RTLM broadcast political propaganda and death warrants, targeting individuals and groups and encouraging the killing of Tutsis. "It is time to gather in the harvest," it told its listeners, helping set off the bloodshed that resulted in the deaths of over 1 million people and the loss of homes for many more. Encouraging the massacres to continue, it later announced, "The baskets are only half full. They should be filled to the brim." The station went as far as to read over the air individual names of people to be targeted.

Later in Burundi, Tanzania, and Zaire, broadcasts from extremist Hutu mobile stations urged more than 2 million refugees to remain in their camps until the day of reckoning. Many refugees, hearing of the broadcasts, remained in the refugee camps afraid for their lives if they tried to return to their homes.

The problem of hate speech, or hate media, also featured prominently in the war in the former Yugoslavia. State-owned media were extensively used as tools for spreading nationalist propaganda and retaining power by the warring factions on all sides to further their aim, and they were widely blamed for the resulting massacres and ethnic cleansing. Confrontations between the stabilization force peacekeeping troops and Serb hard-liners for control of television stations in Bosnia's Srpska Republic illustrate how valuable broadcasting can be in a conflict situation. In conflict situations, one of the first targets of the opposite side is to try to destroy a country's communication lines and to take control of independent media outlets within one's own country.

Those using hate speeches exploit their rights to freedom of speech in order to spread their messages of hatred. The difficulty recognizing those who use hate media is that they often operate in remote areas or use local languages, not easily recognizable, thereby escaping international attention until it is too late.

Media reports can be used to spread conflict, but they can also be used to foster tolerance and postconflict reconciliation. Many ideas have been put forward as a means of counteracting hate media and hate speeches; one of these is to find solutions to improve the efficiency and operations of "peace media."

PEACE MEDIA

Peace media could be defined as promoting peaceful conditions of life and resolution of conflict, or countering hate media by presenting issues fairly, offering alternative sources of information and broadcasts nullifying or mitigating messages of hate media. Peace media seeks alternative viewpoints that could turn public sentiment toward a peaceful resolution of a conflict. Open communications are important to maintain or re-establish stability and orderly change. Peace media is a conscious attempt to take a role in conflict prevention, conflict resolution, or moderation.

Developing effective broadcasting strategies for resolving conflict was a major topic at a conference jointly sponsored by the U.S. Institute of Peace and the Voice of America (VOA). Colonel Mike Seidl, with the U.S. Army's Psychological Operations Division, and Neguisse Mengesha, with VOA's Kinyarwanda/Kirundi Service, said that in practically every conflict that was aggravated by a humanitarian crisis, simply providing information on when and where food would be distributed, where separated family members could be found, and where medical services could be obtained drew the biggest audience in the region—and away from a warring faction's propaganda.

Coordination between peacekeeping forces, nongovernmental organizations (NGOs), and independent radio stations is crucial to the success of peace operations. Bill Yaeger, with the U.S. Agency for International Development's Office of Transition Initiatives, at the same conference, also said that programming resources should focus on the most critical tasks in efforts to recover.

The media have an essential role in the rebuilding of civil society, and it is often, once active conflict has ended, that the media may be most effective. By making available space or air time for expression of grievances, the media encourage an essential part of the healing process. During the period of reconciliation and rehabilitation, the media can also serve to empower groups that had previously been voiceless. Television, radio, and print material can provide specific support for categories of people who have become disenfranchised during the war.

Although controversial among journalists, for it goes against the grain of remaining neutral in reporting, there are many incidences where the media were utilized and directly involved in some form of mediation between parties, which produced positive results. Though many journalists resist the role of mediator and feel that it is outside the bounds of their profession, it has in many instances played an important role in conflict resolution or in helping to rebuild a society after a crisis is over.

MEDIA AS MEDIATORS

Capitol to Capitol, the live, interactive broadcast between lawmakers in Washington and Moscow that was aired in 1986, at a time of considerable superpower tension, was notable for the way it placed leaders from the two countries in direct touch with each other in a nonconfrontational setting, allowing them to respond to each other. By virtue of witnessing this humanizing exchange, the large audiences in each country were, like their leaders, expected to understand more about their country's adversaries and presumably come away from the spectacle both better informed and less antagonistic.[3]

In South Africa, a "video dialogue" was broadcast on *Peace Cafe* in the case where parties to the communal conflict in the community were not even willing to come to the table themselves. Members of both groups spoke independently to the cameras, and edited versions of each group's case were shown to the other group in a process that eventually spiraled into direct engagement of the parties through the mediating power of the video image.

Other projects have directly involved local journalists and media people from different ethnic backgrounds successfully working together in their own country, thereby helping to rebuild society and relationships torn apart by conflict.

MEDIA ROLE IN REBUILDING PEACE

Since 1982, Search for Common Ground (SCG) and Common Ground Productions (CGP), its media production arm, have produced or been part of dozens of media projects aimed at making a positive impact on conflict. In countries like Macedonia, Bosnia and Burundi, different techniques were used to promote positive change, with techniques geared specifically to particular conflict situations.

In Burundi, Search for Common Ground (SCG)/Common Ground Productions (CGP) built studio Jambo ("wise words" in Kirundi), a production studio staffed by Hutus and Tutsis. The project was launched in 1995, on the heels of the genocide in neighbouring Rwanda. Creating a safe haven where Hutus and Tutsis could work together and doing it with radio, where millions could come to recognize the multi-ethnic sound of Ijambo, offered Burundians a clear and resounding "voice of hope." Since then Ijambo journalists have worked in multi-ethnic teams, reporting on the war in their country and on the current fragile peace. They produce news as well as features that highlight issues of importance to Burundians interested in peace and progress. They also make a point of checking out rumours and do not report anything, which they have not verified. They have gained a reputation as perhaps the most reliable source of information in Burundi and were recently awarded the coveted ECHO (European Community Humanitarian Office) radio awards for "humanity in the midst of war."[4]

In the former Yugoslav Republic of Macedonia, a pilot program was designed for journalists that could help minimize ethnic tensions and build understanding and cooperation between ethnic communities with the aim of keeping ethnic tension from becoming violent or destabilizing. The "Inter Ethnic Team Project" brought together journalists from different ethnic news organizations to work together on stories concerning the country as a whole that were then published in identical form in each of the newspapers. Conducting their interviews in mixed ethnic teams, reporters were able to talk to sources they otherwise would not have had access to and avoided stereotyping each other's group.

On a corporate level, with the emphasis on profits, it is, perhaps, unrealistic to expect that commercial media outlets will make huge changes that interfere with profit making. If "good news" is "no news," the media—both international and local—will be less than interested in "no news" items. If the media is to be utilized in a positive way, a better understanding of the role of the media and the ways in which it can be used positively is needed not only by journalists but by the various organizations vying for media attention. To alter the behavior of not only the media but also the public in general who purchase the news, options and initiatives should continue to be explored.

INITIATIVES

Some initiatives have been explored and discussed by various agencies, governmental and private enterprises, NGOs, peacekeepers, and multilateral institutions, as well as the media, in order to promote better journalism or peace media. These are ideas that should be explored in response to the challenges where conflict looms or has already occurred and perhaps could be brought to bear if there were the interest and the will to do so.

At a conference in the Ugandan capital of Kampala, a workshop was organized by the African Bureau of Inter Press Service, the Kenya Human Rights Commission, and the Human Rights and Peace Center at Kampala's Makerere University. The conference took place between mainstream media and human rights organizations on ways in which the media and human rights groups could cooperate more closely.

> During the conference it became clear that a gulf existed between the media and human rights organizations in terms of understanding and communication. Human rights organizations complained about the media's inadequate and sometimes reckless coverage of human rights issues, while journalists criticised the lack of relevant and newsworthy information being provided to them by their human rights counterparts. For their part, media delegates agreed to help their colleagues in the human rights sector to package their information in a way more suited to use by the media, while the human rights organizations undertook to campaign more vigorously on media freedom issues.[5]

As of June 1995, the International Center for Humanitarian Reporting and Crosslines Global Report have begun compiling and entering information that will serve as a basis for a quality and regularly updated database of humanitarian contacts that will provide a service for the international aid community. The database will include media groups and journalists who have a special interest in international humanitarian relief, aid, human rights, development, peacekeeping, security, the environment, and other related issues. It will also allow media personnel to contact journalists in a specific location (during war or another humanitarian crisis) for eyewitness accounts, articles, camera work, and interviews. The database will enable journalists to have more ready access to relief agencies and other aid organizations operating in the field.

RECOMMENDATIONS

How can organizations tackle the problem of hate speech or hate media in volatile situations and help promote better reporting in conflict situations? Proper independent national and international bodies need to regulate the use of broadcasting bands and society as a whole must be aware of the dangers and implications of the misuse of freedom of speech via hate speech.

Promote laws that monitor and ensure that the media are not used to undermine democracy and individual freedoms, violate human rights, or incite violent conflict. Jamming hate radio broadcasts is one alternative, although some believe this infringes on the right to freedom of speech. Others state that this argument fails when radio broadcasts directly violate Article 3c of the United Nations Genocide Convention, "direct and public incitement to commit genocide."

The possibility of jamming RTLM was apparently discussed at the U.S. Department of Defense but not seriously considered, yet the United Nations Assistance Mission in Rwanda commander in Kigali, Major General Dallaire, said that if he had been equipped with proper jamming devices, many lives might have been spared in Rwanda.

Encourage international sanctions against those using hate speech via the media. Journalists can take steps to penalize others in their profession who contribute to disseminating hate propaganda. In 1995 the International Federation of Journalists (IFJ) condemned the misuse of the media in the countries of former Yugoslavia to spread national and religious hatred against other peoples and communities. The IFJ is also establishing an international commission to investigate war propaganda and hate media. The commission will investigate journalists, media organizations, and media authorities who have published or broadcast war propaganda or promoted ethnic hatred and is also organizing an international seminar on journalism ethics.

Promote peace media to help prevent or reduce conflict. Promotion of peace media can discourage the use of radio and other media to promote ethnic and political conflict by supporting efforts to deliver accurate, timely news and information in a manner that can counter the distortions broadcast by hate media.

Develop independent organizations to keep track of rumors circulating in a country. This should take place particularly in situations where it is apparent that conflict looms or other atrocities are imminent or under way, then use the media to refute the rumors and disseminate the truth as widely as possible.

Provide a forum for moderate voices to ensure they are heard in the media. International organizations such as the UN could install and operate a radio station prior to a full-blown crisis situation. Broadcasting in indigenous languages would enable a broad segment of the population to receive and understand the messages.

Tailor the training of the media to local needs. This practice can keep the media organizations from contributing to the escalation of a conflict. The media should make sure that news coverage includes early warning of looming conflicts and reports on conflicts that have erupted in defiance of diplomatic efforts.

CONCLUSION

The media's role in conflict resolution and peacebuilding is significant and is likely to spread in years to come as it becomes recognized as another tool available to help prevent, limit, or solve conflicts. Success will depend not only on the media doing a better job of analyzing and utilizing information but also on the ability of governments, international agencies, and humanitarian agencies to react swiftly, preferably at the outset of a crisis, and to call on the full scope of available preventative and reactive measures. Proper monitoring of the media in conflict zones and better promotion of peace media are essential in order to achieve this aim.

NOTES

1. Lindsey Hilsum, "Where Is Kigali?" Autumn 1995, 148.
2. Noam Chomsky (1997), *Media Control in the Spectacular Achievements of Propaganda* (New York, N.Y.: Seven Stones Press), 5.
3. U.S. Institute of Peace, Virtual Diplomacy Paper, Washington, D.C.
4. Sheldon Himmelfarb, Executive Producer of Common Ground Productions, "Impact Is the Mantra" from "The Common Ground Approach to Media."
5. Media and human rights, press release, 23 February 1997.

SUGGESTED READING

Marthoz, Jean-Paul. (1999). *Et maintenant, le monde en bref: Politique étrangère, journalisme global et libertés.* Bruxelles: GRIP.
Minear, Larry, Colin Scott, and Thomas G. Weiss. (1996). *The News Media, Civil War, and Humanitarian Action.* Boulder, Colo.: Lynne Rienner.
Rotberg, Robert I., and Thomas G. Weiss, eds. (1996). *From Massacres to Genocide: The Media, Public Policy, and Humanitarian Crises.* Cambridge, Mass.: World Peace Foundation.
Shaw, Martin. (1996). *Civil Society and Media in Global Crises: Representing Distant Violence.* London: Pinter.
Strobel, Warren P. (1997). *Late-Breaking Foreign Policy: The News Media's Influence on Peace Operations.* Washington, D.C.: USIP.

Seeking Truth and Minimizing Harm

Bettina Peters

> The real culprits in this long list of executions, assassinations, drownings, burnings, massacres and atrocities furnished by our report are not, we repeat, the Balkan peoples. . . . The true culprits are those who mislead public opinion and take advantage of the people's ignorance to raise disquieting rumours and sound the alarm bell, inciting their country.[1]

This conclusion of an inquiry into the Balkan conflict eighty years before was echoed by UN envoy Tadeusz Mazowiecki in his report in 1995 on the role of the media in the origins of the recent Balkan war. Similar statements have been made about the role of Radio Mille Collines, which broadcast hate messages against the Tutsi before the Rwandan genocide. They are a chilling reminder that a combination of ruthless political leadership and a passive community of journalists makes it all too easy for media organs to become instruments of propaganda and conflict.

It is not unusual in conflicts to find mass media recruited to support political objectives, often at the expense of professional credibility. Indeed, this holds true for almost all wars. But as people of one county turn against each other in ethnic conflict, journalists find themselves facing the grotesque choice of respecting their professional commitment to truth-seeking or risk being branded a traitor. In conflict situations there is always the danger that the media are conscripted by undemocratic politicians to inspire, provoke, and underwrite national fears and hatreds. Journalists who lend themselves to this process abandon their professional status and become propagandists.

Ethnic conflict and strife are not a new phenomenon, but in recent years we have seen an ever increasing fragmentation of human society. As Harold Isaacs put it in his book *Idols of the Tribe:*

> We are experiencing . . . an ingathering of people in numberless grouping of kinds—tribal, racial, linguistic, religious, national. It is a great clustering into separateness that will, it is thought, improve, assure, or extend each group's power or place, or keep it safe or safer from the power, threat or hostility of others.

But this willful exclusion of one community from another is a dangerous step along the road to conflict. Even before the media become weapons of war, journalists are often pressured to promote the process of fragmentation, and if they do not comply, they face censorship.

HATE SPEECH: THE LIMIT OF FREE EXPRESSION

> We must define the limits of tolerance and to do this we must first know what is intolerable.
>
> —Umberto Eco

The Universal Declaration on Human Rights grants the right to freedom of expression but the UN has also aimed to define what is intolerable and has outlawed the dissemination of ideas based on racial superiority or hatred. The International Convention on the Elimination of All Forms of Racial Discrimination states in Article 4:

> States Parties condemn all propaganda and all organisations which are based on ideas or theories of superiority of one race or group of persons of one colour or ethnic origin, or which attempt to justify or promote racial hatred and discrimination in any form, and undertake to adopt immediate and positive measures designed to eradicate all incitement to, or acts of, such discrimination. . . . [States] declare an offence punishable by law all discrimination of ideas based on racial superiority or hatred, incitement to racial discrimination, as well as all acts of violence or incitement to such acts against any race or group of persons of another colour or ethnic origin, and also the provision of any assistance to racist activities, including the financing thereof.

Although a large number of states have ratified the Convention, it is clear that governments and political groups in many countries disregard it. And though incitement to racial hatred and war is a criminal offense in many countries, the dilemma facing most journalists is based on ethical not legal considerations.

Codes of ethics normally place three duties upon journalists: to seek after truth, to be independent, and to minimize harm. The issue of hate speech forces journalists to balance the first of these duties against the third. Journalists must always seek the truth, but it is a finely judged decision about whether to pursue that objective if the consequences may be unduly harmful. To confront the hate speech dilemma with confidence, journalists need to be as free as possible from pressure to follow a particular line. The line journalists should follow is that dictated by their own conscience.

In African media, journalists often have to pay a high price for following their own conscience. As one Kenyan journalist put it: "As much as you want to keep your freedom, there is a limit beyond which you cannot go."[2]

This limit is defined by the pressure and harassment faced by journalists who report truths that those in power do not want to hear.

ETHNIC TENSIONS AND
THE CHALLENGE TO JOURNALISM

Ethnicity or diversity reporting, understood as covering different and sometimes strongly antagonistic communities, poses a daily challenge to journalists. Will reports on ethnic violence incite more violence? How does one avoid being misused for political objectives in an environment where most sources are biased? How can we report accurately and fairly on different communities and the tension between them? In some countries the reality of ethnic conflict is being denied as if silence could mask a problem or heal it. Editors, journalists, and publishers have been condemned for reporting on ethnic tensions and accused by doing so of fanning the flames of tribal or communitarian conflict.

The issue is often linked to that of political transition to multiparty democracy. "We have said it in the past that when a multi-party system is introduced, it will create tribalism, divisions and hatred," declared President Daniel arap Moi in September 1993. "This has now taken place." This reasoning shows that pluralism is defined by some governments as divisive. It is often used as an excuse for banning the publications of certain groups.

At the same time, there is evidence that some governments in Africa have deliberately promoted ethnic tensions for their own survival. Some papers, a journalist from Tanzania has argued, have been created specifically to foster the interests of a particular ethnic group against other groups in society.

African journalists must portray the diverse reality of the society they live in without creating division and sectarianism. At the same time, they have to avoid the pitfalls of "development journalism" and "nation-building journalism," which have been used to get journalists to refrain from critical reporting in the interests of the country as a whole. As a result, the media have often just toed the line and forgotten their role as watchdog of public and private institutions.

The challenge of reporting diversity is not just an African one; journalists around the globe face it. An interesting example of the difference a journalist's perspective makes to a story comes from a coverage of the Rwandan conflict in the Kenyan media. According to Macharia Gaitho of the *Economic Review* in Nairobi, although Rwanda borders Kenya, until very late in the conflict, the only coverage available to Kenyans came from reports from the Western news agencies. Through their correspondents (overwhelmingly American or European), Kenyan readers were getting a Western perspective on the Rwandan crisis. The agencies that did have Kenyan staff were not sending them to Rwanda to cover the story, unless it was to act as assistants in camera crews. Only three months into the conflict did the Kenyan newspapers send their own people to Rwanda. Macharia Gaitho writes:

> I don't think I am being jingoistic when I say that the reports coming out of those brief visits were far superior, at least in the local context, to all the reports from western agencies. The papers were able to bring angles to their stories that were of much interest to local readers, angles which western writers could never conceive.[3]

It is worth asking the question, If Western agencies had used African instead of European or American reporters, might their reporting not have been more incisive, more contextual?

*   *   *

> The journalists shall be aware of the danger of discrimination being furthered by the media and shall do the utmost to avoid facilitating such discrimination based on, among other things, race, sex, sexual orientation, language, religion, political or other opinions, and national or social origins.
> —Paragraph 7, International Federation of Journalists (IFJ)
> Declaration of Principles on the Conduct of Journalists

It should be said from the outset that ethical codes will not solve all the problems of media intolerance, but they may help journalists focus on their own responsibility and help them resolve dilemmas. By setting out the ideals and beliefs that underpin independent journalism, they encourage journalists to do what is essential in all areas of their work—to act according to their conscience.

Codes of ethics begin with sweeping generalities but tend finally to require specific attention to the local context and particular facts. That is how, in the end, ethical dilemmas are resolved. In matters of tolerance, journalists must place the broad sweep of aspirations and values set out in ethical codes firmly in the context of their day-to-day work. They must constantly remind themselves that regulating ethics is the collective business of journalists, not principally of the corporations that commission and carry their work and especially not of governments.

Governments have a legitimate role in regulating media structures to try to ensure the diversity necessary for freedom of expression to flourish and for local culture to flower. But journalists' ethics are a content issue, and governments have no role in media content.

Ethics, then, require active support. Journalists have to act ethically, not merely memorize and parrot ethical codes. The standards or rules of such codes are useful and they work most of the time. But sometimes genuine conflicts arise between values, and ethical decisionmaking is required. This difficult skill is like all the other skills of journalism: it takes training, time, and effort to become good at them. Individual journalists, employers, local journalists' associations, and international organizations of media professionals have a specific responsibility to encourage good practice.

The ethical dilemmas facing journalists referred to earlier in this article—the conflict between the need to seek the truth and to minimize harm—cannot be satisfactorily addressed unless journalists' unions, publishers, broadcasters, and industry regulators do much more to raise awareness among journalists of the potential impact of their work.

There are many different models, but all ethical codes and codes of practice focus on the fundamental aims of the journalistic mission. They can be used like a checklist, even when journalists are working close to a deadline. They direct thinking and permit conscious decisionmaking, which can be explained later if and when controversy arises about decisions.

One model, by Joann Byrd, *Washington Post* ombudsman, suggests the media must ask some simple, yet essential, questions before going public:

- Have we done good reporting?
- What do we know, and how do we know it?
- Who are the sources, and what is their stake in it?
- Have we verified the information?
- Is it reasonable to conclude the truth based on what we know, or do we still know nothing more than some facts?
- Will the story have impact? If so, what kind?

The final question in the list is particularly helpful in dealing with issues of ethnic conflict by helping to clarify the harm that will be caused, which must be weighed against the benefits of publication.

TOWARD AN ACCURATE
PORTRAYAL OF ALL GROUPS IN SOCIETY

The media are often criticized for being only a "bad news" industry. Minority groups, especially, rightly complain about media stereotypes: that racial, religious, or cultural minorities are too often reported either as a problem or as helpless victims of unexplained hostility. If the media are to meet the challenge of diversity reporting and achieve a fair and accurate portrayal of different groups in society, professional and quality journalism is the key. And the basic tools of journalism may help to improve coverage in this area.

Sources: The Key to Quality Journalism

Journalism is only as good as the sources that reporters and writers use to gather their material. In many areas, the sources of information are extensive, but there is always room for improvement. Often, there is criticism that journalists rely too much on "official" sources (police or political authorities and their press office services) without subjecting their statements to enough scrutiny. It is also the case that often the reporter's contacts do not extend very far into the network of organizations and expertise that exists within any minority community. Journalists should have at hand a wide range of expert sources who can strengthen and validate the process of reporting so that all stories, even the most negative in content, can be placed in their proper context. Doing this will bring journalism closer to all sections of the community.

Digging Deep: The Case for More Investigation

The issue of more background information and more reflection in reportage generally is a primary concern for all in the media. Cuts in newsroom budgets generally have seen a decline in the resources available for investigative journalism. The tendency to rely more on agency copy and less on local investigation and follow-up means that quality can suffer. It is certainly the case that reporting of social conflict involving ethnic and religious minorities requires time be set aside to ensure that the story can be covered properly.

Newsrooms should ensure that journalists have the time to verify, to study, and to be inclusive. This may mean that more resources should be made available for coverage of such stories. Inevitably, the complexities of social relations in diverse communities need more time and effort on the part of news gatherers.

Dialogue: Journalism in Conversation with Society

One of the tragedies of the lack of confidence that exists within many communities is that some people never expect the media to perform other than in a negative, unreliable, and insensitive manner. There is very little feedback, and this reinforces the notion that the problem "doesn't exist." For their part, journalists and news gatherers need to review their own performance and analyze how issues are taken up. A regular process of internal review will also strengthen coverage and confront difficulties in newsroom practice.

NOTES

This article originally appeared in *The Courier,* no. 168 (March–April 1998): 83–85. It is reprinted here with permission from the European Commission.

1. Report of the International Commission into Balkan Wars of 1912 and 1913, quoted by Mark Thompson, *Forging War,* Article 19, 1995.

2. Kenyan participant at the IFJ Media for Democracy conference, Ethnic Conflict and Political Change, Arusha, September 1994.

3. "The Rwanda Conflict in the Kenyan Media," in IFJ Media for Democracy publication, *Reporting Ethnic Conflict,* 1995.

Journalists as Mediators

Melissa Baumann and Hannes Siebert

Journalists mediate conflict, whether they intend to or not.

This is the premise we started with in 1990, when we began the work that became the bedrock for the Media Peace Center, founded in 1992 as part of the peace accord structures. When we launched the Mediation Project for Journalists (MPJ) in 1990, journalists in South Africa largely came from mouthpiece or adversarial traditions. The state-run and much of the liberal press operated under the guise of objectivity and the illusion of bearing the absolute truth. Journalists from the alternative media had an open agenda of "giving voice to the voiceless" and offsetting the official versions. The MPJ challenged all that.

Journalists as mediators? Not exactly. But journalists have a unique opportunity to impact a conflict—preemptively, in its midst, and restoratively—to intervene as mediators do. Since 1990, the MPJ has offered nearly 100 journalists—in South Africa and overseas—training in mediation and other conflict handling/covering skills, and posited new journalistic paradigms. At the heart of the project lies this conviction: that journalists can and should help manage conflict rather than exacerbate it.

How to do this, however imperfectly? The MPJ imparts to journalists a set of skills borrowed from mediation, which basically underwrite sound journalism skills and practice:

Bringing parties to the table. Journalists have nearly unparalleled access to parties in a conflict, and often the power to bring them to the table to begin dialogue around conflictual issues in the media and presumably off the record. Key considerations are drawing parties in inclusively and representatively (the "right" sources). The Truth and Reconciliation Commission (TRC) hearings tabled a collective history, and journalists played a key role, along with the commission, in deciding whose stories got told.

Active listening. Journalists can help engage parties in better listening through practicing it themselves and paraphrasing parties' points of view. Conflicts often persist because people aren't really heard. In covering the TRC, journalists enabled people to be heard, but the questions arose: Has the public turned a deaf ear to the litany of atrocities? and How do we represent them differently?

Moving parties off positions, toward interests. This basic tenet of mediation has application for journalists. Journalists needn't reiterate parties' hardened positions with the time-worn "X said Y said" formula. Instead, they can explore interests underlying those positions, possibly identifying common ground between the parties. One of the major gaps in reporting on the TRC was digging for context. The typical reports repeated the gruesome narratives of violence and inhumanity. What drove people to such desperate acts of destruction? We have to uncover the fear, hatred, hunger for power, and the illusion that apartheid trapped us in. Without unfolding and sharing of these underlying interests, our memories will suffocate in the stories of pain and horror; we will never enter the common human space where healing can start.

Agenda setting. Agenda setting harks back to the call for more proactive journalism. What were, for instance, the critical issues emerging from the TRC that warranted the attention/action of government, those involved, and the nation at large? Can we not see the forests of trees—the hundreds of testimonies, though valid in themselves, all adding up to patterns and blocks of sociopolitical insight that need to be analyzed and addressed?

Dispelling misperception and stereotype. Antagonists generally hold rigid (mis)perceptions of each other—of the "other"—reinforced by and generating fear. Journalists can explore these misperceptions with the parties on both sides, and in uncovering them, may help dispel them. Was the media coverage of the TRC dispelling or reinforcing stereotypes?

Questioning assumptions. A good journalist questions his/her own assumptions in reporting, as well as those of others. Many assumptions have presented themselves in the course of the TRC hearings; for one, Does the truth set you free?

Laundering language. Language has enormous power; we use it intentionally and unwittingly. Words can do a lot of damage, creating and perpetuating stereotypes and division. Watch out for binary combinations such as the TRC's "victim" and "perpetrator," for labeling for euphemism. They tend to lock us and our readers into narrow mindsets.

Joint problem solving. This is the best-case scenario—when through the process of reporting and creating/facilitating dialogue around a conflictual issue journalists can help move parties into action, into managing or resolving the conflict at hand. A critical prerequisite to this phase, of course, is helping to structure the conflict, through reportage, and identify key problem areas to be addressed. The media can also support joint problem solving by spotlighting instances where it works, and the process the parties took to get there.

In the course of the TRC and in its spirit, a number of victims and perpetrators have met in an attempt for reconciliation. Although not exactly joint problem solving, it was a joint working through of the past—in spiritual terms, of guilt and forgiveness. The danger in reporting these reconciliations, and in the reconciliations themselves, is that it is done facilely; the evil of these deeds cannot be obliterated in a handshake.

NOTE

This article is a reflection of the media coverage of the Truth and Reconciliation Commission (South Africa). This is a slightly adapted version of "A Paradigm Shift: Points for a New Kind of Journalism," originally published in *Rhodes Journalism Review*, no. 14 (May 1997): 5. It is reprinted with kind permission from the publisher.

CHAPTER 12

Dealing with the Past and Imaging the Future

■ 12.1

Amnesty, Truth, or Prosecution?

Luc Huyse

WAYS OF DEALING WITH THE PAST

When a country makes the transition from an authoritarian state to a more democratic order, the question inevitably arises as to what to do about the crimes of the old regime. In principle, many options are open. Strategies have ranged from unconditionally closing the book to massive criminal prosecution of the supporters of the previous order. All policy choices involve addressing two key issues: whether to remember or forget the abuses and whether to impose sanctions on the individuals responsible for these abuses.

Some of these policies are offender oriented (amnesty, prosecution, and lustration); others are victim oriented (compensation and symbolic measures). Truth commissions are directed toward both offenders and victims.

The catalog of available strategies is not a question of either/or choices. There are cases where a combination of several options is chosen. South Africa combined truth-telling and amnesty-giving. In Ethiopia, the Dergue trials contained a strong element of creating a historical record of the abuses committed by the previous regime.

The granting of *absolute amnesty* is at one end of the spectrum. In some cases the unrestricted pardon is the result of the self-amnesty that the outgoing elites unilaterally award themselves before the transition gets under way. In other instances impunity is the outcome of negotiations between old and new leaders. In Uruguay, for example, the government that succeeded the military dictatorship enacted, under pressure from the military, an amnesty law (1986). Post-Franco Spain is an example of a third route toward impunity: almost all democratic forces agreed to confer immunity to individuals who committed crimes defending or opposing the Franco regime.

Sometimes amnesty is not unrestricted. Categories of crimes and of perpetrators may be excluded from the pardon. In postapartheid South Africa, amnesty is granted but only after the applicants have satisfied strict conditions (complete information and confession) before a truth commission.

Forgiving but not forgetting is the substance of a third major policy choice. Its usual format is the national or international truth commission. The first goal of such a commission is to investigate the fates, under the preceding regime, of individuals and of the nation as a whole. Its aim is not to prosecute and punish. A truth-telling operation, including full disclosure of all human rights abuses, must ensure that the facts are not forgotten but remain alive in the memory of the collectivity. Well-known examples are the Chilean National Commission on Truth and Reconciliation (1990), the South African Truth and Reconciliation Commission (1995–1998), and the UN-sponsored International Truth Commission in El Salvador (1991).

Lustration or disqualification of the agents of the secret police and their informers (of judges, teachers, civil servants, and military personnel) is a fourth way to address the question of reckoning for past wrongs. It sometimes includes the loss of political and civil rights. In some of the postcommunist countries of Eastern and Central Europe the screening of officials has been the only policy step.

By far the most radical interpretation of acknowledgment and accountability is to be found in the outright criminal prosecution of the perpetrators. This task can be taken up by an international body, as in the case of the International Criminal Tribunal for the Former Yugoslavia. National courts also perform this function. A prominent example is Ethiopia where some 5,000 officials of the fallen Mengistu regime have been named for trial. By contrast, as a strategy for dealing with the past, criminal prosecution has encountered almost no support in post-1989 Eastern and Central Europe and in the postauthoritarian regimes of Latin America.

Prosecution and/or general knowledge of the truth might be seen as an incomplete dealing with the crimes of the previous regime. Additional steps may include *compensation* by the state (monetary reparation, free medical and psychological treatment, reduced interests on loans for education and home building) and the *establishment of permanent reminders* of the legacy of the past, such as monuments, museums, public holidays, and ceremonies. In South Africa such measures are seen to provide channels for the nonviolent expression of pain and anger.

Note that very often dealing with the past is a case of *impunity* in its purest form, namely, minor and major violations of human rights do not prompt any reaction. It is estimated that there were more than a hundred domestic armed conflicts in the period 1982–1996. In only forty of them did the crimes committed (including frequent cases of genocide) give rise to legal repercussions: there were two international courts (The Hague and Arusha), one national prosecution (Ethiopia), nineteen truth commissions, and on a couple of occasions the penalty was disqualification from a profession. Twenty or so countries enacted amnesty legislation, sometimes after receiving a report from a truth commission.

POST-TRANSITION JUSTICE: PRO AND CONTRA CRIMINAL PROSECUTIONS

In the ongoing public debate over post-transition justice, political leaders, academics, and journalists are divided on numerous points. But by far the most divisive question is how to balance the demands of justice against the many, mainly political, factors that make prosecution a major risk to the new regime.

The Case for Prosecutions

Those who emphasize the beneficial effects of prosecution bring forward two crucial reasons. First, punishing the perpetrators of the old regime advances the cause of building or reconstructing a morally just order. The second reason has to do with establishing and upholding the young democracy that succeeds the authoritarian system.

Justice needs to be done.   Putting back in place the moral order that has broken down requires that "justice be done," the proponents of prosecutions argue. They believe that the successor government owes it, first of all, as a moral obligation to the victims of the repressive system. Postauthoritarian justice serves to heal the wounds and to repair the private and public damage the antecedent regime provoked. It also, as a sort of ritual cleansing process, paves the way for a moral and political renaissance. Asked by Adam Michnik, a prominent leader of the Polish opposition to communist rule, what he thought of such cleansing, the German writer Jurgen Fuchs answered: "If we do not solve this problem in a definite way, it will haunt us as Nazism did. We did not de-Nazify ourselves, and this weighed on us for years."[1]

Strengthen fragile democracies.   A second argument in favor of a judicial operation against the advocates of the old regime is that it strengthens fragile democracies. In the first months after the transition, it is said, the survival of the successor regime depends on swift and firm action against pro-authoritarian officials and their following. Such action is seen as a necessary protection against sabotage from within. Moreover, if the prosecution issue remains untouched, other forms of social and political disturbance may be triggered, with perhaps a risk of vigilante justice with summary executions; or unbridled screening of political personnel, journalists, and judges may be instigated as happened in postcommunist Poland.

What a new or reinstated democracy needs most, however, is legitimacy. Failure to prosecute and lustrate may generate in the population feelings of cynicism and distrust toward the political system. This is precisely what happened in several Latin American countries.

Some analysts believe that prosecutions also advance long-term democratic consolidation. Opponents of impunity argue that amnesty endangers the inculcation of codes of conduct based on the rule of law. They claim that a discriminatory application of the criminal law, privileging certain defendants (such as military leaders), will breed cynicism toward the rule of law.

Prosecutions, finally, are seen as the most potent deterrence against future abuses of human rights.

The Case Against Prosecutions

Other participants in the debate have argued that prosecuting those alleged to bear responsibility for the crimes of the past is not without considerable ambivalence. There is no guarantee, they say, that its effects will be merely beneficial for democracy. They argue that partisan justice always lurks from behind the corner and that prosecutions can have highly destabilizing effects on an immature democracy. Raoul Alfonsin, Argentina's first elected president after the collapse of the military regime, wrote: "In the final analysis, punishment is one instrument, but not the sole or even the most important one, for forming the collective moral conscience."[2]

Legitimacy of the new regime.   Young democracies affirm that they highly value the rule of law and human rights. But post-transition justice involves a number of decisions that may trespass on those very legal principles. Dealing with the past by prosecutions, some analysts argue, therefore holds a sizable risk. It may force the successor elites to violate rule of law principles today while judging the undemocratic behavior of yesterday. This can, as a consequence, considerably weaken the legitimacy of the new regime.

The principles of the separation of powers and of judicial impartiality are at stake when answering the question of who will be the judges of the authoritarian regime. Political pressure, time constraints, and the unavailability of sufficient judicial personnel may incite the post-transition elites to create special tribunals in which lay judges play a prominent role. This, the opponents of prosecutions argue, makes lapses from important legal norms almost unavoidable. Such special courts can, indeed, become instruments of partisan vengeance because nonprofessional judges are easier targets for pressure by the executive, the media, and public opinion. This is what happened in postwar Belgium and France some fifty years ago.

Justice after a transition must take place within a temporal frame. This frame consists of answers to two questions. The first one is: Do we accept ex post facto criminal legislation? It is the *nullum crimen sine lege, nulla poena sine lege* principle that is at stake here. This principle means that no conduct may be held punishable unless it is precisely described in a penal law, and no penal sanction may be imposed except in pursuance of a law that describes it prior to the commission of the offense. The second question involves the problem of eventually lifting or upholding the existing statute of limitations. This question is particularly acute in the postcommunist countries. Atrocities against the life and property of men and women took place primarily in the late 1940s and during the 1950s. In most cases, as in Hungary, where a thirty-year statute of limitations exists, criminal proceedings for the most reprehensible human rights abuses are thus precluded by reason of the lapse of time. Those who disapprove of prosecutions assert that post-transition trials ultimately will result in changing the rules of the game after the fact, either by applying retroactive legislation or by recommencing the statute of limitation once it has run out.

Another argument of those who disapprove of prosecutions is that post-transition justice tends to be emergency justice—particularly if it comes in the early phases of the transition. The climate is then seldom well suited for a scrupulous sorting out of all the gradations in responsibility for the abuses of the past.

Survival of the democratic process. A new or reinstated democracy is a frail construct. For that reason impunity or, at least, tolerance in the handling of past abuses might be a prerequisite for the survival of the democratic process.

There is, first, the risk of a destabilizing backlash. Military leaders who feel threatened by projected prosecution may try to reverse the course of events by a coup or a rebellion. This problem especially haunts the young democracies of Latin America.

A prolonged physical and social expulsion, based on criminal court decisions, of certain sections of the population may obstruct democratic consolidation in yet another way. It could drive the supporters of the previous regime into social and political isolation. This in turn could result in the creation of subcultures and networks, which in the long run will become hostile to democracy.

Criminal prosecutions may also preclude the reconciliation required for a democracy to function. The need for closing the ranks is one of the main arguments of advocates of amnesty laws. See Uruguayan president Julio María Sanguinetti's justification of an amnesty law pardoning abuses of a previous military regime: "The 12 years of dictatorship have left scars which will need a long time to heal and it is good to begin to do so."[3]

The viability of a young democracy depends, too, on its efficacy. A far-reaching purge of administrative and managerial manpower can be counterproductive as it endangers the badly needed political and economic development of the country. Prudent considerations of the problematic consequences of dismissals from civil service and high industrial jobs have been heard regularly in postcommunist East and Central Europe.

LESSONS LEARNED: A DEVIL'S CHOICE

1. *There are neither universal nor miracle solutions for dealing with a repressive past.* Many policy suggestions on dealing with the past depart from the premise that postauthoritarian elites can actually make choices. However, the first lesson is that the actions of such elites are a function of the circumstances of the journey to democracy. The second lesson is that there are no miracle solutions to the question of how to deal with a repressive past.

2. *Memory is the ultimate form of justice.* In almost all cases the passage of time has not fully exorcised the ghosts of this past. Too much forgiveness undermines the respect for the law, induces the anger of those who suffered, and is an impediment to an authentic reconciliation and an invitation to recidivism. That is why most analysts argue that if the balance of forces at the time of the transition makes a negotiated mildness inevitable, a truth-telling operation with full exposure of the crimes of the former regime is the least unsatisfactory solution. The truth is both retribution and deterrence, and undermines the mental foundation of future human rights abuses.

3. *Dealing with the past is an inescapable task for new democratic regimes.* Successor elites may be put off by the many delicate and explosive aspects of such an assignment. G. O'Donnell and P. Schmitter suggest in *Transitions from Authoritarian Rule: Prospects for Democracy* that, in the case of Latin America, this issue remains an almost insoluble problem. But the worst solution here, they write, would be to try to ignore the problem; the costs of such a cover-up are simply too big.

J. Zalaquett, a member of the Chilean truth commission, adds this warning: "Leaders should never forget that the lack of political pressure to put these issues on the agenda does not mean that they are not boiling underground, waiting to erupt. They will always come back to haunt you. It would be political blindness to ignore the fact that examples of this abound world-wide."[4]

One of S. Huntington's guidelines to democratizers reads: "Recognize that on the issue of 'prosecute and punish vs. forgive and forget,' each alternative presents grave problems, and that the least unsatisfactory course may well be: do not prosecute, do not punish, do not forgive, and, above all, do not forget."

4. *Crimes against humanity cannot be left unpunished.* A major problem is that some of the arguments in the debate on pardon versus punish are quite contradictory. That is certainly the case with the argument that a young democracy cannot establish itself without reconciliation. For some, reconciliation requires a process of forgiving and forgetting. Others, on the contrary, claim that impunity impedes reconciliation.

The same ambiguity lies in the argument that criminal prosecution can seriously threaten the viability of a new democracy. Too many risks are apparently attached to it, such as a military counterrevolution. The idea that the dragon on the patio must not be provoked has acquired considerable following among those in authority in Latin America. In general they make, however, two exceptions. They say that self-amnesty is not admissible, and the second exception is that every state is obliged to prosecute serious violations of internationally acknowledged human rights.

The idea that crimes against humanity cannot be left unpunished lay behind the trial of the French collaborators, Touvier and Papon, almost fifty years after the end of World War II. Opponents of amnesty claim, however, that the survival of a new democracy depends on legal action being taken, as it provides the best assurance against the return of authoritarian methods.

5. *Reconcile ethical imperatives and political constraints.* Most political leaders, journalists, and academics seem to agree that the crucial challenge is to strike a balance between the demands of justice and political prudence. This is no easy enterprise. It entails a difficult and, on occasion, tortuous cost-benefit analysis. All costs and gains, political and moral, of pardoning and punishing, must be balanced against each other.

NOTES

Excerpted from Luc Huyse, "Justice After Transition: On the Choices Successor Elites Make in Dealing with the Past," *Law and Social Enquiry* 20, no. 1. It is reprinted with the kind permission of the University of Chicago Press.

1. J. Fuchs, cited by Adam Michnik, "Justice or Revenge?" *Journal of Democracy* 4 (January 1993): 20, 25.

2. Raoul Alfonsín, "'Never Again' in Argentina," *Journal of Democracy* 4 (January 1993): 15–19.

3. Diane Orentlicher, "Settling Accounts: The Duty to Prosecute Human Rights Violations of a Prior Regime," *Yale Law Journal* 100 (1991): 2537–2542.

4. J. Zalaquett in A. Boraine, J. Levy, and R. Scheffer, eds., *Dealing with the Past: Truth and Reconciliation in South Africa* (Cape Town: IDASA, 1994).

SELECTED BIBLIOGRAPHY

"Accountability for International Crimes." (1997). Special issue of *Law and Contemporary Problems*. Duke University.

Huntington, S. P. (1991). *The Third Wave: Democratization in the Late Twentieth Century*. Tulsa: University of Oklahoma Press.

Jongman, A. J., ed. (1996). *Contemporary Genocides: Causes, Cases, Consequences*. Leiden: PIOOM.

Kritz, N. J., ed. (1995). *Transitional Justice: How Emerging Democracies Reckon with Former Regimes*. Vol. 1, *General Considerations*. Vol. 2, *Country Studies*. Vol. 3, *Laws, Rulings, Reports*. Washington, D.C.: United Institute of Peace.

"Law and Lustration: Righting the Wrongs of the Past." (1995). Special issue of *Law and Social Inquiry*. Journal of the American Bar Foundation.

O'Donnell, G., and P. Schmitter, eds. (1986). *Transitions from Authoritarian Rule: Prospects for Democracy*. Baltimore: John Hopkins University Press.

Van den Wijngaert, C., ed. (1996). *International Criminal Law: A Collection of International and European Instruments*. The Hague: Kluwer Law International.

■ 12.2

Restorative Justice

Howard Zehr

As it seeks to end a variety of long-term conflicts, the world longs for a justice that will address wrongdoing and at the same time promote law and peace. But what does "real" justice look like? Is it compatible with healing or are the two mutually exclusive?

Domestically, many nations are preoccupied with crime. What does justice mean in this situation? The United States' response has been to crank up the machinery of punishment to unprecedented levels. One of the world's highest incarceration rates is rapidly becoming higher, with foreboding consequences. Public funds are being diverted from essential social services and education to build new prisons, without any discernible effect on crime. Norwegian criminologist Nils Christie has warned that the United States is creating a huge crime control industry with no built-in limits, an industry with a self-propelled dynamic of expansion that threatens the foundations of a democratic society.[1] The justice we choose has enormous consequences.

Faced with wrongdoing, society must choose between the three "R's" of justice. If society does not respond adequately, people take justice into their own hands—as in the justice of *revenge*. But as we have seen in Rwanda and the former Yugoslavia, revenge is a deadly spiral, incompatible with organized society. Two other "R's" of justice offer themselves to the world today.

One is the justice of the Western legal system. Its strengths—such as the encouragement of human rights—are substantial. Yet it has important weaknesses. Criminal justice tends to be punitive, conflictual, impersonal, and state centered. It encourages the denial of responsibility and empathy on the part of offenders. It leaves victims out, ignoring their needs. Instead of discouraging wrongdoing, it often encourages it. It exacerbates rather than heals wounds. In fact, *retributive* justice often assumes that justice and healing are separate issues, perhaps even incompatible.

An alternative approach to justice is more reparative in focus. It puts both victim and offender in center stage. Victims' needs and rights are central, not peripheral. Offenders are encouraged to understand the harm they have caused and to take responsibility for it. Dialogue—direct or indirect—is encouraged, and communities play important roles. *Restorative* justice assumes that justice can and should promote healing, both individual and societal. Restorative justice is an older form of justice than retributive justice. It is the dominant justice of African customary law, of the indigenous Maori culture of New Zealand, of the aboriginal people of North America. For those of us from European backgrounds, it is the justice of our foreparents as well. The idea that victims do not have standing in justice, that focus should be on guilt and punishment, is, in fact, relatively recent.

Although space here is too limited to explore them further, the assumptions and characteristics of retributive justice and restorative justice are outlined in Exhibit 12.2-1 and in the appendix at the end of this article.

Exhibit 12.2-1   Assumptions and Characteristics of Restorative Justice and Retributive Justice

	Restorative Justice	Retributive Justice
Problem	Defined relationally as a violation of people Overall context relevant People as victims	Defined narrowly, abstractly, a legal infraction Only legal variables relevant State as a victim
Actors	Victim and offender primary	State (active) and offender (passive)
Process	Participatory, maximizing information dialogue, and mutual agreement Focus = needs and obligations Empathy and responsibility encouraged	Adversarial, authoritarian, technical, impersonal Focus = guilt/blame "Neutralizing" strategies encouraged
Outcome	Making things right by identifying needs and obligations; healing, problem solving Harm by offender balanced by making right Oriented to future	Pain, suffering Harm by offender balanced by harm to offender Oriented to past

They appear here as two polar opposites. Realistically, though, they are perhaps best viewed as "ideal types" on the opposite ends of a continuum. On the one end is "pure" retributive justice; on the other is "pure" restorative justice. Our goal should be to build upon the strengths of the criminal law process, the retributive model, but to move it as far as possible toward the restorative end.

This restorative perspective should be our framework as we look to alternatives within the context of the criminal law system. The United States has a long history of alternatives to prison, which have not been alternatives to prison at all; in fact so-called alternatives have tended to widen and strengthen the net of control and punishment. To avoid that, we need to consider alternative values more than alternative punishments; we need to look at justice through a different, restorative "lens." Our primary search should be for processes that meet the needs of victims and hold offenders truly accountable. Where options like imprisonment are unavoidable, we should seek to make them as restorative as possible to both victims and offenders.

A variety of approaches around the world today are offering forms of restorative justice within the framework of the Western legal system. We will give two examples here, Family Group Conferencing and the Victim Offender Reconciliation Program.

FAMILY GROUP CONFERENCING

One innovative justice model, Family Group Conferencing (FGC), emerged in New Zealand (and soon was adapted in Australia) in the late 1980s as a response, in part, to the concerns and traditions of the indigenous Maori population. The Western-style juvenile justice system was widely recognized to be working poorly, and many Maori argued that it was antithetical to their traditions; it was oriented toward punishment rather than solutions, was imposed rather than negotiated, and left family and community out of the process.

In the juvenile system, which was adopted in 1989, all juvenile cases with the exception of a few very violent crimes are diverted from police or court into FGCs. As a result, judges report substantial drops in case loads as high as 80 percent. New Zealand judge Fred McElrea has called it the first truly restorative approach to be institutionalized within a Western legal framework.[2]

Instead of a court hearing, a youth justice coordinator (employed by the social service system, not the justice system) facilitates a meeting that provides a forum for feelings to be expressed, facts to be explored, and settlements to be negotiated. Offenders are held accountable, and victims are provided opportunities to have some of their needs met.

Families of the offender are an essential ingredient in the FGC concept. This may include both immediate and extended family members. In broken or dysfunctional families, more distant relatives or other significant people may be involved. Caregivers involved with the family may be invited, and a youth advocate—a special attorney—is included to look out for the legal concerns of the offender. Victims too may bring family or supporters. Moreover, the police (who are the prosecutors in this legal system) take part in the meetings. So the meetings are not only large but include parties with divergent interests and perspectives.

That in itself may seem radical, but there is more: this group is expected to come up with a recommendation for the entire outcome of the case, not just restitution, and they must do this by a consensus of the group! Even more startling, they manage to do so in most cases.

FGCs are working well enough that some judges and other practitioners are calling for their adaptation to the adult system in New Zealand. To be sure, the approach has needed some fine-tuning. Restitution follow-up is sometimes inadequate, for example, and the initial legislation did not adequately recognize the central role of victims. In spite of such glitches, however, the evidence emerging from five or six years of experience is impressive.

FGCs are not a panacea, of course, but the evidence so far is very hopeful. In my visits to new Zealand, I have heard many dramatic stories and often from players who I would not expect to be easy converts: judges, police officers, and lawyers.

VICTIM OFFENDER RECONCILIATION PROGRAM

A North American initiative that has a longer history of working alongside the formal justice system is victim-offender reconciliation, or mediation, often called VORP (Victim Offender Reconciliation Program). VORP has taken many forms since the first case in 1974 and has spread to many other countries. In its classic form, it is operated in cooperation with the courts but often housed in separate nonprofit organizations. Upon referral of a case by the court or probation service, trained volunteers separately contact victim and offender to explore what happened and determine their willingness to proceed. If they agree, victim and offender are brought together in a meeting facilitated by the volunteer mediator who serves as a neutral third party. In this meeting, the facts of the offense are fully explored, feelings are expressed, and a written restitution contract is worked out.

This contract and a brief report then go back to the court or referring agency. If it is to become part of a sentence, it must receive final approval of the court, then it becomes a condition of probation. The contract is monitored also, however, by VORP staff, who troubleshoot if the agreement breaks down later.

In this classic form, VORP has predominantly handled property offenses such as burglary. Increasingly, however, programs are receiving cases of violence, some including offenses such as rape and homicide. Offenses like that, of course, require special precautions and procedures and so VORP is today taking many forms in many countries. Some of those working at the upper end of the "tariff" focus more on healing journeys than on impacting sentences.

The list of approaches could go on. Sentencing circles in aboriginal communities of Canada, for example, are providing a way to operationalize culturally appropriate, community-based restorative processes within a legal context. Popular justice institutions in South Africa could provide another.

Crime is likely to be a predominant issue in most countries for the foreseeable future. As we develop our responses, it is imperative that we seriously reconsider our assumptions about justice, the lens we look through, and develop approaches that do not simply repeat the past but offer hope for the future. That hope, I believe, lies in a vision of justice that puts healing and reparations central, holds offenders genuinely accountable, and gives victims an important role. The future is in recapturing some of the best of our traditions: a justice that aims at restoration.

APPENDIX: RESTORATIVE JUSTICE SIGNPOSTS

We are working toward restorative justice when we do the following:

- Focus on the harms of wrongdoing more than the rules that have been broken.
- Show equal concern and commitment to victims and offenders, involving both in the process of justice.
- Work toward the restoration of victims, empowering them and responding to their needs as they see them.
- Support offenders while encouraging them to understand, accept, and carry out their obligations.
- Recognize that although obligations may be difficult for offenders, they should not be intended as harms and they must be achievable.
- Provide opportunities for dialogue, direct or indirect, between victims and offenders as appropriate.
- Involve and empower the affected community through the justice process, and increase its capacity to recognize and respond to community bases of crime.
- Encourage collaboration and reintegration rather than coercion and isolation.
- Give attention to the unintended consequences of our actions and programs.
- Show respect to all parties including victims, offenders, and justice colleagues.

NOTES

This article was originally published in *Imbizo,* Research in Progress Series, Issue 2/1996. It has been reprinted with the kind permission of the editor.
1. Christie 1994.
2. McElrea 1994.

REFERENCES

Christie, N. (1994). *Crime Control as Industry: Towards a Western Gulag.* New York: Routledge.

Consedine, Jim. (1995). *Restorative Justice: Healing the Effects of Crime.* Lyttelton. New Zealand: Ploughshares Publications.

McElrea, F. W. N. (1994). In J. Burnside and N. Baker, eds., *Relational Justice: Repairing the Branch.* Winchester, England: Waterside Press.

McElrea, F. W. N., and B. J. Brown. (1993). *The Youth Court in New Zealand: A New Model of Justice.* Auckland: Legal Research Foundation.

Mika, H., ed. (1995). "Victim Offender Mediation: International Perspectives on Theory, Research and Practice." Special issue of *Mediation Quarterly* (spring 1995).

Zehr, H. (1995). *Changing Lenses: A New Focus for Crime and Justice.* Scottsdale, Pa.: Herald Press.

A bibliographical packet on restorative justice, victim-offender reconciliation, and family group conferences is available from the Mennonite Central Committee, 21 South 12th Street, Akron, Pennsylvania 17501, USA (e-mail: mailbox@mcc.org).

Reconciliation

Hizkias Assefa

In this article we shall look at various conflict handling mechanisms, examining their meaning and application, their relationship to one another, and their comparative effectiveness.

If we were to look at the degree of mutual participation by the conflict parties in the search for solutions to the problems underlying their conflict, we could place the various commonly used approaches to handling conflict in a spectrum as follows:

Exhibit 12.3-1   Spectrum of Conflict Handling Mechanisms

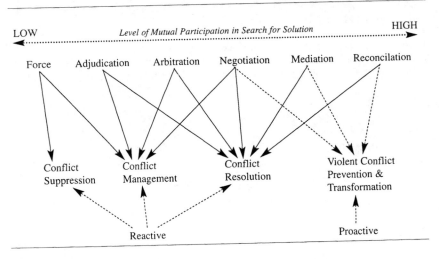

At the left end of the spectrum, we find approaches where mutual participation is minimal. The *use of force* by one of the parties to impose a solution would be an example of a mechanism that would be placed at this end of the spectrum. Further to the right of the spectrum, we could place mechanisms such as *adjudication*. Here a third party, instead of an adversary, imposes a solution to the conflict. However, the mutual participation of the parties in the choice of the solution is comparatively higher here than in the first. In the adjudication process, at least the parties have an opportunity to present their cases, to be heard, and submit their arguments for why their preferred solution should be the basis upon which the decision is made. Nonetheless, the choice of the solution is made by a third party, and the decision is backed by force (enforced), which ensures that the winning party complies.

Arbitration is placed further to the right of adjudication. Here, the participation of the parties is even higher because both adversaries can choose who is going to decide the issues under dispute, whereas in adjudication the decisionmaker is already appointed by the state. The parties in conflict can sometimes identify the basis upon which their case will be decided and whether the outcome will be binding or not. Although the mutual involvement of the parties in the decisionmaking process is much higher than in adjudication, the solution is still decided by an outsider and, depending on the type of arbitration, the outcome could be imposed by the power of the law.

Further to the right on the spectrum we find *negotiation*. Here the participation of all the involved parties in the search for a solution is very high. It is the parties themselves who have to formulate the issues and find a resolution that is satisfactory to all of them. In this situation, however, particularly in bargaining-type negotiations (as opposed to problem-solving negotiations),[1] the final choice of the solution might depend on the relative power position of the adversaries rather than on what might be the most satisfactory solution to everyone involved. The party with the higher bargaining leverage might end up getting the most out of the negotiations.

Mediation is a special type of negotiation where the parties' search for mutually satisfactory solutions is assisted by a third party. The third party's role is to minimize obstacles to the negotiation process including those that emanate from power imbalance. Unlike adjudication, however, in the final analysis it is the decision and agreement of the conflicting parties that determines how the conflict will be resolved.

Toward the far right of the spectrum we find *reconciliation*. This approach not only tries to find solutions to the issues underlying the conflict but also works to alter the adversaries' relationships from that of resentment and hostility to friendship and harmony. Of course, for this to happen, both parties must be equally invested and participate intensively in the resolution process.[2]

Before we move on to examine the insights that emerge from this spectrum, let us quickly glance at one more issue of definitions and distinctions: the conflict handling mechanisms illustrated in the spectrum can be categorized into three groups that we will call *conflict management, conflict resolution,* and *conflict prevention* approaches.

Conflict management approaches generally tend to focus more on mitigating or controlling the destructive consequences that emanate from a given conflict than on finding solutions to the underlying issues causing it. However, conflict resolution approaches aim at going beyond mitigation of consequences and attempt to resolve the substantive and relational root causes so that the conflict comes to an end. Although conflict management and resolution are reactive (they come into motion once conflict has surfaced), conflict prevention tries to anticipate the destructive aspects of the conflict before they arise and attempts to take positive measures to prevent them from occurring.

Most of the mechanisms identified on the left side of the spectrum are conflict management approaches. The uses of military force for deterrence or in peacekeeping (separating the conflict parties from each other so that they do not keep inflicting harm on each other) are typical conflict management strategies. To the extent that adjudication, arbitration, and bargaining negotiations do not resolve conflicts, they become mere stop-gap conflict management measures. But they do provide an opportunity to work out not only differences on substantive issues and negative relationships.

OBSERVATIONS

We notice that as we move from the left to the right on the spectrum, that is, as the participation of all the parties in the search for a solution increases, the likelihood of achieving a mutually satisfactory and durable solution also increases. We know that solutions imposed by force will last only until the vanquished are able to muster sufficient force to reverse the situation. Unless the loser gives up, solutions imposed by adjudication and arbitration can always be frustrated by the latter's endless appeal or lack of cooperation in the implementation process. If, however, the parties are engaged earnestly in the search for solutions and are able to find resolutions that could satisfy the needs and interests of all involved, there could be no better guarantee for the durability of the settlements, for it would be in the interest of everyone to see to it that they are fully enforced. This is what we believe problem-solving negotiations, mediation, and reconciliation can do.

What is noteworthy, though, is that as we move from the left to the right end of the spectrum, although the likelihood of effectiveness and durability of the solutions increases, our knowledge and understanding of the approaches to be utilized become sketchy, less developed, and unsystematic. Our knowledge and methodology of conflict management approaches (the mechanisms on the left side of the spectrum) such as the use of force, adjudication, or arbitration are quite advanced. They are highly developed disciplines with institutions that command high respect and resources devoted to training and practice. Military and police science, jurisprudence and legal studies, as well as entire military and police academies, law schools, ministries of defense and justice, police departments, courts, and prison systems are examples of these disciplines and institutions that advance the practice of these approaches.

In contrast, conflict resolution approaches such as problem-solving negotiation and mediation are less developed, and institutions and resources devoted to their training, advancement, and practice are meager. Whatever is in place is voluntary and ad hoc. Then, when we come to reconciliation, let alone establish procedures and institutions charged with the application of the concept, there is not even much understanding of what it means, especially among social scientists. Religious people and theologians are a bit better equipped to discuss the concept. But even there, there is a great gap between articulation and translation of the ideas into practice.

THE NEED FOR HEALING AND RECONCILIATION

Despite the lack of knowledge about how to operationalize reconciliation, there is, however, no question about the tremendous need for it. In fact, it could be said that the need in today's world is much greater than at any other time in history.

One reason is that conflict management strategies are not adequate to deal with the kinds of contemporary conflicts raging in many parts of the world. Especially since the end of the Cold War, civil wars have replaced interstate wars as the most predominant large-scale social conflicts. To a certain extent, interstate conflict strategies aimed merely at separating the conflicting parties might suffice. Even if the underlying issues of the conflict are not resolved, the separation could help avoid the recurrence of the conflict. Because states tend to isolate themselves from each other by their national boundaries, the task of separating them by peacekeeping forces is relatively easier.

However, in civil war situations the relationship between the protagonists is much more intimate and complex. In most cases, the parties share the same geographic area and even community; there might be strong interdependence between them; and they usually have all sorts of social ties among each other, including intermarriages. In these instances it is quite difficult to separate the protagonists because the boundaries between them are complicated to draw. Even if it is possible to do it for a short while, it is not feasible to think of conflict management strategies such as separation as a long-term solution. For that matter, even decisions imposed by adjudication or other such processes will not be solutions, as the winning party cannot expect to enjoy its victory without facing the consequences of the loser's wrath.

Therefore, in civil war situations conflict management strategies are not adequate. One has to move toward conflict resolution and reconciliation processes where not only the underlying issues to the conflicts are resolved to everyone's satisfaction but also the antagonistic attitudes and relationships between the adversaries are transformed from negative to positive.

Moreover, even in interstate relations, we are increasingly realizing that the components of the modern international system are no more the nineteenth-century autarchic states. The globe is shrinking, and the fates of people worldwide are becoming more and more inextricably intertwined. Thus, it would be increasingly difficult to expect unilateral approaches to handling conflicts such as the imposition of solutions by force as viable approaches.

In an interdependent and closely interconnected world, even those who are supposedly weak can have their own way of subverting or undermining the imposed order. Therefore, those groups must be somehow enabled to participate in the search for solutions in their conflicts even with the more powerful actors. In fact, the democratic values that the current international order is trying to promote as a universal value in all the societies of the world necessitates movement increasingly toward integrative negotiation, mediation, and reconciliation as the predominant ways of dealing with conflict instead of unilateral measures that involve coercion.

THE RECONCILIATION PROCESS

Reconciliation as a conflict handling mechanism entails the following core elements:

- Honest acknowledgment of the harm/injury each party has inflicted on the other.
- Sincere regrets and remorse for the injury done.
- Readiness to apologize for one's role in inflicting the injury.
- Readiness of the conflicting parties to let go of the anger and bitterness caused by the conflict and the injury.
- Commitment by the offender not to repeat the injury.
- Sincere effort to redress past grievances that caused the conflict and compensate the damage caused to the extent possible.
- Entering into a new, mutually enriching relationship.

Reconciliation then refers to this new relationship that emerges as a consequence of these processes. What most people refer to as "healing" is the mending of the deep emotional wounds (generated by the conflict) that follow the reconciliation process.

A very important aspect of the process of reconciliation and one that distinguishes it from all the other conflict handling mechanisms is its methodology. In most of the conflict handling mechanisms such as adjudication, arbitration, and for that matter even negotiation and mediation, the method used for establishing responsibility for the conflict or its consequences is adversarial. In these processes, the parties present their grievances and make a case for the adversary's fault or responsibility, therefore demanding that it should be the latter that should make amends. Each party begins by defending its own behavior and denying its own guilt or responsibility until the opponent proves it otherwise to his or her satisfaction or to the satisfaction of outside observers, be they judges or mediators. In such a process, one's behavior is always explained as a reaction to the behavior of the adversary. The typical pattern of the interaction is: "I did this to you because you did such and such a thing to me!" The aim is to get the adversary to change his or her future conduct by proving the person's guilt. Of course the expectation is that both parties will change each other in this way and will eventually transform their relationship from negative to positive.

In contrast, the essence of reconciliation is the voluntary initiative of the conflicting parties to acknowledge their responsibility and guilt. The interactions that transpire between the parties are not only meant to communicate one's grievances against the actions of the adversary but also to engage in self-reflection about one's own role and behavior in the dynamic of the conflict. In other words, in this kind of dialogue, as much as one attributes guilt and responsibility to the adversary for the damage generated by the conflict, one has to also be self-critical and acknowledge responsibility for his or her own role in the creation or perpetuation of the conflict and hurtful interaction. The aim of such interaction is that in the final analysis, each of the parties acknowledges and accepts his or her responsibility and out of such recognition seeks ways to redress the injury that has been inflicted on the adversary, to refrain from further damage, and to construct new positive relationships.

It is true that in both reconciliation and other conflict resolution mechanisms, the process of dialogue is expected to generate change and transformation. In reconciliation, however, the forces for change are primarily internal and voluntary, whereas in other approaches they are external and to a certain extent coerced. Where the source is external, it is possible that it might be the adversary's skill in marshaling and presenting its arguments; its strong will and intransigence; or its capacity to manipulate, exert pressure, or administer punishment that might intimidate the other party into accepting responsibility and settlement. Under such circumstances, therefore, it is questionable to what extent reluctant acceptance of guilt can serve as a force for significantly altering the future conduct and relationship between the adversaries.

This is not to imply that it is not possible to induce change in behavior and relationships by forces outside the person, nor that every person changes his or her behavior and relationships willfully or voluntarily. The point here is that unless the need for change is internalized, the change is likely to be only temporary. The relationship would not have been significantly altered, and the conflict would not have found enduring solutions. It would emerge again as soon as the circumstances change. More enduring transformation is likely to emerge when motivated by an internal need to change, especially when it emanates from self-reflection and criticism. The role of the third party in reconciliation, then, is to create an environment where the parties are assisted to move from simply finger pointing and attempting to change the adversary to a situation where they reflect upon their own behavior and make changes in themselves as they are expecting to change the protagonist.

In short, reconciliation is probably the most effective and durable way of resolving and preventing destructive conflicts. However, its processes are complex and require addressing the cognitive and deeply affective as well as the rational and nonrational dimensions of the conflict among the protagonists.

NOTES

1. See Roger Fisher and William Ury, *Getting to Yes* (Boston: Houghton Mifflin, 1981) for the distinction between the bargaining type (distinctive) and the problem-solving type (integrative) of negotiation approaches.

2. Of course these categories are neither exhaustive nor watertight. There are many more mechanisms that mix the various types and fall somewhere in between. One example is a mechanism that has come to be known as "med/arb," where the process starts as mediation with the voluntary and full participation of the parties, but if that fails in resolving the problem, the solution is determined by a third party, an arbitrator. There are also other nonformal processes such as *advocacy* by interest groups and *political mobilization* at the grassroots level in order to put pressure on leaders, and these can be placed at various points of the spectrum. Advocacy operates in the adjudication framework, although the body to whom the appeal is done might be the courts of national or international public opinion instead of the regular courts of law. *Political mobilization* could be seen as a tactic in the negotiation process in which the adversaries are marshaling their forces to improve their bargaining leverage or capacity to be heard and be taken seriously.

■ 12.4

Coping with Trauma

Hugo van der Merwe and Tracy Vienings

Trauma is a term that defines a response to an extraordinary event. It is a response to an event that overwhelms the individual's coping resources, making it difficult for him or her to function effectively in society. Traumatic situations are those in which the person is rendered powerless and where great danger is involved. Trauma generally includes events involving death and injury or the possibility of death or injury. The word *trauma* is generally used to include both natural catastrophes (such as hurricanes, floods, or fires) and man-made violence (such as war, concentration camp experiences, torture, and other forms of victimization). For example, traumatic events may include:

- A threat to one's life or physical integrity.
- A person's response of intense fear, helplessness, or horror.
- Serious threat or harm to one's children, spouse, or other close relatives or friends.
- Sudden destruction of one's home or community.
- Seeing another person who has recently been, or is being, seriously injured or killed as the result of an accident or physical violence.

Unresolved trauma has dire consequences, both at the personal and at the community level. Field diplomacy, as a new paradigm, emphasizes the importance of attention to *deep conflict*. In his paper, "Field Diplomacy: A New Conflict Prevention Paradigm," Luc Reychler argues that war engenders a mental environment of desperation in which fear, resentment, jealousy, and rage predominate. Consequently, building peace requires not only attention to the hard layers of the conflict but also to the softer layers of the deep conflict. These softer layers would include reconciliation at the psychological and emotional levels.

Dealing with trauma is dealt with most effectively when all three levels of healing are considered: the national level, the community level, and the individual level. For the healing of trauma on a national scale, structures such as Truth and Reconciliation Commissions (TRCs) can be effective if their aims are structured to uncover truth and deal with perpetrators. On the community level there are many creative ways in which communities deal with the past. Rituals or ceremonies that symbolically pay tribute to the suffering of the past, or that remember those who have died and the loss the community has suffered, are successful in dealing with community traumas. Building memorials to commemorate pain and suffering has been used by many communities over the years.

It is at the individual level that dealing with trauma has certain limitations. The method for dealing with individual trauma is largely practiced through psychological one-on-one counseling, and this has obvious limitations when a large number of people have been traumatized and counseling is unavailable or constrained due to numbers.

After prolonged and extensive social traumas like civil strife, the damage to both the social structure and to individuals requires intervention. The legacy of civil conflict can permeate all aspects of civil society and government institutions for years after the conflicts, often resulting in further forms of violence. Authoritarianism and resultant human rights violations by the police, despite the instatement of democratic governments and even with some state investigations into the past, are still common in countries like Brazil, Argentina, and Chile.[1] As much as the authoritarianism of past regimes can live on for many years, so, too, can the psychological effects of large-scale traumas.

A person suffering from trauma is usually left with intense feelings and sensations that negatively influence his or her mental well-being. These feelings and sensations make it difficult for that person to resume his or her normal, everyday activities. Part of (re)building peace is to rebuild the social fabric of society that is so often destroyed by war. Strong family units that operate effectively as nurturing and moral environments, and which can effectively contribute to rebuilding community structures, require the rebuilding of interpersonal relationships based on trust. A person suffering from trauma will find it difficult to relate to friends and family and will more than likely not be able to contribute meaningfully to initiatives to rebuild families and communities after violence or war.

But failure to deal with trauma may have even more dire consequences than effectively disabling individuals; if ignored, certain victims of past violence are at risk for becoming the perpetrators of retributive violence or displaced social and domestic violence.[2] This phenomenon has also been observed in child victims of violence. Children exposed to violence will more readily become perpetrators of violence themselves. Similarly, studies have found that women who were beaten are at least twice as likely to beat their children than mothers who were not abused.

Therefore, in the case of victims of violence or war, victim empowerment and effective support can break the cycle of violence and be viewed as preventative and as part of the conditions necessary for building peace.

Trauma counseling and a range of other interventions to deal with trauma can be considered effective in alleviating and preventing the consequences and effects of violent victimization.

THE PSYCHOLOGICAL EFFECTS OF TRAUMA

In order to deal with trauma, it helps to understand the broad psychological effects of trauma. These vary according to the victim's beliefs, expectations, and assumptions about the world.

R. Janoff-Bulman asserts that the experience of trauma shatters four basic healthy assumptions about the self and the world: the belief in personal invulnerability ("it won't happen to me"); the view of the self as positive (trauma affects victims by making them feel weak, powerless, guilty, or ashamed); the belief that the world is a meaningful and orderly place and that events happen for a reason; and the trust that other human beings are fundamentally benign.[3]

These four assumptions allow people to function effectively in the world and to relate to others. After an experience of violence, the person is left feeling vulnerable, helpless, and out of control in a world that is no longer predictable. Interventions to deal with trauma, therefore, aim to reframe the trauma so that the individual can see that his or her responses to it are normal responses to an abnormal event. Interventions aim to rebuild the individual's trust in themselves and in the world around them.

POST-TRAUMATIC STRESS DISORDER

People who have been victims of trauma may develop symptoms of post-traumatic stress disorder (PTSD). Not many people develop full-blown PTSD. More commonly, individuals will develop some symptoms of PTSD but not enough to fill all the diagnostic criteria for PTSD. There are three main symptom clusters in PTSD. First, the *intrusive* cluster. Intrusions can take the form of repeated, unwanted, and uncontrollable thoughts of the trauma and can include nightmares and/or flashbacks. Second, the *avoidant* cluster. These symptoms consist of the person's attempt to reduce exposure to people or places that may elicit memories of the event (or intrusive symptoms). This also involves symptoms such as social withdrawal, emotional numbing, and a sense of loss of pleasure. The third category is termed *hyperarousal* and refers to physiological signs of increased arousal such as hypervigilance or an increased startle response.

What will a person experience after a traumatic event and how can you help them? The process of trauma has three main phases. These phases do not follow any strict pattern; rather, they are characterized more by the behavior of the person.

Phase One: The Impact Phase

This phase can last from a few seconds to up to two or three days after the traumatic incident. In this phase the person appears emotionally numb, disorientated, confused, irrational, and disorganized. The person is in a state of shock and may not be entirely aware of the reality of what has happened. Some people show a lot of emotion and may scream or cry. Others are completely calm, as though nothing has happened. This does not mean the person has been unaffected by the trauma; it is merely a coping mechanism. The person may seek reassurance and direction. He or she is usually temporarily helpless in this phase, and their low level of functioning can be compared to that of a very young child.

What kind of help does a person in this phase require? As a helper, you need to be "parental" at this stage: stay calm and be reassuring. The person needs to be in a safe environment, if possible, with structure and support. As a result of the temporary helplessness, the person may need practical assistance, for example, in finding relatives or seeking medical attention. Allow the person to tell their story, but do not force them if they are not ready. Tell them that their reaction to the trauma is normal and will pass with time.

Phase Two: The Recoil Phase

In this phase the person begins to realize the traumatic nature of the experience that they have been through and to express emotion, most likely anger, sadness, and guilt.

What kind of help does a person in this phase require? Most of the traumatic stress symptoms begin to develop at this point and many victims begin to want to talk about the experience. Tell the person that he or she is not weak or going crazy, that their responses are a normal reaction to an abnormal event. It is at this point that the person should go for counseling.

In most conflicts and wars, however, there are no counseling facilities. Even if there were, the number of victims usually substantially outweighs the number of counselors. There are traditional ways that communities have dealt with trauma over generations, but these mechanisms are usually destroyed during the conflict or war, making it more difficult to rely on them.

Using critical incident debriefing is one way of working with trauma that has affected entire groups of people. In this process, the victims are encouraged to share their stories with other members of the group and in that way go through a process of reframing and releasing the trauma. Other methods include symbolic ceremonies where the trauma is remembered and where people have an opportunity to express their grief, anger, and guilt. Community members can hold these ceremonies themselves, and there are many creative ways in which communities have done this.

There are three key elements in helping a person to deal with trauma:

1. *Getting the person to talk about what happened to them, to tell their story, in detail.* This effectively results in the victim verbalizing a horror—and discussing it with someone else, in words and language, renders it less fearsome and less out of control.

2. *Reframing the victim's perceptions of his or her role in the event.* Victims often blame themselves or feel guilty, particularly when they feel they could have done something to save a loved one or friend who died in the incident. The victim needs to be reassured that they did the best they could under the circumstances. They might wish that they had died instead of a relative, and by going over the story, they need to come to terms with the loss and realize that the event was something out of their control. They need to understand that there might not be a logical or reasonable explanation for what happened.

3. *Developing and sustaining coping mechanisms.* The victim of trauma will feel powerless and unable to deal with daily life tasks. You need to help them re-establish their coping mechanisms—not by doing things for them but by getting them to develop ways that they can possibly deal with things.

Phase Three: The Integration Phase

In this phase, the person begins to be able to live with the trauma as a memory that is not overwhelming. Ideally they return to their previous level of functioning and experience themselves as intact. Although trauma does change the individual and is likely to leave emotional scars, the person can learn to live with the experience in a functional way. Some people may be able to draw new strengths and insights as a result of having coped with the trauma.

What support does a person in this phase require? In this phase, the person's trust in others starts to get rebuilt. The person also has an increased ability to relate emotionally to people around him or her and to invest in and engage with life. This should be encouraged and supported.

Although the reactions to trauma are disturbing, particularly for the victim, they are considered to be normal responses to abnormal events. Trauma symptoms are to some extent adaptive, and Baldwin argues that they originally evolved to assist the individual to recognize and avoid other dangerous situations. In some cases these symptoms resolve within a few days or weeks of a traumatic experience. It is only when symptoms persist for weeks or months or when they are extreme and debilitating that the diagnosis of PTSD is made.

There are cases where risk to PTSD is increased. When a victim has to go back into war or is exposed to ongoing conflict, he or she is likely to struggle more to overcome the trauma. There is also evidence that early traumatic experiences during childhood, especially if these are prolonged or repeated, may increase the risk of developing PTSD after traumatic exposure as an adult.

It must also be remembered that there may be many other psychological issues that may confront the individual when dealing with trauma. B. Hamber and S. Lewis show how the individuals who testified at the South African TRC provide a useful example of the complexities of dealing with trauma. A plethora of psychological symptoms and signs have been observed in those who have testified. On the whole, most individuals have presented with a mixture of issues related to social, psychological, and medical problems.

Uncomplicated post-traumatic stress has not been a common feature, mainly because, in most cases, individual past traumas (being tortured, abuses by the police) have been overshadowed by present psychological and social problems. Furthermore, the ability to draw direct causative links between their initial trauma and the present difficulties experienced by most survivors has generally been complicated by the protracted time that has passed since most violations occurred. In some cases, survivors and families have testified about violations that took place in the 1960s.

Dire social circumstances in the present make it difficult for most individuals to deal with or prioritize past psychological traumas. At times, so-called present difficulties, such as occupational problems, substance abuse, or relationship breakdowns, are symptoms of long-term traumatization that has been compounded by impoverished living conditions. However, at other times, the impoverished living conditions, from overcrowding to hunger, have heightened the primary trauma and have also in themselves caused a range of new psychological difficulties and problems.

Classic therapeutic interventions for PTSD were originally developed in relation to soldiers of war. The model thus assumes that the traumatic event has passed and the emphasis is on helping victims to deal with the trauma through retelling the story and reframing the events without self-blame or guilt. The intervention helps strengthen coping skills in the present daily lives of the victims, yet it becomes far more complex when the traumatic event is ongoing (as in protracted civil war) or when the victim is forced to live in a situation where there is continuous stress and trauma.

For example, G. Straker and the Sanctuaries Counseling Center assert that the term *post-traumatic stress disorder* is a misnomer in the South African context and that this could be true in many other countries that also experience continuous high levels of violence.[4] The center was referring to individuals living in South Africa's black townships, which were subject to continuous stress. This stress was attributed to the high levels of violence in the townships, characterized by confrontations between the South African Defense Force and police and various sectors of the community; black anti-apartheid groups and right-wing vigilantes who were more supportive of the status quo; and intergroup fighting among rival anti-apartheid groups such as the United Democratic Front and the Anzian People's Organization. In terms of therapeutic interventions for PTSD, the most serious difficulty was the inability to protect the individual from further trauma.

TYPES OF VICTIMS

A victim of violence is often mistakenly presumed to be the person who was directly affected by a trauma or violent incident. In reality, the traumatic experience of a direct victim may also adversely affect many other individuals with whom they may have contact. This process has been labeled "secondary victimization."[5] The traumatic nature of violence means that any contact with the traumatic materials— through witnessing or hearing of the event—can also have a deleterious effect.

Indirect victims can include witnesses to the event, as well as families and relatives whose loved ones have been victimized or murdered. Those who in some way have contact with narratives of violence or trauma, including journalists, aid workers, and those in the helping professions, can also be traumatized and may be considered victims if they experience any adverse reactions. Many people are traumatized vicariously by reading, hearing, or even seeing footage of violent incidents.

Other types of vicarious traumatization can include "second generation" trauma survivors who are most often the relatives or children of those who have been traumatized. Those vicariously exposed to trauma can suffer from symptoms similar to those of direct victims. Symptoms that have been documented can include feelings of exhaustion and hopelessness, health problems, paranoia, and early burnout. Emotional and relationship problems as well as substance abuse may also occur. At times those vicariously traumatized can act out victim-aggressor patterns and overidentify with victims. Broad existential questions with respect to the meaning of life can also trouble humanitarian and care workers.[6]

It is important not to adhere to a static view of victimization. An individual can assume multiple roles over a period of time, and over a short period of time in the case of war. For example, a person may have been a victim, a perpetrator, and a witness to violence in a short space of time. When considering the emotional response to trauma, all of these factors must be considered. Furthermore, traumas are not always isolated, and they can be prolonged—for example, surviving torture or extended incarceration during a hostage drama. Often individuals may be traumatically wounded, while at the same time they witness another person being killed. Other individuals live in a state of continuous trauma as in war situations.

Dealing with trauma on its own is obviously not enough. Dealing with trauma has to be parallel to measures taken to restore faith in the state institutions of safety, security, and justice, as well as measures to instill a renewed sense of safety and hope in the lives of those who have suffered as a result of violence and trauma.

NOTES

1. Hamber 1996.
2. Hamber and Lewis 1996.
3. R. Janoff-Bulman 1985.
4. G. Straker and the Sanctuaries Counseling Center 1987.
5. R. Janoff-Bulman 1985.
6. Pergamenchtchik 1996.

REFERENCES

Hamber, B. (1998). "Dealing with the Past: Issues to Consider and Recommendations for Countries in Transition." Unpublished paper, Center for the Study of Violence and Reconciliation.
———. (1997). "Living with the Legacy of Impunity: Lessons for South Africa About Truth, Justice and Crime in Brazil." Center for the Study of Violence and Reconciliation.
Hamber, B., and S. Lewis. (1997). "An Overview of the Consequences of Violence and Trauma in South Africa." Center for the Study of Violence and Reconciliation.
Janoff-Bulman, R. (1985). "The Aftermath of Victimization: Rebuilding Shattered Assumptions." In C. R. Figely, ed., *Trauma and Its Wake*. New York: Brunner Mazel Publishers.
Jelin, E. (1994). "The Politics of Memory: The Human Rights Movement and Construction of Democracy in Argentina." *Latin American Perspectives* 21, no. 2: 38–58.
Niebuhr, H. R. (1941). *The Meaning of Revelation*. New York: Macmillan.
Pergamenchtchik, L. A. (1996). Search of Life Meaning in a Post-catastrophe Period. University of Sheffield.
Reychler, Luc. (1996). "Field Diplomacy: A New Conflict Prevention Paradigm." Paper presented at the Brisbane conference of the International Peace Research Association.

Straker, G., and the Sanctuaries Counseling Center. (1987). "The Continuous Traumatic Stress Syndrome—The Single Therapeutic Interview." *Psychology in Society* 8: 48–49.

van Boven, T. C. F., F. Grunfeld, and I. Westendorp, eds. (1992). Seminar on the Right to Restitution, Compensation and Rehabilitation for Victims of Gross Human Rights and Fundamental Freedoms. Netherlands Institute of Human Rights, Maastricht, March 11–15.

■ 12.5

Dealing with the Past in Latin America

Sabine Kurtenbach

Torture, murder, or becoming "missed" are traumatic experiences not only for the suffering individuals but also for societies as a whole. Their effects and consequences persist for a long time after the end of gross human rights violations. Although there might be the wish to put the past to rest, there are no fast ways to heal or overcome the consequences of personal or collective suffering. Coping with the past has legal, moral, and historic aspects; the process will always be conflict-ridden because it forces both victims and perpetrators to explain and legitimize their actions or omissions in the past and because the definition of the historic "truth" is at stake. Victims not only demand documentation of their plight, but justice and redemption; perpetrators mostly try to justify or deny their individual responsibility, saying they acted under orders.

Latin American societies experienced gross human rights violations in the 1970s and 1980s. The military regimes of the 1970s in the Southern Cone (Argentina, Brazil, Chile, Uruguay) fought "dirty wars" against the civilian opposition, targeting mainly the leaders of labor unions, human rights groups, and left-wing political parties. The perpetrators were members of the military, the police, intelligence units, or paramilitary death squads. The Argentine military claimed to fight the active opposition first, their sympathizers second, and finally the indifferent ones who did not support their regime. Their country had the most violent dictatorship with a toll of 8,960 people missing, according to the Sabato Commission, though human rights groups claim 30,000 people are missing. In comparison, the case of Argentina's neighbor Uruguay is an example of a rather soft dictatorship (*dictablanda*) where "only" 150 people disappeared.

The persecution of the so-called communist subversion had a regional component as well as the different military regimes that cooperated under the Condor Plan. Members of the Chilean military secret service, for instance, are accused of having killed the ex–army commander, General Carlos Prats, who had been loyal to the socialist government of Salvador Allende during the 1973 coup, in his Argentine exile in 1974. They could not have done so without the knowledge or help of their Argentine colleagues. Further military cooperation is documented not only on the regional level between the armed forces of Guatemala, El Salvador, and Honduras but also on the hemispheric level, as the Argentine military sent groups of "specialists" in antisubversive tactics as advisers to Central America.

In the civil wars in Colombia, Peru, and Central America, the case of Guatemala is the most violent with more than 200,000 people dead in the longest war fought in the region. The Salvadoran war had a toll of 70,000 killed, and the Nicaraguan revolution and the Contra war in its aftermath led to 30,000 violent deaths. In Peru the death toll has been 30,000, and in Colombia, war and violence are ongoing. In all cases only a small number of the victims lost their lives during open combat between the warring factions of military and guerilla forces. As in the Southern Cone, most of the victims came from the civil society—leaders or members of labor unions, land cooperatives, human rights groups, center or left-wing political parties, or those working as journalists.

Although the context and the cruelty of violence differs between countries, the problem of coping with the past is the same all over Latin America. The manner in which these societies have dealt with the legacy of torture, violent deaths, and people missing allows us to draw some interesting conclusions and lessons for future cases: dealing with the past reflects the balance of power between perpetrators and victims; international actions can be decisive; patience is necessary; and conciliation must be based on the truth.

DEALING WITH THE PAST REFLECTS THE BALANCE OF POWER BETWEEN PERPETRATORS AND VICTIMS

In all of Latin America the manner of dealing with the past depended very much on the way in which a specific violent regime came to an end. In most cases there were negotiations between the warring factions or the military and its civil opponents. Argentina was the only case where the military had to retreat, discredited after a lost war on the Falkland/Malvinas Islands. Argentina could therefore not only document the extent of the violence in the report of the Sabato Commission, "Nunca Más" (Never Again), but it could also bring to trial junta members and send them to prison for a few years.

Although comparatively weak, the military did not accept the trials, however, and by a military rebellion led by Lieutenant Colonel Aldo Rico in April 1987 demanded the end of the persecution of past human rights violations through the civil justice system. At first President Raúl Alfonsín was unable to find a military commander willing to crush the rebellion, and after only two days of massive public protests by political parties, labor unions, and other organizations of the civil society, the rebels left the barrack they had taken. It remains unclear if the government made any secret concessions, but the military regained part of its autonomy during the government of Alfonsín (1983–1989).

In the following years many courts ruled that the accused acted under orders. In 1989, under the presidency of Carlos Meném, parliament passed a law ending the prosecution, and at the end of 1990 President Meném pardoned all the convicts including the junta members. Argentina returned to the Latin American mainstream of impunity for murderers and torturers.

In all other countries the military could not only negotiate but mostly dictate the conditions of power transfer. An amnesty for past human rights abuses and the renunciation of legal persecution was the price for the transition to more open and democratic forms of government. But although the military could maintain a high degree of autonomy, democratization allowed the public to continue its demands for information about the past and the prosecution of the perpetrators. These demands led to a variety of commissions examining the worst cases of past human rights violations and recommending a more efficient protection of human rights for the future. The commissions, consisting of national and in some cases international experts, were installed by governments (Argentina, Chile) or human rights organizations (Bolivia, Brazil, Paraguay, Uruguay, Honduras, Colombia, Guatemala) and led to the documentation of human rights violations. In El Salvador and Guatemala the establishment of the "Truth Commissions" was a central part of the peace treaties. In Peru there were different inquiries into spectacular cases of human rights violations, like the disappearance of a university professor and eight of his students.

Uruguay was a special case insofar as the population was called to a referendum in 1989 where they could vote yes or no on an amnesty law passed by parliament. A majority of 56 percent approved the law, while 41 percent of the Uruguayans voted for its rejection.

INTERNATIONAL ACTIONS CAN BE DECISIVE

In spite of the above-mentioned problems, victims and human rights organizations did not end their efforts for justice and rehabilitation. They kept the problems on the public agenda, gathered information and evidence on individual cases, and prepared legal documents. In view of the balance of power at the national level, international help for further action was crucial all over the hemisphere.

The principle of national sovereignty is the main obstacle for international action in the human rights area. After issuing an amnesty, states and governments usually reject international demands for the legal prosecution of human rights violations, claiming that this is an unlawful intervention in their internal affairs and a violation of national sovereignty. Latin America has a long and very strict tradition of nonintervention in the internal affairs of other states. In 1988, when there was a basic reform of the charter of the Organization of American States (OAS), the principle of promoting representative democracy was explicitly submitted with the principle of nonintervention. Only three years later at the summit in Santiago, Chile, in 1991, did the OAS issue a declaration that obliged its members to install democratic political systems. Haiti was the first case where the OAS imposed a trade embargo.

In the field of bringing past human rights violations to justice, foreign governments tried to exert influence by working on cases where their own citizens or people with double citizenship were involved. The torture, murder, or disappearance of Spanish, French, or German citizens in Argentina or Chile led to charges against junta members. The most famous is the case brought by the Spanish judge Baltasar Garzón against General Augusto Pinochet, who was arrested in London in October 1998 but released in March 2000. Other examples are charges against Guatemalan military leaders in Spain and against Argentine junta members in Germany.

The situation with respect to Central America is more complicated: first, there have not been many cases of foreign citizens as victims of repression; second, most of the foreign victims have been U.S. citizens, such as Michael Devine in Guatemala; and third, the United States has been involved more or less directly at least in the training of the military forces. U.S. archives opened under the Freedom of Information Act give evidence of the knowledge of gross human rights violations. In the case of the murder of U.S. nuns in El Salvador in 1980, there have been charges against top military leaders in U.S. courts.

PATIENCE IS NECESSARY

The wish for justice and the victim's rehabilitation cannot be satisfied entirely in the immediate aftermath of violent regimes. Lessons from Latin America show that patience is crucial for victims and human rights organizations. The case of General Pinochet shows how long it can take just to be able to begin legal proceedings against the formerly powerful. The arrest of the general led not only to broad discussions all over the Western Hemisphere but intensified efforts for justice in other countries.

Patience is also crucial for the gathering of evidence. In 1995—twelve years after the last junta surrendered power in Argentina—an ex–military officer, Adolfo Francisco Scilingo, was the first to break the silence of the perpetrators. Talking to a journalist he described how the military treated its victims. After being tortured, they were sedated and thrown out of aircrafts over the Atlantic Ocean. The interview led to a broad public discussion of the past, culminating in a televised speech of the army commander in chief, General Balza, asking the Argentine people for forgiveness and declaring that immoral orders should not be obeyed by soldiers and subordinates. In 1999—ten years after the end of the Pinochet dictatorship—an officer talked about similar methods of the Chilean Army. Whether this will lead to similar experiences as in Argentina remains to be seen.

Breaking the silence is crucial not only for the gathering of evidence in individual cases but also for the rehabilitation of the victims whose suffering and history are recognized at last. The public recognition of what happened is not only important for historians but is the basis for overcoming the individual and collective trauma.

CONCILIATION MUST BE BASED ON TRUTH

Although there have been few cases of direct revenge, conciliation has been difficult all over Latin America. The arrest of General Pinochet in London shows how unresolved the old conflict has remained in the first decade of democratization, how deep the feelings still are, and how much the military fears their deeds being exposed. Another example, including violence, is Argentina: the leader of the German Coalition against Impunity traveled to Buenos Aires in November 1998. He gathered evidence in cases that should lead to accusations of former junta members and officers in German trials. After having talked to Nobel Peace Price laureate Adolfo Perez Esquivel, he took a taxi that, after a few moments, was surrounded by two black cars. Two men entered the taxi, beat him up, stole all his legal documents, and threw him out at a remote point of the city.

The murder of Bishop Juan Gerardi in Guatemala two days after he presented the report of the church's Project of Historic Remembrance in April 1998 is another example of the sometimes fatal difficulties in the search for truth.

Nicaragua is the only case in Latin America where the government of Violeta Barrios de Chamorro (1990–1996) explicitly favored a policy of national reconciliation between Sandinistas and their opponents. Although human rights violations in Nicaragua occurred to a lesser extent than in other parts of Central America and although there has been some success, the old polarizations still prevail.

In spite of all the difficulties, truth is the basic requirement for the difficult process of conciliation between victims and perpetrators and in the society as a whole. Without truth, conciliation will not be possible. Truth is not only the basic condition for overcoming the past but also the basic condition for developing a nonviolent perspective for the future.

People working in postwar or postauthoritarian societies should be aware of the importance of these problems. At first sight, coping with past atrocities might not have a direct effect on their work, but it will influence everything they do. Working in these societies requires a lot of sensibility for persisting conflicts and respect for the victims. International cooperation can play an important role in creating a space for discussion and providing a neutral place where victims and their families can talk about their experiences without fear. In Guatemala the international cooperation helped finance a project of the Catholic bishops' conference under the name of REMHI (Recuperación de la memoria histórica). During four years, the project not only helped to document past atrocities at the local level but was a place where victims and perpetrators could tell their versions of the past. The results of the project were first gathered at the national level and then brought back to the communities so that there was the possibility to reflect on the past on a broader level.

REPORTS OF TRUTH COMMISSIONS

Arquidiocese de São Paulo. (1985). *Brasil nunca mais. Um relato para a história.* Petrópolis.

Arzobospado de Santiago. Vicaría de la Solidarida. (1979). *¿Dónde están?, Santiago de Chile Leo Valladares, 1993: Los hechos hablan por si mismos.* Tegucigalpa.

Centro Nacional de Cooperación al Desarrollo. (1992). *El terrorismo de Estado en Colombia.* Brussels.

CIPAE (Comité de Iglesias para Ayudas de Emergencia). (1990). *Nunca Más. La dictadura de Stroessner y los Derechos Humanos.* Asunción.

Comisión de la Verdad para El Salvador. (1992). *De la Locura a la Esperanza. Informe de la Comisión de la Verdad.* New York: UNO.

Comisión de Esclarecimiento Histórico. (1999). *Memoria del Silencio.* URLs: http://www.hrdata.aaas.org//ceh and http://www.c.net.gt//ceg.

CONADEP (Comisión Nacional sobre la Desaparición de Personas). (1984). *Argentina Nunca Más.* Buenos Aires.

Oficina de Derechos Humanos del Arzobispado de Guatemala, ed. (1998). *Guatemala—Nunca Más.* Guatemala.

Servicio Paz y Justicia de Uruguay. (1989). *Uruguay Nunca Más. Informe sobre la violación de Derechos Humanos (1972–1985).* Montevideo.

■ 12.6

Dealing with the Past in South Africa

Luc Huyse

HISTORY OF THE TRUTH AND RECONCILIATION COMMISSION

In early 1990 the white government of South Africa took the first formal steps in the direction of a transition. As of February 2, 1990, the African National Congress (ANC) was no longer banned and was even accepted as a negotiating partner. On February 11, 1990, Nelson Mandela was released. The question was immediately raised as to how to deal with the legacy of the past after an eventual transition.

The National Party (NP) and the government of F. W. de Klerk that it had formed, first tried to introduce a de facto amnesty through Indemnity Act No. 35. That pushed the ANC and many nongovernmental organizations (NGOs) to enter into internal debates on this issue. Within the ANC, the majority wanted one or another form of amnesty, albeit bound to full exposure of the crimes committed under apartheid. In the autumn of 1992, the ANC went a step further and gave an international commission the assignment to investigate whether violations of human rights had been committed in the camps of this organization. De Klerk's Further Indemnity Act No. 151 of November 9, 1992, which again introduced new forms of impunity, substantially sharpened the differences of opinion between the NP and the ANC. Nevertheless, after stormy talks a provision was included at the end of the interim constitution of November 1993, which opened the door for amnesty. It prescribed the following:

> In order to advance reconciliation and reconstruction, amnesty shall be granted in respect of acts, omissions and offenses associated with political objectives and committed in the course of the conflicts of the past. To this end, Parliament under the Constitution shall adopt a law providing the mechanisms, criteria and procedures, including tribunals, if any, through which such amnesty shall be dealt with at any time after the law has been passed.

In the third quarter of 1994 it became clear that the operationalization of the promised amnesty would come in the form of a Truth and Reconciliation Commission (TRC). On December 15, 1995, the commission members assembled. The first meeting was the day after, not coincidentally, Reconciliation Day, an official holiday.

MANDATE OF THE TRC

The commission had a fourfold task:

1. To draw up an inventory of the causes, nature, and extent of the violations of human rights committed between March 1, 1960, and December 5, 1993. The violations relate to those committed both in the name of apartheid and in the struggle against apartheid.
2. To grant amnesty to persons who satisfy the set conditions.
3. To allow victims the opportunity to give their version of the facts and to make proposals that could provide a certain reparation for the damage suffered.
4. To produce a final report "providing as comprehensive an account as possible of the activities and findings of the commission and containing recommendations of measures to prevent the future violations of human rights" (from the Promotion of National Unity and Reconciliation Act No. 34, July 19, 1995).

A period of eighteen months was originally provided for this assignment (plus three months for reporting), eventually increased by six months. In other words, this arrangement anticipated the end of activities on June 15 or December 15, 1997. It quickly became clear that a time extension was necessary. Ultimately, the mandate of the TRC was extended to June 1998. The final report was presented to President Mandela on October 29, 1998.

INSTRUMENTS OF THE TRC

The work of the TRC has been divided among three committees: the Human Rights Violations Committee (HRVC), the Amnesty Committee, and the Reparation and Rehabilitation Committee. An investigative unit supported the three committees. In addition, there was support from a media department, a legal department, and a witness protection department. This apparatus—the three departments and the three committees—was also regionally distributed: the head office was in Johannesburg, and there were regional offices in Cape Town, Durban, East London, and Johannesburg. Information from and about the TRC was distributed via leaflets, news bulletins, and the Internet. There was also continual close attention from the

South African and foreign media. The TRC had around 700 employees and members of its staff. At the end of December 1997 more than £30 million had been invested in it.

The Human Rights Violations Committee

The HRVC was the most public of the three committees on account of the often emotional confrontations between victims and perpetrators. Over fifty public hearings were held at which victims have told their stories to the nation. Such sessions were supplied by reports from statement takers who collected statements over the entire country, and by the documentation from domestic and foreign NGOs. In total more than 21,000 statements have been taken. They relate to around 35,000 violations of human rights. A major information campaign preceded these accounts being taken. Hundreds of thousands of leaflets about the TRC were distributed throughout the country in the eleven official languages of South Africa.

A second remarkable activity of the HRVC involved the hearings with representatives of political parties, trade and industry, the bar association, the judiciary, medical bodies, the press, unions, and NGOs. The committee also provided legal assistance to victims for the preparation of their testimony. An important instrument for the HRVC was the right to require individuals to appear before the committee. The committee also had powers of search and seizure.

The Amnesty Committee

This committee was established to consider the amnesty applications. Its deliberations must be public if major violations of human rights are involved.

To qualify for amnesty a person has to satisfy a number of conditions: the application, on an official form, had to reach the committee between December 15, 1995, and May 10, 1997; the relevant crimes had to be committed between March 1, 1960, and December 5, 1993 (a period later extended to May 10, 1994, the day of Mandela's inauguration); the applicant had to give a complete and open account; and the crime must have been of a political nature (a series of criteria have been set to assess that, based on the Norgard principles).

As of June 18, 1998, 7,060 amnesty applications had been submitted. At this time, the committee had granted 125 amnesties and refused 4,571 other demands. Most of the remaining cases concern gross violations of human rights and require public hearings. It is expected that the committee will not complete its task before the summer of 2000.

The Reparation and Rehabilitation Committee

The Reparation and Rehabilitation Committee investigated the acute needs of witnesses, and when necessary, provided immediate help and made recommendations on possible compensation for the material, physical, and/or psychological damage that the victims suffered.

PROBLEMS OF THE TRC

The massive nature of the operation was considered a crucial fact right from the start. There were nevertheless serious miscalculations in the planning. The Amnesty Committee, in particular, quickly became overwhelmed by the flood of applications. The delays that arose in this committee took on dramatic proportions.

The clause in the provisional constitution on amnesty and the act that brought about the TRC were supported by a relatively wide agreement. That has changed since the commission came into effect. The NP and the Inkatha Freedom Party (IFP) of Chief Mangosuthu Buthelezi have turned against the TRC, convinced that the commission was not or could not be impartial. This hostility has substantially hampered the objectives of the TRC. In addition, operations have been continually set up by the NP and the IFP aimed at damaging the TRC or its staff.

The TRC was particularly dependent on the cooperation of bodies such as the army, the police, and the judiciary, who in their composition and culture still exude the spirit of the old order. Their staff often contained individuals who were responsible, in part, for the crimes of the apartheid regime. Obstruction of the commission's work, for example, by destroying or concealing evidence, has been the result of this.

Problems have also been created by opponents of the old order. Members of victims' families (the widow of Steve Biko, for instance) have contested the legality of the TRC before the Constitutional Court, arguing that by granting amnesty, the victims are denied the right to obtain compensation from the perpetrators in a civil action. The court rejected these applications, but they nevertheless delayed the work of the commission and damaged its credibility.

EVALUATION OF THE TRC

What is remarkable about the South African Truth and Reconciliation Commission is the original mix of ingredients in its objectives. Its aim was both justice (and the associated cleansing process) and reconciliation. The first task was operationalized via an inventory of what violations of human rights took place between March 1960 and May 1994. The second task, reconciliation, should be facilitated by the possibility of granting amnesty. Through this combination of truth and reconciliation, the TRC, in contrast to what has been the case in earlier truth commissions, was aimed at both victims and perpetrators and simultaneously the past (truth) and the future (reconciliation).

All these objectives are linked to one another to a certain extent. With amnesty as the inducement, the commission not only wanted to reconcile those responsible for the apartheid regime with the new order but also wanted to prompt them to open the books, as full disclosure is one of the conditions for obtaining amnesty. Thus, the TRC got closer to the truth, which in turn provided victims with a certain atonement that could possibly lead to a more peaceful relationship with the apartheid past.

Justice and reconciliation can also be linked in another way, albeit specific to the South African context. Archbishop Desmond Tutu, chairman of the South African TRC, has played a crucial role in making a link between the two. Justice, he says, should not only be aimed at retribution but also at restoring a damaged relationship. It is the difference between *retributive justice* and *restorative justice*. The second form of justice is based on the African standard concept of *ubuntu*, the tendency to restore a victim's dignity through forgiveness.

However, these two objectives do not always fit together. They call on divergent rationales, a duality reflected in the composition and the problems of two of the three committees of the TRC. Drawing up an inventory of what happened in the past (the task of the Human Rights Violations Committee) is a fact-finding enterprise. But the decisionmaking on amnesty, the assignment of the Amnesty Committee, in a way closely resembles criminal proceedings.

A second remarkable characteristic of the South African TRC is the flexibility with which the preset scenario has been handled. Examples of this can be found in our short historical review. The act stipulated that amnesty could not be requested for crimes committed after December 5, 1993. The intention was not to pardon the violence that mainly came from the extreme right in the run-up to the elections. In an attempt to reconcile the NP and IFP with the TRC, this restriction was withdrawn and the date extended to May 10, 1994. Voices have been heard asking to include even more recent crimes that were committed in Kwazulu-Natal as qualifying for amnesty. The act also stipulated that amnesty applications had to be submitted by December 15, 1996, at the latest. This date was not maintained either.

In itself this flexibility can be seen as a positive development. Nevertheless, it does hold risks. Much of the violence of recent years has been ordinary crime. But it has been artificially defined as political, for the purpose at hand. This politicization of criminality and its transfer to the TRC Amnesty Committee risks reintroducing the culture of impunity into South Africa, which is precisely what the TRC is trying to avoid.

A third characteristic is the substantial depth of the public debate that preceded the creation of the TRC. The act of May 19, 1994, the composition of the commission, and the recruitment of the main staff were subject to many vigorous debates. As a result the TRC operation was quite well rooted in broad cross-sections of society.

Civil society played an important role in that debate through the media and the NGOs. Nevertheless, the relations between the TRC and civil society in general, and the NGOs in particular, were very problematic for much of the time. The TRC kept the NGOs at a distance through the fear that the mobilization of movements that had predominantly arisen in the fight against apartheid would give it a biased appearance. As a result, many opportunities have not been seized: the educational potential of the NGOs in announcing information about the TRC, the databases that they built up over time, and the networks through which evidence could be collected.

It has been pointed out that the TRC has also created positive spin-offs in sectors and areas that are outside the scope of the commission. There are local initiatives aimed at reconciliation between whites, coloreds, and blacks. And there are many self-help groups for victims of apartheid.

Many questions remain regarding the degree of truth and of reconciliation that the TRC has produced. "Yes," TRC's chairperson Desmond Tutu writes in the July 1998 issue of *Truth Talk* (the official newsletter of the TRC). "We believe the TRC has contributed to healing and to reconciliation, or has provided the setting where confession, forgiveness and reconciliation have happened. . . . The TRC has helped to uncover much truth."

But Piers Pigou, a former investigator for the TRC, wrote in *The Sunday Independent* of June 7, 1998:

> It is, however, clear that many thousands of violations have not been reported. . . . It is also evident that most perpetrators have not come forward. . . . In spite of all the TRC has achieved, I fear that it has only just begun to scratch the surface of past violations. What happens next is therefore crucial. The limitations of the process must be acknowledged and recommendations that the work continue will provide a powerful impetus to address the many unattended matters. . . . Investigative and research processes must continue, not necessarily with a primary objective of securing prosecutions. This process should retain current powers of search, subpoena and access to relevant state information.

A last consideration concerns the possible export of the South African form of the truth commission to other countries where an authoritarian regime gives way to a democratic order. Considerable caution is required in this respect. The transition in South Africa is of a very specific nature. This country can draw on resources (manpower, expertise, and public money) that are often lacking elsewhere. There are plenty of NGOs and, though they have only been involved in the operations of the TRC to a limited extent, they played a key role in bringing it about. This element is often not present in many postauthoritarian countries. Finally, there is the effect of the inclination to forgive, as rooted in African mores and in Christian churches.

NOTE

This text is a redrafted summary of part of a policy research paper written on behalf of the Belgian Department for International Cooperation, Brussels, October 1998.

BIBLIOGRAPHY

Asmal, K., et al., eds. (1996). *Reconciliation Through Truth: A Reckoning of Apartheid's Criminal Governance.* Cape Town: David Philip Publishers.
Boraine, A., et al., eds. (1994). *Dealing with the Past: Truth and Reconciliation in South Africa.* Cape Town: IDASA.
Boraine, A., et al., eds. (1995). *The Healing of a Nation?* Cape Town: IDASA.

■ 12.7

Imaging the Future:
A Tool for Conflict Resolution

Máire A. Dugan

We often refer to conflict resolution as a future-oriented field. Yet we offer disputants little assistance to help them identify or describe a future unfettered by the negative energies associated with their current conflicts. Envisioning contributes to conflict resolution by broadening our skills base, liberating ourselves from the exigencies of the conflict, identifying additional commonalities, clarifying whether the conflict is resolvable, generating new ideas for resolution, and providing criteria for assessing different solutions.

A NESTED THEORY OF CONFLICT

A first important question to explore in analyzing a conflict in order to determine appropriate intervention strategies is the level on which its source lies.[1] In answering this question, I suggest that attention be paid to four levels—the issues themselves, the relationship between or among the conflicting parties, the subsystem structure in which the conflict is located, and the more general systemic level.

An issues-specific conflict is one that arises directly from the issues themselves. Issues-specific conflicts can occur on a variety of topics and among a wide diversity of actors: a married couple may disagree on whether to buy a new car or save money for their children's education; a family may be upset about a neighbor's barking dog; an employee may wish to start and leave work earlier to beat rush-hour traffic, but her boss may want all employees to be available to clients from nine to five; one nation-state may hold another responsible for pollutants entering its waters; a group of nations may have difficulties agreeing on a plan to reduce destruction of the ozone.

If these difficulties, though real and potentially complex and/or crucial, are limited to disagreements on the issues at hand, it is sufficient to approach the conflict by exploring the issues in contention, identifying common ground, and searching for a mutually acceptable solution. Often,

however, conflicts are not simply the result of disagreement about a specified list of issues. I use the term *relational conflict* to describe a situation in
which the relationship between the parties has been damaged. A man may
distrust his wife because of a prior infidelity; two project workers with different styles and strengths may resent each other's approaches to a joint
project; two friendly nations may be suspicious of each other's relationship
with a third.

Sometimes, the source of the conflict lies beyond the particular disputants themselves and is more aptly seen as having its source in the system itself. I divide *structural conflicts* into two general categories: the level
of the *subsystem* in which the conflict is occurring, and the level of the
broader system of which the subsystem is a part.

Every organization and institution (subsystem) has its own rules and
procedures that, at times, will lead to difficulties between their members, or
at least lead to difficulties in resolving a matter that has arisen on a more
personal or issues-specific level. The conflict between the employee and
manager referred to above may have its source in the structure of the particular workplace in which no provision is made for flexible hours; the manager may actually think the employee's plan is a good one but is unable to
support it because of the organization's ethos. In this case, attempting to
approach the conflict as an issue-specific one would not likely result in any
constructive movement; the parties involved are simply not in a position to
respond in a different way to the issues presented.

Some conflicts do not have their source in the structure of any specific
organization or institution but are structured into the community, society, or
even global system. A situation in which UN action is prevented by the disagreement of a Security Council member (no matter how many of the
world's nations support it) might be seen as a subsystem conflict because
the UN can be seen as an organization, and the inattentiveness to the opinion of the majority is a consequence of the organization's own charter.
However, the nation-state system is a global systemic structure, and the UN
charter is merely a reflection of the power differentials that are an endemic
feature of the nation-state system.

The purpose here is not to split hairs over the level on which a particular conflict should be seen as occurring. Perhaps it is helpful to see each
level as a sort of continuum, the end of which overlaps with the next level.
The important thing is how the different levels and the conflicts occurring
within them relate to each other. I see them as a set of nested circles, as
depicted in Exhibit 12.7-1.

The important thing to note is the way in which the levels are hypothe-
sized to be related to each other. We can expect that any conflict on the
structural level will have manifestations in terms of relational difficulties
and that specific issues in contention will emerge. It is also possible for
issues to emerge as conflicts on their own, without being encumbered by

Exhibit 12.7-1   A Nested Model of Conflict

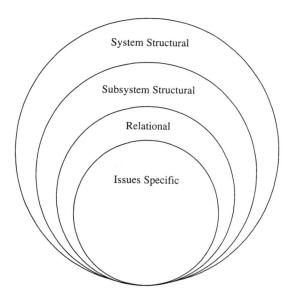

relational difficulties or structural injustices. It is necessary, however, to determine which is happening because treating issues as merely issues-specific problems when they are manifestations of deeper structural injustices creates the proverbial inadequacy of applying a Band-Aid to a cancer and, further, deprives parties of using the opportunity that the issue provides to address the deeper issues.

Inserting the Future in the Conflict Resolution Process

Envisioning is a challenge. In much of Western industrial society, we have not been encouraged to develop our imaginative powers. E. Boulding writes, "The obstacles to imaging lie partly in our social institutions, including schools, which discourage imaging because it leads to visualizing alternatives which challenge existing social arrangements."[2] But this is exactly what we need to do in the case of difficult and intractable conflicts—existing social arrangements are not working; we need to generate proposals for new arrangements.

Issues-Based Conflicts

Parties in conflicts that have their source in disagreements over issues probably do not need envisioning skills to resolve them, although they may help at times. Issues can normally be resolved by analytical mechanisms alone, for even when emotions are high, relationships are not necessarily at stake, and structural change is unnecessary to bring an acceptable solution into being.

Relational Conflicts

Parties in a difficult relational conflict are trapped not only by being locked into their positions but also by their negative feelings. Two questions can help release them, and both are related to the elasticity of the present moment, flexible both because of the impact that the past has on the present and the consequences that actions in the present have on the future. The first question takes the parties back to a point before the conflict began. The second requests them to identify what they wish to have in the future.

Disputants in a mediation, particularly as mediation has developed in the United States, are asked to tell their stories. With this question, disputants go back to the time immediately preceding the development of a conflict, which is now requiring third-party intervention. They are asked to describe their perceptions of the conflict. Although the rest of the mediation session tends to focus on the future, this starting point may not only help them identify and clarify issues and interests, it may also have the adverse impact of catching them up in the negative feelings toward, and judgments of, each other that the conflict between them has created. This is not to suggest that the past should be ignored, just because it is encumbered by negativity.

What I would suggest here is that disputants also be asked what they formerly valued in the relationship. This question can serve to help disputants recognize the loss they have experienced in the deterioration of the relationship, rather than just the anger and/or distrust they feel because of the behavior the other has exhibited during the course of the conflict. Including the recognition of shared good times and the sadness of their loss enables a richer constellation of emotions to be put at the service of resolving the conflict. By calling on these emotions, we also succeed in bringing a broader array of the disputants' capacities to bear on the conflict.

In shifting to the future, another question can be added to the mediation process: What would you like your relationship to be in [ ] years? I leave the number of years blank because the appropriate number depends on both the nature of the relationship and the capacity of the participants to project themselves into the future. For example, to use a ten-year time frame in a dispute between residents of a senior citizens' home would probably be inappropriate in that they may not anticipate living that long. For different reasons, a long time frame may not be appropriate with young children. On the other hand, using a short time frame like one month or one year might inhibit people from doing more than forecasting what is likely.

The intervenor must take such concerns into consideration when suggesting an appropriate time frame.

This second question invites the parties to determine common ground not just on a somewhat abstract sense of common interests or values but on specific similarities of desired states. It broadens the framework within which common ground can be identified and thus multiplies the possibilities of generating mutually acceptable outcomes.

Structural Conflicts

It is at the structural level that envisioning may be most helpful and even necessary, particularly if the conflict is an "ism" conflict at a broad system level. The reason, as indicated above, is that the envisioning process enables us to create a blueprint for a desirable state that does not yet exist. "Futures invention" is one such process that has already been used as a peacemaking tool.[3]

Exhibit 12.7-2   Envisioning Strategies in Conflict Resolution

Type of Conflict	Envisioning Strategy
Issue-Specific	Typically Unnecessary
Relational	Pose Questions: What did you formerly value in the relationship? What would you like your relationship to be in [ ] years?
Structural	Futures Invention: Goal statement; clarification; future present moment; futures history; policy team creation; action planning in the present

SIX STAGES IN THE ENVISIONING PROCESS

1. Goal Statement

In this first stage of the process, participants are asked to work individually, identifying what they wish the situation to be in the arena of the conflict at the future point identified. Participants are encouraged to identify goals that are important enough that they would wish to work for their achievement, to which they can commit themselves, that they "intend." They are asked to free themselves from what they think likely or even possible in order to be free to invent the best possible situation.

2. Clarification

In the clarification stage, participants are divided into small groups of two or three and asked to help each other clarify their goal statements. The purpose here is not to judge or influence but merely to work on the goal statement so that all participants will have the same understanding of exactly what the goal-stater means. In my own first futures invention exercise, I mistakenly assumed that the phrase "world peace" adequately conveyed what I wished for a future twenty-five years from now. Warren Ziegler helpfully pointed out to me that other people would impose their own vision on this generalized statement and that because it meant everything, it really meant nothing. My partners then helped me spin out more of what I actually meant when I spoke of world peace. By the time I finished even this part of the exercise, not only was I more able to convey my meaning to others, I was clearer about it myself.

3. Future Present Moment

This is one of the most exciting parts of the process and also probably the most difficult one for most participants to undertake, at least initially. Participants are asked to put themselves into their desired futures and answer concrete questions like, Where do I live? With whom? How do I spend my day? What happens when I wake up in the morning? What do I fear?

As participants get in touch with their own personal experience in their imaged futures, they become more able to express the future itself in concrete terms and to clarify whether there is anything they would like to change in their goals statements.

4. Futures History

The futures history is the part of the process most difficult to explain to people who have been trained not to use their imaginations and, along with the future present moment, the most difficult to undertake. In this exercise, participants are asked to presume that their desired futures have come into being, project themselves into them, and describe how their futures came into being. The exercise calls for them "to remember" key events, working backward in time, until finally they identify a key event in the time period immediately following the present time in which they are doing the exercise.

5. Policy Team Creation

During this stage of the process, the participants render their goal statements and futures histories to large sheets of papers and display them around the room so that everyone can read them. After having read all materials, the participants engage each other in clarifying conversations, noting with whose visions they have the most in common. They then are asked to group themselves into teams around common visions and to begin the steps described again, this time developing group goal statements and futures histories. The idea is to reduce the general spread of the large group into a smaller number of "scenarios whose proponents *could maintain the integrity of their individual images while at the same time generating a commonly-held future which represent[s] their collective intentioning.*"[4]

6. Action Planning in the Present

Each group is now asked to initiate planning to bring its goal into being. The groups take the key event that they have identified in their futures histories as having occurred nearest in time to the present and make the attaining of that event their short-term goal. They then work together to develop a strategy for bringing it into being. They assess the resources they have at their disposal and identify how they can obtain needed resources not currently at their disposal. Individuals agree to take responsibility for the different tasks and agree on ways they will keep in touch in order to track and monitor their progress toward their goal.

CONCLUSION

Utilizing the Futures Invention process should provide parties, even in deep-seated conflicts, an enhanced possibility of fashioning a way out of their existing turmoil; a more limited set of questions may prove sufficient to those in relational or even issues-specific conflicts. Having put this possibility forward for consideration, much work needs to be done to assess empirically the degree to which envisioning is in fact helpful in a range of types of conflict. As this research is mounted, attention must also be paid to refining the process to be of optimal benefit to parties in conflict.

NOTES

I would like to thank Warren L. Ziegler and Elise Boulding for their groundbreaking work on envisioning upon which much of this article is based.
1. Dugan 1996.
2. Boulding 1989, 109.
3. Ibid.
4. Ziegler 1994, 246 (italics in original).

REFERENCES

Boulding, E. (1989). *Building a Global Civic Culture: Education for an Interdependent World.* New York: Teachers College Press.

Dugan, M. A. (1996). "A Nested Theory of Conflict." *Women in Leadership* 1, no. 1: 9–20.

Ziegler, W. (1994). *Ways of Enspiriting: Transformative Practices for the Twenty-first Century.* Denver: FIA International LLC.

OTHER SOURCES

Fisher, R., and W. Ury. (1981). *Getting to Yes: Negotiating Agreement Without Giving In.* Boston: Houghton Mifflin.

Sherif, M. (1966). *In Common Predicament: Social Psychology of Intergroup Conflict and Cooperation.* Boston: Houghton Mifflin.

Sherif, M., et al. (1961). *The Robbers Cave Experiment.* Norman, Okla.: University of Oklahoma Book Exchange.

■ 12.8

Designing Future Workshops as a Tool for Peacebuilding

Elise Boulding

Recently I was asked to do a daylong workshop with of group of twenty prisoners in a Massachusetts prison, on imaging a nonviolent world, a world at peace. Looking into the intent faces of these men—youthful, middle-aged, and elderly African American, Hispanic, and white long-termers—I wondered how their imaginations could possibly vault the prison walls that enclosed such harsh, discipline-laden, heavily guarded spaces, to visualize a different and better world. I felt hesitant, unsure. But I had promised to do this workshop!

This type of imaging workshop first evolved in the late 1970s, as I began to realize that we peace activists, working to bring about a nonviolent world without war, really had no idea how a world in which armies had disappeared would be functioning.[1] How could we work to bring about something we couldn't even see in our imaginations? Stepping back into the 1950s in my own mind I remembered translating Fred Polak's *Image of the Future* from the Dutch original, a macrohistorical analysis that showed a war-paralyzed and depressed Europe how past societies in bad situations but with positive images of the future had been empowered by their own imaginations to work to bring the imaged future about. Here was a possible answer!

I collaborated with Warren Ziegler and other colleagues to develop a workshop format that spanned thirty years into the future—to a world at peace. The format allowed time for imaginative exploration of how things worked in that future, followed by a remembering, a looking back from this future to the present to imagine how all this peaceableness had come about. The workshops always closed with time for personal commitments to action in the present to help bring about the future that participants had pictured. We found that this type of workshop actually empowered people in their peace activism.

But these workshops had involved participants, who were free, to be change agents in their world. How could prisoners imagine a more caring world, let alone see themselves as change agents to bring those changes about? To make the leap into the future less daunting, I chose ten rather than thirty years as the time span. How would they deal with 2010 in their imaginations?

Well, I found out. After explaining about the failed hopes from peace and justice efforts in the past and the new hopes for peace and justice actions as we stood on the threshold of the twenty-first century, I asked them what they might hope to find in 2010. Through individual reflection and small group discussion, they constructed a list of hopes. The first major theme in their hope was "to be at peace with ourselves and one another and the world in which we live. To recognize, understand, communicate what's going on." Further themes followed: "There should be a peaceful environment for all mankind; no wars, hunger, homelessness, disease, violence, racism, no TV commercials, no pollution." "People listen, respect one another; there is equality, also just laws, freedom from fear." "Life is local, families peaceful; there is a strong community feeling and conflict resolution; people help each other, have fun together."

Those were the hopes expressed for what might be found in the future. The hopes themselves were more well defined than I had expected. What their imaginations revealed when they mentally traveled into the future and then drew pictures of what they imagined was deeply moving. Prison walls had melted away, and all the beauties of nature and the life of free humans stood revealed: open countryside, trees, bushes, flowers, distant mountains, lakes and rivers, and farmlands with houses dotting the landscape and often a church in sight. A few drawings pictured villages, malls with shops, and people walking about in the malls. One of the most striking features of these pictures was the presence of sunlight and other sources of light—lamps, candles, lighthouses, or beacon lights.

Everywhere in these pictures were friendly, often smiling people—walking in couples, bicycling, singing, dancing, playing games, working in small groups, fishing by a lake, growing food, offering a helping hand to each other, walking to church, being seated in meditation or prayer. One picture revealed housing built for the homeless, one the opening up and transformation of a prison. Two pictured bombs dropping on a city with the caption, This Must Not Happen! The absence of cars in these pictures was notable.

The themes of open green spaces, the beauty of nature, sunlight, friendly sociability, and joyful activity had significant similarities to the themes in the pictured futures of workshop participants that I had been collecting for years. Whether the participants were peace or social change activists; members of women's, youth, or church groups; diplomats, soldiers, scholars, or teachers—their pictures suggested a bright, clean, green world, and conveyed the feel of a joyful local community in which people delight in celebrations, in caring for others. Why should I have been surprised that prisoners could imagine that same world? Whatever impacts prison and their before-prison life had on their lives, these men (who had been through Alternatives to Violence training and who now participated in weekly Quaker meetings for worship at Norfolk Prison) had vibrant social and spiritual imaginations.

As we went through succeeding workshop exercises, including developing details of how this future nonviolent society actually worked, remembering history (how it all came about), and choosing specific personal action in the present to bring that future about, I was repeatedly impressed by the creativity and specificity of their responses. Not least regarding what they proposed to do *now* while still in prison. I learned a lot that day.

These are hard times for peace practitioners and activists. Stories of local criminal violence, the violence of war—internal and interstate, genocide, and widespread rape and torture—fill our newspapers. It is getting harder to imagine a nonviolent future, but more necessary than ever. The imaging workshops that in the past have empowered discouraged peace activists now also need to be carried out with very different groups: victims and perpetrators of genocide, soldiers and guerillas, victims and perpetrators of rape. Perhaps most of all they need to be carried out with the traumatized children for whom violence has become an everyday experience.

Of course, traumatized women, men, and children cannot simply be walked into imaging workshops. All kinds of healing settings, experiences of compassionate listening and dialogue with the "other," and explorations of forgiveness and possible reconciliation need to take place. (The prisoners of Norfolk had important healing experiences before entering my workshop.) But serious consideration should be given to the introduction of imaging a world at peace workshops at an appropriate point as part of the longer-range healing experience that victims and perpetrators need to go through. The recovery of hope is crucial to the healing process. Releasing the basic human capacity to imagine the other and better—humankind's special gift as a species that Polak was inspired to identify in the depths of the suffering of World War II—is a key to that healing. This kind of workshop cannot be casually undertaken and should be led only by people with broad experience in both healing and imaging activities, but can be thought of as a significant potential contribution to the complex of activities that will be part of the UN International Decade for the Culture of Peace and Nonviolence for the Children of the World.

NOTE

1. A description of and protocol for this workshop is in chapter 6 and the appendix of Elise Boulding's *Building a Global Civic Culture* (Syracuse, N.Y.: Syracuse University Press, 1988).

CHAPTER 13

Security

■ 13.1

From Peacekeeping to Postconflict Peacebuilding

Winrich Kühne

The fragmentation of states due to an unchecked proliferation of socioethnic, civil war–like conflict has become a fundamental threat to peace and security in the world following the end of the Cold War. These "complex emergencies" or "war-torn societies" may draw entire regions into chaos and bloodshed. Basic standards of the international system, indispensable for ensuring regional and global stability, are eroding. Politics and the international public at large, accustomed to the clear-cut perception of Cold War bipolarity, do not find it easy to understand these new security challenges.

Initially the international community tried to contain and solve these conflicts with an instrument developed in the era of the Cold War: the United Nations' Blue Helmets, or traditional peacekeeping forces. The successful operations in Namibia and Nicaragua in 1989–1990, as well as the later operations in Cambodia and Mozambique, created inflated expectations regarding the future role of the Blue Helmets in conflict management and resolution. These were short-lived. In 1993, the second United Nations Operation in Somalia (UNOSOM II) failed to stop the country's descent into total fragmentation and self-destruction. The United Nations Protective Force (UNPROFOR) in the former Yugoslavia more or less shared UNOSOM's negative fate. The leading global powers and the international community did not provide the UN with the capability and means necessary to successfully conduct such a demanding operation. In 1994 an even greater lack of political will was responsible for the tragic genocide in Rwanda. Almost 1 million people were killed, despite the presence of roughly 2,000 Blue Helmets during the United Nations Mission in Rwanda (UNAMIR). The Security Council was not willing to send additional troops and to change UNAMIR's mandate to prevent this disaster. In fact, most of the Blue Helmets were actually withdrawn.

Apart from the problem of political will, the operations in Somalia, Bosnia, Rwanda, Liberia, and Sierra Leone, among others, revealed the deep conceptual problems of traditional peacekeeping in dealing with the new type of conflict. Traditional peacekeeping was not conceived to operate under such insecure conditions that continued to exist in these countries even after peace agreements or cease-fires had been signed. The use of force became inevitable.

The question that follows is, What is the proper *use of force* in civil war–type conflicts? Traditional peacekeeping doctrine has no answer to this question. Consent and impartiality, like the nonuse-of-force pillar of traditional peacekeeping, are just as difficult to uphold in conflicts where there are no clear geographical front lines and where the warring parties do not divide neatly into two hostile camps. Consent of whom? Impartiality with regard to which parties? Finally, the issue of coordination and joint management obviously becomes much more complicated in operations that have to deal with not only an insecure environment, where there are several parties involved, but also one in which the military, police, and civilian personnel of the UN, humanitarian agencies, and sometimes several hundred nongovernmental organizations (NGOs) have to work together to achieve successful postconflict peacebuilding.

This article will, therefore, try to give an overview, not only of the development from traditional peacekeeping to modern peace support operations (PSOs) and their basic conceptual problems but also the main areas of postconflict peacebuilding.

FROM FIRST- TO THIRD-GENERATION PEACEKEEPING

The so-called first generation of peacekeeping was mostly limited to observing or monitoring cease-fires, like the United Nations Emergency Fund (UNEF) in the Sinai in the mid-1950s, UN Forces in Cyprus (UNFCYP) from the mid-1960s onward, and UN Disengagement Observer Force (UNDOF) on the Golan Heights in the mid-1970s. Consent, impartiality, use of force solely for personal self-defense purposes, free mobility of troops, and a statute of force agreement with the respective country were the basic pillars of this first generation.

In the mid-1980s following the end of the Cold War and unblocking of the Security Council, a second generation developed that was multidimensional and dynamic in character. In contrast to the first generation, the military and its civilian counterparts were no longer limited to the monitoring of cease-fires. Finding political and social solutions to the conflict and removing the need for their presence as quickly as possible became equally important tasks. The operations became much more dynamic and complex in terms of conflict resolution: the United Nations Transitional Assistance Group (UNTAG) in Namibia and the United Nations Observer Mission for the Verification of the Elections in Nicaragua (UNOVEN) from 1989 to 1990, the United Nations Observer Group in El Salvador (UNOSAL) from 1991 to 1995, the United Nations Transitional Authority in Cambodia (UNTAC) from 1992 to 1993, and the United Nations Operation in Mozambique (UNOMOZ) from 1992 to 1994 are showcases for this enlarged, new type of peacekeeping. International civilian police missions (CivPol) and civilians from various professions became important partners of the military.

The unabated violence in cases like Somalia, the former Yugoslavia, Liberia, and Haiti quickly forced additional change on multidimensional peacekeeping. As was already indicated, the solemn signing of peace agreements or cease-fires no longer meant an end to violence. In Somalia, Liberia, and Bosnia hundreds of cease-fire agreements were broken. The peacekeepers and humanitarian organizations were confronted with all kinds of violence. National, regional, and local leaders as well as warlords and armed groups were involved—a difficult mix for the peacekeepers to handle. Establishing and upholding a secure environment for humanitarian aid and socioeconomic and political reconstruction became a primary demand on the soldiers and on the police. The old doctrine of the nonuse of force became untenable. In Somalia, the Security Council consequently felt compelled to provide UNOSOM II with a so-called robust mandate based on Chapter 7 of the UN charter, allowing for the limited use of force. UNPROFOR in the former Yugoslavia, the United Nations Mission in Haiti (UNMIH), the Intervention Force (IFOR) and Stabilization Force (SFOR) in Bosnia, the United Nations Transitional Administration in Eastern Slavonia (UNTAES), as well as the French "Operation Turquoise" in Rwanda, Multi-National Force (MNF) in Haiti, and Inter-African Mission to Monitor the Implementation of the Bangui Agreements (MISAB) in the Central African Republic received similar authorization. The third generation of peacekeeping, now mostly called multidimensional (robust) peace support operations, had come into being.

The "Grey Area" Problem

Robust, multidimensional PSOs are defined in Chapter 7 of the UN charter as multidimensional peacekeeping with consent and impartiality as basic operational pillars, plus the option of the threat or use of limited force for defending or implementing specific elements of the mandate.

Politicians and the military as well as the international public and academia are still struggling with this new concept. There are widespread misgivings about the fact that it is blurring the distinction between traditional Chapter 7–based peacekeeping and military enforcement based on Chapter 8. But academics and traditionalists among peacekeepers who demand strict adherence to this distinction forget that the real-life dynamics of ethnic and similar conflicts have no regard for the written provisions of the charter and its theoretical distinctions. To put it in the blunt terms of a Canadian peacekeeper, speaking in context of the conditions in Somalia and Bosnia: "It was evident that traditional peacekeeping was being made a mockery of. There was almost a total absence of the conditions that are essential for peacekeeping to work."[1]

Ethnic conflict and civil war blur the lines between domestic and international, state, and nonstate actors, as well as that between Chapters 6 and 7. Conflicts in which hundreds of thousands of people are killed or have to flee their country are a threat to international peace and security (Article 39, UN charter) in a highly interdependent world. The Security Council was right to decide as it did in the cases of Somalia, Bosnia, and Haiti and to authorize robust operations on the basis of Chapter 7 of the UN charter.

The Problematic "Use of Force": Arguments and Guidelines

The proper use of force in PSOs still needs a lot of doctrinal and operational clarification. It has to be explicitly stated that, as a rule, the possible use of limited force in the context of peace operations is very different from the massive use of force in war.

Politicians, journalists, and the general public are confused. For most of them, using force is synonymous with going to war and taking sides in a given conflict. The military still struggle with the question of how to use force without getting into a dangerous process of escalation and destroying the entire peace process. In Somalia the confusion about the proper use of force among the military and politicians has led to tragic events and a rushed withdrawal.

There is an urgent need to conceptualize, differentiate, and define the conditions under which the threat or use of limited force apply, in order to promote what continues to be the ultimate goal of peacekeeping: the containment of violence and the resolving of conflicts with the cooperation and consent of the parties concerned. The *ultima ratio* for the threat of or use of force has to be limited to creating a safe environment for the implementation of the mandate and its mainly nonmilitary elements, in particular:

1. The protection of UN and other international personnel and installations.

2. Closing the so-called public security gap, due to the nonfunctioning or one-sided abuse of local security organs on the one hand and the proliferation of small arms in the hands of armed gangs and militias on the other. (The closing of this gap is controversial: it obviously cannot be done by the unarmed CivPol units, which only have a monitoring function. The military, like IFOR in Bosnia, do not consider public security their job, although it is a basic element of creating a safe environment. In Bosnia, therefore, a robust police unit, the Multinational Special Force, based on the concept of the Guardia Civil in Spain and the Carabineri in Italy, was brought in.)

3. Protection of humanitarian aid transports and the necessary infrastructure, such as airports, harbors, and bridges.

4. The resettlement of refugees and internally displaced persons.

5. Deterrence of attacks on declared safe areas and no-fly zones.

6. Disarmament of combatants of the parties to the conflict and other armed groups (probably the most difficult task, judging from experience in Somalia and Bosnia).

Obviously, more tasks could be added to this list, in particular, the maintenance of cease-fires and the prevention of mass killing and "ethnic cleansing." In the final analysis, however, the overriding purpose will always be to bring the warring parties back to the negotiating table and to contain the destructive, violent dynamics of conflict. This can only be done if *consent* and *impartiality* continue to be guiding principles of PSOs.

Consent and the Use of Force

As far as traditional peacekeeping was concerned, according to the rule of international law, only the consent of the governments of the countries involved in the conflict was actually required. This rule was then extended to include the one or two dominant, clearly defined parties to the conflict, like the South-West African People's Organization (SWAPO) in Namibia or the Khmer Rouge in Cambodia.

In socioethnic conflicts, this rule has become difficult to apply. As was mentioned before, the lines of conflict as well as the numbers of parties fighting each other are fragmented and in flux. Peacekeepers have a hard time deciding which actors' consent is relevant or not. In Somalia and Bosnia this became an almost impossible task. Violent groups acquired a great deal of leverage over the peacekeepers by denying consent.

British peacekeeping doctrine was the first to approach this problem more profoundly. The concept of *wider peacekeeping* was developed based on the experience in Northern Ireland and then Bosnia. Its innovation was the distinction between "operational/strategic" and "tactical/local" consent.

With regard to the first aspect, consent continued to be unchallenged as an absolute rule. If consent was withdrawn at this level, peacekeepers also had to withdraw. At a tactical level, however, they could use force or threaten the use of force if consent for the implementation of the elements of the mandate (for instance, delivering humanitarian aid) was denied by a local party. As a result of lessons learned in Bosnia, the British military has abandoned this doctrine as impractical. The relationship between consent and the use of force remains a difficult one, and in terms of doctrine and clear rules of engagement, many unsolved problems remain.

Lessons learned: There is a direct relationship between the level of international military power in the field and the solidity of the consent by the parties to the conflict. As a rule of thumb one may state that the stronger the international capability, the better the prospect of consent not being withdrawn. The need to use force will actually be reduced. This is obviously a forceful argument for going in with oversized rather than undersized forces at the beginning of a PSO.

Consent-promoting techniques become very important to make the use of force an ultima ratio regum. These techniques demand much skill from each and every military and civil peacekeeper, particularly at the leadership level. There exists a wide spectrum of consent-promoting instruments, some of which involve behind-the-scenes pressure, sticks and carrots, economic and other sanctions, psychological operations, the use of the media, and the show of force (also often used in the past by Blue Helmets).

Indeed, the option of robust PSOs to use force as the big, final stick enhances the chance that these nonviolent instruments will be effective and that the open use of force will not have to be brought into play.

Impartiality Versus Neutrality

The 1995 UN General Guidelines for Peacekeeping Operations provide a valid definition of impartiality:

> Impartiality must not promote inaction. On the contrary, peace-keepers must discharge their tasks firmly and objectively, without fear or favour. Neither side should gain unfair advantages as a result of the activities of a peacekeeping operation. . . . Impartiality should not be interpreted as *equidistant* between the mandate and the party's newly revised position. It is the *Security Council mandate* which manifests the legitimate will of the international community.

In the practice of modern peacekeeping operations, however, impartiality faces problems very similar to those of the principle of consent: Impartiality with regard to which parties to the conflict? Which parties are relevant and which are not? There is also a widespread assumption among politicians, journalists, and academics that the use of force is incompatible with impartiality. The moment that peacekeepers use force beyond the purpose of self-defense, they become accused of taking sides. This is a flawed understanding of impartiality.

Impartiality is not equal to neutrality or passivity. The UN charter is not neutral—it demands respect for certain basic values and norms (see, e.g., Articles 1 and 2), nor are the mandates given by the Security Council neutral. Undertaking activities toward the implementation of mandates, including the use of force, does not automatically equal taking sides, even if the activity happens to be to the detriment of one of the parties. If, for instance, in the case of an armed bank robbery, the police were to free the hostages, nobody would accuse the police of taking sides; the police merely would have fulfilled their public mandate.

The crucial issue is whether the activities are in conformity with the mandate and are undertaken in an evenhanded way with regard to its violation by other parties to the conflict. In addition, there is a further fundamental problem with regard to impartiality and the use of force. Mass murder, rape, ethnic cleansing, and genocide have become frequent patterns of socioethnic and similar conflict. They are not accidental but part of the military-political strategy of one or the other of the warring factions. Any action by the peacekeepers and their civilian counterparts to prevent such crimes is bound to pit them against one side or the other. Old concepts of neutrality or static impartiality cannot deal with such perpetrations, although they concern the very rationale behind why the international community is sending peacekeepers in.

Lesson learned: A dynamic, normative definition of impartiality is needed, taking *erga omnes* norms of international law (genocide, massive violations of humans rights, etc.) into account. Security Council mandates and rules of engagement need to be formulated accordingly.

FROM PEACE OPERATIONS TO POSTCONFLICT PEACEBUILDING: FACTS, CONSTRAINTS, AND LESSONS LEARNED

In modern, multidimensional peace operations, postconflict peacebuilding has become of strategic importance. The concept, therefore, figured prominently in UN Secretary-General Boutros Boutros-Ghali's Agenda for Peace of 1992. It was further developed in the supplement to an Agenda for Peace in 1995 and explicitly welcomed by the Security Council and the General Assembly of the UN in a number of resolutions.

The purpose of postconflict peacebuilding is to prevent violent conflict from re-emerging and to rebuild the capabilities of a society to resolve conflict without fighting. Thus, the essence of postconflict peacebuilding is that of a political undertaking, even if it compromises activities that transcend the political domain, like development cooperation, humanitarian assistance, protection of human rights, and institution building. Postconflict peacebuilding is different from development cooperation inasmuch as it includes, inter alia, emergency assistance, demobilization and reintegration of former combatants, and the restoration of public order and security.

Time as a Constraint

Time constraints within which postconflict peacebuilding operates are *short and medium term*, as opposed to the long-term perspective of cooperation. Indeed, lack of time is characteristic of postconflict peacebuilding.

Lesson learned: Short-term concerns should not be allowed to undermine long-term goals.

The Emergency-to-Relief-to-Development Continuum

Lessons learned: The so-called emergency-to-relief-to-development continuum is only a useful basis to work from if approached in an integrated manner. For example, the short-term necessity to prevent combatants, by whatever means, from taking up their arms again, may well clash with long-term development objectives demanding their integration into productive occupations as participants in the national economy. However, relief projects have to take the long-term development focus into consideration. Furthermore, emergency, relief, and development activities often need to take place simultaneously. In some postconflict societies, it is even necessary to adapt an area-based approach, allowing rehabilitation/development work in some parts of the country, while in other parts only relief aid will be possible.

Postconflict peacebuilding has to start as early as possible. It seems natural to think that postconflict peacebuilding should start only after a cease-fire has been agreed upon. However, experience in Cambodia, Mozambique, Haiti, Angola, Rwanda, the former Yugoslavia, and other places demonstrates the importance of an early beginning of postconflict peacebuilding in order to limit the damage caused by violence and to lay the foundations for a more vigorous peacebuilding effort in the future. Inasmuch as postconflict peacebuilding aims at preventing violent conflict from re-emerging, it may appear as a form of preventative diplomacy, and to some extent that is so. Still, the point of departure is different; postconflict peacebuilding applies to situations where the worst has already happened, leaving behind trauma to heal, mine fields to clear, former combatants to disarm, and refugees to repatriate and reintegrate.

Three Fields of Strategic Importance

Apart from the ever-urgent problem of emergency aid and relief activities, it has become clear in recent years that there are three fields of strategic importance for successful peace operations and peacebuilding: (1) disarmament, demobilization, and reintegration (DDR) of combatants and other armed groups; (2) elections and constitution building; and (3) justice and reconciliation.

Lessons learned: Disarmament, demobilization, and reintegration. With regard to DDR, it is important to note that tensions and violence that are at the origin of a conflict do not suddenly disappear as soon as a peace agreement or cease-fire is signed. Progress in the field of DDR and progress in the peace process are highly interdependent. DDR is one of the most demanding elements of peacebuilding. In affluent Western societies, there is a notion that violence does not pay. Yet in ethnic and similar types of conflict, well-considered economic interest is more often than not the dominant reason for rampant and continued violence.

It is therefore extremely important to understand the economics of violence and the economics of war. Warlords represent a sinister combination of military commander, gang leader, businessman, and political leader. Unemployment, particularly among the young, provides a further ground for recruitment. The wide availability of small arms and light weapons in most conflict regions makes it easy and comparatively cheap to arm these youngsters.

Coercive disarmament in the context of these types of conflict carries considerable risk. Consent-based strategies are preferable, but—depending on local conditions—are not always feasible.

Disarmament and demobilization without rigorous programs of reintegration will inevitably fail. Hence, much attention has to be given to the social and economic impact of externally sponsored demobilization programs. Success also very much depends on the extent to which the former warring parties and individuals believe that their physical and economic security will be maintained after relinquishing their arms and abandoning what for many has become a way of life and economic survival.

Weapons buy-back programs may play an important role in disarmament and demobilization, like in El Salvador and eastern Slavonia. In sum, however, their record is mixed. Particularly if connected to money and offered as compensation, buy-back programs can create streams of weapons flowing from one region to another. It may be better to spend these funds on improving the police and judiciary in order to improve the security conditions in the country concerned.

Weapons destruction programs are the most effective way to reduce arms flows and to get rid of collected weapons. If done in public with a ceremony and in the presence of the media, it sends a strong political signal to combatants and to society. The case of Mali and its public burning of collected weapons was a powerful example of this. The *flamme de paix* has become a symbol for a society at peace.

Lessons learned: Elections and constitution building. Elections and constitution building have been a strategic objective in UN peace missions conducted since the end of the Cold War. Internationally monitored elections have become the concluding activity in most cases. They are conceived to be the best mechanism to guarantee an orderly, peaceful, participatory, and transparent succession of governments and to make executive power more accountable to the people. These manifest advantages may be the reason that elections have often been held too soon in conflict-ridden societies and have not terminated the conflicts in the way that had been hoped for. Indeed, elections in fragmented societies may result in increased fragmentation, as, inter alia, the cases of Angola and Sierra Leone demonstrate. *Sometimes elections are simply a continuation of war with other means, particularly in the case of "winner takes all" elections.*

The right timing of elections, therefore, is a central issue in peacebuilding, and, like other elements of peacebuilding, they have to be planned well in advance, ideally two or three years before they take place. *Sufficient demobilization and integration of combatants into the new army, police force, or civil society and a satisfactory restoration of the judicial system and of public administration are necessary preconditions.* Credibility and integrity of the electoral process help to prevent disputes over the outcome and forestall a relapse into violence.

International monitoring should continue throughout the electoral process and even beyond. This is important because of the lasting distrust of the parties to a conflict toward each other. In extreme cases of fragmentation and violence it may even be better to go for power sharing as an interim solution in the general transition from war to peace and democracy. Western-style democracy will not work, at least in the short run; governments of national unity may be the only way to forestall a fall back into fighting. In such cases, the international community should at least try to establish a mechanism to monitor minimum standards of human rights. Finally, one lesson of past democratization processes, inside and outside of peace operations, is crystal clear: elections are only a starting point for democratization, not its successful conclusion. Past international peacekeeping and peace operations by the international community, thus, have been rightly criticized, as having abused elections as a quick-exit option from difficult peace processes. This was particularly the case in war-torn Liberia.

Lessons learned: There will be no lasting peace and stable democracy in war-torn societies without truth, justice, and reconciliation. Mass killing, ethnic cleansing, rape, and other brutal forms of conducting war in ethnic, religious, and similar types of conflict render reconciliation extremely difficult. *Although it is a long-term process, it has to be started as soon as the peace operation and peacebuilding are initiated.*

Different models for reconciliation have emerged. The first one, which may be called "Forgive and Forget," has been frequently practiced in Africa, for instance, in Zimbabwe and Namibia. It is based on the assumption that civil wars have their own dynamic and that its atrocities cannot be judged in normal legal terms. It is reinforced by the assumption that African cultures, in particular, have a great capacity for forgiving. Another more recent model is justice and reconciliation through truth. The South African Truth and Reconciliation Commission has become well known for its endeavors to heal the atrocities of both sides of the anti-apartheid struggle. The Truth and Reconciliation Commission in Guatemala operates in a similar way, whereas the Purification Commission in Mozambique was based on more traditional concepts of healing and reconciliation. Obviously, the commissions in South Africa and Guatemala are based on a Christian understanding of forgiving by confession. In societies in which systematic genocide has occurred, justice, truth, and reconciliation are of even greater importance but even more difficult to achieve.

Rwanda, Bosnia, and Kosovo are cases in point. In Rwanda more than 100,000 perpetrators of the genocide in 1994 are still kept in primitive conditions of detention by the Kigali government. In view of the barely functioning judicial system in Rwanda, one wonders how much justice is needed on the one side and how much can be realistically expected to reconcile the Tutsi and Hutu. How much justice and reconciliation the international criminal tribunals, which have been created by the UN Security Council for Rwanda and the former Yugoslavia, can actually contribute remains an open question. The fact that the accused in Arusha, where the tribunal for Rwanda is based, enjoy a tribunal "deluxe" (with two or three attorneys and not having to fear the death penalty although they are the main perpetrators) puts a severe strain on justice. Those who are dealt with by the barely developed judiciary in Rwanda do not enjoy these privileges. Some of them have already been condemned to death and executed.

In multidimensional peace operations and peacebuilding, the coordination and management of the multitude of military and nonmilitary instruments and actors is of strategic importance for their success. An integrated approach is needed and has to be planned for from the very beginning. This is easier said than done, or as one popular sentence among practitioners goes, "Everybody wants coordination but nobody wants to be coordinated."

During Operation Provide Comfort, in Northern Iraq in the early 1990s, the Allied forces had to cope with about 500 aid organizations, some with more than a hundred employees, some with only three. In Somalia, the number of NGOs was about 200.

Soldiers and NGOs have very different, sometimes downright antagonistic, operational cultures. The military are used to following commands without much questioning. Not so in NGOs, in particular those working on a voluntary basis. To complicate matters still further, the international NGO community itself is extremely heterogeneous. All organizations have their own raisons d'être, peculiarities, and even vanities. Nevertheless, most of them are valuable for rendering humanitarian assistance and peacebuilding. They can do work that military organizations cannot do at all, or at least not as well or as cost-effectively, in particular, with regard to complicated socioeconomic and sociocultural issues. Operation Provide Comfort, UNO-SOM, UNPROFOR, and others have shown that soldiers and NGOs can learn to work together constructively if certain prejudices and psychological barriers are overcome.

Unity not only of purpose, but also of strategy and action are the sine qua non for success. Joint structures for distributing and sharing information to all actors, joint analysis and planning, and implementation mechanisms have proven their effectiveness, as well as joint pre-mission training and regular executive meetings to monitor developments. At all stages the relevant actors— especially the World Bank, the United Nations Department of Peacekeeping, UNICEF, the United Nations High Commissioner for Refugees, the donor community, and NGOs—should be closely involved in the decisionmaking process, led by the UN or a regional organization. *It is essential to earmark a lead agency to take over coordination in the early stages.* And it is of prime importance to enhance and clarify the role and authority of the special representative of the secretary-general or similar leaders of peace operations and peacebuilding as the head of the family and team leader.

CONCLUSION

Robust, multidimensional peace support operations are obviously an extremely demanding task for the military as well as for the civilians involved. Mandates, even when sufficiently clear in the formulation of tasks, cannot be implemented in a rigid manner. Flexibility and an understanding of the consequences of the use of force in a specific situation for the overall mission and, in particular, consent and impartiality, have to be further developed. Peacebuilding has to be started and integrated into the operation at an early point in time. It involves disarmament, demobilization, and reintegration; elections and constitution building; as well as addressing the question of dealing with the past. A lot remains to be done not only in terms of improving doctrine and concept as dealt with in this article but also on such important issues as training, logistics, command, control and communication, intelligence, and equipment.

NOTE

1. Interview with the author.

SUGGESTED READING

Anyidoho, Henri Kwami. (1997). "The Lessons from Peace-Keeping Operations." In G. M. Sorbo and P. Vale, *Out of Conflict: From War to Peace in Africa.* Uppsala: Nordiska Afrikainstitutet.

Biermann, Wolfgang, and Martin Vadset, eds. (1998). *UN Peacekeeping in Trouble: Lessons Learned from the Former Yugoslavia.* Aldershot: Ashgate.

Coulon, Jocelyn. (1998). *Soldiers of Diplomacy: The United Nations, Peacekeeping and the New World Order.* Toronto: University of Toronto Press.

Kumar, Krishna, ed. (1997). *Rebuilding Societies After Civil War: Critical Roles for International Assistance.* Boulder, Colo.: Lynne Rienner.

Peacekeeping and Transitional Administration in Eastern Slavonia

Johan Schoups

Taking part in peacekeeping operations is an exciting experience for any military person. As the commander of the military section of the United Nations Transitional Administration in Eastern Slavonia (UNTAES), this honor was conferred on me. For years, I had been explaining to soldiers and staff the full significance of their choice of career. The reason why we wear uniforms and bear arms is to guarantee security and maintain peace. For that purpose, we train for a variety of skills in the classroom as well as on the shooting range and the drill ground. However, nothing is more gratifying for those of us in the military than putting our know-how and expertise at the disposal of people in distress or communities entangled in a war.

THE SITUATION IN EASTERN SLAVONIA

In June 1991, Croatia declared independence from the Socialist Federal Republic of Yugoslavia. The Serbian Army stationed on Croatian territory reacted promptly: 30 percent of the armed forces, including in eastern Slavonia, in turn, declared themselves independent. The move was regarded by Croatia as a declaration of war. Three regions were given the status of United Nations Protected Area (UNPA): the area surrounding Krajina, western Slavonia, and eastern Slavonia. The latter area borders on the Federal Republic of Yugoslavia, with the Danube River separating the two. In 1995, Croatia retook Krajina and western Slavonia in two surprise attacks. Under international pressure, the government in Zagreb abandoned plans to move into eastern Slavonia, the last Croatian region with a sizable Serbian community. On November 12, 1995, Croatia and the Serbian authorities of eastern Slavonia signed the Erdut Treaty. Under the terms of this treaty, the region would be placed under a transitional UN government for a period of up to two years. On January 15, 1996, the United Nations Security Council approved Resolution 1037, which marked the actual start of this mission.

UNTAES: MANDATE AND ORGANIZATION

Our assignment was quite unique: it revolved around the peaceful reintegration of an area into Croatia. To this end, the region first had to be demilitarized. The only force to be allowed to operate in the region besides UN troops was the police force, whose organization and structure were determined by the governor of the transitional administration. The term of the mission was clearly defined: twelve months with a possible extension of an additional twelve months. The following overview of the seven subassignments of the mandate outlines the full scope of the operation, in which several players shared responsibility:

1. To safely put demilitarized eastern Slavonia under the sovereign rule of Croatia.
2. To safeguard the multiethnic character of the region.
3. To build an atmosphere of trust between the local inhabitants, irrespective of their ethnic origin.
4. To guarantee all refugees and displaced people the right to a free return to their homes and to a safe living environment.
5. To promote respect for human rights and fundamental prerogatives as much as possible.
6. To aim at the economic resurgence and reconstruction of the region within Croatia.
7. To organize free and fair elections within thirty days after the transitional period.

Evidently, a program of such scope can only succeed in such a short term if it is headed by a close-knit multifunctional team to which all parties involved are committed. UNTAES had two essential constituents. On the one hand, there was the civil component, led by a diplomat who headed the transitional administration and had full executive powers. On the other, there was the military constituent, led by myself as commander of the international force. Not only within the military constituent was it of crucial importance to guarantee unity of command; cooperation between the military and civil organizations, too, was an absolute prerequisite for implementing the mandate efficiently.

IMPLEMENTATION OF THE MANDATE

At the beginning of the mandate, we thought that we would require about six months to deploy troops and demilitarize the region. This would leave eighteen months for the transitional administration to implement the civil program. Initially, the operation was almost entirely military in nature, but after the demilitarization, a balance was automatically reached. In the course of the second year, the civil administration gradually gained the upper hand. The more efficient the local multiethnic police force was able to operate, the more easily the tasks of the army could be restricted to maintaining security.

The way in which one deploys a military force and its armory in order to implement a mandate is determined by the rules of engagement. These rules are based upon considerations of international humanitarian law and the political mandate of the mission. They also include possibilities for applying force. As a military commander, I had many options at my disposal, ranging from providing public information about operations to opting for surprise; from using ordinary deterrents to actual use of force; from lightly armed patrols to heavy tank units and the deployment of assault helicopters and aircraft. But it is essential that the commander of the armed forces should be able to assess the consequences and dangers of an operation in relation to the objectives that have been set.

The seven assignments mentioned above illustrate clearly that the most extensive and complex part of the mission had to be realized by the civil constituent—once the safety of both UNTAES and non-UNTAES staff had been secured by the military.

The demilitarization of the region succeeded only because all parties involved were willing to put their trust in the international force. The efforts to inform the people about our mandate, the organization and possibilities of the force, its deployment, and the careful planning that was involved definitely played an important role in this respect. All possible means, including television, radio, local newspapers, and direct contact between the military and the population, were applied to that end.

Also, sufficient attention had to be paid within the command structure to the quality of the mutual contacts. Indeed, my subordinate commanders took care of this on their respective echelons. Clear communication through transparent organizational channels was indispensable, especially in situations where one anticipated friction. As far as the demilitarization was concerned, I—for example—drew up clear instructions that were then discussed with the generals involved. However, I never gave direct orders to Serbian soldiers or officers. Instead, I always made sure that my instructions and guidelines to the 11th Corps of the Serbian Army were channeled through the command chain of the Serbian Army. This also applied to the extremely sensitive order concerning the removal of military insignia and the shedding of uniforms. The basis for this delicate mode of operation was respect for the soldiers' honor and to avoid unwanted publicity, so that no party would feel humiliated. Close cooperation in implementing the agreements was of the utmost importance, and happily this was realized.

However, local criminal gangs and loosely organized paramilitary factions did pose some problems. In order for the entire operation to be credible, they, too, had to be dealt with, but there was no proven way of going about this.

From the beginning, we chose to locate the civilian and military operational headquarters in the same place, namely Vukovar, the regional center. There, the two pillars cooperated closely in drawing up a strategic plan for the transition of the region to Croatia and the follow-up of this plan by means of daily coordination and departmental meetings. An operational center worked around the clock, supported by the military communication network and the operation centers of the units, complemented with UN observers, transitional police, UN civil police, military police, border observers, and de-mining squads. The civil and military logistic support of the mission was centralized at an abandoned airport. As was the case with the four military sectors, the central civil administration in Vukovar was complemented with regional offices. This enabled one to assess the implementation of the projects in the field more accurately.

The sharing of infrastructure meant that very close contacts were maintained between military and civil staff, which was certainly to the benefit of the operation as a whole. The intelligence that the military staff was able to provide proved to be invaluable to all our civilian colleagues on this mission as well as to governmental, nongovernmental, international, and private organizations. It consisted not only in security intelligence but also in information about the actual situation in the field. A force such as the one that I had at my disposal has the capability of being present at many different places and is extremely mobile. Social patrols were deployed throughout the region on a daily basis: these soldiers got in touch with the local population, handed out information leaflets, took note of the needs, and took stock of the available infrastructure and damage caused to homes as well as public facilities. With this information, we were able to be of service to our civilian colleagues in setting up and supporting their numerous projects. Furthermore, we were at their disposal for maintaining security during journeys through this volatile region, for accompanying them into houses and buildings that may have been booby-trapped, for critical and hazardous transportation of fuel, valuable equipment, money, and so on.

Much support was also needed in organizing the elections—a big and significant event that required careful preparation and smooth and safe proceedings. It encompassed registering all inhabitants, distributing valid identity documents, and a great effort on the day of the elections itself, of course. In spite of some difficulties, everything went according to plan.

Maintaining civil order, which is normally a police task, is a constant concern during most peacekeeping operations. However, the credibility of and trust in the police has often been seriously undermined, so that—willingly or unwillingly—the military might have to take care of policing. It is, therefore, crucial that every effort is made to set up an adequate police force as quickly as possible. This cost us a lot of trouble at UNTAES, but eventually we reached a satisfactory result. Employing all means available (including a system of buying up small arms, ammunition, and explosives), we strove to keep eastern Slavonia as safe and peaceful as possible.

As two years is not very long to accomplish all the goals set, we felt that the presence of some 5,000 soldiers should be exploited to finalize as many initiatives as possible under safe circumstances. As such, the military component not only played a part in peacekeeping, but it also made a vital contribution to peacebuilding.

Bringing people together again was the core objective of the mission: to give them hope and the prospect of a better future after years of destitution and needless violence; to boost their self-confidence, willpower, and urge to resume the thread of their normal lives. We felt that we should plot the course to reconciliation and reintegration. Five thousand soldiers from ten different countries with totally different cultural and religious backgrounds, 100 military observers from twenty-five countries, 450 UN civil police officers, and 500 members of the civil transitional administration with divergent professional competencies and subdivided into various organizations were expected to set an example of tolerance, solidarity, and cooperation.

The mine removal program was of crucial importance to making the region livable again. Communication lines between Croatia, the eastern Slavonian region, and Serbia were reopened: telephone, railways, postal services, motorways, and the connection between the Drava River and the Danube were all restored. In all these projects, we invariably tried to involve both parties under the supervision of UNTAES. The Croats were encouraged to recruit demobilized Serbian soldiers into their de-mining squad. After combined clearing activities on the only oil field in the region, locals who had formerly worked there were re-employed. The road from Zagreb to Belgrade, the cranes in the port of Vukovar, the ferry across the Drava at Belisce, and the renewed exploitation of the oil fields were all properly inaugurated.

We felt it was important that the local people were maximally involved in the civil tasks of the mandate. For this reason, the projects not only had to be advertised and explained via all possible media, but it was also our intention to strive toward an active participation on the part of the locals. With each step forward, we would organize a party and an official ceremony to show our appreciation for the commitment and goodwill of the people involved and to urge them to keep on cooperating. Certain events, which I will deal with in a moment, were particularly important in this respect.

In a region with two prevailing religions (Roman Catholic and

Orthodox), we managed to celebrate Easter, All Saints Day, and Christmas. After only two months, and in spite of the high security risks involved, the Easter celebration was used as an opportunity to bring people together again. After eight months, on November 1, we opened up the entire region to allow the Croats to pay a visit to the graves of their beloved at various cemeteries for the first time in five years. And some weeks later, we were once again able to celebrate Christmas in dignity across the war zone.

In addition, toward the end of the demilitarization in June 1996, UNTAES organized a military parade and an air show in Vukovar. Local folk groups and military personnel with artistic inclinations performed side by side in the theater during a cultural evening dubbed "Bridge of Music."

In the demarcation zone between Osijek and Vukovar, a project was set up under the name "Saturday Market." Families from the region, from Croatia and from Yugoslavia, convened there, not only to barter whatever they had brought along but also to chat and socialize. On some days, up to 10,000 people gathered on this spot—without a single security incident.

During winter we were forced to switch to another initiative to encourage a safe restoration of contacts. This is how the sponsorship program came into being. We allowed Croats to enter the zone through several checkpoints so that they could come and pay a visit to local families. The latter were asked to guarantee the safety of their guests, who sometimes stayed over for several nights. After their stay, they had to leave the region through the same checkpoints. Not once was a person unaccounted for.

Gradually, people became convinced that a new start was indeed possible. We achieved this change in attitude by announcing our achievements loudly, louder than the agitators and hysterical television commentators, and more convincingly than the web of lies and deceit that was being spread by newspapers and on the radio, as our words could be tested against our actions.

But the reconstruction process and re-employment drives were delayed. Consequently, the return of the refugees and displaced people did not make sufficient headway. As many people were still full of hate and showing no willingness to reconcile, a considerable proportion eventually left the region of their own free will. Nevertheless, thanks to the commitment of all participants in the mission, I think that we realized as much as was humanly possible in such a short space of time. Indeed, we could not go any further than integrating Croats and Serbs (under the supervision of UNTAES) in all the committees involved in the implementation of the mandate—and, it must be said, these committees did an excellent job.

SUCCESS

To assess a peacekeeping operation meaningfully, one must take into account all of its different aspects. It is not advisable to opt for a one-sided approach in determining the level of success. All aspects—political, military, economic, and humanitarian—should be evaluated together. It is important not only for the region and its inhabitants but also for the members of the mission that the balance of success and failure should be positive. Depending on the circumstances and the point in the mission, the progress made at any given time may be more outspoken in one area than another. Yet it is extremely important that all people involved should identify with the achievements on any particular day rather than concentrate too much on the small setbacks that are inherent in such ambitious operations.

Ultimately, it is important that the people in charge have a strategic plan for the whole undertaking and all its side aspects, so that the criteria for success can be determined per section. At all times should one be able to asses what progress has been made.

Out of sheer curiosity, I returned to eastern Slavonia in April 1999. I met a lot of familiar faces and was delighted to see that significant headway had been made. Clearly, the effort we put into this mission had paid off. These are some of the elements that formed the basis of the success of UNTAES:

- The mandate was based on the Erdut Treaty. The political choice was unequivocal: a peaceful reintegration into Croatia. The duration of the mission was limited.
- The military setup was credible and forceful. One single country was responsible for the military component so that the Belgian commanding officer was assisted by a small staff of capable officers.
- The rules of engagement allowed us to enforce cooperation between the parties involved. Moreover, the decision of whether to deploy NATO air power was decentralized and left to the discretion of the commander of the peacekeeping force.
- UNTAES was able to rely on solid diplomatic support, both during the preparation of the mandate and during its implementation.
- The level of cooperation between the civil and military component was perfect, from the level of the head of the Transitional Administration and the commander in chief down to the most remote corners of the region.
- We succeeded in developing an efficient intelligence system, providing relevant data that allowed us to take the necessary decisions at all levels—civil and military.

- We had UNTAES radio and television transmitters at our disposal and were able to print our own newsletter in Serbo-Croatian and in English. This newsletter was distributed among the population throughout the region by patrolling soldiers.
- We succeeded in commanding the trust and respect of the local population as well as the parties in arms. The local regular command of the 11th Serbian Corps cooperated voluntarily throughout the implementation of the mandate.
- Everybody was committed to making the undertaking a success.

Small Arms—Big Problems

Sami Faltas

War has become unpopular. As Carl von Clausewitz wrote in *On War,* it was once considered an "extension of politics by other means," but today it is seen as a breakdown of diplomacy. The use of force as an instrument of foreign policy is frowned on by public opinion and banned by international law. And it is not only values and norms that have shifted with respect to war. So has the behavior of states. These days, they rarely wage war against each other. This is a remarkable change, but it has not led to world peace. From time to time, states still fight. Often, they engage in arms races, and this can result in greater tension and a higher risk of war. Worst of all, armed violence is on the rise *within* countries. In many countries around the world, crime, domestic politics, ethnic clashes, and class struggles are becoming more violent. For millions of people who have experienced decades of violence in Afghanistan, Angola, Sri Lanka, Sudan, and elsewhere, civil war has become a way of life. We find armed gangs taking over the streets in parts of cities like Rio de Janeiro, Moscow, Johannesburg, Jakarta, and Los Angeles. We also see political and criminal organizations working across international borders, using weapons to achieve their goals.

Of all the small arms and light weapons used in this kind of violence, the most famous is the assault rifle Avtomat Kalashnikov, first made in Russia in 1947. Millions are available to freedom fighters, soldiers, mercenaries, and thugs. The rugged, cheap, and deadly AK-47 has also become an everyday tool to enterprising young men living in hopeless conditions around the world. U.S. peace researcher Michael Klare recently claimed that "the most deadly combat system of the current epoch" is "the adolescent human male equipped with a Kalashnikov."[1] It is easy to see why. In forty-six of the forty-nine regional conflicts that have broken out since 1990, light weapons were the only arms used. The United Nations Development Program has estimated that some 2 million children were killed and more than twice as many disabled in armed conflicts since 1987. Another million have been orphaned, and some 12 million were left homeless. In fact, in most recent wars, most casualties by far are civilians. These wars are rarely fought with tanks, jet fighters, or warships. The weapons used are pistols, rifles, hand grenades, and even machetes. So although major weapon systems in some cases are also a problem in developing countries, we will focus here on the more pressing issue of small arms and light weapons.

THE KALASHNIKOV AGE

There are three categories to consider: (1) military-type revolvers, pistols, rifles, and light machine guns; (2) heavy machine guns and various other kinds of light weapons that can be carried and operated by two persons; and (3) ammunition for the weapons mentioned, hand grenades, and mines. In most discussions of small-arms issues, hunting and sports weapons, traditional weapons, and utensils like the machete are excluded. This is regrettable, because they can cause great bloodshed, as we saw in Rwanda. They are left out mainly because they are less destructive than military-type weapons and more difficult to control.

Controlling small arms is difficult, because they are easy to obtain, use, and hide. To begin with, they are cheap, and they are everywhere. They can be mass-produced at low cost, and prices have been pushed down further by huge stocks of secondhand weapons flooding the world market in recent years. Today, the problem is not so much that unscrupulous manufacturers are exporting these weapons to zones of conflict. Millions of weapons are already there, moving from one trouble spot to the next. This can go on for a long time, as most guns are very durable.

Small arms are also easy to operate and maintain. A teenager can learn to load, aim, and fire an assault gun in an afternoon. Many do. Indeed, in many domestic conflicts, adolescents and children make up a large part of the fighting forces. This helps to explain why most casualties—up to 90 percent—in internal conflicts are civilians, especially children. They are both victims and fighters.

Finally, small arms can be easily dismantled, concealed, and secretly moved around. Even in a state that has well-patrolled borders, efficient customs authorities, and a good police force, it is difficult to prevent illegal transfers of small arms. It is all the harder in the developing countries, where most of today's wars are fought.

However, there are also factors that work in favor of gun control. For instance, the components that kill, such as ammunition, grenades, and shells, can only be fired once. They need to be replaced for armed conflict to continue. If these chains of supply can be broken or controlled, this will help. A gun is not much use without ammunition. Besides, as they are cheap, small, and technically simple, small arms are easier to collect and destroy than major weapon systems.

Then there are political factors that work in favor of gun control. The proliferation of small arms is such an obvious danger to public security and political stability that most governments are quick to see the need for strict gun control. For the same reason, government agencies like the police, the armed forces, and the intelligence services are usually also in favor of it. Of course, companies and workers with a direct interest in the small-arms business are not eager to see their industry curtailed, but they do not represent a powerful lobby. However, in some countries, especially the United States, there is a powerful lobby of gun fans.

We do not know exactly how many small arms and light weapons are in use around the world. Estimates range from 500 million to 1 billion. About 200–250 million of these are in the United States. Although the worldwide trade in arms of all types declined steadily from the late 1980s until 1997, the trade in small arms is thought to have grown. It is believed to be U.S.$5–10 billion a year, or 10–20 percent of the total worldwide trade in conventional arms. These rough estimates are the best we have. Because of the problems outlined above, there are no reliable data on the small-arms trade.

Some kinds of weapons are considered such a risk that they have been banned altogether. This applies to chemical weapons, biological weapons, and anti-personnel mines, but it is not true of small arms and light weapons. Used legally and responsibly by the proper authorities, firearms are seen as tools for the maintenance of public security. That is why there is no global campaign to prohibit small arms. Instead, the advocates of gun control concentrate on fighting what is most problematic about small arms—their proliferation, destabilizing accumulation, undesirable possession, illicit trafficking, and misuse.

WHO BUYS WEAPONS AND WHY

People buy weapons as merchandise, as implements for their hobbies, or to use them against other people. Trafficking arms can be a lucrative business. Almost anywhere in the world, weapons can be legally or illegally exchanged for hard cash. On November 10, 1998, U.S. secretary of state Madeleine Albright pointed out that in many places where it is impossible to find a wholesome meal or a warm bed, it is easy to find a gun or a grenade. In fact, we might add, in situations of chaos and insecurity, a stock of weapons can be better than money in the bank. Often, the trafficking and use of guns is tied up with other illicit activities. In earlier ages, guns were often exchanged for slaves. Today, they are traded against drugs, diamonds, oil, or tropical timber. In fact, they are sometimes used as a kind of currency. The distinction between armed political struggle, gunrunning, the drug trade, and criminal violence is fading or gone in places like Albania, Colombia, Chechnya, Sri Lanka, and Kosovo.

Hunters, marksmen, collectors, and weapons fans also buy guns for pleasure. These people contribute to a culture in which it is considered appropriate and admirable to own and use weaponry.

Finally, of course, weapons are bought to be used—for self-protection, political purposes, or crime. Buyers may believe that they need to be armed in order to protect themselves, their families, and their property. This is understandable in some parts of the world where public security is poorly maintained, but it is undesirable from society's point of view. Only people who are authorized to use weaponry, who are properly trained, and who are strictly controlled should have access to the tools of violence.

Political violence is a frequent occurrence in many countries. In fact, it may be on the rise. This does not necessarily mean that it is held in high esteem. Today, governments are fiercely criticized when they forcibly suppress their critics. Radical movements waging an armed struggle seem to enjoy less support and approval than they might have twenty or thirty years ago. Take the Kosovo Liberation Army (KLA). Although during the Kosovo war it received money and volunteers from various parts of the world, the KLA is widely mistrusted and criticized for its intransigence, its violent excesses, and its involvement in the drug trade.

THE DAMAGE CAUSED BY SMALL ARMS

Small arms and light weapons inflict enormous damage, both on account of their large numbers and because of their destructiveness. A modern assault rifle can fire hundreds of rounds a minute, allowing a handful of combatants to spray a village square and kill or maim everyone in sight. Hand grenades need even less skill. In fact, they are often accidentally exploded by playing children or the heat of a cigarette. Land mines kill indiscriminately, even decades after the conflict for which they were laid is over.

It is with good reason that some peace researchers refer to small arms as today's weapons of mass destruction. The immediate harm they cause is so obvious that we can now move on to their indirect effects.

In the south of Sudan, people say, "Live with a Kalashnikov, and you will live for free." Here, in a nutshell, is the effect of many years of civil war, armed violence, and gun trafficking on a fragile society. Law and order have collapsed. The war has devastated agriculture and cattle farming. Unless you have a functioning farm, it is hard to feed your family legally. However, weapons are widely available—at a price. With an AK-

47, you can appropriate money, food, drink, and anything else available. The rewards are attractive, and the chances of being punished are small. Prosperity, security, prestige, and power come out of the barrel of a gun. They can hardly be obtained any other way. Guns and violence have become an integral part of the economy and the political process. Of course, this is an extreme scenario, but it is safe to say that in most societies, the ready availability and uninhibited use of small arms make criminal and political violence more frequent, more destructive, and more difficult to end. In the long run, the culture of violence caused by the proliferation and misuse of small arms is perhaps just as harmful as the damage caused when the weapons are fired.

PRACTICAL DISARMAMENT AND PEACEBUILDING

One cannot achieve practical disarmament (i.e., removing the tools of violence) without dealing with several related issues. Gun control as a broader effort must address the misuse of weaponry, the demand for weaponry, the undesirable possession of weaponry, and the channels of supply.

Microdisarmament, or practical disarmament, is only one of these four connected points. It can be regarded as the third of four stages, as is illustrated by the peace process in Northern Ireland. Before any progress could be achieved, the killing had to stop. Once that was achieved in the Good Friday Agreement of 1998, confidence-building measures could begin to reduce the demand for weaponry among the hostile communities and militias. To the extent that progress is being made to cut back the demand for weaponry, peacemakers can begin to tackle the sensitive issue of disarmament, which in Ulster is called decommissioning. However, this has not yet started. Of course, at some later stage, the gains of disarmament will need to be consolidated by a rigorous control of the supply routes for weaponry. Otherwise, the hostile factions may rearm, and the availability of arms will increase the risk of the bloodshed starting all over again.

The Ulster story tells us more. Even comprehensive gun control as described above is not enough to make a peace process succeed. Making sure that only the authorized agents of the state have access to the tools of violence is only the first step. These agents of the state must also abide by the law, respect the rights of all members of the population, and be accountable to the courts. This, one supposes, will earn them the trust of the people. In short, the rule of law is essential. The state must reflect the interests, desires, and concerns of all parts of the population. People must have the opportunity to make a living and offer their families a decent life. Finally, society needs to be organized in such a way that people learn to restrain their aggression and settle their differences in nonviolent ways. Most, if not all, of these elements are in evidence in Northern Ireland. Even so, the outcome of the peace process is uncertain.

Asking people to give up their weaponry to promote peace is an attractive notion. It seems a natural, easy, and nonthreatening first step, because it relies mainly on the cooperation of gun owners. This kind of voluntary farewell to arms can also be a powerful symbol of peace, even if only a few weapons are collected.

Of course, in practice, weapons collection is not easy. There are many problems to tackle and pitfalls to avoid. If they are not set up correctly, arms collection programs can promote the arms business. In the United States, Australia, and other countries, there have been cases of people turning in guns to a buy-back program and using the reward to buy more modern weapons. In other instances, when high rewards were offered, people specially bought, stole, or smuggled weapons in order to turn them in. For instance, when the UN disarmed the militias in eastern Slavonia, a Serb enclave in Croatia, weapons were imported from Serbia and sold to the UN, which handed them over to the Croatian government.

There is an even greater danger. Asking people to hand in their weapons can actually harm public security. All other things being equal, if people who are keeping guns for self-protection disarm, while potential aggressors do not, this gives the aggressors an advantage. The result could be more violence, or worse violence.

HOW TO COLLECT WEAPONS AND DISPOSE OF THEM

The first step toward any successful disarmament program is to determine what it is supposed to achieve. If the point is to reduce the number of people injured or killed by small arms in crimes and accidents, then the program may be set up to take all firearms (or particularly dangerous weapons like assault rifles and hand grenades) out of the hands of the population in general. Such a program could also focus on high-risk groups like adolescents. A very different kind of weapons-collection program is often launched after a civil war and a peace agreement, to prevent a return to political violence. This would typically be accompanied by measures to integrate the former combatants as full participants in the economy, the society, and the political process.

People do not give up their weapons easily. Usually, they will want reassurance that someone else will protect their security. Probably, they will expect to be compensated in some way for the value of the weapons they hand in. In most cases, they will also need to be motivated by the fear of being punished if thcy do not disarm during the period of amnesty. So carrots and sticks are both needed.

The right form of compensation is critically important to the success of the program. It is not always a bad idea to buy back the arms, but as we have seen, it can have undesirable effects, especially if high prices are paid. Rewards in kind, such as food, clothing, toys, or entertainment vouchers have been used successfully. In other cases, people giving up weaponry were offered a reward that helped them provide for themselves and their families. Thus, in Mozambique, guns are being exchanged for hoes and other agricultural tools. In Nicaragua, disarmed and demobilized combatants were given microcredits so that they could start businesses of their own. Elsewhere, people surrendering guns have been offered jobs or job training.

Of course, the question is whether people should be compensated at all for giving up guns they held undesirably. Especially if the weapons were stolen (as in the riots of 1997 in Albania and the Central African Republic) or used in acts of criminal or political violence, it may be inappropriate to offer any kind of reward, except perhaps freedom from prosecution during the program of disarmament.

Besnik Alibali, a retired army engineer who runs a disarmament campaign in the Albanian port of Dürres, is opposed to the whole idea of compensating people for giving up illicit weaponry: "I prefer to tell people, if you have guns or grenades in your basement, you have a problem. They are a danger to yourselves, your children and your neigbors. Call us, and we will safely remove them."[2]

The risk of rewarding antisocial behavior is neatly avoided if the reward is given not to the individual but to his or her community. This shows a desire to remedy the effects of gun proliferation and armed violence on the community. Handled properly, it can help mobilize civil society against these dangers. It can even help combat violent crime by improving public security. In the Albanian province of Gramsh, the government authorities are collecting illegally held weapons from the population, while the United Nations Development Program is providing vehicles and mobile radios to the police and installing telephone lines in the province.

Once weapons have been collected, the question arises as to what to do with them. The greatest danger is that they will be sold, stolen, or given away, and end up creating new problems elsewhere. If the arms had originally been stolen, for instance, from government security forces, it may be appropriate to return them to their owner, especially if they are needed to defend the country and maintain public order. Otherwise, the best way to dispose of collected weaponry is to immediately and publicly destroy it in a safe and environmentally friendly way. Various techniques are available, each with its merits and drawbacks. Burning the weapons, dumping them in the sea, or driving a tractor over them is cheap, effective, and spectacular but not good for the environment. Dismantling them and recycling the parts for purposes other than arms is friendlier for the environment but more expensive, less visible, and carries a greater risk of the parts being reassembled again. Other techniques worth considering are cutting the weapons using torches or shredding them. It is interesting to note that with the exception of ammunition and explosives, which are best left to experts, small arms and light weapons are cheap and easy to destroy, using equipment easily available almost everywhere.

NOTES

1. Michael Klare, "The Kalashnikov Age," *Bulletin of Atomic Scientists* 55, no. 1 (January/February 1999): 19.
2. Personal communication, Tirana, October 26, 1998.

SUGGESTED READING

Cameron, Maxwell A., Robert J. Lawson, and Brian W. Tomlin. (1998). *To Walk Without Fear: The Global Movement to Ban Landmines*. New York: Oxford University Press.
von Clausewitz, Carl. (1868). *On War*. Middlesex, UK: Penguin.

Demobilizing and Reintegrating Former Combatants

Kees Kingma

In postwar peacebuilding support efforts, attention should be devoted to the people in the armies who fought the war. Demobilization is often one of the urgent, central, and sensitive postwar processes—be it after a defeat of one of the parties or a peace settlement. Large numbers of combatants (government soldiers and/or opposition fighters) are to be released from the forces and start a new life as civilians. During and after these downsizing operations, policymakers have to deal with a complex set of issues, such as encampment and provision of basic needs, the logistics of resettlement, weapons collection and control, conflict resolution, support for reintegration, employment opportunities, psychosocial problems, and coordination of external assistance. The issues are sensitive because the success of a cease-fire depends on the actual behavior of the armed forces. In some cases it also concerns giving support to what used to be the "bad guys" in times when many others need support as well. This article identifies, on the bases of demobilization experiences in the past decade in Africa and Central America, some of the key issues involved and several general lessons learned.

Demobilization is usually seen as one of the development efforts in postwar situations, along with, for example, economic stabilization, democratization, infrastructural rehabilitation, and repatriation of refugees. But it is often also part of a security sector reform. In most countries the armed forces are totally overhauled, or an entirely new one is established. Often in the cases of demobilization reviewed, there was also a need to reform the police system. In cases such as El Salvador, Haiti, and South Africa, internal security issues during the conflict had largely been dealt with by the army. After the war, or with the change of regime, the decision was made to revert the internal security issues back to the police force. In these types of cases one should question whether a demobilization is really a demobilization or merely a change in the color of the uniform.

The status and standing of the (new) armed forces—and civil-military relations in general—are likely to play a role in peacebuilding processes. An atmosphere of reconciliation in and around the armed forces could make a major contribution. Retraining and reorientation of armed forces personnel and balancing the ethnic and regional composition of the forces might be required. It might strengthen people's confidence in the future if human rights violations of members of the armed forces are dealt with. This could, however, create a dilemma. These people should be appropriately punished, but heavy punishment might also increase tensions between the military and the rest of society.

DEMOBILIZATION, RESETTLEMENT, AND REINTEGRATION

Demobilization and Resettlement

Blueprints for demobilization do not exist. Each case involves a distinct political and socioeconomic context. And decisions to demobilize have been based on specific military, political, and socioeconomic circumstances. In Ethiopia, for example, the defeat of the Derg Army in 1991 led to its total demobilization. In Mozambique, the two parties agreed in 1992 to stop fighting, demobilize, and create a much smaller new national army, consisting of volunteers from both parties. In the case of Uganda, armed conflicts had virtually disappeared several years before the demobilization was initiated, and a considerable number of soldiers of the army of the previous regime had already been absorbed in the new National Resistance Army.

Some countries have opted for first unifying and then demobilizing. For example, after the 1994 elections in South Africa, the old South African Defense Force, Umkhonto we Sizwe (MK—the armed wing of the African National Congress), the Azanian People's Liberation Army (the armed wing of the Pan-Africanist Congress), and the armies of four former "homelands" were integrated in the new South African National Defense Force (SANDF). Subsequently, the number of personnel in the SANDF is being reduced.

Generally, once the decision to demobilize is taken, practical plans have to be worked out and financing ensured. The combatants who are to be demobilized are often brought to assembly areas where they are registered, disarmed, and given an identification card. In other cases soldiers are demobilized directly out of the barracks. In the assembly areas or barracks, they may also receive health care and be assisted with reorientation and counseling. In Uganda, for example, the ex-soldiers and their dependants went through predischarge briefings, providing them details on how to open a bank account, how to start income-generating activities, environmental and legal issues, family planning, and AIDS prevention. At the time of demobilization, a "package" in the way of cash and/or materials is usually provided to assist the ex-combatants in the initial stages of resettlement.

It may include foodstuffs, civilian clothing, household utensils, building material, seeds, or agricultural implements. In most cases, the demobilized receive a cash payment at the time of demobilization and then at subsequent intervals. In Mozambique, the combatants received six months' severance pay at demobilization as well as reintegration subsidies, representing a further eighteen months' pay. A typical postwar demobilization includes the following activities:

- Selection and preparation of assembly areas.
- Planning of logistics, including transport and basic needs supply.
- Resource mobilization (domestic and foreign).
- Selection of those who will be demobilized.
- Cantonment and registration.
- Disarmament.
- Needs assessment.
- Provision of services, such as health care and basic training.
- Predischarge orientation and counseling.
- Discharge and transport to home areas.

Soldiers are considered to be demobilized once they have been disarmed, received discharge papers, and have—officially and de facto—left the military command structure. Considerable support is often required to transport them to where they will resettle. The availability of land is often a critical factor for those returning to rural areas. In many cases, returning refugees and internally displaced people are also in need of land. Land mines in the areas where ex-combatants (and others) would want to start agricultural activities cause one of the constraints for resettlement.

Reintegration into Civilian Life

Once the ex-combatants are demobilized and have settled together with their families in the area in which they want to begin a new life, the reintegration process starts. Although often at least some support is being provided, most of the effort rests on their shoulders. They have to build up a new livelihood and have to reconcile with former enemies. Reintegration is not one general process but consists of thousands of microstories, with individual and group efforts and with setbacks and successes.

Reintegration has economic as well as social and psychological aspects. *Social reintegration* is the process through which the ex-combatant and his or her family feel part of, and are accepted by, the community. The history of the war and the degree of reconciliation between the various groups play a role in how the ex-combatants are received. Other factors such as gifts and rituals could also play a role. In Mozambique, for example, many ex-combatants spent a good part of their initial demobilization money on gifts to village elders. That contributed to acceptance in the villages, becoming part of the "social security" and sometimes being allowed to marry a young woman in the village. Most ex-combatants underwent cleansing rituals. These have an impact both on the acceptance by the community as well as on the state of mind of the ex-combatants. Because the history of Uganda has caused a general fear and disrespect for soldiers, the Ugandan government tried to help ex-soldiers reintegrate, through sensitization of soldiers and communities.

Economic reintegration is the process through which the ex-combatant's household re-establishes its livelihood, through production and/or other types of gainful employment. It is important to note that in some cases, the combatants released are the ones with the worst perspective for (self-)employment because of little skills and education, or health problems such as HIV/AIDS. Despite constraints, such as the availability and accessibility of agricultural land and housing, the experience with reintegration has not always been negative. Research in Ethiopia, for example, shows that the ex-soldiers are indeed generally poor, but they are not significantly worse off than civilians in the same location without a military background.

Psychological adjustments are also important to consider. Military personnel and guerrilla fighters are trained in top-down approaches, which are often not appropriate for management and entrepreneurship in the civilian sector. Ex-combatants go through a personal process of adjusting attitudes and expectations, after losing a predictable environment and a certain social status. In addition, large numbers of the demobilized suffer from serious psychosocial problems due to post-traumatic stress disorder.

DEMOBILIZATION AND REINTEGRATION SUPPORT

It is important to make an analytical distinction between the demobilization and reintegration process, on the one hand, and support programs to facilitate the process, on the other. Often, particularly among international development agencies, these are implicitly used as synonyms. The list below provides an overview of the possible actors in the total process. If those designing and managing support activities are not sufficiently aware that ex-combatants and their families carry the heaviest day-to-day burden of reintegration, support efforts might, in fact, not help reintegration nor lead to local capacity and sustainability of the achievements.

- Demobilized combatants (male and female ex-combatants; ex–child soldiers; ex–government soldiers and ex-guerrillas; associations of demobilized combatants).

- Families of ex-combatants.
- Communities in which ex-combatants resettle.
- Other groups trying to reintegrate (e.g., returned refugees and internally displaced people).
- Local business community.
- Government agencies.
- Armed forces and other security forces.
- Local nongovernmental organizations (NGOs).
- The UN and its agencies.
- Donor agencies.
- International NGOs.

Some people might argue that it is unfair that ex-combatants receive special support. These combatants often created havoc and made development and life impossible. Many other groups of people suffered and should be supported in restoring their livelihoods. When peace returns, ex-combatants are usually not the only group that has to reintegrate. Returning refugees and internally displaced people usually outnumber by far the ex-combatants. However, the justification to support ex-combatants is usually based on one or more of the following arguments:

1. Demobilized soldiers and fighters require support from a humanitarian point of view. Upon demobilization, they are out of a job and often far from their homes. Therefore, they require at least the initial provision of basic needs and physical resettlement.

2. In some cases demobilized combatants have sacrificed several years of their life to improve the development perspectives for their compatriots (e.g., Eritrean People's Liberation Front—EPLF, or MK in South Africa). In other cases, some of the demobilized have been recruited into the armed forces under pressure (e.g., Derg Army in Ethiopia and Renamo and Mozambican National Resistance in Mozambique). In those cases, support could be seen as a compensation for foregone education or other investment.

3. A third argument to support ex-combatants is because of their potential contribution to general development. Their skills and capabilities might bring new economic activities and employment opportunities.

4. Last, but in some cases most important, lack of reintegration support could jeopardize peacebuilding and human development. Without support, demobilized soldiers and guerrilla fighters might have great difficulties re-establishing themselves in civilian life, and frustrated ex-combatants may threaten the peace and development process by getting involved in criminal activities or violent political opposition. They could also try to apply their skills elsewhere. The use of ex-soldiers as mercenaries in offi-

cial and private armies is increasing, and many of them originate from armies that have recently downsized.

In most efforts to support reintegration, policymakers thus face a dilemma on whether to treat the ex-soldiers and guerrillas as a special target group. Support programs have to strike a balance. It is argued that, for example, ex-combatants should not receive more support than necessary to help them attain the standard of living of the communities in which they live. This targeted support might be costly, but long-term costs for society could be even larger if the ex-combatants would not be able to find new livelihoods. It could lead to increasing unemployment and social deprivation, which could again lead to rising crime rates and political instability.

Governments and NGOs have in the various countries designed and used a broad set of instruments to directly support the ex-combatants and facilitate reintegration. These measures are best applied in different combinations, according to the local circumstances, the target groups, and the available resources. Governments could, of course, also take general measures to create an environment that facilitates reintegration. A general environment of economic growth has shown to be one of the most important factors for successful economic reintegration. Possible components of resettlement and reintegration support programs include:

- Cash payments (in installments).
- Foodstuffs (or coupons).
- Health care.
- Civilian clothing and household utensils.
- Building material and tools.
- Seeds or agricultural implements.
- Agricultural extension services.
- School fees for children.
- Counseling.
- Legal and/or business advice.
- Job placement or general referral services.
- Land distribution.
- Housing support.
- Public works and other (temporary) public sector job creation.
- Wage subsidies.
- Credit schemes.
- Managerial and technical training.

In most of the postwar countries implementing demobilization and reintegration programs, economic conditions are such that the activities cannot be funded solely by national resources. Several of the international development cooperation agencies have over the past few years largely overcome their initial reluctance to get involved in development activities that relate to the military and other parts of the security sector. Multilateral, bilateral, and NGO development agencies provide support in many cases of demobilization through the financing of UN operations, demobilization packages, special services during demobilization, technical assistance, and programs to facilitate reintegration.

LESSONS LEARNED

Success of demobilization exercises could generally be assessed in terms of whether the demobilization contributed to peacebuilding and whether the ex-combatants have been able to reintegrate satisfactorily into civilian life. The diversity of demobilization experiences among countries is large. However, with the appropriate care, and always putting demobilization in the specific context of the broader reconciliation, peacebuilding, and rehabilitation processes, some general lessons could be drawn on the basis of recent experiences.

1. *Demobilization is no "magic bullet"— politics comes first.* Demobilization does not automatically take care of the major development and security challenges. The clearest example is the case of Angola, which has unfortunately shown twice that demobilization cannot substitute for political will. Demobilization has little chance to succeed if one of the major parties is not fully committed. This lesson was also learned by the United Nations Operations in Somalia after it tried to demobilize certain armed groups. "Politics" has to come first. Only then, on the basis of a real political solution of the conflict, will demobilization, resettlement, and reintegration support be natural—and often inevitable—components of postwar conflict transformation, rehabilitation, and development.

2. *Balance and opportunity costs should be considered.* Financial resources are limited in postwar situations, even if donor funding is available. Because the overall objectives are peacebuilding and human development, demobilization exercises have the best results if decisions on resource allocation consider the trade-offs with other types of development spending. First, one could ask, What activities are really necessary to prevent violence to restart or address other direct security threats? Demobilization requirements are often pressing and politically sensitive, and soldiers pose a potential threat to the peace. So, there are usually large potential benefits in support to the demobilization itself. But beyond that, funding subsequent reintegration support would have to be considered along with broader development efforts and the needs of others.

3. *Successful demobilization requires a central authority and implementing agency.* Demobilization requires a clear and credible central

authority and implementing agency. If it is the government, it should be able to guide and secure the process with sufficient oversight. Its police force should be able to intervene if the security of the ex-combatants or others is threatened. Following a peace agreement between two or more parties, this role may be played by an independent outside entity. For example, in El Salvador, Mozambique, and Namibia, the UN was the neutral facilitator in sorting out details during the process, and it stepped in and mediated when the demobilization showed delays or was at risk. Clear and active coordination remains very important during the resettlement and reintegration phases.

4. *Planning for demobilization and reintegration support should start early.* Despite the political uncertainty and institutional weakness usually existing in a country emerging from war, there is a need for early and rigorous planning. Important preparatory work includes needs assessment, the mobilization of resources, and sensitization of stakeholders. Programs for reintegration should start soon after the end of the war, because armies might begin to disintegrate ahead of formal demobilization. Clarity about these programs will provide the ex-combatants and their leaders confidence in the peace agreement and in their future in society. Similarly, if the encampment takes too long and the demobilized have to do without information and opportunities to see their relatives, violent activities and rebellion could undermine the demobilization, as well as the peace process.

5. *Sufficient provision of basic needs are needed in the encampment stage.* Demobilization requires effective management and substantial resources for accommodation, registration, transport, and the provision of basic needs. If the provision of basic needs such as water, sanitation, shelter, and food is insufficient at the encampment and discharge stage, frustration is likely to occur. In Angola in late 1991, for example, living conditions and provision of basic needs in some of the camps were extremely poor. This contributed to widespread desertion. As with the previous lesson, quick visibility of the benefits of peace is required.

6. *Careful disarmament of the combatants is crucial.* If the combatants are not properly disarmed and armories not well protected, weapons might remain or fall into the hands of ex-combatants and other people. The availability of these "uncontrolled" light weapons causes dangers at different levels. It increases the risk that disputes are settled with deadly violence because most ex-combatants know little else than using violence to solve problems. These weapons could also fuel banditry; and armed groups could more easily disturb nonviolent, democratic political processes.

The way in which disarmament is implemented during the demobilization differs. It particularly depends on whether the demobilization is after a defeat of one party, right after a peace agreement, or as a result of a decision to downsize the existing army. Disarming soldiers and guerrilla fighters is usually not easy. Many own several weapons. So, if they turn in one, others might be hidden elsewhere. Large stocks might remain unreported if the parties are not sure that the peace will hold—or speculate on future income. However, the disarmament of ex-combatants is not always so difficult. In Uganda the weapons remained in the barracks when the soldiers moved to the demobilization centers. And in Eritrea, all weapons used by the EPLF had been registered during the war.

7. *Support programs must be designed in a participatory way.* To respond to the real needs, reintegration assistance programs could best be designed and adjusted in continuing dialogue with ex-combatants, their families, and communities. Ex-combatants themselves are usually going though a learning process after leaving the military. For example, they have to find out what is possible—whether the sometimes overambitious plans they had while still in the army make sense after they arrive back in the village, town, or city. The reintegration process is also best facilitated if the support is as demilitarized as possible, stressing the new environment and people's own responsibility.

8. *Decentralized implementation of reintegration support is essential.* Actual reintegration usually takes place throughout the country, in different circumstances and environments. The appropriateness of possible support measures varies from case to case. A support program organized in a decentralized way is most likely to provide the appropriate support in a flexible and cost-effective manner. Also the need for joint learning (lesson 7) implies that the actual implementation of the programs should be as decentralized as possible. Good communication with the "center" should ensure that general lessons—positive or negative—are being learned in the future and in other areas.

9. *Reintegration support should benefit the entire community.* The dilemma of targeted support to ex-combatants and the need to balance between supporting them and the other war-affected groups was indicated above. From a short-term point of view, one may be inclined to keep the ex-combatants happy, to forestall a return to arms. From a long-term perspective, ex-combatants should as soon as possible be treated like everyone else. A consensus appears to have developed that special efforts for ex-combatants are necessary during the demobilization and resettlement phase but that reintegration support should be community-based and part of general rehabilitation efforts. Studies have found that support by communities themselves was often critical for the success of the reintegration of the ex-combatants. These findings indicate that support to reintegration processes is more effective if it falls in line with the broad reconciliation and peace-building processes and the creation of an enabling environment in which people are encouraged to take initiatives.

10. *Provide support to female ex-combatants, former child soldiers, and disabled ex-combatants.* Reintegration programs have thus far generally taken too little consideration of the special needs of female ex-combat-

ants, their children, and the wives of ex-combatants. In the Frente Farabundo Martí para la Liberación Nacional in El Salvador as well as in the EPLF in Eritrea, about one-third of the fighters were women. These female ex-fighters as well as other women in war-affected communities have usually acquired new roles during wars and are often expected by men to return to their traditional roles. Thus, reintegration creates tensions. A high divorce rate has, for example, been observed between ex-fighters in Eritrea. In Uganda, wives of returning soldiers, who came from other regions, were very often not accepted by the husband's family and their community.

Special and rapid support is also needed for former child soldiers. Many of them have become adults in the meantime but still require extra care and assistance. Their experiences in the forces have had a profound impact on their social and emotional development. Many are seriously traumatized by the brutal experiences they have undergone and the violent acts committed. Their environment inhibited the development of social values. They usually lack parental care and access to school. At demobilization, they should not undergo assembly. Assistance in family tracing, special care for the orphaned, and physical and psychological rehabilitation may facilitate reintegration. The success of reintegration will also depend on opportunities to gain access to education, training, and employment. Special protection and rehabilitation programs are necessary for girl soldiers, whose existence is often denied and who face multiple problems after demobilization.

Also health care and special assistance to the disabled should be part of reintegration programs. They usually represent a large proportion of the demobilized in Central America and Africa. Incidence of HIV/AIDS is also high among the demobilized in several countries.

11. *International development agencies should be able and willing to provide flexible and coordinated support.* External funding has in recent demobilizations contributed to the speed with which demobilization and resettlement was implemented. To increase their value, international development agencies should be well prepared to deal with unexpected requests for support. Once called upon, they need to be involved in the planning processes early on. Demobilization and reintegration support requires a large degree of flexibility and willingness to actually coordinate at all levels on the side of the donors—even more so than in more traditional development cooperation. Slow procedures and specific rules and regulations on the side of the donors have more than once affected the effectiveness of demobilization and reintegration support. Duplication and conflicting policies and incentives can be prevented. Good communication and transparency on the side of the donors and their implementing agencies facilitates

coordination by the government and the strengthening of its management capacity.

REFERENCES AND SUGGESTED READING

Ball, Nicole. (1997). "Demobilizing and Reintegrating Soldiers: Lessons from Africa." In Krishna Kumar, ed., *Rebuilding Societies After Civil War: Critical Roles for International Assistance.* Boulder, Colo.: Lynne Rienner.

———. (1998). "The International Development Community's Response to Demobilization." In Kiflemariam Gebrewold, ed., *Converting Defence Resources to Human Development.* Proceedings of an International Conference, 9–11 November 1997. Report 12. Bonn: BICC.

Bonn International Center for Conversion (BICC). (1996). *Conversion Survey 1996: Global Disarmament, Demilitarization and Demobilization.* Oxford: Oxford University Press.

Colletta, Nat, J. Markus Kostner, and Ingo Wiederhofer. (1996). *The Transition from War to Peace in Sub-Saharan Africa.* Directions in Development Series. Washington, D.C.: World Bank.

———. (1996). "Case Studies in War-to-Peace Transition: The Demobilization and Reintegration of Ex-Combatants in Ethiopia, Namibia and Uganda." World Bank discussion paper no. 331. Africa Technical Department Series. World Bank, Washington, D.C.

Gebrewold, Kiflemariam, ed. (1998). *Converting Defence Resources to Human Development.* Proceedings of an International Conference, 9–11 November 1997. Report 12. Bonn: BICC.

Kingma, Kees. (1996). "The Role of Demobilization in the Peace and Development Process in Sub-Saharan Africa: Conditions for Success." *African Security Review* 5, no. 6: 33–42.

———. (1998). "Demobilization and Reintegration: An Overview." In Kiflemariam Gebrewold, ed., *Converting Defence Resources to Human Development.* Proceedings of an International Conference, 9–11 November 1997. Report 12. Bonn: BICC.

———, ed. (forthcoming). *Demobilisation in Sub-Saharan Africa: The Development and Security Impacts.* Basingstoke: Macmillan Publishers.

Kingma, Kees, and Kiflemariam Gebrewold. (1998). "Demilitarisation, Reintegration, and Conflict Prevention in the Horn of Africa." Discussion paper. Saferworld and BICC, London.

Spencer, Denise. (1997). "Demobilization and Reintegration in Central America." BICC paper no. 8. BICC, Bonn.

■ 13.5

Democratic Policing

Rachel Neild

The task of rebuilding and reforming police forces and developing internal security practices that comply with democratic norms and international human rights standards is central to peacebuilding efforts. A durable peace requires the creation of accountable and effective police forces that can provide a secure and safe environment for political, economic, and social development. Although the possibilities for developing democratic policing depend primarily on internal factors (in particular, on the commitment to democratic policing of leading political actors), this article focuses on the contributions made by international actors to the process of police reform.

During conflicts, particularly internal conflicts, military forces often take control of internal as well as external security tasks. Police forces may be displaced as military forces take control of extensive areas and responsibilities, or they may be placed under de facto or de jure military control. During conflicts, police work is oriented toward the protection and promotion of a particular regime rather than the provision of safety and order as a service to the disaggregate public. Such "regime policing" has a profound effect on the capabilities, skills, and public legitimacy of the police who are frequently abusive, corrupt, and ineffective at fighting common crime.

CHARACTERISTICS OF REGIME POLICING

- The mission of the police is to support the political regime or government.
- Police are under military, ethnic, or partisan political command and control.
- Police do not require public legitimacy to be effective, and public mistrust of police is profound.
- Police have few, if any, accountability mechanisms and enjoy impunity for abuse.
- Criminal detection capabilities are weak and concentrated in limited areas or on small constituencies (ethnic, racial, religious, wealthy neighborhoods, or business elites).
- Intelligence-gathering structures are focused on enemies of the regime rather than gathering criminal intelligence.

- Police developed to enforce social and political control have little understanding of, and experience in, crime prevention or are poorly developed (little tradition of visible or community policing on which to build).
- Criminal justice systems are underdeveloped, ineffective, and slow.

During peace processes, the role and mission of military forces are generally reformed and restricted to external defense. This typically requires a rebuilding and professionalization of police forces to take full responsibility for public order and law enforcement. Postconflict security reforms are frequently dependent on international expertise and assistance for the design and implementation of police reforms, as national civilian capacity to develop and direct security policies are typically very weak in countries with long histories of military or authoritarian rule. In designing reforms, donors need to incorporate programs and activities to transfer skills and build national capacity to maximize the sustainability of the police reform.

There are a number of different models of policing in the world, and there is no one definition of democratic policing. Each police reform will also reflect particular national conditions. Nonetheless, through international support for police reforms in contexts as diverse as Bosnia, Namibia, El Salvador, and Haiti, experts see an emerging norm of democratic policing. Definitions vary but emphasize that democratic police should:

- Be under civilian rather than active-duty military control.
- Provide a public service within the context of international human rights standards.
- Be ethnically plural and nonpartisan.
- Be accountable to multiple audiences through multiple channels.
- Be part of a comprehensive criminal justice system.

Design of Police Reforms

Public security sector reforms are generally spelled out—in varying levels of detail—in peace accords or other agreements. It is important to achieve as much consensus as possible between the national actors and among donors about the methods, goals, and responsibilities for the reform process. Ideally, agreements should set out the major benchmarks to be achieved in the reform, and it may be useful to establish timelines for the achievement of those benchmarks. Rigid deadlines may present hurdles if progress is lower than anticipated for purely technical or logistical reasons. If, however, failure to progress is due to opposition and obstruction from political parties or other sectors that do not support the reform, deadlines may provide useful opportunities to address problems and demand compliance with agreements.

Planning for the police reform should start as early as possible in the peace or negotiation process. Advance planning should include preparatory missions and consultation with human rights organizations and national civil society sectors as well as with the government and combatants, where that is possible. Given the difficulties of recruiting qualified civilian police personnel for international missions, efforts to identify and recruit personnel with skills matching identified needs should start well in advance of the deployment of international missions. Advance planning processes should also initiate and develop ongoing plans for donor coordination and assignment of responsibilities.

The Interim Security Gap

The interim security gap describes the period between the cessation of hostilities when programs to dismantle old security forces begin and the deployment of the new police force. Former security forces have often committed serious human rights violations and are mistrusted by large sectors of society. Yet it takes some time to select, conduct background checks on, and train a new police force. Security arrangements must be made that can handle basic public order and law enforcement tasks during the transition from wartime policing to democratic policing. Although it is often politically unpopular, the only solution in many countries is to retain old security forces conducting police work under international supervision until the new, reformed police can be deployed.

International civilian police (CivPol) missions play a key role in accompanying and monitoring the conduct of interim security forces. CivPol's presence reassures fearful local populations and may bolster the confidence of the security forces. In Haiti, members of the interim public security force often would not leave their barracks without a CivPol escort, as they feared that hostile communities might lynch them. CivPol accompaniment can also help to overcome the lack of resources and poor policing skills typical of many security forces that have been regime policing.

Changing Uniforms or Recruiting New Police—the "Demobilization Dilemma"

The relation of old military and police forces to the new police is a key and delicate issue in postconflict reforms. As noted above, old police or military forces are often mistrusted by much of the population and rarely have appropriate skills for democratic policing. On the one hand, "rolling over" these personnel into the new police risks undermining the public legitimacy of the new force and retaining inappropriate institutional practices and the bureaucratic culture of former security forces. On the other hand, creating a new police force from scratch is expensive and results in a force with no practical experience of policing. Ineffective law enforcement by inexperienced police can erode the public credibility of the force and even lead to vigilante responses when rising violent crime is a major public concern. Massive demobilization processes also present the possibility that former soldiers or police—who often face under- or unemployment, despite retraining and reinsertion programs—will turn to common crime or add to political instability.

The decision of whether to risk the problems associated with inexperience or those of bad experience will depend on the political and financial constraints of each context. In general, however, few countries can afford to start completely anew. In either case, CivPol missions should provide an extended period of accompaniment, ongoing mentoring, and field training.

In Haiti the reform created an entirely new police force. Although ex-military and police personnel were not barred from the new force, in addition to a screening process to eliminate any persons responsible for human rights abuse, they had to pass the same recruitment tests as civilian recruits, and relatively few military met the requirements. Many reforms retain some number of former personnel—contingent on human rights screening processes—and also recruit civilians.

In El Salvador, the peace accords stipulated that the new National Civilian Police (Policía Nacional Civil, PNC) comprise 20 percent former police personnel, 20 percent former guerrilla combatants, and 60 percent new civilian recruits. All members of the PNC were to receive the same training at the newly created police academy.

In Bosnia-Herzegovina, the police force was to be reduced by nearly half, from 20,000 to 11,500 police posts. All police were required to reapply for their jobs. The International Police Task Force conducted psychological and basic competency tests, followed by background checks. The names of all police were then published to encourage public complaints against any human rights violators. For those who passed this screening, their first year was a probationary period during which they could be removed from the force if evidence arose of past or new incidents of human rights abuse or noncompliance with the Dayton Accords. Police who completed their probationary period were provided with new uniforms and other equipment. The provision of equipment was explicitly conditioned on completion of the vetting process. The uniforms were a visible symbol of approval and valued by many in the new police, as were the cars and radios that supported more effective operations. International negotiators sought to develop a similar package with the Republika Srpska.

When former military or police personnel are rolled over into the new police, their incorporation should be on an individual basis. Agreements should bar the wholesale incorporation of entire police units, despite the temptation to retain specialist training and skills intact. Entire unit rollovers risk creating divisions between old and new personnel in the new police, and they are often subject to influence from former military or police commanders and/or political authorities outside the chain of command of the new police. In the interests of cohesiveness, accountability, and the creation of a new institutional culture, all recruitment—from former security personnel or civilians—should be done on an individual basis. All candidates should have to pass the same tests and receive the same training, and rigorous background checks should be conducted.

Background checks or human rights "screening" or "vetting" processes are especially important when former military and police personnel are included in the new police, particularly if these forces have committed serious human rights abuses during the conflict. International bodies generally take charge of vetting processes. Vetting processes solicit information from a variety of sources. If there is an international human rights monitoring mission in the country, it will provide valuable information and can conduct additional investigations. International sources, including intelligence sources, should provide information for vetting, and local human rights organizations should also be asked to share their data. It may be advisable to publish lists of names in local newspapers and create mechanisms to receive public denunciations. All persons making denunciations must be guaranteed anonymity to protect their security. Local security conditions will affect the level of public cooperation with vetting and must be taken into account in designing these processes.

The standard of evidence required to bar individuals from the police should reflect the level of institutional involvement in past human rights abuse and the quality of information available for vetting. A relatively low standard of evidence is to be preferred when massive and systematic abuses have been committed by security forces during the conflict, even if this risks barring some innocent personnel. For example, a single denunciation could trigger an investigation to verify the information by the resident UN mission or other UN representative. The engagement of the UN or a multilateral international body is often important to the credibility of the process, particularly in countries where individual nations may not be seen as neutral actors. A high standard of proof—such as requiring documented cases and extensive witness or material evidence, which are often scanty and hard to obtain—risks allowing abusive personnel into the new police.

Police Recruitment Processes Must Be Fair and Transparent

Clear recruitment standards must be set, and application processes should be well publicized throughout the country. Publicity must be adequate to assure a good candidate pool, and special outreach programs to schools and colleges may be useful. The salary offered should be adequate to attract appropriately qualified candidates (and provide a decent standard of living to the police, thus reducing incentives for corruption). Ideally, there should be at least three applicants to choose from for each slot in the police. Where ethnic or sectarian differences have driven past conflicts, recruitment for the new police must reach out to communities that have not been represented in the past. If agreements include ethnic or religious quotas, recruitment processes must be designed to meet them. Requirements, including issues such as height, must not discriminate against entire social sectors.

Recruitment standards should emphasize academic criteria and psychological aptitude as well as physical requirements. Education levels of police vary widely from barely literate beat cops in some nations to a trend in developed countries of recruiting more university graduates with a range of skills that facilitate the development of policing practices (including community policing) that call for more discretion and problem solving by individual police. In each context, recruitment standards should be designed to enhance the professional conduct of the police force while maximizing its ability to develop a good relationship with local communities.

Designing Adequate Police Training Programs

Police training should discuss the role of the police in a democracy and incorporate international human rights standards and codes of conduct for law enforcement officials. If possible, a comprehensive assessment to determine the status and capabilities of the police and criminal justice system should be conducted and provide the basis for designing appropriate police training programs. Training should emphasize practical and role-playing exercises, ideally taking real-life examples. There should be extensive training in the use of force and handling of weapons. Additional training should be provided in crowd control and civil disorder management. Training should use models of use of force as a last resort, provide techniques that defuse rather than escalate tense situations, and train police in nonviolent self-defense techniques and mediation skills. Academy training should be open for public observation and monitoring by local human rights organizations. Donors should encourage the creation of fora to bring together police cadets and community representatives to share concerns and encourage police-public dialogue.

Academy training should be complemented by further training and mentoring in the field. Field trainers should reinforce academy teaching and provide feedback on the strengths and weaknesses of academy training. Extended field training and mentoring is invaluable to assist new police in developing experience and skills without resorting to inappropriate or abusive practices. Ongoing in-service training programs can also be developed to confront particular needs that emerge on the ground or to reinforce basic skills. Finally, donors should include a component to build national police training skills through "train the trainers" programs or similar efforts.

Pressures for rapid deployment and shortened training periods should be resisted, as they result in the deployment of ill-prepared police who are more likely to make mistakes and even panic in challenging situations and use deadly force unnecessarily.

Problems in Developing Police Leadership

It is particularly important to avoid recruiting large numbers of commanders from former security forces to maintain the credibility and integrity of police reform processes. In particular, top police executives should be civilian and have a public record of commitment to democracy. Recruiting suitable civilians can be challenging. Civilians with management and leadership skills often command higher salaries and prefer work in the private sector. Promotion through the ranks cannot rapidly fill senior positions that require experience and seniority. New police commanders also require specialized training and should be familiar with the basic training that their subordinates have received.

Police leaders must be recruited, trained, and deployed at the same time as the police under their command. In Haiti, police leadership recruitment lagged behind general recruitment and training, and the first Haiti National Police deployments started work without commanders, which created morale and logistical problems and required CivPol forces to undertake a de facto leadership role. Once deployed, processes should be established to review the performance of police commanders and assure that they have established their authority, are setting appropriate moral and professional standards, and are complying with police procedures.

Putting Resources and Systems in Place

Resources and systems must be implemented at least at a basic operational level as the new police are deployed. Police stations, basic communications and command systems, transport, lock-ups, and office equipment are vital components of police assistance and must be provided promptly. Basic management and administrative systems must also be in place to keep track of personnel and equipment. Valuable equipment may be lost or destroyed if police managers and administrators cannot keep track of what is allocated to whom or if police do not maintain it properly.

Disciplinary systems should be in place by the time the police are deployed to confront any abuse that may occur and avoid erosion of public confidence and inculcation of bad habits in the new force. The inspector general or internal affairs unit must have adequate resources and support from police and political authorities. It should have regional offices as well as a national office, be easily accessible to the public, and be able to react rapidly to incidents of police abuse and misconduct. Police disciplinary manuals should conform with international standards of human rights and codes of conduct for law enforcement officials and clearly establish disciplinary processes and responsibilities. The central office should investigate all police killings and cases of serious human rights abuse and should review the disciplinary practices of regional and local police commanders. Line supervisors and local police commanders should deal with minor infractions and petty offenses.

Establishing the Chain of Command

The chain of command must be clear and unified, delineating a clear line of authority and responsibility from the government authorities (ministries of public security, interior, or justice) to the police chief and on down to regional commanders and line supervisors. Special units or task forces should not be permitted to operate outside the chain of command, as this risks undue political influence and/or unaccountable behavior. Where local authorities control police, accountability mechanisms should exist to assure that police remain nonpartisan.

Police and the Criminal Justice System

Many police reforms have advanced significantly faster than reforms of the judicial system. A number of problems arise when judicial reforms lag behind as a new police force is developed. A failure to prosecute criminals apprehended by police leads to public and political frustration with the weakness of the criminal justice system. Continued corruption in the judicial system not only deepens public cynicism about the potential of reforms but may also lead to police corruption. Police themselves grow frustrated when they believe that incompetent and corrupt judges will release suspects. In such circumstances, police may undertake "preemptive justice," torturing, or even carrying out extrajudicial executions of detainees. In Haiti, local police in the southern region once set up a kangaroo court and tried and punished an alleged criminal.

Additional training in investigative skills should be provided to judicial police or detectives. The track record in El Salvador and Haiti indicates that it takes considerable time to build police investigative skills in countries where past forces relied on confessions, often extracted under torture, rather than building material and witness evidence for trial. Joint training programs for police and prosecutors and judges have helped improve communication and cooperation between police and judicial authorities.

Civic Education and Community Outreach Programs

Building awareness of reform programs and support for democratic policing is vital. In countries with long histories of conflict and/or authoritarian rule, there is often little public understanding of democratic policing and judicial processes. This can lead to misunderstanding and inappropriate demands being made of the police by the public as well as by local authorities and other sectors. Civic education programs about the rights and responsibilities of the police and public are an essential part of the larger effort to improve police services and public cooperation.

The new police force should also take an active role in building trust by reaching out to the community, creating channels for communication and dialogue about local security fears and needs, and seeking feedback on how to improve police services. (In addition to national campaigns, activities at the local level could include such elements as visits to schools and places of worship, participation in local media programs such as radio call-in shows, assisting with sports and youth after-school programs, and an accessible presence at local markets or other community gatherings.) It may be fruitful to explore further practices of community-oriented policing, but care should be taken to evaluate the suitability of different strategies in each national context as many counterinsurgency campaigns and authoritarian regimes have also used initiatives such as neighborhood watches.

ISSUES FOR DONORS AND THE INTERNATIONAL COMMUNITY

CivPol's Human Rights Mandate

Human rights principles are a central element of all contingents of peacekeeping operations. In Bosnia and Haiti, some CivPol personnel have argued that monitoring and raising human rights issues damages their relationship with local police and the ability to mentor and train them and have deferred these issues to international human rights missions or observers. CivPol must be clear that there is no conflict between mentoring and promoting human rights, and that international police monitors should play a key in demonstrating and teaching that human rights principles are at the core of democratic policing. Both international police and human rights monitors should work to overcome contrasting cultures and work styles to build collaborative relationships, communication, and programs in the field. For example, in Haiti, the human rights mission assisted with academy training and worked with CivPol to develop pilot community policing programs.

The Need for Donor Coordination

In general, close coordination and communication between all donors to police reform processes is essential to avoid duplication and waste. At the political level, it is also important that all donors are unified in demanding compliance with goals laid out in agreements and human rights standards. If different donors send different messages, local actors can play them off against each other and try to weaken reforms.

Long-term Engagement Needed

International supporters of police reforms must also understand that police reform is a long-term process. In some settings, donor nations facing domestic pressures to keep the length of peacekeeping operations as short as possible have pushed for rapid deployment of new police forces to take responsibility for internal security in order to withdraw their own troops. Shortcuts such as reducing the length of training, leaving judicial reform to be dealt with later, or failing to build up management and command systems to keep pace with rapid police deployments can create serious problems. Donors should also consider that police reforms need ongoing support beyond the typical two- to three-year period of a peace process. Ideally, donors should coordinate and share the costs of targeted ongoing bilateral support for some years after the international mission has departed.

Transparency and Democracy in International Missions

Donors should reflect values of democracy and transparency in their own practice. International missions should publish regular and detailed public reports and make them widely available. Donors should provide information to local and international media and nongovernmental organizations working with or monitoring the progress of the peace process. Missions should also establish agreed-upon processes to make public statements and issue special reports rapidly following any serious breaches with agreements, human rights violations, or security problems.

ONGOING CHALLENGES OF POLICE REFORM

The Importance of Domestic Political Will

The level of domestic political will is a determining factor for the success of a police reform. Reforms frequently face opposition from political, military, and economic sectors with vested interests in old security arrangements. If confronted by active opposition from the government, a reform process is highly unlikely to succeed, or may only last as long as the international presence is maintained in the country. However, even without the active encouragement of the government, police reforms may advance if they have the government's permission and receive adequate support from donors and the public.

Sustaining Police Reforms Through Building Civilian Capacities

Supporters of police reform need to consider how better to build civilian capacity and public support for democratic policing. Democratic policing is based on accountability upward to the government in all its branches and downward to the people. A democratic police force must provide a service to the community and do so in a fair and transparent manner. Beyond the effort to make the police themselves more professional, this requires that civilian capabilities be built up to direct and oversee public security and law-enforcement policies and practices. Local expertise must be built to take over tasks conducted by international experts. Reform programs must build civilian police leadership and strengthen the oversight and policy-making capacities of legislators and government officials. International policymakers should also try to consult with and incorporate civil society and community groups during the planning and implementation of police reforms and encourage informed national and local debates about security threats and appropriate responses.

The Challenge of Postconflict Crime Waves

Many postconflict settings see significant increases in levels of crime and violence. The demobilization of combatants, the easy availability of arms, and the economic and social legacies of war all fuel rising common crime. At the same time, new police are inexperienced, their leadership may be weak, and key partners in the criminal justice system may be ineffective or dysfunctional. While a new police may enjoy greater political and public legitimacy as a result of reforms, their operational credibility will suffer if they are seen as ineffective in the face of a crime wave. Such discontent can create demands for tough anti-crime measures that infringe on newly regained rights. Donors may need to assist governments and police in developing targeted initiatives that can have a visible effect on certain types of crime while they continue to support the long-term consolidation of democratic policing and a culture of rights.

SUGGESTED READING

Aspen Institute. (1998). *Honoring Human Rights: From Peace to Justice.* Washington, D.C.: Aspen Institute.

Neild, Rachel. (1999). *From National Security to Citizen Security: Civil Society and the Evolution of Public Order Debates.* Montreal: International Center for Human Rights and Democratic Development.

Oakley, Robert, ed., with Michael Dziedzic and Eliot Goldberg. (1998). *Policing the New World Disorder: Peace Operations and Public Security.* Washington, D.C.: National Defense University Press.

United Nations. (1990). *Basic Principles on the Use of Force and Firearms by Law Enforcement Officials.* Adopted by the United Nations Congress on the Prevention of Crime and the Treatment of Offenders, Havana, September 1990.

———. (1979). *Code of Conduct for Law Enforcement Officials.* Adopted by the General Assembly 34/169, 17 December 1979.

———. (1996). *Commissioners' Guidance for Democratic Policing in the Federation of Bosnia-Hercegovina.* Sarajevo: International Police Task Force.

Washington Office on Latin America. (1995). *Demilitarizing Public Order: The International Community, Police Reform, and Human Rights in Central America and Haiti.* Washington, D.C.: WOLA.

———. (1999). *Themes and Debates in Public Security Reform: A Manual for Civil Society.* A series of papers on police recruitment, training, internal disciplinary mechanisms, criminal investigations, external controls, and community policing. Washington, D.C.: WOLA.

■ 13.6

Getting Rid of Mines

Sami Faltas

Antipersonnel mines are hidden explosives that are activated when someone steps on them or otherwise sets them off. They belong to the category
of light weapons but are discussed separately here because of the special
problems they cause. Soldiers disagree about their military usefulness, but
no one disputes their harmful effects on civilians and society:

- Being indiscriminate killers, mines often make unintended victims.
- The mere suspicion of mines can make large areas unusable.
- Mines are dangerous and costly to remove.
- Unless they are of the new, self-destructing type, they remain a
  deadly hazard long after they are no longer needed.

All these problems are made worse by the wide usage of antipersonnel
mines, partly due to their low price.

Because mines cause great suffering to innocent people, there have
been many attempts to ban them. In the late 1990s, this campaign achieved
a breakthrough. The Ottawa Treaty to Eliminate Antipersonnel Mines, also
known as the Mine Ban Treaty, was signed and soon entered into force—
the first time a whole category of conventional weapons was outlawed. The
Mine Ban Treaty has several limitations. One of them is that the world's
leading manufacturers and owners of land mines (the United States, Russia,
and China) have not signed it. So we cannot expect the treaty to rid the
world of land mines soon, but it represents a big step forward. In this article, we look at the damage caused by antipersonnel mines and how to tackle the many issues they raise.

A GLOBAL MINEFIELD

The world is littered with some 60 million antipersonnel land mines, which
are still being planted in some parts of the world. However, a larger number
are being removed, so the total is falling. Antipersonnel mines are hidden in
the land of about sixty-four countries, but most are in only a few.
Afghanistan, Angola, Cambodia, China, Egypt, Iran, Iraq, Mozambique,

Somalia, Sudan, Ukraine, and Vietnam account for more than 90 percent of the world's planted mines. Some were planted a long time ago. For instance, the mines in Egypt's western desert have been there since World War II. Others are new. In 1998 and 1999, mines were laid in Angola, Somalia, and various other parts of Africa, Afghanistan, Turkey, Yugoslavia, and the Middle East. Sometimes, governments were responsible, but frequently, rebel forces planted them. Since the Ottawa Treaty went into force on March 1, 1999, participating states are not allowed to use antipersonnel mines under any circumstances.

As of 1999, sixteen countries have not officially ended the production of land mines: China, Cuba, Russia, Turkey, the United States, Yugoslavia, and ten states in the Middle East and Asia. Another thirty-eight have ended production. Among them are most NATO and Warsaw Pact members. The international trade in land mines has almost disappeared. This is important, because nearly all of the mines planted in the twelve most affected countries came from abroad. It is illegal for states that are parties to the Mine Ban Treaty to transfer antipersonnel mines to other states.

As far as stockpiles are concerned, there are believed to be 250 million antipersonnel mines stored in the arsenals of 108 countries. Belarus, China, India, Italy, Russia, Ukraine, and the United States have the largest stocks. Italy and Ukraine, both signatories of the Mine Ban Treaty, are destroying their stocks, as required by the ban.

DEVASTATING EFFECTS AND HIGH COSTS

We do not know exactly how many people are killed and maimed by mines around the world. According to one rough estimate, 800 persons, mostly civilians, are killed by mines and unexploded ordnance every month, while several thousand are wounded, often very severely. None of the mine-infested countries produce reliable statistics. The Sudanese government has estimated that during the long civil war in the south, 700,000 people have lost limbs as a result of mines exploding. In Cambodia, some 13,000 people were killed and twice as many injured by mines and unexploded ordnance between 1979 and 1997. However, in the past few years, the number of mine-related casualties in Cambodia has dropped from 230 to less than half that figure. There are many reports of tragic deaths and mutilations caused by mines in places like Afghanistan, Bosnia, Croatia, Eritrea, Mozambique, and Somalia. But there are also consistent reports that the number of these casualties is falling. Maybe the tide is finally turning against the use of these dirty weapons.

The direct effect of someone stepping on a live mine is awful. Even if victims are not killed immediately, they may die of blood loss, infection, or

SECURITY

shock. The cost for surgical care and fitting of an artificial limb ranges from U.S.$100 to U.S.$3,000 and above. The direct medical and rehabilitation costs for the world's land mine victims are roughly estimated to be U.S.$750 million. But this only begins to describe the cost and damage caused by mines.

If they survive, mine victims are always maimed and often blinded. In most cases, they will have to face the dual handicap of poverty and disability. This will traumatize and impoverish them, their families, and their wider communities. There will also be wider public health problems, like malnutrition and the spread of diseases. The social and economic development of these communities will suffer, not only as a result of the casualties, but for other reasons as well. The mere suspicion that an area is mined can make large regions useless. The fear of mines will drive people away from their villages and lands and prevent others from returning to their homes. Humanitarian assistance, agriculture, trade, transport, health care, education, tourism, public security, and public life in general will suffer or disappear from the suspect regions. People will crowd into neighboring areas, creating problems there, too. Of course, mines and other ordnance also kill cattle and wildlife. Their carcasses can become a breeding ground for diseases.

Demining is not cheap either. A mine may cost only a few dollars, but the cost of removing it ranges from U.S.$300 to U.S.$1,000. Removing all antipersonnel mines planted around the world will cost at least U.S.$33 billion. In short, the direct and indirect cost of mines to society is enormous.

HUMANITARIAN DEMINING: A WORLDWIDE BUSINESS

As long as mines have existed, the military has been interested in their removal. It is only recently that the lifting of mines for humanitarian reasons is being tackled on a large scale, often using military know-how. Humanitarian demining consists of two different, but complementary kinds of activities. Because of its comprehensive nature, some call it "integrated humanitarian demining." The anti-mine campaign prefers to call it "humanitarian mine action" (HMA).

The first part of HMA is mostly technical. Areas believed to be affected must be surveyed, and any mines detected must be marked for clearance before they are actually removed. Almost all of this work requires technicians with special skills, although untrained people can provide some help. The second part of humanitarian mine action mainly concerns working with people. Victims need assistance, both in the short term and the long, and the population at large needs to be told about the dangers of mines and how to avoid them. Here, too, professionals like doctors, nurses, and educators are needed, but other people and organizations can make a large contribution.

The goal of humanitarian demining, or HMA, is not just to get the hidden killers out of the ground but to do this in a way that promotes social and economic development. This idea is enshrined in the *Bad Honnef Guidelines* adopted by a wide range of nongovernmental organizations (NGOs), as well as UNICEF, in Germany in June 1997. It was also embraced by the United Nations Mine Action Service in 1998. Like other development efforts, HMA programs face the challenge of achieving sustainability. In this case, it means helping the local population to develop their own capacity for anti-mine action.

How to Detect Mines

Mines are hard to detect before you set them off. They may be small and largely made of plastic and other materials that a metal detector will not recognize. Even if you see one in time, it may be hard to identify it. Before you approach it to mark its location, you should know how it works. The oldest and simplest mines are triggered when someone steps on them or stumbles over their trip-wire. Modern types may have either an electric, magnetic, heat, or light sensor. In practice, only specialists using a metal detector with a nonmetallic probe can effectively locate and identify mines. Sometimes, the help of dogs is enlisted. These methods are slow, dangerous, and expensive but reliable. It is the only technique that meets the UN's clearance goal of 99.6 percent. This means that four out of every 1,000 land mines may remain in the ground. Far too many, some would say.

New technologies are also being developed for use in humanitarian demining, but their practical utility is at this stage very limited. One of these projects is trying to replicate in a robot a dog's ability to sniff out explosives. Another hopes to train bees to do the same. However, one of the first and most obvious things to do in a mine clearance program has nothing to do with machines or technology. One needs to tap the knowledge of the local population concerning suspect areas. The danger zones they point out will always need urgent attention, both to remove any mines that remain and to allay the fears of the locals.

How to Clear Mines

Clearing mines can mean removing, destroying, and/or neutralizing them. All this is work for specialists. It is a widely supported principle of humanitarian demining that the weapons should be destroyed, or at least rendered useless as land mines. The most primitive way of clearing mines is to detonate them. Farmers have been known to do this by driving animals over suspect land, but this is both unreliable and cruel. A better way is to drive a mine-proof vehicle over it, or to use rollers, rotary drums, flails, or robots designed for this purpose. In a more sophisticated approach, the mines are collected first, either by hand or mechanically. Various ploughs and rakes have been designed to do this.

Once land mines have been located, identified, and perhaps collected, they must either be destroyed or neutralized. Various techniques have been developed for this purpose. For instance, there are foams that either detonate the mine or mark and encapsulate it, making it harmless. Other chemicals have been developed that penetrate the mine and destroy the explosive without detonation. In any case, disposing of land mines remains a difficult and dangerous job that should only be attempted by professionals.

What Kind of Organization Will Do the Specialist's Work?

Demining specialists can be employed by military agencies, commercial contractors, or humanitarian organizations. Given the right priorities, adequate resources, and careful guidance, all these kinds of organizations can work according to the high standards of humanitarian demining. In practice, most humanitarian demining is done by commercial organizations working for governments or humanitarian organizations. Humanitarian demining has spawned a growing international industry, involving several firms that used to make land mines or are still producing them. It is a disturbing thought that a firm should make money twice on these nasty weapons, first by supplying them and then by removing them. However, the main thing is to get the demining done properly, soon, and at an acceptable price.

How to Assist the Victims

When people are injured by land mines, many different facilities and services are required:

- Emergency medical care.
- Amputation surgery and postoperative care.
- Physical and psychological rehabilitation.
- Prosthetics, wheelchairs, crutches, and other implements.
- Assistance for the blind, the deaf, and the mentally disabled.
- Programs to fight prejudices against disabled people.
- Programs to return the victims to economic productivity and social life.

In the countries where most victims live, these services are inadequate or nonexistent. Researchers of the International Campaign to Ban Landmines

(ICBL) noted in their *Landmine Monitor Report* of 1999 that in Angola, amputees can only rely on their families for help. In Somaliland, mine victims receive no postoperative assistance. Social and economic reintegration programs are virtually nonexistent in Colombia. Even in a more prosperous country like Croatia, there are no prosthesis workshops. They also point out that worldwide, much more money is available for demining than for assistance to land mine victims.

Assistance to land mine victims is not only hindered by a lack of resources, it is also plagued by inefficiency in government and health care, prejudice against the disabled, and a general lack of understanding of what is needed to combat the effects of these injuries. The World Health Organization, the United Nations Children's Fund, the International Committee of the Red Cross, and the Swiss government have drawn up a document called the *Berne Manifesto* to recommend effective action to meet survivors' needs. A group of twenty-five NGOs working with the ICBL in February 1998 drew up *Guidelines for Care and Rehabilitation of Survivors*.

Education for Mine Awareness

On top of everything else, information and education programs are needed to reduce the threat of land mines to affected communities. People in affected areas need to learn what mines are, what they look like, and how to avoid them. They should also be told what to do if they find themselves in a mine-infected area. Above all, no one should be left in any doubt that land mines are cowardly and despicable weapons that no one should use under any circumstances. If land mine injuries can be thus prevented, that is better than having to treat them. It may also be cheaper.

People also need to know how to provide basic first aid when others get hurt. They need to understand the extent and nature of disabilities caused by mines. It should be made clear to them that the crippled, the blind, and the deaf have certain limitations, but that they may be quite capable of working, raising a family, and doing many other things. In such campaigns, as in the technical side of demining, professionals are needed. However, people who have not been formally trained to be educators or journalists may have a key role to play. Village elders, parents, youth leaders, church people, business people, sports heroes, popular musicians, and politicians will need to get engaged.

SUGGESTED READING

The Red Cross has published a good leaflet called *Landmines Must Be Stopped* that provides a first introduction to these weapons and how to fight them.

The Mine Information Center at James Madison University in the United States has a very informative Web site at http://www.hdic.jmu.edu/. Other useful Internet resources are the humanitarian demining Web site of the U.S. Department of Defense at http://www.demining.brtrc.com/, and the one maintained by Canada's Department of Foreign Affairs and International Trade at http://www.mines.gc.ca/english/index.html.

Norwegian People's Aid (NPA) is a development organization active in demining, especially in Angola: http://www.npaid.no/.

For policy documents, see "Guidelines for Mine Action Programmes from a Development-Oriented Point of View." Revised version of integrating proposals made at the International NGO Symposium, Bad Honnef, Germany, 23–24 June 1997. This document is available from medico-international@t-online.de.

On UN policy, see "Mine Action and Effective Coordination: The United Nations Policy," United Nations Mine Action Service, New York, 1998.

Finally, here are three useful reference works:

International Campaign to Ban Landmines. (1999). *Landmine Monitor Report 1999: Toward a Mine-Free World.* New York. Also see the ICBL Web site at http://www.icbl.org.

United States Department of State. (1998). *Hidden Killers 1998: The Global Landmine Crisis.* Washington, D.C. Prepared by the Office of Humanitarian Demining Programs. Download at http://www.state.gov/www/global/arms/rpt_9809_demine_toc.html.

International Committee of the Red Cross. (1998). *Banning Anti-Personnel Mines: The Ottawa Treaty Explained.* Geneva. Also see the Web page on land mines: http://www.icrc.ch/unicc/icrcnews.nsf/.

13.7

Peacekeeping, Peacebuilding, and the Lessons-Learned Process

Leonard Kapungu

By 1995, a number of significant and sad developments coalesced to convince UN senior officials that something had gone terribly wrong with UN peacekeeping as an instrument for the maintenance of international peace and security. These included the horrific ethnic cleansing that occurred in the former Yugoslavia, in the presence of the United Nations Protective Force (UNPROFOR) 1992–1995, the terrifying genocide in Rwanda in 1994 as the bulk of the forces of the United Nations Mission in Rwanda (UNAMIR) withdrew, and an unfulfilled mandate in Somalia following the withdrawal of the United Nations Operation in Somalia (UNOSOM). Was this how UN peacekeeping operations would operate in the future? The then-undersecretary-general of the Department of Peacekeeping Operations (DPKO), Kofi Annan, and the Office of Internal Oversight were in agreement that the time had come for the UN to draw lessons from its experiences in peacekeeping.

LESSONS LEARNED UNIT

It was therefore necessary to establish a Lessons Learned Unit, with basically two functions: (1) to examine past and current peacekeeping operations, draw lessons to be learned, and recommend how the establishment, management, conduct, and support of future operations could be improved; and (2) to establish and manage a resource center, which would serve as an institutional memory of peacekeeping, so that experiences of past operations could be made easily available to planners and managers of new operations.

On April 3, 1995, Kofi Annan established the Lessons Learned Unit in the DPKO. Since that day, the unit has undertaken studies of UNOSOM, UNAMIR, UNPROFOR; the United Nations Transitional Administration in Eastern Slavonia, Baranja, and Western Sirmium (UNTAES); the United Nations Mission in Bosnia and Herzegovina (UNMIBH); the United Nations Mission in Haiti (UNMIH); the United Nations Observer Mission in Liberia (UNOMIL); and the United Nations Angola Verification Mission (UNAVEM I, II, III). It has also undertaken studies on cooperation between the UN and regional organizations in peacekeeping and on disarmament, demobilization, and reintegration of ex-combatants in a peacekeeping environment.

These studies revealed one common element: *today's generation of peacekeeping is multidimensional in nature, encompassing military, political, humanitarian, and human rights elements.* These elements should be regarded as one of the first steps in laying the foundation for sustainable peace in a country emerging from conflict. This could be done through the supervision and monitoring of elections, training of new civil police, demining, disarmament, and demobilization of ex-combatants, as well as beginning the process of reintegrating those ex-combatants into civil society.

These tasks can only be undertaken if the entire international community—the UN and its member states, regional organizations and their member states, and international nongovernmental organizations—was mobilized, together with domestic organizations and civil societies of countries directly concerned. To assure success, the parties to the conflict should be willing to cooperate with the international community and settle their political differences peacefully. This sounds like a tall order for countries that have gone through many years of fighting and for an international community that is suffering from fatigue from assisting people who seem not to be in a hurry to resolve their conflicts.

BASIC GUIDELINES

Experience has shown that success cannot be ensured unless certain basic guidelines are followed. Notable among these are:

1. The objective of peacekeeping missions should be clear and governed by the realization that peacekeeping is the beginning of a long process aimed at attaining sustainable peace. It is not an end in itself.

2. From the beginning, the planning of peacekeeping operations should be as comprehensive as possible, taking into account all the multidimensional elements of the operation, including the various stages the operation would have to undergo: monitoring cease-fires, support of humanitarian activities, elections, demining, disarmament and demobilization, the establishment and training of a police force, the foundation of a judiciary and prison system, the reintegration of ex-combatants, and arrangements for mechanisms that would take over the tasks begun during the peacekeeping phase.

3. It should not be expected that the tasks mentioned in number two

above are necessarily carried out by the peacekeeping forces. Still, most of them should begin during the peacekeeping phase and, thus, must be planned in an integrated manner, taking the long view of achieving a sustainable peace. The organizations that are expected to assist in the implementation of every phase should be consulted at the planning stage and assist the planners in providing information.

4. Leaders of every phase should be committed to the objective of the mission, willing to be *innovative,* and to interpret the mandate in such a way as to meet the objectives and not always falling back on their headquarters for guidance. They should be people who can work well with others and who surround themselves with advisers willing to provide frank and objective pieces of advice.

5. The resources for every phase of the operation should be identified as early as possible and should be adequate to meet the objectives set.

6. As soon as is practicable in the life of a peacekeeping operation, attempts should be made at capacity-building of the local community, to enable the civil society to continue to contribute to the process of rebuilding the nation after the termination of the peacekeeping operation in the country. It may be difficult to do this early in the life of a peacekeeping mission, especially if the civil society is as polarized as the parties to the conflict.

7. An integrated effort at the field level should be made in implementing all the outlined phases, utilizing the comparative advantages of each organization available.

8. Successor arrangements to a peacekeeping mission should be in place before the operation is withdrawn.

Of all the peacekeeping operations the Lessons Learned Unit has studied to date, UNTAES had all the elements stated above, whereas UNMIH had most of the elements.[1] It is illustrative that both missions were crowned with considerable success.

Learning is a process, and institutions and leaders tend to resist the process of learning the lessons that do not fit into their framework. In this context, a state of mind willing to learn is necessary to attain effective results. In this regard, I would like to reflect on two instructive remarks. First, when Kofi Annan appointed me chief of the Lessons Learned Unit during his tenure as undersecretary-general for peacekeeping, he noted that I should consult as widely as possible, but in the end, "Do not be afraid to take the lessons wherever they lead you, even if they lead to me," he added. The second came from Marrack Goulding, the former UN undersecretary-general for political affairs. While examining the lessons-learned process in the UN system for the new Secretary-General, he stated to me that only leaders who were confident of themselves were willing to learn lessons. He further observed that it was easier for men and women to accept only those lessons that seemed to support their disposition, or to drift with existing policies and attitudes, rather than change as a result of lessons learned. Thus, the establishment of lessons-learned units in organizations is generally resisted, and when finally established, they can easily be sidelined unless those who run them are persistent, patient, and able to mobilize resources to sustain the process. Most lessons-learned units, be it in international organizations or in governments, tend to be starved of resources.

Learning is a slow process, especially in international institutions where people of different cultures interact and suspicions abound. For many years, the UN sought to distinguish peacekeeping from any other activity in a country where peacekeeping forces were operating. It was considered almost heresy to mention the word *peacebuilding* in the context of peacekeeping. Some member states resisted the idea that peacekeepers could also be peacebuilders, for fear that they would interfere in the internal affairs of affected countries. It was felt that the involvement of peacekeepers in peacebuilding projects could compromise their impartiality. There was also concern that peacekeeping budgets would be used for development projects, which could unduly prolong the life of a peacekeeping operation.

PEACEKEEPING AND PEACEBUILDING

Fortunately, the United Nations Security Council now affirms otherwise. In its presidential statement of December 29, 1998, the Council stated that it "recognizes the timeliness of exploring further means to prevent and settle conflicts based on the charter of the United Nations and generally recognized principles of peacekeeping, and which would incorporate postconflict peacebuilding as an important component." The Security Council encouraged the UN Secretary-General to explore the possibility of establishing postconflict peacebuilding structures as part of efforts by the UN system to achieve a lasting and peaceful solution to conflicts and in order to ensure a smooth transition from peacekeeping to peacebuilding. To that effect, the Council recognized the value of including, as appropriate, peacebuilding elements in the mandates of peacekeeping operations. It agreed with the Secretary-General that such elements should be explicitly and clearly identified beforehand and, in addition, urged utmost cooperation and the exchange of information between all relevant actors in the field of postconflict peacebuilding.

At long last, the UN accepts that peacekeeping can be the beginning of the peacebuilding process. However, it maintains that peacekeeping operations should not be perceived as a substitute for addressing the root causes of conflict. Those causes should be examined in a coherent, well-planned, coordinated, and comprehensive manner, with political, social, and developmental instruments. Serious consideration should be given to ways in which those efforts can continue without interruption after the departure of peacekeeping elements. This perspective falls within the framework of the guidelines suggested earlier. It can be argued that the lesson has finally been learned that there is a *symbiotic link between peacekeeping and peacebuilding*.

This affirmation bodes well for the peacebuilding process. It means that in future, the force structure of a peacekeeping operation can be configured with actual tasks in mind. Military demining units would be dispatched when needed, and military engineering units would similarly be part of the force when they are required. Gone will be the days when infantry units remained in a peacekeeping mission (notwithstanding that they were no longer needed), playing soccer and other ball games while waiting for a crisis to occur so they could intervene. There are certain tasks the military can begin better than the civilian agencies that would continue the projects when the groundwork has been laid. Gradually we are beginning to see peacebuilding being integrated into peacekeeping. This is the result of lessons learned from bitter experiences of recent peacekeeping operations.

SYSTEMATIC LEARNING

Lessons-learned activities must be organized systematically. There is a difference between information and knowledge. Only when individuals and institutions have converted their experiences to knowledge can lessons be said to have been learned, and that knowledge is then transmitted and institutionalized. This can only be achieved if the process of learning is made almost automatic. The desire to improve and do better is part of human development. Yet there is an increasing tendency to repeat what we did yesterday because it is easier to tackle. To avoid this, the learning process should be systematic. It is axiomatic that no plan ever survives the point of contact. Thus, once a plan is put in place, it must be automatically evaluated after a set period. In lessons-learned terms, we call it a midmission assessment. At the end of the mission, there also must be an automatic assessment—"End of Missions Assessment" or "After Action Reports," as some governments choose to call it. Equally, when middle and senior officials end their assignment, they must not be allowed to disappear with the experience acquired. Automatically, such experiences must be detailed in an End of Assignment Report. Gradually through this process, an "institutional memory" is built. Planners and managers of operations will benefit from that memory. Things will be done better and time saved.

It should be noted that we do not only learn from processes that fail. Ideally, we should also learn from those that succeed, such as the operations in Namibia, Eastern Slavonia, and Haiti. We have a lot to learn on how to plan, manage, and conduct missions, from the peacekeeping to the peacebuilding phase. From the operations in Somalia, Yugoslavia, and Rwanda, we have a great deal to learn from our own mistakes. It should also be said that parties to conflicts, such as those in Cambodia, Angola, Somalia, Yugoslavia, and Rwanda, equally have a lot to learn from their own actions, which caused so much misery to the people they claim to represent. It bears emphasis that no peacekeeping operation can ever succeed if the parties to the conflict do not wish it to succeed.

I conclude with a note of caution. The international community should never think that it could ever build a nation. *The parties to the conflict and the people of those nations are the only ones that can build their nations with the assistance of the international community.* This must always be emphasized in any process that begins with peacekeeping and ends with sustainable peace. This is the lesson of our time.

NOTE

1. See also Lieutenant General Johan Schoups's article, "Peacekeeping and Transitional Administration in Eastern Slavonia," in this book.

PART 3

Surviving in the Field

CHAPTER 14

Managing Stress

Luc Quintyn

Few words in psychology are used so loosely as the word *stress*. Each author seems to hold his or her own definition, depending on whether their viewpoint is physiological, psychological, social, or ergonomic. Evidently, all these definitions describe part of the stress phenomenon. In this article, we shall stick to the definition that is most easily applied within the context of stress prevention for diplomats in the field.

Because of the very nature of their jobs, social workers, policemen, firefighters, personnel of nongovernmental organizations (NGOs), and the like sometimes find themselves in extremely difficult situations that may occasion strong emotional reactions. Such reactions result from psychological strain or stress. Both during actual operations in the field and on returning home, stress reactions may cause problems for the individual directly affected as well as his or her family, friends, and colleagues. In some extreme cases, stress reactions may even pose a serious threat to the positive outcome of the operation as a whole.

In relation to humanitarian operations, one notices that more and more people proceed into danger zones without any psychological preparation or protection. Consequently, they are more prone to the kind of emotional reactions that we will describe later. We should emphasize, though, that these reactions do not belong to the field of psychiatry and that the best protection against any kind of stress consists of good information (cognitive prevention) and the possibility of sharing emotions with colleagues (emotional prevention). It is also true that there is such a thing as positive stress. After all, people tend to voluntarily accept the challenges attendant to a difficult yet rewarding job. Positive stress allows us to function efficiently in exceptional circumstances and makes us cautious and alert. Still, we have to be aware that even this kind of stress, which serves and protects us in critical situations, demands a great deal of energy from our body. If this type of functional stress is sustained too long, it, too, can turn into nonfunctional stress. This, in turn, may lead to total exhaustion, thus totally undermining any efficient performance.

As far as fieldwork is concerned, we discriminate between four main categories of nonfunctional stress: basic stress, dysfunctional stress, cumulative stress, and traumatic stress.

BASIC STRESS

Basic stress is inherent in any individual who is posted abroad, though its manifestations and magnitude do vary from person to person. Its source is our own personality, whose adaptation mechanisms may or may not offer an adequate response to the situation in which we find ourselves. Being far away from one's friends, family, and partner in a foreign country with different customs, climate, culture, religion, and food can be more troublesome than expected. The stress that this causes is often latently present and can build up, as if our body were being slowly poisoned with small doses of venom. At a certain point, it can all get too much—for example, when operations last longer than planned, especially if one has no affective or supportive relations with other staff members.

The causes of basic stress are manifold, including the wrong motivation to go on a mission. A typical example of this is the urge to commit oneself to a greater cause, the so-called Jehovah complex. "This country is doomed without me" is the type of expression that characterizes such an attitude, which might result in exaggerated activity. Another "wrong" motivation that one commonly encounters may be described as an escape into commitment. This often occurs after a shattered relationship or as a result of a seriously disrupted family situation. Not seldom do such people cause severe security incidents by starting a relationship with a member of the local population, for example.

Apart from an impure motivation, a lack of suitable defense mechanisms may also trigger unwanted basic stress. Examples that spring to mind are escapism (into alcohol and drugs or by losing oneself in nonessential tasks) or regression (quitting temporarily or withdrawing from social contacts with colleagues). A less recognizable manifestation of inappropriate defense mechanisms is hyperactivity. It can, in fact, take several days before it becomes obvious that one or more team members is manifesting excessive zeal. Usually, such hyperactivity reveals itself in all possible actions, so that the individual affected is unable to distinguish between priorities and side issues. Consequently, he or she starts doing things simultaneously but will inevitably fail to conclude anything. A good description of such a state is "hyperactivity without creativity." In extreme and rather rare cases, one sometimes refers to individuals suffering from such basic stress as "stickers." These people typically engage their colleagues' attention totally. Although this phenomenon is somewhat rare, it can have quite a destructive impact on an operation as a whole, and it therefore warrants firm action.

Preventative Measures Against Basic Stress

As we have seen in the previous paragraph, basic stress is closely linked to people's own motivation and processing mechanisms. Although we do not mean to disclaim the value of idealism, it should be pointed out that, besides commitment, humanitarian operations require a great deal of professionalism. Intellectual honesty and personal awareness of how one tends to react in stressful situations is part and parcel of such an attitude. In this respect, a thorough recruiting policy with careful selection procedures is certainly not a waste of energy.

Some preventative measures for reducing stress can be taken by anyone:

1. *Prior to departure:* gather thorough information about the mission, the exact assignment, the surroundings and circumstances, the climate, and so forth. More experienced people can assist their less experienced colleagues. The military adage "knowledge is survival" certainly holds here. Though hardly ever applied, a detailed and personalized job description card can be very efficient.

Be aware of one's own limits and realize (or concede) when these limits may have been exceeded. A useful tool in this respect, but one that requires some maturity, is to have an open conversation with a colleague and to discuss each other's limits, weaknesses, and defense mechanisms before leaving on your mission. One could agree, for example, to inform one another (discreetly) if one gets the impression that the other person has exceeded his/her limits. It is, however, also important that one follows up the agreed preventative measures. Simply retreating into privacy for half an hour now and then may, for example, work wonders.

2. *During the mission:* any activity requires an effort from the body. Therefore, it deserves our respect. Make sure to get enough rest and sleep. Sleep deprivation is one of the main triggers of emotional instability and inadequacy. Take your time to eat properly and take care of personal hygiene. If one notices that a colleague is neglecting elementary hygiene, this should be seen as a sure symptom of loss of self-esteem and pride. Also, keep your consumption of alcohol, tobacco, medication, or any other intoxicating substances under control.

The above-mentioned suggestion that one might occasionally want to retreat into privacy for half an hour is also in place here. It helps when you use this solitary moment to run through your own job description card. If such a job description is not available, it usually suffices to ask yourself the following questions: What I am doing here? What is my job? What do peo- ple expect of me? What shall I do after leaving this place? Ideally, every employee in the field should ask himself/herself these questions once or twice a day, regardless of the stress-prevention issue. Experience tells us that this small effort (under normal circumstances, just a couple of minutes should do) to arrive at a more intense awareness is indelibly printed on our memory and sustains its power for many years. In this way, we can analyze our stress, which is much better than simply to endure it.

Nonfunctional stress is an additional weight on the shoulders of the whole team. The best remedy is to discuss our discomfort at the earliest opportunity. Pretending to be tough is altogether wrong. Responsibility for such simple basic stress prevention lies partly with ourselves and it depends partly on the relationships within a group.

A fine example of basic stress prevention is a recently set up military experiment that—as far as we know—produced excellent results for the entire group of individuals involved. The initiative was taken by the organi- zation itself, that is, the leadership of the group. The experiment consisted in weekly meetings of one hour in which all the members of the group got together to discuss whatever they had on their minds. Initially, they seemed uncomfortable with the scheme, but the sessions became increasingly suc- cessful, and after a while the participants actually started to look forward to them. Just to give you an idea of the prevailing atmosphere, suffice it to say that the sessions were soon called the "spitting hour."

The following conditions are of great importance to the ultimate suc- cess of this simple technique: none of the issues discussed should ever be taken outside the group or included in any assessment report; the team leader is responsible for the initiative and should stick strictly to the timing (even though he or she must lay down their rank during the actual ses- sions); nobody is obliged to talk, but everyone should attend the meetings; if an issue has not been resolved or if a heated debate is going on at the end of the session, one should finish, regardless, at the agreed time and contin- ue the discussion during the following session. This technique also proved to be a good antidote against another frequent symptom of widespread but destructive signs of basic stress within a team, namely gossip.

Basic stress is the basis on which all following types of stress are graft- ed or molded. It is, therefore, of great importance that each person should take responsibility in relation to him- or herself and the team as a whole.

DYSFUNCTIONAL STRESS

By dysfunctional stress we mean all stress-reaction patterns and discomfort generated by organizational shortcomings. Unlike with basic stress, the cause is the organization as such. The most common triggers are lack of information and communication problems, physical inconvenience (accommodations, sanitary set-up, etc.), unexpected change, conclusion of or uncertainty about the mission, lack of recognition for the assignment carried out by the organization, and inadequate or insufficient equipment in order to perform the mission properly.

A recently identified source of dysfunctional stress during humanitarian operations is a certain style of leadership in which the expectations of the person in charge are unclear or unspoken. This often finds expression in such statements as, "The boss asks nothing, but he demands everything."

Prevention of Dysfunctional Stress

Prevention of dysfunctional stress is not self-evident. Reality usually forces an unsatisfactory situation upon us. After all, the decision to accept a challenging assignment is taken voluntarily. Once one faces the actual challenge, it is good to recognize the dysfunction as quickly as possible, to look for alternatives and creative solutions together with colleagues, and to accept what cannot be changed. The organization expects the team to carry out the mission as well as possible under the given circumstances.

Typical problems often occur as a result of communication difficulties with the head office of the organization and/or as a result of decisions taken by the head office. They are often regarded as negative or totally wrong in the field. If there are insufficient means of communication with the people in charge on the home front, the information gap is often bridged by conjecture, which more often than not does not correspond to reality. Such a mood is typified by such statements as, "They don't understand a thing." "They ought to come and take a look down here. Then they'd see for themselves." Nevertheless, it is quite likely that one does not have all the necessary information at hand to judge why such and such a decision has been taken, even though it does not meet our expectations. Expressing severe criticism of the leadership of the organization during the operation is often counterproductive and a waste of time.

CUMULATIVE STRESS

This type of stress stems from long-term exposure to various traumatic experiences during the mission. Cumulative stress can be clearly distinguished from traumatic stress, which is triggered by a single occurrence. Factors that may add to cumulative stress are aggression and/or verbalized ingratitude on the part of the local population; a boycott or denial of the mandate by the local authorities; one's own powerlessness with regard to the grief of the local population; security incidents; enforced inactivity or delays; or continuously disruptive behavior on the part of one or more colleagues. If several of these factors coincide or follow one after another, the result is cumulative stress. As is the case with basic stress, the initial symptoms are often psychosomatic and may include backache, headache, stomachache, and more. In addition, they may lead to signs of depression, such as sleep disorders and concentration problems.

Together these symptoms generate a downward spiral that can result in fatigue, better known as burnout. When this stage has been reached, one's ability to judge is severely affected, relationships with colleagues have changed, cynical remarks within the team have become more common, and humor has ceased to have a therapeutic effect. In general, burnout is characterized by a feeling of total fatigue, often linked with exhausting hyperactivity and feelings of guilt, powerlessness, and total lack of efficiency. Evidently in such a situation, one loses the capacity to think objectively about one's own professional abilities. In most cases, it will be necessary to remove the person concerned from the job, either temporarily or not.

TRAUMATIC STRESS

Traumatic stress is a direct result of a gripping and traumatic experience. It is commonly referred to as "critical incident stress." A critical incident (CI) is defined as a *single,* totally *unexpected* event resulting in immense *fear,* in which an individual or his/her immediate surroundings are exposed to *mortal danger,* and against which one is totally *helpless.* Examples of situations that may result in traumatic stress are rape, accidents, or being taken hostage.

Any individual with a normal personality structure who has been exposed to a CI will experience a psychological shock. That is why one speaks of a normal reaction (e.g., crying parents) to an abnormal situation (e.g., dead child). Due to differences in people's personalities and depending on their vulnerability at any given time, traumatic stress reactions can differ according to their intensity, duration, and severity. One can also make a distinction between immediate reactions and delayed reactions, which may emerge weeks or months after the actual incident.

Traumatic stress reactions are an amalgam of strong discomfort, both for the person who experienced the CI and for the surrounding group. In an effort to analyze this discomfort resulting from traumatic stress, crisis psychology distinguishes between four levels of manifestation:

1. *The physical level:* nervous exhaustion, excessive transpiration (especially at night), trembling, difficulty getting to sleep, interrupted sleep, nightmares, and migraines.

2. *The emotional level:* anxiety, despondency, feelings of guilt, and the need to retreat. Sometimes the opposite may occur: irritation, feeling hunted, anger, and hyperactivity. Emotional instability (crying, outbursts) is also a common symptom.
3. *The cognitive level:* one sometimes observes fleeting moments of disorientation and confusion, sped-up or slowed-down flows of thought, concentration problems, or indecisiveness.
4. The above-mentioned feelings of discomfort in turn have an impact on a *behavioral level:* fits of anger, quarrelsomeness, reckless driving, and so on.

Delayed post-traumatic stress reactions may manifest themselves weeks, months, or even years after the actual incident, and in extreme cases may seriously incapacitate the CI victim. These delayed symptoms should not be taken lightly. On the contrary, the condition has been recognized worldwide since 1980 as a syndrome that should be regarded as very serious, indeed. Known as post-traumatic stress disorder (PTSD), it is now described in most reference books for professional social workers.

To diagnose sufferers of PTSD accurately, the following elements must be present: having been the victim of a CI; the insistent urge to relive the traumatic experience in the shape of nightmares and flashbacks; intense emotional outbursts at moments that remind the victim of the trauma; a tendency to avoid all thoughts, emotions, or activities that might evoke the traumatic experience; and neurovegetative hyperactivity combined with severe sleep disorders. All these symptomatic difficulties must persist for at least one month.

Treatment of the condition is a task for specialists, who should ideally work in a multifunctional team. The focus during treatment, which is usually limited in time, is on the traumatic experience itself.

Prevention of Traumatic Stress

The prevention of traumatic stress is based on five principles:

1. *Immediacy:* the sooner the case is tackled, the smaller the likelihood that the stress reactions will cause mental scars in the colleagues affected.
2. *Proximity:* once outside the physical danger zone, immediate preventative action is taken, both on the spot and within the natural setting of the person affected.
3. *Anticipation:* it concerns normal reactions to an abnormal situation. Although one may have witnessed unpleasant reactions in affected colleagues, there is no reason why they should not be capable of

resuming their work speedily after receiving the appropriate treatment.

4. *Simplicity:* most preventative measures are relatively simple and easy to master. However, this does not mean that preventative work after a CI is easy as such. The principle of simplicity also refers to the manner in which one should approach a victim. Victims are always victims of abuse of power. In order of depth of impact, they are the victim of abuse by other human beings, mechanical accidents, and natural disasters. This implies that the basic attitude in approaching a victim must always be humility and, even more so, vulnerability. Victims are inevitably oversensitive to any display of power including titles, uniforms, and symbols.

5. *Uniformity:* each organization should have a general policy on the appropriate preventative measures. Any CI is, by its very nature, a chaotic occurrence, so that uncoordinated preventative measures will only result in greater confusion. A centralized approach is therefore required.

On the basis of these principles, some effective techniques have been developed. One could, for example, respond to a CI by applying the defusing technique as soon as possible. This technique is derived from the more complex Critical Incident Stress Debriefing (CISD), which is applied at a later stage. In simple terms, the defusing technique is based on three so-called F-pillars: Facts/Feelings/Future. First, one analyzes the objective facts, then the personal feelings in relation to these facts, and finally one's outlook for the future.

CISD is slightly more complex. There are more conditions to be met, and those applying the technique must be fully trained.[1] Recent research has shown that misuse and irresponsible or unqualified use of the CISD technique might have a negative impact on the consequences of the CI for the individuals concerned and even for the organization as a whole.

What can CI victims do personally? First and foremost, they should not be afraid to talk about their experience. In a good labor culture, one may expect superiors or colleagues not to judge an individual, let alone condemn him or her for responding to a CI. On the contrary, the incident should not be trivialized. A victim's experience should be recognized, and his or her confidence in being able to get better should be confirmed. It is normal under such testing circumstances to experience unpleasant feelings and diverse reactions, but these will pass. Medications, such as tranquilizers and sleeping pills, and alcohol should be spurned at all cost. Attending preventative activities organized within the working group is, of course, highly recommended.

So what can one do when a colleague has been confronted with an intensely traumatizing experience? Do not judge and certainly do not condemn. Your attitude will often determine whether the afflicted colleague will accept you or not. If one does not know what to do, one should admit it, express it. Such a display of vulnerability and powerlessness may well provide access to the other person. Encourage the victim to express his/her emotions, but without forcing closed doors. Your silent presence and concern already mean a lot. Do not doubt these ways of offering support. Unlike forcefulness, powerlessness will not harm anyone. One should also keep in mind that nobody undergoes a CI without being affected by it. At best, it might even prove an enriching and strengthening experience.

CONCLUSION: STRESS PREVENTION FROM WITHIN THE ORGANIZATION

Within the Western-oriented high-risk-job (HRJ) organizations, it has become common practice in recent decades to pay more attention to the human impact that sometimes extremely stressful missions can have. Almost all HRJ organizations (police, army, firefighters, International Red Cross, Doctors Without Borders) have developed some sort of stress-prevention structure. It goes without saying that setting up these stress teams requires a lot of energy, money, and a great deal of human input.

But why are stress teams so important? The first reason is the human aspect. It is a well-established fact that a properly developed human resources policy not only leads to a more efficient mode of operation but also enhances workers' motivation. A second reason is the safety aspect. Too much stress causes concentration problems. NGO staff in the field with an excessive stress load are noticeably more likely to be hurt in (security) incidents. Because of the official recognition of PTSD as a syndrome, employees who feel they were not sufficiently supported by their employers have increasingly taken legal action in order to gain recognition of the psychological consequences of their HRJ assignments. Today, there are precedents in most Western countries for convicting HRJ organizations, not for being an HRJ organization as such but for failing to provide sufficient support to affected employees. These convictions can have dire financial consequences for an organization. Moreover, staff under contract who have to take sick leave because of incorrectly applied traumatic stress prevention measures will further drain financial resources. Finally, the lack of a stress prevention policy can seriously damage the image and, consequently, the public relations of an organization, especially if employees who feel that their problems are not sufficiently recognized should decide to go public.

Humanitarian operations require proper professionalism. This also applies to the prevention of all types of nonfunctional stress that are inherent in this kind of work. That is why each HRJ organization should have an adequately developed prevention policy in place for the benefit of its staff.

NOTE

1. Jeffrey T. Mitchell and George S. Everly, Jr. (1993). *Critical Incident Stress Debriefing*. Elicot City, Md.: Chevron.

CHAPTER 15

Dialogue and Listening

■ 15.1

Listening

Luc Reychler

THE NEED FOR DIALOGUE

Dialogue plays a very important role in ending violent conflicts and in peacebuilding. The goal is to increase mutual understanding, which helps in finding common ground among longtime enemies. Dialogue is not the exclusive property of those who perform at the world stage. It works at all levels of life in ways large and small. It differs from other types of encounters in several ways.[1] Exhibit 15.1-1 illustrates how it differs from debate.

Exhibit 15.1-1   Debate and Dialogue

Debate	Dialogue
Assuming that there is a right answer and you have it	Assuming that many people have pieces of the answer and that together they can craft a solution
Combative: participants attempt to prove the other side wrong	Collaborative: participants work together toward common understanding
About winning	About exploring common ground
Listening to flaws and making counter-arguments	Listening to understand, find meaning and agreement
Defending assumptions a truth	Revealing assumptions for re-evaluation
Critiquing the other side's position	Re-examining all positions
Defending one's own views against those of others	Admitting that others' thinking can improve on one's own
Searching for flaws and weaknesses in other positions	Searching for strengths and value in others' positions
Seeking a conclusion or vote that ratifies your position	Discovering new options, not seeking closure

Equality must reign, and coercive influences should be absent. In genuine dialogue, there is no arm-twisting, no pulling of rank, no hint of sanctions for entertaining unconventional ideas and attitudes, no coercive pressures of any sort, whether overt or indirect. Deep-rooted assumptions should be brought into the open. In dialogue, participants are invited to examine their own assumptions and those of the other participants. When in the open, the assumptions should not be dismissed out of hand but considered with respect even when participants disagree with them. Participants should listen with unreserved empathy. The capacity to respond empathetically to one another is indispensable to dialogue.

LISTENING

Listening is essential for establishing rapport with the parties, for making a good diagnosis, and for generating a more effective transformation of conflicts. The ability to listen carefully enables us to seek the truth in any interaction. It helps people to overcome their fear of change. The natural response in a crisis or conflict situation is to push things forward to get things done, an asset in some cases but a definite liability when it comes to listening. Listening does not come easy. The average person remembers only about 25 percent of what he or she hears because we don't pay attention; our minds wander. Because most people speak about 125 words a minute and our brains process information three times that fast, we have a lot of lag time, which we usually fill up by tuning out, daydreaming, or rehearsing our response.[2]

LISTENING TO INTERESTS, PERCEPTIONS, DESIRES, AND FEELINGS

Conflict is not only about so-called substance but also about feelings. Escalating struggles typically generate heavy emotions such as anger, resentment, and frustration. These emotions have to be dealt with effectively. There are, however, some assumptions about emotions that stand in the way and need to be overcome. Some people believe that emotions are bad, irrational, and irritating obstacles; that they are irrelevant and only "substance" counts; that if we ignore feelings, they'll eventually go away; and that the feelings behind a destructive action are as wrong as the action.[3] Conflict transformation requires that feelings are elicited and effectively responded to. If not, they will prevent the de-escalation of the conflict.

Although most people think of communication as being a verbal exercise, it is equally true that body language serves as an indicator of what the parties are thinking and feeling. In most cases the parties are unaware of their nonverbal communications. Nonverbal messages could be expressed through posture and body position, facial expressions, and voice volume and speech. Paying attention to verbal and nonverbal behavior makes it possible to watch for contradictions and to discuss them with the parties.

CONFLICT ESCALATION AND LISTENING

When a conflict escalates, communication is increasingly less accurate. Increased intensity and emotional involvement corresponds with a decreased ability to listen and communicate. Experience suggests that there is a maximum level of conflict and emotional intensity that can be handled productively. In Exhibit 15.1-2,[4] point B represents the ideal. Here communication and understanding is at its highest. Lower and higher conflict intensity corresponds with a decreased ability to listen and communicate. Point A suggests that low conflict awareness results in little communication and mutual understanding. In other words, increased conflict helps us to think and understand that there is a problem that needs to be resolved. Point C signifies a high intensity and emotional involvement and a complete inability to listen, communicate, or understand.[5]

Exhibit 15.1-2   Conflict Escalation and Listening

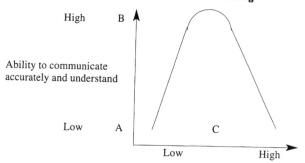

Conflict intensity and emotional involvement

GOOD LISTENING

Good listening is important in all interactions and can be a powerful key to an effective transformation of conflicts. Good listening aims at:

- Encouraging: show interest in what the speaker is saying.
- Validating: affirm the worth of the speaker, and even the validity of his or her ideas or feelings.
- Restating: briefly paraphrase the main points to let the speaker know that you have heard and understood.
- Reflecting: briefly restating the feelings you are hearing
- Clarifying: brief questions can help you to make sure you understood and give additional information.
- Centering: centering questions can bring the speaker back to what is most important to them, or help the speaker stay on track.
- Attending: pay attention to the speaker. Don't let yourself be distracted. Focus on the speaker rather than your own thoughts and possible responses.[6]

HABITS THAT UNDERMINE GOOD LISTENING

- Advising: What you should do is . . .
- Commanding: You had better . . .
- Diagnosing: Your problem is that you . . .
- Discounting: Cheer up, it will get better.
- Judging: This was not a good idea.
- Lecturing: Don't you know that . . .
- Preaching: How many times do I have to remind you . . .
- Threatening: If you do, I'll . . .[7]

COMMUNICATION AND LISTENING SKILLS

A useful typology of listening and communication skills can be found in Karl Slaikeu's practical guide to mediating disputes.[8] These skills can also be used for different purposes and in different circumstances. Two types of skills are distinguished.

Level 1 skills are essential for building rapport and gaining needed information from the parties. They include *active listening, self-disclosing,* and *questioning.*

- Active listening is a method through which one focuses entirely upon the speaker's communications and internal frame of reference (views and feelings) and then reflects back to the speaker what has been heard to check understanding of what has been said. In active listening, the focus is not on the listener's view or opinion but rather on the content of the speaker's message. The focus is on interests, feelings, perceptions, and desires. The listener plays back or paraphrases. It is about reflecting in one's own words the essence of what the speaker has said. "So you felt . . . You are saying . . . You believe . . . " This is the most useful skill for demonstrating one's commitment to understanding.

- Self-disclosing is a communication skill that focuses on the speaker's feelings, thoughts, or beliefs. It uses "I statements" to communicate "my" interests, views, and feelings. It deliberately gives the listener more information about yourself, as when, for example, you tell him/her that you are angry and why.
- Questioning is a basic communication skill aimed at eliciting and clarifying data. There are three basic types of questions and three time dimensions: (1) open-ended questions (who, what, where, why, when, and how) can be used to generate data; (2) closed-ended questions (those yielding to a yes or no answer) can be used to refine and clarify statements and test commitment; and (3) both types of questions can focus on the past, the present, and the future.

Level 2 skills can be used to translate, expand, and channel the information. They include *reframing, brainstorming,* and *confronting.*

- Reframing involves changing the wording, concept, or description of a piece of information to make it easier to understand or accept. It a technique for: making the content more palatable to the other side or more conductive to collaborative problem solving; moving from position to interests; and for unloading or defusing intense situations by using a different word or term to describe something that one party may have stated in an obnoxious fashion. For example, one might reframe "The guy's an absolute jerk" into "By that you mean, he is often late, he interrupts people."
- Brainstorming aims to generate possible solutions to a problem that has already been defined in terms of interests and other supporting facts. It asks "what if" questions; it allows ideas to be put forward without critique; and it is particularly useful for creating integrative solutions that might satisfy the interests of the parties involved in the conflict.
- Confronting is a communication skill used by mediators to encourage one or more parties to stop a particular negotiating behavior that is destructive to the process. Confrontations that attack tend to lead to defensive behavior of the other side and to counterattack. A more constructive way of confronting each other consists of using a "when-I-because" sequence. This formula includes three elements of behavior (what the other person is doing that bothers the speaker,

the speaker's reaction to the behavior, and the reason for the reaction). In this sequence, the mediator encourages a party to cover the following points:

When: "When you came in late to those meetings . . ."

I: "I get upset."

Because: "Because it looks to me like you don't care about what we are trying to do here."

CROSS-CULTURAL DISSONANCE OR HARMONY

Culture is not anymore the hidden dimension in conflict transformation. By now most scholars and practitioners agree that culture matters. When trying to end a destructive conflict, it is important to have some understanding of the culture of the conflicting parties. Such knowledge helps a negotiator or mediator to identify what the parties really want, what are their hot buttons, or what they are prepared to do.

The record provides persuasive evidence of the practical consequences of cultural disharmonies and incompatibilities. In some cases they resulted in a failure of the negotiation process; the achievement of less favorable terms than they might have otherwise; a loss of credibility and damage to the relationship; and the inability to foresee future moves and hence to take necessary preventive or remedial action. If cross-cultural dissonance can harm a relationship, the opposite should be equally true: that cross-cultural harmony based on careful attention to the other side's cultural needs should prove beneficial. This has been proven true. However, one should add that cross-cultural knowledge is a necessary but insufficient condition for success. Unless there are shared interests in an agreement, no amount of cross-cultural sensitivity will help. In an excellent book on negotiating across cultures, Raymond Cohen provides ten recommendations for the intercultural negotiator.[9]

1. Prepare for a negotiation by studying your opponent's culture and history and not just the issue at hand. Best of all, learn the language. Immerse yourself in the historical relationship between the two nations. It may explain more than you expect.
2. Try to establish a warm, personal relationship with your interlocutors. If possible, get to know them even before the negotiations get under way. Cultivating contacts and acquaintances is time well spent.
3. Do not assume that what you meant by a message—verbal or nonverbal—is what representatives of the other side will understand by it. They will interpret it in the light of their cultural and linguis-

tic background, not yours. By the same token, they may be unaware that things look different from your perspective.

4. Be alert to indirect formulations on nonverbal gestures. Traditional societies put a lot of weight on them. You may have to read between the lines to understand what your partners are hinting at. Do not assume that they will come right out with it. Be ultra-careful in your own words and body language. They may read more into them than you intend.

5. Be aware of the emphasis placed by your opponents on matters of status and face. At a personal level, establish them as equals. Avoid the unmasked exercise of pressure. Do not express criticism in public. Do not lose your temper. Avoid confronting them with prearranged solutions. Do not go over their heads. Avoid unpleasant surprises. Anything that leads to the loss of face is likely to be counterproductive.

6. Do not overestimate the power of advocacy. Your interlocutors are unlikely to shift their positions simply in response to good arguments. Facts and circumstances speak louder than words and are easier to comply with.

7. Adapt your strategy to your opponent's cultural needs. On matters of inviolable principle, attempt to accommodate their instinct for prior agreement with your preference for progress on practical matters. Where haggling is called for, leave yourself plenty of leeway. Start high, bargain doggedly, and hold back a trump card for the final round.

8. Flexibility is not a virtue against intransigent opponents. If they are concerned to discover your real bottom line, repeated concessions will confuse rather than clarify the issue. Nor is there merit in innovation for its own sake. Avoid the temptation to compromise with yourself.

9. Be patient. Haste will almost certainly mean unnecessary concessions. Resist the temptation to labor under artificial time constraints; they will work to your disadvantage. Allow your opponent to decide in his or her own good time. Their bureaucratic requirements cannot be short-circuited.

10. Outward forms and appearances may be as important as substance. For face-conscious negotiators, an agreement must be presentable as a prestigious outcome. However, symbolic gains may compensate them for substantive losses.

Some practitioners criticize such lists of do's and don'ts. They say that such checklists are making too much abstraction of the contexts and tend to assume that culture is something like a "trait list," timeless and a stable thing. They stress that to know an actor's culture is to know all her cultures (she is a professor, she has been educated in Korea and the United States, spiritually she is an eclectic, etc.); and to be aware that cultures change. Culture, as a way of satisfying universal needs, is reinvented and revalidated by each generation. There is an Arab proverb to this effect: "Men resemble their times more than their fathers."

Experienced peacebuilders are used to learning about culture. Training courses, however, are useful to sensitize and shorten the learning curve of neophytes about the culture in general and the conflict culture in particular. Such courses could also help mediators learn how to draw out (elicit) the commonsense knowledge of disputants in order to facilitate the creation of new, culturally appropriate models for handling conflicts constructively.[10]

NOTES

1. Daniel Yankelovich, *The Magic of Dialogue* (New York: Simon and Schuster, 1999).

2. See Diane Dreher, *The Tao of Personal Leadership* (New York: Harper, 1997).

3. Carolyn Schronk-Shenk, *Feelings in Conflict, in Mediation, and Facilitation Training Manual: Foundations and Skills for Constructive Conflict Transformation*. 3d ed. (Akron, Ohio: Mennonite Conciliation Service, 1995).

4. John Paul Lederach, "Understanding Conflict: The Experience, Structure, and Dynamics," in Bob Gross, ed., *Mediating Interpersonal Conflict* (North Manchester, Ind.: Education for Conflict Resolution, 1995).

5. Ibid.

6. Bob Gross, *Mediating Interpersonal Conflict*.

7. Ibid.

8. Karl Slaikeu, *When Push Comes to Shove: A Practical Guide to Mediating Disputes* (San Francisco: Jossey-Bass Publishers, 1996).

9. Raymond Cohen, *Negotiating Across Cultures: International Communication in an Interdependent World* (Washington, D.C.: U.S. Institute of Peace, 1997).

10. Kevin Avruch, *Culture and Conflict Resolution* (Washington, D.C.: United States Institute of Peace Press, 1998); and John Paul Lederach, "The Elicitive/Prescriptive Spectrum," in Jim Stutzman and Carolyn Shrok-Shenh, eds., *MCS Mediation Training Manual* (Akron, Ohio: Mennonite Conciliation Service, 1998).

Breaking the Ice

Pat Patfoort

To be effective in the field, workers need first and foremost to be accepted by the people they work with and, then, to make these various people accept the presence of each other. These tasks require effective communication skills built on open-mindedness, trust, flexibility, and inner strength.

OPEN-MINDEDNESS

A field-worker's work environment can vary to a great extent from situation to situation. Physical conditions (e.g., housing, means of transport, food, climate, hygiene) and psychological conditions (e.g., culture and cultural practices, habits, relational structures, leisure concepts) vary from one society to another. To cope effectively with these widely varying conditions, the following guidelines might be of use:

1. Field-workers should not use their own cultural values as a standard measure. Field-workers need to be cautious not to judge every situation on the basis of the norms and rules of their own cultural values. The reverse would imply a field-worker considering a foreign culture less important than his own.

2. Give an empty space to a new cultural environment. Field-workers should be prepared psychologically well in advance before leaving home. This means trying to know as much as possible about the society he or she is going to work in, such as the history of the country, its geography, and its customs. This may be done by reading articles and books on the country and by meeting with and talking to others who have lived or worked in that specific society. A field-worker can better prepare her-/himself for the unknown if they understand that they will be confronted with situations they either would not have expected or could not have imagined.

3. Positive thinking is important. The conditions faced in the field are often difficult, such as lack of enough water to take a bath and lack of toilet paper for hygienic purposes. It is helpful, therefore, to think positively to be able to deal with these hardships. Remember that the people in a particular society have lived through these hardships all their lives and that they

have adapted to it, while you as a field-worker are there for only a short while.

4. Refrain from judging, but show interest. *Patience* is the key word here. Often, things may seem to take much longer to move toward the desired direction. Field-workers should not judge the people they work with as "lazy," "ineffective," or "incompetent" just because things are moving slower than in their own society. To work effectively and integrate in a host society, one must adapt to its rhythm of life and appreciate the advantage of not being rushed. Field-workers should avoid considering themselves as being superior to, or more developed than, the people they work with. At least, they should show some interest in the lifestyle of the people in their host society: participate in their social, traditional, and cultural activities, eat their food and drinks, read their literature, listen to their music, and avoid criticizing them. This not only enriches the understanding and knowledge of the people, but it also makes it easier to fit in, be accepted, and therefore work more effectively.

TRUST

Trust and acceptance are the most important aspects needed *before* beginning to work as a field-worker. Involving the local people and the society as a whole from the beginning of the project helps boost and build trust. Field-workers should not only strive to gain acceptance, they should also help the people trust them to work and live in their society.

Impartiality is an essential and fundamental basis for building trust. It is, however, not easy to realize and certainly not in an apparent situation of offender against victim. It is vital that all the involved parties feel fully respected as equal human beings and that one group does not receive more attention than another. In order to build trust, the start of a mediating process could involve holding preliminary separate dialogue sessions with the different groups to give each group a chance to express themselves and to be listened to in a free and unbiased environment.

It is important to have *a clear working code highlighting the basic principles, objectives, and methods* that will be used to achieve the desired goals. Specific written materials given beforehand help clarify the aims of the work sessions.

Sincerity builds and gives trust in return. Sincerity doesn't necessarily mean saying everything one thinks. It implies that one thinks and feels what one says.

When beginning a presentation on violence and nonviolence in my workshops, I usually include personal examples and experiences. Particularly when I work on interethnic conflicts, I tell about my own personal experience in my childhood. I was brought up in a small French-speaking community that lived among the Flemish majority in Flanders. As a teenager I became more aware of the subtle patterns of domination, humiliation, and pushing around of one community by the other. When I tell such personal stories, I am naturally quite emotional. This helps people believe in my sincerity and my commitment.

Expressing one's feelings nonverbally is an important element of communication. When people narrate their experiences (individually or in a group) to me, I often feel and show much empathy. My eyes mist, I do not and cannot hide my emotions. A profound closeness is build between us in this way. There are many more ways of communicating other than verbal communication, which are often perceived as deeper, more intensive, and more reliable. Sharing feelings through laughing, listening to music, dancing, eating and drinking, and playing games are deep ways of communicating with one another.

FLEXIBILITY

The more open a field-worker is to a host society, its culture, and its people, the more he or she will be able to understand and accept particular situations, and even look beyond these. However, there will be moments when things won't go as intended or as planned. Some things that seem obvious to us, may not be to other people, such as expecting participants to be present throughout a workshop and not just visit for a short while. Flexibility, therefore, means being patient, open to criticism, and creative.

Patience: In every unexpected situation, field-workers have to remain kind and patient because sometimes people do things unintentionally or unconsciously; often people are ready to put things right once they realize their "mistakes." But sometimes, of course, they simply don't know how.

Openness to criticism: People in a group often have needs that one may not know about or easily perceive. For a field-worker, it is important to create a favorable atmosphere to make it possible for the people they are working with to express their needs easily and freely without feeling hindered.

At the beginning of a workshop I always allow some time for people to get to know each other better. I organize some exercises/games to help them learn and remember each other's names, careers, interests, and jobs easily.

I worked with a Rwandese group once, and after having allowed some time for this acquaintance, I started with a theoretical presentation, highly spirited as usual. After going on for about fifteen minutes, someone suddenly interrupted me, expressing his need to first get to know the members of the group better before starting the presentation. My enthusiasm was abruptly broken, but I quickly relaxed, opening myself to the need of this person. I also checked if more people in the group had the same need, and we therefore had to continue with the acquaintance for a while longer before starting the theory again.

During the evaluation session at the end of the workshop, the person who had interrupted me pointed out that he had very much appreciated my openness and flexibility, and felt that I had practically proved the theory that I taught.

Creativity: Every time a field-worker is confronted with a new situation, he or she should consider all the elements of the new situation as well as the elements of his or her own culture in order to come up with a solution for the new situation.

INNER STRENGTH

Field-workers need a lot of inner strength and self-confidence. The people a field-worker meets in the field often feel powerless and helpless; they also may expect quite a lot. The field-worker needs to have a strong will, to be able to persevere even when things seem hopeless and people are skeptical.

When I worked in Kosovo in 1997, there was an Albanian in the workshop who was very skeptical from the first day. After I had explained my views on violence and nonviolence and on constructive conflict management, he replied that all this was very nice theoretically but that he could not do anything with it in daily life. It surely wasn't the first time that I heard such comments. Still, it always requires strength, self-confidence, and positive thinking to remain committed. I didn't begin to argue with him. I just asked him if he could wait for a few days to have a discussion about this and to give the whole workshop with its exercises a try. If afterward he still had the same feelings, I told him I was ready to discuss it then. I still remember the last day when he stood up to say how much the workshop had changed him and his way of thinking. "I became a new man," he said.

Of course the more I have experiences of people being skeptical at the beginning of a session and who grow so much just after a few days, the easier it is for me to have confidence in myself.

Field-workers also need a lot of strength to develop most of the abilities mentioned above, including openness, positive thinking, impartiality, nonjudgmental behavior, sincerity, patience, and openness to criticism. To enable one's inner strength to grow, here are some important factors to consider:

Self-consciousness: One should search his or her inner self and grow in understanding and acceptance of oneself. This can be done through a variety of ways, including reflecting, writing, listening, meditation, and being open to feedback from others. It is particularly important to be as conscious as possible of one's emotions, like irritation, powerlessness, pain, and fear.

Processing one's emotions: One need not suppress one's emotions but "process" them. If one feels like crying or expressing emotions in any other way (talking, writing, moving, singing), one should do exactly that. Look for ways and create favorable circumstances to do this harmlessly. A very effective tool here is having a support group, in which one can feel safe, listened to, and unconditionally accepted, despite one's shortcomings.

Self-affirmation: One needs to feel as self-confident as possible, being aware of the good qualities one possesses and having a positive sense of oneself. A support group is a good tool for this, too.

APPENDIX: SUGGESTIONS TO PROMOTE "ICE BREAKING"

- Create an empty space to a new culture.
- Do not use your own culture as a standard measure for other cultures.
- Avoid being judgmental; adapt and appreciate the advantages of what is different.
- Develop and show interest for the different culture and cultural habits.
- When faced with difficult situations, be creative in developing positive thoughts.
- Be cautious of sympathizers of the community you will work with.
- Have clear and specific basic principles and working methods.
- Be impartial and avoid getting too close to certain people; show respect and try to understand *all* people.
- Never accuse or make anyone feel guilty.
- Express and share your emotions whenever possible.
- Have patience in listening to people's emotional experiences.
- When you sense appreciation, ask questions to get a deeper understanding of their stories.
- Show a lot of understanding and concern when people narrate their painful experiences to you.
- Use nonverbal communication (facial expressions, empathy, etc.).

- Make use of informal situations to have people share their personal feelings.
- Never give the feeling to some people that you think they are right and others wrong.
- Be prepared for the unexpected.
- Appreciate people's efforts.
- Be open to criticism and opposing ideas.
- Do not feel demoralized when people do not agree with you.
- Be immensely creative and innovative to come up with solutions.
- Persevere and be energetic, even when things seem hopeless.
- Be conscious and master your emotions.
- Appreciate and be happy with yourself.

SUGGESTED READING

Patfoort, Pat. (1995). *Uprooting Violence, Building Non-violence.* Freeport, Me.: Cobblesmith.

■ 15.3

Rumor Control

Luc Reychler

Rumors tend to be overlooked in the study of violence prevention despite the fact that they can escalate or de-escalate conflicts considerably. Rumors give us a picture of the deeper structure of public opinion. They also provide us with an insight into conflict dynamics. Rumors build animosity and thus serve as a barometer of the tensions within a conflict region. A rumor can be described as a communication process as well as a product; one that is easily started and disseminated but may be difficult to stop; and one that is constructed around unauthenticated information.[1]

Rumors are descriptions, forecasts, or explanations of events that are largely shaped in informal encounters and are seriously entertained by a substantial portion of an interested collective body. Rumors frequently precede short-term outbursts, such as panic, crazes, and riots; they play a part in long-term disturbances such as revolutionary and religious secessions.[2] Rumor-mongers can even use them for deadly purposes. However, not all rumors have bad effects. Wish rumors could, under special conditions, hasten the completion of a desired event. Exemplary was the whirlwind of rumors about the cessation of hostilities on the eve of World War II.

TYPES OF RUMORS

Rumors can be classified according to their impact on the conflict (positive or negative); the extent to which they are planted or have a more spontaneous character; and the type of emotional needs they tend to satisfy: fear, hostility, and wishes.

The *fear or bogey rumor* is essentially derived from fears and anxieties about the future. It can range from a rumor with a dour and pessimistic quality all the way to a panic rumor. A typical example is, "Several thousands bodies including women and children have been found in the forest."

The *hostility rumor,* also called the wedge-driving or the aggression rumor, divides groups and destroys loyalties. Its essential motivation is aggression or hatred. The prelude of genocide in Bosnia is full of hostility rumors.[3] Hostility rumors range from the attribution of negative qualities to another group to the instigation of hate. Two examples of such rumors in the commercial world are the conspiracy and contamination rumors.[4]

Neil Smelser distinguishes four stages in the process leading to a hostile outburst.[5] First, for a period of time before the outbreak there are murmurs of unrest. These murmurs take the form of stories featuring discrimination, insults, or misdeeds ascribed by each group to their opponents. They are hostile and accusatory stories. In the next phase, danger is indicated when rumors assume a threatening form. "Something is going to happen at the market!" Third, often, though not invariably, the spark that ignites the powder keg is itself an inflammatory rumor. These rumors exaggerate an event. "A Muslim woman has been thrown off the bridge by the Serbs." Fourth, during the heat of riot, rumors spread faster and reflect acute fanaticism. Sometimes they are hallucinatory. Tortures, rapes, and murders are recounted in a frenzied manner to justify the violence under way and to speed up the process of vengeance.

The *wish rumor,* also called the pipe dream or peace rumor, expresses the wishes and hopes of those among whom it circulates. A wish rumor can also be referred to as wishful thinking.

RUMOR-MONGERS

To understand conflict dynamics one has to identify the conflict entrepreneurs and the spoilers of the peace process. Also, rumors have people who can make a difference; they can plant rumors and make them more vigorous. Although the motivation for passing on a rumor may be complex, there are a few patterns worth noting.[6]

Exhibitionism is one of the prime motives. The insecure person may often resort to rumor-mongering as a means of heightening his or her personal status among associates. By disseminating rumors the individual conveys the impression that he or she has access to information and knowledge not available to others.

Bestowing a favor. In the case of many rumors, particularly panic rumors, the strong impulse to transmit them arises from the desire to inform others of impending menace or danger.

Reassurance and emotional support. Here the rumor is told primarily for the purpose of sharing one's own anxiety with another. If one is terrified by an alarming rumor and persuades another of its truth, then the very mutuality of fear is a relief.

Aggression. As with most aggression rumors, it is obvious that hostility is the driving motive.

Projection of internal conflicts. It has long been observed that people will treasure any device that will externalize fears, wishes, and hostilities that have been repressed. Passing rumors provides an excellent means for achieving this end. The telling of a rumor can be an act of catharsis.

A THREE-STAGE PROCESS

Rumors tend to follow a roughly three-stage process.[7]

Stage 1: Creation of a story. It may be deliberately spread as a trial balloon, or a person may plant malicious gossip, or it can erupt spontaneously.

Stage 2: Diffusion. Once interests have focused attention on the issue, and rumors have spontaneously erupted or been methodologically planted, the report should begin to travel. Frequently rumors will be passed from person to person in the hope of acquiring a credible confirmation or denial. In this phase, the story will also become distorted. It concerns especially three types of distortion: leveling, sharpening, and assimilation. *Leveling* refers to the elimination of some details. As a rumor travels it tends to become shorter, more concise, more easily grasped and told. *Sharpening* is defined as the selective perception, retention, and reporting of a limited number of details from a larger context. The whole rumor becomes structured around one or more details. In *assimilation* the story is tuned into the habits, interests, and sentiments of the listeners. This gives the rumor a powerful, attractive force. The intensity of rumors is influenced by the importance of the issue, the ambiguity of the situation, and the critical sense of the recipients. These ingredients have been condensed in a rumor formula: Rumer = Importance x Ambiguity x 1/Critical Sense.[8]

Stage 3: Ending. This is the terminal stage in the rumor process. Some stories die a natural death. People can grow weary of an issue. New events may refocus attention. Efforts can be undertaken to deny the story and to convince people that the story is false and not to pass it on. Rumor-control units could be established to provide anti-rumor services, such as monitoring, evaluation, and communication of the truth.

RUMOR CONTROL

The control of rumors is not easy. Where possible, one should opt for prevention. As the conflict grows, informal communication modes supplement and may even replace formal media. This results from an increased demand for information by more people who are alerted and involved.[9] Rumor, slander, innuendo, and inaccurate data tend to aggravate the conflict. The sense of threat increases between the parties as their communication channel deteriorates and as they become more secretive. What are the intentions of the other party? The worst is imagined. Information that contradicts threatening images is filtered out. In handling of conflicts, Mohandas Gandhi paid a great deal of attention to countering the distortion of information. His campaign techniques and tactics were openly discussed. Steps in the campaign are made known to opponents beforehand. He used the mass media to acquaint everyone with movement plans. Misinformation and secrecy were eliminated. This helped to reduce perceived threats among the opponents and lessened public fear and ignorance.[10]

When prevention has failed, there are different ways of responding to rumors. Each of these options, listed by F. Koenig, has strengths and weaknesses.[11]

Do nothing. The first option is to ignore the rumor and hope that it will fade away. This prudent or cautious response is a favorite among public relations people in the business world, among whom it is almost a tradition to feel that anti-rumor campaigns are dangerous and should be avoided except as a last resort. One of the reasons for choosing not to do anything is the possibility that an anti-rumor campaign will call attention to the rumor itself. There is the risk that a media rebuttal campaign gives the story a wider audience. There is also the risk of the "convergent rumor process," where calling attention to one rumor can make the company susceptible to other rumors.

Do something—but discreetly. The second approach deals with rumors obliquely. It may be that one recognizes the widespread threat of a rumor and wants to do something about it, but does not want to talk about it specifically as a rumor problem. The negative content of the rumor is never mentioned. This approach involves, for the most part, a public relations campaign focused on the opposite side of the content of the rumor message. This approach is a compromise in which it can be said that one is doing something about the rumor without being committed to going all-out against it. Another technique is to threaten or actually bring lawsuits against rumor perpetrators. This could convince the public that one means business against this "outrage."

Do something all-out. This strategy confronts the rumor directly by going to the public with a refutation, using all the media resources available. The offense can be directed against the source, the content, or the recipient of the rumor. The source of the rumor and/or the rumor itself can be discredited. When a rumor hurts, one should treat the rumor as a fire, put it out, and not waste time. One's single most important concern is to end the rumor forcefully, as completely and as soon as possible. Another action that could reduce the virility of rumors is the dissemination of public information about the nature of the rumors. People who understand the dynamics and motivations of the rumor process are less likely to become involved in irresponsible and destructive hearsay and more likely to develop a critical mindset toward rumors.

In several rumor-prone environments systematic efforts have been undertaken to prevent or cope with rumors. They may involve the engagement of a communication manager or even creation of a rumor-control center. Rumor-control centers and similar anti-rumor services have, for example, operated in Northern Ireland and England to stem social unrest intensified by rumor-mongering. In the pioneering Rumor Clinic, inspired by Gorden Allport in Boston shortly after the outbreak of World War II, more than fifty volunteer rumor wardens were located throughout the community. This team was composed of college professors, businessmen, and media people. Their function was to monitor and evaluate rumors and gather and disseminate accurate information.

In rumor control, four steps can be distinguished: (1) an alert procedure for monitoring rumors systematically, (2) an assessment of the possible or real impact of the rumors on the conflict process, (3) an objective evaluation of the story, and (4) the construction of an appropriate strategy to end the rumor effectively.

Because rumors entail conflict management, they are of importance to students and practitioners dealing with peacebuilding. Far from being pathological, rumors are an integral part of conflict transformation, an important aspect of the continuing efforts to cope with the ups and downs of life.[12]

NOTES

1. Ralph Rosnow, "On Rumor," *Journal of Communication* 24 (1974): 26–38.

2. Neil Smelser, *Theory of Collective Behavior* (New York: Free Press, 1962).

3. Robert Knapp, "A Psychology of Rumor," *Public Opinion Quarterly* 8 (1944): 23–37.

4. Fredrick Koenig, *Rumor in the Marketplace: The Social Psychology of Commercial Hearsay* (Dover, Mass.: Auburn Publishing Company, 1985).

5. Smelser, *Theory of Collective Behavior.*

6. See Knapp's chapter in, *Rumor in the Marketplace: The Social Psychology of Commercial Hearsay* (Dover, Mass.: Auburn Publishing Company, 1985), 34–35.

7. See Rosnow, "On Rumor."

8. A. M. J. Chorus, *Grondslagen der sociale psychologie* (Leiden, 1953), 103.

9. James Coleman, *Community Conflict* (New York: Free Press, 1957).

10. Paul Wehr, *Conflict Regulation* (Boulder, Colo.: Westview Press, 1979).

11. Koenig, *Rumor in the Marketplace.*

12. T. Shibutani, *Improvised News: A Sociological Study of Rumor* (New York: Bobbs Merrill, 1966), 580.

Dealing with Stereotypes

Clem McCartney

One of the difficulties facing third parties who try to help those in conflict is that they often find it hard to understand why the conflicting parties cannot adopt an obvious solution or way out of the problem. This article looks at this phenomenon and, in particular, the part played by stereotypes in lowering expectations of a satisfactory outcome to the conflict and justifying resistance to the conflict-resolution process. It describes one example of how participants in the Georgian/Abkhazian conflict were helped to understand these processes and the importance of taking them into account if the parties were to engage meaningfully in effective conflict resolution.

THE RISKS IN DEALING WITH CONFLICT

To an outsider it seems so clear that there are better, simpler alternatives than continued conflict. It is assumed that conflicting parties have more room to maneuver and should be able to take initiatives that would help. Therefore, their unwillingness to move and even to enter into negotiations can be interpreted as a sign of intransigence and used as a confirmation that they have no interest or intention in finding a way out of the conflict.

It is important to understand the way opposing parties see the conflict and why they stay in the conflict rather than take up solutions that may seem obvious to others. We often say "there is a solution to every problem," but we can turn that expression around in relation to people in conflict for whom, as was once said, "there is a problem to every solution."

Understanding the difficulties of the conflicting parties is not the same as accepting their interpretation of the conflict. But looking at current perceptions of the situation, or "where people are at," is the most viable starting point for dealing with the problem. It is no help for a third party to say what each side should do and what solution they should accept, and it is even less helpful for one party to tell their opponents what they should do.

It is true that sometimes in mediation under duress the third party may be strong enough or persuasive enough to convince one or all parties to accept a proposed solution. And such an achievement may in some instances provide a breathing space in an inflamed conflict for longer-term progress to be made. But in most cases third parties do not have that kind of leverage, and even when they do, a settlement based on coercion often leaves the existing grievances and resentments unresolved and ready to break out again when circumstances change.

Nongovernmental organizations (NGOs), with little coercive power, often adopt an alternative approach and try to avoid the skepticism and distrust that exist and accentuate the positive potential of conflict resolution. They hope that by the force of argument they can negate the resistance and reservations the parties have about moving away from their uncompromising and intransigent stances. Again such an approach may work for a time, and the parties may even agree to participate in a process of conflict resolution that is proposed by the third party. But invariably in these circumstances, there seems to be little meaningful acceptance of alternatives to confrontation, and there may be little tangible change as a result of the efforts of the third party. Indeed on some occasions one or more parties may agree to take part in a proposed process of dialogue with opponents only to subvert the process by withdrawing at a late stage, or sending lower-ranking representatives, or hedging their participation with a variety of reservations.

Consequently, it is generally recognized that it is better that the parties are able to approach negotiations in a positive manner having acknowledged and come to terms with their reservations about the risks of dealing with their opponents. And it is important for third parties who intend to help with negotiations to understand the kind of reservations that exist and appreciate why many groups in conflict find it a safer option to maintain the conflict rather than try to resolve it. One aspect that all the parties, including third parties, need to consider is the motivating forces influencing each side and then test how helpful (or unhelpful) they actually are. If these considerations are explained and understood, then all the parties can feel more positive about constructing an inclusive way forward.

STEREOTYPING AS A MECHANISM IN MAINTAINING CONFLICT

In a seminar involving Abkhazian people, ideas were explored on the way stereotypes are used in both maintaining conflict relationships and discouraging attempts at conflict resolution. Any communities living in close proximity will understand themselves through their relations with each other, and so their customary images or stereotypes of themselves and of the other helps to explain why relationships are the way they are. For example, if one group is more dominant or it is feared that they could be more dominant, the communities will look for some explanation that gives a positive image of one's own group and justifies their standing in society. The more successful group can explain their achievements as the result of their industry and willingness to take initiatives and their more modern and sophisticated outlook, while they will describe the less successful group as lazy and bound by tradition. However, the less successful group will emphasize their own qualities in other ways and explain the success of the other group as being due to aggression or individualist disregard for others or because they had external help or patrons. In this particular situation, the Abkhaz believed that the Georgians were advantaged by the power of Stalin, a Georgian.

Stereotypes are, in effect, a source of strength. They provide ways of dealing with underlying concerns: the sense of superiority and inferiority in relation to others or the need to keep distance or reach greater closeness to the other community. Stereotypes express fears, hopes, and needs. A community has preoccupations, and one way in which they are expressed is through stereotypes. This connects naturally into other social constructs such as identity and myths of origin, all of which contribute to an emphasis on difference.

These preoccupations and their expression become the reality, and often that reality maintains the conflict situation. In turn, the sense of a conflictual relationship reinforces the importance and correctness of the initial preoccupations and is used to explain events. Any information that cuts across the assumptions and stereotypes is ignored, and the historical experience is used to support them. The stereotypes of each society often mirror those of the other and give further justification for keeping them.

It is, in general, much easier to maintain our preconceptions than allow them to be challenged. If one feels psychologically comfortable with the situation, there is little incentive to want to change it even if it has uncomfortable consequences in a material sense. If one starts a process of change, it therefore exposes one to the possibility that other people may also have truth on their side that will have to be acknowledged. It might even give an enemy the possibility to attack. Once an enemy is created through processes like stereotyping, it is difficult to abandon that image. Thinking becomes very self-limiting.

In the Georgian/Abkhazian seminar, a five-stage circular process was posited using the examples given during the discussion: (1) the group's perception of its situation was explored; (2) policies and strategies were adopted to deal with the perceived reality; (3) ideological underpinning was applied to explain the perceived reality; (4) historical and value references were used to justify the group's perceptions; and (5) current events were interpreted in light of perceptions, which reinforce the existing social construction of reality.

On the basis of this analysis, it is fairly straightforward to recognize how each party may view the impact of contact differently and how they need to build a justification for their stance in relation to contact. Their stance can range along a continuum from total intransigence to a desire for unconditional friendly contact. It is evident that the stance adopted by a party will be a direct reflection of the group's assessment of its situation and how to improve it. Intransigence is often a response to the fear of assimilation. A willingness to have open contact is also often instrumental in the hope that issues can be submerged and the new relationships will advance the interests of that party. Sometimes in a conflict the establishment of friendly relations with the other side is already a part of the victory. While there is a denial of the opponent (they are known well enough and there is no need to know more) there is at the same time curiosity and an impulse to know more about the others, whether they are changing and how genuine these changes are.

Once there is an awareness that assumptions and stances are functional and that stereotypes of one's own group and others are functional (in that they justify our positions), then it becomes more evident that it cannot be assumed that parties in conflict are looking for a settlement and are willing to change in order to get it. Changes will occur if the perceptions of the situation change, and perceptions of one's needs in the situation change. Where does that change come from?

It may be helpful to look at how these issues were considered and used in a particular seminar involving people from a conflict situation. But first it may be necessary to give a little background on the situation.

THE GEORGIAN/ABKHAZIAN SITUATION

The context for the seminar was the conflict related to Abkhazia. The Abkhaz people live on the Black Sea to the south of the Caucasus. Although they are on the southern side of the Caucasus, they feel that they share much with the people of the north Caucasus culturally, ethnically, and religiously, having a shared Islamic tradition. Nonetheless, in the former Union of Soviet Socialist Republics, Abkhazia was an autonomous Soviet republic within the Soviet Socialist Republic of Georgia; during this period many Georgians settled in Abkhazia, so that the Abkhaz became a very small minority within the republic—of the total Georgian population of 4 million, only 100,000 were Abkhazians.

With the breakup of the Soviet Union, Abkhazia saw the opportunity of separation from Georgia, and as a result of a Georgian action in 1992, Abkhazia responded with force. At first the Abkhazian forces were weak and much territory was lost, but with the help of Russia, the Abkhazians drove out the Georgian forces and declared their independence in 1993.

Since then, there has been something of a stalemate. Abkhazia's independence has not been recognized, and in fact, it has been placed under an embargo that has created social and economic hardship and made it very difficult to create a sense of normality. However, Georgia has been unable to exercise authority over the territory. There are also outstanding issues especially in relation to displaced people, mostly Georgians, who are currently living in Georgia. The situation has had a good deal of international attention and third-party interventions, but the Abkhazians have been reluctant to enter into negotiations, and the Georgians have been reluctant to give credibility to the Abkhaz administration and its aspirations by treating them as an equal party to Georgia, a sovereign state.

Taking an active interest in the situation have been the Confederation of Independent States (CIS) (mainly the Russian Federation), the UN, and the Organization for Cooperation and Security in Europe. The CIS and UN have provided a joint peacekeeping force. NGOs and academic institutions have also been accepted and have organized various meetings and conferences to explore the issues.

THE GEORGIAN/ABKHAZIAN SEMINAR

Context

The seminar was one of a series organized by an NGO active in the area to develop links and understanding between the Abkhaz and Georgians with a view to building confidence in the possibility of a negotiated settlement. This meeting had a similar format to the previous meetings they had organized.

Aims and Purpose

This seminar had two parallel foci. It had been intended to have a more reflective session at the midpoint of the program, which overall had a more action orientation in developing opportunities for cooperation. It had originally been thought that it would be helpful to look at the nature and impact of stereotypes, as they played a part in maintaining the conflict. It was felt that the Georgian and Abkhaz societies have well-developed stereotypes of each other that greatly influenced the behavior of the two communities, and it was thought that it would be useful to make these explicit and examine them.

It also seemed an apt time to look at the obstacles and difficulties the two parties experienced in entering into negotiations. There was a good deal of expectation that both sides should sit down and reach a solution to the conflict. At the same time it was clear that the parties were reluctant to take such a step, fully recognizing the dangers and risks involved. However, neither side seemed to be able to appreciate the difficulties that faced the other side, and some intermediaries seemed unaware of the reasons for the caution.

As we have noted, in these circumstances parties in the conflict generally tend to build up their arguments against engaging with their opponents and negotiating with them. It therefore seemed important to spend some time looking at and understanding these patterns. Because one aspect of this process is building up and maintaining stereotypes, by looking at stereotypes as originally envisaged, the broader issues of wariness and caution could also be tackled. A seminar on this theme would allow one intermediary to acknowledge their awareness of these concerns and, more important, it made it possible for people from both communities to talk to each other about them.

Participants

The number of participants was small—four from Georgia and four from Abkhazia—because it seemed that small numbers would allow for more direct and reflective communication, and this turned out to be the case. As has already been touched on, there was no intention that the participants would reach any agreement on future action, so it was not important that the participants should be representatives and could speak directly on behalf of their communities. Their important attributes were that they were typical of the wider population and had sufficient status and authority to be able to introduce into their society the thinking that was exposed during the seminar.

The individual participants had multiple roles in their societies, and between them they represented people active in politics and government, the NGO sector, journalists, academia, and the displaced, and they were mixed in age and gender. Almost all of them had been involved in previous meetings.

Process and Working Method

To achieve the aims of the seminar, it was important to create and sustain a working method that would encourage open exploratory interaction and achieve a greater awareness of the perspectives and concerns of each other. It is perhaps difficult to envisage the process that can reach this level of exchange and understanding when we are dealing with relations between identity groups and other large communities in conflict, whereas it is easier to identify with the kind of interpersonal communication that would be appropriate to individuals in dispute. For example, in the latter situation we can think of the technique of giving "I messages," which is a means of expressing the speaker's own feelings about a situation. They are generally easier to listen to and accept than statements about what others are doing wrong and what they should do differently.

We can also think of the technique of active listening through which the listener tries to hear not only the words but reaches for the feelings and meaning behind the words and tries to convey back an understanding of what they have heard before commenting or disagreeing with it. We know how much more productive communication can be if we can avoid judging the attitudes and actions of others. We also know that this does not mean we condone or approve of their actions but that we can use these communication techniques to make these distinctions clear.

These approaches are helpful in any communication. Yet to achieve meaningful dialogue between representatives of larger entities, it is often more effective to focus not on how the conflicting parties could cooperate with each other but rather to assist them in appreciating and acknowledging the difficulties they each had in entering into dialogue and working toward an agreed solution.

Participants did not bring prepared presentations into the seminar but explored issues raised by the facilitator and developed and shared ideas and speculations as they arose. The small numbers of people present also meant that communication could be kept direct and informal. It was seldom necessary to break into smaller groups, or even into nationality or ethnically homogeneous groups. Because it was made clear that the purpose of the meeting was joint exploration of the problems of engaging with opponents and that there was no intention to draw up a plan for future action. it was easier to talk frankly and speculatively in the manner of a problem-solving workshop.

The seminar operated on two levels. One was direct dialogue between the parties to the conflict when participants articulated the positions and explained the perceptions held on each side; the other was an attempt to step back and, in a more detached way, to reflect and analyze the underlying processes and their implications, and generalize from the particular examples. This requires considerable self-discipline because when one is involved in the argument it is difficult to step back and reflect on what is happening and its significance.

The way discussion was structured was also designed to assist in a more measured dialogue and a fuller understanding of the underlying processes through which conflict is maintained. The facilitator's function was not only to raise issues and move the analysis forward through a series of phases but also at regular intervals to systematize the discussion and provide conceptual frameworks that participants could reject or use to advance the analysis.

For each topic participants first described current thinking and assumptions in their communities and then gave their reactions and those of their community to the stances and attitudes in the other community. They were then asked to consider and try to explain the reasons for these views and positions, and in a joint discussion they tried to draw out their significance and meaning for a community involved in conflict. In effect, the participants were carrying out a process of deconstruction on the views and statements of the parties in order to understand what they indicated about their basic concerns. Recurring questions were: Why do you/the other side think like this? What motivates your/their thinking? What role does this opinion play in maintaining your/their community?

As has already been noted, consideration of the operation of stereotyping in Georgia and Abkhazia was the way into the wider issues and obstacles to an inclusive negotiation process. The discussion was planned and developed through five stages:

1. Participants described and explained their stereotypes of themselves and others.
2. The meanings of their stereotypes were discussed.
3. Participants examined the consequences of the stances of each group toward their opponents and their impact on the possibility of finding an agreed settlement.
4. Both the desirability and feasibility of changing those stances were explored.
5. Steps were formulated to initiate changes in stances.

Concurrently, the discussion also operated at four levels of analysis that can be characterized as follows: description; reactions; implications; and significance, meaning, and purpose.

The Application of the Process: The Outcomes of a Seminar

To help to flesh out the process of communication and analysis, the rest of this article describes some of the content and conclusions of the specific discussion.

To open communication, each group was asked to present a picture of the stereotypes they held, both about themselves and their opponents. It was stressed that they needed not only to think of stereotypes about the other but the stereotypes each community had of themselves. The stereotypes were expressed fairly readily perhaps because, from the beginning of the discussion, it was stressed and accepted that such attitudes do exist in every community.

Once the images had been presented, each group was then invited to comment, not so much to confirm or deny them but to talk about the impact they had. In particular, they were asked to indicate which were seen as positive and which were seen as negative and to indicate which three aspects of the picture were most hurtful.

There was, in fact, a kind of a pattern to the images, with the negative image perceived by one side having a counterbalancing positive aspect on the other, and these images together captured something of the actual nature of relations between the two groups. For example, both groups focused on some similar aspects of the Abkhaz traditions. But the Georgians were more aware of the image of a traditional warrior with his knife, while the Abkhaz themselves were more inclined to take pride in their lineage and roots in the area. So the very features that were a key element of self-image can appear a criticism in the image held by others.

Next, the discussion turned to the question of the importance of the stereotypes and the function they have for those who hold and promote them. Fear is often an element that encourages a negative stereotype of the other. In the example just given, it was recognized that the image of the warrior with a knife had the effect in Georgia of justifying the need for vigilance. Equally they can be a way to deal with threats. For the Abkhaz the recognition of their roots and rights through their ancestors was a way of protecting them from the fear of being displaced or assimilated by Georgians.

In the current situation, the Abkhaz are concerned that they will be assimilated into the more dominant Georgian state and so are cautious about negotiations and prefer to retain some social distance, while Georgians hope that the development of good relations will diminish the Abkhaz demand for independence and that the old status quo could more or less return. Not surprisingly, as in many conflicts, this means one side wants to agree to a settlement and then they will be willing to work at improving relationships, while the other is keen on improving relationships and then feels that a settlement will be easier to achieve.

Having identified in each society the dominant ethos about conflict and the other community, and understanding its function for the society, it was possible to pursue the issue further and try to tease out how this ethos arose and was maintained and, consequently, how it might change. The participants explored the role of intellectuals and the media in generating perceptions and myths but also acknowledged that these formulations of ideas were only effective when they responded to something in the feelings and concerns of the wider community and provided what the society wants to hear.

There is often a climate in society that is crystallized by certain events, articles, or books. It is actually easier to connect to the more negative feelings that exist because the population has more need to justify or explain their concerns and the means to overcome them than they need to understand their more positive feelings.

In a conflict, a key issue is the dynamics between the leaders and the masses, and stereotypes are a factor in this relationship. The leaders may know that popular perceptions, assumptions, and stereotypes are often shallow, ungrounded, and unsubstantiated. They know the situation and cannot afford the luxury of stereotypes. Nor can they ignore popular assumptions, and they will use them to justify their stances. There is sometimes an illusion that the leader can act completely independently to pursue war or agree to a peace settlement, but in effect even authoritarian regimes have to operate to a greater or lesser extent within the views and sentiments of the general public.

Responding to Stereotypes and Suspicions

It was apparent that the most effective way forward was for existing concerns to be dealt with and for opportunities and prospects to be clarified so that the risks could be assessed, as was happening in the seminar. However, it is generally the case in ongoing conflict situations that concerns are expressed but not dealt with and that opportunities are suppressed because they are too dangerous. Therefore, solutions can seldom be found by an effort of will by either or both parties or by a third party, and the third party should not assume the conflicting parties can make that effort of will. We need to understand the underlying motivations and processes.

Awareness of these processes and dynamics in their conflict does not resolve the problems or make any party change its stance. In the seminar when the parties were asked what would make a difference and help the other side to overcome its resistance and suspicion and build up its confidence in the possibility of working with their opponents, they still proposed the same preconditions and demands that have been made in the past and to which it has proved difficult to respond (such as the ending of the embargo). An important discussion followed, but it did not address the type of issues raised in the seminar about how the concerns and interests of the other side could be acknowledged and incorporated into future negotiations. Nonetheless, there was a greater realization that the stance of opponents was quite reasonable from their perspective and was not likely to change until they themselves saw a reason to change.

It was difficult for some of the participants to cope with the fact that participants from the other side presented themselves as opponents, especially if their own image of themselves was that they were naturally very peaceful and conciliatory. They saw the value in good personal relations and found it difficult to accept that others might see things differently. However, ultimately they all recognized that without accepting these constraints a resolution of the situation would be even harder to find.

■ 15.5

Overcoming Sentimental Walls: Antisectarianism in Northern Ireland

Ken Logue

Antisectarianism is community relations in action—a positive, life-affirming concept that promotes the acceptance of diversity in our divided society. Based on the experience of working in community relations and community development over the past fifteen years, this article examines the meaning of antisectarianism—and of sectarianism and nonsectarianism—in the context of Northern Ireland.

Sectarian attitudes, behavior, and structures have been a feature of Northern Ireland life, and in cultures and societies far from Northern Ireland, for a considerable time. Few, if any, parts of Northern Ireland life and society escape from the sectarian attitudes and behavior that exist in that society. Many of those involved in business and public life, however, seek to distance themselves and their organizations from these attitudes and behavior. This article examines whether and how far nonsectarian attitudes and behavior can be taken toward something we describe as *antisectarian*.

SECTARIANISM AND ANTISECTARIANISM

The definition of what we mean by *antisectarianism* depends on what we mean by *sectarianism*. It is not fully possible to entrap the nuances of feelings, passions, intellectual niceties, or gut reactions conjured up by a discussion of sectarianism. It is not just the bigotry and prejudice, the dehumanized, emotionless, ruthless cynicism that leads to sectarian murder. It is also the ghost at the feast of much polite society in Northern Ireland. While it can and often is the reality of life in working-class housing estates, it is equally present in the leafy and apparently more "civilized" suburbs. It is ingrained into the fabric of society. But what is it?

It is not possible to examine the roots of sectarianism in any detail here. However, the dispute in Northern Ireland is not at heart religious. It is rather about allegiances: one community to "Britain" and "Britishness" and the other to "Ireland" and "Irishness." Clearly religion is a major part of the identity of the two communities, but it is much more important as a label.[1] It is a major apparent difference between the two communities and the difference that conveniently labels each one. Other commonly recognized labels include where you live, what your name is, what sports you are interested in, and what school you went to. People only "recognize" these labels because of the social significance that is already placed on assumed or real differences. Attaching importance to these labels already constitutes a form of sectarianism.

Sectarianism thus depends, in part, on a popular culture that invokes religion as a way of distinguishing between the two communities. For those of a Unionist/Loyalist persuasion or belief, sectarianism is generally something to do with the personal—one individual Protestant discriminating in practice or in their attitude against individual Catholics. For those of a more Nationalist/Republican turn of mind, sectarianism is an integral part of state power—in Northern Ireland a Protestant state actively and inevitably discriminating on a sectarian basis against those whose loyalty is suspect. The truth is perhaps more complicated than that.

Definitions

Sectarianism in the context of Northern Ireland is discrimination arising from political or religious prejudice leading to relationships of distrust between the two major politico-religious communities. Sectarianism is not just a matter of economic, social, or political consideration; nor is it simply a question of personal attitude or behavior. It is a historical and cultural phenomenon arising out of religious and political differences and perpetuated by groups and self-interests.

Nonsectarianism is a neutral position recognizing the existence of sectarianism in society. This position does not accept the validity of sectarianism and regards it as wrong and destructive. Nonsectarianism does not, however, imply the need to take any active steps to reduce or challenge sectarianism. Many organizations that espouse a nonsectarian position operate across the politico-religious divide and may actively encourage and participate in cross-community work and discriminate against no one. They do not, however, actively take steps to examine issues of sectarianism and balance in their organization and practices.

Antisectarianism seeks to challenge those personal and group attitudes, culturally and socially formed, that result in sectarianism. It tries to address the resulting lack of knowledge about the other side, fear of the unknown, sectarian behavior, intolerance of "differences," bigotry, and lack of human respect. Antisectarianism addresses attitudes and practices beyond those already covered by existing antidiscrimination and equal-opportunities legislation and aims to decrease sectarianism at individual, group, and institutional levels. For organizations it refers to those actions, procedures, and programs that are specifically aimed at challenging and countering discriminatory attitudes and practices between communities with different religious or political perspectives.

Levels and Continuums

There is a gradation of meaning and weight attached to notions of nonsectarianism and antisectarianism, with considerable areas of gray in between. It becomes helpful to see this as a continuum:

Sectarian   →   *Nonsectarian*   →   *Antisectarian*

The implications for antisectarianism of the notion of a continuum of sectarianism operating at three distinct but also clearly linked levels is that organizations and individuals wishing to make an impact on sectarianism and adopt an antisectarian position can afford to be flexible and still hope to achieve some of their objectives. There is not a clear distinction between sectarian and antisectarian but a gradual move at varying paces at different levels along a continuum.

Sectarianism is a very complex phenomenon even if its outcomes are too often brutally simple. In order to begin to clarify meanings, it is helpful to look at sectarianism in terms of who is practicing it and what is being practiced. John Brewer's useful analysis of sectarianism is one that most closely analyzes the definition suggested above and takes it a few useful steps further.[2] This unpicks some of the complexities and identifies at least three levels within the idea of sectarianism: personal beliefs, individual and group behavior, and structural. At the first level this refers to the myths and demonology that people believe about the "other side" and about themselves; the second is the level at which people act on these beliefs by harassing and intimidating individuals or small groups from the other community and by discriminating at a personal or individual level against those from the other side. The third level is that of institutionalized, structural discrimination against a community.

Clearly these levels do not exist independently of each other. Institutionalized discrimination is not independent of the personal beliefs of individuals or society, nor is the harassment of a person from the other side entirely divorced from the policies that may have been carried out by state agencies. They are different facets of a whole while retaining their own particular characteristics. These levels can be applied to both nonsectarianism and antisectarianism as well as to sectarianism.

For sectarianism the levels can be seen as:

- *Ideas:* myths about the origins of the other community, demonology, about incidents in relationships between the two communities, and personal beliefs about the practices, aspirations, and ideology of the other side.

- *Behavior:* harassment of individuals and groups at work; intimidation of people from the other side in the community; personal discrimination against individuals for goods or services.
- *Social structure:* social and economic advantage experienced by one community at the expense of the other; institutionalized discrimination for jobs or housing; unequal access to rights and justice.

When we look at nonsectarianism, the levels can be seen as follows:

- *Ideas:* acceptance of cultural diversity and the need for equal treatment; neutrality, as regards the experience of the other side (no bias but open-mindedness toward the experience of the other side).
- *Behavior:* rejection of harassment and intimidation; commitment to equal treatment and opportunity.
- *Social structure:* supporting equal resources for both communities and not discriminating because of culture.

In terms of antisectarianism, the levels referred to would result in the following:

- *Ideas:* depoliticizing cultural beliefs; private/public domains separate; multiculturalism; shared cultures; right to hold contrary beliefs and accord the same to others.
- *Behavior:* nonacceptance and nonconsciousness of differences in personal relationships; challenging the same in others; not acting out discrimination; not using derogatory terms; not stigmatizing.
- *Social structure:* challenging at the official level discriminatory practices and structures and implementing programs to counter these; outlawing and stopping intentional and nonintentional discriminatory practices; overcoming patterns of advantage.

WHAT CAN ORGANIZATIONS DO ABOUT SECTARIANISM?

Antisectarianism needs to permeate through all of society, challenging existing structures. We need to look for sectarianism in ourselves and encourage an open, accepting ethos in our organizations. A model for an organization is to recognize any existing sectarianism within the organization, move to establish a mission statement, and then move on to practical work. This involves both training and awareness raising and attention to such things as recruitment policies.

Awareness

For many organizations the nonsectarian mode is often confused with a more proactive one that actually addresses the sectarian issues in Northern Ireland society. One of the hallmarks of an antisectarian position is that it recognizes that active moves must be made among all of the people involved internally in an organization—staff and management—to raise awareness about sectarian attitudes and practices. The latter are clearly within the remit of the organization, for they are concerned with the way staff deal with the public, with the nature of membership, and the ethos of the direction of the organization.

The kind of work that can be done internally within organizations ranges from information about sectarianism through nonchallenging discussions about the experience of sectarianism in the context of the organization to a more searching personal examination of individual beliefs, attitudes, and practices. Clearly the parameters of such activities, the expectations of the organization, and the support that individuals receive in this process must be carefully agreed upon in advance. If, for instance, it is agreed to explore sectarianism in the context of a nonchallenging discussion, then care must be taken to ensure that the discussion does not inadvertently stray into more personal areas, or that individuals do not expose themselves emotionally in an inappropriate and potentially damaging way. If the latter does occur in spite of care, then confidentiality must be ensured and support guaranteed, even if it means bringing in additional help.

Policy Statement

It is important to look at developing and adopting a policy statement on antisectarianism after working on awareness, because the process of adopting and then implementing a policy should be a collective exercise that can and should flow from the consideration and discussion mentioned above. A policy statement on antisectarianism is important because it commits an organization to a particular path and provides the organization with a benchmark against which to judge its performance in this area. Without such a statement, it is all too easy to slide into unacceptable practices and to take the line of least resistance. This statement should include an overall statement of the organization's commitment to antisectarianism; the expectations that the organization has of its staff, its members, and its board in relation to the antisectarian policy; and an indication of the steps it intends to take to implement the policy.

Openness

The openness of an organization (to people and experiences with diverse origins and backgrounds) is important, and the perception that it is so is both more important and more difficult to achieve. It is also the case that some businesses and branches of public bodies are physically based in one community or another, and their openness (or otherwise) is seen as almost irrelevant because few, if any, from the other side have easy access to it. This applies especially to those organizations that are based in a particular building and/or are established to serve a particular, physically determined, local area. Organizations, then, should consider any centers they use in the community in terms of their openness to both communities.

Having said that, openness, especially in terms of physical resources like buildings, raises other issues. When is the display of flags and emblems sectarian and when is it simply a question of celebrating local or cultural identity? One answer is almost certainly that it is in the eye of the beholder: if I feel threatened by such displays or actively excluded by them from a particular location, then they are sectarian and efforts should be taken by any organization seeking to be antisectarian to remove them or, at least, present them in a way acceptable to me.

The other, potentially contradictory, answer is that it is, in fact, a question of intent. Are the symbols intended to threaten me or make sure I as a member of the other community do not want to be in a particular center? Posing the questions, particularly in the light of the suggestion earlier that sectarianism was based on perceptual cues that themselves indicated a sectarian beholder, points to the levels and layers of sectarianism that our society has to address and peel away.

Promoting Antisectarianism in the Community

What an organization does internally and how it presents itself to the outside world are crucially important steps in reducing sectarianism in our society. Being even more proactively antisectarian and promoting such attitudes and practices in the wider community is more difficult. Not only can it be, at one extreme, life threatening, but it can in less direct ways threaten the credibility of an organization. Community values and fears may be able to absorb some moves toward the promotion of antisectarian attitudes and practices if the credibility of the organization and its staff is high, and if the steps taken do not threaten too much, take people along a particular road too fast, and are sensitive to the prevailing climate.

Any external steps must acknowledge the close relationship between pride, a sense of belonging, and the legitimate espousal of political views, on the one hand, and sectarian attitudes and behavior, on the other. One of the objects of taking an antisectarian stand is to reduce tensions and inter-community strife—not to increase it or import it into a community. Thus, the most appropriate ways of challenging and addressing sectarianism in the community are by example: "This organization doesn't allow sectarian behavior or displays because we want to be open about our beliefs and make contact over common problems (and possibly differences) with people from all communities."

Other methods include public education sessions—workshops, exhibitions, talks—and informal contact with user groups, youth groups, pensioners' clubs, and mother and toddler groups. Methods of this sort can and should be addressed in the course of awareness raising within the organization and in the process of developing a policy statement on antisectarianism. As suggested above, however, organizations must be careful that they do not (by implication or by directive) expose either the staff or management to threats from less well-developed members of the community. Any requirement on organizations, whether imposed or suggested from outside or self-generated, to adopt a proactive antisectarian stance must be measured and stress that appropriate and constructive methods must be employed.

Recruitment

There are broad requirements on organizations of a certain size to conform to fair employment and equal-opportunities legislation. It is assumed that all organizations of such a size will so conform. In the context of an antisectarian policy, organizations are encouraged and may be expected to go further by adopting, where appropriate and when not infringing on the legislation, a policy of affirmative action in recruitment of staff. This may be done by actively encouraging applications from the underrepresented community by advertising in that community or stating that applications from all communities are welcome and that the organization operates an antisectarian policy.

Many businesses operate a policy of employing local people as part of their commitment to increasing local employment. Although this is understandable and laudable, care should be taken that by doing so applications from areas where employment opportunities may be even lower are not excluded. In this context, consideration should also be given to the possibly positive (and antisectarian) effects of employing a "mixed" workforce. Many organizations are involved in funding work in the community. If such funding bodies agree that antisectarian principles are important, how far can they go in asking or demanding a similar commitment from bodies they support?

A Signal of Intent

The importance of the policy statement mentioned above is that it is a signal of intent. There need to be opportunities for all to engage in the process of developing a policy and implementing it. Internally a policy debate on sectarianism and antisectarianism could provide a mandate for change. It is important to recognize the fear: undertaking this kind of work can be scary and dangerous. At the same time, a policy statement can lead to procedures that would need to be followed and give a benchmark for evaluation and review. It should be remembered that the value system of an organization underpins its work. It is equally important to build on the positive before addressing the negative; therefore, diplomacy, tact, and skill are required in addressing any issues concerning antisectarianism.

CONCLUSION

Sectarianism is a widespread and serious problem in Northern Ireland society. It operates across a continuum—it is not just a question of sectarian violence; it consists also of everything from apparently harmless attitudes based on stereotypes about people from the other community, and of discrimination in the workplace and elsewhere, to violence and killing on the streets. It operates at the individual, group, and institutional levels. Nonsectarianism has been the dominant mode in our organized society (voluntary and community groups, businesses, the public sector) and has essentially meant trying not to "import" the tensions in society into the workplace or organization. Although this is an acceptable and in some sense a safe option, it does nothing to promote change or to address very serious problems.

Antisectarianism tries to do that: to address sectarian attitudes and behavior within organizations, among staff, and within the community. Antisectarianism is one end of a continuum that begins with negative sectarian attitudes and behavior leading through more progressive and positive nonsectarian positions to something that challenges sectarianism in ourselves, in our organizations, and in society. Moving to antisectarian positions and practices is not without its problems and it does raise anxieties and concerns. Personal concerns exist about the dangers of challenging antisectarianism in the workplace and in organizations generally as well as in society at large.

POSTSCRIPT

In his book, *The Glass Curtain,* Carlo Gebler examined many aspects of life in the "Troubles." He tells this story, which illustrates how, although we know sectarianism and other ills exist in our society, we often find it hard to pin it down or to recognize it in ourselves. He writes about the "house with the blue door":

"If you believed what you read in the papers," she said "you'd think civil war was raging everywhere in Northern Ireland. But if you live here, and you think of trouble, you think of it as happening in certain towns. And if you live in those certain towns, you think of it as happening in certain districts. And if you live in those certain districts, you think of it as happening on certain housing estates. And if you live on those certain housing estates, you think of it as happening in certain streets. And if you live in those certain streets, you know that the trouble is being caused by the man at the end of the road in the house with the blue door."[3]

It is all too easy to attribute the problem of sectarianism to somewhere safely "elsewhere," behind the blue door. It is, unfortunately, not so easy and sectarianism in all its forms is something we in Northern Ireland—and beyond—must address.

NOTES

1. More accurately a "stereotypical cue." Religion has been described as "a social marker through which conflict is articulated rather than as a source of conflict in its own right. . . . Sectarianism operates whenever religion is invoked to draw boundaries and to represent or reduce patterns of inequality and social conflict" (John Brewer, "The Parallels Between Sectarianism and Racism: The Northern Ireland Experience," in *One Small Step Towards Racial Justice,* report of CCETSW National Steering Group, London, 1991, 101).

2. Brewer, "The Parallels Between Sectarianism and Racism."

3. Carlo Gebler, *The Glass Curtain—Inside an Ulster Community* (London: Hamish Hamilton, 1991), 73.

The Usefulness of Humor

Sue Williams

War and violent conflict, like other extreme situations, often prompt responses that, to outsiders, may seem eccentric and difficult to understand. A classic response is black humor: often cynical, even twisted, it reveals the twistedness of the situation, and in so doing upholds the human capacity to understand and survive even the incomprehensible.

Its significance in field diplomacy is twofold: (1) humor will be part of nearly every conflict and therefore should be understood both as part of the situation and as a revelation about it; and (2) it will be important, in intervening in such a situation, to convey one's ability to understand the multiple levels and nuances of humor in order to be a credible party to the exchange of views and interpretations. Some of the key uses of humor are described below, followed by a brief elucidation of the possible uses in field diplomacy.

HUMOR AS ADAPTATION

A principal function of humor is to facilitate adaptation to difficult situations and to point out the adaptation. A classic form of this involves celebrating what one can still do while recognizing that this, too, may soon become impossible. A story of this type made the rounds of the very small expatriate community of humanitarian workers in Uganda during the civil war there.

> A new recruit to the emergency services proudly defied the prevailing wisdom and drove a colleague home across the city late at night. Both soon returned on foot, the novice shrieking that she had been held up at gunpoint by a soldier who hijacked her Range Rover. Her colleague commented dryly: he was really only waving to ask for a lift, you know, and imagine his astonishment to have the car and all your money thrust at him!

This use of humor will often be especially noticed by outsiders and new arrivals who may not understand it at all and, indeed, may be the butt of the joke. This is simply a sign that they are "normal," they have not yet made these adaptations, and as they do so, they may begin to laugh.

HUMOR AS A LIMIT TO ADAPTATION

There is the old riddle: How do you boil a frog if you have no cover to prevent the frog from jumping out of the pot? Begin with lukewarm water, and heat it up very gradually so that the frog never notices when it is in danger.

Because humans are almost infinitely adaptable, we have a tendency to adapt to changes in circumstances, however dreadful. Humor can be a way to point out, to ourselves and others, that we are accepting the unacceptable and adapting to something that may cost us our lives. Jokes can re-establish the capacity for scandal and indignation as justifiable and even pragmatic responses to untenable circumstances. In so doing, they are a reminder that something better is possible and is, indeed, what one is due.

Jokes can also put things into perspective for us. An example of this: Why did a U.S. court refuse to extradite an IRA man who escaped from prison in Northern Ireland after serving only a small part of his sentence? They knew that life in prison would be intolerable for the poor lad. He'd not be able to get a decaf mocha double espresso latte from one year's end to the next. We may not be normal, but do we really want to be like them?

CHANNELING OTHER EMOTIONS

In many extreme situations, people seem to laugh too much, and inappropriately. This is a reflection of the drastic reduction in the gamut of responses that are pragmatically feasible in the distorted world. Wars are, after all, very dangerous, especially for civilians. Responses that would be more normal, even naive, such as anger or despair, are likely to increase the individual's vulnerability. These emotions are therefore displaced into a form that is more calm, distant, and vigilant, to foster reactions more likely to keep one alive.

TO SOCIALIZE AND HUMANIZE

Humor is, by its nature, a social activity. A joke only becomes a joke when told. Commenting derisively on events tends to draw people together, to emphasize that they are not alone in their exposure, and to make collective action more likely. Jokes are also a way to reassert one's humanity in the face of the inhuman, showing that even if it is not possible to change the situation, humans defy it by understanding and surviving it.

CONVEYING A TRUTH SAFELY

Jokes, and especially cartoons, often make it possible to overcome censorship and intimidation by stating a truth humorously. Because the accusation is not made directly, it need not be proven, and the interpretation implicates the audience as well as the humorist.

A cartoon in Guatemala showed one man in the street saying to another: "You see, we're getting back to normal; even the electrical grid is being repaired." Other man: "You know that's only because the amnesty has been abolished, and generals must be electrocuted with full honors." This double-edged cartoon accuses the generals of capital crimes, including torture using "grids," suggests an appropriate punishment, and at the same time reestablishes the perspective that normal human needs are not the motivation for improvements in society.

SUBVERSION AND VULNERABILITY

Because black humor insists on putting in question what is, it is inherently subversive and threatening to those whose power depends on an unquestioning acceptance of the unacceptable. In Northern Ireland, there was a time when the UK government tried the questionable strategy of marginalizing political parties associated with armed groups by making it illegal to quote their words in their own voices. This led to the use of actors' voices reading the words while the politicians were shown speaking: "A man came out of the voting booth, and a Sinn Fein campaigner demanded to know how he had voted." Response: "I voted for Niall Cusack (a well-known actor); he's the only one making sense around here." Like many examples of humor in conflict, this one ridicules two power-wielders at once (the government for its policy and Sinn Fein for intimidating voters) and does so indirectly.

Humorists and cartoonists have been imprisoned and attacked in many places. This shows the power of humor as well as the vulnerability of the individual. It is impossible to eradicate the joke once told, and the ridicule undermines what would otherwise appear all-powerful.

THE USE OF HUMOR BETWEEN POLITICAL OPPONENTS

In sharply conflicted situations, where opponents may have little or no direct communication, humor can be both negative and positive as a tool.

Opposing sides will ridicule each other and use humor to police the boundaries between one side and the other. As they begin to contemplate even indirect communication across the lines of division, they may use humor to find common ground (ridicule of outsiders, for example). Eventually, they will begin to test each other: Does he understand the subtleties of how we see things? Will he use humor to wound me if I become vulnerable through talking with him? Is he able to accept gentle jokes about himself (suggesting reduced defensiveness)?

Humor is one tool in the process of discovering whether the other side is able to change and whether the opponents can begin to build a shared understanding of each other and of the situation. Field staff wishing to foster indirect or direct communication between opponents must be prepared for this, able not only to appreciate it but to explain it, interpret examples, and reinforce ground gained toward building a shared reality.

IMPORTANCE FOR FIELD DIPLOMACY

This article contains several caveats for field diplomacy, as well as a few possibilities. Minimally, intervenors in conflicts should expect to notice their own discomfort at what seems to them inappropriate laughter and incomprehensible humor, and interpret it as a reflection of their own need to learn. Those who hope not just to survive but to intervene constructively in the conflict should expect to become able to understand the jokes and begin to find them funny. Real involvement in political mediation or encouraging dialogue, at whatever level, requires a sufficient level of understanding to remember humor and convey it in a sufficiently nuanced form to be informative to sophisticated actors in the situation. It is too much to expect that field diplomats will be able to make jokes of their own, and a risky strategy unless one is very sure of doing it delicately and well. But if one happens to have this gift (and test it discreetly on trusted locals), it will be much appreciated by those involved and taken as an indicator of high-level understanding and credibility. At a high level of involvement, field staff should understand the use of humor as part of the process of building dialogue.

As a new arrival to a situation, in a position or with the intention to engage as a field diplomat, one will be tested by local actors. A range of characteristics and aptitudes is expected and accepted, provided that there is no pretension to understand or offer what is patently beyond one's capacities. There is tolerance of the perspective of the outsider, and of a learning curve, a steady progression toward more complete and more sophisticated understanding of the local situation. What is not acceptable is for those who fancy themselves field diplomats to remain outside and either ignorant or judgmental of the local culture and its humor.

BIBLIOGRAPHY

Conners, Joan L. (1998). "Hussein as Enemy: The Persian Gulf War in Cartoons."
    Harvard International Journal of Press-Politics 3, no. 26: 96–114.
Darby, John. (1983). *Dressed to Kill: Cartoonists and the Northern Ireland
    Conflict.* Belfast: Appletree Press.
Navarri, Pascal. (1998). "Humour noir, sublimation: Quelques questions." *Revue
    française de psychanalyse* 62, no. 4: 1163–1172.
Root, Jeraine. (1996). "Is a Picture Worth a Thousand Words? A Methodological
    Study of Political Cartoons." Ph.D. diss., University of Houston. Cited in
    Political Communication 13, no. 3: 363–364.

CHAPTER 16

Dealing with Moral Dilemmas

Hugo Slim

THE CONTEXT OF AGENCY DECISIONMAKING

The notion that "being humanitarian" and "doing good" are somehow inevitably the same is a hard one to shake off. For many people, it is almost counterintuitive to have to consider that humanitarian action may also have a dark side that compromises as well as helps the people whose suffering it seeks to assuage. However, the many difficult situations in which relief agencies have found themselves in recent years have inevitably led members of the relief community to examine this shadow side of humanitarianism. The increasing involvement of relief agencies in the very heat of war and political violence has given rise to a growing sense of moral unease among agency policymakers and field-workers alike. More and more they feel confronted by "moral dilemmas" in their work. To borrow (and distort) a phrase from the poet John Keats, relief workers have increasingly been forced to consider the "negative capability" of humanitarian assistance, as analysts like M. Anderson and J. Prendergast have come up with traditionally Mosaic decimal lists that identify the many ways in which aid can do harm as well as good.[1] This new awareness and these new lists and commandments have given many relief workers a genuine fear that, as well as helpers, they may also become bystanders and colluders in the violence in which they operate.

But this insight and its attendant anxiety are, of course, not new to humanitarianism. For as long as people have felt the urge to help others, they have seen risks and faced dilemmas in doing so. In the fourth century, the Egyptian hermit Abba Paphnutius observed: "I have seen a man on the bank of a river buried up to his knees in mud and some men came to give him a hand and help him out, but they pushed him further in up to his neck."[2] Altruism—the spirit behind humanitarianism—is obviously risky to the helped as well as to the helper. And its risks are perhaps fourfold. First, altruism can risk the physical well-being of the person doing the helping. Second, if misguided, it can also endanger still further the person one is trying to help. Third, whether misguided or not, it can often end up providing succor to the perpetrators of the original evil. And finally, any intervention in the midst of man's inhumanity to man is also likely to threaten the moral integrity of the helper. Getting involved is bound to lead the helper into an encounter with humankind at its worst, as well as at its best. In such situations, helpers soon find themselves dining with the devil. And in doing so, no matter how long their spoon, they will tend to find themselves feeding on moral compromise and getting dirty hands.

This article's main aim is thus to give relief and development workers some common ethical language and basic moral guidelines with which to describe and think through their moral choices and dilemmas. In this way, it hopes to help them to do the right thing. But equally important, it seeks to help agencies to articulate and communicate what they believe to be the right thing. Improved ethical analysis can contribute to morale within agency staff and beyond to the people they are working with. As the word suggests, morale is a moral matter. People only tend to feel good about what they do if they are confident that what they are doing is right. Much poor morale in relief agencies is directly linked to a predominant sense of moral confusion. A moral position that does not gloss over difficulties but sets out a clear and acceptable moral vision within such difficulties can make a great contribution to the morale of the helpers and the helped in any situation.

Before starting, however, it might be wise to sound a note of caution. The international aid community has a tendency to colonize, and this tendency is no less apparent in its moral debates where all too often it has shown signs of making all the moral problems of the world its own. In debates about humanitarian ethics, this has sometimes meant that relief agencies and their critics have tended to overstate the moral burden on humanitarianism—perhaps because it is easier to accuse a relief agency than a warlord these days. But it should never be forgotten that relief agencies are always responding to the violence of others. The difficult moral choices faced by relief agencies usually come about as a result of the immoral choices already made by political leaders and other individuals and groups. In most situations, relief agencies inherit an already uneven moral playing field. It would thus be morally negligent if excessive agonizing by or about relief agencies (the groaning of the white man and his burden) shouted out the accusations of blame, which should be put squarely where they are most obviously due: with the killers, the rapists, the dispossessors, and their political leaders who initiate and sustain the policies of excessive and unjust violence in today's wars and genocide.

MORAL DILEMMAS

Important Characteristics of Moral Dilemmas

S. Blackburn defines moral dilemmas as "situations in which each possible course of action breaches some otherwise binding moral principle."[3] In other words, a moral dilemma is a choice between two wrongs. In the face of such a choice, two attitudes are possible. One can become fatalistic about dilemmas and regard them as essentially no-win situations in which whatever one does will be wrong, which it inevitably will. Alternatively, one can view dilemmas as more of a challenge and try to determine the lesser of two evils in any given situation. If a situation is a true moral dilemma, whatever one does will be wrong and should be regretted. But in responding to a moral dilemma, it is also possible to do something that, while not right, is perhaps the best thing to do in the circumstances.

In the face of moral dilemmas, therefore, it is usual to find oneself operating in the extremely uncomfortable moral zone between various wrongs in search of the least worst. Making ethical decisions in such terrible and constricted moral space is bound to be depressing, and relief agency staff should expect to find their decisions painful in these areas. Neither are such decisions much better once they are made. The usual sense of relief that comes with making a decision seldom accompanies the resolution of a dilemma. Instead, decisions out of a dilemma will by nature continue to be troubling rather than liberating.

Moral dilemmas have their origin in moral systems that have a range of fundamental moral principles, and these can inevitably compete with one another in a particular situation. Moral views that believe in a single golden rule (like J. Bentham's utilitarianism, J. Fletcher's love-based situation ethics, or a belief in natural law) encounter few moral dilemmas. For them the right option in any choice is usually clear. In contrast, as Blackburn has observed, "Any morality with more than one fundamental principle seems capable of generating dilemmas."[4] This characteristic is important because it means that some nongovernmental organizations (NGOs) will have more moral dilemmas than others, depending on the range and number of their fundamental principles. For example, an organization whose mission is focused on the one main principle of saving life may well have few, if any, moral dilemmas. With a purely humanitarian mission, most of its difficult choices are relatively easily decided in terms of which course of action will save the most lives. At the opposite end of the spectrum, an NGO that has built a mission around a wide variety of basic principles encompassing civil, political, and economic rights may find its various principles constantly competing. Organizations that work according to the whole range of human rights face particular problems here. Although in theory such agencies seek to prioritize all types of human rights as first equal (universal and indivisible in the language of human rights advocates), they are frequently faced with situations on the ground that demand that they choose fast between particular rights and so put one principle above another. There is perhaps a rule that the more basic moral principles you have in your mission as an agency, the more moral dilemmas you are likely to face in your practice.

Most relief agencies and relief operations these days can be described as "multi-mandate" because they have a range of values built into their mission statements and objectives.[5] In broad terms, relief agencies seem to have four main competing areas of moral values that can compete with each other in any given situation. The first is the basic humanitarian value, that of preserving *human life* itself. The second is the vast spectrum of values across the economic, social, civil, and political spheres known collectively as *human rights*. The third is the principle of *justice*, which is the moral measure of fair and equal relationships between individuals and groups in any society. Finally, there is the value of *staff safety*, which, almost in contradiction to the other three, appears to value the particular lives of some people over all other lives. Almost every difficult moral decision in relief work seems to involve the collision of competing demands from these four values.

Is It Really a Moral Dilemma?

The terrible characteristics of moral dilemmas make it crucial that any given choice a relief agency is facing is in fact a genuine moral dilemma. Like most people today, relief agency staff may not always use the phrase in its proper sense. In common parlance, the word *dilemma* often means nothing more than a difficult decision, a tough choice. Although tough, however, a choice may not necessarily be a genuine moral dilemma. There are perhaps four other types of choice that often masquerade as moral dilemmas. Distinguishing between real moral dilemmas and apparent moral dilemmas is important because while all options involve a wrong action in a real moral dilemma, there is usually a right course of action in a tough choice. By miscasting a tough choice as a moral dilemma, a relief agency could fail to see that there is indeed a right course of action in a difficult choice and so could fail to take it.

The first type of apparent moral dilemma is a tough choice that wavers on uncertain evidence. J. Childress and J. Macquarrie describe such a choice as when "there is some evidence that an act is morally right and obligatory, and some evidence that it is morally wrong."[6] However, this choice may not be a genuine moral dilemma if it is possible to gather more information that will swing the evidence one way or the other. In such a situation, therefore, and if time and capacity permit, more evidence should be sought before accepting that one faces a genuine moral dilemma.

A second type of tough choice comes about when "the moral reasons for (or against) an act are in conflict with non-moral reasons—such as prudential or political reasons—against (or for) such an act."[7] As will be seen, these choices hinge on judgments about expediency and competing program objectives. Commonly arising as choices between speaking out against human rights abuses or continuing to manage relief programs in silence, this type of tough choice often assails NGO operations. Operational pragmatism and the need to protect staff safety, vulnerable populations, or operational freedom often compete as prudential reasons for not doing an obvious good. Although such a situation might be a tough choice, it is not strictly a moral dilemma when there is no doubt that there is a morally right course of action involved that could be taken but is not taken for prudential reasons.

The third type of tough choice that can also masquerade as a moral dilemma is, ironically, a choice between two goods. As will be seen from the case studies below, relief agencies have sometimes claimed to face a "moral dilemma" when they have been faced by a tough choice between two goods rather than two wrongs. A choice between two good courses of action is not a moral dilemma in the strict sense. These choices are not necessarily the agonizing no-win decisions they have been made out to be but are in fact more like win-win choices in which the agency can perhaps technically do no wrong. The challenge of these tough choices between two goods is to determine the greater good, but the lesser good is not by necessity wrong in itself. Such choices may arise in the selection of target population or in decisions to confine one's mandate to a particular area of work.

Finally, the fourth kind of choice that may appear to be a moral dilemma, but which is not, is the most brutal of all. It has been compared by Blackburn to Sophie's choice in William Styron's book and film of the same name.[8] All too common in war and political violence, these choices, like in *Sophie's Choice,* involve horrific options like a mother being forced to chose within seconds which of her children should live and which should die. Such unbearable choices are not true moral dilemmas, as the choice is not between competing moral principles. Instead, such choices lie more in the realm of torture. They are thus inaccurately described as moral dilemmas and might be better known as hellish choices. Relief workers may well face such hellish choices in their work, particularly related to the inevitable rationing of supplies in situations that surpass all reasonable attempts at triage. Faced with 100,000 starving people but with food for only 10,000 and no realistic possibility of triage, it is hard to see how morality can play a part in guiding such decisions. These options seem to lie in some amoral zone where moral principles no longer even exist to compete with one another.

With tough and hellish choices able to masquerade as moral dilemmas, it is particularly important that relief agencies are sure when a hard choice is actually a genuine moral dilemma between two absolute wrongs. A first step for any agency in its ethical analysis, therefore, should be to determine which type of choice it faces. Having clarified this, the agency may then deliberate on the problem, judge its actions, and gauge its responsibility accordingly. Without doing so, the tendency might be for agencies to simply label every difficult decision a moral dilemma and in turn become fatalistic in their programming. Such an approach is morally lazy on the one hand and makes for bad and irresponsible programming on the other.

Who Is to Blame for a Moral Dilemma?

Moral dilemmas differ in terms of culpability. Sometimes a moral dilemma will be the fault of a relief agency and sometimes it will not. As noted above, one can never do the right thing in a moral dilemma, but can only really hope to do the best thing. Nevertheless, the question of fault still arises. Who is responsible for the evil that results from the eventual choice in any moral dilemma? Although one should always regret such evil, should one also take the blame for it?

Most moral philosophers would argue that if a moral dilemma has arisen in a manner beyond my control then, although technically responsible for the outcome, I can in no way be blamed for it and reckoned as guilty. However, if the dilemma has come about or been manufactured through my own doing, then fault and blame can be laid squarely at my door. This question of fault is obviously an important one for relief agencies and should always be part of their ethical analysis and deliberation over their moral dilemmas. if they themselves are the cause of a dilemma, then any handringing on their part is disingenuous. An element of honesty and transparency about agency knowledge, capacity, and intention is therefore important in any ethical analysis of difficult programming decisions. What were the agency's intentions? Did it know enough to prevent a moral dilemma? Could it have done anything to prevent it?

MORAL RESPONSIBILITY

Actions, Consequences, and Moral Responsibility

The next step for an agency to take in developing its ethics around moral dilemmas is to decide where it stands in the debate about the nature of goodness and the limits of moral responsibility. This debate is essentially the debate between actions and consequences and about who should take responsibility for what. Since time immemorial, moral philosophy has been divided between those who think that goodness lies mainly in the nature of an action that is right in itself and those who think instead that an action is only truly right if goodness emerges as an obvious outcome of that action. Some people believe that certain actions are always good in themselves. Others believe that actions are only ever good when their wider consequences are also good.

These two approaches are known by Greek terms as *deontological ethics* (duty-based ethics) and *teleological ethics* (goal-based ethics). Deontologists believe some actions are simply good in themselves, and so one always has a duty to do them regardless of their consequences. Ethics for them become primarily a matter of identifying these intrinsically good actions and so knowing and doing one's moral duty. For example, as a deontologist I might believe that it is always good, and therefore my duty, to heal a person's wounds if I can. In contrast, people with a teleological perspective are more concerned with the wider consequences of any action. They believe that all actions must be measured as good or bad by virtue of their wider goal or consequences. As a consequentialist, therefore, I might believe that it is not always good to heal some people's wounds if they then return to battle and kill children. Ethics for consequentialists becomes the complicated and uncertain process of anticipating wider outcomes and holding oneself responsible for events well beyond the present time. For deontologists, ethics is more simply a matter of doing one's duty and of dispersing responsibility more widely to others. At the risk of parody, it could be said that the particular humanitarianism of the International Committee of the Red Cross represents the dentological position. Recognizing the essential duty to save all human life, it acts accordingly, seeing the consequences of that action as a matter primarily for others to contend with. In contrast, the more broadly based civil, political, and economic rights agenda of an NGO arguing against all aid to an authoritarian regime might represent the consequentialist position. Its goals are different, and it defines what is good now in relation to what it sees as the best possible outcome in the future.

Within this ethical debate, a relief agency needs to decide where it locates the goodness in its programming. Each agency must decide whether its programs are good simply because they involve good deeds or whether they are good only when they produce good consequences at a much wider level. To test an organization's position on this, it might be useful to ask the following two questions: Is the organization secure in the belief that its actions are always good in themselves? Or does the NGO believe it needs to have a sure grasp of the wider consequences of its programs to be certain of the goodness of its work?

A decision about whether an agency's goodness lies primarily in its particular actions on the one hand or in their wider consequences on the other will also determine how much an agency assumes moral responsibility for conditions and events surrounding its programs. If a food-aid NGO takes a minimalist duty-based approach to its work, then it would take moral responsibility only for feeding people well or badly in relation to the nutritional status of its target population. The NGO would not, however, take moral responsibility for the wider consequences of such actions that might contribute to the sustenance of violence and a war economy. It would believe that such consequences depend on the moral choices made by others in the way they choose to use or abuse the NGO's feeding program. By contrast, another NGO might feel itself responsible for any way in which its feeding program contributed to the nourishment of fighting forces or the development of military strategy in the area and would feel bound to stop its program.

Taking a position in this debate about the primacy of good actions or of good consequences, and the subsequent parameters of moral responsibility, is thus an important step for any relief agency in framing its ethical position around moral dilemmas and tough choices. A difficult decision may or may not be a moral dilemma depending on how much an agency feels morally responsible for the wider consequences of its actions. Agreeing upon the precise location of goodness in its programming and the limits of its moral responsibility will enable an agency to set some moral boundaries to its work. This might help to dispel some of the unease that pervades so many organizations at present. But it would be unwise to expect any stand along the spectrum to be particularly comfortable. A minimalist duty-based approach to the ethics of relief programming will invite the wrath of consequentialist critics whose stinging rebukes will harangue such agencies for their naiveté and irresponsibility. A more maximalist approach that tries to take account of consequences will be plagued with uncertainty, speculation, and endless calculation about possible outcomes, as well as the temptation (to which the Western liberal conscience is already too susceptible) to feel personally responsible for every terrible thing that happens in one's theater of operations.

Factors Affecting Moral Responsibility and Blame

Although a decision about how far an NGO is responsible for the consequences of its actions in the future can be disputed, the field of ethics has always been clear about particular factors that determine whether one is acting responsibly in the present. Western moral philosophy has come up with a number of principles of good practice in this area, which relief agencies would do well to consider more formally in any ethical analysis of their programming. Such principles involve an analysis of intention, motivation, coercion, knowledge, ignorance, deliberation, capacity, and mitigation. All these factors determine how morally responsible and how culpable an agency is in any given situation. They can be grouped around three main aspects of any agency's action: what drives an agency; what informs an agency; and what empowers an agency. In choosing a particular course of action, a relief agency must be prepared to be judged according to these various categories.

What drives an agency are its *intentions* and its *motivation*. An organization's intentions must be good. It must be able to show that it was acting out of the best of intentions in any situation, even if these intentions were not subsequently realized in full. Similarly, it must be able to show that its motives were good. Discerning motives can be complicated. Like most people, most organizations usually have mixed motives for doing things. In relief agencies, such mixed motives often involve instincts like compassion jostling with motives like income, publicity, market presence, interagency competition, growth, and influence. This mixture of motives can often lead to an agency doing the right thing for the wrong reason—something of which it needs to be aware and that may ultimately have a detrimental effect upon the way it operates on the ground. For example, a health agency highly motivated by publicity may tilt its program more toward the camera than to people's needs, compromising the impact of its health work accordingly.

Malevolent outside influence characterized as *coercion* (by fear or force) can also drive an agency and is usually a reason for diminished responsibility in its decisionmaking. This drive is important, as there is little doubt that relief agencies do sometimes feel coerced by warlords, totalitarian regimes, the media, and even by donors and communities. While the reality of such fear or force is usually dismissed, or at least underplayed, by their critics, relief agencies may sometimes have reasonable grounds for pleading an element of coercion in their decisionmaking around moral dilemmas and tough choices.

What informs an agency is also critical, as an agency can only really be deemed fully responsible for a decision on the basis of what it knew when making that decision. Here the key factors are *knowledge* and *ignorance*. An organization must be able to show that it made every effort to garner all possible information relevant to its decision. On this point, moral philosophy distinguishes between *vincible ignorance* and *invincible ignorance*. If an agency did not have all the knowledge at its disposal when making the decision, it must be judged on whether it could have had. If necessary information did exist and the organization could reasonably have been expected to collect it but did not, then it must be held culpable of vincible ignorance—an ignorance, in other words, that could have been overcome.

If, however, pressure of time, lack of access to information, or lack of information itself made the gathering of sufficient knowledge impossible in the circumstances, then an agency must be judged the victim of invincible ignorance—an ignorance that could not have been overcome. Its responsibility is thus much less.

The third area upon which an agency can be judged culpable or not concerns its *capacity*. An agency can only really be held responsible for not doing something if it could have done it but chose not to. For example, I might feel terrible about not being able to save a stranger from being beaten up by a gang of ten armed men when I suddenly come upon the final moments of the incident taking place. I might feel terrible that I could not stop his suffering but I would be wrong to feel morally responsible for not stopping it. I simply did not have the means to stop ten armed men in so short a time. Similarly, capacity is also a critical determinant of moral responsibility in relief work. Considerations of an agency's reasonable capacity must, therefore, be factored into the organization's ethical thinking around tough choices and moral dilemmas.

Two other key factors are essential to good practice in moral decision-making: *deliberation* and *mitigation*. To be acting responsibly in any situation, an organization must be making every effort to deliberate on the matter in hand. In ethics, the verb *to deliberate* implies a serious commitment to the moral question concerned and an applied effort to take counsel, consult, debate, and weigh carefully in mind the various aspects of the problem. Without such an approach, neither an individual nor an organization can be regarded as giving due seriousness to a moral choice. Deliberation in relief agencies is a complicated process. Often short of time, the process of due deliberation is made more difficult when the staff of an international agency is spread across different parts of the globe, frequently preoccupied with other matters, and usually composed of people from a wide cultural mix with different languages and different ethical traditions. Some relief agencies are obviously better than others at ethical deliberation. Feeling uneasy and agonizing about a moral problem is not necessarily the same as deliberating over it. If relief agencies can be criticized in this area, it is most likely to be on the grounds that they mistake unease for deliberation and come from a predominantly activist culture that sometimes values action over deliberation, holding that any action is better than no action, even if that action is sometimes wrong. A more formal commitment to ethical deliberation as part of responsible program design and management might serve to correct these tendencies.

The other key principle of good ethical practice is that of *mitigation*—an idea well-known to the international humanitarian community as it relates to disaster prevention. In matters of morality, mitigation is a must if a person or organization is to act responsibly by maximizing on whatever good there is, and limiting their culpability. Where possible, an agency should always seek out and apply additional knowledge or capacity (however minimal) to seek to minimize the bad where it cannot stop it completely. This principle of damage limitation is particularly important in tough choices, or in moral dilemmas where one is choosing between two wrongs. Indeed, the existence of a mitigation strategy can become the guiding principle that determines which wrong to choose.

CONCLUSION

This article has attempted to set out the particular challenges of moral dilemmas and tough moral choices being faced by relief agencies today. It has also attempted to identify potential principles of good practice for relief agencies in their efforts to develop formal ethical analyses as a more central and rigorous part of their relief programming in political emergencies and wars. We started with a reference to the poet Keats and to his idea of negative capability. Humanitarian aid obviously does have a dark side. Misapplied or not, the provision of help may well have negative repercussions beyond its original intention. The challenge for relief agencies is to determine the proper limits of their moral responsibility for this dark side and then make all efforts to mitigate against it in their programs. In his use of the term "negative capability," Keats referred to his admiration of that rare artist who does not just create a sense of truth and beauty out of the things in this world that are already positive, like a stunning red rose. Such a "positive capability" is not especially admirable. What is truly the mark of genius is the artist who can engage with the negative side of human life and from it create a work of art that is also truthful and beautiful. Although the worlds of poetry and relief work do not often coincide, the real challenge for the relief worker is to develop a negative capability: that ability to be present in the worst of human situations; to be faced with the hardest of choices and yet still to respect and protect human life in a way that constantly challenges evil without colluding in it. This is no easy task.

NOTES

A more extensive version of this article originally appeared as Hugo Slim, "Doing the Right Thing: Relief Agencies, Moral Dilemmas and Moral Responsibility in Political Emergencies and War," in *Disasters* 21, no. 3 (1997): 244–257. Copyright © of the Overseas Development Institute. It has been reprinted with kind permission from the Overseas Development Institute.
    1. M. Anderson 1984, 1986; and J. Pendergast 1995.
    2. Ward 1975, 7.

3. Blackburn 1994, 250.
4. Ibid.
5. African Rights 1994.
6. J. Childress and J. Macquarrie 1986, 156.
7. Ibid.
8. Blackburn 1994, 251.

REFERENCES AND SUGGESTED READING

African Rights. (1994). "Humanitarianism Unbound? Current Dilemmas Facing Multi-mandate Relief Operations in Political Emergencies." Discussion article no. 5. African Rights, London.

Anderson, M. (1994). *International Assistance and Conflict: An Exploration of Negative Impacts.* Issue series no. 1. Local Capacities for Peace Project, Cambridge, Mass.

———. (1996). *Do No Harm: Supporting Local Capacities for Peace Through Aid.* Local Capacities for Peace Project, Cambridge, Mass.

Blackburn, S. (1996). *The Oxford Dictionary of Philosophy.* Oxford: Oxford University Press.

Childress, J., and J. Macquarrie. (1986). *The Dictionary of Christian Ethics.* SCM.

Code of Conduct for the International Red Cross and Red Crescent Movement and the Non-Governmental Organizations (NGOs) in Disaster Relief. (1994). Geneva.

de Waal, A. (1993). *Human Rights, Complex Emergencies, and NGOs.* Save the Children, London. Mimeograph.

Keen, D., and K. Wilson. (1994). "Engaging with Violence: A Reassessment of Relief in Wartime." In J. Macrae and A. Zwy, eds., *War and Hunger: Rethinking International Responses to Complex Emergencies.* London: Zed Books and Save the Children.

Lewer, N., and O. Ramsbotham. (1993). *Something Must Be Done: Towards an Ethical Framework for Humanitarian Intervention in International Social Conflict.* Peace research report, Department of Peace Studies, University of Bradford, UK.

McClellan, J. (1995). *Moral and Ethical Issues.* Presentation to the Symposium on the Role of NGO Emergency Assistance in Promoting Peace and Reconciliation, March, Copenhagen. ICVA Humanitarian Affairs Series no. 8, Geneva.

Macrae, J., and A. Zwy. (1994). "Famine, Complex Emergencies and International Policy in Africa: An Overview." In Macrae and Zwy, eds., *War and Hunger: Rethinking International Responses to Complex Emergencies.* London: Zed Books and Save the Children.

Minear, L. (1995). "New Opportunities and Dilemmas for Independent Agencies." Address to the Seventy-fifth Anniversary Conference of the Mennonite Central Committee, June, Conrad Grebel College, Waterloo, Ontario.

"The Mohonk Criteria for Humanitarian Assistance in Complex Emergencies." (1994). Program on Humanitarian Assistance, World Conference on Religion and Peace, February.

Prendergast, J. (1995). "Minimizing the Negative Externalities of Aid: The Ten Commandments." Article for the U.S. Institute of Peace conference on

Humanitarian Aid and Conflict in Africa. "Providence Principles" as cited in L. Minear and T. Weiss (1995), *Mercy Under Fire: War and the Global Humanitarian Community.* Boulder, Colo.: Westview Press.

Rose, M. (1995). In the biennial CENDEP International Debate at Oxford Brookes University, 13 November.

Tomasevsky, K. (1994). "Human Rights and Wars of Starvation." In J. Macrae and A. Zwy, eds., *War and Hunger: Rethinking International Responses to Complex Emergencies.* London: Zed Books and Save the Children.

Van Hoeylandt, P. (1995). "Ethics of Humanitarian Intervention: The Case of the UN Operation in Somalia." Master's thesis, University of Oxford.

Ward, Sister Benedicta. (1975). *The Sayings of the Desert Fathers.* London: Mowbrays.

Welby, J. (1992). "Can Companies Sin? Whether, How, and Who in Company Accountability." *Grove Ethical Studies,* no. 85.

CHAPTER 17

Coordination and Codes of Conduct

■ 17.1

The Challenge of Coordination and Networking

Paul van Tongeren

Creating networks and improving coordination are among the major challenges in the world of conflict resolution and peacebuilding today. Considering the diversity of people and organizations dealing with conflict resolution and peacebuilding, it would almost seem too far-fetched to come up with the idea of creating more coordination in the first place. Actors engaged in stopping and preventing conflicts are tainted by multiformity. They vary from governments and international organizations such as the UN and the Organization of African Unity to colorful collections of nongovernmental organizations (NGOs). All of these different actors have their own specific background, culture, and interests. The NGOs among them represent, undoubtedly, the most multiform category, as they vary from such diverse sectors as development organizations, academic think tanks, professional conflict-resolution groups, and small spontaneously established groups of unpaid local peacemakers. Many of these organizations may not even be aware of each other's existence. In addition, conflict resolution and peacebuilding are in many aspects still in their infancy stage. No wonder collaboration and coordination are often lacking.

Yet it is obvious to me that coordination is not only desirable but also often close at hand, almost easy to grab. For instance, relief organizations that enter into emergency areas to do their work have good opportunities to coordinate their activities, if only because of their physical proximity.

Fortunately, they and other actors increasingly take opportunities for coordination, both on the local and international level. There are signs as well that this positive development includes the domain of conflict resolution and peacebuilding. In a number of countries, including Canada, Germany, and Finland, national platforms on peacebuilding have been established. These networks are a major step toward creating an infrastructure for collaboration and coordination. In Europe, national networks joined forces in the European Platform for Conflict Prevention and Transformation. Let me elaborate here on the history and objectives of this European network to shed more light on the potential of international coordination.

THE AMSTERDAM APPEAL

In February 1997, the European Conference on Conflict Prevention, the largest conference on preventing conflicts to date, was held in Amsterdam. The meeting was hosted by the Dutch National Committee for International Cooperation and Sustainable Development in collaboration with the Liaison Committee of Development NGOs to the European Union (EU). The conference resulted in the formulation of a plan of action that was dubbed the Amsterdam Appeal. This appeal was presented to the political leaders of the EU as well as to relevant NGOs.

The appeal presented terms for an effective EU approach to preventing conflict and outlined key advocacy issues to be adopted by NGOs. The document stressed the need for joint efforts by a range of actors, including NGOs, and urged for coalition building by NGOs, national governments, and European institutions. At a subsequent meeting of European participants of the conference, the European Platform for Conflict Prevention and Transformation was established.

CREATION OF THE EUROPEAN
PLATFORM FOR CONFLICT PREVENTION

The European Platform is an open network of organizations working in the field of conflict prevention and resolution and aims to include participant organizations of all European countries. Ideally, the platform would consist of national platforms or networks, each of which represents national NGOs. The European Platform supports the establishment of these national networks in countries where they do not yet exist. Apart from national European platforms, the European Platform invited international networks of NGOs to participate.

Objectives

It is relevant to distinguish the different tasks the national and international platforms have adopted, because the establishment of these types of platforms can really help and strengthen peacebuilding.

Clearinghouse.   One of the most useful assets of the national and international platforms is their clearinghouse mandate. It is important to know what other actors are doing in a certain area in order to be able to complement each other. In a clearinghouse, such relevant information can be exchanged. Human rights, peace, development, and humanitarian NGOs are often working within their own discipline, sometimes hardly aware of other sectors' paradigms and practices. However, all these different organizations are increasingly confronted with conflict situations, a fact that confronts them with similar problems.

As a starting point for developing a full-fledged clearinghouse mandate, information should be available about who is doing what in what region. To meet this condition, the European Platform published an international directory, listing about 500 conflict-management organizations and their activities. Several national platforms have published national directories as well, listing the names of organizations and individuals engaged in conflict management.

The European Platform also published surveys on conflict, providing information on the backgrounds of conflicts as well as on conflict-management efforts that already have been undertaken in a particular country or region. These surveys, published both in print and online, are an important tool to help strengthen the capacity of the peacebuilding community. They also are a good starting point for networking and cooperation in certain regions.

Lobbying.   Lobbying is another crucial task of networks. As a comparatively young discipline, conflict prevention and peacebuilding still cope with a rather weak infrastructure and low profile. Collective lobby and advocacy activities can increase the chance of more public resources being invested in conflict prevention and could also give the discipline a stronger profile on the political agenda.

Education and media.   Educational and media activities should be undertaken by the platforms to increase awareness of the potential of conflict prevention and peacebuilding among a broad public. Only if a broad public becomes committed to conflict prevention will it be possible to generate significant political support to increase the resources and expertise necessary for peace work to become more effective.

Disadvantages and Difficulties

It is true that there are always a lot of arguments against cooperation—for instance, collaboration costs, time, and energy. Joint activities come with a certain loss of identity and make it more difficult for individual organizations to profile themselves, which may have detrimental effects on fundraising activities. Difference in mandate and the political profile of organizations are also mentioned as barriers for collective action and coordination. In some cases, the simple fact that coordination means getting together for time-consuming meetings hinders the potential for cooperation to come about.

Other factors may also hold organizations back from cooperating, even if a strong commitment to do so is present. One of these factors is the difference in background and culture, to which I referred earlier. NGOs, churches, governments, and intergovernmental organizations (IGOs) each have their own peculiarities. For instance, peace groups may work with volunteers, whereas development and humanitarian organizations often have paid staff. This kind of difference has an impact on the level of cooperation. Another hindrance can be found in rivalry about the leadership of joint operations as well as about the concept of ownership—the extent to which members of the organizations involved feel they still can shape joint activities.

FUNDAMENTAL ROLES NGOS MIGHT PLAY IN CONFLICT RESOLUTION

- A preventive role by means of early warning.
- Human-rights monitoring.
- Peacebuilding/strengthening civil society.
- Supporting peace constituencies.
- Conflict-resolution activities.
- Advocacy/lobby/education.

Early warning signals are frequently not translated into political action. The early alarms on Somalia, Bosnia, and Rwanda proved to be ineffective. Thus, more concerted political action is required from NGOs.

NGOs embody an internationalist, moral position with a strong involvement directed toward empowerment, peace, well-being, and social and economical justice. In addition, NGOs can do more for less money. In the words of the World Bank, "NGOs work at low cost: they are funded largely by charitable contributions and staffed by volunteers." Collectively, NGOs have the ability to:

- Act without being constrained by narrow mandates of foreign-policy imperatives.
- Achieve access to areas inaccessible to official actors.
- Talk to several parties without losing their credibility.
- Deal directly with grassroots populations.
- Operate in obscurity without media, parliamentary, or public scrutiny.
- Take the greatest risks, given their public-advocacy and social-justice agendas.
- Effectively network, given their longstanding relationships, built on trust, with civil society in the conflict zones.
- Draw upon public opinion to galvanize political will.
- Focus on a longer-term perspective than governments are able to.

FROM EUROPEAN TO INTERNATIONAL NETWORKING

Despite difficulties and disadvantages, the necessity to improve information sharing and cooperation in the area of conflict resolution and peacebuildling becomes increasingly evident. To mention just a personal example, some time ago I attended a session of the Canadian Peace Building Consultation as one of few foreigners. During this session, we had a debate on the strengths and weaknesses of peacebuilding efforts, lessons learned, and conflict-impact assessment, topics that are also under study by European NGOs. It occurred to me there and then that more exchange of ideas and experiences across borders would be very useful.

In our daily practice at the European Platform, we also ran into examples showing the importance of setting up a structure for international cooperation. For instance, we published a book, *People Building Peace*, containing stories on thirty-five cases of peacebuilding. Many of these stories show that in many countries there are numerous small NGOs and peace groups that are not connected to one another. To me, this again showed that it would make sense to build a framework that increased the chance for those organizations to cooperate. Local and national networks should be sustained by international contacts.

I am, therefore, pleading for the establishment of an international network of conflict-resolution and peacebuilding organizations. The question, of course, is how we can accomplish this and what such a network should look like. In other words, how can we set up an international network that really serves the purpose of all parties involved and is user-friendly?

The Need for International Networking

Before addressing that question, let me list the reasons why, in our experience, an international network would be a good way to strengthen international ties and would boost cooperation between actors in Europe and those on other continents:

1. More international exchange of information on conflict resolution and peacebuilding is needed. This concerns both evaluation of initiatives, lessons learned, publication of surveys, and setting up media projects.
2. The domain of conflict resolution and peacebuilding should become stronger and better structured. It is now still too weak and scattered.
3. More information on conflict resolution and peacebuilding should be available and dispersed, both among the general public and organizations working in the issues. There is a lack of awareness about the scope of activities and infrastructure that is already in place.
4. An international network will make it easier for organizations or national platforms to link up with other networks.

Mission Statement

The mission statement of such an international network is to facilitate the exchange of information and experience between organizations, institutions, and individuals in order to stimulate cooperation and action for conflict resolution and peacebuilding.

Objectives

Its objective would be to build a global constituency that is supportive of conflict prevention, conflict resolution, and peacebuilding through networking; providing support to national platforms; encouraging cooperation and exchange of information between members of the network; supporting coordinated advocacy and lobbying activities; initiating innovative activities such as educational, media, and advocacy projects; and strengthening capacity and expertise.

Purpose

The network would function both as a platform and a facilitator of communication. As far as communication is concerned, the Internet can be a great asset. The challenge is to collect and store information in such a way that it is easily accessible for field-workers, academics, and policymakers. The platform purpose would amount to meeting the need for personal contact through organizing seminars and conferences.

Constituencies

The constituency of an international network could consist of two major categories:

1. Established conflict-resolution and peacebuilding NGOs and networks, categorized in geographical terms. These would vary from local peace groups to national coalitions and platforms, from regional coalitions to international/global coalitions.
2. Established issue- or sector-based NGOs, academic institutions, and networks. This refers to categories such as development, human rights, relief, women, media, and church organizations.

Activities

After the range of activities is identified, it would be crucial to establish a task force that would lead the process of establishing the network. Preferably, this task force would be represented by people from one or two leading agencies that are experienced in setting up networks. It seems wise to avoid taking big steps and instead to follow the path of organic growth of the network.

Cooperating Within Zones of Conflicts

An important form of international networking that should be mentioned here, one that could benefit from an all-covering international network, is the setting up of coalitions of actors who live in a specific conflict area and those who operate from abroad. Generally speaking, this comes down to cooperation between people in the North and South. There are numerous NGOs and local groups in zones of conflicts, and there are numerous NGOs and IGOs in the North that deal with conflicts in the South. Links between them are often nonexistent.

Two examples of this type of international coalition are the Horn of Africa Program and the Great Lakes Policy Forum. The Horn of Africa Program, run by the Life and Peace Institute, aims at establishing cooperation between actors in Africa and the North from a ecumenical perspective. Although the program has not yet realized all its plans, it can be seen as a way forward.

The Great Lakes Policy Forum, formerly known as the Burundi Policy

Forum, is an interesting example of informal collaboration between non-governmental and governmental officials, both from Africa and the North. For instance, the forum has organized debates attended by NGO staff and members of the CIA. The participants of the monthly forum meetings discuss sensitive issues in an informal setting, unhindered by hierarchies and procedures that would normally constrain such discussions.

As it went along, the Great Lakes Policy Forum discovered what the added value of a network can be. As participants were discussing the crisis in Burundi, they realized they could also serve as monitors and early warning agents for a wider region. They realized that the ethnic and political situation in Burundi is interlinked with developments in Rwanda and the eastern Congo. This was also the reason to change the name from Burundi Policy Forum to Great Lakes Policy Forum.

Networks such as these could be beneficial for other zones of conflicts as well. They can provide access to local groups in the region, collect early warning signals, help develop relationships built on mutual trust, and give local groups access to foreign governments and NGOs.

REGIONAL CONFLICT-PREVENTION CENTERS

Connie Peck, United Nations Institute for Training and Research program coordinator for peacemaking and preventive diplomacy, strongly pleads in her book, *Sustainable Peace: The Role of the UN and Regional Organizations in Preventing Conflict,* for the creation of UN regional center for sustainable peace. These centers would provide a conflict-prevention mechanism that would build a strategic partnership to assist with dispute resolution and good governance. The centers would link closely with the relevant regional organizations as well as conflict-resolution and governance NGOs and research institutions and think tanks in the region. They should combine the tasks of research, policy advice, training, and offer a meeting place to all people sincerely working for peace in the region.

COORDINATION OF NGO
ACTIVITIES WITHIN CONFLICT REGIONS

During large humanitarian crises, such as in Somalia, Bosnia, or the Great Lakes region, NGOs often jump in by large numbers without much preparation or coordination. This has led to situations in which available resources have not been used optimally. In order to prevent a recurrence of such undesirable situations, many organizations engaged in conflict areas over the past few years have developed strategies to improve coordination and cooperation. This has led to yet another type of networking and coordination.

The UN, through its Administrative Committee on Coordination, developed the concept of strategic frameworks. This concept provides a structure for a wide variety of actors to coordinate their efforts in a particular crisis region. The strategic framework should provide for greater coherence between the political strategies of governments on the one hand and the activities of humanitarian and other NGOs on the other. In practice, such a coherent approach is realized by involving as many relevant actors as possible in outlining a plan of action.

The first effort to implement this strategy has been during the humanitarian crisis in Afghanistan. Since the mid-1990s many assistance programs have been running in this country, varying from projects to reduce opium production to supporting community-based agricultural programs to adopting an anti–land mine initiative. In a promising move, UN agencies, NGOs, and donors tried to develop a common, coordinated strategy to build peace in Afghanistan. After widespread consultations between humanitarian, development, and political actors in 1997, a strategic planning workshop was organized, involving some eighty Afghan and international actors, who formulated a strategic preparatory framework. This framework included a series of interesting principles, such as the agreement to close the gap between political actors involved in the conflict and the world of assistance and development. The framework stated that information should be exchanged between those involved in the political negotiating strategy and those devoted to emergency and recovery activities.

The Strategic Framework for Afghanistan may have been the most far-reaching effort to realize coordination among assisting agents in the field. However, the process also revealed some obstacles these undertakings may run into. Some organizations closely involved in the Afghanistan process, such as Oxfam and Doctors Without Borders, signaled some failures. One mishap mentioned was the alleged absence of a common strategy or strategic vision on where to go to with the country. Without such a grand strategy, it is indeed very difficult to continue on the path toward coordination. Another setback was the tendency among some organizations to retreat to their own responsibilities and mandates in order to preserve their independence and autonomy.

Officials of some organizations, including members of Doctors Without Borders, broke a lance for the legitimacy of adhering to an organization's own mandate, saying that creating a system that joins a wide variety of actors would inevitably harbor conflicting interests and may even aim for unrealistic objectives.

Maybe the experience with the Strategic Framework for Afghanistan tells us that certain limitations to coordination and collaboration should be accepted. It could also be taken as a signal to continue the search for new, creative, and innovative answers to overcome these problems on the road toward coordination. To me, it is clear that efforts such as the Strategic Framework for Afghanistan should be taken as a source of inspiration for further discussion and debate on strengthening conflict resolution and peacebuilding. I am convinced that there is a lot to be won by strengthening coordination, a process that, in its turn, can be boosted by creating strong and vibrant networks.

Enhancing the Quality
of NGO Work in Peacebuilding

Norbert Ropers

> NGOs have the flexibility, expertise and commitment to respond rapidly
> to early signs of trouble. They witness and give voice to the unfolding
> drama, and they provide essential services and aid. Not least, they
> inform and educate the public both at the national level and worldwide
> on the horrors of deadly conflict and thus help mobilize opinion and
> action.[1]

This conclusion by the Carnegie Commission on Preventing Deadly
Conflict highlights the esteem in which the work of nongovernmental
organizations (NGOs) as well as other civil activists in the prevention and
transformation of violent conflicts are held.[2] The increasing involvement of
NGOs in this area is not, however, entirely welcomed. Critical voices point
out that this expansion has its darker sides and that it gave rise to illusions
about the manageability of potentially violent conflicts. The criticism was
initially aimed at the consequences of the "humanitarian interventionism"
as a result of the massive involvement of humanitarian aid organizations in
civil wars and "complex emergencies." It focused on the erosion of regional and local self-help capacities, on the relativity of state responsibilities,
on the voluntary or involuntary siphoning off of aid to the warring factions,
on the competition about media coverage of aid projects (an effective
means for increasing donations), as well as on the considerable detraction
of funds for structurally efficient foreign aid to emergency situations.[3]
Some of this criticism has been dealt with by the organizations concerned
and has led to a new policy for humanitarian aid in the sense of a
Hippocratic oath of aid: Do no harm.[4]

With regard to the considerably smaller funds for direct civic measurements in favor of conflict prevention and transformation, the debate about
its possibilities and limits was, until recently, only a sideline in the discussions about humanitarian interventionism. Practical experience gained in
the meantime, as well as first attempts to perform evaluations in this field,
have led to critical questions about conflict-resolution projects within the
civil society. Some of these questions were raised from the outside, especially in academic circles, whereas others have dealt with this topic in the

traditional sense—as diplomats or representatives of multilateral organizations.[5]

Further questions are the result of experience gathered by NGOs involved in this field, as well as of attempts toward a professionalization of conflict management. These questions, problems, and considerations that arose within and outside the NGOs will be condensed to eight points of criticism in order to determine the possibilities, limits, and needs for further clarification of conflict prevention and transformation by civil activists. For reasons of simplification, we call this whole complex *movement for conflict prevention and transformation.*

1. The movement for conflict prevention and transformation narrows down the problem of violent conflicts to the question of the means of actual conflict and assumes that with sufficient information about the enlightened self-interest, all parties finally can be convinced to agree to a peaceful solution. The activists tend to rule out questions about power and sovereignty and overlook that the violent escalation of conflicts could, from the viewpoint of single activists, be a highly rational and calculated policy.

This criticism assumes with good reason that the causes and effects of acutely or potentially violent conflicts are highly complex and that so far it has not been systematically clarified on which levels and with which means they could be influenced toward a solution or prevention of the conflict. There are only tentative answers to the old question of the social sciences, whether macrosocial transformations can be influenced at all by conscious interventions of single activists. Studies about mediation have given us some evidence that interventions by interested powers, and multilateral organizations applying the tools of power politics on the level of the involved political groups, have the greatest measurable effect. On closer inspection, however, the conditions for this form of mediation in many cases are not given, especially not in ethnopolitical conflicts.[6] From a practical point of view it would thus be irresponsible to ignore the options for action in and through the civil society.

As the activists of the civil society naturally have no authority to enforce things, their efficiency is dependent on the media of communication, interaction, and publicity as well as on the mobilization and donation of material help, consulting, and educational services. These are their strengths and their potential in conflict management. Whether consciously or not, *the activities of NGOs have necessarily to do with power and authority.* There are four ways of dealing with it, of which the first two explicitly and with good arguments refer to these factors, whereas the two latter indeed have some blind spots in regard to power, as some critics rightly point out.

- NGOs try to empower single and/or all parties to deal with the conflict constructively and/or to support them to avoid a violent outbreak. Among other things this means the monitoring and lobbying of human rights and the protection of minorities, capacity building and protective measurements for disadvantaged or endangered groups, negotiation training for strategic activists, and public relations.
- NGOs try to create channels and forums to balance out the influence of power differences, power-political positions, and negotiation strategies in favor of an orientation toward basic interests, the clarifying of relationships, and the enabling of common problem solutions. The underlying assumption of this Track 2 kind of communication, of community and reconciliation work, is that in escalated and especially violent conflicts agreements that have been reached at by power-political measurements alone, a sustainable peace cannot be created. It is much more important to discover deeper common interests and shared needs through communication and learning experiences.
- NGOs help the victims of violent conflicts regardless of interests of power and sovereignty. As mentioned above, this well-meaning approach has been revised as a consequence of the debate about the negative sides of humanitarian interventionism in favor of a Hippocratic oath of aid.
- NGOs contribute to the civilizing of conflicts by promoting skills and capabilities for constructive conflict management to as many individuals as possible. This belief is not altogether wrong, but not sufficient as the one and only approach, because it doesn't consider enough that individual opinions and forms of behavior only become politically powerful in the context of social movements, organizations, and institutions. To achieve such an effect, questions about the organizational development as well as the meso- and macrosocial interconnections have to complement the individual training.

2. The fixation on prevention and/or termination of violence as well as the role of third-party negotiation in conflict management make the movement for conflict prevention and transformation blind toward questions of justice.

This criticism also dates back to an old debate—the one about the relationship between the values of peace and justice. The tension between these two cannot be solved completely. Therefore, it is all the more important in the societal debate about appropriate means of conflict management that both values get considered sufficiently. This initially means to give up the idea that constructive conflict management is primarily the result of third-party mediation. Without the support of legitimate interests of disadvantaged persons and groups, without their empowerment toward capabilities for conflict, without the work of groups for the protection of human rights and minorities, conflict prevention and transformation would be incomplete. Third parties, however, can have an important function in the concentration on improving the communication between the conflicting parties rather than to enforce externally developed solutions. Aspects of justice play a certain role in this, but primarily in regard to the practicalities of the process, for example, in the attempt to create a fair representation of the conflicting parties, which can have an effect on the power balance. We need to mention that a large part of the mediation movement takes it for granted that solutions that are achieved by third-party negotiations are evaluated according to recognized normative standards (e.g., rules for minority protection in international documents).

3. The approach of conflict prevention and transformation tends to psychologize conflicts and to treat all participants as victims.

This point refers primarily to those NGOs that organize training and workshops about conflict resolution with more or less influential members of the conflicting parties but not with the leading groups of the parties. On this level they concentrate either on the training of individual skills or work on aspects of relationships within the conflict (traumas, different patterns of behavior and attitudes, etc.). Therefore, psychological interpretations and explanations of the conflict take up a large space.

Apart from that, some schools of thought base the need for dealing with the psychosocial aspects, especially in protracted conflicts, on the fact that a sustainable solution of the factual controversy is impossible without addressing the often traumatic history of the relationship and the clarification of the basic needs on both sides for recognition of the specific collective identities. The traditional unease between the legal and the psychosocial approaches of responding to violent behavior also needs to be mentioned. Because of their potential for action, the civil activists tend to favor the psychosocial approach for resocialization.

Based on these experiences, emphasizing psychological (and spiritual) aspects of violent conflicts is, therefore, a necessity. Nevertheless, some criticism rightfully points out one weakness in the conflict-prevention-and-transformation movement so far: the underestimation of questions of organizational development and conscious activities on meso- and macrosocial structures, as mentioned above. There are only few concepts and tentative approaches to overcome these weaknesses, like the creation of peace constituencies, but the infrastructure for their application so far has still to be improved.[7]

4. The concentration on activities of the civil society in many transitional and developing societies endangers the necessary strengthening of the state as an effective monopoly of power as well as of its legal control.

Since the 1980s and early 1990s, when the support of the civil society as such was considered an important contribution toward socioeconomic modernization and a guarantee of a peaceful social transformation, critical voices have been on the rise. They point out that this concept often was equalized with the support of the NGOs in developing societies by Western donors who, without a sufficiently social basis, only created a fragmented and artificial society.[8] They claim that in a crisis this might endanger the already weak foundations of state institutions. This criticism has to be taken seriously. It illuminates that the civilization of the conflict potential in transitional and developing societies never can be the task of civil society alone. Dieter Senghaas pointed out that such a process is rather dependent on six different but interrelated achievements: the monopoly of power as well as its legal control; an economy with a high degree of labor division with its resulting interdependency and affect control; and sufficiently democratic participation and social justice as well as a "culture of conflict management," which is also anchored in the (civil) society.[9]

Looking at the importance of the civil society and of NGOs from this viewpoint, one can determine its contribution to conflict management in clearer terms. Not only the capacity for self-regulation of societal activists and the creation of nonparty, nonethnic loyalties is important, but also participation in the support of the other civilizing dimensions. The simple contrasting of measurements for the strengthening of the state as an alternative to the strengthening of the civil society is confusing. This has its origin in the function of the civil society as a counterpart of authoritarian regimes as in Eastern Europe before the transition in 1989–1990. In the same way, however, as one succeeds to democratize state structures, the functions of the civil society have to change. Now it can also be important to support state institutions to offer services as well as a legally controlled monopoly of power.

5. Because of the constant external interference of the movement for conflict prevention and transformation in critical areas, there is the danger that their representatives themselves become part of the conflict, that they tend to reproduce particularly popular recipes for conflict management, and worst, even create the stimulus for the continuation of the conflict—albeit involuntarily.

This argument follows the same pattern as the criticism of humanitarian intervention and its involuntarily counterproductive effects. In the case of interference by external civil activists, one first has to differentiate whether it is an "interested" attempt in favor of a disadvantaged group, or a more or less neutral attempt to prevent or terminate violence or to balance interests. With interested activities, it is obvious to ask the question of how far an empowerment of single parties really contributes to a constructive conflict transformation. This is less obvious with activities of mediation, consulting, and support from a point of view of a neutral or all-party position.

This is understandable when we remind ourselves that in countries undergoing deep social changes with existential consequences for all its members, every substantial intervention from the outside nearly always has consequences for the power and influence of the different groups. For example, the decision that persons and organizations are selected or supported as partners for the conflict management has considerable consequences for their position in society. It can, therefore, be very advantageous to maneuver oneself into the position of a "difficult" and potentially violent party. A known aspect of group dynamics and realpolitik, such behavior attracts attention and is an important factor in the power struggle. Third parties are, therefore, not only reactors, but the more they engage in conflict management, the more influence they have on the conflict itself.

This is particularly noticeable in long-term postconflict reconstruction phases, where a large number of NGOs are at work and a marketplace situation develops, with a demand and supply of conflict-management services. Because of the economic situation, the market is less orientated to the needs in the conflict areas (however defined) but more on the interests and the assessment of the Western donors. This has the consequence that activities get primarily promoted that abide by the rules of the donors for distribution. This may mean short-term education in conflict resolution, which can be evaluated easily by the number of trained multipliers. More difficult in comparison to this is to find support for long-term, complex attempts to establish peace constituencies among strategically important groups.

The debate about humanitarian interventionism has shown that withdrawal as a meaningful and ethically acceptable consequence from these difficulties is no viable option. More appropriate is a conscious consideration of the byproducts of the interference to be expected. The same is true for the movement of conflict prevention and transformation. It is facing the challenge to develop a more self-critical and reflective relationship toward its work. This is helped by forums and opportunities for facilitated self-reflection as well as by a growing participation of local civil activists.

6. Like with other activists within the civil society, the conflict-prevention-and-transformation NGOs are lacking in sufficient legitimacy in regard to their (potential) influence as well as to their own internal structure. The more powerful the NGOs become, the greater is the danger that they prioritize the preservation of jobs rather than self-critically discuss their efficiency.

This issue has in the past been mainly discussed in regard to environmental NGOs, but the insights gained from this can be applied to conflict management, too. In regard to the question of "external" legitimacy, however, this criticism cannot be justified, because NGOs are not capable of collectively binding decisions. One could argue, though, that at least those NGOs that can raise considerable means enabling them to influence the socioeconomic situation in crisis zones, have to face critical questions about their legitimacy. This is not the case, however, with most of the activists in the movement for conflict prevention and transformation. For all other NGOs, this point is reduced to the question of acceptance by their partners as well as their efficiency in the sense of the declared aims of conflict prevention and transformation.

The question of the "internal" legitimacy in conflict management is more difficult. Often efficiency is mentioned to justify decidedly hierarchical NGO structures, which can be appropriate in certain phases of activities and public ventures. For many areas of conflict management, those structures are counterproductive, because sustainable peacebuilding is, after all, based on the increasing competence of persons and organizations to deal cooperatively with arising tensions and conflicts. It is hard to imagine, though, how to achieve this, if it doesn't correspond to the ways the particular NGOs are organized and cooperate with each other.

It is difficult to formulate general statements about the appropriate constitution of NGOs dealing with conflict management because they are rooted in a highly diverse environment. This makes it all the more important to promote the process of self-understanding about standards of quality in this field. This may also be the best way to deal with the unavoidable consequences of the inner dynamic of growing organizations. We cannot emphasize enough that the main problem in this field in the foreseeable future is not the dynamics of powerful organizations but, on the contrary, the contrast between the massive needs for action on the one hand and the mainly underfinanced small organizations that are mainly feeding on idealism and self-exploitation.

7. Similar to the world of development NGOs, the movement for conflict prevention and transformation is influenced by the distinct North-South divide as well as the West-East divide. This concerns the dependencies in the cooperation of NGOs as well as the application of primarily Western concepts in conflict management.

With regard to the extreme, diversely developed civil societies as well as their economic basis in the various parts of the world, the first part of this critical statement is based on a given fact. Whether the divide is as significant as it is in the world of development NGOs are questionable. Many transitional societies have traditional conflict-management mechanisms and cultures, without which the changes would be even less manageable. With the growing pressure for modernization and politicization, they are, however, increasingly under strain. Given these conditions, and also because of their cultural implications, Western forms of communicative conflict management more and more meet with reservations.

It is interesting to note how far the movement in time has managed to narrow the divide by empowering NGOs in the South and East, by creating increasingly partner-orientated structures as well as by integrating non-Western conflict-management approaches. In this regard there are a number of positive indicators showing up in the diversity of the organizations listed in this book. This is comparable with the development of culturally and societally oriented concepts for training. The dynamic development of the movement for conflict prevention and transformation in South Africa and parts of Eastern Europe has furthermore resulted in more partner-oriented structures in these areas.

8. In regard to the immense challenges for conflict prevention and transformation and their limited resources and the labor division among NGOs as well as between NGOs on the one hand, and states and multilateral agencies on the other hand, is surprisingly underdeveloped.

This criticism is based, among others, on the Carnegie Commission on Preventing Deadly Conflict. It suggests the strengthening of connections and encouraging labor division and recommends institutionalizing cooperation, namely in the form of regional conflict forums. Many practitioners in the movement would like to intensify the cooperation with local social institutions and develop local and regional peace constituencies. These demands are frequent and very understandable, because they express the wish for increased efficiency in spite of the presumably ongoing tight financial situation. Nevertheless, it should be taken into account that coordination and cooperation also require energy, money, and time and that they have to be assessed under a cost-benefit perspective, too.

Historically the movement for conflict prevention and transformation is in its seminal stage. Its contributions to sustainable peacebuilding are primarily dependent on how far it succeeds to manage a successful process of self-reflection, to learn from experience, and to contextualize its work in regard to other political, societal, and economic influences.[10]

APPENDIX: EXAMPLES OF CODES OF CONDUCT

Twelve Principles of Multitrack Diplomacy
(Institute for Multi-Track Diplomacy, Washington, D.C.)

1. Relationship. Building strong interpersonal and intergroup relations throughout the fabric of society.
2. Long-term commitment. Making an ongoing commitment to people and to processes that may take years to come to fruition.
3. Cultural synergy. Respecting the cultural wisdom of all the parties and welcoming the creative interaction of different cultural ways.
4. Partnership. Modeling collaborative process by partnering with local parties and with other institutions and coalitions.
5. Multiple technologies. Utilizing a variety of technologies and creating new methods to meet the unique needs of each situation.
6. Facilitation. Assisting parties in taking responsibility for their own dreams and destiny.
7. Empowerment. Helping people become empowered agents of change and transformation within their societies.
8. Action research. Learning from all that we do and sharing that learning with others.
9. Invitation. Entering the system where there is an invitation and an open door.
10. Trust. Building relationships of mutual trust and caring within the system.
11. Engagement. Acknowledging that once we enter a system, we become a unique part of it, an engaged, caring, and accountable partner.
12. Transformation. Catalyzing changes at the deepest level of beliefs, assumptions, and values, as well as behaviors and structures.

Guiding Principles for Conflict
Transformation Work (International Alert, London, 1996)

The core of conflict transformation work is the building of sustainable peace. This involves a process of profound change, transforming situations characterised by violence and fear, thereby creating an environment in which reconciliation, social justice and participative democracy can take root. The principles outlined below are designed to help guide this process.

1. *Primacy of People in Transforming Conflicts.* "We believe that genuine conflict transformation is only possible with the participation and involvement of those most affected by the conflict."
2. *Humanitarian Concern.* "Our primary motivation is the alleviation

of human suffering and our engagement in situations of violent conflict is driven principally by concern for the societies and peoples at risk from such conflicts."

3. *Human Rights and Humanitarian Law and Principles.* "We are committed to the principle and practice of promoting human rights in our work in situations of violent internal conflict. We urge compliance with international humanitarian law and principles and respect for human rights amongst all parties to the conflict."

4. *Respect for Gender and Cultural Diversity.* "We respect the dignity and cultural diversity of all peoples and we make no discrimination on grounds of nationality, race, class or gender or religious, cultural or political beliefs. We recognise and endeavour to build upon the capacities of people to resolve their own conflicts and we support the distinctive peacemaking roles of women in societies affected by violent conflict."

5. *Impartiality.* "We endeavour to be inclusive in our work, seeking access to the relevant parties to the conflict. We do not take sides in conflicts and we derive guidance from our adherence to the principles outlined in this Code which we strive to advance in appropriate ways at all times."

6. *Independence.* "We are an independent organisation, free to formulate policies and operational strategies in accordance with our legally registered aims and the principles expressed in this Code."

7. *Accountability.* "We are morally responsible to those whom we seek to assist and accountable to those with whom we work. We are bound by UK Charity Law through our trustees and accountable through regular reporting mechanisms to our donors. As a means of enhancing accountability, we endeavour to be open and transparent in our work."

8. *Confidentiality.* "Whilst endeavouring to be open and transparent, we are committed to maintaining confidentiality in situations where the effectiveness of our programmes or the security of our staff and partners may be at risk. Furthermore, we believe that, in most cases, conflict transformation work is best done discreetly."

9. *Partnerships.* "We are committed to working in collaboration and complementarity with individuals, organisations, governments and other institutions which could contribute to the prevention and resolution of conflict. In particular, we believe sustainable conflict transformation is dependent upon effective co-operation with individuals and organisations within conflict-affected societies."

10. *Institutional Learning.* "We are committed to building up our collective pool of knowledge, institutional memory and experience through undertaking regular reviews and evaluations of our work

and developing the skills of all our staff. Furthermore, we endeavour to share the lessons we learn with relevant individuals and organisations who may benefit from them and, in turn, learn from the experiences and knowledge of others."

Declaration of Principles, Code of Conduct, and Qualities of a Dispute Resolution Practitioner (Canadian International Institute of Applied Negotiation, 1997)

Registered Practitioners in Dispute Resolution (RPDR) should be honest and unbiased, act in good faith, be diligent, and not seek to advance their own interests at the expense of the parties. Responsibilities to the parties include:

1. A dispute resolution professional should accept responsibility only in cases where s/he has sufficient knowledge regarding the appropriate process and subject matter to be effective. A RPDR has a responsibility to *maintain and improve his or her professional skills.*
2. It is the duty of the RPDR to *explain to the parties at the outset of the process, the bases of compensation, fees and charges,* if any.
3. *Impartiality.* When active as a neutral the RPDR must maintain impartiality toward all parties. Impartiality means freedom from favouritism or bias either by word or by action, and a commitment to serve all parties as opposed to a single party.
4. *Informed Consent.* The RPDR has an obligation to assure that all parties understand the nature of the process, the procedures, the particular role of the dispute resolution practitioner, and the parties' relationship to the dispute resolution practitioner.
5. *Confidentiality.* Maintaining confidentiality is critical to the dispute resolution process. Confidentiality encourages candour, a full exploration of the issues, and a practitioner's acceptability. There may be some types of cases, however, in which confidentiality is not protected. In such cases, the dispute resolution practitioner must advise the parties, when appropriate in the dispute resolution process, that the confidentiality of the proceedings cannot necessarily be maintained. Except in such instances, the practitioner must resist all attempts to cause him or her to reveal any information outside the process. A commitment by the practitioner to hold information in confidence within the process also must be honoured.
6. *Conflict of Interest.* The dispute resolution practitioner must refrain from entering or continuing in any dispute if s/he believes or perceives that participation would be a clear conflict of interest. The

dispute resolution practitioner also must disclose any circumstance that may create or give the appearance of a conflict of interest.

7. *Promptness.* The dispute resolution practitioner shall exert every reasonable effort to expedite the process.

8. *The Settlement and Its Consequences.* The dispute resolution process belongs to the parties. The dispute resolution practitioner has a responsibility to see that the parties consider the terms of a settlement. If the dispute resolution practitioner is concerned about the possible consequences of a proposed agreement, and the needs of the parties dictate, the dispute resolution practitioner must inform the parties of that concern. In adhering to this standard the dispute resolution practitioner may find it advisable to educate the parties, to refer one or more parties for specialized advice, or to withdraw from the case. In no case, however, shall the dispute resolution practitioner violate section 5 above, Confidentiality.

9. The experienced RPDR should participate in the development of new practice in the field and engage in efforts to educate the public about the value and use of alternative dispute resolution.

NOTES

This article was originally presented at the Synergy in Conflict Management conference organized in Strausberg, Germany, on 17–18 June 1998, by the Center for European Integration Studies, Bonn, and the Akademie der Bundeswehr für Information und Kommunikation; the text was further discussed at a codes of conduct workshop organized by the European Center for Conflict Prevention, the Berghof Center, Life and Peace Institute and International Alert, Soesterberg, the Netherlands, 23–25 April 1999.

We are most grateful to Christoph Marthaler (European Center for Conflict Prevention) and Kristel Maasen (Catholic University of Leuven) for their contributions to the Appendix in this article.

1. Carnegie Commission on Preventing Deadly Conflict, *Preventing Deadly Conflict: Final Report,* Washington, D.C., 1997, 114.

2. This is centered on the NGOs. As the boundaries to other parts of the civil society, namely, religious, educational, and scientific institutions and the media, sometimes are not clearly drawn, they will be considered, too, in parts.

3. Tim Allen, "International Interventions in War Zones," *Contemporary Politics* 2, no. 1 (spring 1996): 7–22.

4. Mary Anderson, *Do No Harm: Supporting Local Capacities for Peace Through Aid* (Cambridge, Mass: Collaborative for Development Action Inc., 1996).

5. Eftihia Voutira and Shaun A. Wishaw Brown, *Conflict Resolution: A Review of Some Non-Governmental Practices: A Cautionary Tale* (Uppsala: Nordiska Afrikainstituet, 1995); and Mark Duffield, "Evaluating Conflict Resolution—Context, Models and Methodology," in Gunnar M. Sorbo, Joanna Macrae, and Lennart Wohlgemnuth, *NGOs in Conflict—An Evaluation of International Alert* (Fantoft-Bergen: Christian Michelsen Institute, 1997), 79–112.

6. See Chester A. Crocker, Fen Osler Hampson, and Pamela Aall, eds., *Managing Global Chaos: Sources and Responses to International Conflict* (Washington, D.C.: USIP, 1996); and I. William Zartmann, and J. Lewis Rasmussen, eds., *Peacemaking in International Conflict: Methods and Techniques* (Washington, D.C.: USIP, 1997).

7. See John Paul Lederach, "Conflict Transformation in Protracted Internal Conflicts: The Case for a Comprehensive Framework," in Kumar Rupesinghe, ed., *Conflict Transformation* (London: Houndsmill, 1995), 201–222; Norbert Ropers, "Roles and Functions of Third Parties in the Constructive Management of Ethnopolitical Conflicts" (occasional paper 14, Bergof Research Center for Constructive Conflict Management, Berlin, 1997); and Anja Weiss, "Insider NGOs as a Key to Developing Peace Constituencies in the New Eastern Democracies," in *Peace and Security* (March 1997): 37–45.

8. Luis Roniger and Ayse Guynes-Ayata, eds., *Democracy, Clientelism, and Civil Society* (Boulder, Colo.: Lynne Rienner, 1994).

9. Dieter Senghaas, "Frieden—Ein mehrfaches Komplexprogramm," in Senghaas, ed., *Frieden machen* (Frankfurt: Suhrkamp, 1997), 560–575. He describes this complex as a "civilisatory hexagon."

10. For an exemplary report about such a process, see Judith Large, *The War Next Door: A Study of Second Track Intervention During the War in Ex-Yugoslavia* (Lansdown: Hawthorn, 1997).

PART 4

Conclusion

CHAPTER 18

Peacebuilding:
A Comprehensive
Learning Process

Thania Paffenholz

As the variety of topics in *Peacebuilding: A Field Guide* suggests, peacebuilding is a comprehensive learning process. We feel that we already learned a great deal simply from bringing together the experience and expertise of all the authors who have contributed to this book; we hope the readers will share this sentiment. It is important that we understand that no matter what we do and where we work, we are all part of a bigger picture. In order to build sustainable peace, a range of tasks—many of which have been discussed in this book—need to be accomplished.

Direct peace intervention such as mediation or training of peacebuilders is not the only way in which one can contribute meaningfully to building peace. Almost any initiative in or around existing or possible conflict settings has an influence on war and peace.

However, people working in the field tend to be caught up in the daily management of their specific tasks. Field-workers are often unaware that they are part of the conflict environment in which they are working, finding themselves in the middle of an armed conflict as reporters, doctors, or businesspeople. Consequently, many are also unaware that they can contribute meaningfully to building peace. Therefore, the real challenge is to make people more aware, to make them understand how they can make a constructive contribution to peacebuilding through the specific activities that they are pursuing, be it humanitarian work or development cooperation, reporting, or election monitoring.

Indeed, that was the very aim of this book: to raise the reader's awareness of the bigger picture and provide specific guidelines on how to maximize one's personal contribution to peacebuilding within the context of one's specific line of work.

By way of conclusion, I would now like to take a closer look at the themes that recurred throughout the book; themes that are important conditions for building sustainable peace, no matter where we work or which specific task we are fulfilling.

OPERATING WITH A VISION FOR PEACE

When working in or around a present or potential conflict setting, it is very easy to get lost in the daily management of the specific tasks one is dealing with. The doctor working in a hospital is busy handling new intakes, the journalist reporting from a conflict zone is engaged in timing interviews, the local human rights activist is trying to get the latest reports printed, the ambassador is caught up in meetings, the soldier in a peacekeeping mission is usually busy organizing logistics, the mediator is facilitating training workshops, and everyone is involved in organizing their own security in order to survive. However, if we want to contribute to peacebuilding—no matter what our specific task—we need to link our actions with a vision for peace.

It is hard to blame the individual field-worker for failing to operate permanently with a vision for peace; the immense tasks and challenges in the field often prevent him or her from thinking about the overall objective. Usually, permanent reflection and rethinking of interventions are not included in the tasks of people working in the field.

If one is operating in or around conflict settings, the vision for peace seems to be easy to define: to contribute to a more peaceful society. However, it does not suffice to just identify this vision. It is important to bring to it that this higher goal be translated in terms of our own reality; one needs to reflect on what contribution one can make to achieving a more peaceful society within the confines and possibilities of one's own assignments.

Hizkias Assefa, Hugo van der Merwe, Tracy Vienings, and the other authors who contributed to Chapter 12, "Dealing with the Past and Imaging the Future," make us aware that thinking about the past and envisaging the future can be very useful. We have to examine what elements of the past are worth continuing or revitalizing. Which wounds from the past need to be healed before we can proceed on our way to the future? Máire Dugan and Elise Boulding show us how important it is to look toward the future and ask ourselves: What elements are lacking? What do we need in the future to achieve a more peaceful society?

After these general reflections, it is necessary to translate them into our own reality and to link them to our specific tasks. In other words, we need to discover which elements of the higher vision we can adopt and integrate into our own assignment.

ALL RELEVANT ACTORS NEED TO PARTICIPATE

One major source of conflict is the exclusion of people from decisionmaking, be it at a high political level or at the lowest local level. Thus, including the right people into the decisionmaking process can constitute a significant contribution to building peace. It is, therefore, important in all kinds of interventions in conflict-prone societies that the relevant actors should always be involved in planning and decisionmaking.

Vivien Erasmus describes in his article how aid delivery could be made much more efficient by involving the local communities into decisionmaking and project planning. Manuela Leonhardt and Mary B. Anderson confirm these findings in the article on aid and peacebuilding. Kees Kingma points out that the success of demobilization and reintegration processes for ex-combatants depends on a participatory design of the process involving the families of ex-fighters and the communities.

It sometimes happens that people involved in peacebuilding have a very clear objective and operate with a vision yet fail to involve the relevant people in their activities because they feel they know exactly how to proceed in order to achieve their goals. A journalist, for example, may base an article entirely on conversations held with people who were presented to him or her, simply because this is how it was arranged by an aid agency or one of the parties involved in the conflict, which facilitated his access to the conflict area. The article will inevitably present a one-sided picture, which in turn may influence the readers. Other examples are Western conflict-resolution trainers who apply the same type of training irrespective of the conflict setting, without reflecting on the specific training requirements dictated by a particular situation. Had they prepared the training more adequately and involved local experts into its planning and implementation, this would no doubt have been beneficial to attaining the overall goal of building sustainable peace. Another example shows just how important it is to be very flexible in one's assessment of who is a relevant actor: in many conflict situations, peacemakers try to empower civil society actors, such as peace and human rights activists, who have an interest in peace. However, they often ignore other important groups, such as the business community. Ray Mullan makes us aware that business has a stake in peace, as business does not work properly without institutional and other security.

No matter what kind of activity we perform in an area of possible or existing conflict, it is of extreme importance that we involve the relevant actors into our activities.

GOOD PROCESS

It is not only important to be aware of what we are doing and why, but also how. Ron Kraybill points out that people are usually more sensitive to how a decision is reached than what the decision is about.

Involving all the relevant actors into planning and implementation—as discussed above—is part and parcel of a good process design, as we are well aware that it is nearly impossible to predict in advance exactly how to achieve our goals. It is the actors involved who will outline the necessary actions. Therefore, the most important task for field-workers is to design an adequate process that will lead to the necessary actions being taken in order to achieve our goals.

Rachel Neild asserts in her article on police reform that designing the process for achieving such reform is crucial to its success. Sami Faltas puts forward a similar argument in relation to the problem of controlling small arms.

When I suggested incorporating a good process design into a project proposal for demobilization in a postconflict situation, I was heavily criticized by colleagues. They opted for a detailed plan of action to be described in the project document, arguing that otherwise the donor might refuse to make available the necessary funds for the project, and adding that without such a plan it would be impossible to control the implementing agency. I argued that by the time the donor had finally approved the project, the situation might have changed so much that we would have to implement our plan differently, which would be difficult, seeing that everything is outlined meticulously in the project document. Furthermore, I felt that not all relevant stakeholders could be included in the project design, as we did not want to raise expectations before approval of the project. This might have given an unclear picture of the real needs and appropriate actions. We finally reached a compromise: we merely designed the process, not a detailed plan of action, while incorporating detailed monitoring and reporting procedures for the implementing agency, including a monitoring committee comprising the relevant stakeholders for controlling the development of project activities.

ALLOWING DIFFERENT PERSPECTIVES

Looking at our work from different perspectives may help us to incorporate new elements, which in turn can make us think and act more creatively. The inclusion of a gender perspective, for example, is a familiar theme to most of us. The need to incorporate a different perspective such as gender is obvious: in this way, we will acquire more options in the planning process and incorporate the right themes and actors into our activities. Beth Woroniuk's work is very helpful in this respect, as she has developed a practical guide on how to incorporate a gender perspective into peacebuilding.

Even if we do not possess guides on how to incorporate other perspectives, we should at least think about including people with different views into the peacebuilding process. Rienzie Perera explains how the presence of religious leaders in Sri Lanka helped to reduce the conflict. Ahmed Yusuf Farah recounts how the involvement of traditional leaders paved the way to successful peacebuilding in Somaliland, and Ray Mullan describes the important role of the business community in the Northern Ireland peace process.

While working in Somalia I experienced that external actors, be it aid or conflict-resolution organizations, tended mostly to involve the local actors that were familiar to them. Many aid agencies involved only the community chiefs, whereas most conflict-resolution nongovernmental organizations involved the local human rights or peace activists into their work. However, neither involved the business community. And yet, if one talked to the businesspeople themselves, a very different perspective emerged. They as a group were closely involved in rebuilding Somali society, and as such they had a stake in development and peace. This potential, however, was never explored by the external actors.

IS TIMING RELEVANT?

In many publications on peacebuilding, much of the debate centers on the issue of time. It occurred to me when going through the present book again that timing of interventions in conflict areas was not really a topic. Many authors, including John Paul Lederach, Johan Svensson, Herbert Kelman, and Rachel Neild, do point out that peacebuilding is a long-term process, but they make no suggestions regarding specific time frames for individual peacebuilding actions. It seems, then, that there is no need to time interventions for peace. What is needed is commitment at any given time in order to establish a network for peace through many different local and international interventions. Mari Fitzduff illustrates this within the context of the Northern Ireland peace process. I draw a similar conclusion in my analysis of the peace process in Mozambique, where building peace was only made possible by means of many different interventions at various times in the entire process.

Being prepared to make a long-term commitment in a peace process is not that difficult for internal local actors. However, there are few external actors who are prepared to remain involved forever in a conflict setting, even though some organizations may be prepared. It is, therefore, extremely important that the knowledge acquired by different staff members is preserved and passed on in a coherent manner.

COORDINATION FOR THE SAKE OF EFFICIENCY, NOT FOR THE SAKE OF COORDINATION

We have talked a lot about the comprehensiveness of peacebuilding and the value of each and every single action toward building peace. Paul van Tongeren argues that all these actions—if they are implemented in a coordinated manner—can be made more efficient. He summarizes the advantages of coordination with reference to the creation of the European Conflict Prevention Platform.

These suggestions also make us aware how difficult it is to actually achieve good coordination in the field. Everybody seems to be aware of the importance of coordination, even though in reality few organizations truly coordinate their actions. While reflecting upon my own experiences with coordination, it occurred to me that the objective of coordination must be clear and desirable to every actor involved. The appointment of an executive agency is also conducive to good coordination. Sometimes organizations already lack internal coordination, which severely restricts their ability to attain proper coordination with other actors.

However, in some cases it might be preferable not to establish coordination mechanisms but to rely instead on ad hoc task forces for specific purposes.

OPERATING WITH CODES OF CONDUCT

To cope with moral dilemmas, political challenges, or even stress and other issues that may prevent us from carrying out our activities in and around conflict settings, some authors suggest introducing codes of conduct. Bettina Peters opts for codes for journalists working in crisis areas. She wants her colleagues to minimize harm through seeking truth and proposes that this is best achieved through following existing journalistic codes of ethics.

Norbert Ropers analyzes a range of problems that conflict-resolution NGOs may encounter while working in and around conflict settings. He, too, argues in favor of introducing codes of conduct for organizations working in conflict areas (printed codes of conduct developed by different organizations have been included in his article).

The introduction of codes of conduct for aid delivery in Somalia and Liberia contributed to peacebuilding in these two countries, even though the results achieved were quite different. The code of conduct in Somalia was formulated very generally and mainly denied aid delivery to those regions lacking a minimum of security and administration. The code thereby supported the establishment of zones of peace in various regions and areas in Somalia. In the case of Liberia, many people believe that the introduction of a detailed and substantial code of conduct speeded up the peace process.

PEACEBUILDING AS A LEARNING PROCESS

We feel as if we have already learned a lot merely from bringing together the different experiences and knowledge of the authors contributing to this publication, and we sincerely hope that the reader shares this feeling.

When working in the field, one is often aware that much knowledge and expertise is present. However, lessons are mainly learned individually and not by organizations and institutions. When people leave an organization, the expertise that they have acquired often leaves with them, so that the person succeeding them has to start learning from scratch all over again. Likewise, evaluation units of big organizations accumulate vast amounts of knowledge and expertise but usually only in relation to the specific cases that they evaluate. Very little emphasis is put on collective learning by organizations.

Two authors highlight this aspect in their contributions: Leonard Kapungu shares with us his experiences regarding the lessons-learned process in the United Nations Department of Peacekeeping Operations. By evaluating past peacekeeping missions and transforming the lessons learned from successes and failures, the Lessons Learned Unit in a participatory process of learning with internal mission staff and external advisers was able to produce a number of guidelines for future missions. The recent mission in eastern Slavonia, which incorporated the lessons learned by then, is an example of successful UN peacekeeping. This example shows that—no matter how difficult the process—an institution can learn. It would be a good thing if lessons-learned units could be established for the entire UN system.

Karen Kenny writes about the need to learn lessons from human rights monitoring. She highlights that debriefing is not enough and suggests that a learning resource center be established within the office of the United

Nations High Commissioner for Human Rights in Geneva. The task of such a center would be pooling and screening information from different human rights organizations and incorporating this knowledge into guidelines for monitoring.

ENGAGING THE RIGHT PEOPLE

The need for qualified staff is obvious. All issues tackled in this book and all the themes excerpted from it and discussed above demonstrate just how necessary it is to engage the right people in any activity in conflict areas.

According to Katarina Kruhonja and Margareta Ingelstam, field-workers need to be properly qualified. And, as Jo Wouters and Arno Truger argue, this should be complemented with adequate training. Awareness building in relation to the cultural background of the country of assignment is of tremendous importance, as Angelika Spelten, Ahmedou Ould Abdallah, and Pat Patfoort explain.

However, Luis Enrique Eguren, as well as Katarina Kruhonja and Margareta Ingelstam, confirm that the personal qualifications of people working in the field is at least equally important. Good qualifications are commitment, openness, flexibility, self-confidence, and the ability to adapt. Leonard Kapungu adds to this the ability to work in a team. Professional skills are a necessary precondition; however, without the above personal skills, a field-worker will not be able to cope with the difficult situation of working in or around an existing or potential conflict setting. Merely to rely on professional skills, while leaving personal qualifications to chance, will minimize the likelihood of success and may put field staff at risk.

It was not the fault of the unfortunate doctor, who was sent by a humanitarian aid agency to a hospital in an area affected by armed conflict, that he got killed. He was a competent doctor and did his utmost to save the life of his patient. Nobody told him after the death of a particularly important patient that he should leave the place as soon as possible. The patient had suffered severe gunshot wounds and the doctor was unable to save his life. Two days after the death of the patient, two armed gunmen entered the hospital and killed the doctor. Local inhabitants wondered why the doctor had not left the place earlier. Apparently, he had failed to realize the seriousness of the warnings. Nobody had made him aware that this was the rule of the game.

There are less harrowing examples that illustrate how necessary it is to engage the right staff in conflict situations. During election monitoring missions in Africa, I witnessed a number of such incidents: the young female observer from a European country who was arrested by local authorities because she was wearing a miniskirt, for example. And there was the case of another observer, who was unable to figure out why he never received proper information from the local communities about threats to members of opposition groups. However, it emerged that he always asked people in public whether they had had any problems with the ruling party, so that it was hardly surprising that nobody told him anything. During an internal debriefing, he heard about the interviewing techniques of other colleagues and was astonished how they knew about these methods. When asked, some told him that they had simply handled the situation with common sense, while others conceded that they had gone through extensive training.

I would like to mention one more anecdote, which influenced my thinking about people working in the field. The story concerns a donor agency that had funded a cholera hospital in an area of armed conflict. A monitoring mission from the donor agency was sent to the region because the cholera epidemic could not be brought under control despite the emphasis that had been put on the need for preventative measures such as chlorinating of wells. The mission discovered that the implementing agency, a prominent European NGO, had been conned by the local subcontractors. The contractors took the money for chlorinating the wells but never performed the work because they had no interest in reducing the cholera rates. No cholera, no income—simple as that! The aid agency staff, which was changed every three to six months, never understood this situation.

During the flight back to the neighboring country, I had an opportunity to talk to one of the doctors from the hospital. He had just finished his six-month term and was moving on to another assignment. He was twenty-four years old, had graduated from medical school one year previously, and this was already his second assignment in a war zone. He explained to me that he loved emergencies, "because you have a clearly defined task to perform in a limited amount of time: cholera breaks out, you treat the cholera and off you go to another place." He also mentioned what satisfaction it gave him to work so efficiently. I tried to mention the failure regarding the preventative measures, but his mind was already set on his next assignment. Was it Afghanistan or Sierra Leone? He was not quite sure—but that didn't really matter; he ended the conversation.

The Contributors

Mary B. Anderson is president of the Collaborative for Development Action and director of the Local Capacities for Peace Project. She is based in Cambridge, Massachusetts (USA).

Kent Arnold is the manager of the Senior Government Project for the Center for Conflict Resolution in Cape Town, South Africa. He was the senior trainer for the Burundi training of trainers program.

Hizkias Assefa is professor of conflict studies, Eastern Mennonite University, and a Distinguished Fellow, Institute of Conflict Analysis and Resolution, George Mason University (both USA). He is the founder and coordinator of the African Peace and Reconciliation Network in Nairobi, Kenya.

Melissa Baumann is cofounder of the Media Peace Center, Cape Town, South Africa.

Elise Boulding is professor emerita of sociology, Dartmouth College, Hanover, New Hampshire (USA), and a former secretary-general of the International Peace Research Association.

Máire A. Dugan is the director of the Master of Arts Program in Conflict Resolution at Columbia College in Columbia, South Carolina (USA).

Luis Enrique Eguren is cofounder of the Colombia Project of Peace Brigades International, London. He has accompaniment experience in El Salvador, Sri Lanka, and the Balkans.

Vivien Erasmus is executive director of Aktion Afrika Hilfe. He is based in Nairobi, Kenya.

Sami Faltas is in charge of research and consultancy on surplus weaponry at the Bonn International Center for Conversion, Germany.

Ahmed Yusuf Farah is senior researcher, the War-Torn Societies Project, Somalia. He is based in Nairobi, Kenya.

Mari Fitzduff is professor of conflict studies and director of the Joint Initiative on Conflict Resolution and Ethnicity of the University of Ulster and the United Nations University, Derry, Northern Ireland.

Ellen Gardner is a media consultant. Recent assignments include human rights–related work in Kosovo (1999) and intelligence and media analysis (1995–1998) for the United Nations International Criminal Tribunal for the former Yugoslavia, Antwerp, Belgium.

Luc Huyse is professor of sociology and sociology of law at the University of Leuven, Belgium.

Margareta Ingelstam is program secretary at the Christian Council of Sweden, Stockholm.

Leonard Kapungu is chief of the Lessons Learned Unit, Department of Peacekeeping Operations, UN, New York.

Herbert C. Kelman is the Richard Clarke Cabot Research Professor of Social Ethics and director of the Program on International Conflict Analysis and Resolution at the Weatherhead Center for International Affairs, Harvard University (USA).

Karen Kenny is codirector of the International Human Rights Trust and has advised the European Commission, the European Community Humanitarian Office, the Organization for Security and Cooperation in Europe, and nongovernmental organizations on human rights operations.

Kees Kingma is project leader for demobilization and peacebuilding at the Bonn International Center for Conversion, Germany.

Ron Kraybill is associate professor in the Conflict Transformation Program at Eastern Mennonite University in Harrisonburg, Virginia (USA). He was director of the Mennonite Concilation Service from 1979 to 1988 and director of training at the Center for Conflict Resolution in Cape Town, South Africa.

Katarina Kruhonja is former president of the Osijek Center for Peace, Nonviolence, and Human Rights (Croatia) and is currently director of the center's project "Building a Democratic Society Based on a Culture of Nonviolence—Postwar Peacebuilding in Eastern Croatia."

Winrich Kühne is deputy director of Stiftung Wissenschaft und Politik, the German Research Institute for International Affairs at Ebenhausen, Munich, and adjunct professor at Johns Hopkins University, School of Advanced International Studies, Bologna Center (Italy).

Sabine Kurtenbach is researcher at the Institute of Iberoamerican Studies in Hamburg, Germany.

John Paul Lederach is the founding director of the Conflict Transformation Program at Eastern Mennonite University, Harrisonburg, Virginia (USA), where he is professor of sociology and conflict studies. He is the former director of the International Conciliation Service of the Mennonite Central Committee.

Manuela Leonhardt manages the Peace and Conflict Impact Assessment project at International Alert in London.

Ken Logue has been a freelance consultant working on community relations and community development issues in Northern Ireland over the past fifteen years.

Michael Lund is senior associate at the Center for Strategic and International Studies and Creative Associates International, Inc., both in Washington, D.C.

Clem McCartney is an independent consultant on conflict and community issues. He is based in Northern Ireland.

Ray Mullan is director of communications, Community Relations Council, Belfast, Northern Ireland.

Laurie Nathan is the executive director of the Center for Conflict Resolution in Cape Town, South Africa.

Rachel Neild is a senior associate with the Washington, D.C., Office on Latin America.

Ahmedou Ould Abdallah is the executive secretary of the Global Coalition for Africa in Washington, D.C. He served as the special representative of the UN Secretary-General in Burundi (November 1993–October 1995). He is also a cofounder and board member of Transparency International.

Thania Paffenholz is senior researcher at the Swiss Peace Foundation in Bern, Switzerland, and has worked as a peacebuilding adviser for the European Commission in Kenya for several years.

Pat Patfoort is an author, lecturer, trainer, and mediator, and cofounder and director of De Vuurbloem (the Fire Flower, a center for nonviolent conflict management) in Brugge, Belgium.

Rienzie Perera is research director, Life and Peace Institute, Uppsala, Sweden.

Bettina Peters is director of projects at the International Federation of Journalists; the projects include the Media for Democracy Program. She is based in Brussels, Belgium.

Luc Quintyn is director of the Center for Crisis Psychology, Queen Astrid Military Hospital, Brussels, Belgium.

Luc Reychler is professor of international relations and conflict studies at the University of Leuven, Belgium, and chairman of the Field Diplomacy Initiative.

Filip Reyntjens teaches African law and politics at the Universities of Antwerp and Brussels, Belgium. He is the chairman of the Center for the Study of the Great Lakes Area of Africa at the University of Antwerp.

Norbert Ropers is director of the Berghof Research Center for Constructive Conflict Management, Berlin, Germany.

H. Gajus Scheltema is the personal adviser to the Organization for Security and Cooperation in Europe's High Commissioner on National Minorities based in The Hague, the Netherlands. Prior to this function he was chargé d'affaires and subsequently ambassador in the Slovak Republic.

Johan Schoups, lieutenant general, is chief of staff regional headquarters allied forces in northern Europe and former force commander of the United Nations Transitional Authority in Eastern Slavonia.

Hannes Siebert is cofounder of the Media Peace Center, Cape Town, South Africa.

Hugo Slim is director of the Center for Development and Emergency Planning, Oxford Brookes University. Previously, a relief worker, he has worked for Save the Children Fund and the UN in Ethiopia.

Angelika Spelten is consultant for development cooperation at the head office of the Protestant Association for Cooperation in Development in Bonn, Germany.

Matthias Stiefel was director of the War-Torn Societies Project and is now director of the War-Torn Socieies Project Transition Program, Geneva, Switzerland.

Johan Svensson is regional director of the Horn of Africa Program, the Life and Peace Institute, Nairobi, Kenya.

Arno Truger is deputy of the executive president of the Austrian Study Center for Peace and Conflict Resolution and director of the International Civilian Peacekeeping and Peacebuilding Training Program at the Peace Center Burg Schlaining, Austria.

Stef Vandeginste is a legal researcher at the Center for the Study of the Great Lakes Area of Africa at the University of Antwerp, Belgium. He previously worked as governance officer for the United Nations Development Program in Kigali, Rwanda.

Hugo van der Merwe is a senior researcher at the Center for the Study of Violence and Reconciliation, Johannesburg, South Africa.

Patrick Vander Weyden was a member of different election observation missions and is currently a doctoral assistant at the Catholic University of Brussels, Belgium.

Jan Van Eck is senior consultant and manager of the Great Lakes Program at the Center for Conflict Resolution, Cape Town, South Africa. He has been involved in implementing the project "Burundi: Towards Dialogue" since 1995.

Paul van Tongeren is executive director of the European Center for Conflict Prevention, based in Utrecht, the Netherlands.

Tracy Vienings is manager of the Education and Media Unit at the Center for the Study of Violence and Reconciliation, Johannesburg, South Africa.

Sue Williams is director of the Policy and Evaluation Unit of the Joint Initiative on Conflict Resolution and Ethnicity of the University of Ulster and the United Nations University, Derry, Northern Ireland.

Beth Woroniuk is a principal with the Canadian consulting firm Goss Gilroy, Inc., Ottawa, and works on gender-equality issues in peacebuilding and other areas.

Jo Wouters is head of International Operations, Belgian Red Cross–Flanders. He is based in Brussels, Belgium.

Howard Zehr is professor of sociology and restorative justice at Eastern Mennonite University's Conflict Transformation Program, Harrisonburg, Virginia (USA), since 1996. Prior to that he served for nineteen years as director of the Mennonite Central Committee U.S. Office on Crime and Justice.

Index

About the Book

A milestone in the search for sustainable peace, this handbook highlights the invaluable contributions of people working in the field. The authors clarify how field-workers "fit" in the overall peacebuilding process; provide details of the most effective practices; and offer guidelines for preparing for the field.

Part 1 of the book introduces concepts and tools for sustainable peacebuilding, including chapters on selecting and training field-workers. Part 2 focuses on seven specific peacebuilding activities: mediation, monitoring, linking development aid and peacebuilding, training local peacebuilders, dealing with the media, reconciliation, and peacekeeping. Part 3 addresses the practical and emotional problems that field-workers confront on an almost daily basis. And Part 4 provides an overview of the lessons learned from the previous chapters.

Written for a broad readership, *Peacebuilding* offers a repertoire of concrete methods that researchers and practitioners can use to analyze contemporary conflict dynamics to develop a better peacebuilding architecture and to heighten the synergy of their efforts.

Luc Reychler is professor of international relations and director of the Center for Peace Research and Strategic Studies at the University of Leuven in Belgium. He also serves as chairman of the Field Diplomacy Initiative. His recent publications include *Democratic Peacebuilding: The Devil Is in the Transition* and *Our Burundi: Le défi de la paix*. **Thania Paffenholz** is a senior researcher at the Swiss Peace Foundation in Bern, Switzerland, and has worked for the past four years as a peacebuilding adviser for the European Commission delegation in the Horn of Africa.